Schizophrenia and Related Syndromes

Second Edition

P. J. McKenna

 Routledge
Taylor & Francis Group

LONDON AND NEW YORK

First edition published in paperback 1997 by Psychology Press
27 Church Road, Hove, East Sussex, BN3 2FA

Simultaneously published in the USA and Canada
by Routledge
270 Madison Avenue, New York, NY 10016

Second edition published in 2007 by Routledge
27 Church Road, Hove, East Sussex, BN3 2FA

Simultaneously published in the USA and Canada
by Routledge
270 Madison Avenue, New York, NY 10016

Routledge is an imprint of the Taylor & Francis Group, an Informa Business

Copyright © 2007 P.J. McKenna

Typeset in Times by RefineCatch Limited, Bungay, Suffolk
Printed and bound in Great Britain by TJ International Ltd, Padstow, Cornwall
Cover design by Sandra Heath

British Library Cataloguing in Publication Data
A catalogue record for this book is available from the British Library

Library of Congress Cataloging-in-Publication Data
McKenna, P. J.
  Schizophrenia and related syndromes / P.J. McKenna. – 2nd ed.
    p. cm.
  Includes bibliographical references and index.
  ISBN-13: 978–1–58391–928–6 (hbk)
  ISBN-10: 1–58391–928–7 (hbk)
  ISBN-13: 978–1–58391–929–3 (pbk)
  ISBN-10: 1–58391–929–5 (pbk)
  1. Schizophrenia.   I. Title.
  [DNLM: 1. Schizophrenia.   WM 203 M479s 2007]
RC514.M394 2007
616.89′8–dc22
2006026832

ISBN: 978–1–58391–928–6 (hbk)
ISBN: 978–1–58391–929–3 (pbk)

Schizophrenia and Related Syndromes

Second Edition

This new edition of *Schizophrenia and Related Syndromes* has been thoroughly updated and revised to provide an authoritative overview of the subject, including new chapters on the neurodevelopmental hypothesis, cognitive neuropsychology, and schizophrenia and personality.

Peter McKenna guides the reader through a vast amount of literature on schizophrenia plus related syndromes such as paranoia and schizoaffective disorder, providing detailed and in-depth, but highly readable, accounts of the key areas of research. The book describes the clinical features of schizophrenia and its causes and treatment, covering subjects such as:

- Aetiological factors in schizophrenia
- The neurodevelopmental theory of schizophrenia
- Neuroleptic drug treatment
- Paraphrenia and paranoia
- Childhood schizophrenia, autism and Asperger's syndrome

Schizophrenia and Related Syndromes will prove invaluable for psychiatrists and clinical psychologists in training and in practice. It will also be a useful guide for mental health professionals and researchers working in related fields.

P. J. McKenna is a psychiatrist specialising in the treatment of schizophrenia and has published widely on the neuropsychology of schizophrenia. He has worked as both a clinician and an academic and is currently Professor of Psychiatry at the University of Glasgow.

Contents

Preface to the second edition

If the first edition of this book was a single-author work, the second edition has definitely been written by two people, one a still relatively junior general psychiatrist with an interest in schizophrenia, and the other someone who has worked more or less exclusively with schizophrenic patients for over 15 years, learning much more than he expected to in the process.

There have been no breakthroughs in the understanding of schizophrenia in the 14 years that have intervened between the first and second editions of this book, but it is surprising to discover just how much knowledge has been added incrementally. Perhaps the most significant development has been the rise of the neurodevelopmental theory, which was only touched on in the original version of the book but has since undergone exponential growth, fuelled by birth cohort studies. Another growth area has been brain imaging. The first edition focused on CT scan studies of schizophrenia, which made up the bulk of the structural imaging literature at the time. These have now been replaced by MRI studies, which allow much more detailed analysis of brain structure. Functional neuroimaging has been essentially revolutionised over the same period, and among other things this has made it possible to write a chapter on the so-called cognitive neuropsychology of schizophrenia.

Clinically, less has changed. The same old battles are still being fought about whether schizophrenia is a legitimate category of disease, and arguments continue about the status of schizoaffective disorder and late paraphrenia. Childhood schizophrenia has finally become fully accepted, due in no small part to the work of Rapaport and her colleagues, but there is essentially no more research on delusional disorder than there was when the book was first written. Writing a second edition has, however, given me an opportunity to include a chapter on the relationship between schizophrenia and personality, which I left out of the first edition (mainly because it seemed too daunting), and have felt guilty about ever since.

P.J.M.
Glasgow, June 2006

Preface to the first edition

In 1896 a professor of psychiatry published the fifth edition of a previously unremarkable textbook of psychiatry. The same year he gave a lecture at a meeting of the association of psychiatrists to which he belonged. In both these he annnounced that he had come to the conclusion that a frighteningly large number of patients in insane asylums suffered from a single form of mental disorder. This conclusion derived ultimately from the writings of an earlier psychiatrist whose ideas were so offbeat that he had had to publish them at his own expense. It was also based on a study he had been carrying out, which involved summarising his patients' clinical details on file cards and collating the information during the academic vacations. In some ways, it even grew out of what seemed to be an increasingly natural way of organising the chapter headings in successive editions of his textbook. The psychiatrist's name was Kraepelin and the form of insanity he was referring to he called dementia praecox.

History does not record the response of the audience at Kraepelin's lecture, but elsewhere his proposal was met with what he termed lively resistance, and what in some quarters amounted to derision. Within a few years, however, the concept of dementia praecox had become accepted all over the world. To some extent this success was attributable to the work of another psychiatrist who had adopted Kraepelin's ideas early on. This psychiatrist was Bleuler, and he produced an exceptionally well-written book on the subject incorporating some of the ideas of psychoanalysis, which was just becoming fashionable. Bleuler also coined the term schizophrenia as a less clumsy and potentially less misleading alternative to dementia praecox.

Both the concept and the term were to prove enduring. Schizophrenia has survived attempts to narrow it down almost to the point of non-existence; to broaden it until it became a synonym for any serious psychiatric disturbance, and sometimes for none; and to wish it away altogether. Many psychiatrists have argued that the disorder is an aggregate of several disorders which will eventually be shown to be aetiologically different. Conversely, a number of attempts have been made to demonstrate that the disorder has no real point of demarcation from other forms of functional psychosis, especially manic-depressive psychosis. Nevertheless, in present day psychiatry large numbers of patients are still routinely given the diagnosis of schizophrenia – a striking if grim tribute to the intellectual achievement of Kraepelin and Bleuler.

Although the literature on schizophrenia has become huge, there has only been one further English language textbook on the subject which has been written by a single author from the clinical point of view. This was Fish's *Schizophrenia*, first published in 1962. Although revised and updated by Hamilton twice in an exemplary way, Fish's account of schizophrenia has inevitably become dated. The aim of this book was originally – and still is – to follow in Fish's footsteps and provide a clinically oriented account of schizophrenia suitable for the general psychiatrist, particularly the trainee psychiatrist. The book covers the clinical aspects of schizophrenia in some detail, and tries to cut a path through the large body of research into the disorder. The approach of the book is conditioned by the author's background in experimental psychology, where it is considered essential not just to convey findings, but to describe and criticise the research on which they are based; it is hoped that this is not at the price of sacrificing readability. As it was being written, the book also took on a distinctly historical slant. To some extent this was deliberate, an attempt to communicate the feel of a great deal of high-quality work that has been carried out over the years – some of which has been neglected or distorted. Also, and less consciously, it has undoubtedly been a reflection of the renewed sense of respect with which descriptive psychiatry has begun to regard itself in recent years.

P.J.M.
Cambridge, June 1993

Acknowledgements

Without the unwitting help of four of my teachers, it is most unlikely that this book would have been written. These are Thomas Powell, Eve Johnstone, David Cunningham Owens, and Philip Snaith.

I would like to thank a number of people who have given comments on chapters, provided references, or otherwise made constructive suggestions. These include Paul Bailey, Peter Bentham, Paul Calloway, John Cutting, Carol Gregory, Ann Mortimer, Richard Mindham, Michelle Turner, Christopher Ward, and especially Linda Clare. I would also like to thank Philip Ball who drew many of the figures in the book. I am also indebted to Michael Todd-Jones who obtained numerous obscure articles, arranged for the translation of some of these, and turned a blind eye to several very prolonged book loans. I am similarly indebted to Patricia Allderidge who gave up time to discuss the cases of the artists described in Chapter 12. I am grateful for the secretarial assistance (and also encouragement) of Shirley Easton and Jacqueline Waller. I would also like to thank my editors at Oxford University Press for guidance in developing the idea of the book, and for extreme patience in its execution. On many occasions I was fortunate to be able to access the vast historical knowledge of German Berrios, whose contribution to this book is wholly inadequately reflected in the references to his published work.

Finally, a special debt of gratitude is owed to my wife, Kay.

Acknowledgements for the second edition

Among the people who have unwittingly contributed to this edition of the book is Robin Murray, whose regular invitations to write or talk about challenging topics in schizophrenia provided me with a considerable amount of material for the purposes of cannibalisation. Another is once again German Berrios, this time for the extended series of talks and seminars he organised in his home, where I was exposed to state-of-the-art knowledge about the history of psychiatry, phenomenology, neuropsychiatry and not least statistics. Keith Laws taught me meta-analysis, examples of which are now scattered throughout the book. The framework of the first edition of the book was suggested by a series of lectures I gave to trainee psychiatrists in Leeds. A similar series of lectures I have given to psychology undergraduates in the University of Essex over the last five years gave me the structure for the chapters on the neurodevelopmental hypothesis and the cognitive neuropsychology of schizophrenia.

Thanks are due to Psychology Press, not only for allowing me to test their patience to the limit, but also more importantly for agreeing to publish the paperback edition of the first edition, which caused it to keep selling modestly, and so made a second edition a viable proposition.

1 The cardinal symptoms of schizophrenia

Schizophrenia confronts the clinician with an array of symptoms that is remarkably diverse and disconcertingly large. The symptoms themselves are often quite strange, sometimes extraordinary, and on occasion downright unbelievable. To make matters worse they vary greatly from patient to patient, and in the same patient at different times. In such circumstances their description and classification might be considered to present something of a daunting task.

To a considerable extent this task was accomplished by Kraepelin (1913a) and Bleuler (1911) in the two original accounts of schizophrenia. With an eloquence that has never been equalled, they delineated the full range of symptoms seen in the disorder, brought them to life with examples, and constructed a framework for classifying them that has governed all subsequent thinking. Succeeding decades saw only minor modifications to their scheme, the most important of which was the isolation by Schneider (1958) of a set of 'first rank' symptoms, which he considered to be pathognomonic of schizophrenia. Some further refinement has been achieved in the contemporary era of standardised methods of assessment. A particularly influential contribution in this area has been the rich and phenomenologically rigorous definitions of many schizophrenic symptoms provided in the glossary to a structured psychiatric interview, the Present State Examination of Wing *et al.* (1974), which far outstrips any of its competitors.

The symptoms detailed in this chapter consist of those that would be ordinarily regarded as psychotic rather than neurotic, and would be considered unexceptional in established schizophrenia, or, if they occurred in isolation, would raise the distinct possibility of schizophrenia being the diagnosis. These are divided in the time-honoured way into *abnormal ideas*; *abnormal perceptions*; *formal thought disorder*; *motor, volitional, and behavioural disorders*; and *emotional disorders*. Some members of each category have come to be regarded as prominent, striking, or especially characteristic of schizophrenia and therefore are singled out as cardinal symptoms. Other more minor or non-specific phenomena are grouped together as miscellaneous symptoms. Finally, there are the diagnostically important but otherwise motley collection of *Schneiderian first rank symptoms*, which are given a category of their own.

Abnormal ideas

The cardinal abnormal idea of schizophrenia is of course delusion. This is typically defined as a belief that is judged to be erroneous; is held with fixed, intense conviction; is incorrigible to argument; and is out of keeping with the individual's social, educational and cultural background. Delusions are also usually fantastic, patently absurd or at least inherently unlikely (Feighner *et al.*, 1972); typically they are also justified by the patient in a peculiarly illogical way (Sims, 2002). Abnormal ideas that are not delusions are undoubtedly also seen in schizophrenia, but are very much a mixed bag of individually uncommon phenomena.

Delusions

Always the hallmark of insanity, Kraepelin (1913a) drew attention to the extraordinary frequency with which delusions of many different types developed in schizophrenia, and to the fact that they could be either transitory or permanent. Bleuler (1911) made the point that schizophrenic delusions characteristically lacked systematisation and logical integration. In almost all cases, ideas that were obviously inconsistent with one another were simultaneously entertained; often there was a whole series of senseless and completely contradictory beliefs; occasionally this amounted to what could only be described as a 'delusional chaos'. Both authors considered persecutory and grandiose delusions to be particularly common, but sexual, hypochondriacal, referential and guilty delusions could also be seen.

Contemporarily, delusions are accepted as forming a commonplace, though variable part of the clinical picture of schizophrenia. They may be florid, multiple, and shifting; or alternatively sparse and only elicited on questioning, but persisting in the background for years. The rich variety in the content of schizophrenic delusions continues to be noted (Fish, 1962/ Hamilton, 1984); nevertheless it is striking how regularly particular themes recur. The most detailed classification of delusions according to content is that in the Present State Examination of Wing *et al.* (1974). This is reproduced in a slightly condensed form and with a few minor modifications below.

Delusional mood

Here the subject feels that his familiar surroundings have changed in a puzzling way which he may be unable to describe, but which seems to be especially significant for him. Everything feels odd, strange and uncanny, something suspicious is afoot, events are charged with new meaning. The state may be experienced as ominous or threatening, or there may simply be puzzlement. The state typically precedes the development of full delusions: the patient may fluctuate between acceptance and rejection of various delusional explanations, or the experience may suddenly crystallise into a clear, fully formed delusional idea.

Delusions of reference, misinterpretation, and misidentification

The central experience here is that all kinds of neutral events acquire special significance and refer to the patient personally, but in a more definite way than in delusional mood. What is said has a double meaning, someone makes a gesture that is construed as a deliberate message, the whole neighbourhood may be gossiping about the patient, far beyond the bounds of possibility. He may see references to himself on the television, on the radio, and in newspapers; or feel he is being followed; that his movements are observed; and that what he says is tape recorded. The same phenomenon can extend beyond gestures and words to many other aspects of the environment, so that situations appear to be created and people seem to be acting in ways that have a special meaning. Circumstances appear to the patient to be arranged to test him out, objects are placed in particular positions to convey a meaning to him, whole armies of people are deployed to discover what he is doing or to convey some information to him. The patient sees people he knew from the distant past planted in his way to remind him of something; there are people about in disguise; patients on the ward are not what they seem to be.

Delusions of persecution

Here the patient believes that someone, some organisation, some force or power is trying to harm him in some way, to damage his reputation, to cause him bodily injury, to drive him mad, and so on. The symptom may take many forms, from the simple belief that people are hunting him down, to complex and bizarre plots incorporating all kinds of science fiction. *Delusions of assistance* are a variant of the same phenomenon, where the patient believes the same forces, powers and organisations are endeavouring to help him in surreptitious ways – to direct his life, to enable him to become a better person, and so on.

Grandiose delusions

These are separated in the Present State Examination into *delusions of grandiose ability, delusions of grandiose identity* and *religious delusions*. In delusions of grandiose ability the subject thinks he has unusual talents, he is much cleverer than others, he has invented things, composed music or solved mathematical problems beyond most people's comprehension. Because of these talents he may feel he has a special mission or that he is particularly suited to helping people. The patient with delusions of grandiose identity believes he is famous, rich, titled; he is royalty or some famous person, or is related to prominent people. Although not all religious delusions are grandiose, grandiose delusions commonly have a religious colouring: patients may believe they have a divine purpose, they are saints, prophets, angels, even God.

Hypochondriacal delusions

At its purest, this term is applied to an individual's belief that his body is unhealthy, diseased or rotten. However, the bizarre complaints of bodily change and malfunction in schizophrenia frequently – almost characteristically – go far beyond the relatively unelaborated ideas seen, for example, in depression. Kraepelin described patients who believed that that their lungs were dried up, that their body was full of wax, or that their flesh was coming away from their bones. Contemporary examples in the same vein can be found in the Present State Examination, where Wing *et al.* gave as examples patients who stated that they had a metal nose, or that their liver was turned to lead by X-rays. One of Sims' (2002) patients was convinced that his semen travelled up his vertebral column to his head, where it was laid out in sheets.

Sexual and fantastic delusions, delusional memory and delusional confabulation

Sometimes sexual delusions are intimately bound up with hallucinatory sensations, for example in the genitals; in other cases, however, there are beliefs of pregnancy, in a fantasy lover, or that one's sex is changing, which cannot be attributed to abnormal perceptions. In fantastic delusions, the notable bizarre quality of schizophrenic delusions comes to violate common sense at its most elementary. Patients describe giving birth to thousands of children, walking all over the moon, having hundreds of people inside their body, and so on. One form of delusional memory consists of clearly recalled experiences of past events that equally clearly did not take place. These commonly have a fantastic quality, for instance a patient's recollection that he came to earth on a silver star or that members of the Royal family were present at his birth. In other instances, genuine memories become distorted by delusional significance in much the same way as current events do in referential delusions; for example, a patient realised he was of royal descent when he remembered that the fork he had used as a child had a crown on it (Fish, 1962/Hamilton, 1984)). Delusional confabulation is a rare phenomenon in which delusions – invariably fantastic delusions and delusional memories – appear to be made up on the spot and shift, change and become more elaborate as the patient is questioned about them. An example is shown in Box 1.1.

Box 1.1 Delusional confabulation

Extract from an interview with a chronically hospitalised schizophrenic patient whose main symptoms were auditory hallucinations and mild-to-moderate catatonic phenomena. He was not thought to be currently deluded, but had alluded to 'violent ideas' while being tested by a psychologist.

Q: The main thing I wanted to ask you about today was about what you were telling me on Wednesday about the Carlton brothers. Can you tell me again?

A: OK I'll tell you what happened. In 1978 I shot a man in the back of the head in a shop in Cambridge. I put one cartridge into him. My brother David put about eight into him. I shot a man in the leg called Conrad Carlton.

Q: When was this?

A: About 1978. I frogmarched him from St Neots right into the Midlands with a shotgun pointed at him. It was an empty shotgun.

Q: Was this on foot?

A: Yeah. Right into the Midlands, about 80-odd miles.

Q: Both walking?

A: Yeah, I did. I was on the television.

Q: How did you end up on television?

A: Because I had a shotgun pointed at him, you know. I was sort of notorious, you know, we had a bit of fame – well the wrong sort of fame – but, you know, we got into a sort of contest and he could have lost his life. If I had aimed a few inches higher I could have killed him.

Q: Where did you shoot him?

A: I shot him in the leg.

Q: And you say this was a contest.

A: Yes [laughs]. Only he lost it. In 1979 Richard, Conrad Carlton, Reg Walters and, um, Davis, shot my father in the head with a shotgun in a removal van in Papworth Everard hospital grounds.

Q: What were the circumstances of that, then?

A: Well, the Walters, Richard and Reg Walters and the Wilson brothers got together and they murdered my father in the back of a removal van in Papworth Everard hospital grounds. I think they shot him in the head with a shotgun and Reg and Richard smashed the back of his head with club hammers and axes. And Richard said bring the next one up and Conrad and Paul got hold of me and tried to get me in the back of the removal van and I said you are not going to get me into that and do what you did to my father.

Q: Why were you around there?

A: To visit my father in hospital.

Q: What was the matter with him?

A: He had a lung disease. He had emphysema.

Q: Carry on from there.

A: Then I think Paul then – this was 1979 after me and my brother shot this man in Cambridge – and I think Richard shot me in the head with a shotgun and they couldn't get me into the back of the van, so Richard took me back home in his car, and during the night I was laying in bed and I could feel myself dying – yes, because of the shotgun wound to my head. I said I am not going to die, I am going to get out of this. I went to work the next morning, you know, and the foreman looked at me and said, 'You can't work like that, you have got a hole in your head.'

Q: Where was this hole?

A: [indicates] I think it was on the left-hand or right-hand side of my head. The shotgun split my head open I had about an eight or nine inches split in my skull.

Q: You went to work like that?

A: I did, yeah.

Q: So the foreman said . . .

A: He said you can't work like that, you've got a hole in your head. So he took me down the hospital in his car and they took the shot out of my head and patched me up.

Miscellaneous abnormal ideas

Partial delusions

Jaspers (1959), still the authority on the phenomenology of delusions, criticised the standard definition of delusions on a number of counts, one of which was degree of conviction. As he noted, it is a common clinical experience to encounter schizophrenic patients who express ideas that are not held with complete conviction but are so bizarre that to entertain them at all has to be regarded as abnormal. Although they fail to meet the criterion of fixity, the content of these ideas otherwise resembles delusions in all respects, for example in having typical referential, persecutory or grandiose content. Wing *et al.* (1974) took the step of formally extending the concept of delusion to include what they called partially held delusions – beliefs that are expressed with doubt, or are not yet formed fully but still at the stage of being only one conceivable explanation for some unusual experience.

Obsessions

Repetitive, intrusive ideas that are recognised by the patient as senseless are an established but uncommon finding in schizophrenia. According to Fish

(Fish, 1962/Hamilton, 1984) around 3 per cent of schizophrenic patients experience obsessional symptoms at some time. Typically they appear at the beginning of the illness when they may continue unchanged in content and severity after the diagnosis becomes established, or alternatively transform into delusions (Bleuler, 1911). Sometimes obsessions and compulsions develop later in the course of illness, also said to happen in 3 per cent of cases. Occasionally, schizophrenic delusions (and also hallucinations) assume a repetitive, intrusive quality, but these lack the other phenomenological attributes of obsessions (A. Lewis, 1936). Some chronic patients show ritualistic behaviour involving touching, placing objects in particular positions or doing things like turning the lights off wherever they go; these similarly lack any discernible element of subjective compulsion, and are probably best regarded as complex stereotypies and mannerisms.

Overvalued ideas

Often wrongly used as a term for partial delusions, overvalued ideas are actually isolated, strongly held, preoccupying abnormal beliefs that, unlike obsessions, are not resisted or considered senseless by the patient, and that at the same time seem to lack the bizarre, qualitatively abnormal conviction of delusions (McKenna, 1984). The content of the idea may revolve around an alleged injustice (the querulous paranoid state – see Chapter 12), marital infidelity (morbid jealousy), health (hypochondriasis) or appearance (dysmorphophobia); it can also be argued that the central belief of anorexia nervosa is phenomenologically an overvalued idea. The aetiological settings in which overvalued ideas develop are diverse, but they have been described in schizophrenia. Usually, but not always, they appear as the earliest sign of illness; as the diagnosis becomes obvious, the idea may transform into a delusion, or become lost among other psychotic symptoms. The conceptual distinction between overvalued ideas and delusions is fraught with difficulties, a problem that becomes particularly acute in relation to the diagnostic concept of paranoia. This issue is discussed further in Chapter 12.

Abnormal perceptions

The cardinal phenomenon of this class is hallucination, although a variety of other perceptual experiences make a significant contribution to the clinical picture of schizophrenia. As originally defined by Esquirol (1838), a hallucination is a perception without an object. Other authors have added that hallucinations occur simultaneously with and alongside real perceptions, that they have the force and impact of real perceptions, and that they are outside voluntary control (Jaspers, 1959; Slade, 1976; Sims, 2002). Hallucinations may occur in any sensory modality; however, those of hearing are particularly important and are treated separately from the rest.

Auditory hallucinations

The phenomenon of verbal auditory hallucinosis – hearing voices – was singled out as the characteristic hallucinatory experience of schizophrenia by Kraepelin (1913a) and Bleuler (1911), both of whom also emphasised the almost limitless variety of this symptom. Summing up years of clinical observation, Mayer-Gross *et al.* (1969) pointed out that auditory hallucinations could be the first sign of schizophrenia, or could be absent until chronicity became established. Their frequency could range from only being experienced on a single occasion to persisting for years, overwhelming and tormenting the patient every waking moment. In form, they could vary from an indistinct muttering to elaborate conversations involving several parties. Their source could be unlocatable; or they could be felt to come from all sides; to emanate from a particular point in space; to be within the head; or sometimes the body. Commonly derogatory, schizophrenic voices could also be neutral, observing, reassuring, encouraging or praising. One of the very few verbatim examples of the content of auditory hallucinations is illustrated in Box 1.2.

Auditory hallucinations continue to be regarded as one of the commonest symptoms of schizophrenia, with few patients failing to exhibit them at some stage (Fish, 1962/Hamilton, 1984). Despite their great variability, certain forms of auditory hallucination occur with regularity and are worth distinguishing for phenomenological and diagnostic purposes. The following classification is combined from the accounts of Fish (Fish, 1962/Hamilton, 1984), Wing *et al.* (1974) and Sims (2002).

Elementary (non-verbal) hallucinations

Relatively uncommonly, schizophrenic patients report hearing noises like tapping, scuffling, banging, car engines, or occasionally music. Such experiences are frequently given a delusional interpretation, for instance as a machine being turned on, or as burglars moving around outside the house. Also included in this category by Wing *et al.* (1974) is indistinct whispering, muttering or mumbling where no words can be made out.

Third person and commenting hallucinations

A hallucinating schizophrenic patient may describe hearing a voice or voices speaking about him and accordingly referring to him in the third person. Typically, two or more voices discuss the patient with one another. In the most extreme expression of this phenomenon, one or more voices keep up a continuous commentary on the patient's every thought and action. This symptom forms one class of first rank symptom.

Box 1.2 What schizophrenic voices say (from Kraepelin, 1913a)

Notes made by a patient of what he heard. Statements in parentheses are questions inwardly directed by the patient to his voices.

(Why are you speaking in me?)
'You must eat blood. A. must laugh at you. Because we are poor block-heads. Asylum. We'll bring you later to an asylum. Oh my dear genius! Because we are hypochondriacs. I am your poor marmot. We are the mistresses of the German whipping-club. We inhale you.'

(Why do you torment me?)
'Have you a fate! We think the best of you. Taraxacum! Taraxacum! We thrash Dr S.'s bones bloody for he has become surety for you. Because we are frightfully fond of you. What am I to do? We weep laughing tears. We are differently developed. Oh you my darling little Jesus. Because we ourselves are tormented. Because we morally act perversely. We have christian catholic morality. Every human being must laugh at you. You are mentally ill. Yes, it is so. Because we have to fear your brain grease. Oh wild sheikh Almagro! Whom one loves, one torments. We have no implements of handicraft. You are in many things an absolute child, an absolute fool. We torment you as moral rapscallions.'

(What is your real object?)
'We wish to kill you. You have offended divine providence. Our object is morally irrelevant. M. must laugh at you. Our object is your cleansing. But Absalom! We love and hate you. Our object is terrible establishment of women's regiment. We are silly.'

(Are you human beings or spirits?)
'We are human beings, old topswine. Oh that needs an insane patience! I will show you my last aims. We weep about you. You have been very prudent. We are climbing up Ararat. Now then, little spirits! Little folk, brownies! You are fundamentally insanely deep!'

(Are you near?)
'No, far away. What shall we do contrary to your interests? No, in the middle of your head.'

Imperative hallucinations

These are voices that quite simply command the patient to carry out certain actions. They are said to be not very common (Fish, 1962/Hamilton, 1984) and usually they are easily ignored. Occasionally, however, the patient obeys, with grave consequences.

Functional hallucinations

In this rare phenomenon the patient hears voices superimposed on and developing out of real environmental noises, such as leaves rustling, water running from a tap, cars revving up, and so on.

Extracampine hallucinations

These hallucinations (which may occur in other modalities besides the auditory) are identified by the patient as originating from beyond the limits of normal perception. For example, a patient may describe hearing the screams of children being tortured in another city or hear himself being discussed by his relatives many miles away.

Other hallucinations

Hallucinations can be experienced in all other sensory modalities in schizophrenia. Their frequency is uncertain but they are generally regarded as being considerably less common than auditory hallucinations.

Visual hallucinations

Phenomena ranging from spots, rays and plays of colour, through human figures, to panoramic or apocalyptic scenes, were considered by Kraepelin (1913a) to be common enough, if rather inconspicuous in schizophrenia. Bleuler (1911, 1926) described visual hallucinations as frequent and lively in the acute stages, but otherwise rare. Since then, visual hallucinations have come to be considered so unusual in schizophrenia that they should raise the possibility of underlying organic brain disease being present. Clinical experience suggests that this is not the case, and that they are an unremarkable, if usually minor part of the clinical picture.

Somatic hallucinations

These were given somewhat more prominence by Kraepelin and Bleuler than visual hallucinations. They described sensations of being touched, tickled and pricked in their patients (*haptic hallucinations*), of heat and cold (*thermic hallucinations*), wetness (*hygric hallucinations*) and movement and joint position (*kinaesthetic hallucinations*). Also complained of were pain and sexual sensations, as well as altogether more incomprehensible electric, vibratory, rolling, moving and sliding experiences inside the body. Somatic hallucinations continue to be regarded as quite common in schizophrenia (Fish, 1962/

Hamilton, 1984; Sims, 2002). It has also been observed (Berrios, 1982) that such experiences are not usually reported as such, but instead tend to be combined with a degree of delusional elaboration – in practice the relative contributions of hallucination and delusion to the bizarre bodily complaints of schizophrenic patients are often impossible to disentangle.

Olfactory and gustatory hallucinations

Sometimes simple, or sometimes bound up with delusional interpretations, these were described as a routine part of the clinical picture by Kraepelin and Bleuler, and their occurrence has been noted by numerous other authors. Their frequency, however, is uncertain.

Miscellaneous abnormal perceptions

Perceptual distortions

McGhie and Chapman (1961) gave the first detailed account of a variety of perceptual changes that they claimed were commonly experienced by schizophrenic patients in the early stages of illness. These took the form of transient alterations in the size, distance and shape of objects, and heightened or dulled perception; analogous changes could also be found in the auditory sphere. Subsequent studies have supported the occurrence of such perceptual changes in schizophrenia (e.g. Cutting and Dunne, 1989), but clinical impression suggests that they are seen more in established illness than in the initial stages. As with visual hallucinations, these perceptual distortions are usually a minor part of the picture and are elicited on questioning rather than being described spontaneously.

Pseudohallucinations

This term refers to perceptual experiences that are similar to hallucinations in the sense of being vivid, compelling and involuntary, but that are localised by the individual to inner subjective space (i.e. heard 'inside the head', seen 'with the mind's eye'). The term has unfortunately acquired different shades of meaning (Hare, 1973), and an enduring controversy surrounds the issue of whether pseudohallucinations are perceived as 'real' by the patient (see Sims, 2002). Schizophrenic verbal auditory hallucinations commonly take the form of pseudohallucinations, where they have exactly the same diagnostic value as 'true' hallucinations; indeed, true and pseudo-auditory hallucinations may co-exist in the same patient (Wing *et al.*, 1974). According to Fish (Fish, 1962/Hamilton, 1984) many schizophrenic visual experiences also turn out to be pseudohallucinatory in nature when the patient is questioned closely.

Depersonalisation and derealisation

These symptoms have been considered to be common in schizophrenia, especially in the early stages (Sedman, 1970; Sims, 2002). In established, usually florid schizophrenia they may acquire a delusional interpretation – becoming what Wing *et al.* (1974) refer to as delusions of depersonalisation. The patient states with full conviction that he has no brain, no thoughts, there is a hollow in his skull, his body is a shadow or that he cannot see himself in the mirror. These symptoms blur into Cotard's syndrome of nihilistic and other delusions, which is occasionally seen in schizophrenia as well as in its more familiar setting of psychotic depression (Enoch and Ball, 2001).

Formal thought disorder

The 'formal' of formal thought disorder refers to disturbances in the form of thinking – that is, its structure, organisation and coherence – which manifest themselves as a loss of intelligibility of speech; the listener becomes unable to follow what is being said. Formal thought disorder is a relatively uncommon finding in acute schizophrenia. It is often stated that it becomes more frequent among chronic schizophrenic patients (e.g. Wing, 1978), but those showing severe forms of the symptom are not easy to find even in the chronically hospitalised population. The term encompasses a number of quite disparate abnormalities, which may be seen in more or less pure form or occur in erratic combinations. Perhaps most commonly it is the moment-to-moment, logical sequencing of thoughts that is at fault. At other times, language itself appears to be disturbed, so that the meaning of individual words and phrases is obscured. At still other times, the fault seems to be at a high level: individual words, sentences and short stretches of speech make sense, but there is no discernible thread to longer verbal productions.

Of the many descriptive abnormalities that have been proposed to underlie formal thought disorder in schizophrenia, a relatively small number have come to be regarded as accounting for a disproportionate amount of the phenomenon. These are designated here as the cardinal elements of formal thought disorder. Some of the remainder, designated here as miscellaneous, are uncommon or relatively nonspecific.

Cardinal elements of formal thought disorder

Attempts to define what it was that made schizophrenic speech sometimes difficult to follow largely began, once again, with Kraepelin and Bleuler. Kraepelin (1913a) considered that there was a central process of *derailment*, a continual tendency to be deflected from the point, to glide off into more or less closely related areas. He hypothesised that, operating at different levels, derailment could give rise to a range of abnormalities: a lack of connectedness in the train of ideas; a disturbance in the construction of individual sentences; even a peculiarity of word selection to the point of invention of entirely new words or *neologisms*. Bleuler (1911) proposed a somewhat different unifying explanation. In his view there were two closely related fundamental disturbances: *loosening of associations* and *loss of the central determining idea*. The former caused patients to lose themselves in irrelevant side-associations; as a result of the latter, thoughts remained subordinated to some sort of general idea but were no longer directed by any unifying concept of purpose or goal.

Other classical authors built on Kraepelin's and Bleuler's explanatory constructs and made contributions of their own. The most significant contribution during this era, however, was that of Kleist (1914, 1960; see also McKenna and Oh, 2005), who argued that dysphasia-like abnormalities were discernible in thought-disordered schizophrenic speech, particularly when it was severe. In addition to neologisms, a recognised feature of dysphasia, he claimed he could find evidence of other dysphasic phenomena, including *paraphasias* (erroneous words phonetically or semantically related to the target word), and *paragrammatism* (speech that is fluent but with overproduction of words and phrases, grammatical misuses, and uncompleted linguistic expressions).

Bridging the classical and contemporary eras were two influential studies that sharpened existing concepts and added important new ones. In an analysis of schizophrenic formal thought disorder that largely ignored all previous work, Cameron (1938) concluded that three important abnormalities stood out. In *asyndetic thinking*, a tendency to use loose clusters of related ideas rather than well-knit sequences of concepts, he essentially redescribed loss of the central determining idea. *Metonymic distortion* (word approximation), however, in which imprecise verbal constructions are substituted for commonplace words or phrases (e.g. 'handshoe' instead of glove), was the first succinct identification of a phenomenon that had previously only been referred to obliquely. The eloquent term *interpenetration of themes* described an inability to keep the immediate matter in hand and one's own inner concerns apart; patients showing this phenomenon would blend fragments of what Cameron called 'persistent problems of a personal nature' (usually delusions) into whatever topic was being discussed. Later, Wing and colleagues (Wing, 1961; Wing *et al.*, 1967; Wing *et al.*, 1974) introduced the concept of poverty of content of speech. This described speech that was free and normal in quantity, but that was so vague and contained so little information as to produce an impression of complete emptiness (see also McKenna and Oh, 2005).

As part of the drive to make the diagnosis of schizophrenia and other psychiatric disorders more reliable (see Chapter 4), Andreasen (1979a) pooled the descriptions of these and other authors, extracted their common themes, and was able to arrive at a comprehensive taxonomy of what she termed thought, language and communication disorders. This consisted of 18 different abnormalities, of which four can be considered the most important, by virtue of the emphasis placed on them in the Present State Examination and DSM III/DSM IV. These are described below. Except where otherwise stated, the definitions are those of Andreasen (1979a). The terms in brackets refer to generally older descriptions that are synonymous or at least partially overlapping. Some illustrations are given in Box 1.3.

Box 1.3 Examples of formal thought disorder

Derailment

Interviewer: (Tells the donkey and the salt story and asks patient to recount it in his own words.)

Patient: A donkey was carrying salt and he went through a river, and he decided to go for a swim. And his salt started dissolving off him into the water, and it did, it left him hanging there, so he crawled out on the other side and became a mastodon. . . . It gets unfrozen, it's up in the Arctic right now; it's a block of ice, the block of ice gets planted. . . . It's forced into a square, right? Ever studied that sort of formation, block of ice in the ground? Well it fights the perma frost; it pushes it away and lets things go up around it. You can see they're like, they're almost like a pattern with a flower; they start from the middle and it's like a submerged ice cube that's frozen into the soil afterwards.

(Rochester and Martin, 1979)

Incoherence

Interviewer: (Asks patient to interpret the proverb 'don't change horses in mid-stream'.)

Patient: That's wish-bell, double vision. Like walking across a person's eye and reflecting personality. It works on you like dying and going into the spiritual world but landing in the vella world.

(Harrow and Quinlan, 1985)

Interviewer: Have you been nervous or tense lately?

Patient: No, I got a head of lettuce.

Interviewer: You got a head of lettuce? I don't understand. Tell me about lettuce.

Patient: Well, lettuce is a transformation of a dead cougar that suffered a relapse on the lion's toe. And he swallowed the lion and something happened. The . . . see, the . . . Gloria and Tommy, they're two heads and they're not whales. But they escaped with herds of vomit, and things like that.

(Neale and Oltmanns, 1980)

Poverty of content of speech

Interviewer: Are you feeling unwell?

Patient: It's hard to live on your own in this society. I get fears of violence and death – feeling that I'm all negative inside – you know – I always have a clash with authority. They have too much power to incarcerate me and you. The alternative is death; I would have done myself in. There's no love in an empty flat. . . .

(Author's own example)

Interviewer: Do you ever get the feeling that everybody knows your thoughts?

Patient: Yes, I was thinking that just before I came in here, actually I have the feeling, which I feel is just a sort of creation of myself and I've created, I've formed, a person which is the character, the part of me which is ordinary, the other self which I've shaped as an onlooker, as Fred, or John, or Allan and so on, people I know, and I converse with them a lot of the time.

(Benson, 1973)

Stilted speech

Interviewer: (Asks patient to interpret the proverb 'discretion is the better part of valour'.)

Patient: Pliant rectitude is a trait more appropriate for successful living than hot-headedness, which is either stubborn or crusady.

(Harrow and Quinlan, 1985)

Neologisms, word approximations and idiosyncratic use of words

Neologisms: comforting the bathroot, Vella world, stubborn or crusady, God's tarn-harn

Technical neologisms: Snortie – to talk through walls; Trominoes – tiny people who live in one's body; Split-kippered – to be simultaneously alive in Lancashire and dead in Yorkshire.

Word approximations: Daily reflector – mirror; suction device – cigarette; homing out station – place to take a break from living at home; 'My tongue is exceeding my mouth' – patient describing acute dystonic reaction.

Idiosyncratic use of words: 'Well, there is a frequenting of clairvoyance.' '. . .against such things as America's central cotton wool.'

(Bleuler, 1911; Wing et al., 1974; Harrow and Quinlan, 1985; author's own examples)

Derailment (loosening of associations, asyndetic thinking, knight's move thinking)

This describes a pattern of spontaneous speech in which the ideas slip off the track onto another one that is clearly but obliquely related, or onto one that is completely unrelated. Things may be said in juxtaposition that lack a meaningful relationship, or the patient may shift idiosyncratically from one frame of reference to another. In what is perhaps the commonest manifestation of this disorder, there is a slow, steady slippage, with no single derailment being particularly severe, so that the speaker gets farther and farther from the point. Andreasen partly redefined the related term *tangentiality* to refer to replies to questions that are oblique, off the point or irrelevant from the outset.

Loss of goal (lack of central determining idea, loosening of associations, asyndetic thinking)

This refers to a failure to follow a train of thought through to its conclusion, usually manifested in speech that begins with a particular subject, wanders away from this and never returns to it. The abnormality often occurs in association with derailment, but sometimes no clear-cut instances of this latter phenomenon can be demonstrated.

Incoherence (drivelling, word salad, paragrammatism, 'schizophasia')

This describes a severe disorder where the pattern of speech is essentially incomprehensible at times. Several different mechanisms may contribute, all of which may occur simultaneously. Sometimes the disturbance appears to be at a semantic level so that words are substituted in a phrase or sentence in a way that distorts or destroys the meaning; the word choice may seem to be totally random or may appear to have some oblique connection with the context. Sometimes the rules of grammar and syntax are ignored, and a series of words or phrases seem to be joined together arbitrarily and at random. Sometimes portions of coherent sentences may be observed in the midst of a sentence that is incoherent as a whole.

Neologisms and related abnormalities

Neologisms are completely new words or phrases whose derivation usually cannot be understood. Occasionally patients coin words or phrases to describe otherwise indescribable experiences; this phenomenon is referred to as technical neologism (Fish, 1962/Hamilton, 1984). In *idiosyncratic use of words* (Wing *et al.*, 1974), phrases are used that are composed of ordinary words, but that are incomprehensible as a whole. *Word approximations* are also idiosyncratic uses of words but here the word has been incorrectly built up because of a misuse of existing words and often the meaning will be evident even though the usage seems peculiar, stilted or bizarre.

Poverty of content of speech (woolliness of thought, alogia, empty speech)

Here, although replies are long enough for speech to be adequate in amount, they convey little information. Answers to questions tend to be vague, often over-abstract or over-concrete, repetitive and stereotyped. The interviewer may recognise the abnormality only by observing that the patient has spoken at some length but has not given sufficient information to answer the question. Sometimes the speech can be best characterized as 'empty philosophising'.

Miscellaneous aspects of formal thought disorder

Circumstantiality

This was defined by Andreasen (1979a) as a pattern of speech that is very indirect and delayed in reaching its goal idea. In replying to a question, the speaker brings in a welter of unnecessary detail and explores all sorts of unnecessary avenues before returning to the point. The disorder differs from derailment and loss of goal in that the unnecessary details are clearly related to the main theme, and that the goal idea is eventually reached. Circumstantiality is perhaps the best example of abnormality in thought form that is found in schizophrenia, but that is by no means specific to it. It has been described in some patients with epilepsy, in chronic organic states and in mental handicap. It is also by no means rare among normal individuals (Sims, 2002).

Vorbeireden

This rare phenomenon (literally talking past the point) is also known as *approximate answers* or *paralogia*. It has also been referred to as *Ganserism* as it is the defining characteristic of the Ganser syndrome (Whitlock, 1967). The patient gives replies to questions that are incorrect, but in a way which betrays that the correct answer is known. Sometimes the answers are truly approximate, for instance, a cow is said to have three legs, a pack of cards five suits, and so on; more commonly they are random or absurd. When asked the difference between a fence and a wall, a patient replied 'Well, a wall's made out of wood, isn't it.' Some more of his verbal productions are illustrated in Figure 1.1.

DEPARTMENT OF CLINICAL PSYCHOLOGY
REPORT

Date	
	Name: BARRY XXXXXXXXX **Age:** 24 YEARS
	Hospital Number: XXXXX **Referred by** XXXXX

GENERAL COMMENTS

Barry was first seen on Monday 26th November when he was accompanied by his parents. He slumped into his chair and maintained an inane smile expressing absence of concern for the proceedings. After brief preliminaries the parents responded to my request that they leave and after a further brief period during which I attempted to achieve satisfactory rapport, but with only partial success, the WAIS proceedure was commenced. Barry's reactions to this were reminiscent of the classical dementia praecox - bizarre illogical answers, silences, and inappropriate laughter.

<u>Examples</u>

Information - 8. Weeks in year? "Twenty four" (laughter).

Information - 1 Average Height of women? "Three foot six".

How tall is your mother? "Over five foot"

Is your mother tall, short or average?
"About average".
Then what is the average height of English women?

"three foot six".

(c) Capital of "Italy"? "Spain".
Comprehension - 3. Envelope - "Lick and stick it on"
Repeated. "Take it home.
What would you do with it?
"Keep it".

(d) Similarities -

1. Orange-Banana "Both red".
   Repeated. "Both yellow".
2. Coat-dress "Green".
   Repeated - "Clothes".

Numbers 3 and 4 were correct.

5. North-West "It's like a compass isn't it?
6. Eye-Ear. "Parts of human body".
7. Air-water. It's a balloon.
8. Table-Chair. "Both stools aren't they"-

At this point testing was temporarily discontinued.

Do not write here—margin for securing in folder

Figure 1.1 Vorbeireden in a schizophrenic patient.

Stilted speech

Occasionally, the speech of schizophrenic patients is excessively formal, ornate or pompous. The stilted quality may be a consequence of excessive use of polysyllabic rather than monosyllabic words, over-polite phraseology or stiff and over-formal syntax (Andreasen, 1979a).

Concrete thinking

This term was introduced by Goldstein (1944) to describe an inability to generalise, grasp the essential rather than literal meaning of a statement, and keep in mind different aspects of the situation – in short, to think abstractly. Originally intending it to explain some aspects of schizophrenic thought disorder, Goldstein recognised that concrete thinking occurred in organic brain syndromes as well – his application of the concept to schizophrenic thinking (see Fish, 1962/Hamilton, 1984) was in fact somewhat convoluted. Concrete thinking survives as a sign of dementia, delirium and the frontal lobe syndrome, but it is rarely mentioned in association with schizophrenia anymore.

Perseveration

Like concrete thinking, the inappropriate repetition of words, ideas or themes has long been considered to be a feature of both schizophrenia and organic states, especially the frontal lobe syndrome. Unlike concrete thinking, perseveration was retained as one of Andreasen's (1979a) 18 descriptive abnormalities in thought, language and communication. There is no doubt some patients with schizophrenia perseverate, particularly those with severe, chronic schizophrenia. Whether perseveration is seen particularly in patients with formal thought disorder, however, is an open question.

Motor, volitional and behavioural disorders

Oddities of movement, bizarre behaviour and changes in the level of overall activity are part and parcel of the clinical picture of schizophrenia. The cardinal examples of this class of symptom have to be the exotic phenomena subsumed under the term catatonia. Certain other types of motor, volitional and behavioural disorders are less striking, but far more common in schizophrenia – good examples being the important symptoms of lack of volition and poverty of speech.

Catatonic phenomena

Kahlbaum (1874) gave the first account of catatonia, describing many of the individual symptoms that come to be grouped under the term. Incorporating catatonia into schizophrenia, Kraepelin (1913a) detailed an even wider range of abnormalities. It was, however, Bleuler (1911) who provided the first systematic description and classification of 'peculiar forms of motility, stupor, mutism, stereotypy, mannerism, negativism, command-automaticity, spontaneous automatism and impulsivity'. Classical descriptions were supplemented by Kleist (1943, 1960) whose particular contribution was to enlarge the category of simple motor abnormalities in schizophrenia.

Until recently, the description of catatonic symptoms consisted of Fish's classificatory scheme (Fish, 1962/Hamilton, 1984), which essentially combined the accounts of Bleuler and Kleist. In the last few years, however, the concept of catatonia has undergone a significant degree of reappraisal at the hands of neurologists and neuropsychiatrists, including notably Marsden *et al.* (1975), Lees (1985), Rogers (1985, 1992) and Lohr and Wisniewski (1987). The following account therefore brings together that of Fish with these more recent authors.

Simple disorders of movement

The commonest representatives of this class of abnormality are *stereotypies*, *mannerisms* and *posturing*. Stereotypies are more or less purposeless motor acts that are carried out repetitively and with a high degree of uniformity. They include simple movements like rocking, rubbing hands and tapping objects, as well as more complicated, 'gymnastic' or 'contortionist' phenomena. In mannerisms, everyday goal-directed acts like washing, dressing and eating come to be executed in idiosyncratic ways; for example, while eating a patient may hold the spoon by the wrong end, put his hand round the back of his head to bring the food to his mouth, or drop the food back on to the plate several times between each mouthful. *Manneristic gaits* feature mincing, over-precise or alternatively extravagant qualities and sometimes incorporate stooping, twisting, grotesque limb movements, walking on the toes, interpolated actions, and so on. *Posturing* is the modern term for stereotypies and mannerisms of posture: patients sit hunched and constrained, often in a way that seems to express a turning away from the world; in some cases bizarre, statuesque, 'pharaonic' poses are adopted (Sims, 2002).

In practice, it is usually difficult to separate stereotypies, mannerisms and posturing from one another; patients show movements and actions that are abnormal by virtue of varying degrees of repetitiveness, purposelessness and stiltedness of execution. Exactly analogous motor abnormalities may affect facial expression and are collectively referred to as *grimacing*.

Other catatonic abnormalities at this level take the form of impairments rather than embellishments of movement. In *blocking* and *freezing*, a purposive act becomes interrupted in mid-sequence; the movement may become fixed at this stage or the limb may gradually sink back to a resting position. In *waxy flexibility* (catalepsy) the patient allows his limbs or torso to be placed in any position, which is then maintained for minutes or occasionally much longer. This disorder is rare but maintenance of uncomfortable positions for a few seconds (*Haltungsverharren*) and so-called *psychological pillow*, where the patient lies with his head two to three inches off the bed, can be quite commonly observed among chronically hospitalised patients.

Kleist used the term *parakinesia* to describe movements reminiscent of chorea, athetosis and tics, but distinguishable from these by a certain emotional colouring, a motivated quality not ordinarily seen. Such patients were said to grimace, twitch and jerk continuously, carry out voluntary movements in an abrupt way, and speak in short, sharp, disjointed bursts. Whether such movements were genuinely different from the tardive dyskinesia-like involuntary movement disorders that are now recognised to occur in untreated schizophrenia (see below) is a moot point.

More complex disorders of volition

Although expressed in motor acts, these abnormalities appear to involve a disturbance in the will behind the movement rather than in the movement itself; at the same time the disorder conveys the compelling impression of being outside conscious control. Figuring prominently at this level are disorders of cooperation, including *negativism* and a variety of abnormalities characterised by over-responsiveness and excessive compliance, which Lohr and Wisniewski grouped together as *positivism*.

According to Bleuler the term negativism encompasses a spectrum of phenomena. At the simple, motor end of this is the phenomenon of *gegenhalten* (opposition), where the patient resists all passive movements with exactly the same degree of force as that exerted by the examiner. At a somewhat higher, volitional, level patients do the reverse of whatever is asked of them; they hold their breath when asked to breathe deeply, violently resist attempts to get them to stand up, only to continue to resist when it is requested that they then sit or lie down.

The term positivism conveniently groups a number of phenomena previously separated into *mitgehen*, *automatic obedience* and *echopraxia*. In *mitgehen*, the patient appears to wish to anticipate the intention of the examiner. There is scarcely any resistance to passive changes of posture, and limbs elevate themselves at the slightest touch like an anglepoise lamp. Requests to move are complied with in an abrupt, exaggerated way that may overshoot the mark or even unbalance the patient. When requested to perform a particular act, the patient repeats it unnecessarily, or copies one limb movement with another. Such phenomena shade into automatic obedience where any and every suggestion (even one that is merely implied) is mindlessly obeyed; and echopraxia, where gestures and actions are copied, sometimes with a certain amount of modification or elaboration.

Other volitional catatonic phenomena include *ambitendence*, where a patient appears to simultaneously try to and prevent himself from carrying out actions: he may move his hand from his body with obvious intent, then stop, start and stop again until finally giving up altogether. In *handling* and *intertwining* (also known as *hypermetamorphosis*) the patient seems impelled to touch and manipulate everything within reach, and so kneads objects and continually adjusts his clothes, and approaches and picks up any object in the vicinity.

Very complex disorders of overall behaviour

At this level, the drives that underlie behaviour as a whole become disturbed in ways that carry the bizarre and pointless stamp of catatonia. Some stereotypies and mannerisms were considered by Bleuler to be expressed at this level: the patient's whole daily routine may assume a monotonous rhythmicity; every action is carried out with an almost photographic sameness. Gestures and demeanour become affected, pompous, a caricature of some cultural or subcultural style. Similarly, negativism, according to Bleuler, gives way by degrees into an all-pervading contrariness of attitude: patients insist on staying in bed when they should be getting up, and vice versa; they resist going for a meal and then refuse to leave the table once they have been taken there; they demand baths at unconventional temperatures and then complain that attempts are being made to scald or freeze them. The converse phenomenon of positivism probably also has its corresponding higher echelons: For example, Fish (Fish, 1962/Hamilton, 1984) described *advertence* where the patient always turns to the examiner when approached and begins talking, usually nonsense, until he is cut short, for example by walking away.

Catatonic stupor, *excitement* and *impulsiveness* also affect the patient's entire behaviour. In catatonic stupor the patient sits or lies motionless, expressionless, mute and often incontinent, and sometimes in a contorted posture. Typically the state is associated with other catatonic phenomena like grimacing, waxy flexibility and gegenhalten; occasionally the patient can be lifted up bodily without any alteration in position. Although unresponsive, there is evidence that the patient is aware of his surroundings; he may tense or blush when someone enters the room, or follow their movements around the room with his eyes. Sometimes such a patient, having been otherwise completely mute, will suddenly speak as the interviewer is leaving the room, the so-called *reaction of the last moment*.

Catatonic excitement consists of aimless overactivity, destructiveness and violence, from which the patient seems strangely disengaged and out of contact with the environment. Such patients run about naked, masturbate openly, bite crockery, destroy furniture, strip beds, embrace and kiss other patients only to violently assault them a second later. Manneristic and stereotyped actions, often of a complicated kind, are typically also woven into the presentation.

Catatonic impulsiveness refers to sudden, incomprehensible and often very violent acts that the patient can give no real account of. Often in a setting of stupor, the patient will suddenly rouse himself, knock over furniture, throw objects, strike another patient, set fire to his hair. Explanations like 'I had a sort of feeling to do that', and 'because it was desired' are given, or none at all.

Catatonic speech disorders

Speech, like any other motor activity, can be affected by catatonia, and once again the abnormalities can range from the simple to the highly complicated. In the simplest cases, speech may be interrupted by hawking, grunting, or other vocalisations. Or it may be *aprosodic*, with normal delivery being replaced by a flat monotone, peculiar scanning or affected intonations. Speech stereotypies and mannerisms are also seen: a word or phrase may be repeated over and over again (*palilalia*), the patient may speak in all kinds of accents, in infinitives and diminutives, or add -ism or -io to ever word. In *verbigeration* speech is replaced by more or less incomprehensible mumblings, among which a few repetitive words and phrases can be made out. *Echolalia* is the verbal counterpart of echopraxia. Finally, *mutism* often accompanies other catatonic symptoms.

Miscellaneous motor, volitional and behavioural disorders

Involuntary movement disorders

In the original description of catatonia, some of Kahlbaum's (1874) patients exhibited various spasmodic phenomena that would nowadays be classified as chorea, athetosis and dystonia. Kraepelin (1913a) also thought that some schizophrenic patients showed 'peculiar, sprawling, irregular, choreiform, outspreading movements'. Initially, Bleuler (1911), considered chorea and athetosis to be rarely if ever seen in schizophrenia, but later in 1930 (cited by Rogers, 1992) he came round to the view that there were some schizophrenic symptoms 'which are likewise found in various diseases of the basal ganglia'. Other convincing descriptions of similar involuntary movements in the days before neuroleptic treatment have since been collected (see Waddington, 1984; Rogers, 1992; Cunningham Owens, 1999).

These surprising observations have now been confirmed in contemporary studies. In the first of these, Owens *et al.* (1982) found, in the course of a survey of 510 chronically hospitalised patients with schizophrenia, 47 who had never been treated with neuroleptic drugs (this was mostly because they had been under the care of a psychiatrist who did not believe in drug treatment). The prevalence of tardive dyskinesia-like involuntary movements in these patients was found to be 43 per cent, a figure that was only slightly lower than that for the neuroleptic-treated patients in the study. McCreadie *et al.* (1996) found a prevalence of dyskinesia of 38 per cent in untreated chronic schizophrenic patients in rural India, one of the few areas where it is still possible to find such patients. Data from a number of studies of first episode schizophrenic patients who have not been exposed to neuroleptic treatment also suggest that spontaneous dyskinesias can be found, although at a much lower rate of approximately 4 per cent (Fenton, 2000).

Lack of volition

What Kraepelin (1913a) described as a 'permanent weakening in the main-springs of volition' continues to be recognised as one of the key negative symptoms of the disorder (see Chapter 2). Patients get up late, go to bed early and do little in between. They no longer bother to wash or shave, change their clothes only sporadically and let their teeth decay. There is no inclination to socialise, to follow former pursuits, and above all to work – unemployment is the rule in chronic schizophrenia. In extreme cases the patient may just sit in a chair all day, live in squalor, become infested, and so on. *Poverty of speech* can be regarded as the same disorder affecting speech, resulting in anything from a slight degree of taciturnity to something that shades into mutism. Nothing has equalled Kraepelin's (1913a) description of this symptom: 'The patients become monosyllabic, sparing of their words, speak hesitatingly, suddenly become mute, never relate anything on their own initiative, and let all answers be laboriously pressed out of them. They enter into no relations with other people, never begin a conversation with anyone, ask no questions, make no complaints, give their relatives no news.'

Non-specific abnormal behaviours

Fish (Fish, 1962/Hamilton, 1984) gave a graphic account of certain charac-teristic patterns of behaviour seen in chronic schizophrenic patients. One of these was incessant letter-writing. The letters themselves could be well laid out, or cover the paper in a scrawl with additions made longitudinally in the margins. Collecting and hoarding were also common. The pockets of male patients and the handbags of female patients could often be found to be full of rubbish – pieces of stale food, wood, matchsticks, grass, stones, dead insects, pieces of string, pieces of toilet paper and scraps of soap. One patient killed cats and other small animals, then wrapped them in cloth and stored them in her room; another caught and killed birds and then carried the carcasses around in her clothing. Wandering is another well-known occur-rence; at least a third and probably more like half of vagrants are chronic schizophrenics (Priest, 1976).

Emotional disorders

For psychiatric purposes, emotion is broken down into affect and mood. Although these terms are often used interchangeably, *affect* strictly refers to moment-to-moment emotional responses that are responsive to circumstance and environment. *Mood* on the other hand traditionally refers to longer-term, prevailing feeling states that tend to colour the individual's whole mental life.

Many clinicians also use the term affect to refer to emotionality as judged objectively by the interviewer, and mood to describe the patient's subjective account of his or her emotional state. Disorders of both affect and mood are recognised in schizophrenia; as affective flattening and inappropriateness, the former are particularly important and so are given the status of cardinal symptoms here.

Affective flattening and inappropriateness

Affective flattening, the core affective disorder in schizophrenia, eludes easy definition. According to Sims (2002), the subtleties of one's emotional state are constantly, and largely unintentionally, signalled to others, by facial expression, tone of voice, gesture, posture and 'body language'. This is registered by the other person and evokes reciprocal responses, so that a kind of emotional dialogue accompanies any verbal interaction between people. It is this that is diminished, lost or altered in schizophrenia. When mild, the effect is discernible, if somewhat intangible: there is, as Jaspers (1959) put it 'something queer, cold, rigid and petrified there'. When it is more marked, a restriction of the normal breadth of emotional expression and a definite lack of responsiveness to emotive topics can be pinpointed. When the disorder is severe, all emotional expression becomes impoverished and the patient exhibits a uniformly blank, withdrawn or peculiar manner.

For Kraepelin (1913a), affective flattening was, along with lack of volition, one of the two major components of the destructive effect of schizophrenia on the personality. Bleuler (1911) elevated affective flattening to the status of a fundamental symptom in schizophrenia (see Chapter 4), one which was 'present in every case and at every period of the illness', even if it could not always be recognised with certainty. Both these latter authors were at pains to point out that affective flattening had a range of different manifestations. These included coldness, indifference, shallowness, loss of delicacy of feeling, and lack of conviction of emotions when they were expressed.

Complicating and interrupting affective flattening, Kraepelin and Bleuler observed the appearance of sudden, intense emotional states, which were out of keeping with events or even completely causeless. Patients would fall into uncontrollable laughter or become inconsolably sad for no reason; they would laugh while recounting suicide attempts; become miserable or irritated on occasions for happiness; sometimes they could even seem to be simultaneously laughing and crying.

Affective flattening has been found to be present in between a third to two-thirds of acute schizophrenic patients (Andreasen, 1979b; Boeringa and Castellani, 1979); inappropriateness, however, is uncommon. Both become considerably more common in chronic schizophrenia. Authors interested in developing scales for assessing affective flattening (Abrams and Taylor, 1978; Andreasen, 1979b; Andreasen and Olsen, 1982; Mortimer *et al.*, 1989) have also rediscovered the point made by classical authors, that the phenomenonon is multifaceted. Based on their studies the following tentative classification of schizophrenic affective abnormality is offered.

Affective unresponsiveness

Perhaps the most important element of affective flattening, this refers to a narrowing or constriction in the range of emotions expressed during normal conversation or in the course of an interview. The patient fails to smile in response to social cues; other facial expressions, gestures and expressive postures are reduced in range or completely absent; and there is an apparent indifference to emotive topics. When severe, the abnormality is easy to recognise, but at the mild end of the spectrum experienced clinicians often disagree over whether or not it is present. The usual rule of thumb is that it can be regarded as being present when a patient discusses what would normally be distressing experiences (usually but not always delusions or hallucinations) with obvious lack of concern.

Emotional withdrawal

This was repeatedly alluded to by classical authors and describes an aloofness that is easily recognisable but difficult to describe. Sometimes there is nothing more than a certain lack of the normal rapport that is established when two people converse. When more severe, the patient seems wrapped up in his own concerns, distracted, or alternatively cold and detached. The abnormality tends to be seen in association with affective unresponsiveness.

Inappropriate affect

This describes a tendency to express emotions incompatible with the subject under discussion. In practice it almost always takes the form of smiling or laughing while discussing distressing topics, such as persecutory delusions, derogatory auditory hallucinations or suicidal ideas. The term is often also extended to include unprovoked, causeless laughter. The available evidence indicates that inappropriate affect occurs independently of affective unresponsiveness and emotional withdrawal (it is part of the disorganisation rather than the negative syndrome – see Chapter 2).

Shallowness, coarsening and blunting of affect

This term groups together, partly for convenience, disorders where emotional expression lacks subtlety, refinement and sensitivity, or appears to be without depth or conviction. Blunting of affect is often used as a synonym for affective flattening, but this and the closely similar coarsening of affect are conceptually quite different from affective unresponsiveness and instead refer to what Kraepelin described as the 'loss of the delicacy of emotion'. For example, Sims (2002) described a schizophrenic woman who, with obvious relish for the sensational effect, took her visitors upstairs to view the corpse of her mother who had been dead for two days.

Retardation of affect

This was originally described by Bleuler (1911), and a similar term *stiffening of affect* was used by Fish (Fish, 1962/Hamilton, 1984). Both terms refer to a slowing of changes in emotional expression and the maintenance of any given affect for too long. This affective disorder has since been largely neglected in the literature, and is almost certainly uncommon.

Miscellaneous abnormalities of mood

Mood colourings

Drawing a distinction from affective flattening, Bleuler (1911) described the occurrence of certain 'basic moods' in schizophrenia. These were seen particularly in chronic patients and took the form of a monotonous bonhomie, moroseness, irritability, querulousness or some other emotion, which formed a backdrop for the expression of all other symptoms. The moods could be fairly transient, but more commonly tended to persist without much variation for years or decades. Inevitably, the prevailing mood was one of depression or elation in a proportion of cases. In such patients, Bleuler maintained that the quality of the mood change could be distinguished from that seen in manic-depressive psychosis. The question of just how far depression and elation can be considered to form part of schizophrenia is discussed further in Chapter 13.

Perplexity

This is typically seen in schizophrenia at the beginning of an acute exacerbation. The patient appears to be in a bemused state, sometimes tinged with anxiousness, suspiciousness or rapture, and searches the environment restlessly asking repetitive questions. The disorder is closely associated with delusional mood and has been argued to be the objective counterpart of this (delusional mood can, however, be described by a patient without there being any obvious evidence of perplexity). Perplexity is not specific to schizophrenia and can occur in organic confusional states, major depression and also in normal individuals following exposure to severe emotional stress.

Schneider's first rank symptoms

Out of the many symptoms of schizophrenia, Schneider (1958) put eight in the 'first rank of importance'. These were all subjectively described experiences and comprised: audible thoughts; voices heard arguing; voices heard commenting on one's actions; the experience of influences playing on the body; thought withdrawal and other interferences with thought; diffusion of thought; delusional perception; and all feelings, impulses (drives) and volitional acts that are experienced by the patient as the work or influence of others. Schneider made no claim that these symptoms were new; many of them had in fact already been described by Kraepelin and Bleuler. Nor, in his view, did they have any particular contribution to make to the understanding of schizophrenia, although he speculated that some first rank symptoms might have a common phenomenological basis in a 'lowering of the barrier between the self and the surrounding world'. Instead, their value was diagnostic: in the absence of any organic illness, Schneider considered the presence of any one of them to be decisive evidence for a psychosis being schizophrenic.

Concepts of what constitute first rank symptoms and how they should be classified have evolved and changed since Schneider's description (see Koehler, 1979). The following account is a synthesis of the descriptions of Mellor (1970), Wing *et al.* (1974) and Sims (2002). Some examples, which are taken from Mellor (1970), are shown in Box 1.4.

Box 1.4 Examples of first rank symptoms (from Mellor (1970), First-rank symptoms of schizophrenia. *British Journal of Psychiatry*, 117, 15–23. Reproduced with permission from the Royal College of Psychiatrists)

Special forms of auditory hallucination
Patient who heard a quiet voice with an Oxford accent and immediately experienced whatever the voice was saying as his own thoughts. When he read the newspaper the voice would speak aloud whatever his eyes fell on (*audible thoughts*). One voice, deep in pitch, repeatedly said to a patient 'G.T. is a bloody paradox'. Another, higher in pitch said 'He is that, he should be locked up'. A female voice occasionally interrupted, saying 'He is not, he is a lovely man' (*voices arguing*). Patient who heard a voice from across the road describing everything she was doing in a flat monotone. 'She is peeling potatoes, got hold of the peeler, she does not want that potato, she is putting it back because she thinks it has a knobble like a penis, she has a dirty mind.' (*thought commentary*).

Passivity experiences
Patient who felt X-rays entering her neck, passing down his back and disappearing into his pelvis. These were accompanied by warmth, tingling and then coldness and prevented him from getting an erection (*somatic passivity*). Patient who felt that others were projecting unhappiness and other emotions onto her brain (*made feelings*). Patient who stated 'when I reach

my hand for the comb it is my hand and arm which move and my fingers pick up the pen, but I don't control them. I sit there watching them move, and they are quite independent . . . I am just a puppet who is manipulated by cosmic strings' (*made volitional acts*).

Alienation of thought
Patient who felt that Eamonn Andrews (a British TV personality) treated her mind like a screen and flashed his thoughts on to it 'like you flash a picture' (*thought insertion*). Patient who stated, 'I am thinking about my mother, and suddenly my thoughts are sucked out of my head by a phrenological vacuum cleaner, and there is nothing in my mind, it is empty' (*thought withdrawal*). Patient who said, 'As I think, my thoughts leave my head on a type of mental ticker-tape. Everyone around has only to pass the tape through their mind and they know my thoughts' (*thought broadcasting*).

Delusional perception
At breakfast, a patient felt a sense of unease, that something was going to happen. One of his fellow lodgers pushed the salt cellar towards him, and as it reached him he realised that he must return home 'to greet the Pope who is visiting Ireland, to see his family and reward them because Our Lord is going to be born again to one of the women. And because of this they are all born different with their private parts back to front'.

Special forms of auditory hallucination

Audible thoughts (*gedankenlautwerden, echo de la pensée, thought echo*) are auditory hallucinations that speak the patient's thoughts aloud. The experience may precede, occur simultaneously with, or follow the thought, but the content of both is the same; symptoms such as voices answering thoughts, talking about them or saying the opposite of them may additionally be present. In *voices arguing*, two or more voices discuss the patient. In *thought commentary*, one or more voices comment on the patient's actions, describing them as they occur, and often providing a running commentary with derogatory asides. In these latter two first rank symptoms, the voices typically refer to the patient in the third person. As a consequence any form of *third-person auditory hallucinations* have come to be regarded as a first rank symptom.

Passivity experiences (made experiences, delusions of control)

Somatic passivity is Schneider's experience of influences playing on the body. The patient describes bodily sensations, heat, pain, sexual excitement, and so on, as being imposed on him by some external agency in an immediate and vivid way. The same phenomenon can apply to emotions, as *made feelings*; to irresistible urges as *made impulses*; and most importantly to movements and speech as *made volitional acts*. Schneider considered all these experiences to be first rank in nature, but not all subsequent authors have agreed (see Koehler, 1979). Wing *et al.* (1974) referred to made volitional acts as *delusions of control*. They specified the essence of the symptom as the experience of one's will being replaced by that of some other force or agency, and included as examples the belief that someone else's words are coming out using the patient's voice, that what he writes is not his own, or that he is the victim of possession – a zombie or a robot controlled by someone else.

Thought interference (thought alienation, disorders of the possession of thought)

In *thought withdrawal*, the subject feels that his thoughts are being taken from his mind, typically leaving it completely empty. Wing *et al.* (1974) consider this symptom to be a delusional interpretation of another symptom, also considered by some (see Koehler, 1979) to by a first rank symptom, *thought block*, where the patient reports that all thinking suddenly and unexpectedly comes to a complete halt; such patients typically say they have no thoughts in their head for minutes or hours at a time. *Thought insertion* refers to experiencing thoughts in one's mind that lack the quality of being one's own. Usually, but not always, some outside agency is invoked to account for this. *Thought broadcasting, diffusion or sharing* describes a patient's feeling that his thoughts are not contained within his mind, that they are made public and often that they are projected over a wide area. The symptom differs from the more common and non-first rank delusion of thoughts being read by virtue of being indiscriminate – the patient feels that his thoughts are freely available to all and sundry. In many, but according to Wing *et al.* not all, cases the phenomenon appears to be a delusional explanation of audible thoughts.

Delusional perception

Schneider (1949, 1958) applied this term to a variety of experiences in which abnormal, self-referential significance became attached to environmental events, among which he clearly included delusions of reference and misinterpretation. As these phenomena are not generally accepted as being diagnostic of schizophrenia, various refinements of his definition have been proposed with the aim of making it more restrictive. In one such attempt, it has been argued that, whereas in a delusion of reference significance is merely triggered off by perception of neutral events in the environment, in delusional perception the significance is somehow contained within the perception itself (see Koehler, 1979). This argument is difficult to follow by anyone other than mid-twentieth-century German psychopathologists, and so a more mundane alternative has been developed by British psychiatrists (Fish, 1962; Mellor, 1970; Wing *et al.*, 1974). They suggest that the sense of meaning, which is vague and unspecified in delusions of reference, becomes explicit and immediate in delusional perception. On perceiving a neutral event, a delusional interpretation of it, which is usually elaborate, drops fully formed into the patient's head.

Conclusion

This listing of schizophrenic symptoms is far from exhaustive. A number of special forms of delusion, for instance the Capgras syndrome, and a variety of abnormalities in perception, of the body, of self and of time, are recognised to occur in schizophrenia and cannot be done justice to in a single chapter. In addition to psychotic phenomena, a wealth of neurotic, depressive and non-specific symptoms are commonplace among schizophrenic patients and form an important source of their suffering. A more detailed account of these other symptoms can be found in textbooks on psychopathology, notably that by Sims (2002).

The ways in which schizophrenic symptoms combine with each other are just as erratic and complicated as the phenomena themselves. Virtually any symptom may occur in complete, or perhaps more accurately, almost complete isolation. Alternatively, there are undoubtedly patients who can be found to be experiencing an exceptionally wide range of delusions and hallucinations, who also exhibit significant formal thought disorder, affective flattening and even a smattering of catatonic phenomena. While it is probably safe to assume that any particular schizophrenic symptom can be seen in association with any other, certain groupings nevertheless appear with regularity. It is these recurring themes in the clinical presentation of schizophrenia that form the subject of the next chapter.

2 The clinical pictures of schizophrenia

Schizophrenia, as brought into being by Kraepelin in 1896 (see Cutting and Shepherd, 1987), was the synthesis of three converging lines of argument. First, he made the observation that three existing forms of insanity, catatonia (described by Kahlbaum in 1874), hebephrenia (described by Kahlbaum's follower, Hecker in 1871, see Sedler, 1985) and dementia paranoides (described by another of Kahlbaum's followers, Kraepelin himself), were all characterised by a course that led inexorably to deterioration. Second, he argued that the features of the three disorders were not sharply demarcated from one another and transitional forms were regularly encountered. Finally, he observed that the disorders all had other features in common: they all tended to develop in early adult life, there was no notable depression or elation of mood, and indicators of the ultimate poor outcome were present from the earliest stages. Kraepelin therefore concluded that the three forms of insanity should be brought together into a single disorder, dementia praecox, a series of outwardly divergent states, whose common characteristic was 'a peculiar destruction of the internal connections of the psychic personality', and which followed a course ending in 'a more or less well marked mental enfeeblement'.

Renaming dementia praecox as schizophrenia, Bleuler (1911) felt that the diversity of its presentations was so great that it might be more proper to speak of a group of schizophrenias. Possibly in an attempt to reconcile this wide range of symptomatology with the concept of a unitary disorder, he went out of his way to describe a series of subdivisions of the clinical picture. To the paranoid, hebephrenic and catatonic forms distinguished by Kraepelin, he added a fourth variety, simple schizophrenia (which Diem in 1903 had recently described as a separate disorder, simple dementia). He highlighted the fact that the course could be chronic or marked by intermittent attacks, and described the different presentations of the latter in detail. Finally he proposed that on theoretical grounds schizophrenic symptoms themselves were divisible into two types, *fundamental*, which were always present and specific for schizophrenia, and *accessory*, which could come and go and were seen in other forms of psychosis as well.

Contained in Kraepelin's and Bleuler's accounts were the seeds of all later approaches to the subclassification of schizophrenia. The distinction between intermittent attacks of symptoms and the development of permanent disability has been preserved as acute and chronic schizophrenia. The differentiation of paranoid, hebephrenic, catatonic and simple forms of schizophrenia has, via a circuitous series of modifications, also survived. Finally, it is not stretching the truth too far to maintain that Bleuler's proposal of a broad division of symptoms into fundamental and accessory types has as its legacy the contemporary positive:negative dichotomy in schizophrenia.

Acute and chronic schizophrenia

Viewing schizophrenia from a longitudinal perspective, Kraepelin (1913a) and Bleuler (1911) felt that only two statements could be made with certainty. The first of these was that in many cases the disorder began with a discrete attack of symptoms, which was followed by improvement and then further exacerbations. The second was that that sooner or later a state of permanent, relatively immutable deterioration was reached. Acute attacks tended to be commoner in the first few years, although they were not unknown later in the course of illness. Signs of deterioration became unmistakeable in the majority of cases within two to three years. It was in this rather uncertain way, hedged with reservations and qualifications, that the distinction between acute and chronic phases of schizophrenia was first drawn.

Acute schizophrenia

This was given its first detailed description by Bleuler (1911). Under the heading of acute syndromes, he detailed a series of presentations of new symptoms or worsenings of existing ones. These could set in out of the blue or after a prodrome of non-specific symptoms, and could last from as little as a few hours to as long as several years. Most commonly such episodes were characterised by delusions and hallucinations. These could be accompanied by pronounced mood colourings, formal thought disorder and catatonic phenomena especially of a hypo- or hyperkinetic kind. Rather less frequently the picture was predominantly one of dreaminess, abstraction, clouding, or torpor. Occasionally, an episode could consist of little more than fits of anger or attacks of screaming.

The term acute schizophrenia, and closely related terms like exacerbations, thrusts, shifts and phases soon became part of the vocabulary of schizophrenia. The connotation of development of new symptoms or worsening of old ones was retained, and the implication of fairly recent onset of illness became virtually a prerequisite. But beyond this the literature on acute schizophrenia remained nebulous – clinicians were familiar with the clinical pictures encountered, but descriptions of them remained sparse and insubstantial. Acute schizophrenia became little more than a convenient label for any change in a patient's condition that required treatment or hospitalisation.

In the 1970s, however, a formal reassessment of the meaning of acute schizophrenia took place. This was as a by-product of a large-scale investigation, the International Pilot Study of Schizophrenia (WHO, 1973), which was undertaken to determine whether schizophrenia existed and could be reliably diagnosed across different cultures (this study is described in detail in Chapter 4). The patient sample consisted of over 1200 referrals to hospital psychiatric services, all of whom received an extremely detailed clinical assessment using a version of the Present State Examination. All the patients were required to have had an onset of illness within the last five years, to have experienced persistent symptoms for less than three years, and to have spent overall less than two years in hospital. Out of this group, 811 were given a consensus diagnosis of schizophrenia.

In this group of operationally defined cases of acute schizophrenia, virtually every class of schizophrenic symptom was found. The 15 most frequent of these are shown in Table 2.1. The commonest symptom was lack of insight, which was present in over 80 per cent of cases. Delusions and 'predelusional' symptoms like suspiciousness and delusional mood were present in around half, and auditory hallucinations were only slightly less frequent. Flatness of affect and poor rapport were also common, at just over and just under 50 per cent of cases, respectively. Thought alienation was the only class of first rank symptoms to feature among the 15 most frequent symptoms, being present in approximately a third of cases.

Formal thought disorder was an uncommon symptom in this study, being present in only 7.6 per cent of cases. Catatonic symptoms were present at a similar low frequency (5 per cent were rated on in 'qualitative psychomotor disorder', consisting of negativism, overcompliance, stereotypies, grimacing,

Table 2.1 15 most frequent symptoms in 811 acute schizophrenic patients

Symptom	Frequency (%)
Lack of insight	84.1
Inadequate description	64.5
Suspiciousness	60.2
Unwilling to cooperate	57.5
Ideas of reference	54.8
Flatness of affect	51.9
Delusions of persecution	51.8
Delusions of reference	49.6
Delusional mood	48.7
Poor rapport	47.0
Auditory hallucinations	42.3
Verbal hallucinations	38.0
Voices speaking to patient	35.6
Thought alienation	34.2
Gloomy thoughts	32.9

Source: WHO (1973). *The International Pilot Study of Schizophrenia.* Geneva, World Health Organization, 1973, Table 10.5. Reproduced by permission.

posturing, mannerisms, waxy flexibility and also hallucinatory behaviour, and 8 per cent on 'quantitative psychomotor disorder', comprising overactivity, retardation, stupor and repetitive movements). Depression, elation, and anxiety were all present in less than 20 per cent of patients. Another non-psychotic symptom, derealisation, was present in just over 20 per cent of patients.

Chronic schizophrenia

If credit for delineating acute schizophrenia belongs to Bleuler, that for chronic schizophrenia has to go to Kraepelin (1913a), who provided the first, and what has subsequently proved to be the only, detailed account of the clinical pictures encompassed by this term. He separated a number of different states from each other on the basis of their severity and special characteristics. While he considered that these were to some extent distinct, he also recognised that all kinds of transitional forms could be seen, and that in individual cases transformations from a milder to a more severe presentation could sometimes take place.

Kraepelin termed the mildest form of chronic schizophrenia *simple weak-mindedness*. After the florid phenomena of an acute episode had subsided, the patient was left odd, stiff, constrained, awkward and sometimes eccentric in manner. A degree of affective flattening was noticeable, often overlaid with mood colourings of suspiciousness, moroseness, irritability, and so on. Lack of volition showed itself in an inability to manage at a previous level of occupation or in a disinclination to do work of any kind. A degree of poverty of speech was also common. Thinking was narrowed and impoverished, and a certain weakness of judgement manifested itself when complicated decisions had to be made. An example of such a case, which was quite severe and is also notable for its description of orofacial dyskinesia before the introduction of neuroleptic drugs (see Chapter 1), is presented in Box 2.1.

Box 2.1 Kraepelin's 'simple weak-mindedness' (from Kraepelin, 1905)

The patient, a 21-year-old man, had become unwell some time previously. He believed his illness was a result of masturbation, which was a sin against the sixth commandment. As a result his power of working was reduced, he felt languid and miserable, and he had become a hypochondriac. He was concerned that he had a rupture and was suffering from wasting of the spinal cord. He had stopped seeing friends because he believed that they knew about this and were making fun of him about it.

The patient was 'delicate' as a child and was described as reserved and stubborn. He had become more and more solitary over the previous few years, and was preoccupied with the belief that he was ugly and laughed at by his brothers and sisters. Although he did quite well at school, he failed to complete university entrance examinations. He then began crying a great deal, masturbated, ran about aimlessly, was occasionally excited and disturbed at night, played senseless tunes on the piano, and began to write obscure observations on life.

In hospital he was in a state of excitement for several days, during which he chattered in a confused way, made faces, ran about, wrote in disconnected scraps, which were crossed and recrossed with flourishes and meaningless combinations of letters. After this a tranquil state ensued. The patient would lie in bed for weeks and months, or sit around without feeling the slightest need to occupy himself, or at best turning over the pages of a book. He would stare ahead with expressionless features, over which a vacant smile would occasionally play. When he had visitors he would sit without showing any interest, did not ask about what was happening at home, hardly ever greeted his parents, and went back indifferently to the ward. Occasionally he wrote a letter to the doctor, expressing all kinds of distorted half-formed ideas, with a peculiar and silly play on words. For example he begged for 'a little more allegro in the treatment', and 'liberationary movement with a view to the widening of the horizon', and 'nota bene for God's sake only does not wish to be combined with the club of the harmless.'

When interviewed, the patient gave a correct account of his past experiences. He knew where he was and how long he had been in hospital, but was only very imperfectly acquainted with the names of the people around him, and said that he had never asked about them. He made all statements about his earlier symptoms in an indifferent tone of voice, without looking up or troubling about his surroundings. His expression betrayed no emotion; he only laughed for a moment now and then. There was occasional wrinkling of the forehead or facial spasm. Round the mouth and nose a fine, changing twitching was constantly observed. He made his statements slowly and in monosyllables, not because his wish to answer met with hindrance, but because he felt no desire to speak at all. All his movements were languid and expressionless. There was no sign of emotional dejection, such as one would expect from the nature of his talk, and the patient remained quite dull throughout, experiencing neither fear nor hope nor desires. He was not at all deeply affected by what was going on around him although he understood it without any difficulty. It was all the same to him who appeared and disappeared, or who talked to him and took care of him, and he did not even once ask their names.

He was returned to the care of his family unchanged.

The degree of deterioration could vary considerably. Some patients would merely seem a little quieter than before, more absent-minded, but remain steady, careful and precise workers in jobs that did not require any responsibility. Others would do nothing, 'absolutely refuse to work', or just sit staring. There were also qualititative variations in the state. Some patients became taciturn, shy, withdrawn, or avoided people. Others were over-familiar, talked too much, displayed signs of slight excitement, acted impulsively or became promiscuous – one of Kraepelin's patients, previously a respectable girl, gave birth to three illegitimate children in five years, one of which she smothered through carelessness.

In *hallucinatory* and *paranoid weak-mindedness*, the above changes were complicated by the continuing presence of hallucinations, delusions or both. These symptoms, however, tended to be much less preoccupying than during the acute phase. Even though auditory hallucinations might be as frequent as before, the patient no longer talked openly about them; they were no longer distressing, merely irritating. Delusions, especially persecutory, remained firmly held, and even became more fantastic and nonsensical, but were recited in a monotonous, unelaborated way; peculiarly stoic or inconsequential attitudes were adopted to the imagined persecution. The patients remained lucid on the whole, but when they touched on their delusions they could become incoherent. Other minor symptoms, such as mannerisms, the stereotyped repetition of questions and stilted speech, could sometimes be seen.

More severe chronic states took a multiplicity of presentations. Kraepelin recognised five main types, which he called *drivelling*, *dull*, *silly*, *manneristic*, and *negativistic dementia*. The common denominator of these states was marked affective flattening and impairment of volition, coupled with a striking impoverishment of all mental life. Such patients showed a complete emotional indifference, or alternatively a rigid inaccessibility, which was interrupted by causeless silly laughter, tearfulness, fits of anger, and so on. Many would do nothing or lie in bed all day. Others might be temporarily rousable to carry out some kind of simple work, but if left to themselves, would soon sink back into a state of complete apathy. Some were mute or nearly so.

Sometimes delusions, hallucinations, and formal thought disorder were far in the background, and made only a minor contribution to a clinical picture dominated by severe apathy and self-neglect. In other cases delusions and hallucinations, or formal thought disorder, or both, remained continuously present, often in a very florid form. Such patients would express a wealth of fantastic delusional beliefs, be hallucinated in all modalities, or show completely incoherent speech. Catatonic phenomena, in the form of minor stereotypies, mannerisms, echophenomena, and so on, or sometimes as a more pronounced feature, became common among all such patients. Sometimes catatonic symptoms dominated the picture, as manneristic or negativistic deterioration.

Sometimes, in what Kraepelin called silly dementia, the picture was one of impulsiveness and weak susceptibility to influence rather than apathy. Such patients were active and kept themselves occupied, albeit with aimless and repetitive activities. They would do things like decorate themselves, play with dolls, pull faces, 'chat casually about intimate matters', and speak in an affected way. They were also childish, thoughtless, impulsive, easily led, completely lacking in judgement, and sometimes showed a restlessness which drove them to all kinds of foolish and reckless behaviour. Their mood was often one of cheerful confidence, but they were also prone to sudden excitements and outbursts of rage and agitation. Active psychotic symptoms were often entirely lacking in these patients.

Since Kraepelin's account, next to nothing has been written about chronic schizophrenia. Mayer-Gross et al. (1969) spoke of the schizophrenic patient coming, as the years went by, to an arrangement with his illness. As a degree of stability was achieved, apathy, flattening of affect and mannerisms grew to rule the clinical picture, and behaviour, thought and attitudes became narrow and inflexible. Delusions and hallucinations, if they did not fade away altogether, became colourless, repetitive and lost much of their emotional impact. On the other hand formal thought disorder tended to become a more conspicuous part of the clinical picture. Wing and co-workers (Wing and Brown, 1970; Wing, 1978), as discussed below, were the first to draw attention to a common thread of symptoms and behaviours in chronic schizophrenia – affective flattening, slowness of thought and movement, underactivity, lack of drive, poverty of speech and social withdrawal – which they termed the 'clinical poverty' syndrome. The writings of Fish (1962/ Hamilton, 1984) are noteworthy for his accounts of the very degraded ways in which many chronically hospitalised patients behave: he described them becoming very filthy, smearing faeces, spitting on other patients, and stealing food and cigarettes from them. Fish was one of the very few authors to acknowledge that chronically hospitalised schizophrenic patients are sometimes incontinent.

Some objective confirmation of the picture of chronic schizophrenia comes from two contemporary studies. One of these is, once again, the International Pilot Study of Schizophrenia. Two years after the initial survey, 543 of the original 811 schizophrenic patients were re-examined (WHO, 1979). Although the interval between the two assessments was relatively short, clear differences in the pattern of symptoms had emerged. The 15 most common symptoms at this time are shown in Table 2.2. The frequency of delusions and auditory hallucinations was much lower, and three other florid symptoms, delusional mood, voices speaking to the patient and thought alienation, had dropped out of the list altogether. Replacing them were symptoms like apathy, restricted speech and autism (emotional withdrawal), corresponding to a picture of evolving deterioration.

At the more severe end of the spectrum, Owens and co-workers (Owens and Johnstone, 1980; Owens et al., 1985a) surveyed 510 patients meeting diagnostic criteria for schizophrenia who had been continuously hospitalised for more than a year, and whose average duration of stay was 26 years. Approximately a third showed active psychotic symptoms, just under a third showed marked flattening of affect and/or lack of volition, and a third showed both. A picture of ongoing very florid symptoms was not uncommon – just under 20 per cent scored maximally on the delusions and hallucination

Table 2.2 15 most frequent symptoms in 543 schizophrenic patients two years after acute presentation

Symptom	Frequency (%)
Lack of insight	42.5
Flatness of affect	27.1
Poor rapport	26.3
Inadequate description	25.2
Suspiciousness	25.2
Unwilling to cooperate	24.5
Apathy	18.8
Ideas of reference	18.0
Delusions of reference	14.2
Restricted speech	12.9
Autism (emotional withdrawal)	12.7
Delusions of persecution	12.7
Hypochondriacal/neurasthenic complaints	12.7
Auditory hallucinations	11.6
Verbal hallucinations	10.7

Note: The absolute rates for symptoms are generally lower than for acute patients because of the high proportion of patients with few or no symptoms of any kind.

Source: Adapted from WHO (1979).

items of the rating scale used and 7 per cent scored maximally on incoherence of speech. Disturbed and deteriorated behaviour were very common, and a sizeable minority of patients were 'only able to conform to the rudiments of acceptable behaviour'. A final surprising finding was that, despite requiring chronic hospitalisation, 7 per cent of the patients surveyed appeared to be free of all active psychotic symptoms and exhibited no marked deterioration.

The classical subtypes of schizophrenia

Schizophrenia was the outcome of a merger between four disorders previously thought to be independent entities, Kahlbaum's catatonia, Hecker's hebephrenia, Kraepelin's dementia paranoides and Diem's simple dementia. One of the reasons Kraepelin (1913a) felt that these could be combined was that 'between them there are such numerous transitions that in spite of all efforts it appears impossible at present to delimit them sharply'. To which Bleuler (1911) added that each form had the potential to transform into another: 'a case which begins as a hebephrenic may be a paranoid several years later'. Nevertheless, both authors felt that a sizeable proportion of cases retained their paranoid, hebephrenic or catatonic stamp throughout the course of their illness. This distinctiveness was typically most marked at initial presentation, but it was also evident in the manner of progression, and was even discernible as subtle differences in the severity and character of the terminal state.

The following descriptions of the classical subtypes of schizophrenia are based on those of Kraepelin (1907, 1913a) and Bleuler (1911), which remain unmatched in richness of detail. Following their format an idealised form of each subtype is presented first and this is followed by some of the variants that tend to be met with in practice. (It should be remembered that the symptoms and courses are those of schizophrenia as unmodified by treatment.)

Paranoid schizophrenia

In this form, delusions and hallucinations are to the forefront of the clinical picture continuously or for long periods of time.

The typical first sign is a feeling of change that may or may not amount to delusional mood. This gives way to suspiciousness and ill-formed persecutory and grandiose delusions. Gradually, or in some cases suddenly, these then go on to acquire complete conviction. Later, derogatory verbal auditory hallucinations set in, and become incorporated into what by this time is a complex delusional system involving plots, conspiracies, and the like. Other hallucinations, particularly somatic hallucinations, may follow. The patient becomes increasingly withdrawn and isolated and he may not dare to leave his home; alternatively he may move repeatedly on the basis of imagined persecution.

Sooner or later disturbed behaviour, squalid living conditions, or a violent act based on delusions precipitates admission to hospital. The persecutory delusions are by now very florid and hallucinations may be present in all modalities. Formal thought disorder can also be a prominent feature at this stage.

Once the patient is in hospital, improvement takes place. The florid symptoms clear up completely or nearly completely, and there appears to be little in the way of residual disability. Nevertheless, once discharged the patient does not manage outside hospital for very long. Attempts to get re-established in work fail: the patient may not apply himself, or fails to turn up regularly, or is simply no longer able to get along with his co-workers. Active symptoms recur at some point and further hospitalisation becomes necessary. This time recovery is slower. The delusions and hallucinations do not recede completely, and signs of lack of volition become more obvious.

Ultimately a more or less stable end state is reached. The overall severity of this may vary dramatically, but is most commonly one of mild or moderate deterioration. The patient's delusions lose their force and no longer exert any influence over his behaviour. Lack of volition and self-neglect are readily apparent, but affective flattening may be only slight. Typically, the patient is indifferent, apathetic and lives from day to day without ambition or goals. He may manage to carry on some work in hospital, but only mechanically and without initiative. In favourable circumstances he may even maintain himself outside hospital. Just occasionally, the chronic state is marked mainly by persistent delusions and hallucinations, with any deterioration being so far in the background that the patient remains capable of steady work, even, it is said, notable achievements.

Commonly, this pattern is not adhered to and the illness follows a more irregular course. Florid symptoms may appear suddenly, out of the blue, or emerge only after a prolonged prodromal phase of non-specific symptoms. Rather than there being a more or less smooth development of symptoms, the course may be one of swings and oscillations with returns to near-normality in between. The delusions may be predominantly grandiose, religious or hypochondriacal rather than persecutory. Instead of being relatively fixed they can be fluid and constantly changing. Some patients experience only delusions; others only hallucinations. Catatonic phenomena of every kind can intrude into the clinical picture.

Hebephrenic schizophrenia

In this form the leading symptoms are formal thought disorder coupled with affective flattening and incongruity, which become superimposed on a particularly severe form of deterioration.

In most cases symptoms develop gradually, even insidiously, over many years, but in a minority the onset is acute or subacute. The first symptoms tend to be vague: absentmindedness, dreaminess or forgetfulness; the patient complains of lassitude, nervousness, or irritability; performance at school or work falls off. More serious abnormalities then appear: he stands around, stares into space, talks to himself. Behaviour becomes increasingly bizarre; aimless purchases are made, money is squandered, and all kinds of pointless and childish pranks are engaged in.

Sooner or later the diagnosis is clarified by the appearance of delusions. These tend to be multiple, ill formed, poorly sustained and often fantastic. Hallucinations are usually only present to a minor degree and may be absent altogether. They are also commonly visual or somatic rather than auditory. Formal thought disorder, on the other hand, is a prominent feature, especially poverty of content of speech and stilted speech. The emotional state may or may not be in keeping with the delusions that the patient expresses, but is shallow, coarsened and subject to sudden fluctuations; the patients laugh and cry for no reason and break out into obscenities on trivial provocation. Catatonic phenomena may complicate the picture, but usually only to a minor extent.

In a few cases this form of schizophrenia follows a fluctuating course punctuated by periods of considerable improvement. In the majority, however, there is a more or less smooth progression to a state of deterioration that is usually more severe than that of paranoid schizophrenia and against the background of which formal thought disorder, inappropriate affect and bizarre behaviour remain conspicuous. Some cases merely show a uniform dull affective flattening; in others catatonic phenomena become more prominent. Few of these patients are able to survive outside hospital, and hebephrenic end states are commonplace among the institutionalised populations of mental hospitals.

Hebephrenic schizophrenia was originally considered to appear early, at around the time of puberty. Age, however, did not figure in Kraepelin's later descriptions and was dismissed as irrelevant by Bleuler. This latter author also extended the concept of hebephrenia to include virtually all cases in which there was no distinct paranoid or catatonic colouring. In his view, hebephrenic schizophrenia was characterised by deterioration where hallucinations, delusions, formal thought disorder and even catatonic symptoms could complicate the clinical picture without ever dominating it.

Catatonic schizophrenia

This form of schizophrenia is characterised by the presence of multiple motor, volitional and behavioural disorders of the kind described in the previous chapter, which almost invariably develop against a background of stupor, excitement or alternations between the two.

Catatonic schizophrenia may commence abruptly, evolve over weeks or months, or have a more insidious onset. In the latter cases an essentially non-specific prodrome, of quietness, withdrawal, absentmindedness, and so on, gives way at some point to florid delusions, hallucinations and formal thought disorder. At this stage bizarre acts or self-neglect are frequently disproportionately prominent. The catatonic nature of the disorder then declares itself by the appearance of stupor or excitement. This often has an abrupt onset, but stupor may evolve quite slowly. Stupor and excitement tend to alternate, but in a wholly irregular way; sometimes one or the other phase may be no more than a brief interlude; occasionally a mixed state of stupor and excitement is seen, as in patients who dance about mute or lie motionless singing. As well as the entire range of individual catatonic phenomena, extravagant delusions, hallucinations of all types and formal thought disorder of an extreme kind may be incorporated into the clinical picture.

At some point, often unexpectedly, improvement then sets in. The excited patient becomes quiet, the stuporose patient gradually starts to take up activities again. At this stage the outcome can be favourable, and some patients show degrees of improvement approximating to full recovery. In other cases an otherwise excellent remission is spoilt only by the continuing presence of minor stereotypies and mannerisms. But in at least half of all cases the remission is clearly incomplete.

Subsequently, sometimes only after several years have elapsed, further attacks follow. After one attack, signs of deterioration become obvious and go on to worsen with each subsequent episode. The terminal state is one of severe deterioration – the most profound of any of the subtypes according to Kraepelin – in which remnants of stereotypies and mannerisms can be discerned and which are often pervaded by a continuous mild stupor or excitement.

For Kraepelin, stupor and/or excitement were always evident in catatonic schizophrenia, even though the hypo- or hyperkinesia could be quite subtle. Bleuler, however, included presentations that had a catatonic flavour from the outset, and finally developed into a state with negativism, mutism and other clear-cut catatonic phenomena, but in which stupor or excitement never featured.

Simple schizophrenia

This form, which did not form part of Kraepelin's original concept of schizophrenia, but whose inclusion Bleuler successfully argued for, consists essentially of a slowly progressive impoverishment of mental life without development of florid symptoms.

The onset can often be traced to adolescence; occasionally it seems to go back even earlier. A student begins to fail in his studies; an officer leaves the army to start a string of unsuccessful businesses; a well-qualified teacher takes up a succession of temporary positions and engages in disastrous financial dealings. Hand in hand, there is a change in temperament, with depression, irritability, stubbornness or hypochondriacal concerns. There is a narrowing of interests and the patient becomes cold, unsympathetic and estranged from his family. As the disorder evolves, the fall-off in capacity becomes ever more noticeable. Work becomes impossible. The patient sits around for days on end, or whiles away his time in bars, and makes no plans for the future. Some patients wander, become vagrants, or fall into alcoholism, prostitution or petty crime.

The course of this type of schizophrenia invariably extends over several years, if not decades. There may be clinical standstills as well as more or less abrupt worsenings. The ultimate outcomes vary greatly. At its mildest there may be only a slight decline accompanied by minor peculiarities of conduct, which is perceptible only by the contrast to the individual's former self. Kraepelin considered that progression to a really profound state of deterioration did not occur, but Bleuler described some patients who became completely apathetic and required long-term institutional care. Often enough, according to Kraepelin, a presentation of simple schizophrenia can last for many years before finally transforming into one of the other forms of schizophrenia and clarifying the diagnosis.

Both Kraepelin and Bleuler speculated on the likely existence of subclinical and variant forms of simple schizophrenia. As Kraepelin (1913a) put it: 'Who cannot call to mind companions of his youth who at first gave just ground for certain, perhaps brilliant, hopes but then from some point of their development onwards failed in an incomprehensible way?' Bleuler (1911) considered that there were many simple schizophrenics among eccentrics, philosophers, world reformers and vexatious litigants. He also gave the example of a woman who married at 20 and lived happily for more than five years. She then gradually become increasingly irritable, gesticulated while talking, quarrelled with neighbours incessantly and became unbearably demanding at home. The suspicion of schizophrenia was raised by her complete indifference to her children and the fact that she had become unable to manage her household, making all kinds of silly mistakes and useless purchases.

Kraepelin's and Bleuler's four-way subtype classification of schizophrenia was never meant to be sacrosanct. Bleuler (1911) felt that it was largely of practical usefulness and could only reflect any true aetiological groupings in the broadest and crudest way. Kraepelin (1913a) came to consider the classification unsatisfactory and ultimately increased the number of subtypes to nine. Paranoid schizophrenia was divided into two groups with mild and severe outcomes ('paranoid dementia mitis' and 'paranoid dementia gravis'). Three new groups were added, in which depression, elation or alternations between the two were prominent features and which progressively approximated to catatonic schizophrenia. A final group ('confusional speech dementia') consisted of a small number of cases that, after an otherwise unremarkable course, gave way to a stable state characterised by severe formal thought disorder against a background of unusually well-preserved behaviour and ability to work.

Given this latitude, later authors had no hesitation in making major alterations. Kleist and his follower Leonhard proposed a massively expanded form of subtyping (see Fish, 1957, 1958a; Leonhard, 1979). In their view, as the initially somewhat amorphous presentations of schizophrenia evolved towards chronicity, they crystallised into a large number of stable states – 19 in Leonhard's classification – which were individually distinctive and did not overlap to any significant degree. In each form the picture was dominated by one or a few symptoms, such as formal thought disorder, affective flattening or one particular type of catatonic phenomenon. Such a minute, rigid dissection left no room for the transitional forms recognised by Kraepelin and Bleuler, and despite a number of studies claiming that it was possible to categorise chronic schizophrenic patients in this way (e.g. Fish, 1958b; Astrup, 1979), the scheme simply failed to find favour with the vast majority of clinicians. It is now only of historical interest.

Some countries, such as France (Pichot, 1982) and the USSR (Calloway, 1993) evolved their own, quite individualistic classifications of schizophrenia. These became and have remained standard in their own countries. Although superficially these depart substantially from Kraepelin's and Bleuler's original classification, it is fair to say that close examination generally reveals that the similarities are greater than the differences. For example, the French concept of schizophrenia has a strict requirement of deterioration, and accordingly separates off a number of chronic delusional and paranoid hallucinatory states. Some of these latter disorders would simply be classified with schizophrenia in other countries, whereas others would fall into the categories of paranoia and paraphrenia (see Chapter 12).

A different kind of problem has concerned the particular concepts of catatonic schizophrenia and simple schizophrenia. There is no doubt that nowadays acute catatonia is rare to the point that it has 'largely disappeared from the modern psychiatric unit' (Mahendra, 1981), and this has led some authors to question whether it was ever really part of schizophrenia in the first place. According to this argument, some of Kahlbaum's and Kraepelin's original patients were really suffering from neurological disorders such as tertiary syphilis or encephalitis lethargica (Marsden *et al.*, 1975; Mahendra, 1981; Boyle, 1990), and others would nowadays be diagnosed as having manic-depressive illness (a claim that is examined further in Chapter 13). It is difficult to sustain such arguments, given that 53 of the 811 rigorously diag-nosed schizophrenic patients (6.5 per cent) in the International Pilot Study of Schizophrenia were given a subtype diagnosis of catatonic schizophrenia. This figure did conceal undeniable evidence for a low frequency of acute catatonic schizophrenia in developed countries, where the rate ranged from 1 to 3 per cent, although in developing countries the rate was 8 to 22 per cent. Another difficulty for the claim that catatonia is not part of schizophrenia is that there is ample evidence for the continuing presence of catatonic symp-toms up to and including the full catatonic syndrome in chronically hospital-ised patients (Pfohl and Winokur, 1982; Rogers, 1985; Lund *et al.*, 1991).

The existence of simple schizophrenia has always been controversial. Even as he incorporated it into schizophrenia, Bleuler (1911) stated: 'In spite of serious attempts of some very competent investigators, the concept . . . is still not generally accepted'. A steady stream of criticism continued afterwards (N.D.C. Lewis, 1936; Kant, 1948; Stone *et al.*, 1968). Once again, however, some patients in the International Pilot Study of Schizophrenia were given a diagnosis of simple schizophrenia, although this was only in 31 of 811 (4 per cent) cases. Some authors have also presented well-documented series of cases who developed typical schizophrenic deterioration from early adult life, but in whom no florid symptoms seemed ever to have been present (Galderisi *et al.*, 1999; Serra-Mestres *et al.*; 2000; Suzuki *et al.*, 2005). But possibly the most convincing evidence that simple schizophrenia exists comes from an epidemiological survey of schizophrenia in an Irish county by Kendler *et al.* (1994). Out of 282 individuals with a clinical diagnosis of schizophrenia, 126 met DSM-III-R criteria and most of the remainder could be assigned other DSM-III-R diagnoses including schizoaffective disorder, schizophreniform disorder, atypical psychosis and affective illness. However, there were 11 (3.9 per cent of the total sample) who had no place in the DSM-III-R framework. They met all the criteria for schizophrenia, except the first relating to delusions, hallucinations, incoherence of speech or catatonic symptoms. In the ten patients who were still alive at follow-up on average 16 years later there was no change in their presentation. Kendler *et al.*'s description of one of their cases is reproduced in Box 2.2.

For better or worse, Kraepelin's and Bleuler's original four-way subtyping has stood the test of time. Beyond this, there has been a small amount of empirical investigation of its validity. Carpenter *et al.* (1976) used the detailed clinical information in the International Pilot Study of Schizophrenia to

Box 2.2 'Sitting by the fire', a case of simple schizophrenia (from Spitzer *et al.* (1989), *DSM-III-R Case Book*. American Psychiatric Press. © American Psychiatric Publishing, Inc. Reprinted by permission)

Paddy O'Brien is a 26-year-old bachelor, living with his mother and two older brothers on the family farm in the west of Ireland. He is interviewed as part of a family study of mental disorders being conducted in Ireland.

Paddy is described by his mother as having been a 'normal' youngster up until the age of 14. He was average to slightly below average in his school-work. He had friends he played with after school, and he helped his brothers and father with the chores around the farm. When he was 14, he began to 'lose interest' in his schoolwork. His teacher noted that he was 'staring into space' while in class, and rarely followed the work. Soon thereafter, his mother noticed that he no longer played with his friends after school, but would just come home and sit in front of the turf fire. It also became harder and harder to get him to do the farm chores. Sometimes he would come in and say the work was finished. Only hours later would they notice that only some of the cows had been milked, or only some of the eggs collected.

When he was 16, because his condition had become progressively worse, Paddy was withdrawn from school and was admitted to the county psychiatric hospital. The hospital records indicate that he was socially withdrawn and had a flat affect. It was not possible to interest him in ward activities. No psychotic symptoms could be elicited. Paddy has been in psychiatric care intermittently ever since that time. For the last year and a half, Paddy has been attending the local day centre two days a week.

When interviewed by the research team, Paddy is observed to be an obese, rather dishevelled young man. He replies to most questions with a 'yes', 'no', or 'could be'. He denies any psychotic symptoms, feelings of depression or elation, or difficulty with appetite or energy. He does, however, admit to unspecified problems with his 'nerves', and problems in sleeping. On probing, he admits to feeling uncomfortable around 'people', except his family. Eye contact is poor: he looks at the floor during most of the interview. His affect is flat. Despite all attempts, the interviewer is unable to establish rapport with him.

According to Paddy's family, when he is not at the day centre, he sits all day in front of the fire at home. Occasionally, he can be encouraged to help with a farm chore, but he usually stops after about 15 minutes and returns to his chair by the fire. Unless prompted, he will not wash or change his clothes. He refuses to attend any social functions, and his childhood friends have long ago stopped calling at the house for him.

At the day centre, Paddy sometimes works for brief periods of time at simple tasks in occupational therapy, but then soon quits and goes to sit by himself in the day room. Both the family and staff note that he is quite aware of what is going on around him, as reflected by an occasional perceptive comment. Neither his family nor any of the psychiatric staff who care for Paddy has ever been able to elicit any psychotic symptoms.

In the *DSM-III-R Case Book*, where the case was taken from, this patient was given a diagnosis of schizotypal personality disorder. However, the authors noted that the marked change in functioning he experienced at about the age of 14, and the profound deterioration with typical residual symptoms of chronic schizophrenia, are not characteristic of this disorder. Rather, they considered that his illness corresponded to the traditional concept of simple schizophrenia. They felt that simple schizophrenia should be considered as a possible addition to DSM-IV, although not as a subtype of schizophrenia and perhaps called simple deteriorative disorder.

examine the validity of the paranoid, hebephrenic, catatonic and simple subclassification further. They averaged the ratings on 27 types of symptom shown by patients who had been given a clinical diagnosis of paranoid ($N = 325$), hebephrenic ($N = 87$), catatonic ($N = 53$) and simple schizophrenia ($N = 31$), and plotted the scores to form a 'profile'. Inspection of these profiles revealed that the different subtypes were all roughly similar in the pattern and level of psychopathology displayed. The differences between the paranoid and hebephrenic profiles were minimal, although they were in the expected direction: the paranoid schizophrenics had higher scores on persecutory, but not other delusions and lower scores on the items relating to affective flattening. The profiles of the catatonic and simple groups showed more substantial differences from the paranoid schizophrenics, but these were still overall modest, and not always in the predicted places. For example, some of the highest scores in patients with catatonic schizophrenia were on symptoms not especially associated with this subtype, such as visual hallucinations and unkempt appearance. The four profiles are illustrated in Figure 2.1.

Carpenter *et al.* then went on to apply cluster analysis to 600 patients with subtype diagnoses of paranoid, hebephrenic, catatonic and simple (and also acute and schizoaffective) schizophrenia. This mathematical technique (discussed further in Chapter 4) has the effect of partitioning the subjects into groups showing the most homogeneity among their symptoms. They found that four clusters accounted for almost all the patients. The first cluster was characterised by poor insight, persecutory delusions, auditory hallucinations, passivity, flattened affect and social withdrawal. Carpenter *et al.* termed this 'typical schizophrenia', and it obviously resembles paranoid schizophrenia. The second cluster shared many of the characteristics of the first, but was also characterised by aberrant, agitated or bizarre behaviour, incomprehensibility of speech, unkempt appearance and incongruent and flattened affect. Carpenter *et al.* termed this 'flagrant schizophrenia', but it is also reminiscent of hebephrenic schizophrenia. Cluster three was characterised by neurotic symptoms and preservation of insight, as well as delusions and hallucinations. The final cluster was characterised by high ratings on somatic

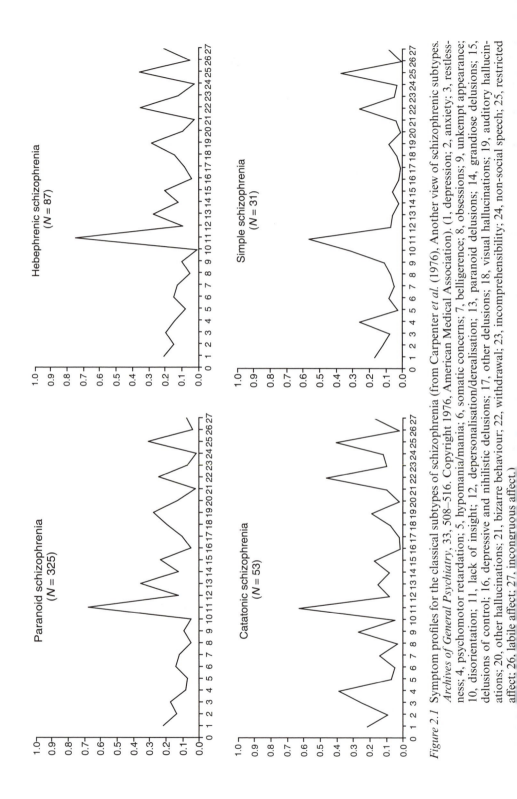

Figure 2.1 Symptom profiles for the classical subtypes of schizophrenia (from Carpenter *et al.* (1976). Another view of schizophrenic subtypes. *Archives of General Psychiatry*, 33, 508–516. Copyright 1976, American Medical Association). (1, depression; 2, anxiety; 3, restlessness; 4, psychomotor retardation; 5, hypomania/mania; 6, somatic concerns; 7, belligerence; 8, obsessions; 9, unkempt appearance; 10, disorientation; 11, lack of insight; 12, depersonalisation/derealisation; 13, paranoid delusions; 14, grandiose delusions; 15, delusions of control; 16, depressive and nihilistic delusions; 17, other delusions; 18, visual hallucinations; 19, auditory hallucinations; 20, other hallucinations; 21, bizarre behaviour; 22, withdrawal; 23, incomprehensibility; 24, non-social speech; 25, restricted affect; 26, labile affect; 27. incongruous affect.)

concerns, neurotic symptoms and visual hallucinations. These two clusters were considered to show little correspondence to catatonic and simple schizophrenia.

Subsequent cluster analytic studies (Farmer *et al.*, 1983; Dollfus *et al.*, 1996; Lykouras *et al.*, 2001) have all isolated clusters reasonably consistent with typical/paranoid and flagrant/hebephrenic schizophrenia. Two of them (Dollfus *et al.*, 1996; Lykouras *et al.*, 2001) also isolated a group of patients showing predominantly flattening of affect, social withdrawal, poverty of speech, motor retardation and mannerisms and posturing, although it would be dangerous to identify this with simple schizophrenia as these were cross-sectional studies which could take no account of the presence of past symptomatology. But, as in Carpenter *et al.*'s study, these studies all produced further clusters with no obvious clinical counterparts.

The positive:negative dichotomy and Liddle's three syndromes

According to Berrios (1985, 1991), the concept of positive and negative symptoms originated in 1857 when Reynolds, a physician, used the terms to divide neurological signs into two different types. Symptoms like spasms and convulsions could be understood as 'the excess or alteration of vital properties'. In contrast, symptoms such as paralysis and anaesthesia seemed to represent the 'the negation of vital properties'. The application of this distinction to the symptoms of insanity was made somewhat later by the distinguished neurologist Hughlings Jackson. However, in his hands the terms acquired more than a little additional theoretical baggage and lost some of their original 'productive' and 'deficit' sense.

Neither Reynolds' nor Jackson's concepts of positive and negative symptoms is known to have had any direct influence on Kraepelin and Bleuler. Nevertheless, ideas that were not entirely unrelated ran through their thinking. In order to define schizophrenia, Kraepelin (1896) essentially separated and then coupled together on the one hand a set of florid symptoms and on the other a characteristic deterioration. Bleuler (1911) explicitly distinguished what he termed accessory symptoms, which included most of the florid symptoms of schizophrenia, from fundamental symptoms, some but not all of which were deficits. He considered this distinction to be of crucial diagnostic and aetiological importance, but purely phenomenological considerations, if there were any, were lost in a wealth of theoretical speculation.

Berrios (1985, 1991) identified a number of authors in the early and middle twentieth century, including notable figures like de Clérambault (1942) and Ey (1952), who used the terms positive and negative in connection with the symptoms of schizophrenia. In all cases, however, the usage was casual and lacked any attempt to specify what the defining features of each class of symptom were. It was Wing and his co-workers who, in a series of papers culminating in Wing and Brown (1970), finally distilled these ideas into the modern concept of positive and negative symptoms. On the basis of a number of lines of evidence he argued that the intrinsic symptoms seen in chronic schizophrenic patients (i.e. those that could not be understood as arising as a reaction to being ill or in response to the unfavourable social consequences of illness) fell into two independent clusters. One was a constellation of florid or positive symptoms that included delusions, hallucinations, formal thought disorder, overactivity and various forms of odd behaviour. The other was his 'clinical poverty' syndrome described earlier in this chapter – social withdrawal, affective flattening, lack of volition and poverty of speech, and also slowness and underactivity.

Subsequent authors added the finishing touches to the concept. Strauss *et al.* (1974) made the crucial phenomenological distinction: positive symptoms were those that were distinguished by the presence of an abnormal phenomenon, whereas negative symptoms represented the absence or diminution of a normal function. Andreasen (1982) developed a rating scale for negative symptoms, the Scale for the Assessment of Negative Symptoms (SANS), which gave a full and detailed description under the headings of alogia (poverty of speech and poverty of content of speech), affective flattening, avolition-apathy, anhedonia-asociality and attentional impairment. Finally, in an influential paper, Crow (1980) realised that the distinction had potentially wide implications. Positive symptoms could relapse and remit, tended to fluctuate in severity, and were most obviously responsive to neuroleptic drugs (see Chapter 10). Negative symptoms, on the other hand, were relatively enduring, more resistant to treatment, and seemed to underlie much of the chronic disability of schizophrenia. This suggested that positive and negative symptoms were the manifestations of two different pathological processes in the brain, one associated with acute schizophrenia, which was potentially reversible and possibly had a basis in neurochemical abnormality; and the other defining a group of illnesses with a graver prognosis, and which Crow speculated might reflect irreversible structural changes in the brain.

The positive:negative dichotomy was immediately influential and continues to cast its shadow across almost all areas of theory and research in schizophrenia. At its heart, nevertheless, the distinction is a phenomenological one, and it is on phenomenological grounds that its validity has to be judged. If positive and negative symptoms are two separate constellations of symptoms in schizophrenia, then the presence of one positive symptom should be associated with the presence of other positive symptoms. The same should also be true for negative symptoms. The two classes of symptom should, however, be unassociated with each other.

Correlational studies of positive and negative symptoms

A series of studies using a variety of different scales soon established that negative symptoms such as lack of volition, affective flattening, poverty of speech, impoverishment of thought and self-neglect were all significantly intercorrelated, usually highly so (e.g. Andreasen and Olsen, 1982; Bilder *et al.*, 1985; Kulhara *et al.*, 1986; Mortimer *et al.*, 1989). Two studies (Andreasen and Olsen, 1982; Kay *et al.*, 1986) also found that negative symptoms had a high internal consistency, using a statistical measure of this (Cronbach's alpha).

Three studies (Andreasen and Olsen, 1982; Kulhara *et al.*, 1986; Mortimer *et al.*, 1990) also examined the correlations among delusions, hallucinations and formal thought disorder. They all found strong positive correlations between delusions and hallucinations. However, the correlations of these two symptoms with formal thought disorder was either non-significant or significant but weaker than that between delusions and hallucinations. Other symptoms like bizarre behaviour and catatonic symptoms, which might reasonably be considered to be distinguished by the presence of abnormality, were also found to correlate poorly with other positive symptoms (Andreasen and Olsen, 1982; Mortimer *et al.*, 1990).

The correlation between positive and negative symptoms has been examined at least eight times in studies on acute and chronic schizophrenic patients, with sample sizes ranging from 32 to over 500 (Owens and Johnstone 1980; Andreasen and Olsen 1982; Lewine *et al.*, 1983; Rosen *et al.*, 1984; Pogue-Geile and Harrow 1985; Kay *et al.*, 1986; Kulhara *et al.*, 1986; Mortimer *et al.*, 1990). Without exception, no significant correlation was found.

At the same time, these early studies made it clear that some findings did not fit into the positive:negative framework very well. One of these was the above unexpectedly weak correlation between formal thought disorder and other positive symptoms. Another concerned the symptom of inappropriate affect, which Andreasen (1982) included in her scale for negative symptoms, despite finding that it correlated poorly with other measures of affective flattening such as unchanging facial expression, poor eye contact and emotional unresponsivity. It was later found not to correlate significantly with positive symptoms either (Mortimer *et al.*, 1989). What were originally perceived as minor irregularities assumed more significance when a more powerful technique for exploring the pattern of correlations among symptoms began to be employed – factor analysis.

Liddle's three syndromes

Liddle (1987a) applied factor analysis (described in detail in Chapter 4) to the symptoms shown by a group of 40 stable chronic schizophrenic patients. As shown in Table 2.3, this resulted in three rather than two factors. Two of the factors were immediately recognisable as negative and positive symptoms. The former (which Liddle termed 'psychomotor poverty') loaded heavily on poverty of speech, decreased spontaneous movement, unchanging facial expression, paucity of expressive gestures, affective non-responsivity, and lack of vocal inflection. The latter (which Liddle termed 'reality distortion')

Table 2.3 Results of factor analysis of symptom ratings in 40 chronic schizophrenic patients

Symptoms	Factor 1	Factor 2	Factor 3
Psychomotor poverty syndrome			
Poverty of speech	0.80	−0.01	−0.03
Decreased spontaneous movement	0.95	−0.04	−0.03
Unchanging facial expression	0.85	−0.01	0.05
Paucity of expressive gesture	0.97	0.02	−0.04
Affective non-responsivity	0.82	0.02	0.00
Lack of vocal inflection	0.90	−0.20	−0.05
Disorganisation syndrome			
Inappropriate affect	0.19	0.84	0.09
Poverty of content of speech	−0.08	0.57	0.01
Tangentiality	−0.05	0.94	0.03
Derailment	−0.05	0.94	0.04
Pressure of speech	−0.10	0.61	0.08
Distractibility	0.00	0.81	0.01
Reality distortion syndrome			
Voices speak to patient	0.04	−0.07	0.67
Delusions of persecution	−0.19	0.06	0.51
Delusions of reference	0.13	0.04	0.84
Somatic delusions	−0.03	−0.03	0.03

Source: Liddle (1987a), The symptoms of chronic schizophrenia: a re-examination of the positive–negative dichotomy. *British Journal of Psychiatry*, 151, 145–151. Reproduced with permission from the Royal College of Psychiatrists.

had high loadings on auditory hallucinations, delusions of persecution and delusions of reference. The third factor loaded on thought disorder items, tangentiality, derailment, pressure of speech, poverty of content of speech and distractibility, and also inappropriate affect. Liddle termed this the 'disorganisation syndrome', a term that, unlike reality distortion and psychomotor poverty, has been universally adopted.

Numerous further factor analytic studies have been carried out, using both acute and chronic schizophrenic patients, a range of different symptom scales, and in some cases sample sizes considerably larger than in Liddle's original study. These have generally confirmed Liddle's findings (reviewed by Thompson and Meltzer, 1993; Andreasen *et al.*, 1995; see also McKenna and Oh, 2005). When more than three factors have been found the additional factors isolated have usually reflected depression or elation (e.g. Bell *et al.*, 1994; Lindenmayer *et al.*, 1995), or have simply split the positive or negative factor in some way (e.g. Shtasel *et al.*, 1992; Arora *et al.*, 1997). Confirmatory factor analyses, which mathematically test the goodness-of-fit of different models, have invariably reached the conclusion that more than two factors are needed to satisfactorily account for the correlations among schizophrenic symptoms, and have found little to choose between three- and four-factor models (Brekke *et al.*, 1994; Peralta *et al.*, 1994; Dollfus and Everitt, 1998).

Taking advantage of the fact that it is possible to statistically combine correlations, Grube *et al.* (1998) and Smith *et al.* (1998) meta-analysed some of the studies, and once again found that the existence of three factors was upheld. These two meta-analyses are summarised in Box 2.3.

Box 2.3 Two meta-analyses of factor analytic studies of schizophrenic symptoms (from Grube *et al.*, 1998, and Smith *et al.*, 1998)

Grube *et al.* (1998) pooled data from 10 studies (total N = 896), which rated negative symptoms using the SANS and positive symptoms using either the SAPS (Andreasen's rating scale for positive symptoms) or the closely similar Schedule for Affective Disorders and Schizophrenia (SADS). The correlations reported in the studies were pooled for each of the five SANS subscale scores: affective flattening, alogia, avolition, anhedonia and attentional impairment, and each of the four SAPS/SADS subscale scores: delusions, hallucinations, positive formal thought disorder and bizarre behaviour. These pooled values were then used as the correlation matrix for principal components analysis. This resulted in three factors with eigenvalues greater than 1: positive (delusions and hallucinations), negative (the five SANS subscale items) and disorganisation (positive formal thought disorder and bizarre behaviour). The total variance accounted for was 63%.

Symptom	Factor 1	Factor 2	Factor 3
Affective flattening	0.77	−0.04	−0.02
Alogia	0.73	−0.16	0.33
Avolition-apathy	0.79	0.06	0.00
Anhedonia	0.79	0.09	−0.15
Attentional impairment	0.63	−0.04	0.35
Hallucinations	0.08	0.80	0.12
Delusions	−0.09	0.83	0.12
Formal thought disorder	0.01	0.29	0.75
Bizarre behaviour	0.07	0.05	0.77
Variance accounted for	32.3%	19.8%	11.3%

The separation of the factors was clear apart from the finding that alogia and attentional impairment loaded on disorganisation in addition to the negative factor at 0.33 and 0.35 respectively. Grube *et al.* speculated that these ratings might be 'impure', incorporating items that are not homogeneous to the construct. They noted that the alogia item poverty of content of speech had been found to load on disorganisation in several studies.

Likewise, attentional impairment might not just be a deficit symptom, but could be produced by lack of distractibility, manifest clinically as formal thought disorder.

Smith *et al.* (1998) carried out a similar procedure to Grube *et al.*, but extracted correlations from 24 studies that employed a wider range of rating scales. They then used confirmatory factor analysis to test the goodness-of-fit of one factor, two-factor and three-factor models. Liddle's three-factor model was the most satisfactory. However, the fit was at best mediocre and three factors did not capture the structure among schizophrenic symptoms well.

Conclusion

One of the most enduring controversies surrounding schizophrenia has been whether it is one or a group of disorders. The message of this chapter is that schizophrenia resists sharp divisions of any kind; it has not become possible, as Bleuler hoped, to speak of the group of schizophrenias. No one would suggest that acute and chronic schizophrenia are distinct forms of illness. It has always been at least as clear that the classical subtypes of schizophrenia are not sharply demarcated from each other, but are instead connected by innumerable transitional forms. Here, though, there are some grounds for believing that they carve schizophrenia at its natural joints. Cluster analysis has consistently honoured the distinction between paranoid and hebephrenic schizophrenia, and while it is true that such studies have been much less successful at isolating forms of presentation corresponding to catatonic and simple schizophrenia, it has to be remembered that cluster analysis is designed to generate mutually exclusive subgroups of individuals and so might not be an entirely appropriate technique (a problem that surfaces again in the distinction between schizophrenia and manic-depressive psychosis – see Chapter 4).

There is a robust way of subdividing schizophrenia, but this is into groups of symptoms rather than groups of patients. A late entrant into the subclassification field, the positive:negative dichotomy has gone from strength to strength and is currently one of the key organising principles in schizophrenia research. But even this is an oversimplification. The existence of a third disorganisation syndrome in schizophrenia seems as inescapable as that of the two original ones of positive and negative symptoms. This would seem to entail accepting yet another pathological process in schizophrenia, which somehow causes neither productive symptoms nor deficits, but in the words of Liddle (2001) disjointed thought, emotion and behaviour.

A corollary to this conclusion is that the different ways of subcategorising schizophrenia are in some tantalising and as yet ill-understood way complementary. The concepts of acute and chronic schizophrenia overlap with those of positive and negative symptoms, which in turn have some kind of connection with the paranoid and simple subtypes of the disorder. In the same way, the conjunction of formal thought disorder, inappropriate affect and bizarre behaviour, which make up the disorganisation syndrome, clearly echoes the concept of hebephrenia, and an apparent splitting and fragmentation of mental functions was originally recognised by Kraepelin as 'intrapsychic ataxia', and is enshrined in the very word schizophrenia by Bleuler.

3 The natural history of schizophrenia

The basic epidemiological facts about schizophrenia are reasonably well established. As summarised by Jablensky (1997), the general picture to emerge from studies carried out between the 1930s and the 1970s is one of a disorder with a relatively low incidence (range 0.17–0.57 per 1000 of the population), a relatively high point prevalence (range 2.4–6.7 per 1000), and a lifetime risk in the region of 1 per cent (range 0.38–1.87 per cent). Some of the variation in these figures can be attributed to methodological differences among the studies, but the International Pilot Study of Schizophrenia also found evidence of variations in frequency in different parts of the world, with significantly higher rates in India and some other third world countries than in the western world (see Jablensky, 1987). These were confirmed in a later worldwide incidence study, the Determinants of Outcome of Severe Mental Disorders (Jablensky *et al.*, 1992). However, in both cases, the variation was markedly reduced when strict diagnostic criteria were applied.

The demographics of schizophrenia are at least as well understood (e.g. Eaton *et al.*, 1995). It develops most commonly in early adult life, and decreases in frequency in both directions outside the age bracket of 20 to 35. Broadly speaking, men and women are affected equally, but the age distribution differs so that the peak age of onset is 5 to 10 years later for women compared to men. Schizophrenia is associated with single status and reduced rates of reproduction, and is also disproportionately represented among lower socioeconomic classes. The available evidence suggests that these findings are consequences of the disorder rather than being of causal significance (Shur, 1988).

An area where hard facts are more difficult to come by concerns the course of schizophrenia. In spite of follow-up studies that can be numbered in the hundreds, and reviews of these that have been only slightly less numerous, what the future holds for an individual who has been diagnosed as schizophrenic remains uncertain and a matter of serious dispute. A degree of order can be brought to the large and sometimes unruly literature on this question by breaking it down into its three constituent parts. These are *the pattern of course of schizophrenia, its long-term outcome*, and *its prognosis*.

The pattern of course of schizophrenia

While maintaining that the trajectory of schizophrenia was always towards deterioration, Kraepelin and Bleuler were the first to acknowledge the many different routes the disorder could follow in its downhill course. Kraepelin (1913a) observed that some cases progressed very slowly and insidiously, whereas in others symptoms broke out suddenly and resulted in an incurable decline within a few weeks or months. But most commonly, the progression was interrupted by remissions of greater or lesser degrees of completeness, which could last days, weeks, months, sometimes years, and occasionally decades. According to Bleuler (1911), advances, halts, exacerbations and remissions could be seen at all stages. The evolution could be smooth, along a regular flat curve, or take place in a series of steps, or via an irregular series of thrusts, or supervene all at once. Sometimes deterioration appeared early and sometimes late in the course of the disease.

The detailed cataloguing of the different patterns of schizophrenic course fell to later investigators. These studies (reviewed by WHO, 1979; see also Ciompi, 1980; Harding, 1988) all arrived at remarkably similar conclusions. One of them, however, stands head and shoulders above the others, in terms of its numbers, depth of analysis, and meticulous attention to detail. This is the monumental personal follow-up of over 200 schizophrenic patients that Manfred Bleuler (Bleuler's son) carried on for over 20 years (Bleuler, 1974, 1978).

Bleuler's sample consisted of 100 men and 108 women admitted to a single hospital over an 18-month period between 1942 and 1943. All the patients were known personally to him: he admitted the patients, took an active part in their assessment, treated them himself and advised many of their relatives. The diagnosis of schizophrenia was made in a rigorous way that anticipated present day approaches. He included only patients 'who have gone through a severe psychotic phase at least once in their life', and he excluded 'borderline cases which could be described just as well as eccentrics, as schizoid personalities, as psychopaths, as neurotics or pseudo-neurotics, or as latent schizophrenics'. He considered that, by virtue of showing at least three different classes of symptoms, 185 of his 208 patients would also be likely to be diagnosed as schizophrenic by other schools of psychiatry. Of the 23 in whom the diagnosis might be open to debate, 9 had 'serious manic-depressive manifestations'; in 3 the illness began at the age of 60; and in 11 alcoholic hallucinosis, reactive psychosis or paranoid psychosis was a realistic differential diagnosis.

The follow-up period lasted between 21 and 23 years, during which contact was lost with only 8 of the original 216 patients. What Bleuler termed 'objective and complete' data were obtained on the patients' further hospitalisations, their functioning outside hospital, their domestic circumstances, whether and how successfully they were employed, how well relatives and carers judged them to be, and how well Bleuler himself judged them to be.

'Non-objective and incomplete' information consisted of impressions gained about the patients' relationship with their relatives, how these relationships were affected by the patient's illness, and the influence of various life events on their mental state and functioning.

On the basis of these findings, Bleuler came to three broad conclusions. The first concerned the very prolonged course that schizophrenia tended to run. Years or even decades after they became ill, patients still occasionally underwent acute exacerbations of florid symptoms. Not infrequently, there were also more gradual trends towards overall improvement or further deterioration. Sometimes the patient merely became generally more agitated or tranquil, or showed improvement or deterioration in dressing, eating, personal hygiene, and so on.

Bleuler's second conclusion was that, notwithstanding these fluctuations, a substantial majority of cases eventually reached a certain stability in their condition. Twenty years after the follow-up began, three-quarters of the 208 patients had reached a position where their clinical state had persisted relatively unchanged for at least 5 years. In such patients it was rare to encounter any marked change subsequently, although minor changes could and did take place, more often than not in the direction of improvement.

Finally, Bleuler concluded that schizophrenia could not be considered to be a progressive disorder in the strict sense of the term. A more accurate view was that it tended to evolve over a period of on average 5 years, and afterwards showed no further deterioration, and if anything a tendency towards improvement. Even this statement was only true in the statistical sense: after 5 years a nearly a third of the sample continued to experience worsenings of their condition, but these were matched by an equivalent number who showed improvement. There was, as it were, a dynamic equilibrium, so that the ratio of improved to unimproved patients was the same at 20 years as it was at 5 years, although the patients in the improved and unimproved groups would not all be the same.

Additionally, Bleuler found that in over 90 per cent of cases the course of schizophrenia adhered to one of seven patterns. Typically, the course became established within a few years, and although one type of course could change into any other, such conversions were the exception rather than the rule. The different courses could be conveniently classified into two main types, simple (i.e. continuous) and undulating (i.e. intermittent), each of which had a number of subtypes. A small proportion of cases showing miscellaneous patterns were grouped together as atypical courses. These disease courses are described below, and are illustrated schematically in Figure 3.1.

Simple (continuous) courses

Psychoses in this group could begin abruptly or insidiously, but were characterised by a steady progression with little or no remission.

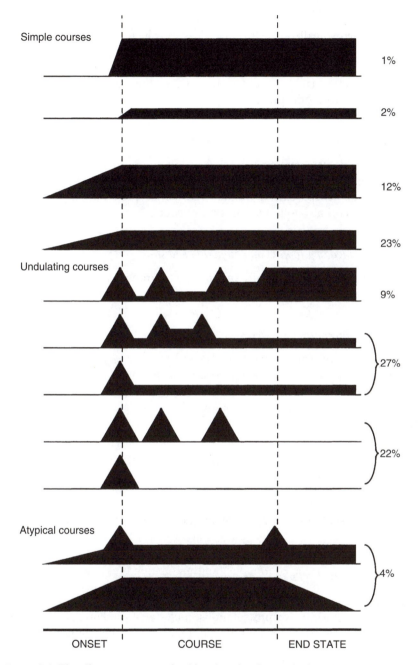

Figure 3.1 The disease courses of schizophrenia (from Bleuler (1978), *The schizo-
phrenic disorders: Long-term patient and family studies* (trans. S.M.
Clemens), New Haven: Yale University Press. Copyright 1978 Yale
University Press. Reproduced with permission.

Acute onset leading to severe, moderate or mild end states

These included so-called catastrophic illnesses, which were very uncommon and accounted for only 1 per cent of cases. Slightly more frequent at 2 per cent were cases that began abruptly and proceeded rapidly with no remission to mild or moderate end states. The patients in this subgroup mostly had hebephrenic or catatonic presentations.

Chronic onset progressing to severe end states

Illnesses in this category evolved slowly and smoothly to chronic, severe terminal states, and accounted for 12 per cent of cases. They consisted principally of hebephrenic, paranoid and simple presentations, but some catatonic patients also followed this type of course.

Chronic onset leading to mild and moderate end states

This group consisted principally of late onset paranoid schizophrenias and accounted for 23 per cent of the sample.

Undulating (intermittent) courses

These consisted of illnesses where a more or less acute onset was followed by incomplete recovery, or complete recovery was followed by further episodes with incomplete recovery. There were also a significant number of cases showing one or more acute episodes from which a complete recovery was made each time.

Undulating course leading to mild, moderate and severe end states

These included patients with hebephrenic, catatonic and paranoid presentations. They accounted for 36 per cent of cases (9 per cent progressing to a severe end state and 27 per cent progressing to moderate or mild end states).

Undulating course leading to recovery

These 'benign' or 'phasic' psychoses were composed principally of acute catatonias, schizoaffective presentations, and states presenting with 'acute delirious' features. At 22 per cent of cases they were not uncommon.

Atypical courses

Various other types of evolution could occasionally be seen. These accounted for just under 5 per cent of cases overall, and as Bleuler put it: 'They are so different, and each individual type is so unusual, that it is not worth the effort to subdivide them further.' The most common example of this type of course was the patient who started to experience acute exacerbations after a previous prolonged simple chronic course.

One further finding of Bleuler's study deserves comment. This was the phenomenon of late improvement in illnesses that had hitherto pursued a severe course lasting many years. Some patients, who had not uttered coherent sentences for years, would start to speak normally on certain occasions. Others took up social activities when they had previously always been apathetic. Still others would suddenly begin to behave in a normal way on leave, during hospital entertainments, or while suffering from a physical illness. Bleuler considered that such improvements took place in 45 of his 208 patients, and were usually, in his words, 'delicate'. Occasionally, however, something approximating to recovery could be seen. Bleuler described eight such patients, six of whom had previously shown chronic forms of illness. After 28 years of illness culminating in chronic hospitalisation, a female patient improved to the point where the diagnosis of schizophrenia was 'no longer applicable'; she was left, however, with a moderate memory impairment. Twenty-one years after his illness began, and after he had developed severe deterioration accompanied by stereotypies, a male patient began to take interest in many things, spoke to his relatives, read newspapers, and attended church. From the age of 30 a female patient gradually became more and more deluded and developed increasingly disturbed behaviour until she required institutional care. At the age of 65 she unexpectedly improved, showed no trace of self-neglect, and became devoted to her grandchildren. Nevertheless, she remained in hospital and showed no insight into her illness. Two patients with more episodic illnesses also showed prolonged remissions after stormy courses. In one of these latter two cases the improvement was due to a spectacular response to neuroleptic treatment 14 years after he had become chronically hospitalised. Otherwise, neuroleptic treatment (which was introduced in Bleuler's hospital in the middle of the follow-up period), could not be considered relevant.

The concept of late improvement in schizophrenia receives some contemporary support in a study by Harrison *et al.* (2001) who analysed the 15-year follow-up data of 644 patients in the WHO International Study of Schizophrenia (which combined data from the International Pilot Study of Schizophrenia, the Determinants of Outcome of Severe Mental Disorders and other WHO studies). They found that 15.7 per cent of patients whose previous course was classified 'continuous', in Bleuler's above sense of the term, fell into Bleuler's 'recovered' category at follow-up (which includes both full recovery and social recovery – see below). Murray *et al.* (2004) have also documented two cases of improvement in severe, chronic illness that could not be attributed to neuroleptic drug treatment, and where cognitive function also improved. A further celebrated example is that of the Nobel Prize winning mathematician John Nash, who underwent a remarkable degree of spontaneous improvement after nearly 30 years of illness. His case is described in Box 3.1.

Box 3.1 Late improvement in schizophrenia: The case of John Nash (from Nasar, 1998)

As a child, John Nash showed traits of immaturity and social awkwardness, and terms used to describe him as a young man included, solitary, cerebral, weird, socially inept, eccentric and dreamy. However, he had a number of close emotional relationships throughout his life, and, particularly after he became successful, he could be sociable and charming.

His mathematical talent showed itself early – at school he would often produce simple and elegant proofs to problems that were better than those of his teachers. While doing postgraduate work in Princeton he became interested in game theory. He applied himself to the problem of proving that a solution existed for all games with more than two players, which the leading authority in the field, Von Neumann, had been unable to solve. In his first paper, published at the age of 21, he used an ingenious mathematical argument to show that, if certain axioms held, a unique solution existed which maximised the product of the players' utilities. Initially regarded as too simple and too narrow to be widely applicable, the Nash equilibrium went on to become one of the great classics of modern economics.

He continued to work on game theory, and also produced papers on other mathematical topics, which attracted comments like audacious and original. His embedding theorem, which required 2 years single-minded work, was described as 'one of the most important pieces of mathematical analysis in this century'. All this work was completed while he was still in his twenties.

At the age of 30, he started making remarks about world affairs and licence plate numbers, and hinted to junior colleagues that he had been asked to play some extraordinary role in the world. One day he walked into the common room at the Center for Advanced Study and announced that abstract powers from outer space, or perhaps foreign governments, were communicating with him through a story in the corner of the front page of the New York Times. When he was later offered a prestigious chair in Chicago, he replied that he would have to turn it down because he was scheduled to become emperor of Antarctica.

He was admitted to hospital after his behaviour became increasingly erratic. At this time he believed there was a military conspiracy to take over the world and he was the leader of a peace movement and was going to form a world government. He was diagnosed as schizophrenic and treated with psychoanalysis and milieu therapy, but also received chlorpromazine. He improved over a matter of weeks and was discharged, but then almost immediately began behaving erratically again. He travelled to Europe, tried to renounce his American citizenship and spent his time writing endless letters, petitions, and applications.

He spent most of the 1960s in a chronically psychotic state. He was often to be seen on the Princeton campus with shoulder length hair, a bushy beard, wearing a Russian smock-like garment, and carrying around a scrapbook entitled 'Absolute Zero' in which were pasted things like a map of the Princeton area cut out from the cover of a telephone directory. He talked nonsense about numerology, dates, and world affairs, and wrote cryptic messages on the blackboards of lecture rooms. He had further admissions to hospital where he was treated with drugs, ECT and insulin coma therapy. When on neuroleptic treatment he would improve and interact with people again. During one such period, after he had been ill for 6 years, he produced another groundbreaking paper. He refused to take medication after 1970.

He remained consumed by numerology and would perform elaborate calculations to link birthdays, bar mitzvah dates, social security numbers, etc. He developed an interest in computing and became extremely proficient at writing programs using the university mainframe computer. A colleague who saw him nearly every day in the computer centre during the 1970s and 1980s said: 'In the early stages he was making up numbers out of names and being worried by what he found. Gradually, that went away. Then it was more mathematical numerology. Playing with formulas and factoring. It wasn't coherent math research, but it had lost its bizarre quality. Later it was real research.'

By 1985 a visiting professor at Princeton who knew him from 10 years before was struck by his improvement – whereas previously he had asked for help in factoring a number derived from Rockefeller's name, now he seemed to be interested in real mathematics. Another colleague, a programmer, noted that Nash's programs were 'startlingly elegant'. In 1990 he asked for a copy of a lecturer's paper on the Riemann Hypothesis. A few days later he began a series of discussions with him, bringing with him a sheaf of computer printouts. He appeared perfectly rational, although he did not look at him the first time he asked him a question. His remission was noted by several other Princeton mathematicians at this time.

In 1994, with two others, he won the Nobel prize for economics for his work on the Nash equilibrium. He was not asked to give the customary hour-long Nobel Lecture in Stockholm but gave a lecture in the University of Uppsala on the problem of developing a mathematically correct theory of a non-expanding universe that was consistent with known physical observations. He spoke without notes, clearly and convincingly, starting with tensor calculus and general relativity. His ideas went against the consensus view that the universe is expanding, but they made sense, were interesting and were expressed with the appropriate degree of scepticism.

He currently lives with his wife and spends time in Princeton University, where he now has an office. He described his improvement as a gradual tapering off in the 1970s and 1980s. He has told people he is still plagued by paranoid thoughts, even voices, but that the noise level is lower. He has compared rationality to dieting, a constant, conscious struggle. His son, John, also became schizophrenic.

The outcome of schizophrenia

While Kraepelin and Bleuler considered schizophrenia to be a disorder that led inexorably to deterioration, they also recognised that the ultimate degree of this could vary from the slight to the very profound. On the question of whether full recovery ever took place, their views were marked by equivocation and paradox: Kraepelin (1913a) found spontaneous improvement to the point where the patient could be regarded as 'completely well without reservation' in about 3 per cent of his patients. This lasted more than 5 years in four of these patients, and in one it lasted 29 years, but in each case there was ultimately a return of symptoms followed by the development of deterioration. He therefore preferred to talk of remissions rather than recovery. Nevertheless, if the disease process could remain quiescent for nearly 30 years, he felt that the possibility of permanent recovery could not be denied. Bleuler (1911) stated flatly that he had never released a patient in whom distinct signs of the disorder were not still present. However, in describing what he referred to as far-reaching improvements, he gave examples of patients who between episodes became poets, judges and academics; one patient qualified as a doctor, and another maintained an international scientific reputation.

Kraepelin (1913a) was also at pains to point out the pitfalls associated with trying to establish the recovery rate of schizophrenia. When patients who appeared to have been cured were found, there was always a lingering doubt about the diagnosis, especially if there had only been a single episode of active symptoms. Another problem was defining what exactly was meant by recovery. The dividing line between complete mental well being and a personality change that might be missed on casual examination but was obvious to the patient's relatives, and between this and mild but definite deterioration, was not always clear, and might, in the final analysis, be arbitrary. Conversely, abnormalities might have been present before a patient became ill, which could later be wrongly be ascribed to the effects of the illness. Finally, the length of the follow-up period was a crucial factor. If this was too short an artificially favourable picture would be painted.

Many follow-up studies of schizophrenia have since been carried out. Despite being subjected to critical review at regular intervals (e.g. Blair,

1940; Stephens, 1978; WHO 1979; Ram *et al.*, 1992), these have produced no consensus on the figures for outcome. Possibly their most important result has been to clarify what the requirements for such studies are – often by not fulfilling them themselves. The ground rules that have emerged seem to comprise the following:

1   The sample size needs to be large enough to permit a meaningful analysis to be made.
2   The patients need to be representative of the whole spectrum of schizophrenia, and should not, for example, consist only of those who have been discharged from hospital.
3   The diagnosis should not just be taken from the hospital case-notes, official records and the like, but should be made independently and in a critical way.
4   The ascertainment of cases should be made early in the course of the illness. This is to ensure that the diagnosis is really made on the basis of the presenting clinical picture and is contaminated as little as possible by information about the course subsequently pursued.
5   The follow-up should be by personal interview with the patients in as many cases as possible, and at the very least in all those who are not chronically hospitalised. The use of labour-saving devices like postal questionnaires (and more recently telephone interviews) is grounds for immediate disqualification.

If only studies meeting these minimal requirements are considered, their numbers are reduced to a handful. The studies described below have the following features in common. First, they all included at least 100 patients at the point of entry. Second, while making allowances for changes in diagnostic fashion, the diagnosis was made independently and was based on the presence of characteristic symptoms in a way consistent with modern concepts of schizophrenia. Third, the follow-up was by personal interview, at least with those patients who were out of hospital. It would also have been desirable to restrict the study population to first admissions. This was not included as a requirement because it has been criticised as impracticable (for example by Bleuler, 1978). Instead a stipulation is included that either the studies stated (or clearly implied) that their patients are early in the course of their illness, or that they examined a subgroup of first admissions separately.

The studies selected fall naturally into three groups according to when they were carried out. The first group comprises those carried out in the days before the introduction of neuroleptic drugs. The second consists of one study which bridges the preneuroleptic and neuroleptic eras. The third group consists essentially of contemporary studies in which neuroleptic drug treatment, criterion-based diagnosis, and prospective design have become a fact of life. The findings are summarised in Table 3.1.

Table 3.1 Outcome studies in schizophrenia

	Percentage rates			
	Complete recovery	Social recovery	Improved	Unimproved or worse
Preneuroleptic era				
Langfeldt (1937) 100 followed up 7–10 years	17	4	13	66
Malamud and Render (1938) 160 followed up 6–8 years	15	9	12	64
Holmboe and Astrup (1957) 255 followed up 6–18 years	29	9	20	42
Johanson (1958) 82 followed up 10–18 years	2	9	26	63
Bridging neuroleptic era				
Bleuler (1978) 152 followed up 21–23 years	← 20 →		33	47
Neuroleptic era				
WHO (1979) 543 followed up 2 years	26	25	20	29
WHO (Sartorius et al. 1987) 513 followed up 5–7 years	← 61 →		← 39 →	
Shepherd et al. (1989) 107 followed up 5 years	16	32	9	43

The outcome groups are somewhat variable between studies, but typically include some or all of the following:

Complete recovery: No active symptoms, no signs of deterioration, working at previous level, no or minimal social impairment, only one episode of illness.

Social recovery: No or minimal active symptoms, minimal signs of deterioration, for example in affect, working, no severe social impairment, may have been more than one episode of illness.

Improved: Ongoing active symptoms and/or obvious signs of deterioration, may or may not be able to work at lower level, out of hospital.

Unimproved or worse: Moderate or severe ongoing active symptoms and signs of deterioration, unable to work, may or may not require long-term hospitalisation.

Studies from the preneuroleptic era

Two very early investigations are included here: Langfeldt's (1937) study of 100 patients followed up for 7–10 years, and Malamud and Render's (1938) study of 160 patients followed up for 6–8 years. Out of a number of large-scale studies by Astrup and co-workers, that of Holmboe and Astrup (1957) is selected as the one from which overall outcome figures can be most easily extracted. Finally, the careful study of Johanson (1958) is included even though it was restricted to male patients.

In these studies the diagnosis of schizophrenia was generally based on Bleulerian fundamental symptoms, but the presence of florid symptoms such as delusions and hallucinations was also explicitly or implicitly required. All the patients in each study were diagnosed by a single clinician, either one of the study investigators or the director of the hospital at the time. In each of the studies attempts were made to exclude diagnostically doubtful cases and cases with organic brain disease; Johanson, however, included some patients with low intelligence. The patients in the studies of Holmboe and Astrup and Johanson were all first admissions, and a lack of chronicity was clearly implied in the other two studies.

Two studies that have regularly featured in other reviews are not included. The study of Mayer-Gross (1932) is excluded because nearly half the sample died of starvation in the First World War, which intervened during the follow-up period (Stephens, 1978). The often-cited study of Eitinger *et al.* (1958) separated the patient sample into 'schizophrenic' and 'schizophreniform' groups in a way that did not permit their recombination.

The findings of two of the studies (Langfeldt, 1937; Malamud and Render, 1938) are in close agreement. In both, slightly over a fifth of the patients were in the two best outcome groups, with most falling into the completely recovered category. Similarly, somewhere in the region of two-thirds were found to be unimproved or worse in both studies. The other two studies both found somewhat lower percentages of patients in the worst outcome groups, and they also diverged considerably on the proportion showing a good outcome. In Holmboe and Astrup's study over a third of patients were considered to have made complete or nearly complete recoveries. In Johanson's, the corresponding figure was 11 per cent, and most of these patients fell into the category of social recovery rather than complete recovery.

In spite of these differences, it can be concluded that in the days before any effective treatments were available, the outlook in schizophrenia was not nearly as gloomy as Kraepelin and Bleuler thought. After several years of illness, approximately 20 per cent of patients – certainly no less than 10 per cent and no more than 30 per cent – could be expected to present a picture of full or at least social recovery.

Studies bridging the preneuroleptic and neuroleptic eras

Of the studies carried out during this period, the outstanding example is that of Manfred Bleuler described above. His diagnostic criteria were, for the time, exemplary. All the patients were diagnosed by Bleuler himself and followed up by him personally. Not all of his sample of 208 patients were first admissions – in fact some had long prior durations of illness – however, he separately analysed the 68 patients who entered the study at the time of their first hospitalisation. As mentioned above, neuroleptic drugs were introduced in Bleuler's clinic midway through the follow-up period, and for the last 9–10 years were in common use. However, in all cases treatment was only given intermittently, when the patients were actively psychotic: 'Not one single patient living outside the clinic for years or permanently, in a state of recovery or improvement, ever took medication over extended periods of time' (Bleuler, 1978).

Several other studies date to this era, but are excluded for one reason or another. The study of Huber *et al.* (1975, 1980) is simply too difficult to evaluate: these authors employed an idiosyncratic method of categorising outcome and it is difficult to be sure what they meant by remission. Much of the detail of this study is also not available in English. In the study of Stephens (Stephens and Astrup, 1965; Stephens, 1970, 1978) the sample was based on patients discharged from hospital, and so suffers from ascertainment bias. Additionally, the diagnosis was taken from the case-notes, and it was not specified in what proportion of cases the follow-up was made by personal interview. The study of Tsuang *et al.* (1979) has also been excluded, but this is essentially for technical reasons: the patients were divided into only three outcome groups, recovered, improved and unimproved, and the very long duration of follow-up (30–40 years) meant that only 93 of the 186 patients could be traced and interviewed.

In Bleuler's study 152 of the 208 patients were considered to have reached a stable end state of at least 5 years duration by the end of the 20-year follow-up period. Of these, 20 per cent fell into his recovered category, which corresponds to the complete and social recovery groups of other studies. Nearly half were unimproved or worse. The findings in 68 patients who entered the study at the time of their first hospital admission were slightly better but overall not markedly different.

These results are much the same as those of earlier studies. Particularly striking was the finding that the same proportion of cases, one-fifth, was found to have either fully or socially recovered. This is despite the longer follow-up period in Bleuler's study, and the availability of neuroleptic treatment for some of the time.

Studies in the neuroleptic era

Recent work on the outcome of schizophrenia is dominated by the very large scale, diagnostically sophisticated 2 and 5–7 year follow-up studies undertaken as part of the International Pilot Study of Schizophrenia (WHO, 1979; Sartorius *et al.*, 1987). The only other study that can be included is the smaller, but otherwise equally rigorous, 5-year follow-up of 107 patients by Shepherd *et al.* (1989).

A number of studies have been excluded. The study of Bland and Orn (1978) was too small, consisting of only 50 patients, of whom 7 could not be traced. The study of Biehl *et al.* (1986) was methodologically superior, but again too small with 70 patients at the point of entry. Small numbers and other methodological idiosyncrasies also make several other recent studies unusable (Carone *et al.*, 1991; Breier *et al.*, 1991; Marengo *et al.*, 1991). The study of Brown *et al.* (1966) followed large numbers of patients and was meticulous in design, but the focus was on social outcome to the exclusion of all else: the follow-up interviews were carried out by a social worker rather than a psychiatrist, who interviewed a relative in preference to the patient. Perhaps the most surprising omission is the WHO Determinants of Outcome of Severe Mental Disorders Study (Jablensky *et al.*, 1992), which was similar in design to the International Pilot Study of Schizophrenia and was undertaken specifically to confirm some of its findings concerning outcome (notably the apparently better outcome of schizophrenia in developing as opposed to developed countries). However, this study provided neither overall outcome figures for its 2-year follow-up, nor figures for the subset of patients diagnosed as schizophrenic.

In both the International Pilot Study of Schizophrenia and the study of Shepherd *et al.*, the diagnosis of schizophrenia was made on clinical grounds, but with the benefit of detailed mental state information from the Present State Examination. Neither study was restricted to first admissions. However, the International Pilot Study included only patients with a total duration of symptoms of 5 years or less, and Shepherd *et al.* analysed the outcome separately for their 49 first admissions. In contrast to earlier studies, the overall outcome groupings were based on detailed clinical and social ratings, which were combined according to a fixed scheme.

The results of the two studies were highly consistent. In the International Pilot Study 51 per cent of the patients at 2 years, rising to 61 per cent at 5 years, were in the best two outcome groups. In the Shepherd *et al.* study 48 per cent were in the best two outcome groups; this changed slightly to 55 per cent if only first admissions were considered. There was also a measure of agreement between the studies that somewhere in the region of a fifth of all patients (26 per cent and 16 per cent respectively) made a complete recovery, experiencing only a single episode of illness and showing no more than minimal social or occupational impairment. In the International Pilot Study there was a shift of outcome away from the most severe end of the spectrum. This is not evident in the study of Shepherd *et al.*; however, the poor outcome groups in the two studies are not strictly comparable because of methodological differences in the way they were specified.

These two contemporary studies suggest that schizophrenia appears to have undergone a substantial lessening in severity over the last 30 years. This conclusion is also supported in a meta-analysis of 320 studies carried out over virtually the whole of the twentieth century (Hegarty *et al.*, 1994). This found that between the 1920s and the 1970s the number of patients rated as clinically improved approximately doubled (see Box 3.2).

Box 3.2 Meta-analysis of outcome studies in schizophrenia (from Hegarty *et al.* (1994), One hundred years of schizophrenia: A meta-analysis of the outcome literature. *American Journal of Psychiatry*, 151, 1409–1416. Figure reprinted with permission from the American Journal of Psychiatry, Copyright 1994. American Psychiatric Association)

The authors searched the world literature between 1895 and 1991 for studies meeting the following criteria: (a) they reported data on patients with a diagnosis of schizophrenia (studies which included schizoaffective patients were excluded); (b) they had a follow-up period of at least 1 year; (c) less than 33% of the sample were lost to follow-up and there were at least 15 patients at the end of the study period; (d) subjects were not selected a priori for good or poor outcome; (e) explicit numerical data on clinical social or vocational outcome were included from which outcome groups could be derived; and (f) treatment throughout the follow-up period was specified.

From a total of 821 studies, 320 studies met these inclusion criteria. These represented 51,800 subjects in 368 cohorts. Countries included the UK, the USA, Scandinavia, Germany, Switzerland, Japan, China, Canada, and India, among others. Just under half of the studies included neuroleptic treated patients. Because of the difficulty of accurately defining clinical outcome in schizophrenia, clinical, social or vocational data were used to define a general criterion of improvement based on attainment of substantial levels of functioning and freedom from psychotic symptoms. Patients considered improved had to have been described as recovered, in remission, well without residual symptoms, minimally or mildly symptomatic, improved without significant deficit, socially recovered, or working or living independently.

The average proportion of patients showing a favourable outcome was 40.2%. As shown in the figure, a decade-by-decade breakdown of studies with 10 or more years of follow-up (314 of 368 cohorts) indicated that the outcome had improved over the course of the century ($p < .0001$)

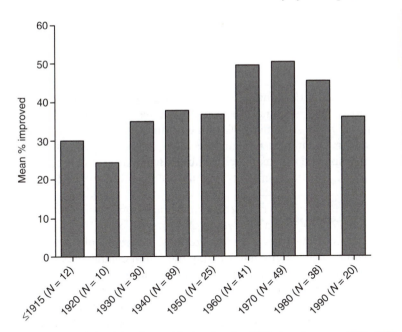

Decades are defined by their midpoint, i.e. the 1950 decade spans 1946–1955. Figures in brackets refer to number of studies.

Examination of moderating factors revealed that the likelihood of a favourable outcome declined with longer periods of follow-up, but only slightly and non-significantly. There was also a significant effect for treatment: both neuroleptic treatment and convulsive therapy were associated with a better outcome than no treatment (or lobotomy).

In order to examine the potential moderating effects of the different ways in which schizophrenia was diagnosed, the studies were assigned to either a narrow 'Kraepelinian' category, where there was an implication of poor long-term course, or a broad 'non-Kraepelinian' category. The former required at least six months of illness whereas the latter were more symptom-based and cross-sectional, with no duration requirement or less than a month of illness. Studies using broad criteria had significantly better outcomes than those using narrow ones, and this held throughout the century.

Whatever else this improvement has been due to, it is probably not the relatively short follow-up period of the two contemporary studies. Two of the studies from the preneuroleptic era (Langfeldt, 1937; Malamud and Render, 1938), in which the outcome was much poorer, had relatively short follow-up periods (up to 10 years). Duration of follow-up also was not a significant factor moderating outcome in Hegarty *et al.*'s meta-analysis. One obvious explanation for the improvement is the introduction of neuroleptic drugs in

the 1950s. Another, less obvious, possibility is that changes in diagnostic practice over the years have given rise to improvement that is more apparent than
real. Harrison and Mason (1993) made the point that Kraepelin and Bleuler
both incorporated poor outcome into the concept of schizophrenia, and
argued that that this doctrine of 'incurability in principle' could well have
seriously biased early studies of course and outcome – believing that recovery
almost precluded a diagnosis of schizophrenia many authors would have
tended to rediagnose patients who showed this as some other form of psychotic disorder. These issues remain unresolved, but Hegarty *et al.* found in their
meta-analysis that both neuroleptic treatment and the use of broad as opposed
to narrow diagnostic criteria were significant predictors of good outcome.

The prognosis of schizophrenia

It is clear from the preceding two sections that schizophrenia pursues an
erratic course to issue ultimately in anything from complete recovery to profound disability. In these circumstances it would obviously be useful to be
able to make predictions about the long-term course from features present at
the early stages. The effort devoted to finding such prognostic factors has
been intense – for a period of up to 40 years it was one of the major preoccupations of schizophrenia research – and the fact that it has been so hints
at the surprising difficulty the search has faced. The relevant literature is most
easily considered in the three historical successive stages it can be regarded as
having fallen into.

The era of clinical impression

The authoritative classical views on prognosis were those of Kraepelin and
Bleuler, both of whom were frustratingly reticent on the matter. Kraepelin
(1913a) singled out a number of symptoms whose appearance often
announced the end of any hope for improvement. These included flattening
of affect, fixed mannerisms and stereotypies, especially when simple, and the
onset of abrupt episodes of excitement or moodiness. Regarding other factors, only insidious onset stood out as definitely unfavourable. Age and sex
affected outcome only indirectly: being female and having a late age of onset
were associated with a paranoid presentation of illness, and in general these
cases did not progress to very severe terminal states.
    Bleuler (1911) had little to add on the prognostic value of individual
symptoms. He agreed that affective flattening conferred a poor prognosis,
as did catatonic symptoms, although not all of them – in his experience waxy
flexibility and negativism were not necessarily sinister signs. Grandiose delusions were sometimes but not always an indicator of poor outcome. Bleuler
also examined the way in which subtype diagnosis affected the prognosis
more thoroughly. He found that paranoid schizophrenics had the best outcome, showing a high frequency of mild deterioration (65 per cent) and a low

frequency of severe deterioration (19 per cent). Hebephrenics were next in order, showing slightly less in the way of mild deterioration (58 per cent) but no difference in the rate of severe deterioration (20 per cent). Catatonic schizophrenics showed the worst outcome: the rate of mild deterioration was much the same as for hebephrenics (57 per cent), but severe deterioration was considerably more common (30 per cent). Nevertheless, it was striking how small all the effects were: 'Heredity (in its present broad sense of the term), age, sex, intelligence, number of degenerative stigmata, state of health, individual type of disease, individual symptoms and their various groupings – all these have so little bearing on how far the disease will go toward deterioration that they scarcely can be considered in establishing the prognosis.'

The era of schizophreniform psychosis

The second and longest phase of prognostic thinking was ushered in by Langfeldt (1937). As part of the follow-up study of 100 schizophrenic patients described earlier in this chapter, he took the trouble to examine the initial presentation of each of the patients as it had been documented in the case-notes. In addition to the usual paranoid, hebephrenic and catatonic cases, and those showing mixed forms of presentation, he found 13 patients who were difficult to classify. The diagnosis was 'unmistakeable schizo-phrenia' in these patients, and they all had florid symptoms, showing one or more of delusions, auditory hallucinations and catatonic phenomena. Never-theless, the picture tended to be distinctive. In several, while it would have been difficult to construe the overall presentation as affective, there was a pronounced expansive, religious, guilty or nihilistic theme to the psychosis; sometimes both grandiose and depressive delusions were simultaneously present. Typically, the delusions also had a vague and shifting quality and the hallucinations lacked a 'massive' (i.e. bizarre and alien) quality. A degree of clouding of consciousness was present in some cases. In a few there were hysterical or hypochondriacal features.

On follow-up 7–10 years later, 11 out of these 13 atypical cases were found to fall into Langfelt's 'fully recovered' category. The other two were con-sidered to be 'cured with defects'. This was in contrast to the 87 typical patients, of whom only 6 could be regarded as completely recovered and 2 cured with defects. The outcome of the atypical patients was so radically different from the rest that it almost seemed as if schizophrenia contained a small group of patients who were quite different from the majority, both in terms of presenting symptoms and long-term prognosis. Langfeldt coined the term 'schizophreniform psychosis' to describe this group of patients. A description of one of his original cases is reproduced in Box 3.3.

Shortly afterwards and working along different lines, Kant (1940, 1941a, b), independently concluded that schizophrenic patients with good and poor prognosis could be distinguished at the time of their initial presentation.

Box 3.3 One of Langfeldt's schizophreniform cases (from Langfeldt, 1937)

Case G. K. born 7/4/1890. Admitted 4/4/28. Discharged home 17/4/28

Family: The mother has had a depressive illness.

Temperament and character in childhood and youth: Sociable, gentle, chatty, liked to associate with people. Often strikingly excited, conceited.

Onset of the disease: 7 years prior to admission to the Clinic he became depressed, anxious, frightened of people, nervous about the future, now and again wished he had never been born, but was not suicidal. The last three years did practically no work, went about in a continual state of restlessness and was somewhat fearful.

At the Psychiatric Clinic: Orientated, quite clear and easy to deal with. Hears whispers a long way off. Various fancies come to him, e.g. that he has been loved by an unmarried woman in the district. He fights on two flanks against powers of good and evil. Often afraid of being poisoned. Has had a feeling that someone followed him in the lanes with the intention of maiming him. Felt he was being libelled. The whispering voices say both good and bad things. Has, inter alia, conceived the idea that he is to preach the word of God. States that since the age of 20 he has had periods of despondency. During the past 7 years he has nearly always been despondent, had some religious doubts accompanied to some extent with ideas of eternal death. Says that he has seen many strange things during these years. 'There was something from the other side which he saw in a dream'. During his stay he showed no sign of hallucination or feeling of passivity. The ideas that people wished to injure him completely disappeared, he believed that they only wished to keep an eye on him if they could.

Further course: The patient himself writes on 20/5/33. 'I am much better. The nervousness with which I was afflicted has disappeared. I have worked practically every day for two years.' The County Medical Officer writes that since the patient ceased to be under public care on 15/8/31 he has been quite well.

Mental state in 1936 (at home): Quite open and approachable, talkative. Full insight into the period of his disease which he remembers very well. Believes that to a great extent the cause of his illness lies in financial worry during the past years. He began to worry and became sleepless. Remembers that he had an aversion to mixing with people and that he had a feeling that people followed him. Remembers that he believed people wished to do him harm. During the past 4–5 years he has been quite rid of these thoughts. But now and again he has brief periods in which he is deprimated.

> He now works as a master builder and has more than enough to do. At the mental examination he appeared somewhat dull in thinking, his memory was also slightly weakened. Moreover, it proved somewhat difficult for him to interpret proverbs, but he showed no disorder in thinking otherwise. Apart from this he revealed no mental defects.

Langfeldt's, Kant's and a number of other studies were reviewed by Vaillant (1962), who concluded that some or all of six features were repeatedly associated with recovery: family history of affective illness (usually depression), normal premorbid personality, acute or relatively acute onset, presence of a precipitating event, confusion or disorientation during the episode of illness, and presence of affective symptoms, particularly depression. These, along with Langfeldt's lack of 'massiveness' of the delusions and hallucinations (which became converted into the concept of their being 'understandable'), became the defining characteristics of schizophreniform, or good prognosis schizophrenia.

This work left unsettled the nature of the relationship between schizophreniform psychosis and schizophrenia proper. The radical view, which was implied by Langfeldt but only stated openly by Robins and Guze (1970), was that it was not simply a matter of severity of illness; they were different disorders. Others, including Vaillant (1962) and also Langfeldt himself in his later work (e.g. Langfeldt, 1956), took a more cautious position. Their statements were generally to the effect that while the features of schizophreniform psychosis, as a group, appeared to separate recovered from non-recovered schizophrenics to a considerable degree, none of them possessed great specificity in the individual case.

These competing interpretations are susceptible to testing. All that is necessary is to identify clear-cut cases of schizophrenia and schizophreniform psychosis at the time of initial presentation, and to follow their subsequent progress. If the two disorders are distinct, then their separation at follow-up should remain absolute (or nearly absolute as the initial clinical differentiation cannot be expected to be perfect): most of the schizophreniform patients should show full recovery, or at worst minor residual symptoms, whereas the schizophrenic group should show a wider spectrum of outcome, although always with some degree of deterioration being detectable. If on the other hand the concept of schizophreniform psychosis merely embodies a cluster of individually unrelated prognostic variables, then the groups of schizophreniform and schizophrenic cases should show substantial overlap at follow-up, and there should be representatives of the best and worst outcomes in both groups.

A number of studies with this type of design have been carried out, and have been reviewed by Stephens (1978). The results of those that examined outcome in much the same rigorous way as the outcome studies described earlier in this chapter are summarised in Table 3.2. It is clear that

Table 3.2 Outcome in patients diagnosed as schizophrenic and schizophreniform at initial presentation

	Percentage rates					
	Schizophreniform			Schizophrenia		
	Recovered	Improved	Unimproved	Recovered	Improved	Unimproved
Achte (1967) (N = 57 and 89)	70	21	9	15	30	55
Eitinger et al. (1958) (N = 44 and 110)	75	14	11	2	10	88
Astrup and Noreik (1966) (N = 304 and 271)	26	46	28	6	10	84
Stephens (1970) (N = 116 and 90)	35	61	4	7	39	54

Source: Adapted from Stephens (1978).

the second rather than the first hypothesis is supported. Patients designated as 'schizophreniform', 'reactive' or 'good prognosis schizophrenia' at an early stage certainly tend to fare better in the long term than those considered to have 'true', 'process' or 'poor prognosis' schizophrenia. However, in every study the differences are relative rather than absolute, and in all cases some schizophreniform patients are found in the poorest outcome category.

The era of empirical investigation

The third and current wave of research has been marked by a systematic search for individual variables that might be of prognostic significance in schizophrenia. This era can also be considered to have begun with Langfeldt, whose 1937 study included an examination of the various features of the illness held to be of prognostic significance by Kraepelin, Bleuler and some other classical authors. He was able to confirm the unfavourability of insidious onset and the presence of catatonic symptoms. He also found that presence of a 'schizoid' personality (see Chapter 16) before the onset of illness was associated with a poor outcome. Presence or absence of a family history of psychosis, however, was irrelevant. However, in a later replication and extension of this study (Langfeldt, 1956), he found that the relationship of factors like age, sex, intelligence, previous personality, family history of schizophrenia, rapidity of onset, precipitating stress and individual symptoms to prognosis was, in almost every case, less clear-cut than he had originally thought.

The need was apparent for a thorough reappraisal using modern diagnostic techniques and a prospective design. The opportunity for this has been afforded, once again, by the International Pilot Study of Schizophrenia (WHO, 1979). This study had the benefit of large numbers (543 of the original 811 patients were followed up), and the advantage that both the initial evaluation and the re-evaluation were standardised and detailed. Its main disadvantage has been that to date only the 2-year follow-up data have been analysed.

Initially, a set of 47 'predictor variables', which the previous literature had suggested might be of prognostic importance, was examined. These covered sociodemographic factors like age, sex and educational level; past history factors, including mental illness in relatives and previous physical and psychiatric illness; and finally a number of factors pertaining to the presentation of the illness itself, including type of onset and some rather broad clinical variables such as personality change and the presence of affective flattening.

The main finding was that no single factor, nor any combination of them, accounted for a large proportion of the variation in course and outcome. Even when the factors that individually had the greatest predictive power were combined, only 26 per cent of the outcome variance could be explained. These are shown in Table 3.3. The addition of other predictor variables resulted in relatively small gains.

Table 3.3 Best predictors of 2-year outcome in schizophrenia (general)

Sociodemographic characteristics
Social isolation (poor)
High educational level (poor)
Widowed, divorced or separated (poor)
Professional, managerial or clerical occupation (good)

Past history characteristics
Past psychiatric treatment (poor)
Poor psychosexual adjustment (poor)
History of behaviour symptoms (poor)
Unfavourable environment (poor)
Previous contact with other agencies with psychiatric problems (good)

Characteristics of inclusion episode
Long prior duration of episode (poor)
Insidious onset (poor)
High score on flatness of affect (poor)
High score on psychophysical symptoms (good)
High score on indications of personality change (poor)

Source: Adapted from WHO (1979).

The next step was to examine the predictive power of the initial clinical picture in more detail. In order to do this, all 129 individual symptoms assessed at initial evaluation were entered into a predictive calculation. This time the amount of variance that could be explained rose to 68 per cent, indicating that patients with the best and worst outcomes at 2 years had initial patterns of symptoms that were, to a significant extent, distinguishable. This is well illustrated in discriminant function analysis (see Chapter 4) performed on the 127 patients in the best and 78 patients in the worst outcome groups, which indicates that their initial clinical features separate clearly. This is shown in Figure 3.2.

Individual symptoms that were found to be predictive of good and poor outcome at 2 years included some that were reminiscent of schizophreniform psychosis: perplexity, derealisation, and affective symptoms such as depression and lability of affect. Some of those predictive of poor outcome, in contrast, pointed to insidious onset of illness dominated by negative symptoms: flatness of affect, haughtiness, personality change, social withdrawal, and changes in interests and sexual behaviour. In other respects, though, the picture was less clear. Some delusions, such as delusions of persecution, were associated with a good outcome, whereas others, such as fantastic delusions, were associated with a poor outcome. Hallucinations showed no obvious affiliations, nor did first rank symptoms – some types of each were represented among the good and poor predictors. Overall, there was no obviously interpretable pattern, as can be seen from Table 3.4, which shows the 20 best predictors of outcome.

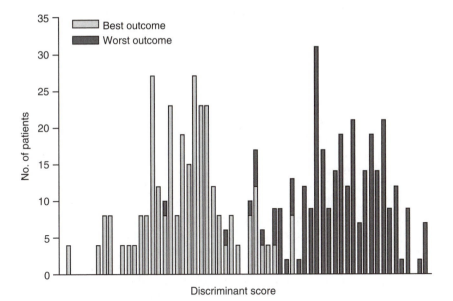

Figure 3.2 Discriminant function analysis of clinical features at initial presentation
in patients who were in the best and worst outcome groups at 2-year
follow-up (from WHO (1979), *Schizophrenia: An international follow-up
study*. Copyright 1979, John Wiley and Sons Limited. Reproduced with
permission).

Table 3.4 Best predictors of 2-year outcome in schizophrenia (clinical)

Good outcome	Poor outcome
Early waking	Suicidal thoughts
Overactivity	Flatness of affect
Ambivalence	Worries
Negativism	Change in sex behaviour
Derealisation	Mutism
Speech impediments	Repetitive movements
Mannerisms	Fantastic delusions
Lability of affect	Speech dissociation
Delusions of persecution	Situational anxiety
	Haughtiness
	Social withdrawal

Source: WHO (1979). *Schizophrenia: An international follow-up study*. © 1979 John Wiley and
Sons, Ltd. Reproduced by permission.

Conclusion

The message of this chapter is that a number of misconceptions about
the natural history of schizophrenia need to be avoided. One of these is
that it follows a remorselessly progressive course. The phenomenon of late

improvement, which Manfred Bleuler was the first to document, makes it clear that a much more sophisticated view needs to be taken, one which may in fact have no parallels in the rest of medicine. Manfred Bleuler's findings also suggest that the view that schizophrenia ultimately reaches a static, unchanging end state is an oversimplification: even after 20 years of illness nearly 25 per cent of patients were still experiencing quite severe worsening and improvements. As Owens *et al.* (1985a) put it, 'the idea of "burned out" schizophrenia is no longer acceptable, referring as it does more to the clinician's interest than to the realities of the established disorder'.

A second pitfall to be wary of is the concept of recovery in schizophrenia. The figures of around 50 per cent full or social recovery quoted in recent outcome studies will always include patients who may have no active psychotic symptoms, are able to work, and seem quite normal to their doctors, but who have undergone an unquestionable decline – that their relatives will often touchingly describe. These studies make one wonder just how much the astute clinical judgement of an earlier generation of studies has been sacrificed to the objectivity of rating scales covering symptoms and social function. The findings of one contemporary outcome study by Johnstone (1991, 1994), which could not be included in the studies reviewed in this chapter because it did not calculate overall outcome figures, tell their own story. Less than 20 per cent of the patients were in full-time work, less than 50 per cent were regarded as fully independent by their relatives, 60 per cent were single, and 60 per cent had no confiding relationship. More than 20 per cent had not had any visitors in the last six months, 44 per cent had not attended any social gathering or place of entertainment in the preceding month, half lacked interest in current affairs, and 60 per cent had no strong interest or hobby.

But it is in the area of prognosis that the most caution has to be exercised. Research in this area has come full circle from guarded statements by Kraepelin and Bleuler, through bold claims for the existence of subgroups of good and bad prognosis cases, to the hotchpotch of clinical features identified in the International Pilot Study of Schizophrenia. It is sobering to realise how insubstantial terms like 'benign', 'good prognosis', 'reactive' and 'schizophreniform' turn out to be when they are subjected to close scrutiny, and how frustrating an exercise it can be to try to pin down the pattern of prognostic factors that is undoubtedly there.

4   The diagnosis of schizophrenia

Identifying diseases by means of their characteristic symptoms and signs is one of the cornerstones of medicine whose value is usually taken for granted. It therefore comes as something of a surprise to find that the concepts of disease and diagnosis are fraught with difficulties and uncertainties (e.g. see Kendell, 1975; Clare, 1980). Every attempt to capture the essential nature of disease – as suffering, as presence of a lesion, as biological disadvantage, and so on – has been found to be unsatisfactory; like health, disease eludes easy definition. Diagnosis is also a rather less straightforward process than it might appear. The theoretical classification of disease, just like the classification of any natural phenomena, can never hope to be perfect, and there will always be areas of dispute. The practical act of making a diagnosis is less perfect still, being subject to human error and, rather more than might be wished, to the vagaries of medical fashion.

In most branches of medicine, any such reservations about disease and diagnosis are brushed aside. In psychiatry, however, they cannot be ignored. The concept of disease begins to show signs of strain when it is applied to disorders such as depression, anxiety and personality disorder, and it falters badly when it is faced with aspects of the human condition like alcoholism and sexual deviation. Psychiatric diagnosis is also complicated at the practical level by the need to rely on a set of symptoms which do not lend themselves to precise description. Worse still, making a psychiatric diagnosis tends not have the clear-cut implications it does in the rest of medicine – the prognosis can generally be counted on to range from complete recovery to permanent disability, and treatment all too often runs the gamut of psychotherapy, tranquillisers, neuroleptics, antidepressants, and ECT. Psychiatry runs the risk of – and is regularly accused of – merely giving patients labels that are meaningless if not pejorative.

More than any other psychiatric disorder, it is schizophrenia at which such criticisms have been levelled. The reasons for this are not hard to find: its symptoms are legion, its presentations are diverse, its cause is unknown, and its response to treatment is far from satisfactory. In the 1960s and 1970s these criticisms reached extraordinary heights, when as the 'sacred symbol of psychiatry', the antipsychiatry movement singled out the disorder for particular vilification and attack. This movement ran its course and abated, but it left a legacy of disquiet about the nature of schizophrenia, its status as a distinct entity, and the foundations on which its diagnosis is based. One way of considering the various nosological issues that have been raised over the years is to ask, in order, three questions. These are: *Does schizophrenia exist?; Is it separable from manic-depressive psychosis?*; and finally *Can it be diagnosed cross-sectionally?*

Does schizophrenia exist?

In the half-century or so after its introduction, schizophrenia made the transition from comfortable respectability to being of distinctly unsavoury reputation. The reasons for this decline are difficult to reconstruct and were undoubtedly multiple. They ranged from purely academic concerns about the apparent lack of definite boundaries between it and other psychotic disorders, to, at the other extreme, a social and political stand against what was perceived as the incarceration and barbaric treatment of individuals who deviated from society's norms.

But perhaps the most important factor was historical, in the shape of an extraordinary sequence of events that unfolded in the USA. As documented by Blashfield (1984) and Shorter (1997), in this country psychoanalysis and the psychodynamic tradition became mainstream psychiatric thought. Under the influence of leading figures like Meyer and Menninger, the medical model of mental disorders was more or less openly rejected, diagnosis on the basis of presenting symptoms was disdained, and clinical decision-making, so far as there was any, came to rest on intuition and interpretations of patterns of interpersonal relationships. In the words of another historian of this chapter in American psychiatry history, Paris (2005):

> After the Second World War, psychoanalysis dominated academic psychiatry. Forty years ago, the most influential departmental chairs in North America were trained psychoanalysts. Many prominent teachers in psychiatry belonged to an even more exclusive inner elite: training analysts who supervised candidates at independent 'institutes'. For a time, psychiatry as a discipline became almost indistinguishable from psychoanalysis. Graduates of the top residency programs aspired to become either psychotherapists or fully trained analysts.

American psychiatry retained the diagnostic concept of schizophrenia, but it was broadened drastically. This appears to have been at least partly on the basis of a statement made in passing by Bleuler (1911), that individuals with latent forms of schizophrenia, who showed far less in the way of manifest symptoms, were many times more frequent than fully developed cases. As a result, anyone and everyone could and often did receive the diagnosis. The term schizophrenia became used so loosely as to be virtually meaningless.

Eventually the credulity of some was strained too far and attempts were made to put American diagnostic practice to the test. In one study Katz *et al.* (1969) showed an audience of American and British psychiatrists a filmed interview with a young woman who described symptoms of anxiety and depression, and also gave an account of relationship difficulties and the frustrations of trying to make it as an actress in New York. A third of the American psychiatrists, but none of the British, gave her a diagnosis of schizophrenia. In another study (Rosenhan, 1973) eight volunteers posed as patients and sought admission to 12 American psychiatric hospitals of varying prestigiousness. Each complained of a single symptom – hearing voices saying single words like 'empty', 'thud' and 'hollow'. Otherwise, apart from falsifying their names and employment, they gave an entirely truthful history. The 'pseudopatients' were all admitted to hospital, whereupon they behaved as normally as they could. At first they took notes secretly, but soon they were able to do this openly as it became clear that the staff were not taking any interest in this activity. In 11 of the 12 cases, they were given a diagnosis of schizophrenia; the twelfth received a diagnosis of manic-depressive psychosis. In no cases was the deception detected by the hospital staff. By contrast, 35 out of a total of 118 patients on the same wards made statements like 'you're not crazy', 'you're a journalist', 'you're a professor' and 'you're checking up on the hospital'. The implication of this finding perhaps ought not to be spelled out.

In the wake these and other fiascos, a general uneasiness began to be felt about the way schizophrenia was diagnosed, and just how responsibly those making the diagnoses were acting. The opposition that built up can perhaps best be described as taking strong and weak forms. In the strong form, the whole concept of schizophrenia was attacked. The two luminaries of the antipsychiatry movement, Laing (1964, 1965, 1967) and Szasz (1960, 1971), and some lesser lights (e.g. Sarbin and Mancuso, 1980) argued that schizophrenia did not in fact exist, that it was an invention, a myth. To diagnose an individual as schizophrenic was a spurious attempt to 'medicalise' patterns of behaviour that were better understood in social or cultural terms. In the extreme form of these views, to label a person as schizophrenic was essentially a political act, designed to marginalise, victimise and persecute someone who was merely reacting understandably to the ills and hypocrisies of contemporary society.

The antipsychiatry position on schizophrenia cannot be done justice to here. A detailed and balanced account is given by Clare (1980) and a flavour of it is conveyed in Box 4.1. The important point, however, is that the claims made were essentially non-scientific in nature. The arguments advanced by antipsychiatry were passionate, polemical and sometimes just plain ill-informed, but they were not susceptible to any kind of confirmation or refutation, no alternative hypotheses were offered and no formal testable predictions were ever presented.

The weak form of the argument against the existence of schizophrenia, as

---

Box 4.1 The antipsychiatry position on schizophrenia (from Laing and Esterson (1964), *Sanity, madness and the family* (2nd edn), London: Tavistock Publications. Reproduced with permission)

When a psychiatrist diagnoses schizophrenia, he means that the patient's experience and behaviour are disturbed *because* there is something the matter with the patient that causes the disturbed behaviour he observes. He calls this something schizophrenia, and he then must ask what causes the schizophrenia.

We jumped off this line of reasoning at the beginning. In our view it is an assumption, a theory, a hypothesis, but not a *fact*, that anyone suffers from a condition called 'schizophrenia'. No one can deny us the right to disbelieve in the fact of schizophrenia. We did not say, even, that we do *not* believe in schizophrenia.

If anyone believes that 'schizophrenia' is a fact, he would do well to read critically the literature on 'schizophrenia' from its inventor Bleuler to the present day. After much disbelief in the new disease more and more psychiatrists adopted the term, though few English or American psychiatrists knew what it meant, since Bleuler's monograph, published in 1911, was not available in English until 1950. But though the term has now been generally adopted and psychiatrists trained in its application, the fact it is supposed to denote remains elusive. Even two psychiatrists from the same medical school cannot agree on who is schizophrenic independently of each other more than eight out of ten times at best; agreement is less than that between different schools, and less again between different countries. These figures are not in dispute. But when psychiatrists dispute the diagnosis there is no court of appeal. There are at present no objective, reliable, quantifiable criteria – behavioural or neurophysiological or biochemical – to appeal to when psychiatrists differ.

We do not accept 'schizophrenia' as being a biochemical, neurophysiological, psychological fact, and we regard it as palpable error, in the present state of the evidence, to take it to be a fact. Nor do we assume its existence. Nor do we adopt it as a hypothesis. We propose no model of it.

---

articulated by Bentall (1990, 2003) and Boyle (1990) requires more serious consideration. This accepts that mental illness exists, but maintains that it is wrong to split off a category of schizophrenia. Put more formally, the position taken is that the diagnosis of schizophrenia is so lacking in reliability and validity that it should be abandoned altogether. Such a view is perfectly amenable to testing, and in fact has always faced a certain amount of investigation along these lines. Between the 1930s and the 1970s, a number of studies of the reliability of psychiatric diagnosis were carried out (see Kendell, 1975; Blashfield, 1984). There were also a few attempts to test the validity of psychiatric diagnosis over the same period (see Bentall, 1990). Of all the studies, however, one, the International Pilot Study of Schizophrenia (WHO, 1973, 1979) stands out as being by far the largest, as being thorough, and also as being devoted specifically to schizophrenia. Accordingly, this study is focused on here and its findings are described in detail.

Reliability

Although it does not in itself establish validity, the demonstration that clinicians can agree on diagnosis is customarily regarded as a prerequisite for this.

The first phase of the International Pilot Study of Schizophrenia (WHO, 1973) consisted of an examination of 1202 patients who had been referred to psychiatric services in nine different countries. Patients were included on the basis that they showed abnormalities of mental state or behaviour that raised the possibility of a psychotic diagnosis. A detailed history was taken, and they underwent structured mental state examination using an early version of the Present State Examination. The participating psychiatrists then used all sources of information to make a diagnosis. It is important to note that the International Pilot Study of Schizophrenia was carried out in the days before criterion-based approaches to diagnosis like DSM III came into being, and beyond the fact that the psychiatrists were all schooled in the descriptive phenomenological approach, they were under no constraints in the way they made their decisions.

As part of the study, the participating psychiatrists interviewed five patients in pairs, but made their diagnoses independently. These diagnoses were then compared with each other. All told, 190 patients were so examined, 122 of whom were subsequently given a consensus diagnosis of schizophrenia. Complete diagnostic agreement was found in 131 (69 per cent). In many of the cases where there was disagreement, this was between one or another subcategory of schizophrenia. These involved particularly 19 patients who were diagnosed as 'schizoaffective' by one or other of the pair. There was disagreement over whether the diagnosis should be schizophrenia and affective psychosis in two cases. Only in five cases was there disagreement over a psychotic as opposed to a non-psychotic diagnosis.

This degree of inter-rater reliability may not appear outstandingly high, but it compares favourably to those of an earlier generation of reliability studies (see Kendell, 1975). The issues surrounding schizoaffective disorder are not trivial (see Chapter 13), but if it is accepted that differences of opinion within the overall category of psychosis are less important than those between psychotic and non-psychotic categories, then the level of serious disagreement falls to less than 3 per cent.

Validity

Of the many approaches to establishing validity, the psychologist Zubin (1967) has enumerated four that are particularly appropriate to psychiatry. *Content validity* merely requires that diagnosis depends on the clinical features that are alleged to define the condition, rather than being made on the basis of some other factor, for example overall severity of illness. *Concurrent validity* is the demonstration that clinical diagnosis can be corroborated by methods other than the clinical, for example scores on a rating scale or a psychological test. *Construct validity* is similar to concurrent validity, but here it is necessary to show that the clinical diagnosis is associated with some objectively measurable variable – an example would be measures of autonomic arousal in anxiety states. *Predictive validity*, which according to Kendell (1975) is by far the most important type, consists of determining that diagnosis is associated with a particular outcome, for example good or poor prognosis, mortality, or response to a particular treatment.

The concept of construct validity cannot be applied to schizophrenia, since no reliable marker for the disorder, biological or otherwise, has yet been found. However, some findings from the International Pilot Study (WHO, 1973, 1979) can be brought to bear on the remaining three aspects of validity, with the proviso that the fit is at times a little forced.

Content validity

Of the 1202 potentially psychotic patients recruited in the International Pilot Study, 811 were given a consensus diagnosis of schizophrenia. In these patients, as described in Chapter 2, the commonest symptoms were lack of insight, suspiciousness, flattening of affect, poor rapport, together with ideas and delusions of reference, delusions of persecution, auditory hallucinations, especially verbal, and alienation of thought. Much the same pattern was observed in each of the nine centres in different countries. The patterns of symptoms among the patients in the International Pilot Study who were given diagnoses of mania or psychotic depression were quite different. For mania, the most common symptoms were elated thoughts, lack of insight, observed elated mood, increased interests, delusions of persecution, delusions of grandeur, poor cooperation, sleep problems and early waking; for psychotic depression, they were depressed mood, gloomy thoughts, hopelessness, early waking, feels worse in morning, sleep problems, delusions of self-depreciation, anxiety, lack of insight and retardation.

The diagnosis of schizophrenia thus appeared to be firmly based on the presence of the cardinal symptoms of the disorder. While this statement might appear somewhat tautological, it has to be remembered that, as mentioned earlier, the psychiatrists taking part were not working to any explicit set of rules when making a diagnosis of schizophrenia; they could and did make significant numbers of diagnoses of simple, latent, residual and schizoaffective schizophrenia.

Concurrent validity

The requirement here, that independent methods of assessment converge to give the same diagnosis, is not easy to fulfil; no means of diagnosing schizophrenia other than the clinical has yet been devised. Something approximating to this test of validity was, however, achieved in the International Pilot Study, by virtue of the comparison it made between clinical diagnoses and diagnosis as generated by computer. The computer program employed, CATEGO, applied a standard set of rules to information from the mental state examination in order to arrive at an overall diagnostic classification. In order to do so, individual ratings of symptoms were first combined into 35 'PSE syndromes' of intuitively related phenomena, for example *nuclear syndrome* (first rank symptoms), *grandiose delusions*, *hypomania*, *simple depression* and *special features of depression* (biological symptoms). The PSE syndromes themselves were then combined into six descriptive categories according to further fixed rules (e.g. simple depression + depressive delusions = psychotic depression), with each being assigned its own degree of certainty. Finally, by utilising differential weights, systems of priorities, hierarchies and decision points, an overall diagnostic classification was generated for each patient.

Of 876 patients with a clinical diagnosis of schizophrenia or paranoid psychosis, 786 were also assigned by the CATEGO program to one of its three schizophrenic groups, 'S' (schizophrenic, i.e. psychoses with first rank symptoms or second person auditory hallucinations), 'P' (paranoid, where there were delusions of any type without auditory hallucinations but including any other type of hallucinations) and 'O' (other, mainly patients who showed only catatonic symptoms or symptoms such as talking to themselves). This gave a concordance of 89.7 per cent, considered by the investigators to be more than acceptable.

Predictive validity

In the absence of firm aetiological findings or of an outstanding response to treatment, the aspect of schizophrenia by which the diagnosis stands or falls is its tendency to poor outcome. Even this approach faces difficulties, as psychiatric outcome is not simple to measure and the differences among different disorders are not especially great. This aspect of validity was examined by the International Pilot Study (WHO, 1979) in a 2-year follow-up study of the original cohort of patients. This addressed what might be termed both quantitative and qualitative aspects of outcome, that patients with schizophrenia should be expected to show not just evidence of decline from a previous level of functioning, but also a particular kind of deterioration not seen in other diagnostic groups.

Table 4.1 Two-year outcome for schizophrenia, mania and depression in the International Pilot Study of Schizophrenia

Outcome measure	Schizophrenia (N = 543)*	Depression (N = 53)*	Mania (N = 73)*
Psychotic at follow-up (%)	37	14	26
Length of episode of inclusion >18 months (%)	27	9	2
In psychotic episode for more than 75 % of follow-up period (%)	28	9	4
Still in episode of inclusion at follow-up (%)	26	7	2
Severe social impairment (%)	23	10	9
In worst overall outcome group (%)	18	7	2

* Numbers varied slightly across the analyses.

Source: Adapted from WHO (1979).

Quantitatively, social functioning was assessed at the end of the 2-year period, as were a number of clinical course indicators such as percentage of follow-up period spent psychotic, frequency of active psychotic symptoms at follow-up examination, and numbers of patients still actively psychotic at the end of the follow-up period. Table 4.1 shows the percentages of patients with diagnoses of schizophrenia, depression and mania falling into the worst outcome groups on these clinical and social measures. Twenty-three per cent of the schizophrenic patients were found to show severe social impairment, more than twice the rate seen in any other diagnostic group. All the other measures similarly distinguished the schizophrenic patients from other two groups. The differences were significant in every case except for between the percentages of schizophrenic and manic patients still psychotic at follow-up.

Qualitatively, the 15 commonest symptoms in the schizophrenic patients at follow-up were compared to those of the patients with mania or depression. As shown in Table 4.2, the pattern was clearly different in each case. Patients diagnosed as schizophrenic, but not the other two groups, displayed a clinical picture instantly recognisable as chronic schizophrenia.

In one way, however, the predictive validity of schizophrenia left something to be desired. During the 2-year follow-up period, 177 of the 811 patients with an initial diagnosis of schizophrenia experienced one or more further episodes of illness. While the vast majority of these episodes could be characterised as schizophrenic or probably schizophrenic, in 16 per cent of cases the presentation was one of depression or mania. In a small but significant number of patients, the course of schizophrenia did not seem to run true.

In summary, having been subjected to very close scrutiny in the International Pilot Study, the reality of schizophrenia emerges as clearly established.

Table 4.2 15 commonest symptoms at 2-year follow-up in patients initially diagnosed as schizophrenic, depressed and manic

	Frequency of symptom (%)	
Schizophrenia	Depression	Mania
Lack of insight (42.5)	Worse in morning (30.6)	Lack of insight (27.4)
Flatness of affect (27.1)	Lack of insight (19.4)	Elated thoughts (19.6)
Poor rapport (26.3)	Early waking (16.3)	Early waking (19.6)
Suspiciousness (25.2)	Gloomy thoughts (15.3)	Elated mood (15.7)
Inadequate description (25.2)	Hypochondriacal (15.3)	Worse in morning (13.7)
Unwilling to cooperate (24.5)	Hopelessness (13.9)	Ideas of reference (11.8)
Apathy (18.8)	Situational anxiety (13.9)	Self-depreciation (11.8)
Ideas of reference (18.0)	Lability of affect (13.9)	Verbal hallucinations (11.8)
Delusions of reference (14.2)	Obsessive thoughts (9.2)	Voices speak to patient (11.8)
Restricted speech (12.9)	Delusional mood (8.3)	Auditory hallucinations (11.8)
Delusions of persecution (12.7)	Anxiety (8.3)	Depressed mood (11.8)
Hypochondriacal (12.7)	Sleep problems (8.3)	Sleep problems (11.8)
Autism (12.7)	Inadequate description (8.3)	Unwilling to cooperate (11.8)
Auditory hallucinations (11.6)	Flatness of affect (8.3)	Flight of ideas (9.8)
Verbal hallucinations (10.7)	Social withdrawal (8.3)	Pressure of speech (9.8)

Source: Adapted from WHO (1979).

The diagnosis can be made at least reasonably reliably, and the disorder shows evidence of validity in each of the admittedly rather limited ways that can be devised to test this. There is only one reservation to this conclusion: a minority of patients diagnosed as schizophrenic will have later relapses that are affective rather than schizophrenic in character. This raises the curtain on the next question about the nosological status of schizophrenia, that of how far it and manic-depressive psychosis can be considered to be separate from one another.

Can schizophrenia be separated from manic-depressive psychosis?

As important as the controversy about its existence was, most psychiatrists have never been in any doubt that patients showing the requisite clinical features were all too frequent and obvious. A far more significant and possibly less futile debate has been whether schizophrenia is a distinct clinical syndrome, or whether, as authors like Bentall (1990, 2003) maintain, it spuriously separates a group of cases from what is in reality a continuously varying matrix of functional psychosis. As the other main variety of functional psychosis is manic-depressive psychosis, this question reduces to whether the disorders are separate or whether they lie at opposite poles of a continuum with no sharp point of demarcation in between.

This issue is by no means new. In the nineteenth century (and traceable back even earlier), one school of psychiatric thought held that there was only one type of insanity – *Einheitpsychose* – which took endlessly varying forms in different individuals (see Berrios, 1987; Beer, 1996). After Kraepelin separated schizophrenia and manic-depressive psychosis, the concept of unitary psychosis was eclipsed, but it never completely disappeared. A version of it has provided a longstanding undercurrent to discussions about the status of schizoaffective psychosis (see Chapter 13), and it regularly surfaces in discussions about the alleged overlap in the genetic basis of psychotic disorders (e.g. Crow, 1986; Craddock and Owen, 2005).

Debates on where schizophrenia and manic-depressive psychosis stand in relation to one another have invariably had recourse not only to their presenting features, but also to their course, their outcome, their family history, and even their treatment (e.g. see Kerr and McClelland, 1991; Bentall, 2003). However, the obvious approach – and arguably the only one that is ultimately meaningful – is to judge their separation at a clinical level. If schizophrenia is a valid syndrome it should be characterised by a set of symptoms that tend to run together, and a relative lack of symptoms of other disorders should be evident; and the same should hold true for manic-depressive psychosis.

The patterns of aggregation and segregation among psychotic symptoms can be examined in a relatively straightforward way by applying the techniques of multivariate statistical analysis. This requires, first, the collection of a sample of patients with both disorders, which should be both large and unselected. Then all the patients' symptoms need to be rated, preferably in detail and when they are acutely ill. The symptom scores can then be subjected to factor, cluster or discriminant function analysis. If schizophrenia and manic-depressive psychosis are separate entities, two distinguishable patterns of symptomatology should emerge. In practice, a number of obstacles lie in the way of achieving this aim. One of these is the statistical techniques themselves (particularly cluster analysis as will be seen below), which are not always appropriate for disorders whose symptoms overlap substantially. In addition, many of the relevant studies in this area are also less than ideal for examining this issue, most commonly because their samples have not been restricted solely to psychotic patients. The best studies are described below.

Factor analytic studies

This set of related techniques (see Blashfield, 1984) works by mathematically transforming a large number of variables that show all degrees of correlation with each other into a series of new variables, or factors, that are uncorrelated with each other. These factors have 'loadings' of +1 to –1 on the original variables, and a few of them often account for a substantial proportion of the original variance in the sample. As applied to psychiatric classification, the initial variables are scores on different symptoms, and the factors translate into syndromes – items with high loadings on a particular factor represent highly associated constellations of symptoms. It is accepted (though often seemingly forgotten) that there is no necessity for the number of factors isolated to correspond to the number of hypothetical underlying sources of variation; that is, the syndromes themselves should not be taken as intrinsically meaningful. It should also be borne in mind that factor analysis can only isolate groups of related symptoms and not groups of patients, and so its bearing on the separation of schizophrenia and manic-depressive psychosis is conceptually somewhat indirect.

Among a number early factor analytic studies of psychiatric populations (reviewed by Blashfield, 1984), those of Lorr *et al.* (1963) stand out at probably the most exhaustive and also the most appropriate, being carried out on samples made up only of patients with functional psychosis. From a series of their own and others' samples, Lorr *et al.* (1963) concluded that 10 factors had validity. These were: *excitement* (conforming closely to manic symptoms), *hostile belligerence* (essentially the attitudes and behaviours of hostility), *paranoid projection* (persecutory, referential and other delusions, and passivity), *grandiose expansiveness* (grandiose ideas, delusions and behaviours), *perceptual distortion* (mainly various modalities of hallucination), *anxious intropunitiveness* (a constellation of depressive symptoms), *retardation and apathy* (objective signs of retardation), *motor disturbances* (principally catatonic phenomena), *conceptual disorganisation* (formal thought disorder) and *disorientation* (as commonly understood).

Lorr *et al.* then proceeded to factor analyse the 10 factors themselves to produce a set of second order factors. When this was done, three factors emerged: one was a bipolar factor containing all the first order factors that would might be expected to be associated with manic-depressive psychosis, with the exception of *grandiose expansiveness*. The second factor loaded on *grandiose expansiveness* and on the two delusion and hallucination factors, and was considered to correspond fairly closely to paranoid schizophrenia. The third of the second order factors, which loaded on *disorientation, motor disturbances, conceptual disorganisation* and *retardation and apathy*, was considered to combine elements of hebephrenic and catatonic schizophrenia.

These studies were all carried out in America in the days before DSM III, using scales that were not perhaps ideally suited to capturing psychopathology. Table 4.3 summarises nine more recent factor analytic studies that (a) used phenomenologically oriented structured interviews to rate symptoms; (b) examined unselected groups of psychotic patients; and (c) entered individual symptom scores into the analysis rather than overall measures such as global delusion or negative symptoms scores. This last requirement was included in order to avoid the criticism made by Stuart *et al.* (1999) that use of scores for entire categories of symptoms rather than for the individual symptoms themselves would necessarily constrain the number of factors that could be produced.

All the studies isolated unquestionable mania and depression factors. Schizophrenia was invariably represented by more than one factor, but

Table 4.3 Factor analytic studies of unselected psychotic patients

Study	Sample	Psychopathology ratings	No. of factors	Variance accounted for (%)	Positive symptoms	Negative symptoms	Disorganisation	Mania	Depression	Other	Comment
Kitamura et al. (1995)	584 consecutive admissions	Authors' own structured interview	5	Not stated	✓			✓	✓	Negative symptoms/ disorganisation Catatonia	Patients with drug abuse, mental handicap, organic brain disease included
McGorry et al. (1998)	509 first episode patients	MIP	4 and 6	Not stated	✓	✓		✓	✓	Negative symptoms/ disorganisation/ catatonia	Negative symptom factor appeared in six factor solution
Van Os et al. (1996)	672 inpatients with chronic psychosis	CPRS	4	26.4	✓	✓		✓	✓	—	—
Van Os et al. (1999)	448 inpatients with chronic psychosis	OPCRIT	5	41	✓	✓	✓	✓	✓	—	—
Rosenman et al. (2000)	978 patients in epidemiological survey	OPCRIT	5	55.4	✓	✓	✓	✓	✓	Negative symptoms/ disorganisation	Substance abuse factor also identified
Cuesta and Peralta (2001)	660 consecutive acute admissions	AMDP	10	54	✓ (2 factors)	✓	✓	✓	✓	Positive catatonia/ restlessness Negative catatonia/ perplexity Dysphoria/ irritability Lack of insight	Delusions and hallucinations/ thought interference in separate factors

Study	Sample	Instrument								Notes
McIntosh et al. (2001)	204 acute admissions	OPCRIT	4	39	✓	✓	✓	✓	—	Single negative symptom included (restricted affect) loaded on disorganisation factor
Serretti et al. (2001)*	2241 consecutive acute admissions	OPCRIT	4	47.1	✓	✓	✓	✓	—	Negative symptoms loaded on disorganisation factor
Murray et al. (2005)	387 patients in epidemiological survey	OPCRIT	4	29.2	✓	✓	✓	✓	—	Negative symptoms loaded on disorganisation factor

* Includes patients of Serretti et al. (1996).
MIP: Royal Park Multidiagnostic Instrument for Psychosis; CPRS: Comprehensive Psychopathological Rating Scale; AMDP: Manual for the Assessment and Documentation of Psychopathology; OPCRIT: Detailed checklist for use with interview and case-note information.

these were broadly consistent with Liddle's positive, negative and disorganisation syndromes (see Chapter 2): all the studies isolated a factor (or in one case two factors) consisting of delusions and hallucinations, and there were factors that were immediately recognisable as negative symptoms and disorganisation (sometimes combined into a single factor). Other factors were isolated in some studies but, as in Lorr *et al.*'s earlier study, these were for the most part clinically intuitive, for example catatonic symptoms and lack of insight.

Cluster analytic studies

This disparate group of techniques (over 150 methods have been developed) aims to subdivide heterogeneous populations into more homogeneous subgroups of its members (Kendell, 1975; Blashfield, 1984). In order to achieve this, the individual members of the sample are partitioned and re-partitioned into groups of varying size, which are then examined according to some criterion of within-group similarity or between-group dissimilarity until an optimum is reached. Cluster analysis has advantages over factor analysis for psychiatric classification because it isolates groupings of patients rather than groupings of symptoms. However, the technique faces difficulties of its own. One of the most important of these is that a hierarchy of solutions is always generated, from a single cluster that takes in the whole population to one that has a cluster for each individual member. An intermediate solution must be chosen from somewhere between these extremes, either intuitively or on the basis of a variety of mathematical devices, none of which is without its critics. Another problem, which might be particularly important for psychiatric classification, is that cluster analysis generates mutually exclusive subgroups of individuals within a population; subjects can only belong to one cluster and those showing mixed forms cannot be accommodated within the model.

Cluster analysis in one or another of its forms has been applied to psychotic patients many times (see Blashfield, 1984). Unfortunately many of the studies have used inappropriate material (e.g. scores on psychological tests), or had other shortcomings, notably not being restricted to patients with psychosis. For example, the otherwise scrupulous study of Everitt *et al.* (1971) contained only just over 309 psychotic patients in a total sample of 500. Only two studies stand out as being of a high standard methodologically, and even these for one reason or another are not ideal.

Lorr *et al.* (1966) clustered profiles of symptoms in 547 acute admissions to hospital, almost all of whom had a clinical diagnosis of schizophrenic or affective 'reaction'. The analysis was carried out independently on the male and female patients in the sample. Nine clusters were isolated, of which seven met the anthors' criterion of validity, that of being common to both men and women. No direct comparison with clinical diagnosis was made (which was probably a good idea in the USA in the 1960s); however, one cluster seemed clearly to consist of patients with mania, and another of those with depression, including those both with and without psychotic features. Four 'paranoid' clusters were identified; these contained patients with persecutory delusions variously in combination with grandiose delusions, hallucinations or disturbed behaviour. However, the remaining clusters, which contained patients with disorientation, motor abnormalities, and anxiety accompanied by psychotic phenomena, had no obvious clinical counterparts.

A cluster analysis was also carried out as part of the International Pilot Study of Schizophrenia (WHO, 1973). This was performed on all 1202 patients most, though not all, of whom were ultimately given a psychotic diagnosis. Based on rather opaque reasoning that the most interesting division of patients was likely to fall between 6 and 12 groups, the 10-cluster solution, which seemed both the mathematically best structured of these, was chosen. The results were much less clear than in Lorr *et al*'s study; clinically diagnosed schizophrenic and manic-depressive patients were found to be distributed across all 10 clusters. The distribution, however, was highly significantly non-random and patients with particular clinical diagnoses were over-represented in a small number of clusters.

These two studies were not conspicuously successful in separating schizophrenic from manic-depressive patients. However, it could be asking too much of the technique to do this, because of the problem alluded to above. Cluster analysis always generates mutually exclusive subgroups of individuals based on their features, and this is arguably inappropriate for disorders where the diagnosis commonly rests on the relative prominence of different classes of symptom, as well as their phenomenological nuances – the quality of the mood change, the congruence or incongruence of delusions and hallucinations, and so on. This problem is avoided in a recently developed form of multivariate technique, Grade of Membership analysis (Woodbury and Manton, 1989). Like cluster analysis, this assigns subjects to what are called 'pure types', which are intended to be similar to prototypical or 'textbook' cases. Unlike cluster analysis, it permits 'fuzzy' class membership: the individual subjects need not be assigned to a single diagnostic class and the analysis generates a value for the degree to which each subject belongs to each pure type.

Manton *et al.* (1994) applied Grade of Membership analysis to the 1065 patients out of the 1202 in the International Pilot Study of Schizophrenia for whom sufficient data were available. They used current symptoms elicited in the diagnostic interview, plus information about symptoms during the current episode as obtained from an informant. An eight pure type solution was found to give the best fit. Its findings are summarised in Table 4.4. Two of the pure types corresponded to mania and depression. Three pure types were considered to be related the diagnostic concept of schizophrenia. One was a psychotic syndrome characterised uniquely by auditory hallucinations, but that also featured other hallucinations, first rank symptoms, persecutory delusions and flattening of affect, all shared with other pure types. The

Table 4.4 Symptom profiles of schizophrenic and affective pure types generated by Grade of Membership analysis

A. Schizophrenic pure types

Pure type I	*Pure type II*	*Pure type III*
Unique features		
Verbal hallucinations (1.00)	Changed appearance (1.00)	Apathy (1.00)
Voices speak to patient (1.00)	Distorted time perception (1.00)	Restricted speech
Frequent auditory hallucinations (1.00)	Looking at self (1.00)	(1.00)
Voices speak full sentences (1.00)	Break of self-identity (1.00)	Negativism (0.61)
Voices discussing patient (1.00)	Depersonalisation (1.00)	
Non-verbal auditory hallucinations (0.99)	Sexual delusions (1.00)	
Voices commenting on thoughts (1.00)	Gustatory hallucinations (0.83)	
Auditory pseudohallucinations (0.48)	Nihilistic delusions (0.77)	
Hallucinations from body (0.42)	Sexual hallucinations (0.45)	
	Delusions of impending doom (0.44)	
Shared features		
First rank symptoms	First rank symptoms	Autism
Delusions of persecution	Many positive psychotic	Flatness of affect
Tactile, visual and olfactory	phenomena	Self-neglect
hallucinations		Decreased interests
Flatness of affect		Speech
		dissociation
		Stereotypies,
		ambivalence

The two paranoid pure types contained shared symptoms only, including suspiciousness, delusions of persecution, delusional system, ideas of reference, verbal and physical aggression, overactivity and agitation, bizarre behaviour and visual hallucinations (pure type VI); and suspiciousness, delusions of persecution, delusions of reference, delusional mood, ideas of reference, unwilling to cooperate and poor rapport (pure type VII). Figures in brackets are lambda$_{kj}$ values, the probability that a symptom will be expressed by a pure type.

second was characterised chiefly by psychotic forms of depersonalisation and derealisation (changed appearance, experience of looking at one's self from outside, experience of a break in the identity of the self and distorted time perception), but also by many other psychotic symptoms which were shared with other types. The third consisted almost exclusively of negative symptoms and the attributes of chronic and residual schizophrenia – autism, stereotypies, ambivalence and negativism. The two remaining pure types were similar to each other and were considered to reflect paranoid psychosis. They contained patients with persecutory delusions, ideas of reference, suspiciousness, irritability, aggression and bizarre behaviour. The final pure type was an asymptomatic type.

Discriminant function analysis

This technique, described in detail by Kendell (1975), is conceptually rather different to factor and cluster analysis. It is carried out in a number of stages.

B. Affective pure types

Pure type IV	Pure Type V
Unique features	
Depressed mood (1.00)	Observed elated mood (1.00)
Hopelessness (1.00)	Lability of affect (1.00)
Worse in morning (1.00)	Demonstrative (1.00)
Special quality of depression (1.00)	Flight of ideas (1.00)
Decreased energy (1.00)	Pressure of speech (1.00)
Retardation (1.00)	Sudden changes in direction of interests (1.00)
Decreased libido (1.00)	Mood swings (1.00)
Suicidal tendencies (1.00)	Perseveration (0.93)
Delusions of self-depreciation/guilt (1.00)	Suggestibility (0.89)
Decreased interest (1.00)	Change of interests (0.88)
Indecision (0.85)	Ecstatic mood (0.70)
Worse in evening (0.58)	Klang associations (0.50)
Shared features	
Delusions of guilt	Delusions
Suicidal thoughts	Hallucinations
Obsessive thoughts	Autism and ambivalence
Retardation	Others

Source: Manton *et al.* (1994), Symptom profiles of psychiatric disorders based on graded disease classes: An illustration using data from the International Pilot Study of Schizophrenia. *Psychological Medicine*, 24, 133–144. Reproduced with permission from Cambridge University Press.

First, a sample (i.e. psychotic patients) consisting of two identified subpopulations (i.e. those with schizophrenia and manic-depressive psychosis) are rated on a set of variables that are considered relevant to the distinction between them. Next, a way of weighting each of these variables is calculated which achieves the maximum possible degree of separation of the two alleged subpopulations. In the final stage, the scores on all the weighted variables are summed for each individual and the results plotted as a histogram. If the two subpopulations are genuinely distinct a bimodal distribution with well-separated means will be the result; if not the distribution will be unimodal.

Discriminant function analysis avoids many of the problems of factor and cluster analysis. Probably the most important difficulty it faces lies in the determination of whether the final distribution is bimodal or not: the decision rests ultimately on scrutiny of the histogram, for a central 'point of rarity'. This can be supplemented by one of several mathematical validators, for example testing whether the distribution differs significantly from a normal distribution, but the superiority of these methods over visual inspection is debatable.

Discriminant function analysis has been applied to the distinction between schizophrenia and manic-depressive psychosis twice, on both occasions in large-scale and rigorous studies. The first of these was a well-known study by

Kendell and co-workers (Kendell and Gourlay, 1970) and the somewhat less well-known follow-up study of the same patients by Brockington *et al.* (1979). The second is an almost universally ignored series of analyses performed in the International Pilot Study of Schizophrenia.

Kendell and Gourlay (1970) used clinical assessments on 292 acutely ill patients, 146 with a diagnosis of schizophrenia and 146 with a diagnosis of affective psychosis, which included both manic and depressed patients. The sample was drawn from the British and American patients in a study that compared psychiatric diagnosis in New York and London (Cooper *et al.*, 1972), and in all cases the diagnoses had been made by the same team on the basis of detailed history and mental state information. Out of the many hundreds of clinical ratings available, a preliminary analysis found 90 that differed significantly in frequency of occurrence between the groups. From these, 14 history and 24 mental state items were selected as the best potential discriminators. Some of these, like 'blunting of affect' and 'hears voices nearly every day', followed clinical intuition; others such as 'difficulty relaxing' and 'always nervous or highly strung', and also age and sex, were more surprising choices. The discriminant function had a distribution that was significantly different from a normal (i.e. unimodal) distribution, but, as shown in Figure 4.1, appeared trimodal rather than unimodal.

Five to eight years later, Brockington *et al.* (1979) carried out a further discriminant function analysis on 128 of the 134 British patients in the sample, this time including follow-up information. This time the distribution obtained was unequivocally bimodal. The findings of this study are also illustrated in Figure 4.1.

A number of discriminant function analyses were also performed in the International Pilot Study of Schizophrenia (WHO, 1979). These were carried out on groups of over 500 patients, and they differed from the studies of Kendell and co-workers in that schizophrenic patients were compared separately with those diagnosed as manic and with those diagnosed as depressed. The most important analysis, in which patients with clinical diagnoses of schizophrenia and mania or depression were compared on the basis of the symptoms they exhibited at initial presentation, is also illustrated in Figure 4.1. Both for schizophrenia and mania, and for schizophrenia and depression, the distributions were clearly bimodal, and the overlap between the two groups of patients was small.

Figure 4.1 Discriminant function analyses of groups of schizophrenic and manic-depressive patients (from Kendell and Gourlay (1970), The clinical distinction between the affective psychoses and schizophrenia. *British Journal of Psychiatry*, 117, 261–266; Brockington *et al.* (1979), The distinction between the affective psychoses and schizophrenia. *British Journal of Psychiatry*, 135, 243–248. Reproduced with permission from the Royal College of Psychiatrists; WHO (1979), *Schizophrenia: An international follow-up study*. Copyright 1979, John Wiley and Sons Limited. Reproduced with permission).

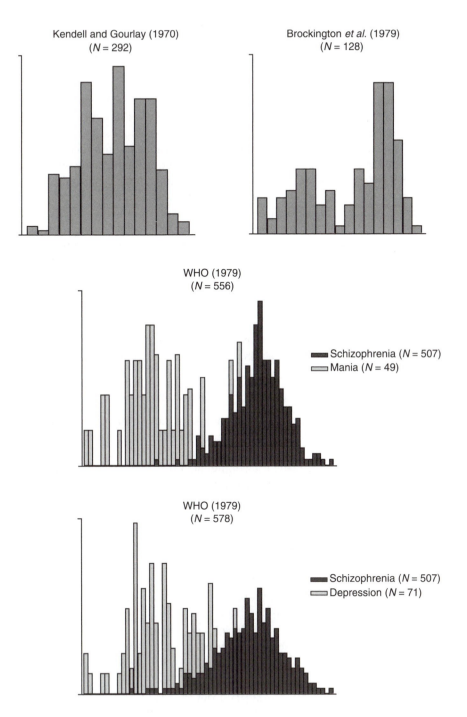

Figure 4.1

The minimal conclusion that can be drawn from studies using multivariate statistics is that schizophrenia and manic-depressive psychosis are not a single disorder. Factor analysis has always isolated groupings of symptoms that are obviously identifiable with depression and mania. Schizophrenia certainly emerges from these studies as a syndrome with a complex internal structure, but this approximates to Liddle's positive, negative and disorganisation division, which is not widely regarded as having diminished the disorder's unitary status. The cluster analytic findings seem at first sight damning, but this evidence might be inadmissable on a technicality – the requirement for mutual exclusivity of clusters makes the technique unable to deal with the fuzzy sets of psychiatric diagnosis. Grade of Membership analysis, which was designed with fuzzy sets in mind, partitions mania and depression from schizophrenia startlingly well, although it hints at unexpected subdivisions within the schizophrenic syndrome itself. Contrary to the strong interpretations later placed on it, Kendell and co-workers viewed the findings of their original discriminant function study as ambiguous. By the time of their second study, which incorporated follow-up information, there was no longer any room for doubt: the distribution was unequivocally bimodal. The findings of the International Pilot Study, which concentrated firmly on cross-sectional symptomatology, on the other hand, are unqualified: the clinical classification of patients as schizophrenic as opposed to manic or depressed reflects measurable differences in their patterns of symptoms.

Can schizophrenia be diagnosed cross-sectionally?

At the heart of the concept of schizophrenia is the coupling of a characteristic clinical picture and a certain kind of outcome. As a way of defining a disease, this is entirely legitimate. As an approach to diagnosis, however, it contains a whiff of tautology: schizophrenia, a disorder defined in part by a deteriorating course, can only be said with certainty to be present when signs of deterioration become apparent. If the diagnosis of schizophrenia is not to be confounded with what was historically its main purpose, that of prognosis, it follows that it should be capable of being made at an early stage, as it were cross-sectionally rather than longitudinally.

It was Bleuler (1911) who, probably not with exactly this intention in mind, made the first attempt to articulate a set of principles for the foolproof diagnosis of schizophrenia. He proposed that there were a number of what he called fundamental symptoms in schizophrenia, which were 'present in every case and at every period of the illness even though, as with every other disease, they must have attained a certain degree of intensity before they can be recognized with any certainty'. These comprised *association disturbance*, or formal thought disorder; *affective disturbance*, especially flattening and inappropriateness; *autism*, the tendency to consider inner life more real than the outside world; and *ambivalence*, the ability of patients to hold completely contradictory feelings, wishes and beliefs simultaneously.

Bleuler was not entirely clear about the extent to which fundamental symptoms could be used in the service of diagnosis. Nevertheless, they were seized on for this purpose, to some extent in Europe (see Hoenig, 1983), but above all in the USA. As psychiatrists in this latter country broadened the concept of schizophrenia to the point of meaninglessness, it was on the alleged presence of mild fundamental symptoms that the diagnosis came to be based. After this approach to schizophrenia collapsed, as described above, fundamental symptoms found themselves taking much of the blame, being criticised as too soft and too subjective to be diagnostically useful. Even if these criticisms were overstated, it had become abundantly clear that basing the diagnosis of schizophrenia on symptoms that were difficult to define and not sharply demarcated from normality was never going to be viable.

Two other approaches to the cross-sectional diagnosis of schizophrenia have arisen out of the failure of fundamental symptoms. The first originated in the attempt by Schneider (1958) to identify a set of pathognomonic, or first rank symptoms. The second approach is essentially that taken by current criterion-based diagnostic schemes, and might be referred to as the concept of schizophrenia as non-affective functional psychosis.

Schneider's first rank symptoms

Recognising that psychiatric diagnosis 'must be based on the presenting situation and not on the course taken by the illness', Schneider (1958) proposed that certain symptoms were of special diagnostic importance for schizophrenia. As described in Chapter 1, these were certain types of auditory hallucinations, thought withdrawal, insertion and broadcasting, passivity experiences and delusional perception. These symptoms were not always present or even especially frequent in schizophrenic patients, but when they were there, and when there was no evidence of organic brain disease, according to Schneider the diagnosis could be made with certainty. In their absence, diagnosis had to rest on symptoms of second rank importance – other delusions and hallucinations, affective changes, and exceptionally the presence of formal thought disorder alone.

Schneider arrived at his concept of first rank symptoms from his own clinical experience and their pathognomonicity was supported only by his clinical authority. It was left to subsequent investigators to determine how useful they were in practice, or to put it another way, how sensitive and specific they were to schizophrenia.

What was to all intents and purposes the sensitivity of first rank symptoms was examined in a spate of studies of their prevalence among schizophrenic patients, carried out in the 1960s and 1970s. These were reviewed by Koehler *et al.* (1977), whose table is reproduced in Table 4.5. This makes it clear that first rank symptoms are a far from universal finding in schizophrenia: at most 72 per cent of patients will exhibit one or more of the relevant phenomena at any given point in their illness, with around 50 per cent being a more realistic

Table 4.5 Frequencies of first rank symptoms in schizophrenia

Type of study	Number of patients	% with first rank symptoms
Case record		
Huber (1967)	195	72
Taylor (1972)	78	28
Abrams and Taylor (1973)	71	34
Koehler (1979)	210	33
Prospective		
Mellor (1970)	166	72
Carpenter *et al.* (1973)	103	51
Carpenter and Strauss (1974)	801	57

Source: Koehler *et al.* (1977), First rank symptoms in Schneider-oriented German centers. *Archives of General Psychiatry*, 34, 810–813. © 1977, American Medical Association.

figure. As a means of diagnosing schizophrenia cross-sectionally, first rank symptoms leave a lot to be desired.

If they were specific to schizophrenia, first rank symptoms would still be a valuable aid to diagnosis. Two studies, however, suggested that this was not the case. Taylor and Abrams (1973) and Carpenter *et al.* (1973) examined groups of patients with affective disorder and found one or more first rank symptoms could be elicited in 11 per cent of manic patients and 23 per cent of both manic and depressed patients respectively. Although these studies went on to be widely quoted, they are both open to criticism. Taylor and Abrams employed their own diagnostic criteria for mania, which even at the time were notorious for being loose. None of their patients had been given a clinical diagnosis of mania and a significant proportion also displayed catatonic symptoms. The findings of Carpenter *et al.*'s study, where the diagnosis of affective psychosis was based on a wealth of clinical material, including structured psychiatric interview, are more difficult to dismiss. Nevertheless, this study also found that that 2 of 23 patients (9 per cent) with diagnoses of neurosis or personality disorder also showed first rank symptoms, a finding that few psychiatrists would find easy to swallow.

Two further studies have had more sober findings. Wing and Nixon (1975) reviewed all the patients in the International Pilot Study of Schizophrenia who had been rated as having first rank symptoms. They found that in 95 per cent of cases the patients had been assigned a clinical diagnosis of schizophrenia or paranoid psychosis. The frequency of first rank symptoms among other diagnostic groups was 7.5 per cent overall, and it was only in patients diagnosed as manic that the rates were anything like substantial (13 of 79 cases). The remaining ratings were scattered among patients with depressive diagnoses (9 of 176 cases) and neurosis and personality disorder (1 of 53 cases). When the mental state interviews for the 13 manic patients were examined, it was found that in most cases the justification for the first rank symptom being present was either inadequate or not given. Only in two patients were there were some grounds to believe that the symptom may have been present and even here there was room for doubt.

O'Grady (1990) suspected that some of the conflicting findings might reflect how broadly or narrowly first rank symptoms were defined. He examined 99 acute admissions to hospital using a structured psychiatric interview. First rank symptoms were rated according to wide or narrow criteria, based on proposals previously made by Koehler (1979). For example, the narrow definition of thought withdrawal involved thoughts ceasing in the subject's mind due to the direct influence of an outside agency, whereas the wide definition was thought block without the experience of their being interfered with by an outside agency. Four of 34 patients meeting diagnostic criteria for major depressive disorder were found to show first rank symptoms. Two of these only met a wide definition but two met the narrow definition. None of 12 manic patients showed first rank symptoms, but one who received a diagnosis of schizoaffective mania did.

The disputes about the findings in this area cannot be fully resolved. However, a reasonable synthesis might be that first rank symptoms will be encountered in between a fifth and a quarter of manic-depressive patients. Some of these patients will show enough other schizophrenic symptoms to warrant a diagnosis of schizoaffective psychosis (see Chapter 13). Taking a rigorous phenomenological approach may reduce the frequency further (to 4 per cent in O'Grady's study). But this will not banish the phenomenon altogether and there will always be some patients who show first rank symptoms as part of an otherwise unexceptional picture of mania or psychotic depression.

Schizophrenia as non-affective functional psychosis

In this approach, diagnosis is achieved, quite simply, by weighing up the various different elements of the clinical picture at the time of initial presentation, disregarding – in theory, if not always in practice – the longer-term course. In these circumstances the differentiation of schizophrenia from manic-depressive psychosis turns on whether or not there is significant mood change, whether this mood change has the unique features of mania or depression rather than merely being the kind of schizophrenic mood colouring described in Chapter 1, and whether it is present to a degree that an affective diagnosis makes intuitive sense. If there is a functional psychotic state in the absence of these features, then the diagnosis must, by default, be schizophrenia.

The origins of this method of diagnosis can probably be traced back to Kraepelin (1913a) who felt that, while no individual symptom was characteristic of schizophrenia, the composition of the entire picture was often, though not always, decisive. Schneider (1958) took a similar position when he stated that in the absence of first rank symptoms diagnosis had to depend wholly on the coherence of the rest of the clinical features. But by far the most important influence on the development of this approach was the so-called neo-Kraepelinian movement in American psychiatry which culminated in DSM III.

As described by Blashfield (1984) and Wilson (1993), a small number of American psychiatrists took stock of the appalling diagnostic disarray in this country, and, with a certain amount of conspiracy, set out to re-establish psychiatric diagnosis on the basis of symptoms and signs. The first step was Feighner *et al.*'s (1972) development of a set of reliable operational criteria for selected psychiatric disorders; this was ostensibly for the purposes of research. Then Spitzer *et al.* (1978) developed a more refined and elaborate version of these criteria, the Research Diagnostic Criteria (RDC). By this time, although research was the stated purpose, it was clear that issues of classification and diagnosis were beginning to be confronted for their own sake. It was natural that Spitzer should then head a task force set up to revise the slim and nondescript American psychiatric diagnostic manual, as required by a treaty with the World Health Organization, which was updating its own *International Classification of Diseases* (ICD). The result was the 567-page *Diagnostic and Statistical Manual of Mental Disorders*, 3rd edition, or DSM III. Closely modelled on the RDC, this based all diagnoses on the presence of rigorously defined symptoms, which had to be present in certain combinations for certain periods of time. It represented a landmark in American psychiatry which, as its authors noted in the preface, was met with 'interest, alarm, despair, excitement and joy' – and probably a certain amount of wailing and gnashing of teeth from the psychodynamic establishment, which found itself on the losing side of a coup d'état.

The approach to the diagnosis of schizophrenia is much the same in the Feighner *et al.*, RDC and DSM III approaches, its successors DSM-III-R, DSM IV, and also ICD 10. At least two different types of positive symptom are required to be present, and there has to be an absence of marked affective symptoms. Different degrees of importance are attached to different classes of schizophrenic symptom, so those that are not always easy to agree on, such as formal thought disorder, are given a low weighting, whereas those like delusions and hallucinations, especially when both are present, are valued more highly. First rank symptoms are also incorporated into the scheme, where they are given over-riding or near over-riding importance. Schizophrenic mood colourings (see Chapter 1) can be accommodated by making only the absence of a full affective syndrome an exclusion – that is, mood changes which are accompanied by the specific concomitants of mania (increased vitality accompanied by overactivity, overspending, decreased need for sleep, etc.) or depression (anhedonia, biological symptoms, self depreciation, etc.).

The RDC criteria for schizophrenia, the purest example of criterion-based diagnosis, are illustrated in Box 4.2. Other criterion-based approaches also stipulate that the course of the disorder up to the time of evaluation should be taken into consideration. In DSM III and its successors the requirement is six months of illness and a decline in social and occupational functioning.

Box 4.2 Research Diagnostic Criteria for schizophrenia (from Spitzer *et al.* (1978), *Research diagnostic criteria for a selected group of functional disorders.* Biometric Research, New York State Psychiatric Institute. Reproduced with permission)

A through C are required for the period of illness being considered.

A. During an active phase of the illness (may or may not now be present) at least two of the following are required for definite and one for probable:

(1) Thought broadcasting, insertion or withdrawal (as defined in this manual).
(2) Delusions of being controlled (or influenced), other bizarre delusions, or multiple delusions (as defined in this manual).
(3) Somatic, grandiose, religious, nihilistic, or other delusions without persecutory or jealous content lasting at least one week.
(4) Delusions of any type if accompanied by hallucinations of any type for at least one week.
(5) Auditory hallucinations in which either a voice keeps up a running commentary on the subject's behaviours or thoughts as they occur, or two or more voices converse with each other.
(6) Non-affective verbal hallucinations (as defined in this manual) spoken to the subject.
(7) Hallucinations of any type throughout the day for several days or intermittently for at least one month.
(8) Definite instances of marked formal thought disorder (as defined in this manual) accompanied by either blunted or inappropriate affect, delusions or hallucinations of any type, or grossly disorganised behaviour.

B. Signs of the illness have lasted at least two weeks from the onset of a noticeable change in the subject's usual condition (current signs of the illness may not now meet criterion A and may be residual symptoms only, such as extreme social withdrawal, blunted or inappropriate affect, mild formal thought disorder, or unusual thoughts or perceptual experiences).

C. At no time during the *active* period (delusions, hallucinations, marked formal thought disorder, bizarre behaviour, etc.) of illness being considered did the subject meet the full criteria for either probable or definite manic or depressive syndrome (criteria A and B under Major Depressive or Manic Disorders) to such a degree that it was a *prominent* part of the illness. (See criteria for Depressive Syndrome Superimposed on Residual Schizophrenia.)

This dilutes the cross-sectionality of the diagnosis, but is a defensible manoeuvre for what is after all a practical procedure.

The criterion-based approach has been phenomenally successful, being universally adopted at once and remaining the benchmark for diagnosis for over 20 years. But despite this, its validity needs establishing just as much as that of its predecessors. This is no easy matter because the approach is not susceptible to the kind of sensitivity and specificity analysis applied above to first rank symptoms. A basic aim of the criterion-based approach to diagnosis, which derives ultimately from its origins in use for research purposes, is to capture those patients who unequivocally have the disorder, rather than those in whom it is the most likely diagnosis. This automatically guarantees that its sensitivity will always be less than clinical diagnosis. With regard to specificity, this can only realistically be judged against manic-depressive psychosis, and since presence of manic-depressive mood change is an exclusion criterion, the argument becomes unbreakably circular.

In the face of these constraints, interest has turned to a form of predictive validity, similar to that described earlier in the chapter, which might be termed the sensitivity and specificity of outcome. The aim here is to demonstrate that use of diagnostic criteria performs as well as – or preferably better than – clinical diagnosis in predicting poor outcome in schizophrenia, and that it misdiagnoses patients who later turn out to show a picture more consistent with manic-depressive illness to no greater an extent.

Brockington and co-workers (Brockington *et al.*, 1978; Kendell *et al.*, 1979) carried out the pioneering studies of the predictive validity of different ways of diagnosing schizophrenia. Utilizing detailed history and mental state data gathered on 134 patients with functional psychosis, they made diagnoses of schizophrenia according to several different definitions. All the available information, both the presenting symptoms and the course of the illness up to the time of assessment, was used to make a clinical diagnosis. The patients were also diagnosed according to RDC criteria which, as mentioned above, depend exclusively on the clinical picture at the time of examination. Diagnosis was also made on the basis of whether first rank symptoms were present. A number of other diagnostic systems were also applied.

On average 6.5 years later, as many as possible of the 134 patients were traced and re-interviewed by an investigator unaware of the original diagnosis. Ratings of symptomatology and social functioning were made, and corroborative information from hospital records and interviews with relatives and carers was obtained. All these new sources of information were used to formulate an outcome diagnosis that was made blind to the original diagnoses. The results are shown in Table 4.6. On the whole, it is striking how minor the differences between any of the diagnostic approaches were. Diagnosing schizophrenia according to the RDC (or according to presence of first rank symptoms) was as good as diagnosing it clinically in terms of predicting incomplete recovery, persistent delusions and hallucinations,

Table 4.6 Predictive validity of different diagnostic systems in schizophrenia

Outcome measure	Clinical diagnosis (N = 45)*	Research Diagnostic Criteria (N = 34)	First rank symptoms (N = 38)
Incomplete recovery	22 (49 %)	19 (56 %)	16 (42 %)
Persistent delusions and hallucinations	15 (33 %)	14 (41 %)	13 (34 %)
Defect state	8 (18 %)	8 (23 %)	7 (18 %)
Social isolation	25 (49 %)	22 (65 %)	22 (58 %)
Outcome diagnosis of affective psychosis	5 (11 %)	4 (12 %)	8 (21 %)

* The fact that more patients were classified as schizophrenic clinically was largely due to the inclusion of patients with residual schizophrenia (i.e. without active symptoms at initial evaluation).

Sources: Brockington *et al.* (1978); Kendell *et al.* (1979).

development of a defect state and social isolation. Both the RDC and clinical diagnosis also misdiagnosed patients to much the same extent: slightly over 10 per cent of cases diagnosed as schizophrenic clinically or by RDC subsequently turned out to show symptoms more consistent with manic-depressive psychosis. First rank symptoms, however, misdiagnosed manic-depressive patients at nearly twice the rate of the other diagnostic systems.

Twenty years later Mason *et al.* (1997) obtained roughly similar findings in a study with a longer duration of follow-up. Their sample consisted of the 99 patients in the UK sample of the Determinants of Outcome of Severe Mental Disorder Study (Jablensky *et al.*, 1992), one of the successors to the International Pilot Study of Schizophrenia. The patients in this study had all made a first contact with psychiatric services with a possible diagnosis of psychosis, and they were all assigned a consensus clinical diagnosis. Follow-up information was obtained on 96 of the 99 patients on average 13 years later; this involved interviews with the patient and an informant and obtaining information from family doctors and hospital records (nine had died but enough follow-up information was available from these other sources for them to be included). At this time one of the investigators also reviewed the original assessments under blind conditions and assigned DSM-III-R and ICD 10 diagnoses. It also proved possible to derive a diagnosis which relied heavily on Schneider's first rank symptoms (CATEGO category S+) from the information originally collected. At the 13-year follow-up the patients who were given an initial diagnosis of schizophrenia were broadly found to have higher levels of symptoms and disability than those who had been given other psychotic diagnoses. The differences were significant for patients diagnosed according to DSM-III-R and ICD 10, and were marginally significant for disability but not for symptoms for those diagnosed clinically. However, diagnosis according to presence of first rank symptoms did not distinguish between the schizophrenic and non-schizophrenic patients 13 years later.

The logic of the methods that need to be used to test the validity of criterion-based approaches to diagnoses is quite convoluted, but their findings are clear. Making the diagnosis of schizophrenia according to a simple formula, presence of psychotic symptoms plus absence of manic-depressive mood change, is as accurate as a more judicious weighing of history and mental state information, experience and probably clinical intuition as well. Incorporation of the latter undoubtedly allows cases of schizophrenia to be picked up which would otherwise be missed; but even so the gains are relatively minor. Both approaches are almost certainly better than relying on the presence of first rank symptoms.

Conclusion

A largely unspoken distinction running through the work reviewed in this chapter has been that between two different senses in which the term 'diagnosis' is used. In its theoretical sense, diagnosis refers to a method of classifying disease, a way that may or may not be valid. In its practical sense, diagnosis describes an act of clinical decision-making; this cannot be either valid or invalid, it can only be performed with greater or lesser degrees of acumen. Some of the controversy that has surrounded the diagnosis of schizophrenia over the course of the twentieth century seems to have been due to the confusion between these two uses of the term.

At the theoretical level, it is difficult to see what all the fuss was about. Diseases will always need to be classified according to some kind of scheme, and the one which isolated the entity of schizophrenia has clearly survived a quite searching examination of its reliability and validity. With respect to the practical sense of the term, it has to be said that the record of psychiatrists in diagnosing schizophrenia (and other psychiatric disorders) has not always been good. However, the important question here is not whether schizophrenia *is* diagnosed reliably, but whether it *can* be diagnosed reliably. The evidence reviewed in this chapter suggests that it is possible to achieve this both with an acceptable degree of accuracy and before it becomes a self-fulfilling prophecy.

There remains a minor anomaly in that a small number of psychotic patients stubbornly resist being diagnosed as either schizophrenic or manic-depressive at the time of presentation, or fail to stay in their designated category as their illness progresses. How these patients should be regarded is discussed at length in Chapter 13. Partly for this reason, and no doubt partly for others, the question of whether or not schizophrenia should be regarded as a disease in the strict medical sense of the term will continue to be debated. Meanwhile it goes on being one of the great scourges of mankind.

5 Aetiological factors in schizophrenia

The first and most important fact about the cause of schizophrenia is that it remains unknown. Nearly a century ago Bleuler (1911) pointed out that the illness gives no indications as to where its origins might lie – there were no obvious signs of an underlying physical pathology, and nothing much to suggest that it was related in any obvious way to emotional trauma, childhood deprivation, or any of the other vicissitudes of life. The only thing that was known with certainty at the time was that mental diseases were more common in the families of patients with schizophrenia than in those of the healthy. Over ninety years on, not all that much has changed. Many lines of investigation have been pursued and a handful of abnormal findings have been thrown up, but most if not all the leads have turned out to be slender and there has invariably been dispute, if not about the findings themselves then about the construction that should be placed on them.

A second fact which is abundantly clear is that the aetiology of schizophrenia is a battleground, disputed territory over which long and bitter campaigns have been fought. The two sides in this struggle have consisted quite simply of those who believe schizophrenia to be a biological brain disorder, and those who maintain that it can only properly be understood psychologically, as the result of mental trauma, or as a manifestation of inner conflicts or the end result of disturbed emotional relationships. One or other of these camps has held the upper hand for decades at a time while the other has been forced underground and has only been able to engage in guerrilla warfare. From time to time there have been attempts at reconciliation, but the relationship between the two sides continues to be more in the way of a fight to the death than an accommodation.

The most obvious result of a sizeable, protracted, and well-diversified research effort in schizophrenia has been the accumulation of a forbidding body of literature. It is not possible to weave this into any kind of a coherent synthesis – this is a futile quest in the present state of ignorance. Nor is it possible to review the evidence in a way that does justice to all the avenues that have been or are currently being explored with promising results – this cannot be done in a chapter, perhaps not even in a whole book. Instead the aim of this chapter is to take a critical look at the overall status of the psychodynamic and biological schools of thought as applied to schizo-phrenia, a strategy which ensures that the main themes of research in recent memory will be touched on.

Psychodynamic approaches

Psychanalysis and psychodynamic psychiatry began with Freud, and although he and his immediate circle paid considerably more attention to neurosis than psychosis, it is to them that the first orthodox psychoanalytic accounts of schizophrenia can be traced. Over the course of time these views have undergone considerable change and evolution, as of course has the psychoanalytic tradition as a whole. Nevertheless, within the many variations there has been a constant theme in the interpretation of schizophrenic symp-toms in terms of personality development and the forces acting on it. This set of approaches can be referred to as *individual theories* of schizophrenia.

The history of psychodynamic psychiatry has also been one of rivalry, schism, and the setting up of schools that have strayed far from Freud's original approach. One result of this was the emergence in the 1940s of a movement that shifted the emphasis away from the individual to the family. This gave rise to a number of theories about schizophrenia that were couched in quite different terminologies from each other, but collectively came to exercise unprecedented influence over psychiatric thought. These are usually referred to as *family theories* of schizophrenia.

Individual theories

Arieti (1974), in one of the surprisingly few scholarly overviews of the field, considered that three figures had made outstanding contributions to the psy-choanalytic understanding of schizophrenia. The first of these was, naturally, Freud. He established a key explanatory principle behind delusions and other classes of what would now be called positive symptoms. This was the mental mechanism of projection, whereby the individual's own unbearable sexual ideas and wishes became displaced on to others in an inverted or otherwise disguised form. He also explained what would now be called negative symp-toms as being due to a withdrawal of the libidinal energy that is normally invested in the outside world. Later, he applied his formulation of ego psych-ology to schizophrenia. The central idea here was that in the face of an intolerable conflict, regression took place to a very early (pre-oral) stage of development. This allowed the unconscious id to become able to intrude into consciousness where it partially usurped the rational functions of the ego with its irrational, childlike mode of functioning.

The two other psychiatrists who exerted a major influence departed some-what from the strict Freudian tradition. Like Freud, Jung also believed that under stress or prolonged conflict the unconscious started to overwhelm normal conscious life. However, he was more concerned to try to make sense of the bizarre world of the schizophrenic. He argued that the alien, autonomous quality of schizophrenic symptoms was a consequence of a process he called complex formation, in which a set of emotionally charged ideas were repressed and proceeded to take up a more or less independent existence in the unconscious. At some point they then re-entered consciousness in an uncontrolled and uncorrectable way as delusions, hallucinations, and other psychotic symptoms. Jung was also struck by the primitive, often mythic themes that dominated schizophrenic experiences, and it was this that led him to his well-known theory of the existence of a collective unconscious.

Sullivan's contribution was to establish the importance of interpersonal relationships in schizophrenia. He argued that the alteration which Freud believed took place between the individual and the outside world was specifically a change in the individual's relationship with people in the world. According to Sullivan, all thoughts and fantasies were about people, real and imaginary, and were built up in childhood from what he termed reflected appraisals of parents or parent figures. Like Freud and Jung he believed that traumatic experiences – but interpersonal ones causing blows to self-regard – were excluded from consciousness. These 'not-me' processes then went on to distort the interpretation of subsequent interactions with people, giving rise to a vicious circle of interpersonal difficulties. Once again the repressed material ultimately returned to consciousness and gave rise to schizophrenic symptoms.

In the way of psychodynamic psychiatry, these theories are not notable for their scientific rigour, or even for being framed in such a way as to permit the extraction of testable hypotheses. As a group, however, they share a current of thought which places them within reach of the scientific method. A key proposition of all the theories is that psychological stress, by causing a regression to take place or by overburdening already strained coping mechanisms, triggers a sequence of internal changes whose outward expression is psychotic symptoms. The stress itself may be more of a prolonged conflict than a single disturbing experience; or it may be objectively minor but have special psychological implications for the individual; or it may exert its effect by virtue of acting on an already distorted personality structure. But there is no getting away from the fact that the theories propose that stress precipitates schizophrenic breakdown. This can be construed as a prediction, one that can be tested relatively easily by examining the frequency of stressful life events in patients over the weeks and months before they become schizophrenic.

The first and most famous study of life events in schizophrenia was carried out by Brown and Birley (Brown and Birley, 1968; Birley and Brown, 1970). They established a set of eight classes of events that seemed likely on common sense grounds to provoke emotional reactions of either a positive or a negative kind. The events selected were typically personal, concerning the individual or his close relatives, and involved danger, significant changes in health, status, or way of life, the promise of these, or important fulfilments or disappointments. For the purpose of the study Brown and Birley only included events that could be dated with accuracy, and those that were not obviously a result of the individual's own actions – for example losing a job because of strange behaviour at work. As an additional safeguard, the events were broken down further into those that were 'definitely independent' – those that were for all practical purposes outside the subject's control, for example a relative's serious illness or a burglary – and those that were 'possibly independent' – events where claims for full independence could not be made, but where there was no evidence to suggest that they had been related to the subject's unusual behaviour, for example losing a girlfriend, or changing job.

Fifty patients with acute schizophrenia were selected by screening admissions to a number of psychiatric hospitals. The diagnosis was based on structured psychiatric interview with a forerunner of the Present State Examination. Only patients with an acute onset were included. This was defined as a sudden and marked change in behaviour accompanied by the public expression of schizophrenic symptoms, which had to be dateable to within one week as judged by the patient's own and independent accounts. Life events were rated over the three-month period prior to onset. A control group of 325 normal individuals matched for age, sex and educational level were also assessed using the same procedure.

The schizophrenic patients were found to have experienced on average nearly twice as many life events as the controls in the three months before they became ill (1.74 vs 0.96), a difference which was highly statistically significant. Brown and Birley concluded that this represented reasonably sound evidence that environmental factors can precipitate a schizophrenic attack, and the hypothesis of stress as an aetiological factor in schizophrenia was therefore supported.

Or was it? For a number of reasons, the finding was not as strong as it first appeared. In the first place, a marked difference in the occurrence of life events was only found for the minority of 'possibly independent' events (0.72 vs 0.25); there was an increase in the considerably larger number of 'definitely independent' events (1.02 vs 0.71), but this did not reach significance. Second, the differences were confined to the three weeks immediately prior to onset; for the bulk of the three-month period the frequency of life events was similar in the schizophrenics and the controls. Third, the majority of the sample consisted not of patients who were experiencing their first attack of schizophrenia, but those with established illnesses who were undergoing a relapse: only 24 of the 50 patients were first admissions and only 15 of these were experiencing their first episode of illness. Fourth, it was dubious whether the life events rated always preceded the development of schizophrenia. In 15 patients the onset was not onset of illness but a move from mild to severe schizophrenic symptoms; and in 8 the change was from non-specific symptoms such as depression or withdrawal to florid psychosis. But the most serious methodological flaw was that the study was not carried out under blind conditions, despite the fact that the decision as to whether an event was possibly independent rather than non-independent might be expected to be sometimes quite subjective.

The eight further studies of life events in schizophrenia are shown in Table 5.1. Any hopes that these would overcome the shortcomings of Brown and Birley's study are quickly dashed. Most of the studies defined onset similarly to Brown and Birley, including exacerbations as well as the first appearance of symptoms; one study (Canton and Fraccon, 1985) used what is agreed to be an unacceptable criterion of onset, admission to hospital. Only three of the studies (Jacobs and Myers, 1976; Malzacher *et al.*, 1981; Gureje and Adewunmi, 1988) were carried out on first admissions and only one of these (Gureje and Adewunmi, 1988) specified that the patients were experiencing their first episode of illness. Only a single study (Chung *et al.*, 1986) made the assessment of life events under blind conditions. Even so, the findings are not strong: only one study (Bebbington *et al.*, 1993) found an overall significant increase in independent life events.

Family theories

The way in which the view developed that schizophrenia was the outcome of abnormal parent–child interaction has been described by Hirsch and Leff (1975). Thinking along such lines began with Hadju-Gaines (1940) who, in the course of an orthodox analysis of four schizophrenic patients, concluded that they had in common the experience of a cold, rigorous, sadistically aggressive mother and a soft, indifferent, passive father. A few years later Fromm-Reichmann (1948) coined the term 'schizophrenogenic mother'. In the 1950s, four analytically oriented authors, Bateson, Lidz, Wynne and, above all, Laing, elaborated these ideas into a series of theories whose common theme was that schizophrenia is a way of thinking and behaving inculcated during childhood by the individual's parents. Bateson (Bateson *et al.*, 1956) proposed that a parental tendency to communicate ambiguous and conflicting messages – the so-called double bind – had enduring effects on the child's capacity to focus attention and extract the meaning of what was being said. In Lidz's theory (Lidz *et al.*, 1957a, b), 'skew' and 'schism' in the parental relationship provided the model for a pattern of coldness and ambivalence in the child's later interactions with others. Wynne (Wynne *et al.*, 1958; Wynne and Singer, 1963) argued for a central role of abnormalities in the parents' communication, which in turn affected the child's style of thinking and caused social difficulties as an adult. Laing (Laing, 1965, 1967; Laing and Esterson, 1964) placed such ideas in the framework of existential philosophy. For him, abnormalities in the family relationship undermined the child's sense of self until he was no longer able to maintain any sense of being in the world.

Explanations of symptoms like formal thought disorder, affective flattening, and possibly some forms of delusion flow naturally from such accounts.

Table 5.1 Studies of life events in schizophrenia

Study	Subjects	Diagnostic criteria	Stage of illness	Definition of onset	Period of analysis	Findings
Jacobs and Myers (1976)	62 patients 62 controls	Authors' own (similar to RDC)	First admissions	Emergence or exacerbation of symptoms	12 months	Significant excess for all life events, but not for independent events
Malzacher et al. (1981)	33 patients 33 controls	Clinical	First admissions	Emergence of psychotic symptoms	6 months	No excess of life events
Canton and Fraccon (1985)	54 patients 54 controls	DSM III	Not all first admissions	Not given	6 months	Significant excess of life events in 3 out 10 categories
Al-Khani et al. (1986)	48 patients 62 controls	PSE/CATEGO	Not all first admissions	Normal to psychotic Neurotic to psychotic Minor to major psychotic	6 months	No excess of life events
Chung et al. (1986)	24 patients 24 controls	DSM III	Not clear if any first admissions	Normal to psychotic Normal to prodromal Residual to psychotic	6 months	No overall excess of life events Significant excess of threatening events in schizophreniform pts
Dohrenwend et al. (1987)	66 patients 197 controls	DSM III (non-affective psychosis)*	21 first episode	Not given	12 months	No overall excess of life events Significant excess of 'non-fateful events'
Gureje and Adewunmi (1988)	42 patients 42 controls	RDC	First episode	Not given	6 months	No excess of life events
Bebbington et al. (1993)	52 patients 207 controls	DSM III	Unspecified number were first admissions	Normal to psychotic Neurotic to psychotic Exacerbation of psychotic symptoms	6 months	Significant excess of life events, including definitely independent events

* Included patients with schizophrenia, schizophreniform disorder, brief reactive psychosis, schizoaffective psychosis and atypical psychosis.

It is also easy to see how social withdrawal could be a reaction to the interpersonal difficulties that resulted. The theories can even explain why schizophrenia tends to develop in early adult life – this is the time when an individual's relationships with family members begin to be replaced with significant relationships with other adults.

Hirsch and Leff (1975) found in their review that the investigation of the parents of schizophrenic patients had been surprisingly thorough. The first study was carried out in the 1930s and research continued until, as described below, their own study brought it to an abrupt end in 1971. Although methodologies tended to be flawed and the findings were frequently contradictory, they concluded that a number of statements could be made that were reasonably well supported by evidence. These are summarized in Box 5.1.

Hirsch and Leff also found that one set of results stood out from what was otherwise a welter of generally weak and non-specific findings. This was Singer and Wynne's series of studies designed to test their proposal that the parents of schizophrenic patients showed abnormalities of communication. In the first of these studies, Singer and Wynne (1965) transcribed the speech of the parents of 20 schizophrenic patients, 6 neurotic patients, and 9 patients with a diagnosis of borderline personality disorder (the speech concerned was actually their responses to the Rorschach test). These were then rated, under blind conditions, for presence of abnormalities in language and communicative style. Based purely on analysis of the *parents'* speech, the correct diagnosis was assigned to the *patients* in 17 of 20 of the schizophrenic cases, 4 out of 6 of the neurotic cases, and 7 of the 9 borderlines. Subseqently, the same authors (Singer and Wynne, 1966; Wynne, 1968, 1971) developed a manual for scoring communication deviance, and were able to demonstrate that there

---

Box 5.1 What can be considered established about the parent–child relationship in schizophrenia (from Hirsch and Leff, 1975)

1. More parents of schizophrenic patients are psychiatrically disturbed than parents of normal children and more of the mothers are 'schizoid'.
2. There is a link between 'allusive thinking' in the parents of schizophrenics and in their children, but this is also true of normal people in whom it occurs less frequently.
3. The parents of schizophrenics show more conflict and disharmony than the parents of other psychiatric patients.
4. The pre-schizophrenic child more frequently manifests physical ill health or mild disability early in life than the normal child.
5. Mothers of schizophrenics show more concern and protectiveness than mothers of normals, both in the current situation and in their attitudes to their children before they fell ill.

was very little overlap between the performance of parents of schizophrenics and those of normal or neurotic parents – only 22 per cent of normal subjects' parents scored above a cut-off defined as the lowest score for any of the schizophrenic patients' parents.

After commenting that Wynne and Singer's studies were 'the most important work to date supporting theories which set out to link the development of schizophrenia to the presence of specific abnormalities in parents which act through specific environmentally transmitted mechanisms', Hirsch and Leff (1971) went on to try to replicate their findings. They collected a group of 20 patients with acute schizophrenia, diagnosed using the Present State Examination. These were matched with a control group of 20 patients with neurotic diagnoses, who were similar in age, sex, and social class. They then interviewed the parents of both groups under blind conditions and rated their speech using the manual developed by Wynne and Singer. Close liaison with Wynne's group throughout the course of the study ensured that both the interviewing and the scoring were carried out in the same way. As in Wynne and Singer's studies, the deviance scores (calculated as the total number of deviances divided by the number of responses) of the schizophrenic patients' parents were significantly higher than the neurotics' parents: 1.33/response versus 0.88/response. However, as shown in Figure 5.1, the overlap between

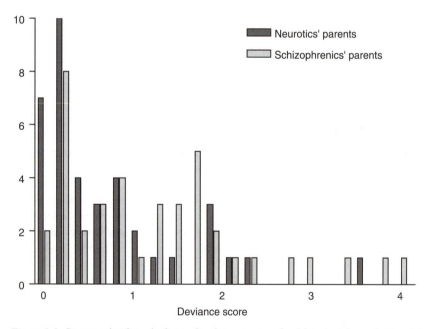

Figure 5.1 Communication deviance in the parents of schizophrenic patients and neurotic controls (from Hirsch and Leff (1971), Parental abnormalities of verbal communication in the transmission of schizophrenia. *Psychological Medicine*, 1, 118–127. Reproduced with permission from Cambridge University Press).

the two groups of parents was considerably greater than Wynne and Singer had found: 40 per cent of the parents of schizophrenic patients scored below the median and 40 per cent of the parents of neurotic patients scored above it. It was also evident that a large proportion of the parents in both groups showed very little or no abnormality of speech, and that the difference was almost entirely accounted for by 5 of the 40 parents of the schizophrenic patients who showed unusually high scores. Further analysis revealed that the parents of the schizophrenic patients used significantly more words than the parents of the neurotics (the deviance score was a proportional measure, but it corrected only for the number of responses made, not the number of words used). When this potential confounding factor – the more words spoken, the more opportunity there would be for a deviance to be rated – was corrected for, the difference between the groups disappeared.

Biological approaches

The earliest aetiological hypothesis about schizophrenia was that it was an organic disease of the brain. Kraepelin (1913a) took this as a foregone conclusion, and it was under his direction that the first genetic and neuropathological studies of the disorder were undertaken. Bleuler (1911) took a somewhat watered down organic position: he considered that, while most or all of his secondary schizophrenic symptoms were psychological in nature, only a concept that included anatomic or chemical disturbances of the brain could do complete justice to the fundamental symptoms of the disorder.

Thereafter, biological research in schizophrenia did not exactly proceed apace. For several decades the rate of advance was slowed by the relatively crude methods available for studying the brain in life. For nearly as long a period all progress was held up by the ascendancy of psychodynamic psychiatry in America. A turning point was the discovery of chlorpromazine and other antipsychotic drugs, which pointed plainly to the possibility that at least some of the symptoms of the disorder might be biologically determined. Later, the development of brain imaging gave additional momentum to what was already fast becoming a worldwide renaissance of interest in the biological basis of schizophrenia. Ironically, the making-up of lost time has been most apparent in America.

Leaving aside biochemical research and the neurodevelopmental hypothesis, which are given chapters to themselves, the two most productive areas of biological schizophrenia research have been genetics and neuroimaging; these are discussed below. A number of other lines of investigation have been followed that have resulted in only minor, equivocal or contested findings. Probably the most important of these has been the question of whether there is a neuropathology of the disorder, so this is also given a section.

Genetics

The first study to investigate the apparent tendency of schizophrenia to run in families was undertaken by Rudin (1916), working in Kraepelin's department. Investigations of the parents, twins, siblings, children, and other relatives of schizophrenic patients have since formed the main output of some of the most distinguished of several generations of schizophrenia researchers. This work has been reviewed and updated many times, first by the daughter of Rudin (Zerbin-Rudin, cited by Slater, 1968); and later by many other authors (for example Kallman, 1938; Slater, 1968; Gottesman and Shields, 1982; McGuffin, 1988; Riley *et al.*, 2003). However, possibly the best and certainly the most readable of all the accounts remains that of Gottesman (1991), and what follows covers the same ground as his account, although with a few embellishments and changes of emphasis.

By pooling the results of around 40 of the better studies carried out in Britain, Europe and Scandinavia (but not the USA) between 1920 and 1987, Gottesman was able to produce a table of risks for developing schizophrenia in first-degree, second-degree, and third-degree relatives of patients with the disorder. His summary of these data is reproduced in Figure 5.2. It makes a compelling case that the risk rises more or less steadily with increasing consanguinity to reach a peak of nearly 50 per cent in monozygotic twins and the offspring of two schizophrenic parents.

It does not take long to realise that these findings do not by themselves establish that hereditary factors operate in schizophrenia. This is for the reason that families share the same environment as well as the same genes. As Gottesman pointed out, juvenile delinquency and adult criminality show significant degrees of familial clustering, and measles has a high rate of concordance in

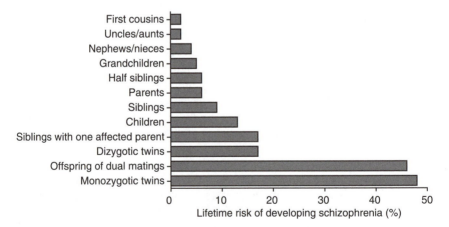

Figure 5.2 Pooled data for rates of schizophrenia in increasingly consanguinous relatives of schizophrenic patients (from Gottesman (1991), *Schizophrenia genesis: The origins of madness*. Copyright © 1991 by Irving I. Gottesman. Reprinted with permission of W.H. Freeman and Company).

monozygotic twins; yet few would care to defend the genetic basis of these disorders. In order to exclude a spurious reason for the family studies' findings, and satisfy the ever-present critics of any biological finding in schizophrenia, it is necessary to unconfound the part played by genetics from the part played by environment. Two strategies have been employed to achieve this.

The first method has been to compare the concordance rates for monozygotic and dizygotic twins. The genetic differences between the two are substantial (the former are genetically identical whereas the latter are no more closely related than siblings), whereas the environmental influences would be expected to be closely similar in both. The results of 10 studies of twin pairs with one schizophrenic member are summarised in Table 5.2, which is based

Table 5.2 Twin studies in schizophrenia

(a) Classical studies

	Sample	*MZ concordance (%)*	*DZ concordance (%)*
Luxenburger (1928)	19 MZ 13 DZ	58	0
Rosanoff *et al.* (1934)	41 MZ 53 DZ	61	13
Essen-Moller (1941)	11 MZ 27 DZ	64	15
Kallman (1946)	174 MZ 296 DZ	69	11
Slater (1953)	37 MZ 58 DZ	65	14
Inouye (1961)	55 MZ 11 DZ	60	18

Note: Concordance is calculated pairwise.

(b) Contemporary studies

	Sample	*MZ concordance (%)*	*DZ concordance (%)*
Gottesman and Shields (1963)	22 MZ 33 DZ	58	15
Kringlen (1967)	55 MZ 90 DZ	45	15
Pollin *et al.* (1969)	164 MZ 277 DZ	31	6
Fischer (1973)	21 MZ 41 DZ	56	27

Note: Concordance is calculated probandwise, which gives higher values.

Sources: (a) Slater (1968); (b) Gottesman (1991), *Schizophrenia genesis: The origins of madness.* Copyright © 1991 by Irving I. Gottesman. Reprinted with permission of W.H. Freeman and Company.

on the reviews of Slater (1968) and Gottesman (1991). All the studies found a higher concordance rate in monozygotic twins, and so supported the genetic hypothesis.

One study originally provided an exception to these findings. Tienari (1963) found a concordance of zero in a series of 16 monozygotic twin pairs. However, when the twin pairs were followed-up up a decade later (Tienari, 1975), it turned out merely to prove the rule – by this time the concordance rates had become a respectable 36 per cent, more than twice the rate in a comparison group of dizygotic twins of 14 per cent.

The second way of disentangling familiality from heredity is to examine children with a schizophrenic parent who have not been brought up by their families. The classic study of this type was carried out by Heston (1966). He tracked down and interviewed the adult offspring of 47 American women who had been hospitalised with a diagnosis of schizophrenia at the time of giving birth. In accordance with state law, all of these children had been taken away from their mothers within three days of birth and raised in orphanages or with non-maternal relatives. Also traced and interviewed were a control group of 50 children of healthy mothers who had been adopted away shortly after birth. Five (10.4 per cent) of the schizophrenic mothers' offspring were found to be suffering from schizophrenia, as diagnosed by a consensus of three clinicians, in contrast to none of the controls. Heston also found a wealth of other kinds of psychopathology in the children of the schizophrenic mothers, among which neurosis and sociopathic personality disorder figured prominently, and even those with no psychiatric diagnosis often had colourful life histories.

These studies placed the existence of a significant genetic contribution to schizophrenia beyond reasonable doubt. Or did they? Every one of the studies cited above was carried out before the days of criterion-based approaches to diagnosis, most of them at a time when psychiatric diagnosis was at its zenith of unreliability. The index cases of schizophrenia were invariably diagnosed clinically, and even where safeguards were built in, for instance requiring a consensus between two or more clinicians, some patients would almost certainly have been included who would not meet present-day diagnostic criteria. When it came to diagnosing the relatives, there was a widespread tendency to include as schizophrenic 'borderline', 'latent', and 'pseudoneurotic' cases, so-called schizophrenia spectrum disorders. Could, as Gottesman put it, the earlier overwhelming evidence for familial clustering of schizophrenia have been falsely generated by biased psychiatrists making unreliable clinical judgements under non-blind conditions?

This problem was brought out into the open by an attempt to replicate Heston's study of the adopted-away offspring of schizophrenic parents, the Danish–American adoption study (Rosenthal *et al.*, 1968, 1971). Ostensibly carried out with meticulous attention to detail, it produced results that were broadly in line with those of Heston. Ten years after it was published it was singled out for an attack by one of the proponents of an earlier generation of family theories of schizophrenia, Lidz (Lidz *et al.*, 1981; Lidz and Blatt, 1983). His criticisms were as vitriolic as they were accurate. In the first place, although Rosenthal *et al.* claimed that 31.6 per cent of the adopted-away offspring of 76 patients in their index group had diagnoses 'in the schizophrenia spectrum', only two had been given a definite diagnosis of schizophrenia – the remainder all had diagnoses such as 'borderline schizophrenia', 'simple schizophrenia;' 'significant paranoid tendencies', '?beginning paranoid schizophrenia' and 'almost pseudoneurotic schizophrenic'. Second, Rosenthal *et al.*'s index sample included, explicitly for comparison purposes, a group of seven patients with a diagnosis of manic-depressive psychosis (plus six more in whom it was uncertain whether the diagnosis was manic-depressive psychosis or 'reactive schizophrenia'). However, when it came to the rates of schizophrenia spectrum disorders in the offspring, the two groups were muddled together in a way that was by any standards sloppy.

Fortunately, further family history studies have followed, where schizophrenia was diagnosed according to DSM III or other modern diagnostic criteria. The results of seven large studies that employed normal controls and where the diagnoses in the relatives were made under blind conditions are summarised in Table 5.3. In all but one the rates in the first-degree relatives were significantly higher than the control rate. Mostly in the range of 4–6 per cent, these rates were lower than the figure of approximately 10 per cent found in earlier studies, but this is a widely accepted consequence of the use of diagnostic criteria, and the rates in the control relatives were correspondingly lower, clustering around 0.5 per cent.

A number of twin studies using modern diagnostic criteria (reviewed by Cardno and Gottesman, 2000) have also continued to find the same monozygotic:dizygotic concordance discrepancy as earlier studies. Finally, a single further adoption study (Tienari *et al.*, 2000) found 6.7 per cent of the adopted-away offspring of schizophrenic mothers had a DSM-III-R diagnosis of schizophrenia, compared to 2 per cent of the offspring of control mothers.

The lack of 100 per cent concordance in monozygotic twins, combined with statistical modelling of the rest of the pattern of risk, establishes with near certainty that schizophrenia follows a non-mendelian mode of transmission. In fact, its pattern of inheritance aligns it closely with disorders like diabetes mellitus, disseminated sclerosis, and pernicious anaemia, where liability is a complex trait, determined by genes, environment, and their co-action or interaction (Riley and McGuffin, 2000). It is likely that a large numbers of genes are involved, with or without the action of a small number of genes of major effect. To date, however, no genes have been identified and there are no well-replicated findings of particular chromosomal loci for such genes.

Structural brain abnormality

There have always been hints that the structure of the brain is not normal in schizophrenia. Mild cerebral atrophy was reported in some early

Table 5.3 Family history studies of schizophrenia using diagnostic criteria and employing controls

Study	Numbers	Diagnostic criteria	Percentage of first-degree relatives with schizophrenia	
			Patients	Controls
Tsuang *et al.* (1980)	200 patients/ 375 relatives 160 controls/ 543 relatives	Feighner	5.3	0.6
Baron *et al.* (1985)	90 patients/ 376 relatives 90 controls/ 374 relatives	RDC	5.8	0.6
Kendler *et al.* (1985)	253 patients/ 723 relatives 261 controls/ 1056 relatives	DSM III	3.7	0.2
Frangos *et al.* (1985)	116 patients/ 572 relatives 116 controls/ 694 relatives	DSM III	4.5	0.9
Maier *et al.* (1993)	146 patients/ 589 relatives 109 controls/ 419 relatives	RDC	3.9	0.5
Kendler *et al.* (1993a)	126 patients/ 342 relatives 123 controls/ ?no. of relatives	DSM-III-R	6.5 (MR)	0.5 (MR)
Varma and Sharma (1993)	162 patients/ 1018 relatives 106 controls/ 812 relatives	RDC	9.9 (MR)	1.4 (MR)

MR – Morbid risk

post-mortem studies, and a number of studies using the technique of air encephalography to examine the brain in life claimed to find cortical atrophy accompanied by ventricular dilatation (see David, 1957; Haug, 1962). But the studies were few in number, their findings were inconsistent, and they made little impression on mainstream psychiatric thought.

All this changed dramatically in the 1970s. Johnstone *et al.* (1976), using one of only two computerised tomography (CT) scanners then in existence, reported that a sample of 13 chronically hospitalised schizophrenic patients had significantly larger lateral ventricles than 8 normal controls, made up of hospital staff. This was followed by an avalanche of replications, most of which supported the finding. For example, Andreasen *et al.* (1990) noted that 35 out of 48 studies which compared schizophrenics and normal individuals under blind conditions found a significant increase in lateral ventricular size, and most of the negative findings were in studies with small sample sizes or with other shortcomings of design.

At the same time, it became clear from an early stage that the degree of ventricular enlargement in schizophrenia was for the most part modest. In the first study with a large sample size Weinberger *et al.* (1979) found that 60 per cent of a group of 58 chronic schizophrenic patients had lateral ventricles that were within the control range, and only in 10 of the cases could the presence of clinically significant ventricular enlargement be agreed on, where in most cases it was described as mild or borderline. This rendered the CT scan findings in schizophrenia vulnerable to a methodological problem concerning the choice of controls. Several of the early studies employed 'medical' controls – that is, patients with scans that had been reported as normal by radiologists – a practice that can all too easily lead to those individuals who have lateral ventricles at the extreme upper end of the normal range being excluded, as their findings will often have been reported as questionable. This would then tend to lower the control group mean, and so in turn give rise to spuriously inflated values for lateral ventricular enlargement in a schizophrenic group. The possibility of such a systematic bias was raised by Smith and Iacono (1986) who compared a number of CT scan studies with positive and negative results and found evidence that the differences in the former studies did not reflect larger lateral ventricular sizes in schizophrenic patients, but smaller ones in the controls!

It was clear that lateral ventricular enlargement would need to be demonstrated in a well-controlled CT scan study for it to be able to avoid the kind of criticisms levelled at other biological findings in schizophrenia. This was provided by Andreasen *et al.* (1990), who compared 108 patients meeting DSM III criteria for schizophrenia with 75 prospectively ascertained normal volunteers. The two groups were matched not only for age and sex, but also for height, weight and level of education. Potential control subjects were interviewed and excluded if they had a history of significant medical disorder, head injury, substance abuse or psychiatric illness. The ventricle:brain ratio (VBR), the customarily used measure of lateral ventricular size in CT studies, was found to be significantly greater in the schizophrenic group than in the controls, although the magnitude of the difference was small (6.6 vs 5.7; $p = .04$). When only patients and controls under the age of 50 were considered (ventricular size increases disproportionately after late middle age, which could have tended to obscure any differences), the difference remained and the level of significance became somewhat higher despite the reduction in numbers (6.5 vs 5.4 $p = .01$). Even so, as shown in Figure 5.3, there was a substantial degree of overlap between the two groups. In fact, the difference in mean VBR between schizophrenic patients and controls under the age of

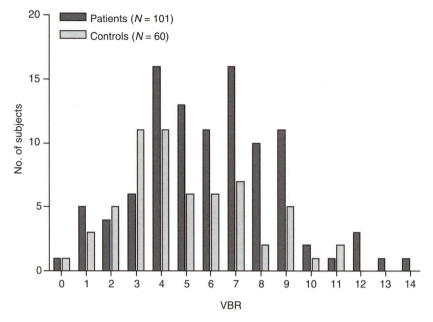

Figure 5.3 Lateral ventricular size (VBR) in schizophrenic patients and controls aged under 50 (from Andreasen *et al.* (1990), Ventricular enlargement in schizophrenia evaluated with computed tomographic scanning. *Archives of General Psychiatry*, 47, 1008–1015. Copyright 1990, American Medical Association).

50 of 1.1 VBR units was of approximately the same magnitude as that found between normal females and normal males in the study (5.9 vs 4.8).

This and a similar study by Jones *et al.* (1994b) established the existence of a small but significant degree of lateral ventricular enlargement in schizophrenia beyond reasonable doubt. The issue then arises of what this means. Owens *et al.* (1985b) carried out a large study examining the relationship of lateral ventricular size to a wide range of clinical variables in 112 chronically hospitalised schizophrenic patients. As can be seen from Table 5.4, the only significant associations were with presence of tardive dyskinesia and impairment of current behaviour – this latter reflecting mainly reduced activity and poor social behaviour. Particularly noteworthy were the lack of any relationship between ventricular enlargement and negative symptoms or intellectual impairment. Reviewing this and numerous other studies, Lewis (1990) concluded that 'for most clinical variables mooted at one time or another to be related to ventricular enlargement, there is little in the way of convincing replication'.

Another question is whether ventricular enlargement predates the development of schizophrenia or whether it appears as the disorder progresses. In his review, Lewis (1990) found that almost all studies failed to find evidence of a relationship between lateral ventricular size in schizophrenia and factors

Table 5.4 Correlates of lateral ventricular size in schizophrenia

Feature	Correlation with VBR	Comment
Positive symptoms	NS	–
Negative symptoms	NS	No differences between groups matched for defect state vs no defect state
Abnormal behaviour	$p < .05$	Largely due to impaired social function and reduced activity
Intellectual impairment	NS	Curvilinear relationship with excess of impaired patients at both extremes of ventricular size
Academic record	NS	No differences between groups matched for high vs low achievement
Involuntary movements	$p < .01$	Found with two different scales and with various cut-offs for abnormality
Insulin treatment	NS	No differences between groups matched for none vs much
Electroconvulsive therapy	NS	No differences between groups matched for none vs much
Neuroleptic treatment	NS	No differences between groups matched for none vs much

Source: Owens *et al.* (1985b), Lateral ventricular size in schizophrenia: Relationship to the disease process and its clinical manifestations. *Psychological Medicine*, 15, 27–41. Reproduced with permission from Cambridge University Press.

such as age and prior duration of illness. Several studies (e.g. Weinberger *et al.*, 1982; Schulz *et al.*, 1983; Turner *et al.*, 1986) also found ventricular enlargement to be present in young patients and those undergoing their first episode of psychosis. Five studies carried out repeat scans on schizophrenic patients up to 9 years after they were originally performed. Four found no change (Nasrallah *et al.*, 1986; Illowsky *et al.*, 1988; Reveley *et al.*, 1988; Sponheim *et al.*, 1991), but in one (Kemali *et al.*, 1989) there was evidence of progression. The CT findings thus favour lateral ventricular enlargement being 'neurodevelopmental' rather than 'neurodegenerative'.

Magnetic resonance imaging (MRI) has now largely replaced CT in structural imaging studies of schizophrenia. This technique gives superior resolution, and its ability to provide thin slices with good delineation of sulci and gyri enables the 3-D reconstruction of the whole brain and regions such as the frontal and temporal lobes It also has the advantage of being able to differentiate grey and white matter, allowing the volume of subcortical structures such as the hippocampus, amygdala and basal ganglia to be measured. MRI studies of schizophrenia have also tended to be of a high standard methodologically, typically using prospectively ascertained volunteer controls and matching their samples for age and sex, and either matching for or

Box 5.2 Meta-analysis of volumetric MRI studies in schizophrenia (from Wright et al., 2000)

The authors meta-analysed 58 MRI studies that used volumetric brain measurements and compared schizophrenic patients to normal controls. Studies in which the controls were the unaffected relatives of the patients were also included. Studies reporting findings in early onset schizophrenia were included, but those where the mean age of the patients or controls was greater than 40 were excluded.

The CT scan finding of lateral ventricular enlargement was confirmed, with the mean value representing an increase of 26% over normal. In contrast, whole brain volume was only slightly reduced, to 98% of normal. Relative volumes of whole brain grey matter (6 studies) and white matter (5 studies) were approximately in line with the whole brain volume reduction.

Brain structure	No. of studies	Total N	Effect size (d)	% of normal volume (confidence interval)
Left lateral ventricle	18	1053	0.51	130 (120–141)
Right lateral ventricle	18	1053	0.39	120 (113–128)
All ventricles	30	1896	0.49	126 (120–132)
Whole brain	31	1867	−0.25	98 (97–99)
Left frontal lobe	13	762	−0.34	95 (92–98)
Right frontal lobe	13	762	−0.36	95 (93–97)
Left temporal lobe	25	1362	−0.18	98 (96–99)
Right temporal lobe	25	1362	−0.24	97 (96–98)
Left hippocampus– amygdala	15	731	−0.24	95 (92–99)
Right hippocampus– amygdala	15	731	−0.28	94 (92–97)
Left hippocampus	24	1298	−0.42	93 (90–97)
Right hippocampus	24	1298	−0.38	94 (91–96)
Left amygdala	7	283	−0.72	91 (87–94)
Right amygdala	7	283	−0.69	91 (87–95)

The temporal lobe volume reductions were in line with the whole brain differences, while those for the frontal lobes were possibly greater, but there were relatively few studies in this latter analysis. Larger reductions were found for both components of the hippocampus–amygdala complex. There was no significant gender effect for the majority of structures studied.

controlling for a range of other factors including height, educational level, socioeconomic status and ethnicity.

Wright *et al.* (2000) meta-analysed volumetric MRI studies comparing schizophrenic patients and normal controls. The findings are summarised in Box 5.2. Lateral ventricular enlargement was supported, with an effect size in the medium range and corresponding to a mean volume increase of 26 per cent. This was not associated with anything close to an equivalent reduction in brain volume: the effect size for whole brain volume was in the small range, and corresponded to only a 2 per cent difference between schizophrenic and normal subjects. At 2–5 per cent, the reductions in the size of the frontal and temporal lobes were not clearly of greater magnitude than those for the brain as a whole. However, the reductions in the hippocampus and amygdala were somewhat greater, with the effect size approaching the large range on some measures.

Contrary to a frequently stated view, there was little evidence from this meta-analysis to support particular reductions in grey matter as opposed to white matter. The former showed a pooled volume reduction of 4 per cent, and the latter 2 per cent, but the confidence interval was closely similar in both.

MRI studies have also revisited the question of progressive structural change in schizophrenia. Seven such studies have been carried out, which have re-scanned patients and matched controls over periods from 1 to 5 years. In all but one of the studies the patients were scanned at the time of first admission (the remaining study was made up of mixed first episode and chronic patients). The findings are shown in Table 5.5. Mostly they are negative: only one study found progressive increase in lateral ventricular volume, with another finding an increase on the left in the setting of no overall change. Decreases, no change and, in one study, an increase relative to controls were found for overall brain or grey matter volume. There were only scattered findings of change in the frontal and temporal lobes and hippocampus and/or amygdala.

Functional brain abnormality in schizophrenia

As with brain structure, early studies of brain function in schizophrenia had to rely on a crude technique, in this case electroencephalography (EEG). Early EEG studies of schizophrenia claimed that slowing and other abnormalities could be seen in up to 80 per cent of patients. However, a critical review of this literature (Ellingson, 1954) plus two more recent surveys (Itil, 1977; Shagass, 1977) made it clear, first, that the rates of all abnormalities were considerably lower in studies that employed proper controls, and second, that the abnormalities seen consisted exclusively of non-specific phenomena that also occurred with substantial frequency in normal individuals.

Then, once again in the 1970s, the investigation of brain function in schizophrenia was transformed by the development of a much more powerful

Table 5.5 MRI studies examining progression of lateral ventricular volume and brain structure changes over time in schizophrenic patients

Study	Sample	Interval	Lateral ventricles	Whole brain/ cerebral cortex	Frontal lobe/cortex	Temporal lobel cortex	Hippocampus/ amygdala	Comment
DeLisi et al. (1997)	50 patients 20 controls	3–5 years	NSD	More than controls	–	NSD	NSD	–
Lieberman et al. (2001)	36–53 patients 13 controls	2–3 years	NSD	Less than controls	–	–	Less than controls	–
Gur et al. (1998)*	40 patients 17 controls	30 months	NSD	NSD	?NSD (see comment)	Less than controls		Left frontal lobe decrease in patients, but not significant compared to controls
Mathalon et al. (2001)	24 patients 25 controls	4 years	?More than controls on left (see comment)	–	NSD	NSD		Patients showed greater increase in lateral ventricular volume on left, but not significant overall
Cahn et al. (2002)	34 patients 36 controls	12 months	Increased	More than controls				Greater decrease in whole brain volume in patients due to grey matter decrease
Ho et al. (2003)	73 patients 23 controls	3 years	NSD	NSD	?More than controls (see comment)	NSD	–	Frontal lobe differences borderline significant
Kasai et al. (2003)	13 patients 14 controls	18 months	–	–	–	More than controls on Left (superior temporal gyrus)	NSD	–

* Only half the sample were first episode patients. All other studies were of first episode patients.

tool, functional imaging. This was first applied to schizophrenia in 1974 by Ingvar and Franzen. Using the relatively crude technique of [133]Xenon inhalation to measure regional cerebral blood flow, they compared 15 normal individuals (actually abstinent alcoholics), 11 patients with dementia and two groups of chronic schizophrenic patients, one consisting of 9 chronically hospitalised patients and the other of 11 younger chronic patients. Whereas the demented patients showed significantly reduced cerebral blood flow in all areas, in the schizophrenic patients global blood flow was not significantly different from the controls. There was, however, a changed regional pattern of flow in both groups of schizophrenic patients, with a reversal of the normal pattern of greater flow in anterior as compared to posterior regions – or hypofrontality as Ingvar and Franzen christened it.

Beginning with Buchsbaum *et al.* (1982) and Mathew *et al.* (1982), the first of many replications began to appear, some using Ingvar and Franzen's original [133]Xenon technique, and others using single photon emission computed tomography (SPECT) or the considerably more sensitive technique of positron emission tomography (PET). Unfortunately, while these studies have been marked by spectacular advances in technological sophistication, this has not always been matched by corresponding increases in methodological rigour – many of the studies have had sample sizes of less than 10 and control groups have sometimes been lacking or inappropriate. Chua and McKenna (1995) reviewed 27 studies that included 12 or more schizophrenic patients and met other basic methodological requirements. Only 10 of the 27 studies found statistically significant hypofrontality. They concluded that hypofrontality could not be regarded as a robust finding in schizophrenia. In the same year, in an editorial entitled 'Hypofrontality in schizophrenia: RIP', Gur and Gur (1995) argued that the finding was a shibboleth that had only meagre experimental support.

At least partly in order to account for the poor record of these studies, Weinberger *et al.* (1986) proposed that hypofrontality might be more consistently demonstrable in schizophrenia when cognitive demands were made on the prefrontal cortex. They carried out functional imaging using the [133]Xenon technique in 20 chronic schizophrenic patients and 25 age and sex matched controls, both at rest and during performance of the Wisconsin Card Sorting Test, a prototypical frontal/executive task. The schizophrenic patients showed only a trend to hypofrontality at rest, but markedly and significantly failed to activate the prefrontal cortex during task performance. In contrast there was no difference in the pattern of activation between the patients and the controls during performance of a non-executive task involving number matching. They also found that the degree of failure of prefrontal cortex activation correlated with the severity of the impairment in task performance.

Once again, however, task-related or activation hypofrontality has not been consistently replicated in schizophrenia. Chua and McKenna (1995) also reviewed the seven studies of task-related or activation hypofrontality in schizophrenia available at the time. Five of these examined schizophrenic patients during performance of executive tasks and the other two used memory tasks, which are also known to activate the prefrontal cortex. Only three of the studies found significant differences between patients and controls, with two more having equivocal findings.

As a finding that has been not consistently supported, and where it has often been argued that factors such as medication status, stage of illness, and the imaging technique used might be important confounding factors (eg Andreasen *et al.*, 1992), hypofrontality in schizophrenia is a suitable candidate for meta-analysis. Hill *et al.* (2004) meta-analysed approximately 100 studies that used the so-called region-of-interest approach (where values for blood flow/metabolism are obtained across a defined area such as the prefrontal cortex) and can therefore be meta-analysed by the conventional method of pooling effect sizes (see Box 5.3). In line with Ingvar and Franzen's original study, there was little overall support for a reduction in whole brain cerebral blood flow/metabolism in schizophrenia: the effect size was in the small range and was significantly moderated by neuroleptic treatment, which seemed to account for most or all of the reductions found. In contrast, resting hypofrontality was supported with a medium effect size. Here, the differences between patients and controls did not appear to be attributable to drug treatment. This was found to moderate the effect size in studies that measured absolute frontal blood flow/metabolism, but not studies that corrected for whole brain blood flow/metabolism – exactly what would be expected with an effect of drug treatment on global flow/metabolism. Interestingly, there was little to suggest that activation hypofrontality was of greater magnitude than resting hypofrontality, as originally proposed by Weinberger *et al.* As shown in Box 5.3, the meta-analysis also suggested that hypofrontality is a function of chronicity of illness, a possibility that had certainly been mooted from time to time but had not previously emerged clearly from the literature.

Studies using the region-of-interest approach have now been largely replaced by those using voxel-based techniques such as Statistical Parametric Mapping (SPM). Many of these have been devoted to the issue of hypofrontality, and the examination has almost always been under conditions of neuropsychological task activation. Because such studies use voxel-by-voxel comparisons across the entire brain and identify clusters of significant difference between patients and controls, they cannot be meta-analysed using conventional methods. Nevertheless, using a statistical technique for examining the distributions of peak activation foci (the centre of clusters of significant activation), Hill *et al.* were able to combine the data from a number of these studies and found no support for the view that patients with schizophrenia show a different pattern of frontal activation from normal.

Box 5.3 Meta-analysis of studies of hypofrontality in schizophrenia (from Hill *et al.*, 2004).

The authors located 103 region-of-interest studies that compared whole-brain and frontal blood flow/metabolism in schizophrenic patients and normal controls. Studies included those carried out at rest and under conditions of neuropsychological task activation, using tasks known to activate the prefrontal cortex (i.e. executive, working memory, long-term memory and vigilance tests). The roles of a number of potential moderator variables such as age, medication status and stage of illness were examined. The studies employed a variety of different imaging techniques, including ^{133}Xenon, SPECT and PET, and measured hypofrontality in two main ways: absolutely and relatively, i.e. correcting for whole-brain blood flow/metabolism. The influence of these factors was also examined.

A significant reduction in whole-brain blood flow/metabolism in schizophrenia was found, which fell in the 'small' range. Neuroleptic medication was a significant moderating factor and appeared to account for at least some of the differences between patients and controls. In contrast, the effect size for resting hypofrontality was greater. This held true for studies using both absolute and relative measures of hypofrontality. The former effect size was significantly moderated by neuroleptic treatment but the latter was not – as would be predicted on the basis of medication having an effect on global flow/metabolism only.

	No. of studies	Total N	Effect size (d)	Approx. degree of non-overlap (%)
Whole brain	22	795	−0.26 (−0.40/−0.11)	20
Resting hypofrontality (relative)	38	1474	−0.32 (−0.43/−0.21)	25
Resting hypofrontality (absolute)	25	950	−0.55 (−0.68/−0.41)	33
Activation hypofrontality (relative)	17	685	−0.37 (−0.53/−0.22)	25
Activation hypofrontality (absolute)	10	347	−0.42 (−0.65/−0.20)	30

Note: No. of studies, total Ns and effect sizes are for homogeneous subsets of the studies in each analysis.

Differences in technique did not produce markedly different effect size for hypofrontality, although there was a non-significant tendency for SPECT studies to be associated with less hypofrontality than [133]Xenon and PET.

An unexpected finding was an apparent association with chronicity of illness. Studies examining first episode patients or patients with a mean duration of less than two years showed no hypofrontality, whereas studies carried out on mixed or purely chronic patient groups showed progressively more evidence of this.

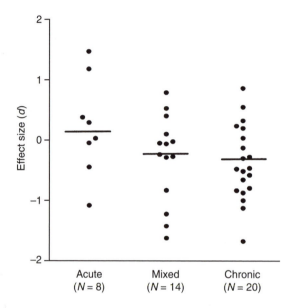

Activation or task-related hypofrontality was also supported, with a similar effect size to resting hypofrontality.

Voxel-based activation studies cannot easily be used to calculate effect sizes for hypofrontality. What can be meta-analysed is the pattern of activation found across these studies. For this, peak activation foci for schizophrenics and controls in 14 studies (7 PET and 7 fMRI) were plotted onto a rendered brain, and their pooled distributions were compared using a 3-dimensional version of the Kolmogorov-Smirnov test. In both patients and controls wide areas of the prefrontal cortex bilaterally showed significant activation. Comparison of the two distributions in the prefrontal cortex revealed no significant difference (KS3 statistic = 0.16, p = .94). There was also no difference between the non-frontal distributions of peak activation foci (KS3 statistic = 0.14, p = .98).

The neuropathology of schizophrenia

So convinced was Kraepelin (1913a) that schizophrenia was an organic brain disease, that he persuaded a psychiatric colleague, who was about to leave to become director of an asylum, to retrain in neuropathology and establish the post-mortem brain pathology of the disorder. This colleague's subsequent endeavours revealed that there were no obvious macroscopic brain abnormalities, and the microscopic findings were also rather slim – although this did not deter Kraepelin from interpreting them as evidence of severe and widespread cortical disease. However, the efforts of this colleague – whose name was Alzheimer – turned out not to be entirely wasted.

The claims made by Alzheimer, Nissl and a number of other investigators for histological abnormality in schizophrenic post-mortem brain included, but were not limited to: cell loss, cell shrinkage and ballooning, dwarf cells, metachromatic bodies, cellular inclusions, demyelination and gliosis. Notwithstanding the confident way in which they were reported, the findings often gave the impression of being minor, widely scattered throughout the brain, and not very consistent from study to study. After a careful review of the literature, David (1957) felt there were grounds for dismissing all of the alleged abnormalities on the grounds that they were either fixation artefacts, or were not well replicated, or had also been documented in the post-mortem brains of normal individuals. By the time of the first International Congress of Neuropathology in 1952, schizophrenia had acquired a reputation as the graveyard of neuropathology.

The renewal of interest in the brain in schizophrenia rescued neuropathology from this much quoted status, but it was also clear that any microscopic pathology was going to be subtle, and likely to take the form of quantitative differences in cell numbers, density or size rather than some unique histological abnormality. In such circumstances, as described by Benes (1988), Dwork (1997) and Heckers (1997), methodological considerations loom large. Age and sex matching with controls needs to be rigorous. The cause of death, the duration of the agonal period, the length of post-mortem delay, the amount of time spent in fixative, and numerous other factors, can all introduce systematic bias and so also need to be comparable in patient and control groups. Another important consideration is quantitation, where there are issues concerning the differentiation of neurons from glia, the effects of tissue shrinkage, and the use of measures of cell density versus cell number. It goes without saying that the diagnosis of schizophrenia needs to be made according to diagnostic criteria, particularly given that several post-mortem studies have utilised series of schizophrenic brains collected in the first part of the twentieth century, when clinical information was liable to have been poor and accessory diagnoses such as mental handicap, alcohol abuse or brain injury may not always have been recorded.

It has to be said that, by and large, contemporary post-mortem research on schizophrenia have not risen to this challenge, and the field continues to be dominated by studies whose sample sizes are often less than 10, where matching for the above variables is often dealt with cursorily, and whose findings do not go on to be replicated. A case in point is the most well-known finding in the field, hippocampal pyramidal cell disarray. This was first reported by Scheibel and Kovelman (1981; Kovelman and Scheibel, 1984) who compared the left hippocampus in 10 clinically diagnosed schizophrenic patients and 8 age matched controls under non-blind conditions and found a disturbance of the normal orderly palisade-like arrangement of the pyramidal cells and irregularity of their dendritic domains. In a later study, the same group (Altshuler *et al.*, 1987) found no significant difference in the degree of hippocampal cell disarray between seven schizophrenic patients and six controls. Later still, the same group (Conrad *et al.*, 1991) found significantly more hippocampal pyramidal cell disarray in an overlapping series of 11 patients and 7 controls (age matched, not sex matched and using no diagnostic criteria). In this study, however, it was noted that disorganisation was also common in the controls, and there was a large variation in both groups. Four independent studies (Christison *et al.*, 1989; Benes *et al.*, 1991; Arnold, 1995a; Zaidel *et al.*, 1997) all failed to replicate the finding.

Harrison (1999) has critically reviewed other contemporary histological studies in schizophrenia. Noting that controversy surrounds nearly every point, he concluded that only three findings could be regarded as being reasonably well established. In descending order of robustness these were: absence of gliosis, which has been widely replicated and is usually taken to support the neurodevelopmental hypothesis of schizophrenia (see Chapter 7); decreased neuronal size in the hippocampus, which has been supported in three studies counting large numbers of neurons; and finally reduced numbers of neurons in the dorsal thalamus, which is based on only two studies. Harrison considered that all other abnormalities, including cytoarchitectonic disorganisation, especially in the parahippocampal gyrus and frontal cortex; decreased neuron number in the frontal cortex, anterior cingulate gyrus, entorhinal cortex and hippocampus; and maldistribution of cortical subplate neurons have not been reliably reproduced from study to study, or are suspect for other reasons.

Conclusion

Psychodynamic theories of schizophrenia have a seductive appeal and held sway over psychiatric thinking for a long time. But no matter how passionately advocated and plausibly argued, the truth is that they have never managed to attract more than feeble experimental support. The case for stressful life events precipitating schizophrenic episodes is not persuasive, and there is no evidence at all that they can cause a first attack of schizophrenia. When Wynne and Singer's finding of deviant parental communication could not be independently replicated, and lack of scientific rigour seemed at least partly to blame, the whole edifice of family interaction in schizophrenia came crashing down.

At the same time, as the sorry state of neuropathological research demonstrates, a healthy scepticism needs to be maintained regarding biological research in schizophrenia. Nevertheless, two findings have withstood all attacks to emerge as established beyond any conceivable doubt. One of these is that there is a genetic component to the aetiology of schizophrenia. A little ground has to be given in that the hereditary predisposition seems to express itself in disorders that go beyond schizophrenia, and are often in the realm of personality, a finding that is taken up again in Chapter 16. The other incontrovertible finding is lateral ventricular enlargement. The caveat here is that the degree of enlargement is small, and, given that it seems to be of the same order of magnitude as the difference between normal men and normal women, it almost certainly cannot play any direct causal role. Its significance must presumably lie in its being a trait marker for schizophrenia, some kind of a by-product of the genetic or other pathological process that directly causes the disorder. This conclusion is reinforced by the fact that no one has succeeded in relating lateral ventricular enlargement to any feature of schizophrenia, clinical or demographic.

Otherwise, the vastly more sophisticated technique of MRI appears to have left few survivors among the other candidates for structural brain abnormality in schizophrenia. Any reduction in overall brain size in schizophrenia is trivial, and there is little to suggest that it affects grey matter more than white matter, or that there is disproportionately greater volume loss in the frontal or temporal lobes. The evidence does, however, become slightly stronger in the case of two temporal lobe structures, the hippocampus and the amygdala.

With respect to functional brain abnormality, hypofrontality has had a nothing if not chequered career, but can be regarded as being saved from a verdict of non-replication by meta-analysis. This also suggests that some of the inconsistencies in the literature are due to an association with duration of illness. If this can be trusted, then unlike lateral ventricular enlargement, hypofrontality appears to be a state rather than trait marker in schizophrenia.

6   The neurochemistry of schizophrenia

Accepting a biological basis for schizophrenia still leaves an explanatory gap: it is not readily apparent how an abnormality in brain structure or function might become translated into the many and varied symptoms of the disorder, most if not all of which are quite different from the usual signs of brain disease, not to mention being prone to erratic fluctuations in a way not at all reminiscent of neurological disorders. The usual way of bridging this gap has been to postulate an intervening variable in the shape of a neurochemical disturbance. Such a disorder could easily be the expression of a genetic fault, such as one affecting the regulation of a neurotransmitter; and it is not difficult to imagine it in turn giving rise to a derangement of brain function, of a rather subtle kind, resulting in disorders that are primarily in the realm of thinking, feeling and perception. Nor is a neurochemical disturbance completely incompatible with structural brain abnormality – for example, insidiously evolving damage in certain key areas might trigger off pathological fluctuations in neurotransmitter levels.

Precedent certainly exists for the idea of alterations in brain chemistry giving rise to abnormal mental states. From the ancient religious usage of psilocybin and mescaline, through the plagues of ergotism of the middle ages, to the opium-induced pipe dreams of Victorian England, drugs have always been known that have the ability to induce mental changes every bit as remarkable as the symptoms of schizophrenia. However, it was probably the synthesis of LSD in 1947 and its subsequent widespread illicit use that first concentrated the minds of researchers on biochemical hypotheses of schizophrenia. The first wave of theories proposed some inborn error of metabolism – a 'pink spot' in the urine, an aberrant form of the copper transporting enzyme, abnormal transmethylation of biogenic amines – which led to the production of a chemical with mind-altering properties. For one reason or another these theories did not stand the test of time (see Iversen, 1978; Smythies, 1983). Shortly afterwards they were replaced by another biochemical theory which went on to show remarkable tenacity: the hypothesis that some schizophrenic symptoms are due to an excess of brain dopamine.

Every psychiatrist is familiar with the observations on which the dopamine hypothesis of schizophrenia was originally based. Somewhat less well known is the ingenuity and resourcefulness that went into establishing that dopamine rather than any other neurotransmitter played the crucial role. Less widely appreciated still has been the methodical series of steps that were then taken to provide a direct test of the dopamine hypothesis. These culminated in what was arguably the most important experiment in the history of psychiatry, one that to the dismay of many had negative findings. The resulting neurochemical vacuum has since been filled by another transmitter, glutamate, which has come to be widely regarded as a worthy heir to the dopamine hypothesis.

Origins of the dopamine hypothesis

Ideas not totally removed from the concept of a neurochemical disorder in schizophrenia ran through the minds of classical authors. Kraepelin (1907) stated that the underlying brain pathology was potentially and to a limited extent reversible. Bleuler (1911) came closer when he speculated that some toxic agent – for example an endocrine abnormality or an infectious process – might both produce the symptoms of schizophrenia and then go on to cause permanent changes in the brain.

The dopamine hypothesis was later foreshadowed in a remarkably prescient way by Mettler (Mettler, 1955; Mettler and Crandell, 1959). He, like a number of other authors, had been struck by the occurrence of abnormal movements reminiscent of those seen in extrapyramidal disorders in (untreated) chronic schizophrenic patients (see Chapter 1). This led him to speculate that the pathology of the disorder might involve the basal ganglia. However, since schizophrenia was a disorder of exacerbations and remissions, it seemed unlikely that this pathological process could be one that caused permanent damage to basal ganglia structures. Since dopamine had not yet been discovered, he had to fall back on the rather unsatisfactory proposal that some form of vasospasm led to an intermittent compromise of the function of this part of the brain.

But this was all preamble. The dopamine hypothesis proper burst onto the scene in the 1960s, as the result of two symmetrical and more or less contemporaneous observations. The first of these was the antipsychotic action of neuroleptic drugs; the second was the psychosis-inducing properties of amphetamine and related drugs.

The antipsychotic effect of neuroleptic drugs

Chlorpromazine was discovered in 1952 and its therapeutic effects were immediately recognised. As described in more detail in Chapter 10, over the next 15 years or so the effectiveness of this and a number of other drugs was placed beyond doubt by a large number of well-designed studies.

How chlorpromazine and other neuroleptics exerted their therapeutic effect, however, remained a mystery for considerably longer. Eventually, several lines of evidence converged to suggest that dopamine receptor blockade was the important pharmacological action. Reviewing these, Seeman (1980) noted four findings as crucial: (1) Chlorpromazine and other drugs effective in treating schizophrenia were found to accelerate the metabolic turnover of dopamine. (2) In animal behavioural studies, the drugs also induced a state similar to human Parkinsonism, as well as reversing the effects of dopamine agonist drugs such as apomorphine. (3) In neurophysiological studies the drugs were found to inhibit the effects of dopamine on the firing rate of neurons in the basal ganglia. (4) The molecular structure of all the drugs revealed a clear conformational relationship with dopamine.

This evidence was all circumstantial and did not prove that neuroleptic drugs exerted their therapeutic effect by virtue of dopamine receptor blockade. Furthermore, almost all the drugs in clinical use at the time had other actions besides dopamine receptor blockade: most blocked noradrenaline and serotonin receptors, and some blocked histamine and other receptors as well. Before it could become one of the two pillars of the dopamine hypothesis of schizophrenia, it was first necessary to establish what might be termed the dopamine hypothesis of neuroleptic action beyond doubt. In order to do this, three questions needed to be answered. These were as follows.

Do all antipsychotic drugs block dopamine receptors?

The receptor blocking actions of different neuroleptics have been summarised by Hyttel *et al.* (1985), and his representation of these as pie charts is shown in Figure 6.1. It can be seen that some neuroleptics, such as chlorpromazine, thioridazine and fluphenazine, block multiple receptor types, but always including dopamine. Others, for example haloperidol and trifluoperazine, exert their main effect on dopamine receptors and have only minor actions at other receptor sites. Still others are highly selective for dopamine receptors, a good example being pimozide (which is no longer in wide use due to cardiac side-effects). Finally the receptor blocking effect of one drug, sulpiride, is to all intents and purposes specific for dopamine receptors.

Blockade of dopamine receptors thus seems to be a prerequisite for therapeutic effectiveness in schizophrenia. Another drug, reserpine, which does not block dopamine receptors, but has a functionally equivalent effect of reducing dopamine availability by depleting synaptic stores, has also shown clear evidence of therapeutic effectiveness in schizophrenia (see Chapter 10). No drug that lacks dopamine antagonistic effects has ever been found to be effective as a treatment for schizophrenia.

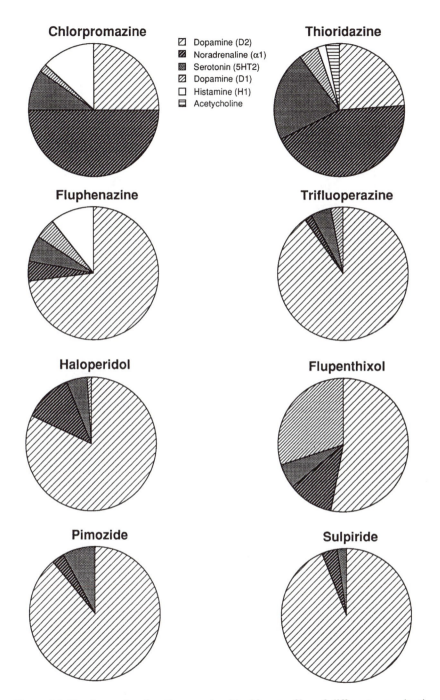

Figure 6.1 Pie charts showing the receptor blocking profiles of different neuroleptic drugs (from Hyttel *et al.* (1985). Receptor-binding profiles of neuroleptics. In D.E. Casey, T.W. Chase, A.V. Christensen, and J. Gerlach (Eds.), *Dyskinesia – research and treatment*, Psychopharmacology Supplementum, No. 2, pp. 9–18. Copyright 1985, Springer-Verlag GmbH and Co. KG. Reprinted by permission).

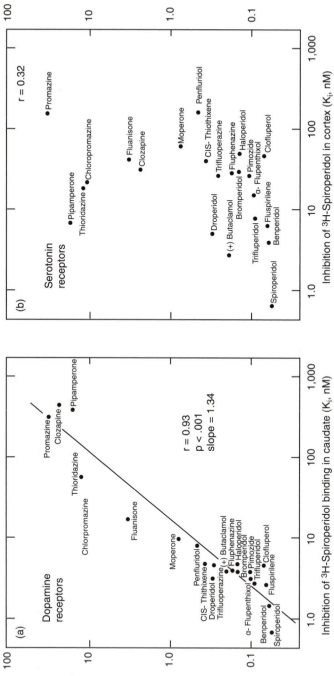

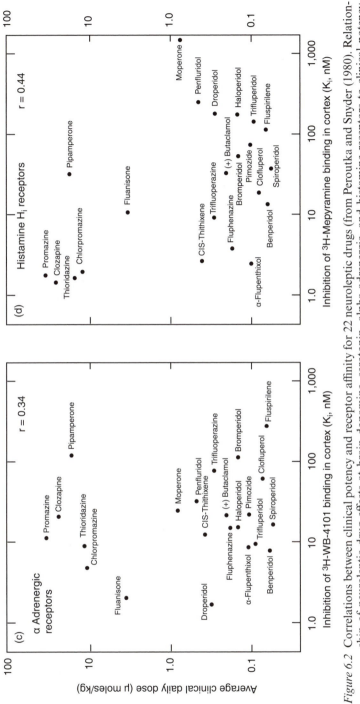

Figure 6.2 Correlations between clinical potency and receptor affinity for 22 neuroleptic drugs (from Peroutka and Snyder (1980). Relationship of neuroleptic drug effects at brain dopamine, serotonin, alpha-adrenergic, and histamine receptors to clinical potency. *American Journal of Psychiatry*, 137, 1518–1522. Copyright 1980, the American Psychiatric Association. Reprinted by permission).

Is antipsychotic effectiveness related to the effectiveness of
neuroleptics in blocking dopamine receptors?

In an early study Janssen (1967, cited in Iversen, 1978) found that a correlation existed between the average daily dose necessary to control schizophrenic symptoms and the dose necessary to reverse the behavioural effects of dopamine agonist drugs in animals. Later, when a direct assay for dopamine receptors was developed, a similar correlation continued to be found, but a major discrepancy became apparent concerning the butyrophenone group of drugs, for example haloperidol (see Seeman, 1980). This discrepancy was resolved when two independent groups of investigators (Creese *et al.*, 1976; Seeman *et al.*, 1976) employed a new, direct and highly accurate method of assaying dopamine receptor binding and found that the correlation between average daily dose of all drugs including butyrophenones and ability to block dopamine receptors was exceptionally high at around 0.9. It was as a direct result of this experiment that the existence of two types of dopamine receptor, D1 and D2, was recognised.

It could still be argued that neuroleptic drugs might show similar clinical: pharmacological correlations for other classes of receptor, but this possibility was excluded by Peroutka and Snyder (1980). They plotted the clinical potency of 22 neuroleptic drugs against their in vitro receptor blocking effects for dopamine (D2), serotonin, noradrenaline and histamine receptors. Their findings are illustrated in Figure 6.2, from which it is clear that while the relationship with dopamine receptors was virtually linear, the corresponding correlations for serotonin, noradrenaline and histamine receptors were insignificant or even inverse.

Does the antipsychotic effect of neuroleptics depend solely on
dopamine receptor blockade?

While the preceding studies leave no room for doubt about the importance of dopamine receptor blockade for the antipsychotic effect, they do not rule out the possibility that blockade of further receptors might make an additional contribution. It could be that the effectiveness of a neuroleptic is related more to the breadth of its actions than just to action on dopamine receptors; the more receptors types blocked, the better. A remote chance also exists that a pharmacological action on some as yet undiscovered neurotransmitter system might be responsible for the antipsychotic effect, possibly one coupled to the dopamine system in some way.

These possibilities were put to the test in an elegant study by Johnstone *et al.* (1978). They took advantage of the fact that the neuroleptic flupenthixol exists in two forms, the alpha (cis) isomer and the beta (trans) isomer. The slight structural difference between the two is enough to confer different biological actions; in particular, the alpha isomer has dopamine blocking effects, whereas the beta isomer does not. Otherwise, the receptor blocking

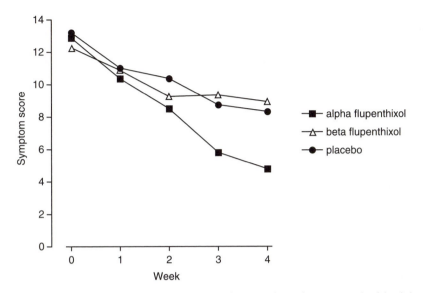

Figure 6.3 Clinical improvement in acute schizophrenic patients treated with alpha flupenthixol, beta flupenthixol or placebo (from Johnstone *et al.* (1978), Mechanism of the antipsychotic effect in the treatment of acute schizophrenia. *Lancet*, i, 848–851. © by the Lancet Ltd, 1978).

profiles of the two drugs are reasonably well matched (although the beta isomer also lacks serotonin blocking effects). Johnstone *et al.* randomly assigned 45 acute schizophrenic patients to treatment with either alpha flupenthixol, beta fluopenthixol or placebo for four weeks, under double blind conditions. The findings are shown in Figure 6.3. All three groups showed some improvement, but only in the alpha flupenthixol treated group was this significantly greater than with placebo.

This study makes it difficult to argue that anything other than or additional to dopamine receptor blockade underlies the antipsychotic actions of neuroleptics. The difference in serotonin receptor blocking properties of the alpha isomer could conceivably have played a part, but as Johnstone *et al.*, pointed out, there was (and still is) very little evidence to suggest a role for serotonin in either psychosis or antipsychotic drug effects. To attribute antipsychotic action to some unknown chemical action is equally problematic – it would have to be assumed that alpha flupenthixol just happened to have such an effect and beta flupenthixol just happened to lack it.

The psychosis-inducing effects of amphetamine and other stimulant drugs

Three years after the stimulant drug amphetamine was introduced, Young and Scoville (1938) reported the apparent complication of schizophrenia-like psychosis in three patients who were taking it for narcolepsy. By 1969 over two hundred cases of amphetamine psychosis had been reported worldwide (Kalant, 1966). It had also become clear that similar psychotic states could occur with use of other stimulant drugs including cocaine, phenmetrazine and methylphenidate, and even the milder ephedrine and diethylpropion (Angrist and Sudilovsky, 1978). Abusers themselves gave the informal impression that psychotic symptoms – 'speed paranoia' – were a routine hazard to be faced in any period of indulgence (Rylander, 1972; Schiorring, 1981).

Despite this, the idea that amphetamine and other stimulants could actually cause a schizophrenia-like state was resisted for a long time (e.g. see Rylander, 1972; Angrist and van Kammen, 1984). One issue that regularly surfaced was whether what was being seen was merely latent schizophrenia being released, or incipient schizophrenia being hastened, in individuals whose predisposition or evolving illness also led them to the fringes of society and so to drug use. Another was whether the psychosis occurred in clear consciousness or whether it was really an acute confusional state. A variant of this latter criticism was that amphetamine psychosis did not reproduce the full picture of schizophrenia, only a state characterised by delusions and hallucinations – in fact, the view that amphetamine psychosis always takes form of a paranoid-hallucinatory syndrome without formal thought disorder or negative symptoms persists to the present day.

These doubts were laid to rest in two large and meticulous studies. Connell (1958) collected a series of 42 patients who developed psychotic states while taking amphetamine. Thirty-four had been taking the drug regularly, but in eight only a single large dose had been consumed. In four patients the amphetamine abuse was accompanied by excessive alcohol intake, and another 16 had a previous history of alcohol abuse, but this did not seem to be a contributory factor at the time of presentation. There was little to sug-gest that the patients were particularly predisposed to develop schizophrenia: an assessment of premorbid personality revealed no excess of schizoid traits and a family history of schizophrenia was found in only one case.

The psychosis typically took the form of delusions of reference and per-secution plus, in some but not in all cases, auditory hallucinations. Visual hallucinations were uncommon and were never a prominent part of the picture. Occasionally there were hallucinations in other modalities. Formal thought disorder was evident in some of the cases Connell described in detail, but there was no reference to catatonic phenomena. For the most part, there was a striking absence of signs of clouding of consciousness. Disorientation – for time only – was present in three cases, two of whom had independent reasons for this, for example a recent suicide attempt by drug overdose. However, reference was made in some of the patients' case-notes to short periods of confusion.

The duration of the disorder was exceptional in comparison to schizo-phrenia. In 77 per cent of cases recovery took place within a week, and almost all the remaining cases remitted within 2–4 weeks; only two episodes lasted longer than this. In nearly all cases the psychosis later recurred, but it was not possible to determine whether or not this was in the setting of further drug use.

Tatetsu (1964) examined a large series of methamphetamine abusing individuals in Japan. Out of 492 chronic abusers, 92 per cent showed some form of psychiatric disorder. This was mostly minor, but in 19 per cent it took the form of a schizophrenia-like state. As in Connell's series, Tatetsu's patients exhibited delusions and hallucinations, and he also described various first rank symptoms and formal thought disorder. Unlike Connell, he also noted lack of volition, shallowness of affect, solitariness and catatonic phenomena up to and including stupor. On the whole, however, these latter abnormalities appeared to be less frequent and less striking than in true schizophrenia.

In Tatetsu's series, as in Connell's, improvement tended to take place rapidly after cessation of the drug. In many cases, however, full recovery was not attained, and in his experience after a month any further progress tended to be slow or absent. Only half of his cases could be discharged in less than six months and 14 per cent were still in hospital 5 years after admission. In some cases active symptoms continued for up to 13 years after withdrawal from methamphetamine; others showed relapses and remissions or fluctuations in severity that could not be attributed to further drug abuse.

Amphetamine and related drugs, and also cocaine, are known to cause a functional excess of brain dopamine. In the case of amphetamine, this is achieved via multiple mechanisms, including enhancement of synaptic release, blockade of re-uptake and reduction of degradation by inhibition of monoamine oxidase (Biel and Bopp, 1978; Moore, 1978). There is also no doubt that these drugs can induce a psychotic state essentially indistinguishable from schizophrenia. Once again, however, these facts do not in themselves provide conclusive evidence for what might be termed the dopamine hypothesis of stimulant drug-induced psychosis. One obvious problem is that the immediate effects of these drugs are euphoria and increased alertness and energy rather than psychosis, and it therefore needs to be established whether psychosis is an inevitable, and hence presumably direct pharmacological effect, or whether it develops unpredictably and so might depend on other factors. A second question is whether the psychosis is attributable to increased brain dopamine: amphetamine produces a functional excess not only of brain dopamine but also the other monoamine transmitter noradrenaline, and so the psychosis could be attributed to either pharmacological action, or conceivably to both. These questions have not been addressed anywhere near as systematically as the corresponding questions concerning the dopamine hypothesis of neuroleptic action, but they are answerable to some extent.

Does amphetamine invariably induce psychosis?

Griffith *et al.* (1968) managed the ethically somewhat tricky task of determining whether amphetamine sooner or later induces psychotic symptoms in everyone, by testing four regular users of the drug, none of whom had a previous history of psychosis. They were each given 10 mg of amphetamine hourly. After around 50 mg had been given the initial euphoria disappeared in all four subjects and was replaced by depression, lack of interest, hypochondriacal complaints and 'adoption of dependent attitudes' to the investigators. From the subjects' retrospective accounts it was also clear that they were entertaining abnormal ideas at this time. After one to five days, paranoid and referential delusions began to be discussed openly. The subjects started talking about being secretly photographed or discussed on television. One felt that the entire study was a subterfuge; another believed that an assassin had been hired to kill him; a third became aware of a giant oscillator placed in the ceiling to control his thoughts and the behaviour of others. When this occurred the drug administration was stopped and recovery then followed over a few hours, or three days in one case.

Angrist and Gershon (1970) carried out essentially the same experiment on four further drug-user volunteers. Two developed clear-cut psychotic states, with one showing obvious formal thought disorder. The sequence of mental changes in this latter patient is described in Box 6.1. The other two patients, however, showed, at most, only changes in the direction of psychosis, for example becoming hostile and suspicious but not frankly deluded, or experiencing minor hallucinations like hearing their name being called.

Box 6.1 Evolution of mental changes with continuous amphetamine administration (reprinted by permission of Elsevier Science Inc. from Angrist and Gershon (1970), The phenomenology of experimentally induced amphetamine psychosis – preliminary observations. *Biological Psychiatry*, 2, 95–107. Copyright 1970 by the Society of Biological Psychiatry)

Clinical notes recorded during administration of 5–10 mg amphetamine hourly to a volunteer. The individual concerned abused heroin, which he typically dissolved in the contents of an ampoule of methamphetamine. Although considered to have a personality disorder and subject to chronic complaints of depression, he had not previously shown psychotic symptoms.

After 5 hours: Mild pressure of speech

After 6 hours: Mild grandiosity, 'If I felt this way I'd be a teacher. I've learned the truth through suffering and pain', etc.

After 7 hours: Slight headache. Talking about manliness and Thomas Wolfe, 'He had being a man in the palm of his hand. That book was his guts', etc.

After 8 hours: Emergence of emotional lability and primitive material in content of speech. Tearfully discusses mother's promiscuity, abandonment by parents and grandfather, wife's infidelity and homosexual attacks by relatives.

After 17 hours: Hostile to nursing staff and feels that their attitude is disparaging.

After 26 hours: Agitated philosophic diatribe with riddles that make little sense. 'One man goes to school, the other can't. Then the other cuts out, says "Fuck you, buddy" ' – interpreted to mean there is no brotherhood in the world.

After 32 hours: Less pressure of speech and irritability. Diminution of feelings of profundity to ideas.

After 34 hours: Returns from patients' movie after a half-hour, frightened. Feels he can judge at a glance which patients are dangerous and 'sensed the presence of danger'.

After 37 hours: Speaking of revelations but is unable to explain what has been revealed. He 'has received new understanding not given to everyone in this cycle'.

After 40 hours: Writing and talking excitedly, constantly. 'My consciousness in the form of what you know as human. My feeling which I receive from him. I bring the answer to the unknown and yet. They who do not hear or show laugh or murder my love. In my human form He might let me act human for the rest must still wonder at my actions which make them doubt my having been used to enlighten. Every thought that stops me accepting all knowledge more than man has ever known.'

After 43 hours: Preaching aloud constantly. Content as above.

After 46 hours: Preaching at maximum vocal volume. Content and form as above. Unable to cooperate with interviews or psychological testing. Amphetamine cut.

After 50 hours: Diminution of agitation. Ideation unchanged.

After 54 hours: Feelings of profundity, but coherent. 'Different races are a source of beauty in the world', etc.

After 60 hours: Sleeps five to six hours. Awakes hostile and demanding.

Next 31 hours: At first depressed and dishevelled but returns to normal.

Is amphetamine psychosis attributable to dopamine?

One line of argument supporting this view is that almost all of the behavioural effects of amphetamine in animals appear to be due to its actions on dopamine rather than noradrenaline. As described in Chapter 10, amphetamine induces a state of behavioural hyperactivity that is initially accompanied by and eventually gives way to a syndrome of stereo-typed motor responses. Pharmacological experiments (see Kokkinides and Anisman, 1981; Mason, 1984) have established that these effects are also produced by other drugs with dopamine agonist effects, but not by drugs with noradrenergic agonist effects. It is, in fact, difficult to provoke any behavioural change at all in animals by manipulation of noradrenaline levels (Mason, 1984)

The second line of argument is that dopamine agonist drugs other than amphetamine can also induce psychotic states in man. Almost all the relevant evidence here concerns Parkinson's disease. In a review of the psychiatric complications of the drugs used to treat this disorder (including not just L-DOPA, which has noradrenergic as well as dopaminergic agonist effects, at least theoretically), Cummings (1991) found visual hallucinations were the most common psychiatric symptom, occurring in approximately 30 per cent of cases, but delusions, euphoria, mania/hypomania, anxiety and sexual changes could also be seen. All these symptoms could occur in clear con-sciousness, and Cummings considered that delirious states were typically a feature of anticholinergic treatment of Parkinson's disease (although their occurrence with dopaminergic drugs had also been documented).

Marsh *et al.* (2004) carried out structured psychiatric interviews on 25 patients with Parkinson's disease who had experienced delusions and/or hallucinations in clear consciousness over the preceding month; patients in whom delirium as the sole cause of psychotic symptoms were excluded. Although visual hallucinations were the most common type of psychotic symptom, occurring in 21 of the 25 (84 per cent), auditory hallucinations were present in 15 (60 per cent). These included musical hallucinations, hearing one's name being called, whispering and voices talking, including in threatening tones. In most cases auditory hallucinations were accom-panied by visual hallucinations. Delusions were present in 16 of the 25 patients (64 per cent) and encompassed systematised beliefs (ie single delusions with multiple elaborations, or a group of delusions related to a single theme), delusions of spousal infidelity, sexual delusions, somatic delusions and first rank symptoms, as well as what the authors termed non-specific paranoid ideation. Delusions and hallucinations were commonly both present: nine patients had only hallucinations and two had only delusions.

Direct tests of the dopamine hypothesis

The evidence that dopamine antagonist drugs improve schizophrenic symptoms appears incontrovertible. The case for dopamine agonist drugs inducing schizophrenic symptoms, if not watertight, is at least defensible – there is no doubt that amphetamine can induce a psychosis closely resembling schizophrenia, but the fact that it, and especially other dopaminergic drugs, appear to do so relatively infrequently remains something of a problem. But however strong and convergent this evidence is, it is circumstantial, and a functional dopamine excess in the brains of patients with schizophrenia still needs to be confirmed by direct investigation.

A functional excess of brain dopamine can only be achieved in a limited number of ways. One of these is *increased synaptic availability*, via increased synthesis of dopamine, increased synaptic release, decreased metabolic degradation, blockade of neuronal re-uptake, or a combination of these. The consequences of this increased synaptic availability should be easily detectable as raised levels of dopamine in dopamine-rich parts of the brain and/or raised levels of the metabolic products of dopamine in the cerebrospinal fluid. The second major mechanism is *post-synaptic receptor supersensitivity*. Here, the effects of normal synaptic release of dopamine become multiplied because there is a greater than normal density of post-synaptic receptors. The phenomenon is analogous to denervation sensitivity where acetylcholine receptors at the motor end plate proliferate in response to injury to the nerve supplying the muscle, and is widely accepted as occurring in the central nervous system. Other potential ways of inducing a functional dopamine excess exist, all of which revolve around the idea of an *anomalous dopamine agonist*, for example an abnormal substance in the general circulation which gains access to the central nervous system and mimics the action of dopamine or stimulates its release from nerve terminals. Alternatively, it has been proposed, based on an analogy with thyrotoxicosis, that there could be an autoantibody to post-synaptic dopamine receptors that for some reason has stimulatory rather than blocking actions (Knight, 1982). These last two mechanisms remain hypothetical.

Increased synaptic availability of dopamine in schizophrenia

Heritch (1990) reviewed 12 studies that examined the metabolic turnover of dopamine in drug-free schizophrenic patients by measuring its principal metabolite, homovanillic acid (HVA), in the cerebrospinal fluid. Seven found no significant difference compared to normal individuals, or patients with neurological disorders, or patients with a variety of psychiatric diagnoses. Four studies reported lower levels of HVA in the schizophrenic group. Only one study found higher levels.

Heritch also reviewed seven studies that took the more direct approach of measuring brain levels of dopamine in schizophrenic post-mortem brain.

Table 6.1 Studies of dopamine levels in schizophrenic post-mortem brain

Study	Caudate nucleus	Putamen	Nucleus accumbens/ olfactory tubercle	Amygdala	Septal area
Bird *et al.* (1977, 1979)	Normal	Normal	Increased	—	Normal
Owen *et al.* (1978)	Increased	Normal	Increased	—	—
Crow *et al.* (1979)	Increased	Increased	Normal	Normal	—
Mackay *et al.* (1982)	Increased	—	Increased	—	—
Toru *et al.* (1982)	—	—	Normal	—	Normal
Bird *et al.* (1984)	Normal	—	Increased	Normal	—
Bridge *et al.* (1985)	—	—	Increased	—	—

Source: Heritch (1990).

This time the findings were less uniformly negative. As shown in Table 6.1, although the majority of the studies reported no increases in dopamine in the majority of brain regions examined, all but one of the studies reported a significant elevation of dopamine levels in at least one brain area, and for two regions, the caudate nucleus and the nucleus accumbens (along with the olfactory tubercle part of a ventral extension of the caudate–putamen complex, the so-called ventral striatum) the balance of evidence favoured an increase.

The patients in these studies had all been exposed to neuroleptics in life and few of them were drug free at the time of death. The changes found might therefore have been due to treatment, even though it is not definitely established that neuroleptic drugs affect brain levels of dopamine (Carlsson, 1977). One further finding is, however, difficult to reconcile with such an explanation. Reynolds (1983) found that the level of dopamine in the amygdala of a series of post-mortem schizophrenic brains was nearly double that found in normal controls, and more detailed examination revealed that the differences were due to a selective increase in the left amygdala. It is possible to envisage neuroleptic drugs having asymmetrical dopaminergic effects in a particular individual (for example, Parkinsonian side-effects are sometimes more pronounced on one side), but hard to see how the left side could be preferentially affected by treatment across a whole series of patients.

Increased dopamine receptor sensitivity

As the lack of any marked abnormality of dopamine metabolism became apparent, attention turned to the possibility of post-synaptic receptor super-sensitivity as the most likely candidate for the putative functional dopamine excess in schizophrenia. The focus of this research has been the dopamine D2 receptor. The reason for this was largely historical: at the time the relevant studies were beginning to be undertaken, pharmacologists had persuaded themselves that the D2 receptor was the main mediator of dopamine's post-synaptic effects – quite wrongly as it turned out (see Waddington, 1989). In addition, a simple and accurate method for measuring D2 receptors was available, whereas assays for the other dopamine receptor known to exist at the time, the D1 receptor, were indirect and crude.

Three key studies of dopamine D2 receptor density in post-mortem schizophrenic brain were published in the same year. The studies all restricted the examination to the basal ganglia, where the brain dopamine innervation is at its richest. Two of them (Lee *et al.*, 1978; Owen *et al.*, 1978) found evidence of substantial increases compared to normal controls; the third (Mackay *et al.*, 1978) found no differences, but this study then confirmed the increase in a larger sample (Mackay *et al.*, 1982). The increases were found in all the basal ganglia nuclei studied, including the nucleus accumbens. Seeman (1987) reviewed these and a handful of further studies and found near-unanimous agreement that dopamine D2 receptors were increased by 60 per cent to 110 per cent in post-mortem schizophrenic brain.

Unfortunately, the very thing that gave rise to the dopamine hypothesis was destined to be the fatal flaw of these studies. By the time the patients in these studies died, almost all of them had been on neuroleptic treatment for up to 20 years. Over this period it had been established that chronic neuroleptic treatment itself led to a compensatory proliferation of post-synaptic receptors (e.g. Burt *et al.*, 1977), by virtue of it producing a func-tional equivalent of dopamine denervation. A valiant attempt to unconfound the finding was made by Lee and Seeman (1980), who managed to collect a series of 11 brains from schizophrenic patients who had received no or negligible amounts of neuroleptic medication during life. The D2 receptor densities in these patients were not significantly different from those of 26 treated patients (although they were slightly lower), and they continued to show a highly significant elevation compared to controls. But the attempt was doomed: Mackay *et al.* (1982) subsequently found that increases in dopamine receptor numbers were restricted to those patients who were on drug treatment at the time of death; in those who had been drug free for one month or longer before death there were no significant differences from controls.

The decisive test of the dopamine hypothesis

Just when the task proving or disproving the dopamine hypothesis seemed hopeless, a way out of the impasse was suddenly found. In 1983 Garnett *et al.* combined administration of radioactively labelled L-DOPA with functional imaging to produce a visual map of dopamine innervation in the living human brain. It was immediately apparent that the technique could be easily adapted to visualise dopamine receptors instead. A study of dopamine receptor numbers in schizophrenic patients in life, and before they were exposed to neuroleptic treatment, had become a realistic possibility.

In principle, such a study is easy to carry out. All that is necessary is, first, to radioactively label a drug that binds to dopamine receptors (i.e. a neuroleptic); to administer it to a group of never medicated, 'drug-naive' schizophrenic patients and controls; and to use functional imaging to quantify receptor numbers in relevant brain areas. In practice the obstacles to this kind of study are formidable. One of these is that the amount of radioactivity involved makes it difficult to carry out a series of assays with different concentrations of radioligand, which is the accepted way of establishing receptor density in animal studies. Instead, simplified methods have to be used that make many assumptions and are vulnerable to factors such as changes in the affinity state of the dopamine receptor and levels of presynaptic dopamine. Another problem is that until recently the available techniques (both scanning and radioligands) meant that only the dopamine-rich basal ganglia could be studied; the low density of dopamine receptors in extrastriatal regions has prevented the relatively small signal being detected above the level of non-specific binding.

The net result has been that the definitive experiment to test the dopamine hypothesis has only been carried a few times. The first two of these were the most technologically sophisticated and had high-profile findings. The first was by Wong and 16 co-authors at the Johns Hopkins School of Medicine in America (Wong *et al.*, 1986), and the second was by Farde and his colleagues at the Karolinska Institute in Sweden (Farde *et al.*, 1987).

The Johns Hopkins study

The authors examined 10 drug-naive schizophrenic patients and 11 age- and sex-matched controls. The patients were on the whole a rather exceptional group, for whom the statement 'only in America' springs to mind. Most of the patients had expressed longstanding reluctance to accept a psychiatric diagnosis or take psychotropic medication; some had undergone prolonged investigation for physical complaints that had all along been delusional; and prior to the study psychotherapy had been their main form of treatment – one patient had been in analysis for 10 years. As a result they had on average a 5-year duration of illness. They all met DSM III criteria, however, and their symptoms were typical of chronic schizophrenia.

Wong *et al.* used 3-*N*-methylspiperone, an early prototype for a dopamine D2 receptor radioligand. This drug has significant serotonin receptor blocking actions in addition to its effects at the dopamine D2 receptor. It also binds irreversibly to D2 receptors, and on injection continuously accumulates in the basal ganglia without coming to an equilibrium. This meant that the rate of increase of radioactivity in the basal ganglia was the only index that could be used, and since this also depends on blood flow to the same brain region, there was a confounding factor. The way in which the authors decided to correct for this involved carrying out two PET scans some days apart, the second of which was after administration of a single dose of (unlabelled) haloperidol. This enabled the effects of blood flow to be covaried out. Calculation of D2 receptor numbers was based on a complicated mathematical model, which made a large number of assumptions.

Wong *et al.*'s findings were unequivocal. The mean density of D2 receptor binding sites (customarily referred to as B_{max}) was 41.7 pmol/g of basal ganglia tissue in the schizophrenic group, whereas that for the controls was 16.6 pmol/g – a more than twofold increase.

Over the next few years the authors managed to increase their sample sizes to 20 drug-naive schizophrenics and 14 controls (Tune *et al.*, 1993). The increase in D2 receptor numbers continued to be found, although its magnitude became somewhat smaller (B_{max} 33.1 vs 14.4). It also became evident that there was a great deal of variability in the finding, with some patients showing normal dopamine D2 receptor densities but others exhibiting marked increases.

The Karolinska study

Six months after Wong *et al.*, Farde *et al.* (1987) published the preliminary results from their study. Their patient group consisted of 15 first episode patients, all of whom had been ill for more than six months and met DSM III criteria for schizophrenia. Drug-naivety was accordingly easy to establish. They were compared with 14 normal controls who were matched for age and sex.

In this study, the radioactively labelled neuroleptic used was raclopride. Unlike 3-*N*-methylspiperone, this is highly specific for dopamine D2 receptors and binds reversibly rather than irreversibly to D2 receptors, enabling something approximating to the standard method for determining receptor density to be followed. Two PET examinations were carried out. In the first, a tracer dose of raclopride was injected and equilibrium was allowed to be reached. Some days later a saturating dose was given. The values for specific versus non-specific binding at the two different saturations were then plotted in a so-called Scatchard diagram, in which the intercept yields the figure for B_{max}. The method of analysis employed was much simpler than that employed by Wong *et al.* However, it had the disadvantage that the Scatchard diagram had to be based on a plot containing only two points.

Farde *et al.*'s findings were in complete contrast to those of Wong *et al.* The dopamine receptor binding (B_{max}) for schizophrenic patients was 25.1 pmol/g and 24.6 pmol/g for the controls, a non-significant difference. The results were unchanged when the authors subsequently increased their sample size to 18 patients and 20 controls (Farde *et al.*, 1990).

Three more studies were carried out in the aftermath of these conflicting findings (Martinot *et al.*, 1990; Pilowsky *et al.*, 1994; Hietala *et al.*, 1994). These all employed drug-naive, or mainly drug-naive, schizophrenic patients and they all failed to find overall increases in D2 receptor numbers. There has also been one recent study of D2 receptors outside the basal ganglia: Suhara *et al.* (2002) found these to be significantly lower in drug-naive patients with schizophrenia than in controls.

All of a small number of studies have failed to find evidence of alterations of D1 receptors in the striatum (Okubo *et al.*, 1997; Abi-Dargham *et al.*, 2002; Karlsson *et al.*, 2002). Cortical D1 receptors have been found to be reduced (Okubo *et al.*, 1997), normal (Karlsson *et al.*, 2002) or increased (but only at trend level) in certain brain areas (Abi-Dargham *et al.*, 2002). The only area where the findings seem at all hopeful concerns amphetamine-induced synaptic release of dopamine. Laruelle *et al.* (1996) found that a single dose of amphetamine produced more than twice as much reduction in post-synaptic striatal D2 receptor binding in 15 drug-free schizophrenic patients than in 15 normal controls, implying that there was a greater release of dopamine from presynaptic terminals. This finding has been replicated in a second sample (Abi-Dargham *et al.*, 1998) and by an independent group (Breier *et al.*, 1997). So far, however, only seven of the patients in these studies have been drug naive (Laruelle *et al.*, 1999). More than these will be necessary to convince sceptics.

Beyond the dopamine hypothesis: Glutamate

Finding a credible alternative to the dopamine hypothesis is an uphill struggle. No drugs improve schizophrenic symptoms in the dramatic way that neuroleptics do. Nor are drugs that can induce a state resembling schizophrenia easy to come by. LSD and other hallucinogens produce striking alterations in perception, thinking and feeling which have been the subject of many fascinating descriptions, particularly by the users themselves (e.g. Wolfe, 1971). However, these same descriptions make clear the lack of similarity to the symptoms of schizophrenia: delusions are very uncommon and the perceptual changes do not consist of auditory hallucinations, but take the form of heightening of perception, illusions and kaleidoscopic visual patterns superimposed onto the environment or projected onto the back of the closed eyelids. Cannabis is accepted as being able to induce psychotic states with delusions and hallucinations, but most documented cases have been in the setting of a toxic confusional state, and it remains uncertain whether such symptoms are ever seen in clear consciousness (Rathod, 1975; Johns, 2001).

There is also increasing evidence that heavy cannabis use is a risk factor for the development of schizophrenia. However, the risk is small: Arseneault *et al.* (2004) reviewed five prospective studies employing population-based samples and concluded that cannabis use confers an overall twofold increase in the relative risk.

The picture is different for one further drug, phencyclidine. This was introduced in the 1950s as an anaesthetic, but was later withdrawn, partly because it was found to cause neuronal changes up to and including cell death in rats, but also partly because of the frequency of adverse mental effects associated with its use. Johnstone *et al.* (1959) gave a vivid account of the early days of its use in clinical practice. When given for pre-operative sedation, the patients became sleepy but rousable. Some were happily euphoric, and several sang or recited poetry in a drunken manner. Others were restless and agitated, or showed a state of maniacal excitement. One patient believed he had become a grub and another was convinced he had been shot into space in a sputnik. Within a few minutes of being given the drug as a general anaesthetic, the patient typically lapsed into a state Johnstone *et al.* described as catatonic stupor or akinetic mutism. The muscles became moderately relaxed, and there was no reaction to painful stimuli. The eyes often remained wide open, staring fixedly into infinity with unimpaired or sluggish pupillary reflexes. At lower doses, the patients could usually respond weakly to instructions and several appeared to be in ecstatic trances, whispering such words as 'heavenly', 'beautiful' or 'lovely'; two believed they were in the presence of God. On emergence from anaesthesia, the patients could be euphoric and excited, or alternatively aggressive and violent, for several hours. Some also described 'vestibular and proprioceptive hallucinations with distortion of vision'.

Hypothesising that phencyclidine might mimic the symptoms of schizophrenia, Luby *et al.* (1959) administered the drug intravenously in subanaesthetic doses to nine normal volunteers (and also to nine chronic schizophrenic patients). This was followed by marked subjective mental changes. All of the normal subjects reported body image disturbances, accompanied by what the authors called 'a loss of ego boundaries' – impaired ability to distinguish between self and non-self, feelings of depersonalisation and a sense of unreality. Some of the normal subjects' descriptions of these experiences are reproduced in Box 6.2. All subjects also showed objective changes in thinking. This was described as typically taking the form of inability to maintain a set, loss of goal ideas and impairment of the abstract attitude. Some patients were considered to show blocking, neologisms, word salad and echolalia, although no examples of these abnormalities were actually given. Seven of the subjects became hostile, stubborn and even 'negativistic'. The other main abnormality, found in three normal subjects, but more common in the schizophrenic patients was the occurrence of repetitive movements, including rocking, head rolling and, less frequently, grimacing. These changes developed against a background of drowsiness and apathy and, in some cases a feeling of

Box 6.2 Study of a new schizophrenomimetic drug – sernyl (from Luby *et al.*, 1959)

Sernyl (phencyclidine) was given intravenously over 12 minutes to 9 normal subjects and 9 patients with schizophrenia. Marked reactions began after 3 minutes and lasted up to 1 hour. Psychological effects included the following.

Body image changes: These were the earliest and most characteristic reaction to the drug. They were reported by all the normal subjects and the 7 schizophrenic patients who were able to communicate adequately. The body image disturbances were accompanied by impaired ability to distinguish between self and non-self stimuli, feelings of depersonalisation, and a sense of unreality. A normal subject reported: 'I was standing but I didn't feel like I was standing. I didn't know where my feet were and I didn't get myself up.' Another stated: 'My arm feels like a 20-mile pole with a pin at the end.' Also described were alternate contraction and expansion of body size, feelings of 'selflessness', being an 'empty nobody'; one subject stated 'I am small . . . not human . . . just a block of something in a great big laboratory.' A disturbing sense of unreality accompanied the body-image distortions. A normal subject felt as though the examiner were at a 'great distance' from him.

Estrangement: There was a commonly experienced profound sense of aloneness or isolation. The sense of being completely detached from all environmental objects and tensions was reported by several subjects directly and implied by others. This was not always accompanied by fear or anxiety. The subjects sometimes appeared to become passive and relaxed.

Disorganisation of thought: Consistent deficits in organisation and direction of thought were seen in all subjects. Most striking was the inability to maintain a set, frequent loss of goal ideas and impairment of the 'abstract attitude'. Some subjects showed blocking, neologisms, word salad and echolalia. To obtain information at the height of the drug effects, the examiner was forced to ask extremely simple and direct questions. Proverbs were interpreted in a fragmentary, concrete manner, or were simply repeated as though this implied meaning. The loose and asyndetic quality of thinking is illustrated by the following response to TAT Card 8BM: 'Oh, there is a doctor and a surgeon and a boy and a gun and a boy, boy, boy, boy, boy, boy, knife, gun, man, card, surgeon . . .' The performance of serial 7's became an impossible task for most subjects.

Negativism and hostility: These reactions were seen in many subjects. Oppositional behaviour varied from subtle expressions of hostility in the normal subjects to child-like negativism and catatonic-like reactions in the more naive and characterologically immature patient subjects.

Drowsiness and apathy: All subjects exhibited progressively increasing drowsiness. At times some appeared to fall asleep but remained responsive to questions. Retrospectively, they recalled being able to hear and comprehend what was expected of them but felt no special need to comply with the examiner's requests. They verbalised this as an 'I don't care' attitude.

Hypnagogic state: Both patients and normal subjects reported dream-like experiences which they experienced while awake and usually had a basis in the subject's past. The subjects reported feeling as though they were in some specific setting and were able to describe it in detail. As in dreams, multiple shifts occurred in the settings, sometimes in rapid succession.

Feelings of inebriation: Occasional euphoria was seen, where subjects would smile vacuously and compare their feelings to those resulting from several Martinis: 'This is a cheap hangover'; 'I feel half-plastered'.

Repetitive motor behaviours: Body movements of a rhythmic type were demonstrated by both normal subjects and patients. These included rocking, head-rolling, and, less frequently, grimacing. Instances of repetitive, chanting speech were observed in several subjects. A normal subject reported in his retrospective account: 'I kept shaking the bottles up and down because it felt good. Then I discovered that it also felt good to make my arms move in a figure eight.'

Neurological changes: Diminution of pain, touch and position sense occurred uniformly. All subjects displayed rotatory nystagmus and ataxic, slapping gait. Some subjects showed diplopia. There were a slight increase in muscle tone and minimal to mild impairment in motor strength. There was also a mild diminution in auditory and visual acuity.

euphoric inebriation. All subjects displayed rotary nystagmus and an ataxic gait.

The phencyclidine model of schizophrenia gained further ground when the drug started to find its way onto the street as 'angel dust'. Numerous case reports (reviewed by Pearlson, 1981; Javitt and Zukin, 1991) documented the development of florid psychotic states in illicit users of the drug. By far the most common presentation was one of delirium, where delusions and hallucinations, especially visual hallucinations, and bizarre and sometimes violent behaviour were present in the setting of obvious confusion. Less frequently, psychotic states resembling schizophrenia were described, which could last up to several weeks. Manic states were also recorded. McCarron *et al.* (1981) described a further presentation where patients appeared to be in a catatonic state, standing motionless and stiff, eyes open staring blankly, with their arms or head in bizarre positions. Many were mute, and some would hear a word or phrase and repeat it continuously, or show verbigeration or echolalia.

The major pharmacological effect of phencyclidine was found to be on glutamate, where it blocks one of several classes of post-synaptic receptor, the N-methyl-D-aspartate (NMDA) receptor. In this way, the phencyclidine model of schizophrenia became the glutamate hypothesis: the proposal that abnormal glutamatergic function – this time a deficiency – is the neurochemical abnormality underlying schizophrenia. Just as with the dopamine hypothesis, the evidence needs to be subjected to close scrutiny and, once again, the pertinent questions are, first, whether the effects of phencyclidine and other glutamate antagonist drugs faithfully reproduce the clinical features of schizophrenia; second, whether glutamate agonist drugs conversely improve schizophrenic symptoms; and finally, whether there is direct evidence for a functional deficiency of glutamate in the schizophrenic brain.

Does the effect of glutamate antagonist drugs resemble schizophrenia?

In a highly influential review, Javitt and Zukin (1991) argued that phencyclidine provided a better model of schizophrenia than amphetamine psychosis, because it not only induced positive symptoms but also caused negative symptoms and thought disorder. This, however, is not established convincingly from the studies cited above. Luby *et al.*'s observations of the effect of phencyclidine on normal volunteers were uncontrolled, and were made at a time when the definition of what constituted schizophrenic symptoms was very different from now. The descriptions of florid psychotic states in abusers of the drug seem compelling, but some of these reports failed to make any kind of distinction from delirium, and in others it was not clear that it was phencyclidine rather than some other street drug that had been taken.

It is no longer possible to investigate the effects of phencyclidine in normal volunteers, but a number of controlled studies have been carried out using ketamine, a weaker NMDA receptor blocker than phencyclidine, which continues to be used as an anaesthetic in children. In the first study of this type, Krystal *et al.* (1994) administered ketamine at two dose levels or placebo under double blind conditions by continuous infusion to 19 subjects. At the higher dose level, ketamine, but not placebo, produced significant increases in scores on both the positive and negative symptom subscales of the Brief Psychiatric Rating Scale (BPRS). The subjects experienced alterations in perception, although none of them described hallucinations. For example, one person felt that his legs were floating in the air when they were resting on his bed. Another perceived that music quietly playing in another room sounded inordinately loud. Several subjects developed ideas of reference and paranoid thought content, for example about staff in neighbouring rooms talking about them in ominous ways. Formal thought disorder was also noticeable on high-dose ketamine, with loosening of associations, derailment and stilted speech, among other abnormalities.

Several other studies have also found ketamine-induced increases in positive symptom scores (Adler *et al.*, 1998; Newcomer *et al.*, 1999) in normal volunteers and, less consistently, increases in negative symptom scores (Newcomer *et al.*, 1999). All these studies, however, were criticised by Deakin (2000) who pointed out that body image disturbances and illusions would tend to be rated on the 'hallucinatory behaviour' item of the BPRS, and feelings of detachment on the negative symptom items of this scale, even though their relationship to schizophrenic symptoms seemed distant. Thinking might become tangential and circumstantial on ketamine, but this could be said of many drugs with intoxicating effects.

Pomarol-Clotet *et al.* (2006) carried out a further similar study where ketamine was administered to 15 volunteers under double blind conditions, and in which symptoms were assessed using a structured psychiatric interview (a shortened form of the Present State Examination). Thirteen of the patients gave descriptions of a wide range of perceptual changes including heightening, dulling, distortions, illusions, feelings of unreality, depersonalisation, derealisation and changed perception of time. However, as in the study of Krystal *et al.*, none of them described hallucinations in any modality. Poverty of speech was evident in eight of the subjects, but only two subjects showed any other rateable abnormality of thought form. The speech of these two subjects did not resemble formal thought disorder, but was merely vague and muddled, and was also affected by poor recollection, in a way immediately recognisable as the effects of intoxication. The only obviously schizophrenia-like symptom was referential thinking, which 7 of the 15 subjects developed. This sometimes seemed classifiable as ideas of reference and sometimes as partially held delusions of reference and/or misinterpretation, and in one or two cases they seemed classifiable as delusional mood. Some examples are shown in Box 6.3.

Box 6.3 Examples of subjects' descriptions of referential ideas (from Pomarol-Clotet *et al.*, 2006)

Subject 4
I feel so enclosed, I almost feel as though I'm in a cage or . . . it's almost like a big brother type thing, people watching . . . I know people aren't looking at me, but I feel as though people could be looking at me . . . as though there's cameras or something like that.

Subject 5
Some of the questions when I was in the scanner, it was like they were saying one thing but what they're actually trying to do is discover what's going on somewhere else. People saying what they're supposed to say. People seem to be saying things for effect, instead of saying what they actually want. Some of the questions in the scanner seemed like they were specially put to make you think about something else. [As] if one's doing

something for a reason but trying to make it look like they don't mean to do it. Things specially arranged beyond the experiment . . . It's like someone wants you to think something and so they make you.

Subject 9
I feel they may talk about me. I think that they're thinking that I'm the centre of the world, although I know they're probably not. Laughing, not critical. I feel like a puppet, I feel guided by people around, to say things.

Also retrospectively described that she thought the interviewer was controlling her replies to questions by looking at her. 'People at the scanner were maybe spies. I was convinced.'

Subject 11
I feel paranoid that people are [looking at me] but I know that they're not, 'cause I'm in an experiment, so I know that they're not. I feel like I've not got control over what I'm saying, so I feel like what I am saying is not right, and then people are just looking at me and . . . OK. I feel as if people's reactions are different to me, reacting differently to me, but I don't feel people are gossiping about me. They just seem to be giving me a lot more attention, a lot more time, everything seems a lot slower. It's like that film [the Truman Show].

I feel things have been specially arranged beyond the experiment. I've got that feeling but I know they haven't.

It feels like something's happening but I'm not quite sure what's going on, I don't quite know what it is.

I feel like I'm the focus, everyone is watching me, which obviously you are doing. I feel like there's more to it than what's actually happening. I feel like I'm not being told everything. Something going to happen and haven't been told.

Subject 14
During second (placebo) interview: I suppose I did [feel self-conscious during the first session]. Maybe people were looking at me longer than they would normally. A bit, definitely . . . I think it could have been because of my concentration – I couldn't really make out what they were saying, and so maybe I then thought they were talking about me, and maybe judging me, judging my reaction to it. At the time maybe I thought they were a bit critical.

Subject 15
It feels as if I'm on stage being watched by an audience. Things are not as they should be. People might be laughing at me because I'm not myself.

Do glutamate agonist drugs improve schizophrenic symptoms?

Glutamate is one the two major transmitters mediating fast excitatory neurotransmission in large areas of the brain. Direct agonist drugs have been developed but are too rapidly metabolised to be useful, and also have the potential to cause neuronal damage through an excitotoxic action. However, the NMDA receptor is known to require co-activation by glycine as well as glutamate. This permits a way of enhancing glutamate function safely, by orally administering glycine, or other drugs such as D-serine and D-cycloserine, which also interact with the NMDA receptor in the same way.

Deakin (2000) reviewed 12 trials of glycine and cycloserine (and one using milacemide, which is converted into glycine in the brain) in schizophrenia, most of which were open label studies. These studies provided no support for a therapeutic effect on positive symptoms, but several of them found clinically important improvements in negative symptoms. A subsequent meta-analysis of 18 double blind, placebo-controlled trials (Tuominen *et al.*, 2005) confirmed the lack of an effect on positive symptoms, but supported a therapeutic effect of glycine and D-serine on negative symptoms, with a medium effect size of 0.66. Cycloserine, however, was found to have no significant effect.

Unfortunately, meta-analysis can sometimes be treacherous. In what has to be regarded as the definitive clinical trial, Carpenter *et al.* (2005) examined the effect of glycine and cycloserine on negative symptoms. In this study 171 schizophrenic patients with persistent negative symptoms were treated with one of the two drugs or placebo for 16 weeks under double blind conditions. All three groups showed slight improvement over the course of the trial, but there was no evidence of significant superiority for either drug over placebo.

Is there evidence of functional glutamate deficiency in the schizophrenic brain?

Paralleling the dopamine hypothesis, there has been some investigation of glutamate levels in the cerebrospinal fluid (CSF) of schizophrenic patients, and in schizophrenic post-mortem brain. However, most investigation has focused on post-synaptic glutamate receptors. These latter studies have only been carried out in post-mortem brain; as yet there are no suitable radioligands available for studies in life.

An early study (Kim *et al.*, 1980) found that CSF levels of glutamate were reduced by almost 50 per cent compared to controls in a sample of 20 schizophrenic patients. However, this finding was not subsequently replicated (Korpi *et al.*, 1987; Gattaz *et al.*, 1985; Perry, 1982). A small number of studies also failed to find to find reductions in the level of glutamate in schizophrenic post-mortem brain (Perry, 1982; Toru *et al.*, 1992; Kutay

Table 6.2 Studies of NMDA receptor numbers in post-mortem schizophrenic brain

Study	Sample	Assay	Prefrontal cortex	Temporal cortex	Hippocampus	Striatum
Kornhuber et al. (1989)	6–13 patients 3–12 controls	[3H]MK-801	Normal	Normal	Normal	Increased
Kerwin et al. (1990)	7 patients 8 controls	[3H]glutamate	—	—	Normal	—
Weissman et al. (1991)	44 patients 11 controls	[3H]TCP	Normal	Normal	—	Normal
Simpson et al. (1992)	13 patients 14 controls	[3H]TCP	?Increased	—	—	—
Toru et al. (1992)	14 patients 10 controls	[3H]MK-801	Normal	Increased	—	Normal
Ishimaru et al. (1994)	13 patients 10 controls	[3H]glycine	Normal	Normal	—	—
Ulas and Cotman (1993)	4 patients 12 controls	[3H] glutamate	—	—	Normal	—
Akbarian et al. (1996)	15 patients 15 controls	mRNA	Normal	Normal	—	—
Humphries et al. (1996)	12 patients 7 controls	mRNA	—	Normal	—	—
Noga et al. (1997)	6 patients 8 controls	[3H]MK-801	—	—	—	Normal
Aparicio-Legarza et al. (1998)	8–13 patients 5–12 controls	[3H] 689,560	—	—	—	?Increased
Sokolov (1998)	21 patients 9 controls	mRNA	Decreased	—	—	—
Gao et al. (2000)	12–18 patients 13–19 controls	mRNA	—	—	Normal	—
Dracheva et al. (2001)	26 patients 13 controls	mRNA	Increased	—	—	—
Mueller et al. (2004)	15 patients 15 controls	mRNA	Increased	Normal	—	—

Note: ?increased means significant differences were found in some but not all the subregions of the area in question.

et al., 1989). Recently, though, Tsai *et al.* (1995) examined glutamate levels in eight regions of post-mortem brain in 12 patients meeting DSM-III-R criteria for schizophrenia and 11 normal controls. They found significant reductions in the prefrontal cortex and hippocampus, but not in the para-hippocampal gyrus, putamen, cingulate cortex, amygdala, parietal cortex or cerebellum.

Glutamate receptors fall into two main classes, ionotropic or ion-gated, of which there are three kinds, and the slower-acting metabotropic receptors, of which there are at least eight types. Studies of NMDA receptor numbers in schizophrenia, the most frequently examined type, are summarised in Table 6.2. The results are inconsistent, but taken together there is no clear support for changes in any of the main regions studied; while one or two studies have found decreases, others have found increases and in the majority there was no change. The findings for the smaller numbers of studies of the two other main kinds of ionotropic glutamate receptors, kianate and AMPA (alpha-amino-3-hydroxy-5-methyl-isoxasole proprionic acid), are not shown, but the balance of positive and negative findings is no better. Only two studies have examined metabotropic glutamate receptors. Ohnuma *et al.* (1998, 2000) found increases in three areas of prefrontal cortex that did not reach signifi-cance, and no differences in the hippocampus. Richardson-Burns *et al.* (2000) failed to find significant differences between patients' and controls' receptor numbers in the thalamus.

Conclusion

The dopamine hypothesis defined an era of biological schizophrenia research. Unfortunately, even though the circumstantial evidence on which it was based has never been overturned, the search for proof in the form of dopamine D2 receptor supersensitivity in drug-naive patients came back empty handed. The theory can still cling on to tenability in the (replicated) finding of increased amphetamine-stimulated dopamine release. As a last resort, it could be argued that the basal ganglia are the wrong place to look for a dopamine receptor excess in schizophrenia, and that the limbic and cortical sites of dopamine innervation are more likely sites of dysfunction. But the mere handful of studies that have been carried out is a telling comment on the lack of enthusiasm for these possibilities.

If the dopamine hypothesis is not able to outlive its obituarists, the glu-tamate hypothesis looks distinctly weak and sickly as a successor. Here, the evidence on which the theory rests turns out to be not nearly as strong or as convergent as its advocates have claimed. The mental changes produced by glutamate antagonists do not provide as good a model of schizophrenia as amphetamine psychosis. Drugs with glutamate agonist properties have never been found to have any therapeutic effect on positive symptoms and it is now clear that they have no effect on negative symptoms either. Confusion reigns in the post-mortem studies of glutamate receptors, but the most frequent finding is of no abnormality. Such findings are not a solid foundation on which to base a neurochemical theory of schizophrenia.

Somewhat lost in the trials and tribulations of the dopamine hypothesis and the rampant theorising that has been the trademark of the glutamate hypothesis – which has invoked other transmitters (including dopamine), structural brain abnormality, cognitive impairment and neurodevelopmental factors – is a point which was originally so obvious that it hardly seemed worth stating. This is that, if schizophrenia has a biological basis, it is difficult to imagine many of its symptoms as being due to anything else beside a neurochemical disturbance. There is just no other way of accounting for symptoms that come and go, respond to drugs, and whose closest counterparts outside schizophrenia are the effects of drugs. If and when this neurochemical disorder is uncovered, it may not prove to be located primarily in dopamine systems, but it might be surprising if the dopamine hypothesis turns out to be completely wrong.

7 The neurodevelopmental theory of schizophrenia

From time to time schizophrenia research has witnessed movements that have risen from humble experimental origins to become a dominant force, not only giving rise to a great deal of investigation, but also reorienting thinking about the nature of the disorder. Some such movements have faded away and later it is difficult to reconstruct what it was that made them so influential. But sometimes they have gone on to become a permanent fixture, a set of incontrovertible findings that any theory has to reckon with. The most recent example of this phenomenon has been the extraordinary rise of the neuro-developmental hypothesis.

At its simplest, the neurodevelopmental hypothesis states that the origins of schizophrenia go back to early childhood, birth or even before. Put like this, it is not a particularly novel or original idea. The season of birth effect, discussed below, and the idea that schizophrenia often develops in individuals who have always shown schizoid or schizotypal traits, described in more detail in Chapter 16, both imply a causative role for factors operating at the time of birth or at any rate a considerable period of time before overt symptoms appear. What makes the neurodevelopmental hypothesis more interesting and powerful is that it also claims that the process which ultimately gives rise to schizophrenia is not necessarily completely silent in the intervening period, and that there are more subtle manifestations before then. Beyond this, accounts vary: some versions of the theory propose that there is a life-long fixed, static brain lesion that remains quiescent until it interacts with normal brain maturational processes around the time of puberty, whereas others envisage some more intrinsically developmental process, akin to developmental disorders like autism, but with a more complex trajectory. But the common feature is always that some individuals are destined to become schizophrenic from an early age.

The neurodevelopmental hypothesis is simple but has had a complicated evolution, from neuropathological findings such as lack of gliosis, through a proposed classification of current schizophrenia into familial and sporadic forms, to an almost unbelievable amount of current speculation about central nervous system (CNS) embryology, brain development during childhood, and the possible interactions of neurotransmitters like dopamine (and glutamate) with such processes. Weaving in and out of the story, leading the debate, and generally seeming to drive the experimental investigation – if not always in the direction advocates of the theory have wished – has been the question of an increased rate of obstetric complications in schizophrenia.

The antecedents of the neurodevelopmental hypothesis

The factors that seem to have played a role in the historical development of the neurodevelopmental hypothesis are many and various. They can be traced back to an argument by Rosanoff (1914) and Southard (1915) that the neuropathological abnormalities claimed at the time to have been found in schizophrenia were 'early hypoplasias' rather than being atrophic changes. Much the same idea cropped up again later in modern post-mortem studies as the well-replicated finding of absence of gliosis, as well as the claims of disarray and maldistribution of neurons that have not stood the test of time (see Chapter 5).

Another factor that is often cited is the venerable tradition of the season of birth effect in schizophrenia. The observation that more than expected schizophrenic patients appeared to have been born in the winter months was first made by Tramer in 1929. Since then this finding has been confirmed, repudiated, considered to be established, and dismissed as an artefact, but overall has maintained its profile in schizophrenia research and continues to be mentioned in virtually all textbooks and many review articles. Bradbury and Miller (1985) reviewed the evidence and found that around 12 of 37 studies carried out in the northern hemisphere could be considered to have avoided major methodological shortcomings. Nine of these reported a seasonality effect, which was restricted predominantly or exclusively to the winter months. The effect was small, of the order of a 5–15 per cent excess, and in some of the studies it spilled over into spring and even early summer. In the southern hemisphere, where the seasons are reversed, the balance of evidence was less favourable: only two of six studies found any effect (both reporting excesses in the winter months), and neither of these were methodologically sound. Despite this, Bradbury and Miller concluded that the season of birth effect could be regarded as genuine.

According to Lewis and Murray (Murray *et al.*, 1988; Lewis, 1989), two of the architects of the neurodevelopmental hypothesis, other factors included the observation that the long-term sequelae of brain injury in animals were not only less severe when the injury was sustained in early life, but could lie dormant for a long time. Goldman and Galkin (1978) gave this finding added value when they found that monkeys who were given prefrontal lesions at or before birth could show few obvious behavioural changes until as late as sexual maturity. Weinberger (1987), the other main architect of the neurodevelopmental hypothesis, added a clinical dimension to such findings. He pointed out that brain injury could produce different clinical symptoms at different periods of the sufferer's life. For instance, hypoxic brain damage sustained at birth may cause cerebral palsy. By 4 years of age athetosis could become a symptom, and later still epilepsy might be a consequence. Sometimes the presence or absence of psychiatric features also appeared to be determined more by the patient's age than by the nature of the underlying pathology. He gave the example of Huntington's disease, where behavioural changes are said to be rare when the onset is in childhood, but are common in adult onset forms of the disorder.

The finding that had the most immediate implications for the neurodevepmental hypothesis, however, was the recognition that lateral ventricular enlargement in schizophrenia was present at the onset of illness and did not appear to progress. This led Murray *et al.* (1985) to make a bold proposal. Their starting point was the inability of simple genetic models of schizophrenia to account for the inheritance of schizophrenia, one interpretation of which could be that there is aetiological heteregeneity in the disorder. Next, they noted the occurrence of schizophrenia-like states in association with certain forms of organic brain disease (see Chapter 14); such patients were often found to lack a family history of schizophrenia. Were such cases infrequent, or were they the tip of an iceberg of a form of schizophrenia caused by a type of brain damage that was usually too subtle to be detectable by standard techniques? They also noted in passing that a popular explanation of the season of birth effect invoked neonatal viral infections, and that some work had linked birth complications to schizophrenia, both of which could lead to perinatal brain damage. On these grounds they therefore suggested that it might be useful to divide schizophrenia into familial and sporadic forms; the former being a genetically determined type of the disorder and the latter being an environmental 'phenocopy' caused by trauma to the brain, the sequelae of which were known to include lateral ventricular enlargement. These two aetiological factors could operate separately, but the distinction could also be conceptualised as a continuum of genetic and environmental causation and still be valid.

Ingenious as it was, Murray *et al.*'s hypothesis was not destined to survive for very long. Owen *et al.* (1989) compared lateral ventricular size in 23 patients meeting RDC criteria for schizophrenia who had a history of major mental illness in a first-degree relative and an age- and sex-matched sample of 23 similar patients with no family history of major mental illness. No significant difference was found.

Obstetric complications

Rosanoff was, according to Lewis and Murray, the author who first singled out birth trauma as the prime suspect for the kind of brain damage that later caused schizophrenia. After arguing that the post-mortem abnormalities found in the schizophrenic brain represented early hypoplasias rather than an atrophic process, as described above, he and his co-workers (Rosanoff *et al.*, 1934) went on to carry out a detailed analysis of 142 twins who were either concordant or discordant for schizophrenia. Their conclusion was that, in a large proportion of cases, schizophrenia was the result of birth trauma in interaction with genetic factors.

A study comparing the rates of obstetric complications in groups of schizophrenic patients and controls was then carried out by Katz in an unpublished PhD thesis in 1939 (not altogther surprisingly, Rosanoff was his supervisor). This was said to have had findings generally in line with the hypothesis and was followed by a trickle of further studies comparing rates of obstetric complications in schizophrenic patients and control groups consisting variably of siblings, other psychiatric patient groups and normal subjects. These studies were independently reviewed by Lewis (1989) and Done *et al.* (1991), who both agreed that they faced serious methodological problems. Johnstone (1994) pithily summed these problems up:

> Examining this relationship in established schizophrenics involves the scrutiny of past obstetric records which may be of very variable quality if they are available at all or else reliance upon the report of the mother who will, of course, not be blind to the fact that her child has developed schizophrenia.

This was the only thing that Lewis and Done *et al.* agreed on, however, and they came to diametrically opposed conclusions about the findings of the studies. Lewis (1989) considered that, despite wide methodological variations, 7 out of 8 studies found a significant excess of obstetric complications in the schizophrenic group. Done *et al.* (1991), in contrast, found felt that only 3 of 11 studies showed clearly significant increases.

Some more recent studies of obstetric complications have attempted to strengthen their methodology by using large samples of prospectively gathered data from registers of obstetric records (Kendell *et al.*, 1996, 2000; Hultman *et al.*, 1999; Dalman *et al.*, 1999, 2001; Byrne *et al.*, 2000). However, these same studies all then weakened it again by failing to use diagnostic criteria for schizophrenia. These large-scale studies are summarised in Table 7.1. Diagnostic impropriety aside, their findings are at most modest, and they are wide open to the criticism that they would not survive correction for multiple comparisons.

The nadir of this line of investigation was reached in a study by Kendell *et al.* (1996). They identified 115 patients with a clinical diagnosis of schizophrenia born in Scotland between 1971 and 1974, and assessed their pregnancy and birth complications by means of information recorded in a standardised way at the time of birth and held on a national database. The patients were each individually matched with a control subject born within two months. It was found that the schizophrenic patients had had significantly increased rates of complications of pregnancy (34 vs 8) and delivery (18 vs 1), but not of pre-existing maternal illness (5 vs 2) or complications in the early neonatal period (7 vs 3). This finding then had to be retracted when

Table 7.1 Large-scale studies of obstetric complications in schizophrenia

Study	Sample size	Diagnostic criteria	Obstetric database	No. of variables showing significant association with schizophrenia	Type of variables showing significant association with schizophrenia
Hultman *et al.* (1999)	167 patients 835 controls	None	Standardised birth records	3/23	Multiparity Bleeding during pregnancy Late winter birth
Dalman *et al.* (1999)	238 patients 507,278 controls	None	National birth register	7/31	Pre-eclampsia Prematurity Uterine inertia Vacuum extraction Low ponderal index Respiratory illness Malformations
Kendell *et al.* (2000)[1]	296 patients 296 controls	None	Standardised birth records	0/23	—
Kendell *et al.* (2000)	156 patients 156 controls	None	Standardised birth records	2/23	Emergency caesarian section Prolonged labour
Byrne *et al.* (2000)	431 patients 431 controls	None	Maternity hospital records	1/21[2] 1/21	Caesarian section Narrow pelvis
Dalman *et al.* (2001)	524 patients 1043 controls	None	Maternity hospital records	1/14	Birth asphyxia in males (Also marginal increase for indices of foetal growth impairment)

[1] Re-analysed data on enlarged sample of Kendell *et al.* (1996).
[2] Obstetric complications were rated using two different scales covering a slightly different set of items.

Kendell *et al.* (2000) discovered that instead of having being matched with the next baby born, the index babies had inadvertently been matched with the next-born baby who had been entered in the database, and this naturally tended to favour babies whose deliveries had been less subject to complications and discharged earlier. When this mistake was corrected, all the differences between the two groups disappeared.

Birth cohort studies

While one solution to the problems facing studies of obstetric complications in schizophrenia was simply to increase the sample size, another far more elegant one presented itself to Done and his co-workers (apparently by chance, when he attended a lecture). The result was a paper in 1991 that launched an era of rapid expansion in the neurodevelopmental hypothesis and caused it to flourish in all sorts of ways that could not originally have been envisaged.

Done *et al.* (1991) took advantage of the fact that approximately 30 years previously a large-scale systematic survey of birth complications, the British Perinatal Mortality Survey, had been carried out in the UK. This sampled 98 per cent of all the children born in England, Scotland and Wales in a single week in 1958 – nearly 17,000 individuals. The main purpose of the survey was to examine social and obstetric factors associated with stillbirth and neonatal mortality, and information on a wide range of maternal and obstetric variables was recorded in a detailed and standardised way. Thirty years later the individuals in this birth cohort were adults and had passed through most of the age of risk for schizophrenia. By a stroke of luck, another national database (the Mental Health Enquiry) had also been set up, which recorded data on all psychiatric admissions in the UK between 1974 and 1986 (when the project was cancelled). This made it relatively easy to identify all members of the cohort who had had a psychiatric admission between 1974 and 1986, in other words between the ages of 16 and 28.

Out of the 252 members of the cohort who had had a psychiatric admission, the case-notes could be obtained for 235. The information contained in these was used to make a diagnosis, both clinically and using the Syndrome Check List of the Present State Examination, which is designed to be applied to case-note material. A clinical diagnosis of schizophrenia was made in 79 cases, of whom 57 met 'broad' criteria and 37 'narrow' criteria for the disorder. The number of risk factors for perinatal mortality was calculated for the future schizophrenic patients and for 12,946 of the remainder of the cohort who had not had any psychiatric admissions. This figure approximates closely to complications of pregnancy and delivery, but excludes variables that are of insignificant risk or whose contribution to risk has been covered by others already in the analysis. The variables included and excluded are shown in Table 7.2.

The odds ratio for perinatal mortality was found to range from 1.41 (0.66 to 3.02) for narrowly defined schizophrenia, to 1.50 (0.86 to 2.63) for

Table 7.2 Obstetric variables included and excluded in Done *et al.*'s (1991) study

Included	Excluded
Parity	Height of mother
All bleeding	Number of previous premature births
Birth weight	Haemoglobin concentration
Maternal weight	Duration of first stage of labour
Months of gestation	Maternal age
Toxaemia	Foetal distress (cord prolapse/
Duration of second stage of labour	meconium/foetal heart)
Duration membranes ruptured	Social and economic status
Labour induced (yes/no)	Fever/tonsillitis/laryngitis
Method of delivery (normal/complex)	Urinary tract infection
Inhalation anaesthesia	Type of resuscitation
Influenza during pregancy	Prescription of drugs to baby
Gastrointestinal disorders during	Lobelline
pregnancy	Streptomycin
Hydramnios	
Falls and accidents	
Prescription of drugs to baby	
Coramine	
Sedatives	
Antagonists	
Synkavit	
Penicillin	
Other	

Note: Variables were excluded because of covariance with other included variables.
Source: Done *et al.* (1991).

broadly defined schizophrenia, and to 1.77 (0.90 to 3.50) for schizophrenia as diagnosed clinically. As the confidence intervals indicate, none of these increases was statistically significant. When individual maternal and infant variables were compared, only two – low maternal weight and administration of non-routine drugs to the infant in the first week of life – were increased in the future schizophrenic patients, and then only at trend level.

The second birth cohort study, carried out by Buka *et al.* (1993), also failed to find any increase in birth complications in schizophrenia. They used subjects enrolled in the Providence, Rhode Island centre of a very large American birth cohort study, the National Collaborative Perinatal Project. Extensive obstetric data were collected, and the children were followed up to the age of 7 years. Using a different strategy to Done *et al.*, the authors identified those subjects who had experienced birth complications, including the rarer kinds of these such as eclampsia, placental problems and breech delivery, and also selected an approximately equal comparison group without any history of birth complications,. As many subjects as possible were traced at ages 18–27 years using a variety of methods, including searches of electoral rolls, motor vehicle registration lists, and contact with government agencies, as well as information recorded during the age 7 assessment. They were contacted and given a structured psychiatric interview, under blind conditions (85 per cent in person, 15 per cent by telephone). As a result, 1.1 per cent of 373 of those who had experienced one or more complications of pregnancy and delivery were given a DSM III diagnosis of schizophrenia or schizophreniform psychosis, compared to 1.2 per cent of the 320 who had not. None of three subcategories of obstetric complications (chronic foetal hypoxia, prematurity or other complications) significantly distinguished the future psychotic patients from those without psychiatric illness.

The third birth cohort study of schizophrenia was the first to broaden the investigation beyond obstetric complications. Jones *et al.* (1994a) used the Medical Research Council National Survey of Health and Development, which was carried out on a random sample of 5362 of the 13,687 births in England, Scotland and Wales in 3–9 March 1946 (all three British birth cohort surveys to date have utilised children born in this week). Individuals in this birth cohort were assessed 11 times between the age of 6 weeks and 16 years, and thereafter regularly (up to the age of 43 by the time of the Jones *et al.*, study). Cohort members with a potential diagnosis of schizophrenia in adult life were identified from three sources of information: the Mental Health Enquiry, as used by Done *et al.*; information from questionnaires and interviews the subjects in the cohort had completed, some of which enquired into general practice visits, hospital contacts, and subjective descriptions of illnesses; and finally a short form of the Present State Examination that all the cohort members had been administered at the age of 36. Based on information from these sources plus hospital case-notes, 30 members of the cohort (20 men and 10 women) were given a DSM-III-R diagnosis of schizophrenia.

The patients were compared to the remainder of the cohort on 54 variables assessed in the study, which the existing literature suggested might be relevant to schizophrenia. This revealed no evidence to suggest that those with lower social class or poorer home circumstances were at increased risk. There was no difference in birthweight between the two groups. There was no difference in age of acquisition of bowel and bladder control, but the future schizophrenics were generally slower, albeit mostly non-significantly so, to reach the developmental milestones of sitting, standing, walking and talking. Taken together, significantly more future schizophrenics than controls had failed to achieve all of the milestones of talking or sitting, standing and walking alone at 2 years (7.4 per cent vs 1.6 per cent). At age 6 speech problems were also significantly more common in the schizophrenic patients than in the controls (11.1 per cent vs 5.1 per cent).

The future schizophrenics also showed significant differences on a range of social and behavioural measures. This was evidenced by an increased preference for solitary play at ages 4 and 6, plus greater self-reported anxiety at age 13. At age 15 they were also rated as more anxious by teachers. At this age, twitches, grimaces and nail biting were also significantly more common.

The strongest finding to emerge from Jones *et al.*'s study concerned intellectual function. Scores on tests of verbal, non-verbal, mathematical, vocabulary and reading skills were significantly lower in the future schizophrenic patients than in the controls at ages 8 and 15, with similar, but non-significant or trend level findings at ages 11. Converted into IQ scores, the future schizophrenic patients showed a disadvantage of 3–9 points on the different tests, or approximately half a standard deviation. This effect appeared to become stronger with age, being non-significant at age 8, significant at age 11 and even more highly significant at age 15.

Done and co-workers (Done *et al.*, 1994; Done *et al.*, unpublished; Jones and Done, 1997) then completed the initial phase of birth cohort studies by returning to the British Perinatal Mortality Survey. This made four attempts to trace the members of the birth cohort in what became known as the National Child Development Study. Ratings of social adjustment were made at the ages of 7 and 11. Compared with a randomly selected 10 per cent subsample of 1385 controls without psychiatric illness, the 33 subjects who went on to develop narrowly defined schizophrenia showed significantly greater maladjustment at both ages. Boys tended to be more over-reactive, 'anxious for acceptance', hostile to other children and adults, and engaged in inconsequential behaviours. However, there was little evidence of social withdrawal. Girls, on the other hand, were not significantly over-reactive and were significantly more under-reactive at age 11, when they were rated particularly as withdrawn and 'unforthcoming'. The assessment at age 11 also included various psychometric tests, one of which was a general ability test, from which IQ scores can be derived. Similarly to Jones *et al.*, Done *et al.* found that the future schizophrenic patients were on average 10 IQ points below the normal controls on this test.

What then followed can only be described as a boom in birth cohort studies of schizophrenia. As their potential for the neurodevelopmental hypothesis was recognised, birth cohorts were unearthed all over the world and mined for data. The main findings of the studies to date are summarised in Table 7.3. It can be seen that IQ disadvantage is a well-replicated finding across the studies, with differences of approximately half a standard deviation, i.e. 7–8 IQ points, typically being reported. On the other hand, there is only limited support for an increased rate of obstetric complications. As described above, the studies of Done *et al.* (1991) and Buka *et al.* (1993) had completely negative findings. Two more studies had equivocal findings: out of numerous variables examined, Jones *et al.* (1998) found a significantly increased risk only for perinatal brain damage (operationally defined as one or more of neonatal convulsions, low Apgar score, birth asphyxia, intraventricular haemorrhage, admission to a neonatal unit, and neurological evidence of brain damage). Cannon *et al.* (2000) found a significant relationship with what they termed obstetric complications associated with hypoxia, but not for maternal illness during pregnancy or low birth weight. Only one study had unequivocally significant findings: Cannon *et al.* (2002) found an overall

Table 7.3 Summary of findings of birth cohort studies of schizophrenia

Birth cohort	Authors	Number with schizophrenia/total	Obstetric complications	Lower IQ	Delayed milestones	Behavioural abnormalities/social maladjustment	Other
BPMS/NCDS	Done et al. (1991; unpublished) Leask et al. (2002)	35/16,980	×	✓	—	✓	Meningitis and TB Neurological soft signs
NCPP (Providence)	Buka et al. (1993)	8/693	×	—	—	—	—
NSHD	Jones et al. (1994a)	30/5362	—	✓	✓	✓	Speech problems
North Finland	Jones et al. (1998) Murray et al. (2006)	76/11,017	? (see text)	—	✓	—	—
NCPP (Philadelphia)	Cannon et al. (2000) Bearden et al. (2000) Rosso et al. (2000)	72/9236	? (1 of 3 classes only)	✓	—	✓	Speech problems
Dunedin	Cannon et al. (2002)	36*/1037	✓	✓	? (walking only)	? ('internalising' only)	Neurological signs Impaired motor skill Speech problems (receptive only)

* Diagnosis of schizophreniform psychosis rather than schizophrenia (see text on p. 176)
BPMS/NCDS – British Perinatal Mortality Survey/National Child Development Study
NCPP – National Collaborative Perinatal Project
NSHD – National Survey of Health and Development
Dunedin – Dunedin Multidisciplinary Health and Development Study.

increased risk of obstetric complications, as recorded in hospital records, in babies who later went on to develop schizophreniform disorder. The increased risk related to low apgar score, birth hypoxia and being small for gestational dates.

Two findings deserve special mention. Rosso *et al.* (2000) studied 9236 children of 6753 mothers from the Philadelphia centre of the National Collaborative Perinatal Project, which, as mentioned above, followed up the children for the first 7 years of life. In this study, motor disorders, taken from standardised neurological and psychological examinations at 8 months, 4 years and 7 years, were found to distinguish the 72 who were later given a DSM IV diagnosis of schizophrenia from 7941 who had never received psychiatric treatment as an adult and who did not have a sibling with schizophrenia. Differences were not apparent at 8 months, but at 4 and 7 years, unusual movements, consisting of tremors, tics, spasms, or athetoid movements of the head and neck, arms and shoulders, hands, legs and feet, or trunk, were significantly over-represented in the preschizophrenics. Motor coordination (eg finger–nose test, rapid alternation, rapid finger movement, buttoning, writing, etc.) was also significantly poorer on the single occasion it was measured at age 7. The findings are shown in Figure 7.1.

Poulton *et al.* (2000) took advantage of psychiatric data collected in childhood as part of a New Zealand birth cohort, the Dunedin Multidisciplinary Health and Development study (Silva and Stanton, 1996). This longitudinally examined the health, development and behaviour of 1037 children born in the 12 months between 1972 and 1973. The cohort was assessed every 2 to 3

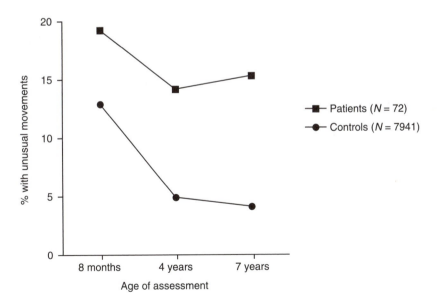

Figure 7.1 Unusual movements in children who developed or did not develop schizophrenia in adult life (from Rosso *et al.*, 2000).

years up to the age of 21, and then again at the age of 26. Uniquely, 789 of the cohort were given a structured psychiatric interview at age 11. Although none of the children had a psychotic diagnosis at this time, 116 (14.7 per cent) responded in the affirmative to one or more of the five questions in the schizophrenia section of the interview. The questions, and some of the examples of the children's responses, taken from notes the child psychiatrist took at the time, are shown in Box 7.1.

A further psychiatric interview, using the adult version of the same structured interview, was carried out as part of the assessment of the cohort at age 26. At this time 25 of the 761 subjects (3.3 per cent) who had also been interviewed at age 11 were given a DSM IV diagnosis of schizophreniform psychosis. This rate was surprisingly high, but corresponded closely to that found in a large American population survey (Kessler *et al.*, 1994). The children who had reported psychotic symptoms at age 11 were significantly over-represented among the adult psychotic patients: 12/107 (11.2 per cent) vs 13/654 (2.0 per cent). Put another way, 42 per cent of those with schizophreniform psychosis at age 26 had reported one or more psychotic symptoms at age 11. Age-11 psychotic symptoms did not predict mania or depression at age 26.

Box 7.1 The five schizophrenia questions children in the Dunedin Birth Cohort were asked age 11, and examples of positive responses (unpublished data from Poulton et al., 2000, with thanks to Ritchie Poulton)

Questions

Some people believe in mind reading or being psychic. Have other people ever read your mind?

Have you ever had messages sent just to you through television or radio?

Have you ever thought that people are following you or spying on you?

Have you heard voices other people can't hear?

Has something ever gotten inside your body or has your body changed in some strange way?

Responses

'Voices call his name when alone'

'Sees things sometimes, looks back and isn't there'

'Teacher knew what he was going to say'

'Knows numbers at bingo'

'Hears buzzing'

'A long time ago, another kid knew what he was thinking'

'Thinks can see people not really there, frequently. Occasionally mistaken identity'

'Occasionally sees things – illusions'

'Friend says same things'

'Sees figures in the sky'

'Friends whisper they may bash her up'

'Knows what friends are thinking'

Beyond birth cohort studies

Use of high-quality prospective data of the kind available in birth cohort studies has paid dividends in confirming – and sometimes also refuting – the importance of developmental factors in the aetiology of schizophrenia. Such studies are, however, always going to be limited by the relatively general nature of their data, which will never have been collected with future schizophrenia in mind. But birth cohort studies have not by any means exhausted the ingenuity of neurodevelopmentally oriented schizophrenia researchers. The same approach can be applied to other datasets, which, while not population based, may be informative for specific questions. What follows is a selection of some of the more interesting findings from a number of studies that have extended the concept of the birth cohort study while remaining true to its ethos.

Childhood home movies

Walker and Lewine (1990) hit on the idea of using home movies, which American parents had been making of their children for decades, to examine the early childhood behaviour of individuals who later went on to develop schizophrenia. In an initial small-scale study they assembled the home movie material available on five children who met DSM-III-R criteria for schizophrenia in adult life. They were able to include footage covering periods from before the first 17 months of life up to at least 4 years of age, and made sure that one, two or three of the siblings were also shown. The movies were shown to six graduate students in psychology and six clinicians, who were informed that they would be viewing sibships in which only one child developed schizophrenia later in life and were asked to identify which one. The raters were able to do this more frequently than chance would predict in all cases, usually but not always significantly so. The factors that influenced the raters' judgements included lack of responsiveness, eye contact and positive affect, and presence of poor gross and fine motor coordination.

In a later study, Walker *et al.* (1994) compared childhood home movies of 30 patients with DSM-III-R schizophrenia, 28 of their siblings and 21 healthy subjects. This time motor abnormalities were assessed under blind conditions by two raters with expertise in motor development, who recorded all instances of observed motor abnormality and impaired motor skill. The children who later developed schizophrenia were found to show significantly more evidence of neuromotor abnormality than their unaffected siblings and the normal controls. The greatest differences concerned extraneous movements in one body part during effortful activity in another body part (e.g. movement of the contralateral arm during unimanual activity), postural abnormalities and choreoathetoid movements. Common postural abnormalities were prolonged fisting, hyperextension of the fingers, wrist hyperflexion, and pronation of the hand, often accompanied by unusual or asymmetric positioning of the arm (two examples are shown in Figure 7.2). Seven of the 30 preschizophrenic children, but only 1 of their 28 healthy siblings showed choreoathetoid movements. These were intermittent, typically occurring in situations where the child's fine or gross motor abilities were challenged (e.g. when presented with a novel or complex object, or during early attempts to stand without support or to walk). The differences were evident only in the period from birth to 2 years, and were mainly on the left. Differences in general quality of movement and motor skill were seen in the older children, but did not reach significance.

The Dutch hunger winter

Between October 1944 and May 1945 a Nazi blockade of western Holland led to widespread famine and the death of thousands from starvation. As well as being associated with marked increases in stillbirths, and perinatal and infant mortality, Stein *et al.* (1975) showed that the famine resulted in an increased frequency of spina bifida, hydrocephalus, and cerebral palsy. (This was one of the studies responsible for establishing the link between low folic acid intake and neural tube defects.) The effect only occurred in those exposed to famine during the first trimester of pregnancy.

Susser and co-workers (Susser and Lin, 1992; Susser *et al.*, 1996) wondered whether this grim natural experiment might also reveal a relationship between first-trimester malnutrition and later development of schizophrenia. Cases of schizophrenia were ascertained using a Dutch national psychiatric registry. Initial findings (Susser and Lin, 1992) suggested an increased risk of schizophrenia in women, but not men, who were exposed in the first trimester of pregnancy. There was no increase in risk for those exposed to famine in the second and third trimesters. A second study (Susser *et al.*, 1996) found a significant increase in both sexes for those exposed in the first trimester when the famine was at its height, but not in the months when it was less severe. The findings are shown in Figure 7.3. It should be noted that in both studies the diagnosis of schizophrenia was based only on hospital discharge diagnoses and there was no attempt to apply diagnostic criteria.

Congenital rubella

Brown *et al.* (2000) investigated whether schizophrenia in adult life could be added to the long list of sequelae of maternal rubella infection in pregnancy. They examined data from a cohort of 243 children with documented exposure to rubella in utero, established in 1964 after a major outbreak in New York. These children underwent psychiatric, intellectual, behavioural and psychosocial evaluations up to the ages of 21–23 years. Many of the members of the cohort had severe and multiple handicaps, often including mental handicap, blindness and deafness in the same individual, but 137 had an IQ over 70 and either no handicaps or only deafness. Of these subjects,

Figure 7.2 Abnormalities of hand posture in preschizophrenic children (from Walker, 1994, with thanks to Elaine Walker).

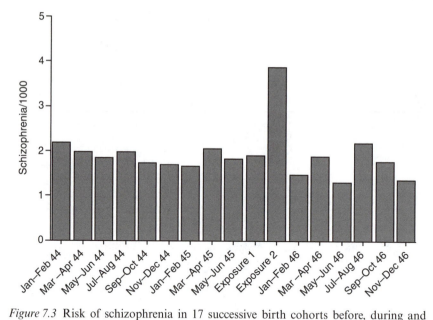

Figure 7.3 Risk of schizophrenia in 17 successive birth cohorts before, during and after the Dutch hunger winter (exposure 1 – conceived August 1–October 14 in the earlier stage of the famine; exposure 2 – conceived October 15– December 31 at height of the famine) (from Susser *et al.* (1996), Schizophrenia after prenatal famine. *Archives of General Psychiatry*, 53, 25–31. Copyright © American Medical Association).

70 were located in adult life and given a structured psychiatric interview. Eleven (15.7 per cent) were given a diagnosis of non-affective psychosis, on the basis of at least one psychotic symptom (delusions and/or hallucinations) for a minimum of six months without evidence of a major affective disorder. This was higher than the rate of 5/164 (3.0 per cent) in an age-matched subgroup of a longitudinal cohort of randomly selected children carried out in the Albany/Saratoga areas of New York State.

The subjects in this cohort also underwent IQ testing at ages 8 and 13. Brown *et al.* (2001) compared the IQ at both time points in eight who had a diagnosis of schizophrenia spectrum psychosis (3 with schizophrenia, 1 with schizoaffective disorder and 4 with psychotic disorder not otherwise specified), and 28 who were free of both schizophrenia spectrum disorders and major affective disorder. The results are shown in Table 7.4. The two groups were indistinguishable at age 8, but those who subsequently went on to develop psychosis showed a mean decline of 10.8 IQ points, compared to 2.7 IQ points in those who did not develop major psychiatric illness.

Table 7.4 IQ in childhood and adolescence in rubella-exposed individuals with and without psychosis in adult life

	N	Mean IQ (SD)	
		Age 8	Age 13
With schizophrenia spectrum psychosis	8	100.3 (19.2)	89.5 (14.8)
Without major mental illness	28	107.4 (13.6)	104.7 (15.2)

Source: Reprinted from Brown *et al.* (2001), Prenatal rubella, premorbid abnormalities, and adult schizophrenia. *Biological Psychiatry*, 49, 473–486. Copyright © 2001, with permission from the Society of Biological Psychiatry.

The Edinburgh high-risk study

One important strand in the history of the neurodevelopmental hypothesis has not so far been mentioned. This is the series of so-called high-risk studies that were begun in the 1960s and are now in their third or fourth decade of follow-up (Erlenmeyer-Kimling and Cornblatt, 1987; Arsanow, 1988; Cannon and Mednick, 1993; Mirsky *et al.*, 1995). These studies had the general design of following a sample of the children born to a schizophrenic parent from birth through to adult life. Although these studies identified emotional, cognitive and motor impairments in such children, they are generally considered not to have realised their potential. This is chiefly because of the small numbers of subjects that have gone on to develop schizophrenia. The long period of follow-up has also meant that the high rates of attrition have been a problem.

One study, however, has modified the high-risk design to provide a uniquely powerful means of investigating subjects in the months and years before they develop schizophrenia. In doing so, the approach has moved a long way from birth complications and early childhood development, but it fills an important gap left by birth cohort studies and in some ways can be regarded as the natural successor to them. This is the Edinburgh high-risk study of Johnstone and her co-workers.

Johnstone *et al.*'s strategy was to recruit a large sample of adolescents and young adults who were at high risk of developing schizophrenia by virtue of having at least two first- or second-degree relatives with the disorder (see Hodges *et al.*, 1999). This necessitated recruiting subjects from all over Scotland, in a process that involved reviewing more than 2500 sets of case-notes and making more than 500 home visits. In the first 5 years of the study it proved possible to recruit 162 high-risk subjects, aged 16–24. These were all considered to be well at the time of study entry. A control group of 33 young people with no known relatives with psychosis was also recruited. The two groups were well matched for age and sex, but were less well matched for education and socioeconomic status.

At initial evaluation the high-risk subjects and controls were rated on measures of childhood behaviour and assessed for schizotypy (see Chapter 16), and were examined for minor physical anomalies, neurological soft signs and dermatoglyphics. At baseline and every 18 months thereafter they were interviewed using the Present State Examination. They were also given a neuropsychological test battery and underwent MRI scanning at the same intervals. (A subset also underwent functional imaging, but these results have not been published as yet.)

At the end of the 10-year duration of the study, 20 of the high-risk subjects had developed schizophrenia (Johnstone *et al.*, 2005). Of the remainder, 67 had never experienced psychotic or possibly psychotic symptoms and 60 had shown partially held or definite but isolated and/or transient symptoms. None had developed non-schizophrenic psychotic illnesses. Johnstone *et al.* were now in a position to determine (a) which of a wide range of factors distinguished those at genetic risk of schizophrenia from the normal population before they became ill; and (b) which of these factors were predictive of actually going on to develop schizophrenia.

Minor physical anomalies and neurological signs

Compared to the normal controls, the high-risk subjects as a group showed significantly more evidence of hypertelorism (Boyes *et al.*, 2001) and significantly elevated rates of neurological soft signs (Lawrie *et al.*, 2001a), but no evidence of increased minor physical anomalies or dermatoglyphic abnormalities (Langsley *et al.*, 2004).

None of these variables, however, were found to distinguish the high-risk subjects who became ill from those who never showed psychotic symptoms. There were no differences for minor physical anomalies, dermatoglyphics and the measure of hypertelorism (Johnstone *et al.*, 2005). Scores on a scale for neurological soft signs were higher in those who became ill, but the difference was not significant (Johnstone *et al.*, 2005).

Behaviour in childhood

Information about the subjects' behaviour prior to age 13 and between the ages of 13 and 16 was obtained from their mothers. This was by means of a standardised questionnaire containing 120 items grouped into eight syndromes: social withdrawal, somatic complaints, anxiety/depression, social problems, thought problems, attention problems, delinquent behaviour, aggressive behaviour and other problems.

Overall scores on the checklist did not distinguish the high-risk subjects as a group from the controls prior to age 13, although the high-risk subjects' scores were numerically higher. Between the ages of 13 and 16, the high-risk subjects continued to have higher overall scores than the controls, but the difference was still not significant. By this time, though, there were significant differences on two of the individual subscales, delinquent behaviour and other problems (Miller *et al.*, 2002a).

In contrast, those high-risk subjects who became schizophrenic had a significantly higher overall score on the childhood behaviour checklist at ages 13–16 than those who never showed psychotic symptoms. The differences were accounted for by higher scores on anxiety/depression and attention problems (Johnstone *et al.*, 2005). The results for childhood behaviour prior to age 13 were not significant.

Schizotypy

On entry to the study all groups were administered two scales designed to rate features of schizotypal personality disorder, the Structured Interview for Schizotypy (SIS) (Kendler and Lister-Sharp, 1989) and the Rust Inventory of Schizotypal Cognitions (RISC). The SIS rates self-reported information on features such as childhood social isolation, ideas of reference, magical thinking and impulsivity, plus interviewer ratings covering, for example, rapport, attention-seeking, grooming and enjoyment of the interview. The RISC is a self-rated questionnaire covering ritualistic thinking, symptoms such as grandiose ideas and auditory hallucinations, and 'defence mechanisms' such as reactions to disturbing ideas. Most of the items in the two scales do not actually measure psychotic or near-psychotic thoughts and experiences (e.g. I never use a lucky charm; Sometimes I get a weird feeling I am not really here).

The high-risk group as a whole showed significantly higher scores than the controls on one of four subscales of the SIS generated by a factor analysis, social withdrawal, but not on the other three, psychotic symptoms, socioemotional dysfunction or odd behaviour (Miller *et al.*, 2002b). There was no significant difference between the high-risk subjects and the controls on the RISC (Miller *et al.*, 2002c).

The findings with respect to schizotypy in those high-risk subjects who progressed to schizophrenia, however, were the strongest in the entire study. The subjects who became schizophrenic had significantly higher total SIS scores compared to those who never showed symptoms; the greatest difference was on the social withdrawal factor of the SIS, and next largest difference was on odd behaviour. Similarly, those who became ill had significantly higher scores on the RISC.

Isolated psychotic symptoms

As mentioned, 60 of the 127 high-risk subjects who did not develop schizophrenia were rated as showing one or more psychotic or possibly psychotic symptoms at some point, many more than the 10 per cent who would be predicted to develop schizophrenia on the basis of their genetic risk (Johnstone *et al.*, 2000, 2005). Four of 26 control subjects also showed psychotic symptoms, mainly isolated hallucinations but occasionally an isolated delusion. These symptoms were rated irrespective of whether the individual belonged to a subcultural group where such experiences could be regarded as acceptable, which was the case in two of the high-risk patients and two of the controls.

At baseline 11 of the 20 who became ill described some psychotic or possibly psychotic symptoms, and 9 did not. This proportion is obviously closely similar to that for the high-risk subjects as a whole.

Neuropsychology

At baseline, the high-risk subjects performed significantly more poorly than the controls on all of a range of tests covering IQ, executive function and memory (Byrne *et al.*, 2003). The differences in IQ were of the order of half a standard deviation (Johnstone *et al.*, 2005). The differences in neuropsychological test scores were of a similar magnitude.

There was no difference in IQ at baseline in the subjects who went on to develop schizophrenia and those who did not. Nor were there any differences on three tests of executive function. Those who became ill, however, performed significantly more poorly than those who did not on one of three memory tests.

Brain structure

Three high-risk subjects were excluded from the analysis because they were found to have incidental structural lesions (arrested hydrocephalus, massive cavum septum pellucidum, and a temporal lobe cyst). The mean brain volumes in the remainder of the high-risk subjects and the controls were closely similar (Lawrie *et al.*, 2001b). There was also no significant difference in lateral ventricular volume in the two groups, although here it was noteworthy that the high-risk subjects had numerically larger ventricular volumes, which were intermediate between the normal controls and a group of age-matched schizophrenic patients. The high-risk subjects and the controls did, however, differ in one region: they showed bilaterally significantly smaller volumes of the amygdalo-hippocampal complex than the normal controls. They also showed smaller thalamic volumes, although here the differences were only significant on the left.

None of these measures were found to differ between the high-risk patients who became schizophrenic and those who remained well (Johnstone *et al.*, 2005).

As to what, if anything, changes in high-risk subjects in the months or years before they become schizophrenic, this remains unknown at the present time. Johnstone *et al.* (2002) have reported that high-risk subjects who underwent an increase in psychotic symptoms after 2 years (including, but not limited to, 10 who had developed schizophrenia at this time) showed evidence of decline in IQ. There was also a decline in memory performance, but this did not reach significance. Lawrie *et al.* (2002) found that 19 high-risk subjects with psychotic symptoms at the time of the second assessment underwent a decrease in temporal lobe volume bilaterally between the first and second assessment, which was markedly greater than that seen in the controls (2.4 per cent vs 0.4 per cent). However, this analysis excluded the seven subjects who had developed schizophrenia by this stage of the study.

Conclusion

The evidence reviewed in this chapter, especially the rich seam opened up by birth cohort studies, leaves one of the two main tenets of neurodevelopmental hypothesis in no doubt. Signs of pathology can be demonstrated in schizophrenic patients long before they develop overt signs of illness. Certainly, these signs are subtle – Poulton *et al.* (2000) commented that the effect sizes of the childhood risk factors identified generally show odds ratios of about 2, which translates into positive predictive values of between 3–5 per cent – but this is what the theory always predicted.

Along the way, however, the other main tenet of the theory, that a brain injury of some kind takes place at around the time of birth, has not fared quite so well. One of the ironies of the neurodevelopmental hypothesis is that it survives and flourishes despite the claim that inspired it in the first place not standing the test of time. No large-scale study of obstetric complications in schizophrenia has produced any evidence that they are over-represented which could withstand the mildest statistical query. Birth cohort studies – which were intended to decide this question once and for all – have had completely negative findings in three out of six cases. Even when the findings were positive they were less than compelling: Jones *et al.* (1998) found an association only with perinatal brain damage; Cannon *et al.* (2000) only with hypoxic complications; and Cannon *et al.* (2002) based their results solely on the information available in hospital obstetric records.

One of what will doubtless be many important findings to emerge from the Edinburgh high-risk study is that, while most of the risk factors or trait markers identified by previous studies distinguish high-risk individuals from the rest of the population, none of them seem to distinguish high-risk subjects who become ill from those who do not. One interpretation of this finding is that what earlier studies picked up was simply the manifestations of carrying an increased genetic burden for schizophrenia, but not the early manifestations of the disorder itself. The one exception is schizotypy, a finding that was not identified particularly clearly in earlier studies.

Still undelivered is the final verdict on a finding that more than anything else was the catalyst for the neurodevelopmental hypothesis – lateral ventricular enlargement. The Edinburgh high-risk study seems to be telling us on the one hand that this is not definitely present in individuals who are at increased genetic risk for schizophrenia, and on the other that those who progress to schizophrenia do not have larger lateral ventricles at initial evaluation than those who do not. These findings appear to constrain lateral ventricular enlargement to a slowly evolving role in the months and years before the onset of illness. The Edinburgh high-risk study has the potential to establish whether or not this is the case, but for the time being the answer remains unknown, or at any rate unpublished.

8 The psychology and neuropsychology of schizophrenia

Whatever causes schizophrenia, it is evident that the pathological process is played out mainly in the domains of higher mental function. As a result there has been a steady stream of attempts to identify a core psychological disturbance or group of disturbances in the disorder. These have ranged far and wide across the different subspecialties of experimental psychology, but overall the application of two broad strategies can be discerned. These might be referred to as, on the one hand, the search for the abnormalities that underlie the presenting clinical picture of schizophrenia, and, on the other, the abnormalities that merely lie behind it.

The psychological abnormalities underlying schizophrenia are those that have the power to account for the occurrence of one or more classes of symptom. The approaches here derive almost exclusively from cognitive psychology and they are typically hypothesis-driven: they proceed from prestated theoretical positions to testing in specially devised experimental procedures which, it is hoped, will reveal convincing differences between groups of patients and controls. Sometimes the theories have been ingenious and powerful. Unfortunately, at least as often they have been vague, abstruse, and have borne little obvious relationship to the phenomena they have sought to explain. Experimentally too, cognitive approaches have generally left a lot to be desired, especially when it comes to demonstrating that the cognitive abnormality found is actually related to the symptom or symptoms it purports to explain.

The abnormalities lying behind the clinical picture of schizophrenia are simply those that are revealed when schizophrenic patients are administered standard psychological tests. Given the nature of standard psychological tests, the approach tends to be neuropsychological in orientation, screening schizophrenic patients for impairment on measures of intelligence, perception, language, memory, attention and so on. Theory is not entirely ignored in the neuropsychological approach, however, for example when the rise of the concept of frontal lobe dysfunction in schizophrenia led to particularly close scrutiny of executive function. The difficulty here is that it has been found that patients with schizophrenia as a group perform more poorly than normal individuals on cognitive tasks, a problem that is particularly marked in chronic patients, who can be relied on to show impairment on virtually any test they are given. In these circumstances it becomes difficult to be certain what, if anything, is specifically abnormal in schizophrenia rather than just forming part of the general pattern of poor performance.

Psychological theories of schizophrenia and particular schizophrenic symptoms abound, and there is if anything an embarrassment of findings of impaired performance on one or another psychological test. In order to review this large and sprawling area of research, a fairly ruthless approach needs to be taken. As a first step, discussion is restricted to studies that are concerned with cognitive function; the assumption is made that work on conditioning, arousal and the like are too far removed from the clinical picture to be able to shed much light on it. In addition, given the credibility problems that have dogged both the cognitive psychological and neuro-psychological approaches to schizophrenia, any findings that emerge are required to pass a 'stringency' test to make sure they are as real and robust as they claim to be.

The cognitive psychology of schizophrenia

Traditionally, the hypothesis-driven experimental psychological approach has regarded its province as the florid, positive symptoms of schizophrenia; explanations of negative symptoms, if attempted at all, are usually tacked on as an afterthought. Both general and specific attacks have been mounted, the former attempting to bring many or all positive symptoms under the umbrella of a single psychological dysfunction, and the latter being directed to one class of symptom such as delusions, hallucinations or formal thought disorder.

Whether general or specific, psychological theories of schizophrenia, like any theories, are only as good as the experimental support they receive. It is at this point that difficulties often arise. The evidence produced for a particular theory invariably consists of a demonstration that schizophrenic patients show impaired performance on what is typically a specially devised test of the psychological function in question. However, since schizophrenic patients are liable to perform poorly on any test, it becomes easy to obtain spurious support for the theory. In order to minimise the influence of this confounding factor, the stringency test that will be adopted is that any alleged abnormal psychological finding should be demonstrable in acute patients, in whom the general tendency to poor performance can reasonably be expected to be less of a problem than in chronic patients. Additionally, for theories of particular symptoms, the abnormality ought to be present in those who show the symptom in question and not in those who do not.

General approaches

There has only ever been one general psychological theory of schizophrenia, or at any rate only one that has generated a significant body of experimental investigation. This is the hypothesis that many of the symptoms of the disorder are the manifestation of a defect in selective attention. Although this theory is over 40 years old, and no fresh studies have been carried out for quite some time, it still has its advocates (e.g. Neale and Oltmanns, 1980; Spring *et al.*, 1991), and it continues to make a cameo appearance in some contemporary integrative accounts (e.g. Gray *et al.*, 1991; Andreasen, 1999).

The background to the selective attention account of schizophrenic symptoms was a surge of interest in the various aspects of normal attention that took place in the 1950s. Broadbent (1958) argued that a crucial aspect of the attentional process was the filtering of sensory information: out of the huge amount of perceptual information that continually impinges on the senses only a tiny amount normally enters conscious awareness at any given moment. Much of the rest of this information, however, is potentially accessible: if desired it is easy to make oneself aware of the watch on one's wrist, the hum of one's computer, noise in the next room, and so on. It follows that there must exist one or more filtering mechanisms that continuously choose a small selection of stimuli for entry into conscious awareness, based either on their novelty or on their significance to the individual at that particular time. Broadbent and others were soon able to adduce evidence that selective attentional processes of the hypothesised type did operate in normal individuals, although the exact details by which the filtering was achieved became the subject of a debate which, in the way of experimental psychology, is still unresolved.

The possible relevance of selective attention to psychiatric disorders was not lost on psychologists. Although the defective filtering approach to schizophrenia had many of the characteristics of an *en masse* movement, the contributions of McGhie and his co-workers (McGhie and Chapman, 1961; McGhie, 1969) stood out. In the course of eliciting retrospective accounts of the onset of their symptoms from young schizophrenic patients, these authors were struck by the descriptions they gave of subjective alterations in the quality of their conscious experience. The changes they described included increased alertness, heightening of perception, exaggerated awareness of the environment, and the capturing of attention by irrelevant stimuli. In some patients, thoughts would sometimes seem to trigger a whole cascade of associations. In others, everyday actions could no longer be carried out automatically, but had to be thought through consciously, step by step.

It was, however, Frith (1979), who parlayed defective selective attention into a fully fledged theory capable of explaining many of the florid symptoms of schizophrenia. The first step in his argument was to specify the location of the breakdown in filtering at the level between conscious and preconscious information processing. Consciousness is where the highest level of cognitive operations take place in full subjective awareness. Such processes are characterised by a severely limited capacity and the tasks undertaken are novel, complex and strategic, and can by and large only be dealt with one at a time.

Preconsciousness, in contrast, deals with the much larger number of cognitive operations that are carried on at any given moment outside awareness, 'without thinking'. Preconscious processes may be highly sophisticated, perhaps nearly as sophisticated as conscious ones, but they are automatic and many operations are routinely performed at the same time. The tasks undertaken are those that are more or less routine, and in which strategic decisions are not required most of the time – examples would include driving, copy-typing and sight-reading music.

Frith argued that if the filter that determines which items of information in preconsciousness should enter consciousness were to break down, then the individual would continually receive an overload of sensory information that was already highly analysed. Accordingly, he would become aware of different potential interpretations of experience. At the same time he would be likely to start experiencing difficulties in selecting and carrying through the right course of action in response to these interpretations. This could give rise to schizophrenic symptoms in the following way.

Delusions

In the normal course of events most of the environmental information available to consciousness fails to reach it; it is irrelevant to any decisions that may need to be made and is not noticed. But if a breakdown in filtering were to cause such inconsequential items of information to be passed up into conscious awareness, because the arrival of such information normally signals that it is important and needs to be acted on, it could acquire a spurious connotation of significance. The seed of an entire class of delusions – referential delusions – could thus be planted. Elaboration into other forms of delusions might then take place through the individual's attempts, using normal reasoning, to explain why he has started to notice all sorts of ostensibly significant events.

Auditory hallucinations

It is reasonable to suppose that when a speech sound is heard, a sequence of hypotheses about its possible interpretations are tested in preconsciousness, before the final result is presented to consciousness as a meaningful message. It also seems inevitable that at least part of the same analysis would have to be carried out on all sounds, with non-speech sounds being rejected at an early stage. In schizophrenia, a defective preconscious:conscious filter could allow incorrect early interpretations of non-speech sounds as speech to enter awareness, and these might then be experienced as voices speaking. The assumption has to be made that there is a steady input of non-verbal environmental sounds to provide the substrate for the erroneous interpretations, but as Frith pointed out, under normal conditions it is seldom that this is not the case.

Formal thought disorder

The process of finding the right words to convert one's thoughts into speech is, like the understanding of speech, likely to involve a complicated search procedure. Various candidate words and phrases need to be accessed and subjected to scrutiny; these operations are effortless and automatic and so take place in preconsciousness. However, if all of the intermediate steps between thought and its expression were to be consciously perceived, it is only natural that a certain amount of distraction and loss of the thread of what one was saying would ensue. That there might also be tendency to slip into using more or less inappropriate words rather than the correct ones, could also easily be envisaged.

The application of the defective selective attention theory to negative symptoms is due primarily to Hemsley (1977). He proposed that schizophrenic patients sooner or later developed one or more deliberate strategies for minimising the constant overload of information they experienced. One way of dealing with the influx of stimuli demanding conscious attention would be to reduce the rate at which all decisions were made; the objective manifestation of this would then be slowness of thought and action. Another would be to raise the threshold for making any response at all; in this case poverty of speech and flattening of affect might be the anticipated result. Finally, the patient might endeavour to avoid any kind of environmental stimulation as far as possible. Plausible consequences of this might be the picture of withdrawal and apathy characteristic of many chronic schizophrenic patients.

While Frith and Hemsley's account of schizophrenic symptoms might have been incomplete and perhaps vulnerable to fairly obvious attack in places, there can be no doubt that overall it had considerable explanatory power. Nevertheless, it is on experimental support rather than plausibility that it has to be judged. In the earliest tests of the theory McGhie and co-workers (see McGhie, 1969), examined the obvious prediction that a breakdown in selective filtering would render schizophrenic patients more vulnerable than normal to distraction. Contrary to expectations, they found that schizophrenic patients showed no greater deterioration in performance than controls when visual or auditory distracting stimuli were introduced during a variety of psychomotor tasks.

By this time, a particular type of distraction experiment had become the stock-in-trade of psychologists investigating Broadbent's model of selective attention. This was the dichotic listening task in which a message such as a series of numbers or a passage of prose is delivered through headphones to one ear, while a different message is delivered to the other ear. The subject has to repeat aloud (shadow) one of the messages, with performance being measured by speed and the number of errors of intrusion from the other message. Although a small industry devoted to dichotic listening in schizophrenia sprang up (reviewed by Neale and Oltmanns, 1980; Cutting, 1985;

Spring *et al.*, 1991) and a substantial number of studies were published, only a few actually compared schizophrenic patients to controls, and used shadowing rather than some secondary measure such as later recall of the message. The fewer still of these which meet the stringency requirement of using acute schizophrenic patients are summarised in Table 8.1. It is clear that their findings have mainly been negative, with only two of the six studies finding significantly poorer performance in the schizophrenic group. In one of these (Rappaport, 1967), half of the patients but none of the controls had been given an injection of sedative medication half an hour before the test. The methodology of the other study (Hemsley and Richardson, 1980) did not have any obvious flaws, but the task was exceptionally difficult – the subjects were required to distinguish prose passages delivered simultaneously to both ears in the same voice purely on the basis of their content.

Defective selective attention as the core psychological dysfunction in schizophrenia was a horse that seemed worth backing on theoretical grounds, but which went on to fall at the first experimental hurdle. It remains possible that such a mechanism underlies some but not all classes of symptom, for example hallucinations (see below). Broadbent's original model has undergone revision over the years, and so it is also possible that the deficit is of a kind that is not unmasked in dichotic listening studies (e.g. Hemsley, 1975; Schwartz, 1982; Gray *et al.*, 1991). But before too many apologies for the theory are made, it has to be remembered that, despite many statements in the literature to the contrary, disorders of attention do not form a conspicuous part of the clinical picture of schizophrenia. In fact, they are much more typical of mania.

Specific approaches

Leaving aside selective attention, there remains an vast amount of research on the psychology of schizophrenia. Some of the bulk of this can be reduced by removing all work that is not cognitive psychological in orientation; and it becomes a lot more manageable when everything that does not address itself to the symptoms of schizophrenia is excluded from consideration. Even so, it only becomes possible to steer a route through the literature by courtesy of the efforts of a few authors such as Cutting (1985), Slade and Bentall (1988), Chapman and Chapman (1973) and Payne (1973), who have taken the trouble to review particular areas thoroughly and critically.

Delusions

Attempts to explain, or even to provide the framework for an explanation of delusions are thin on the ground. There were some tentative explanatory ventures in the classical era (reviewed by Arthur, 1964; Winters and Neale, 1983), for example the proposal, attributed to Gruhle and Griesinger, that

Table 8.1 Dichotic listening studies carried out on acute schizophrenic patients

Study	Sample	Diagnosis	Task	Results	Comment
Rappaport (1967)	90 patients Normal controls	Clinical	Digits One/both ears	Pts significantly worse	Half of patients given IM neuroleptic or barbiturate before testing
Korboot and Damiani (1976)	16 patients Neurotic controls	Clinical	Digits/letters Different ears	NSD	—
Straube and Germer (1979)	24 patients Psychiatric and normal controls	Clinical	Words Different ears	NSD	—
Pogue-Geile and Oltmanns (1980)	8 patients Psychiatric and normal controls	RDC	Prose Different ears	NSD	—
Hemsley and Richardson (1980)	9 patients Psychiatric and normal controls	Clinical	Prose Both ears	Pts significantly worse	Difficult task
Wielgus and Harvey (1988)	20 patients Psychiatric and normal controls	DSM III	Prose Different ears	NSD	—

delusions are a consequence of defective intellect, judgement and powers of reasoning, and Bleuler's (1911) argument that formal thought disorder created fertile ground for the development of abnormal beliefs. These, however, were contradicted by clinical experience, which gave no grounds for supposing that delusions are restricted to intellectually impaired schizophrenic patients or those with formal thought disorder.

A further early view, mentioned by Kraepelin (1913a), Bleuler (1911) and Schneider (1949), was that some delusions are explanations of hallucinations. This idea formed the basis of what was until recently the only formal psychological theory of delusions, that proposed by Maher (Maher, 1974; Maher and Ross, 1984). Normal individuals, Maher's account began, react to the perception of new, novel or unprecedented events in a characteristic way. Initial puzzlement is followed by a search of the immediate environment for related unexpected occurrences. This gives way to the formulation of various potential hypotheses to explain the event, which are then examined in turn against the evidence. Most are quickly discarded or else modified. Sooner or later, however, one hypothesis appears to be credible, and this gives rise to a flash of insight. This initial success is then followed by a phase in which the individual confirms the explanation by means of a series of further tests.

According to Maher, when the environmental events on which this process is brought to bear are abnormal, then the interpretation that is eventually assigned to them must turn out to be abnormal as well – normal cognitive machinery acting on abnormal input can only give rise to abnormal output, or in other words a delusional belief. One obvious class of abnormal perceptual input is hallucinations, which would, according to the theory, go on to elicit delusional explanations. Subtler perceptual disorders might result in the appearance of delusions with correspondingly less obvious antecedents. To account for the occurrence of delusions in the absence of any other obvious psychopathology, Maher postulated that there might be a 'central neuropathology' which gives rise to a free-floating feeling of significance, which could then in turn be elaborated into various classes of referential delusions and might even, in much the same way as Frith (1979) argued, form the core of more elaborate delusional systems.

By invoking the device of central neuropathology, Maher's theory can deal with the problem of how patients without hallucinations can be deluded, but it still predicts that patients with hallucinations should always be deluded, which is not the case. The theory also faces the obstacle that individuals who have abnormal perceptions but are not schizophrenic should be expected to develop delusions. In reality, patients with conditions ranging from tinnitus, migraine and epilepsy to the phantom limb syndrome do not generally become deluded about their symptoms. Maher's account also fails to explain why schizophrenic delusions incline to the bizarre, patently absurd and fantastic – an essentially normal hypothesis-testing machinery should produce explanations that tend to be rational, mundane and plausible. However, the most serious problem of all is that neither Maher nor anyone else has ever put the theory to any kind of experimental test.

Interestingly, Maher's argument works equally well if it is proposed that the cognitive fault underlying delusions lies not in the input to the cognitive machinery of belief, but in the machinery itself. Just such a proposal was made by Hemsley and Garety (1986), who argued that the basis of delusions might lie in a particular form of abnormality in reasoning – probabilistic reasoning bias. Under conditions of uncertainty, where judgement depends on the balance of probabilities, they hypothesised that patients with delusions would essentially jump to conclusions – they would require less information than normal to arrive at a decision, and would be abnormally confident about the decision that they reached.

In the original study to test this hypothesis, they (Huq *et al.*, 1988) employed a task where subjects were shown two jars, one of which the experimenter explained contained 85 red and 15 green beads and the other 85 green beads and 15 red beads. The containers were then hidden from view and the subjects were informed that they would be shown beads from one of the jars until they reached a decision as to which of the two jars it was. One of the containers was then chosen, still hidden from view, and beads were drawn one at a time, replaced, the jar shaken, and another bead drawn, until the subject reached a confident decision. (In fact, the beads were always drawn in the same pre-arranged sequence, which favoured a decision after several draws.) The experimental design is summarised in Figure 8.1. Compared to 15 normal controls, and also to 10 patients with non-psychotic disorders, 15 deluded schizophrenic patients required significantly fewer draws to reach a

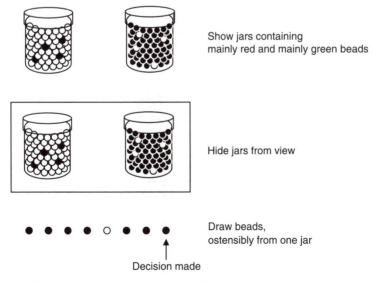

Figure 8.1 Garety and co-workers' probabilistic reasoning paradigm.

decision. Some of the patients came to a firm conclusion after being shown only one bead.

All but one of seven subsequent studies have replicated the finding of 'jumping to conclusions' in schizophrenia (see Garety and Freeman, 1999). It is less clear that the finding overcomes one of the hurdles specified earlier, that of showing that the abnormality is present in acute schizophrenic patients; the patient types were not specified in most of the studies. Nor does it obviously clear the other hurdle, of being seen particularly in patients with delusions. Surprisingly, given experimental psychology's normally fanatical concern with confounding factors, none of the studies felt the need to include a control group of non-deluded schizophrenic patients, and so did not exclude the possibility that probabilistic reasoning bias is a general feature of schizophrenia rather than a function of being deluded.

Two recent studies have now done this: Menon *et al.* (2006) compared 16 schizophrenic patients with delusions, 15 without current delusions and 16 normal controls on the original beads task used by Huq *et al.*, and also a slightly more difficult version where the ratio of beads was 60:40 rather than 85:15. The patient and controls were well matched and the patients were selected for showing relatively preserved overall intellectual function (WAIS-R IQ of 85 or greater). Both patient groups required significantly fewer draws to reach a decision than the normal controls, but there was no difference between those with and those without delusions. The findings are illustrated in Figure 8.2. Moritz and Woodward (2005) also failed to find any clear evidence of differences between deluded and non-deluded patients in a similar study.

Hallucinations

The psychological study of hallucinations has covered considerably more ground than that of delusions. In a review of the literature, Slade and Bentall

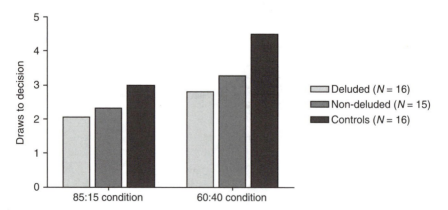

Figure 8.2 Draws to decision in deluded patients, non-deluded patients and normal controls at two levels of uncertainty (from Menon *et al.*, 2006).

(1988) distinguished three separate lines of attack on the problem (and also a fourth which was not cognitive psychological and so is not considered further). The first two of these, referred to by Slade and Bentall as *cognitive seepage* and *abnormal imagery*, are conventional psychological theories with accompanying experimental findings; the third, *subvocalisation*, might be best described as a set of findings in search of a theory.

Cognitive seepage

Theories of this type have sought to explain hallucinations in terms of the entry into consciousness of mental activity that would normally remain preconscious. They are thus just a specific version of the selective attentional account of schizophrenia, which, although seriously dented as a general theory, could still underlie the particular symptom of hallucinations. The theories typically aim to account for auditory hallucinations.

According to the Frith/Slade account, auditory hallucinations are due to preconscious interpretations of non-speech sounds as words. This makes the prediction that the frequency and intensity of the symptom will vary directly with the level of environmental noise to which the patient is exposed. This prediction was tested in a study by Margo *et al.* (1981) in which seven hallucinating schizophrenic patients were asked to rate the duration, loudness and clarity of their hallucinations under various acoustic conditions. These ranged from no stimulation, to white noise, to regular electronic blips, to pop music and passages of prose. There was also a sensory restriction condition, where the patients wore headphones and dark goggles. It was found that increases in both meaningless (e.g. electronic bleeps) and meaningful (e.g. pop music) auditory stimulation had complex effects, but tended if anything to reduce the duration, clarity and loudness of auditory hallucinations (see Figure 8.3). This and a number of other negative findings led Slade and Bentall to reject this approach to auditory hallucinations.

Abnormal imagery

This approach proposes essentially that patients who describe hallucinations are really experiencing mental images that have become so vivid and intense that they are difficult to distinguish from real perceptions. Bearing in mind that schizophrenic auditory hallucinations are commonly reported as being heard inside the head, and that the distinction between true and pseudo-hallucinations has always been one of the most troubled in phenomenology (see Chapter 1), any approach that maintains that imagery and hallucination lie on a continuum has a certain amount of face validity.

The relationship of hallucinations and abnormal imagery has been investigated assiduously since as long ago as the nineteenth century. In a way all too characteristic of experimental psychology, some support for the idea was originally found; subsequently the findings were questioned; then influential

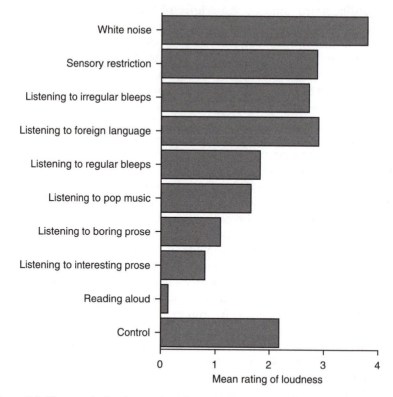

Figure 8.3 Changes in loudness of auditory hallucinations under different auditory
conditions (the pattern was also roughly similar for duration and clarity of
hallucinations) (from Margo *et al.*, 1981).

reviews criticised the validity of measures of imagery used; as a result, studies
with improved methodology were undertaken; these themselves were subjected to further critical scrutiny; and so on up to the present day. Slade and
Bentall concluded, with a note of exasperation, first, that the studies had lent
no consistent support for a link between mental imagery and hallucinations;
and second, that it had become increasingly unclear over time just how much
the vividness and clarity of a mental image was related to judgements about
whether it was real or not.

Subvocalisation

The foundation of this approach is a curious experimental finding which may
or may not be robust, but whose understanding remains sketchy if not completely obscure. In 1949, Gould, an American psychologist, reported a single
case study on a chronically hospitalised schizophrenic woman who was continuously auditorily hallucinated and whom he had noticed also made slight
lip movements when she was not speaking. When he placed a stethoscope on

her larynx, he heard faint sounds. When he then attached a microphone to her throat, words could be made out accompanying her lip movements. The content of the patient's subvocalised speech corresponded closely to her own account of what her voices had just been saying. Gould's transcript of the patient's subvocalisations is reproduced in Box 8.1; there is a noticeable similarity to Kraepelin's description of auditory hallucinations in Chapter 1.

Gould (1948, 1950) went on to carry out two further studies where he documented that electromyograhic (EMG) activity in the speech musculature showed periodic increases in hallucinating, but not non-hallucinating patients, and that the timing of these increases correlated significantly with the patients' reports of the onset of hallucinations.

With more investigation, Gould's finding has in some ways become weaker: Slade and Bentall reviewed a number of subsequent studies that found that only about half of all schizophrenic patients showed increased EMG activity when they were experiencing auditory hallucinations, and that there was no simple temporal relationship with the onset and offset of hallucinations. A further well-conducted study (Green and Kinsbourne, 1990) has done little to clarify matters, finding essentially inconclusive evidence of a temporal relationship between subvocalisation and auditory hallucinations. In other ways, though, it has become tantalisingly stronger: while testing a patient similar to Gould's, Green and Preston (1981), amplified his subvocalisations and played them back to him. This led to a progressive increase in the loudness of the

---

Box 8.1 Subvocalisations recorded from a schizophrenic woman (from Gould, 1949)

At initial recording
'Something worse than this . . . No, certainly not . . . Not a single thing. It certainly is not. Something going on. That's all right. Anything around. Not very much. Something else. Looks like it isn't. It's just what I know. Something funny about it. Anything doing. Anything else. Get near it. Every single thing. No I don't think so. But this one. Society. I don't expect anything.'

At a time when briefer productions were heard on inspiration as well as expiration
Expiration: 'Oh, she is certainly the wisest one in the world.'
Inspiration: 'No, she is not.'
Expiration: 'I don't know if she is on the level.'
Inspiration: 'What is she going to do?'
Expiration: 'I don't know what she is going to do.'

After being given amytal followed by caffeine
'She knows. She's the most wicked thing in the whole wide world. The only voice I hear is hers. He knows everything. She knows all about aviation.'

subvocalisations until a conversation between the patient and his hallucinated voice could be clearly heard!

Despite its lukewarm experimental support, the idea that the schizophrenic patient who hears voices is actually talking to himself and experiencing some cognitive correlate of this remains too intuitively appealing to be dismissed altogether. It resurfaces in a cognitive neuropsychological context in the next chapter.

Formal thought disorder

Attempts to explain what it is that makes schizophrenic speech sometimes difficult to follow have occupied more time and effort than any other schizophrenic symptoms. Two of the major approaches, which have drawn on linguistics and frontal/executive dysfunction, are discussed in the next chapter. A large amount of other research has been completely atheoretical in orientation, simply assessing schizophrenic speech for its statistical properties, informational content, repetitiveness, redundancy, predictibility, and so on. Among the theoretically motivated cognitive psychological approaches, the most empirical investigation has been generated by two proposals. One of these has been over-inclusive thinking, which is now largely of historical interest. The other is increased semantic priming, which is the focus of a great deal of current attention.

Over-inclusive thinking

After defining what he considered to be three key clinical features of thought disorder, asyndetic thinking, word approximations and interpenetration of themes (see Chapter 1), Cameron (1939, 1944) went on to argue that these might all arise from a single underlying abnormality, an inability to select, eliminate and restrict thought to the task in hand – or over-inclusiveness. This could cause concepts to lose their sharp boundaries and allow closely or even distantly related ideas to merge into one another, accounting for asyndetic thinking. It could also affect the selection of the words and phrases in speech, causing them to strike somewhere on the periphery of the target instead of at the bullseye, and so give rise to word approximations. Interpenetration of themes could be another manifestation of the same underlying abnormality, with the failure here being in the normal process of subordination of one theme to another, allowing elements of both to proceed simultaneously.

Cameron never personally tested his proposal, but others did, particularly Payne and co-workers (see Payne, 1973). A series of initial studies found that schizophrenic patients as a group were more over-inclusive than normal controls on a number of purported measures of over-inclusiveness, such as sorting objects or pictures into categories, giving more distantly related synonyms for words, and selecting the appropriate information to be used in a

Table 8.2 Studies of over-inclusive thinking in schizophrenia

Test	Found in schizophrenia?	Independently replicated?	Found in acute schizophrenia?
Giving synonyms for words	✓	✓	—
Rating words as in a category	✓	✓	✓
Giving the gist of a story	✓	—	—
Selecting information for a story	✓	—	—
Interpreting proverbs	✓	✓	✓
Sorting objects into categories	✓	✓	✓
Sorting pictures into categories	✓	✓	—
Changing set	✓	✗	✓
Developing a set	✓	✗	—

Source: Payne (1973).

story (see Table 8.2). By and large these findings were replicated. As also shown in Table 8.2, over-inclusiveness also passed the stringency test of being demonstrable in acute schizophrenic patients. In fact, using a battery of three tests that Payne developed in response to criticisms of the validity of some of the original measures, he found that the 'combined over-inclusiveness scores' were on average twice as high in acute as in chronic schizophrenic patients.

The requirement for over-inclusiveness to be found particularly in patients with formal thought disorder, however, rested on a single study. Hawks and Payne (1971) administered three tests of over-inclusiveness to 36 acute admissions with a clinical diagnosis of schizophrenia, 18 of whom showed thought disorder, and 18 who did not. There were also 18 patients with other diagnoses and 18 normal controls. The thought-disordered schizophrenic patients were found to have a significantly higher mean combined over-inclusiveness score than the non-thought-disordered schizophrenic patients, who did not differ from the non-schizophrenic patients or the normal controls. There were few significant correlations between the combined over-inclusion score and delusions; only that with ideas of influence reached significance. On the other hand, over-inclusiveness correlated significantly with a number of symptoms, including talkativeness, verbal responsiveness, increased motor activity and hostility, which might with greater or lesser degrees of plausibility be regarded as associated with formal thought disorder.

As noted by Chapman and Chapman (1973), over-inclusiveness stands out as the only psychological abnormality that has ever been found to be more characteristic of acute schizophrenia than chronic schizophrenia. Unfortunately, the criticisms that led Payne to develop his second-generation battery of over-inclusiveness tests continued, and rightly or wrongly, eventually brought research in this area to a halt. The occasional study continues to be carried out (see Harrow and Quinlan, 1985), but there is no longer any theoretical interest in the phenomenon.

Increased semantic priming

Maher (1983) introduced his second cognitive theory of schizophrenic symptoms by suggesting that formal thought disorder 'involves an inability to exclude from intrusion into consciousness material from either external stimulation or internally stored associations, that would normally be excluded on the basis of its irrelevance to the task situation in which the patient is performing'. Specifically, he proposed that the associative process was heightened in schizophrenia, or alternatively that there was a failure to inhibit it properly, causing inappropriate associations to be incorporated into speech. For example, in the sentence 'Bees make honey', associations to the word bee would probably include sting, wasp, and hive, and those to honey might include sweet and comb. A statement like 'Bees make sweet', would, however, strike the listener as distinctly odd. The result might be sentences that were merely richer than usual in associations of poetic type or, at the other extreme, a serious compromise in the intelligibility of speech.

Although Maher did not explicitly use the term 'semantic memory', his approach was clearly based on this experimental psychological construct. According to network theories of semantic memory, when a particular item of knowledge, or node as it is often referred to, is activated, for example by hearing, reading or thinking about it, other nodes become activated as well, with the degree of activation being proportional to their semantic distance from the original node. This process of 'spread of activation' plays an important part in the performance of cognitive tasks such as comprehending text and verifying whether propositions are true or false. There is also every reason to suppose that spread of activation takes place while an individual is speaking, where it presumably exerts an influence on what the speaker plans to say next.

As it happens, there is a simple and direct way of testing Maher's hypothesis of heightened associations – or increased spread of activation in semantic memory – in patients with formal thought disorder. This is by means of the semantic priming or lexical decision task. The basic experimental paradigm is summarised in Figure 8.4. Subjects see a string of letters flashed up on a screen and have to decide by a key press whether it is a word or a non-word. Immediately beforehand, a real word – the prime – is briefly shown, which may or may not be semantically related to the target word (if this happens to be a real word). The reaction time for deciding whether the target is a real word has been reliably found to be significantly shorter when the prime is semantically related to the target than when it is not. This facilitation can be explained as the prime producing spread of activation to the target, and hence reducing the degree of activation needed to allow the verification that it is a real word to take place. The period of time over which the prime facilitates lexical decision is short, typically of the order of less than a second.

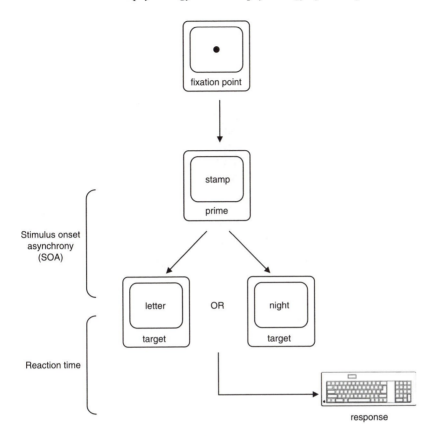

Figure 8.4 The semantic priming paradigm.

In the first study of this type in schizophrenia, Maher and co-workers (Manschreck *et al.*, 1988) tested 12 chronic schizophrenic patients with thought disorder, 12 without the symptom, and 11 normal controls (they also had a further control group of 9 patients with depression). Their priming task employed a short interval between the onset of the prime and onset of the target (commonly referred to as the stimulus onset asynchrony or SOA) of 250 ms. As shown in Figure 8.5, all three groups showed significant priming; that is, the mean reaction time to primed words was significantly shorter than that to unprimed words. However, whereas the mean priming was similar in the normal controls and the non-thought-disordered schizophrenic patients (37 ms vs 36 ms), at 83 ms it was more than twice as great in the thought-disordered patients. Measures of accuracy of identification of words did not distinguish the three groups.

Manschreck *et al.*'s findings were unusual in that the thought-disordered patients were on average faster to respond than the controls in both the primed

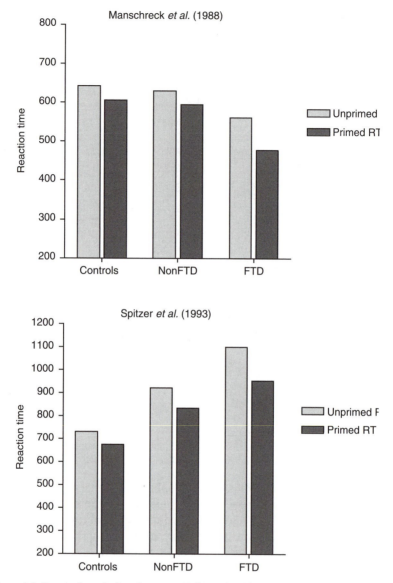

Figure 8.5 Semantic priming in two studies of schizophrenic patients (data from
Spitzer *et al.*, 1993 are for 200 ms SOA, the findings were similar with 700 ms
SOA) (from Manschreck *et al.*, 1988, and Spitzer *et al.*, 1993).

and unprimed conditions, a result that runs counter to the almost universal
finding of slowness of schizophrenic patients on reaction time tasks (e.g.
Schatz, 1998). However, in a later study Spitzer *et al.* (1993) again found
significantly increased semantic priming in 29 thought-disordered patients

but not in 21 non-thought-disordered schizophrenic patients. In this study both groups of patients were overall significantly slower than the controls on all components of the reaction time task. Their findings are also shown in Figure 8.5.

Manschreck *et al.* used a short SOA of 250 ms in their original study. However, it has become accepted that at least two processes contribute to the semantic priming effect in normal subjects. One of these is an 'automatic' process identifiable with spread of activation in the semantic network; this is rapid and seen at short SOAs. The other is a 'controlled' process whereby the subject uses the nature of the prime to generate an 'expectancy set' of potential targets. This is a slower process and only seen with SOAs of greater than about 400–450 ms. Spitzer *et al.* tested the subjects in their study at both short (200 ms) and long (700 ms) SOAs. The patients with formal thought disorder showed significantly increased priming at both SOAs compared to the normal controls; however, compared to the patients without formal thought disorder, the increase was significant at the long SOA but was only at trend level at the short SOA.

Minzenberg *et al.* (2002) reviewed these and further studies of semantic priming in schizophrenia. Many of these studies examined unselected groups of schizophrenic patients; however, of the eight studies that compared thought-disordered patients with non-thought-disordered patients or normal controls, three found increased priming, three found decreased priming, and two found no difference. The findings for schizophrenia as a whole were widely discrepant, but there was a tendency for priming to be normal or increased at short SOAs, whereas all of seven studies using long SOAs found some reduction in priming, although this was not always significant.

Pomarol-Clotet *et al.* (submitted) (see also McKenna and Oh, 2005) subjected these and a number of more recent studies to meta-analysis, with possibly more revealing results. The findings are summarised in Box 8.2. There was no support for increased semantic priming in schizophrenia as a whole. However, semantic priming was significantly increased when studies comparing patients with formal thought disorder to controls were pooled. This increase in semantic priming was only apparent in studies using short SOAs – in other words it reflected increased spread of activation. There was, however, a qualification to this picture of otherwise strong endorsement for Maher's original proposal: the overall slowing of reaction time in schizophrenia was found to significantly moderate the effect size for priming in thought-disordered patients, and so could represent an important confounding factor in the studies.

The neuropsychology of schizophrenia

The neuropsychological approach to schizophrenia makes no attempt to explain the process of symptom formation in schizophrenia. In fact it is

Box 8.2 Meta-analysis of studies of semantic priming in schizophrenia (from Pomarol-Clotet *et al.*, submitted; see also McKenna and Oh, 2005)

To be included studies had to report reaction time data on schizophrenic patients and normal controls in any type of semantic priming paradigm. A search located 31 studies of priming including two unpublished studies.

The studies were subjected to three main meta-analyses, of priming in schizophrenic patients as a whole, and in patients with or without formal thought disorder vs controls. The many minor variations in technique across the studies were ignored.

Schizophrenia vs controls
Several studies reported data on unselected groups of patients, and for this analysis studies reporting findings on separate groups of patients with and without formal thought disorder were combined. The pooled effect size from 31 studies was +0.04 (CI −0.06/+0.14). Excluding 4 outlying studies made little difference to the effect size.

A funnel plot was symmetrical, suggesting that there was no significant publication bias.

Patients with formal thought disorder vs controls
The pooled effect size from 18 studies was +0.16 (CI +0.01/+0.31), indicating just significantly increased priming in the patients. This increased to +0.38 (CI +0.21/+0.55) after 5 studies with outlying effect sizes were excluded.

Patients without formal thought disorder vs controls
Here the pooled effect size from 13 studies was +0.00 (CI −0.15/+0.16). These studies were homogeneous.

The influence of moderator variables
For this, studies were coded as employing a short SOA (≤400 ms) or long SOA (>400 ms). For studies of schizophrenia as a whole, SOA did not significantly moderate effect size: the effect size for 20 studies with short SOAs was +0.06 compared to −0.05 in 17 studies using long SOAs (QB(1) = 1.47, p = .22). However, SOA was a significant moderator in the studies of patients with formal thought disorder: the pooled effect size for 10 studies with a short SOA was + 0.25 compared to −0.14 in 7 studies with a long SOA (QB(1) = 6.33, p = .01).

Age and duration of illness did not significantly moderate effect size. It was not possible to examine medication as a moderator variable, since all but 3 of the studies were carried out on treated patients.

The effect of general slowing of reaction time in schizophrenia

If, as would be expected to be the case, schizophrenic patients were slow to respond on both the unprimed and primed parts of the lexical decision task, this would inflate the value for priming purely for arithmetical reasons – the numerical difference between 900 ms and 600 ms is greater than that between 600 ms and 400 ms, even though the proportional change is the same. In order to examine whether this could be confounding the finding of increased semantic priming in thought-disordered patients, a value for overall slowing in schizophrenia was first derived for each study, calculated as the effect size of the difference between unprimed reaction times in the patient and control groups. This was then entered as a moderator variable in the above analysis. When this was done the significant effect for priming in the studies comparing thought-disordered patients with controls disappeared.

In summary, meta-analysis provides support for increased semantic priming in schizophrenia that is restricted to patients with formal thought disorder. The data suggest that the effect occurs principally at short SOAs, consistent with it being due to increased spread of activation in semantic memory. However, at present the possibility that the finding is an artefact of the general slowing of reaction time in schizophrenia cannot be excluded.

---

not really concerned with the clinical features of the disorder at all. Instead, what is known about the way higher mental functions are affected in various brain diseases is brought to bear on schizophrenic patients, who are quite simply trawled for evidence of similar impairments. Once again, both general and specific approaches can be distinguished. The former approach is directed to the question of whether there is overall intellectual impairment in schizophrenia. The latter examines the question of whether one or more of the traditionally recognised domains of perception, language, memory and executive ('frontal lobe') function are impaired.

The stringency tests that need to be applied to findings of neuropsychological impairment in schizophrenia are necessarily different from those adopted in the preceding section. If poor performance is found on tests of general intellectual function, the obvious requirement is to ensure that the impairment is genuine and not merely attributable to some factors such as poor cooperation, lack of motivation, distraction by psychotic symptoms, and so on. Also included in this category is the frequently rehearsed objection that poor performance is due to treatment. For specific deficits, the requirement is an obvious one, even though it has been ignored with embarrassing frequency in schizophrenia research. This is to demonstrate that the deficit is disproportionate to the overall level of intellectual impairment, in other words that it is not just part of a pattern of general poor performance, which would show itself on any test.

General intellectual impairment in schizophrenia

As well as originating the concept of schizophrenia, Kraepelin and Bleuler were responsible for the view that intellectual function was not affected in the disorder. Kraepelin (1913a) was clear that there was a dementia in the disorder he named dementia praecox, but he went on to state that the injury predominated in the emotional and volitional spheres and that memory and orientation were comparatively little affected. Part of Bleuler's (1911) reason for renaming dementia praecox schizophrenia was that he considered the connotation of intellectual impairment to be misleading. According to him, patients might perform poorly on certain tests at certain times, but this was fundamentally different from dementia and imbecility, and 'even in a very severe degree of schizophrenia all the fundamental functions that are accessible to present tests are preserved'.

These views hardened into the dogma that there was no compromise of intellectual function in schizophrenia, a process that was aided and abetted by the psychoanalytic establishment in America – for whom any hint of brain disease was anathema. Meanwhile, as mentioned earlier, psychological studies were finding that patients with schizophrenia performed more poorly than normal individuals on any and every cognitive task (see Chapman and Chapman, 1973). A typical early American study of this era was carried out by Klonoff *et al.* (1970). They administered the wide ranging Halstead-Reitan battery of neuropsychological tests to 66 chronic schizophrenic patients. Fifty-five (83 per cent) were found to have a composite score below the cut-off for normal. Seven of the patients in the study had undergone leucotomy and six had other associated neurological conditions (including epilepsy and brain damage), but there was no difference between the performance of those with and those without associated neurological conditions. The authors concluded that, at face value, there was evidence of cerebral dysfunction in chronic schizophrenia. However, they went on to state that this conclusion should be treated 'with the utmost caution' and listed psychiatric factors and drug treatment as possible complicating factors.

By just under 10 years later, everything had changed. Three reviews published in the same year (Goldstein, 1978; Heaton *et al.*, 1978; Malec, 1978) found that groups of acute, mixed and chronically hospitalised schizophrenic patients were increasingly difficult to distinguish from patients with brain damage on a wide range of tests, and that for the last group a meaningful differentiation was not possible. Heaton *et al.* went so far as to state that, whatever the underlying reason, 'groups of unselected institutionalised chronic schizophrenics will appear organic on neuropsychological testing because a significant proportion of them are organic' (by this they actually meant that some of the patients might have been suffering from undiagnosed neurological disease).

Six contemporary studies that have applied batteries of neuropsychological tests to groups of schizophrenic patients are summarised in Table 8.3. These all used diagnostic criteria and compared schizophrenic patients to normal controls who were well matched for age, sex and educational level (or parental educational/socioecomonic status, which has been argued to be a better index of educational achievement in schizophrenic patients, who may leave school prematurely because of illness). They include a study by Goldberg *et al.* (1990), which employed what is arguably the best possible comparison group, the unaffected monozygotic co-twins of the patients. It can be seen that every study found some evidence of impairment. In most of the studies this affected most or all of the areas of function examined, but one or two found a more restricted pattern of impairment, in memory and executive function.

These studies provide little support for the view that neuroleptic treatment causes poor neuropsychological performance in schizophrenia. Two of the studies were carried out on drug-free patients (Saykin *et al.*, 1991; Blanchard and Neale, 1994) and one on never-treated patients (Saykin *et al.*, 1994). Such a finding is entirely in accordance with other studies which have found that acute administration of neuroleptics has only minor effects on cognitive function in normal individuals, and higher doses and longer periods of treatment if anything tend to improve cognitive performance in schizophrenic patients (King, 1990; Mortimer, 1997; Mishara and Goldberg, 2004).

Could the impaired performance found in these studies be due to poor concentration, lack of volition and the distracting effects of psychotic symptoms? Since neuropsychological tests are designed with clinical populations in mind, poor performance is not especially easy to ascribe to such factors, but there is still a lingering doubt. For example, doing a whole battery of tests could be considered excessively taxing for schizophrenic patients, or particularly poor performance by a few subjects of dubious testability might have exerted a disproportionate influence on the group as a whole. The effects of motivation and cooperation have occasionally been examined on cognitive performance in schizophrenic patients (Goldberg *et al.*, 1987; Kenny and Meltzer, 1991; Duffy and O'Carroll, 1994), and these studies have not found much to suggest that such factors play a role, but the studies are so few in number that it is difficult to answer this question decisively one way or the other.

Such objections are harder to apply to the simple 'bedside' tests of orientation, memory, language ability and abstract thinking, used by clinicians to screen for the presence of intellectual impairment. These tests may be crude and insensitive, but their brevity and straightforwardness make it difficult to attribute poor performance as representing anything other than genuine intellectual impairment. Owens and Johnstone (1980) examined 510 chronically hospitalised patients meeting diagnostic criteria for schizophrenia using a test of this type. They also tested a control group of 33 patients who required chronic institutional care for physical illnesses. Their findings are

Table 8.3 Studies applying neuropsychological test batteries to schizophrenic patients

Study	Numbers	Diagnostic criteria	Patient type	Matching	Tests	Areas of impairment	Comment
Kolb and Whishaw (1983)	30 patients 30 controls	DSM III	Acute	Age Education	IQ Memory Visual/visuospatial function Executive function Other	Performance IQ but not verbal IQ Memory Executive function	Deficits most marked in memory and executive function
Goldberg et al. (1990)	16 patients 16 controls	DSM-III-R	Chronic	Controls were unaffected MZ co-twins	IQ Memory Vigilance Executive	IQ Memory Some executive tests Vigilance	Affected co-twins performed more poorly than unaffected on all tests, but not always significantly so
Braff et al. (1991)	40 patients 40 controls	DSM-III-R	Chronic	Age Education	IQ Executive Memory Language Visuospatial function Auditory perception Tactile perception Motor skill	All tests except motor skill, visuospatial and language	—

Study	Sample	Diagnosis	Course	Matched variables	Domains tested	Impaired	Notes
Saykin et al. (1991)	36 patients 36 controls	DSM-III-R	Chronic	Age Parental education	IQ Executive function Memory Language Auditory perception Motor skill	All tests except language	All patients drug-free Disproportionately poor performance on memory tests
Saykin et al. (1994)	37 patients 131 controls	DSM-III-R	Acute	Age Education* Parental education	IQ Executive function Memory Language Auditory perception Motor skill	All tests except motor skill	All patients drug-naive
Blanchard and Neale (1994)	28 patients 15 controls	DSM-III-R	Chronic	Age Education	Executive function Memory Language Visual perception Tactile perception Motor skill	Almost all tests	All patients drug-free

* Not matched but differences controlled for in analysis.

shown in Figure 8.6, from which it can be seen that over half of the schizo-phrenic patients were more than two standard deviations below the control group mean. Fifteen per cent of the sample were only able to achieve scores of 20 or less – spectacularly poor performance on a test where knowing one's name, being oriented in time and place and being able to answer elementary general knowledge questions gives a score of 25.

Crow and co-workers (Crow and Mitchell, 1975; Stevens *et al.*, 1978) took this approach to the limit, merely asking chronically hospitalised schizo-phrenic patients to state their age. They found that approximately 25 per cent were incorrect, underestimating how old they were by 5 years or more. They were also able to establish that age disorientation could not simply be attrib-uted to lifelong low intelligence, to exposure to various modalities of treat-ment, or the effects of institutionalisation, and that it typically forms part of a wider pattern of neuropsychological impairment (Liddle and Crow, 1984; Buhrich *et al.*, 1988). Some illustrations of the phenomenon are shown in Table 8.4.

These findings cannot be explained away. It is difficult to believe that

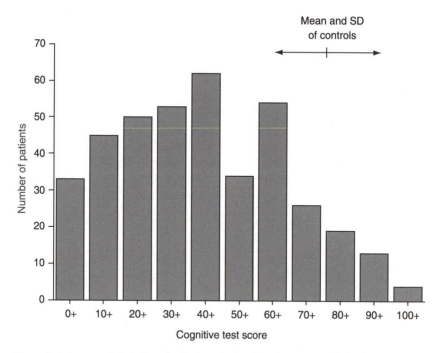

Figure 8.6 Scores of 510 chronically hospitalised patients on a clinical test of intel-lectual function (from Owens and Johnstone (1980), The disabilities of chronic schizophrenia – their nature and the factors contributing to their development. *British Journal of Psychiatry*, 136, 384–393. Reproduced with permission from the Royal College of Psychiatrists).

Table 8.4 Extracts from case-notes of age-disoriented schizophrenic patients

Age at admission	Age when cognitive impairment first noted	Comments in case-notes
20	28	'Confused, not oriented in space or time'
20	26	'100 – 7 = 88'
20	46	'Gives age as 17 . . . does not appear to understand what is being said'
33	56	'Says she is aged 26 years'
22	34	'Answers questions incorrectly. Gives age as 12 years'
20	26	'Dull . . . disoriented'
25	59	'Gives age as 26 years'
22	35	'Dull and confused. Memory shows gross impairment'
28	32	'Very disoriented in time and place'

Source: From Buhrich *et al.* (1988), Age disorientation in chronic schizophrenia is not associated with pre-morbid intellectual impairment or past physical treatments. *British Journal of Psychiatry*, 152, 466–469. Reproduced with permission from the Royal College of Psychiatrists.

withdrawal, distraction, or preoccupation with inner experiences can compromise the ability of chronic schizophrenic patients to answer questions about the day and the date. Nor is it credible to maintain that keeping track of one's age is too demanding a task for chronically hospitalised patients.

Taken together, the findings converge on the conclusion that schizophrenia is accompanied by a variable degree of general intellectual impairment. In acute patients this tends to be minor, but it can be readily demonstrated on neuropsychological testing. In more severe and chronic forms of illness, it becomes prevalent and shows up on 'bedside' tests in a proportion of cases. In a minority of these latter cases it amounts to what is to all intents and purposes a dementia.

Several questions remain unanswered about schizophrenic intellectual impairment, mostly notably concerning when it develops and whether it is static or progressive. Some of the evidence bearing on these issues is summarized in Box 8.3.

Specific neuropsychological deficits in schizophrenia

Establishing that a neuropsychological deficit is specific; that is, that it affects one area of neuropsychological function while leaving others intact, is no easy task in schizophrenia. The background level of general intellectual impairment will tend to depress scoring on all tests to some extent – in fact it is almost certainly this that is the root cause of the well-known schizophrenic tendency to poor performance on all cognitive tests. The most that

Box 8.3 General intellectual impairment in schizophrenia: Where does it come from?

Although the evidence for general intellectual impairment in schizophrenia is persuasive, when it appears and whether it is static or progressive are the subject of much debate.

The birth cohort studies reviewed in Chapter 7 indicate that prior to the onset of illness there is an IQ disadvantage of around 5–10 IQ points. David *et al.* (1997) elegantly confirmed this finding in a study of Swedish army conscripts. Like armed forces recruits the world over, these underwent IQ testing on enlistment at the age of 18. David *et al.* compared IQs of 195 of the recruits who later developed schizophrenia (the diagnoses were made clinically, but a proportion of them were compared with diagnoses made according to DSM III criteria with good agreement) with the remainder of the sample of approximately 50,000. As shown, the distribution of scores for the future schizophrenic patients was shifted to the left by an amount which was statistically significant. Individuals with major neurological abnormality or learning disability were excluded, and the difference in IQ remained highly significant after controlling for socioeconomic status, behavioural and school adjustment, drug abuse, urban upbringing and psychiatric disturbance at the time of testing.

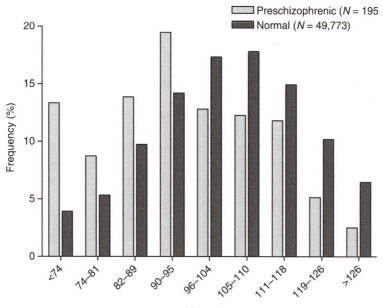

At the same time, the fact that some chronically hospitalised schizophrenic patients show substantial degrees of intellectual impairment suggests that further post-morbid intellectual decline may also take place. In a small minority of such patients the impairment is marked and several authors have documented the existence of patients who appear to warrant an additional diagnosis of dementia. For example, de Vries *et al.* (2001) reported a series of eight non-elderly schizophrenic patients who showed disorientation, memory impairment and other cognitive deficits, low or even mentally handicapped levels of current IQ functioning, and daily living skill failures up to and including incontinence. They had all been educationally normal prior to the onset of schizophrenia and most had either been in higher education or had worked in positions requiring at least average intelligence.

Nevertheless, to date no study has managed to demonstrate direct evidence of intellectual deterioration in schizophrenia. Thus test–retest studies have failed to show IQ decline or worsening of poor neuropsychological test performance over periods of up to 5 years after disease onset (Rund, 1998; Hoff *et al.*, 1999). Furthermore, in a paper provocatively titled 'Schizophrenia and the myth of intellectual decline', Russell *et al.* (1997) traced 34 adults with schizophrenia who had previously had IQ testing in a child psychiatry clinic, in most cases before psychotic symptoms became apparent. They found a mean decline in full-scale IQ over on average 19 years of just 1.9 points. However, since the patients' mean IQ at initial assessment IQ was 84.1, they were far from a representative sample of schizophrenia.

At present there is no easy way of reconciling these findings; the paradox remains that some chronic schizophrenics show cognitive impairment to a degree that is inherently unlikely to have been present throughout life, but all the direct evidence of decline is negative. It has been suggested that the intellectual decline takes place in the months or years preceding the appearance of schizophrenic symptoms, where it might manifest itself as the well-known fall-off in educational or work performance often seen as a prodrome. Caspi *et al.* (2003) examined this possibility in another study of armed forces conscripts, this time in Israel. They traced 44 recruits who became schizophrenic and 44 controls, and retested them on the IQ tests they had been given at enlistment. They found only equivocal evidence of decline.

Another possibility is that a late deterioration takes place in some patients, probably those with the most severe and chronic forms of illness. In support of this, both global intellectual impairment and age disorientation have been found to increase in prevalence with advancing age in the chronically hospitalised population, and approximately two-thirds of such patients over the age of 65 are demented (Davidson *et al.*, 1995; Arnold *et al.*, 1995). Dwork *et al.* (1998) have speculated that a subtle neuronal pathology in schizophrenia reduces the normal 'cognitive reserve' which protects against dementia and lowers the threshold for the appearance of clinical cognitive impairment. This process could be either neurodevelopmental, interacting with normal age-related brain degenerative changes to produce dementia at a higher rate than seen in the normal elderly population; or alternatively might be very slowly progressive and give rise to dementia by itself in a few cases.

can be done is to demonstrate that a particular deficit is disproportionate to the overall level of general intellectual impairment, by methods ranging from covarying out overall intellectual impairment in the analysis, to selecting patients who meet some criterion of overall intellectual intactness, to a highly complicated (and rarely used) regression procedure developed by Chapman and Chapman (1973). A further method, advocated by Shallice (1988) to deal with not dissimilar problems in neuropsychology, is to complement group studies with those using the single case study approach.

This section examines the traditional areas of neuropsychological function in turn: perception (where almost all the work has been on vision), language, memory and executive (frontal) function, with particular reference to whether the deficits found meet the criterion of being disproportionate to the overall level of intellectual impairment. Where possible, findings from single case studies are included, one of the first and most illuminating of which was carried out by Shallice *et al.* (1991) on five chronically hospitalised patients who showed different degrees of general intellectual impairment.

Perception

Cutting (1985) reviewed a number of studies carried out in the 1950s, 1960s and 1970s and concluded that there was little evidence that the early stages of visual processing were impaired in schizophrenia. For example, critical stimulus duration, or the time for which an object has to be exposed in order to permit its correct identification, showed no evidence of slowing in acute or chronic schizophrenic patients. At the higher levels of visual perception, several studies reported that chronic schizophrenic patients had difficulties recognising out-of-focus pictures, figures embedded in other figures, and ambiguous figures. According to Cutting, however, the methodology of these studies was unsound in all cases.

A further visual perceptual paradigm, which has become a focus of some recent interest in schizophrenia, is backward masking. This procedure involves tachistoscopic presentation of an initial stimulus (the target), typically a single letter, for a period that would normally be sufficient for its identification. After a brief interval, a second, 'masking' stimulus is presented; this can be a pattern of overlapping Xs, a meaningful form, or even just a flash of light. If the interstimulus interval is short enough, subjects are no longer able to identify the target. The exact nature of the visual processes that backward masking interferes with remains unclear, but there is agreement that the early stages of visual processing are preferentially affected. A series of studies by Saccuzzo, Braff and co-workers (Saccuzzo *et al.*, 1974; Saccuzzo and Braff, 1981; Braff and Saccuzzo, 1985) and others (Weiner *et al.*, 1990; Weiss *et al.*, 1992; see also Green and Nuechterlein, 1994) have demonstrated that schizophrenic patients, both acute and chronic, require longer interstimulus intervals than normal controls to obtain the same degree of accuracy.

None of these studies, early or recent, made any reference to the issue of whether the impairment found was disproportionate to the overall level of poor performance in the disorder. For this it is necessary to turn to the single case study of Shallice *et al.* (1991). The performance of their five chronically hospitalised schizophrenic patients on eight tests of visual and visuospatial function covering both basic perceptual processes, such as figure–ground discrimination, and higher level processes, such as recognising objects from unusual views and from silhouettes, is shown in Table 8.5. Two patients, HE and HS, were relatively intellectually intact, as measured by a lack of a marked discrepancy between premorbid IQ, estimated by means of the National Adult Reading Test (NART) of Nelson (1982) and current IQ. They showed no failures on any tests. The third patient, RS, showed some evidence of general intellectual impairment – he showed no discrepancy between his estimated premorbid IQ and current IQ, but performed very poorly on another measure of current IQ, Raven's Matrices. He showed two failures on the tests. The last two patients, LE and GT, showed a substantial IQ decline and were grossly impaired on Raven's Matrices. They failed four and five of the tests respectively. This study therefore found nothing to suggest that impairment in visual perceptual processing in schizophrenia is anything other than a function of general impairment.

Language

Much of the large literature on this topic in schizophrenia has been concerned with the relationship between language and formal thought disorder – whether patients with the symptom show intrinsic abnormalities of language, and if so how far this resembles dysphasia. This question is addressed in the next chapter, and the focus here is only on studies that have examined language in schizophrenia as a whole.

Three main studies are usually cited, which administered batteries of aphasia tests to unselected groups of schizophrenic patients (DiSimoni *et al.*, 1977; Silverberg-Shalev *et al.*, 1981; Faber and Reichstein, 1981). These

Table 8.5 Neuropsychological test failures in five chronically hospitalised schizophrenic patients I: Visual, visuospatial function and language

	HE	HS	RS	LE	GT
Age	44	66	55	44	38
Estimated premorbid IQ (NART)	122	111	110	104	94
Current IQ (WAIS)	108	104	100	76	69
Raven's progressive matrices	0	1	3	3	3
Visual/visuospatial tests					
Figure–ground discrimination	0	0	0	3	0
Dot centring	0	0	0	0	3
Dot counting	0	0	0	0	0
Cube analysis	0	0	0	0	2
Unusual views	0	0	3	3	3
Usual views	0	0	3	3	3
Recognition from silhouettes	0	2	2	3	3
Figure copy	0	2	0	0	3
Total no. of tests failed	0	0	1	4	5
Language tests					
Graded Naming Test	0	0	0	1	3
Naming from description	1	0	3	3	3
Modified Token Test	0	0	3	3	3
Total no. of tests failed	0	0	2	2	3

Notes:
Scores 0–3 are impairment indexes derived from normative data. 0 = at or above 25th percentile; 1 = 10–25th percentile; 2 = 5–10th percentile; 3 = below 5th percentile, the usual criterion for failure.
The NART is based on the ability to pronounce words that do not follow the normal rules of pronunciation. This provides an index of whether the meaning of the word was once known that is relatively resistant to intellectual decline.

Source: Shallice *et al.* (1991), Can the neuropsychological case study approach be applied to schizophrenia? *Psychological Medicine*, 21, 661–673. Reproduced with permission from Cambridge University Press.

all found evidence of impairment on some but not all aspects of language performance, but the pattern of this differed substantially across the studies. For example, in the study of DiSimoni *et al.* (1977) the worst affected areas were relevance of expressed speech and comprehension of read material, and naming was found to be unimpaired. In contrast, Silverberg-Shalev *et al.* found that impairment was most marked for naming; comprehension of sentences and paragraphs was also impaired, but comprehension of simple commands, writing and repetition of words were normal. Faber and Reichstein (1981) tested 24 patients, who unlike in the other two studies met diagnostic criteria for schizophrenia, and 28 controls. They used tests from the Boston Diagnostic Aphasia Battery, plus additional tests of naming, and the Token Test, which assesses comprehension of grammar. In this study the patients were separated into groups with and without formal thought disorder, but when combined they performed significantly more poorly than the controls on some of the tests of naming, the Token Test, and also repetition of words and phrases. Most of the differences between the patients and controls were small.

Notable by its absence from all these studies was any consideration of the confounding effects of overall intellectual impairment. Shallice *et al.*'s (1991) single case study, however, included three tests of language, the Graded Naming Test, naming from description, and the Modified Token Test. Their findings are also shown in Table 8.5. Once again, the intellectually preserved patients HE and HS showed little evidence of impairment on these tests. RS, the patient with some degree of overall intellectual impairment, showed more evidence of poor performance, being impaired on 2 out of 3 tests. LE and GT, the patients with more severe general intellectual impairment, failed 2/3 and 3/3 tests respectively.

The emphasis in aphasia test batteries is on comprehension and naming, and expressed speech is typically only assessed qualitatively. However, Morice and Ingram (1982) carried out a linguistic analysis on free speech samples from 34 schizophrenic patients and 18 normal controls, matched for age, education and social class. With the aid of a computer program that identified dysfluencies (e.g. pause fillers and false starts), grammatical complexity, and syntactic and semantic errors, Morice *et al.* found that two main types of variable significantly distinguished the schizophrenic and control groups. The first was a set of items relating to reduced speech complexity. The other main dimension related to integrity of speech – the schizophrenic patients showed fewer well-formed sentences and more sentences containing both syntactic and semantic errors. These findings have been replicated in further studies (Fraser *et al.*, 1986; Hoffman and Sledge, 1988), which found that the errors in speech were more commonly syntactic than semantic. Oh *et al.* (2002) also found the same dysfluencies, simplification of grammar and within-sentence errors in expressed speech in a study of 11 patients using the single case study approach. Unlike impairment of comprehension and naming, in this study these expressive errors appeared to be independent of intellectual impairment. (This study, which included patients with and without formal thought disorder, had more to say about the issue of semantic versus syntactic errors in relation to this symptom and is discussed further in Chapter 9.)

Memory

After reviewing around 30 studies carried out between 1964 and 1981, Cutting (1985) came to what at the time seemed a surprising conclusion. This was that, while memory remained superficially intact in acute schizophrenic patients, poor memory was common in chronic patients and could sometimes amount to marked amnesia. Since then, a number of studies have appeared which suggest that memory is a major area of neuropsychological deficit in schizophrenia (e.g. Calev, 1984a, b; Calev *et al.*, 1987a, b; Goldberg *et al.*, 1989; Landro *et al.*, 1993; Paulsen *et al.*, 1995).

In a study that illustrates the typical pattern of findings, McKenna *et al.* (1990) examined the memory performance of a mixed sample of 60 remitted, acutely ill and chronically hospitalised patients using a relatively brief and undemanding test, the Rivermead Behavioural Memory Test (RBMT) of Wilson *et al.* (1985). As shown in Figure 8.7, whereas less than 5 per cent of a sample of 118 normal individuals originally used to standardise the test achieved a score of 7 or lower, more than 50 per cent of the schizophrenics scored at this level or below. Re-affirming the findings of an earlier generation of studies, the schizophrenics' performance was indistinguishable from that of a group of 176 patients attending a rehabilitation centre for brain injury. Memory impairment was by no means confined to old, chronic or deteriorated patients, and substantial deficits could sometimes be seen in acute or chronic but well-preserved patients, albeit less commonly.

In contrast to perception and language, the question of whether or not memory impairment in schizophrenia is disproportionate to the overall level of intellectual impairment has been explicitly addressed in several recent studies (see McKenna *et al.*, 2002). These, however, have had mixed findings. For example, Saykin *et al.* (1991) compared 36 chronic schizophrenic patients with 36 normal controls on a battery of tests covering memory, overall intellectual function, language, perception, motor performance and executive function. When performance was made comparable by means of z-transformation of the test scores, the schizophrenic patients' mean

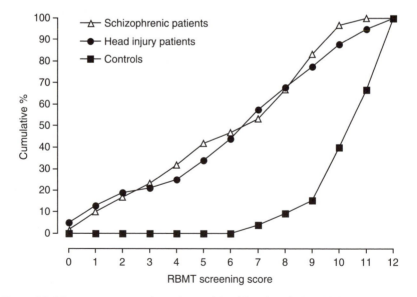

Figure 8.7 Memory test scores in patients with schizophrenia, head injury and normal controls (from McKenna *et al.*, 1990).

scores mostly fell between one and two standard deviations below those of the controls. Only the scores on three memory measures – composite scores for verbal memory, visual memory and learning – provided an exception, performance on these being depressed to nearly three standard deviations below the control group mean. However, this result was only partially replicated in a subsequent study by Saykin *et al.* (1994), which examined an extended group of 102 patients on the same battery. This time the patients showed evidence of a disproportionate deficit on three tests of verbal memory, but not on two tests of visual memory.

The evidence from Shallice *et al.*'s (1991) single case study is likewise equivocal on the point of a disproportionate memory deficit in schizophrenia. It can be seen from Table 8.6 that only one of the two intellectually preserved patients, HE and HS, showed any memory test failures, and these were infrequent. At the same time, RS failed nearly as many of the memory tests as the two intellectually impaired patients, despite having better preserved general intellectual function.

Shallice *et al.*'s study is also noteworthy for its suggestion of a dissociation between short-term and long-term memory performance in schizophrenia – all five of their patients were in the normal range on the prototypical short-term memory test, digit span, whereas three of them showed substantial

Table 8.6 The profile of neuropsychological impairment in five chronically hospitalised schizophrenic patients II: Memory

	HE	HS	RS	LE	GT
Age	44	66	55	44	38
Estimated premorbid IQ (NART)	122	111	110	104	94
Current IQ (WAIS)	108	104	100	76	69
Raven's progressive matrices	0	1	3	3	3
Memory tests					
Digit span	0	0	0	1	1
Story recall (immediate)	3	0	3	1	3
Story recall (delayed)	2	0	3	1	3
Figure recall (immediate)	0	0	1	3	3
Figure recall (delayed)	0	1	1	3	3
List learning (trials 1–5)	3	1	3	3	3
Paired Associates	0	0	3	—	3
Visual reproduction	0	0	0	1	3
Recognition memory (words)	0	0	2	0	1
Recognition memory (faces)	0	0	0	1	3
Total no. of tests failed	2	0	4	3	8

Notes:
1 = 10–25th percentile; 2 = 5–10th percentile; 3 = below 5th percentile, the usual criterion for failure.
Not all the memory tests are shown, due to the large number of these.

Source: Adapted from Shallice *et al.* (1991).

evidence of impairment on the long-term memory tests. This is the pattern that characterises the so-called classical amnesic syndrome (seen for instance in Korsakoff's psychosis). Tamlyn *et al.* (1992) found further evidence in support of an amnesic syndrome pattern in a single case analysis of five schizophrenic patients from the study of McKenna *et al.* (1990), who were selected on the basis that they scored in the moderately or severely impaired range on the Rivermead Behavioural Memory Test, but showed relatively well-preserved overall intellectual performance. None of the patients showed more than minor impairment on a range of short-term memory tests, despite obvious deficits in widespread areas of long-term memory.

Executive function

Although the concept of frontal lobe abnormality has dominated schizo-phrenia research for 25 years, the corresponding neuropsychological ques-tion of whether there is a dysexecutive syndrome in schizophrenia was neglected for some time. It was only after Weinberger *et al.*'s (1986) study finding of task-related hypofrontality that research got underway in earnest. An initial study by this group (Goldberg *et al.*, 1987) demonstrated that chronic schizophrenic patients showed impaired performance on a proto-typical executive test, the Wisconsin Card Sorting Test (WCST), which could not be improved by attempts to teach them how to do it.

Goldberg *et al.* (1988), and many others, went on to show that schizophrenic patients were impaired on other executive tasks besides the WCST, and there is now a long list of studies documenting impairment on tests such as verbal fluency, the Trail Making Test, part B, and the Stroop test, among others (e.g. see Elliott *et al.*, 1995; Velligan and Bow-Thomas, 1999). Another area of cognitive function requiring executive function is working memory, par-ticularly, as its name suggests, the central executive component of this. This has also regularly been found to be impaired in schizophrenic patients (see Keefe, 2000).

Whether executive impairment in schizophrenia is disproportionate to general intellectual impairment, however, is another matter. Laws (1999) reviewed 33 studies comparing schizophrenic patients to normal controls on a range of standard executive tests, and found that while all of these found significantly poorer performance on at least some of the tests used, 14 of them failed to include any non-executive control measures. Of those that did include one or more nominally non-executive tests, none provided unequivocal evidence for a selective deficit.

Laws (1999) also meta-analysed 29 studies using the Wisconsin Card Sorting Test and found that the effect size for impairment on this task was smaller than that for IQ in schizophrenia. This meta-analysis is sum-marised in Box 8.4. Henry and Crawford (2005) later meta-analysed 84 studies of verbal fluency in schizophrenia and reached the same conclusion.

Executive function was the main focus of interest in Shallice *et al.*'s single

Box 8.4 Meta-analysis of studies using the Wisconsin Card Sorting Test in schizophrenia (from Laws, 1999)

The Wisconsin Card Sorting Test (WCST) is the prototypical test of executive function, and is probably the one most widely used to assess executive function in schizophrenia. The author used meta-analysis to quantify the impairment and to compare this with the degree of impairment of general intellectual function in schizophrenia.

Twenty-nine studies were located in a search and included in the meta-analysis. Individual effect sizes were calculated for both the main WCST measures, categories achieved ($N = 23$) and perseverative errors ($N = 28$). After outliers were removed, the pooled effect size for WCST categories achieved was 0.91 (CI 0.76/1.05) (20 studies, 1064 subjects), in the large range, and 0.53 (CI 0.38/0.68) for perseverative errors ($N = 26$ studies, 1516 subjects), in the medium range. However, this latter value increased to 0.69 in studies using absolute measures of perseverative errors (several studies used the proportion of perseverative to non-perseverative or total errors).

WAIS IQ was used as an index of general intellectual impairment, and scores for patients and controls were reported, in 12 of the studies. The effect size for the IQ difference between schizophrenics and controls was 1.23 (CI 1.03/1.43). This was significantly larger than those for both WCST measures.

Laws concluded that, at a minimum, the poor WCST performance found in schizophrenia was neither selective nor disproportionate to the patients' current level of general intellectual functioning.

case study, and this had rather different findings. They administered 10 tests 'held to be sensitive to frontal lobe lesions' to their five chronically hospitalised schizophrenic patients. The findings are shown in Table 8.7. For the first time HE and HS showed convincing signs of impairment, failing 3/10 and 4/10 tasks respectively. This was in the setting of preserved IQ, normal performance on tests of visual perception and language, and only scattered poor performance on memory tests. The other three patients showed even more frequent test failures. Shallice *et al.* argued that impaired executive function was the common denominator of schizophrenic neuropsychological impairment – all five patients were impaired on at least some of the tests, and this stood out relative to the background level of cognitive functioning.

Conclusion

Attempting to explain the symptoms of schizophrenia in cognitive psychological terms has seen the exercise of much theoretical ingenuity but the

Table 8.7 The profile of neuropsychological impairment in five chronically hospital-ised schizophrenic patients III: Executive function

	HE	HS	RS	LE	GT
Age	44	66	55	44	38
Estimated premorbid IQ (NART)	122	111	110	104	94
Current IQ (WAIS)	108	104	100	76	69
Raven's progressive matrices	0	1	3	3	3
Executive tests					
Alternation task	0	0	3	0	3
Cognitive Estimates Test	3	0	3	3	3
Modified Wisconsin Card Sorting Test	3	0	3	1	1
Money's Road Map Test	0	3	3	3	3
Personal orientation test	0	0	3	3	3
Self-ordered pointing	0	3	3	3	3
Stroop: colour naming	2	3	0	3	3
Trail Making Test (B)	3	2	0	3	3
Verbal fluency (FAS Test)	0	1	2	0	0
Weigl-Golstein-Scheerer Sort	0	3	0	3	3
Total no. of tests failed	3	4	6	7	8

Notes: 1 = 10–25th percentile; 2 = 5–10th percentile; 3 = below 5th percentile, the usual criterion for failure.

Source: From Shallice *et al.* (1991), Can the neuropsychological case study approach be applied to schizophrenia? *Psychological Medicine*, 21, 661–673. Reproduced with permission from Cambridge University Press.

generation of few hard facts. There has been no general theory of schizo-phrenic symptoms to replace the discredited approach of defective selective attention. The only theory of delusions that has been tested, probabilistic reasoning bias, is in all probability a red herring; jumping to conclusions is a consequence of being schizophrenic, not of being deluded. All that the study of auditory hallucinations has yielded is a hint – no more – of a relationship with inner speech. It is only in the case of formal thought disorder that there have been anything approaching robust experimental findings. Interestingly, the two most productive cognitive psychological approaches to this syn-drome have revolved around abnormality in words, knowledge and concepts, and so at some fundamental level seem to implicate semantic memory (see McKenna and Oh, 2005).

Comparatively speaking, the approach of screening schizophrenic patients for neuropsychological deficits has on the other hand been wildly suc-cessful. Here, the evidence points to two axes of impairment in schizo-phrenia. One of these is a tendency to general intellectual impairment, which becomes increasingly clinically apparent with increasing severity and chronicity of illness, and whose most extreme expression is frank dementia in a small minority of patients. The other is a pattern of specific – in the sense of disproportionate – deficits that affect long-term memory and executive function. The former axis of impairment is conclusively established, whereas the existence of the latter is perhaps more open to debate, although most people accept that memory and executive deficits can be seen in some patients who show little or no evidence of general intellectual impairment.

The problem with the neuropsychological approach is that it has yielded little in the way of insights into the mechanisms of symptom formation. This has led to a number of attempts to combine elements of psychological and neuropsychological approaches into what is unsurprisingly referred to as the cognitive neuropsychology of schizophrenia. The success of this approach is examined in the next chapter.

9 The cognitive neuropsychology of schizophrenia

The work reviewed in the last chapter culminates in a riddle. How can the abundant evidence of neuropsychological impairment in schizophrenia be translated into a theory of its symptoms, many of which cannot be understood as deficits? Put in a slightly different way, if brain damage causes neuropsychological deficits, why does it not routinely also result in schizophrenic symptoms? One way of solving this riddle is by means of what has become known as the cognitive neuropsychological approach to schizophrenia (Frith, 1992) or cognitive neuropsychiatry (David, 1993; Halligan and David, 2001). The seeds of this approach are in fact contained in the above two questions themselves, both of which are oversimplifications: some symptoms of schizophrenia *are* deficits, and the gulf between other schizophrenic symptoms and the signs of brain damage may not be as wide as customarily thought.

At its most neuropsychological, the cognitive neuropsychological approach simply proposes that certain symptoms of schizophrenia resemble, are perhaps even identical to, particular forms of deficit produced by brain damage. The schizophrenic symptoms concerned are, of course, negative symptoms, and it hardly needs to be stated in light of hypofrontality and some of the other findings discussed in Chapter 5, that the neurological syndrome is the frontal lobe syndrome and its cognitive counterpart, the dysexecutive syndrome.

The most obvious example of brain damage resulting in symptoms that are not simply impairments is fluent dysphasia. Formal thought disorder invites comparison with this, since when it is severe it can give rise to completely incoherent speech accompanied by neologisms. However, the proposal that formal thought disorder is simply a form of dysphasia has more often invited criticism and attack. As a result cognitive neuropsychological approaches have begun to explore other aspects of language such as discourse and pragmatics, or have moved into different areas altogether. The main example of this latter type of approach has once again invoked frontal lobe function, this time arguing that executive impairment is capable of making speech difficult to follow.

It is always going to be difficult to apply concepts like impairment and loss of function to delusions and hallucinations, and these symptoms have few if any close parallels in neurology. At this point cognitive neuropsychological approaches have been forced to propose novel forms of abnormality whose relationship with neurology and neuropsychology is at best distant. Theories of this type have tended to be of the grand unifying variety, drawing on not just cognitive psychology and neuropsychology, but neuroanatomy, neurophysiology and neurochemistry, usually in ways that race far ahead of any established facts. There is just one exception – Frith's (1992) cognitive neuropsychological theory of schizophrenia – which is rigorous and has kept to the psychological level of explanation in an exemplary way. This argues that negative and disorganisation symptoms, plus also certain restricted forms of positive symptom, can all be understood in the by now familiar terms of impaired frontal/executive function.

Negative symptoms as a form of the frontal lobe syndrome

Kraepelin is often cited as the first author to identify the frontal lobes as a possible seat of the pathological process in schizophrenia. He (Kraepelin, 1913a) stated: 'On various grounds it is easy to believe that the frontal cortex, which is specially well developed in man, stands in closer relation to his higher intellectual abilities, and these are the faculties which in our patients invariably suffer profound loss in contrast to memory and acquired capabilities.' However, this was all he said on the subject, and he moved on swiftly to the motor cortex, which he implicated in catatonia, and then to the temporal lobes, which he speculated might be related to both formal thought disorder and auditory hallucinations.

Credit for the frontal lobe theory of schizophrenia really belongs to Kleist (1930, 1960). Way ahead of his time, he believed that the symptoms of schizophrenia were the direct result of focal brain disease. Rather less presciently, he argued that each of the many different subtypes of the ill-fated Wernicke–Kleist–Leonhard classification of schizophrenia (see Chapter 2) were the manifestation of dysfunction in a discrete region of the brain. He specifically implicated the frontal lobes in what would later be called negative symptoms. Thus the clinical picture of the subtype of drive-poor catatonia was dominated by a lack of spontaneity, particularly concerning speech, a symptom that was known to be due to frontal lobe lesions. He also considered that 'a simple affective devastation and an ethical flattening' seen in various of subtypes of hebephrenia was comparable with the changes of character that occurred in injuries and focal lesions of the orbital brain. Kleist (1930) also coined the term alogia. He used this to describe a failure in the thinking process, whose nature was not clearly specified but embodied elements of poverty of speech and lack of productivity of thought, which he believed was similar to symptoms seen in patients with brain damage affecting the left side of the brain, the frontal lobes or the brainstem.

Later Ingvar and Franzen (1974) also commented on the similarities between the symptoms seen in frontal lobe lesions and schizophrenic symptoms in their original functional imaging study of schizophrenia. They speculated that symptoms like reduced spontaneous movement and speech, perseveration, indifference, lack of concern and 'autism' in schizophrenia were the consequence of a decreased level of function in frontal structures, and observed that 'such defects were indeed evident in those of our patients who showed the most pronounced hypofrontality in their rCBF landscape' (Franzen and Ingvar, 1975). Descriptions of this type of schizophrenic symptom had not yet crystallised into the concept of negative symptoms, but when they did a few years later, the idea that these might be the manifestation of frontal lobe dysfunction cropped up in different ways in the work of a number of authors such as Levin (1984), Frith (1987; Frith and Done, 1988), and Liddle (1987b).

The definitive formulation of the frontal lobe hypothesis of negative symptoms was given by Weinberger (1988). Like Kleist and Ingvar and Franzen, he made the point that the negative symptoms of schizophrenia, including emotional dullness, impaired judgement, poor initiative, motivation and drive, decreased concern for personal hygiene, and social withdrawal, seemed similar to the clinical manifestations of frontal lobe disease, especially of the dorsolateral prefrontal cortex. He went on to emphasise a particular form of cognitive impairment that appeared to be associated with negative symptoms, on tests involving planning, problem solving, abstraction, set shifting and novel, non-routinised problem solving, which could be seen despite performance in the normal range on intelligence tests – in other words, a specific executive deficit. Finally, he evaluated the evidence for both these behavioural and cognitive features being due to prefrontal hypometabolism. He was aware of the conflicting findings concerning hypofrontality from the 10 or so functional imaging studies that had then been carried out, but cited his own recent study, which demonstrated prefrontal hypometabolism during performance of the Wisconsin Card Sorting Test (see Chapter 5).

These three elements of the frontal lobe theory of negative symptoms provide a convenient framework for testing it. In a way that serves as a model for the rest of this chapter, the evidence and sometimes lack of evidence for each of the propositions – phenomenological, neuropsychological and functional neuroimaging – is considered in turn.

Negative symptoms as a behavioural equivalent of the frontal lobe syndrome

It is one thing to note similarities between negative symptoms and the signs of frontal lobe disease, but another to show that the similarity is any more than casual and superficial. If nothing else, the frontal lobes form a large region of the brain and patients with the frontal lobe syndrome are quite heterogeneous.

Features of the frontal lobe syndrome with possible counterparts among negative schizophrenic symptoms, drawn from published case studies of frontal lobe damage and frontal dementia, are shown in Table 9.1. For some symptoms there appears to be a one-to-one correspondence: for example, the

Table 9.1 Features resembling negative schizophrenic symptoms described in neurological patients with the frontal lobe syndrome

---

Two patients with bilateral frontal lesions (Blumer and Benson, 1975)

Case 1: Tumour involving the anterior portion of the corpus callosum	Frequently stayed in bed until noon Generally experienced difficulty in getting going Never spoke on her own Slow in answering questions, giving only brief responses when queried Lack of concern for incontinence Extremely apathetic Subjective lack of enthusiasm and energy for almost anything
Case 4: Compound depressed fracture of the left frontal bone sustained in a traffic accident	Quiet and remote Did not initiate either a conversation or a request Speaks when spoken to but then lapses into silence Made no friends on the ward and spent most of his time sitting alone smoking Frequently incontinent of urine, occasionally of stool, which did not bother him Indifferent and unconcerned about his family visiting him on the ward

Patients with frontal lobe dementia (Neary *et al.*, 1988)

Case 1: Frontal lobe dementia	Mental slowing Increased apathy Neglect of personal hygiene and personal chores Bland affect Lacked persistence Did not volunteer conversation, and answers to questions economical and unelaborated Became increasingly apathetic
Case 2: Frontal lobe dementia	Neglect of personal hygiene Ceased to carry out domestic tasks Increasing perseverative and stereotyped speech
Case 3: Frontal lobe dementia	Lacking motivation Neglectful of self-care and personal hygiene Neglectful of domestic responsibilities Speech became more restricted than formerly: did not initiate conversation and answered questions monosyllabically or with maximum economy of mental effort Speech became increasingly repetitive and stereotyped
Case 4: Frontal lobe dementia	Apathetic and lacking motivation Did not initiate conversation, and responses to questions were brief and unelaborated Became totally dependent, making no attempt to wash or dress herself
Case 5: Frontal lobe dementia	Began to neglect his appearance and became increasingly withdrawn

(Continued overleaf)

Table 9.1 Continued

	Apathetic and inactive Displayed virtually no emotion or motivation Motor activity was generally slow Did not initiate conversation and responses were brief and often elicited only by continual encouragement

Four patients with frontal lobe degeneration (Miller *et al.*, 1991)

Case 1: Profound frontal and anterior temporal hypoperfusion	Socially withdrawn Stood immobile and mute at parties Apathetic
Case 2: Frontal and mild left temporal hypoperfusion	Socially withdrawn Apathetic Her elderly mother looked after the household chores
Case 6: Bifrontal atrophy and extensive bifrontal hypoperfusion, more marked in the right than left, with marked hypoperfusion in both anterior temporal lobes	Socially withdrawn Apathetic
Case 8: Bifrontal and bi-temporal atrophy and severe bifrontal and bitemporal hypoperfusion	Sloppy in dress Decreased speech output

Three cases where the area of focal damage lay in frontal regions (Shallice and Burgess, 1991)

Case 1: Extensive bifrontal damage following road traffic accident	Room was untidy with 'hotchpotch' piles of magazines on the floor Shopping, cleaning and laundry are done for him Did not organise any social activities
Case 2: Right frontal depressed skull fracture sustained in a road traffic accident	Untidy Only bathes if going somewhere important Shaving, changing his clothes or undergarments, washing his hair, and having his hair cut are only carried out when his wife tells him Hardly ever spontaneously tackles any domestic chores such as laundry, cleaning, cooking, making repairs or paying bills Wife organises all trips, outings and social contacts with relatives
Case 3: Extensive lesion to the left frontal lobe with atrophy causing enlargement of the frontal horn of the lateral ventricle. Also some atrophy in the left temporal lobe	Undertakes virtually no inessential or novel activities Very untidy, never puts things away Seldom goes out in the evening Others always arrange any social activities

Source: Rice (unpublished PhD thesis).

apathy of the frontal lobe syndrome seems to be similar if not identical to lack of volition in schizophrenia. Laconic speech is seen in the frontal lobe syndrome where it blurs into the syndrome of dynamic aphasia, in which there is little or no spontaneous speech. Poverty of speech is a leading negative symptom of schizophrenia and this similarly shades into complete mutism.

Some differences may be more apparent than real: for example the commonplace self-neglect/poor self-care in schizophrenic patients with negative symptoms turns up as a relatively little-known feature of the frontal lobe syndrome. The frontal lobe sign of perseveration is certainly seen in schizophrenia, although is not usually considered to be a negative symptom – but this could merely reflect the way symptoms are classified in the two disorders.

One area where there is more of a question mark concerns the affective changes seen in the two disorders. Even allowing for the fact that schizophrenic flattening of affect is a multifaceted phenomenon, whether there is any overlap with the emotional changes in the frontal lobe subsumed under terms like blandness, unconcern and coarsening of emotion is open to serious question. It may be that different vocabularies are being used to describe similar symptoms, but there is certainly no guarantee that this is the case. Other 'emotional' features of the frontal lobe syndrome include impulsiveness, irresponsibility and tactlessness, and these have no counterparts in negative symptoms; the restless interfering behaviour and sexual disinhibition described in some frontal patients seem completely incompatible with the concept.

Liddle (1987b), however, was able to suggest a way round this difficulty. He drew attention to a distinction made by Blumer and Benson (1975) (which they in turn attributed to Kleist) between two forms of the frontal lobe syndrome. One was an apathetic or 'pseudodepressed' type, characterised by apathy, slowness, indifference, and unconcern, and the other was a disinhibited or 'pseudopsychopathic' type, in which the patient showed a lack of normal adult tact and restraint and was prone to impulsive behaviour and outbursts of anger. Liddle equated the disinhibited form of the frontal lobe syndrome with the disorganisation syndrome in schizophrenia. In doing so, he echoed Kleist who, as mentioned above, considered that the changes of character and ethical regression of hebephrenia were comparable with focal lesions of the orbital brain.

The association between negative symptoms and executive impairment

One of the first contemporary authors to propose that negative symptoms were due to frontal lobe dysfunction was Liddle (1987b). He did so on the basis of an extension of his pioneering factor analytic study of schizophrenic symptoms described in Chapter 2, in which he correlated the 47 patients' scores on positive, negative and disorganisation syndromes with performance on a range of neuropsychological tests. He found that positive symptoms (reality distortion) did not correlate significantly with impairment on any of the tests. However, negative symptoms did, as did disorganisation, with the pattern of correlations being somewhat different for the two syndromes.

The neuropsychological battery Liddle used in this study did not actually include any tests of executive function, but Liddle and Morris (1991) subsequently had similar findings in a study using four executive tests. The same partially dissociated pattern of correlations was again found in this study, and this led Liddle to propose that the negative and disorganisation syndromes in schizophrenia were associated with – perhaps even resulted from – different executive deficits. The negative syndrome in particular appeared to be associated particularly with impairment in those aspects of executive function governing the self-directed generation of mental activity, whereas there were indications that disorganisation might reflect a specific difficulty in inhibiting inappropriate responses.

The neuropsychological correlates of positive, negative and disorganisation syndromes have been examined in over 20 further studies. Donohoe and Robertson (2003) reviewed a number of such studies that included both executive and non-executive measures, and a slightly modified and updated version of their table is shown in Table 9.2. As per Liddle's original findings, virtually all of these studies failed to find significant correlations between delusions and hallucinations and any neuropsychological measure. Many of these studies found significant correlations between negative symptoms (and disorganisation) and impairment on a range of executive tests. However, Liddle's contention that negative and disorganisation syndromes show different patterns of correlation with different executive tests was not clearly borne out. More seriously, these studies have made it abundantly clear that the neuropsychological correlates of negative symptoms and disorganisation are not specific to executive function. Significant correlations with IQ and memory impairment have often been found, and some studies have found associations with impairment in areas as diverse as sustained attention and visual perception.

Buchanan *et al.* (1994) examined the relationship between negative symptoms and executive function in a way that avoided some of the problems faced by correlational studies, particularly their use of large, unselected groups of schizophrenic patients, which inevitably samples a wide range of the intellectual impairment seen in the disorder. They compared 18 patients meeting their criteria for the 'deficit' form of schizophrenia (by which they meant those with enduring negative symptoms, with or without positive symptoms), 21 meeting their criteria for non-deficit schizophrenia (who showed only positive symptoms), and 30 normal controls. Their measures included four tests of executive function (the WCST, Stroop Test, Trail Making Test and verbal fluency) and four subtests of the Weschler Memory Scale-Revised. All three groups were matched for age and sex, and also for duration of illness. The

Table 9.2 Studies examining the neuropsychological correlates of positive, negative and disorganisation syndromes using a range of executive and non-executive tests

Study	Sample size	Positive symptoms	Negative symptoms	Disorganisation	Not significantly correlated with any syndrome
Brown and White (1992)	48	—	Trails A Trails B Verbal fluency WCST	Digit span	Drilled word span
Moritz et al. (2001)	47	—	Reverse digit span	Stroop Test WCST Trails B Digit span	IQ Trails A Verbal fluency
O'Leary et al. (2000)	134	—	Verbal fluency Trails B List learning Logical memory Paired associate learning Visual memory Circle As test	WCST IQ	Stroop test Continuous Performance Test
Eckman and Shean (2000)/Rowe and Shean (1997)	51	—	Digit vigilance	Trails B Trails A WCST Digit span Digit vigilance Logical memory	—

(*Continued overleaf*)

Table 9.2 Continued

Study	Sample size	Positive symptoms	Negative symptoms	Disorganisation	Not significantly correlated with any syndrome
Basso et al. (1998)	62	—	Trails B Verbal fluency WCST IQ Trails A	IQ Trails A	Positive symptoms correlated with better performance on Trails A and WCST
Norman et al. (1997)	87	Logical memory List learning	Logical memory Verbal fluency WCST	Visual memory	Figure recall Design fluency
Mohamed et al. (1999)	94	—	Verbal fluency WCST Trails A/B IQ Logical memory List learning Visual memory	—	Stroop test Continuous Performance Test Digit span Rey figure copy Rey figure recall
Pollice et al. (2002)	44	—	Digit span	Verbal memory WCST	Continuous Performance Test Tower of London Verbal fluency IQ

Source: Adapted from Donohoe and Robertson (2003).

results are shown in Table 9.3. Both groups of schizophrenic patients performed more poorly than the normal controls on all of the tests. The deficit patients also performed significantly more poorly than the non-deficit patients on two of the four executive measures. In contrast there were no significant differences between them on any of the memory measures.

The interpretation of these findings, which were not particularly strong in the first place, was not straightforward, however. Buchanan *et al.* also found that the deficit patients performed significantly more poorly than the non-deficit patients on one of two tests sensitive to parietal lobe dysfunction (which they included on the basis that previous studies had suggested such a difference). Additionally, the deficit patients had a significantly lower mean IQ than the non-deficit patients, and when this was controlled for the differences between the two patient groups was reduced to trend level on one of the executive tests (the Stroop Test) and became non-significant on the other (Trail Making Test, part B).

Negative symptoms and hypofrontality

Several studies examined the relationship between negative symptoms and hypofrontality using the older region-of-interest technique, with conflicting and overall unclear findings (e.g. Volkow *et al.*, 1987; Andreasen *et al.*, 1992; Tamminga *et al.*, 1992; Wolkin *et al.*, 1992). The pioneering voxel-based

Table 9.3 Performance of patients with deficit and non-deficit forms of schizophrenia on executive and non-executive tests

	Deficit *(N = 18)*	*Non-deficit* *(N = 21)*	*Controls* *(N = 30)*
Executive tests			
WCST % perseverative errors	0.31*	0.24*	0.14
Verbal fluency	29.7*	36.3*	44.3
Stroop Test	9.68*†	4.3	0
Trail Making Test (B)	0.17*†	0.04	0
Memory tests			
WMS-R Logical Memory	27.8*	37.0*	57.5
WMS-R Figural Memory/Visual Pairs	7.1*	8.8*	11.5
WMS-R Verbal Pairs	15.3*	18.0*	20.4
WMS-R Visual Reproduction	27.8*	29.0*	36.6
Other			
Mooney Faces	18.4*†	20.0	20.5
Benton Line Orientation	15.2*	7.8*	5.2

* significantly impaired compared to controls at $p < .05$
† significantly impaired compared to non-deficit patients $p < .05$
Source: Adapted from Buchanan *et al.* (1994).

study was performed by Liddle *et al.* (1992). They carried out resting PET in 30 chronic schizophrenic patients with stable clinical pictures and identified clusters of voxels that correlated significantly with the patients' scores on positive symptoms, disorganisation and negative symptoms. Negative symptoms were found to be associated principally with reduced flow in a large band of the prefrontal cortex, more marked on the left, which predominantly involved the dorsolateral region but also extended round the frontal pole into the medial prefrontal cortex and the anterior cingulate cortex. There was also a relatively circumscribed area of association with reduced flow in the left parietal lobe cortex. There were no regions of cortex where negative symptoms were associated with increased activity (but these were seen subcortically in the heads of both caudate nuclei). The findings are shown in Figure 9.1.

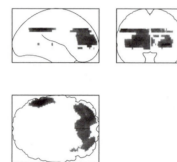

Negative correlations

Psychomotor poverty syndrome

Positive correlations

Figure 9.1 Functional imaging correlates of negative symptoms (psychomotor poverty) in schizophrenia (from Liddle *et al.* (1992), Patterns of cerebral blood flow in schizophrenia. *British Journal of Psychiatry*, 160, 179–186. Reproduced with permission from the Royal College of Psychiatrists).

Seven subsequent voxel-based studies are summarised in Table 9.4. Some of these, like Liddle *et al.*, looked for foci of activation or de-activation that correlated with negative symptom scores, but some compared the functional imaging appearances in patients with deficit and non-deficit schizophrenia. Four provided support for an association between negative symptoms and hypofrontality, in one case strong support: Potkin *et al.* (2002) compared seven (mainly chronic) patients with predominantly negative symptoms and seven with predominantly positive symptoms during performance of a vigilance task, and found that the former showed significantly reduced glucose meta-bolic rates across broad areas of the frontal lobes. The evidence from one study (Perlstein *et al.*, 2001) could be considered inadmissable, since the authors restricted their examination solely to the dorsolateral prefrontal cor-tex on the right. But this still leaves two studies with unequivocally negative findings. Kaplan *et al.* (1993) found no association between negative symp-toms and reduced prefrontal activity, but instead an association with increased flow/metabolism in an area of the left prefrontal cortex in a resting PET study of 20 acute schizophrenic patients. In the study of Honey *et al.* (2003), the significant associations were also with increased flow/metabolism, which were in the frontal lobe but not in the prefrontal cortex.

The cognitive neuropsychology of formal thought disorder

So far, the cognitive neuropsychological approach to explaining symptoms has been exclusively neuropsychological – a schizophrenic syndrome, nega-tive symptoms, is simply argued to be a psychiatric analogue of a neurological disorder, the frontal lobe syndrome. The same simplistic approach can be and has been applied to the symptom of formal thought disorder, as the hypoth-esis that it represents a form of dysphasia. However, there is more to language than what is affected by the crude destructive effects of neurological lesions, and it seems possible, even likely, some of these higher levels of speech might be affected in schizophrenia. The linguistic approach to formal thought dis-order also has a rival in the frontal lobe hypothesis of disorganisation, alluded to earlier. Between them, these approaches start to amount to something that is genuinely cognitive neuropsychological in nature.

Formal thought disorder as a form of dysphasia

The original proponent of this view was once again Kleist (1914, 1930, 1960; see also McKenna and Oh, 2005). In patients with his speech confused subtype of schizophrenia, he stated: 'We are . . . dealing with *sensory aphasic impair-ments* similar to those found in focal brain lesions of the *left temporal lobe*' (Kleist, 1960, italics in original). He argued that some thought-disordered patients showed many paraphasias, a hallmark symptom of fluent dysphasia where a word similar in sound or meaning is substituted for the correct one. He also considered that schizophrenic patients showed other disorders that

Table 9.4 Voxel-based functional imaging studies of negative symptoms in schizophrenia

Study	Sample	Duration of illness (years)	Technique	Associations with decreased flow/metabolism	Associations with increased flow/metabolism	Comment
Kaplan et al. (1993)	20 patients Drug free	4.3	FDG PET resting		l. dorsal prefrontal l. dorsal parietal	—
Heckers et al. (1999)	16 patients Drug treated	17.8	¹⁵O PET during memory task	r. and l. prefrontal r. parietal r. middle temporal gyrus r. superior temporal gyrus		Compared deficit and non-deficit patients
Lahti et al. (2001a)	18 patients Drug free	11.9	¹⁵O PET during auditory discrimination task	l. + r. middle frontal cortex		Compared deficit and non-deficit patients Similar findings in control task
Menon et al. (2001)	11 patients Drug treated	Not stated	fMRI during working memory task	l. + r. posterior inferior prefrontal cortex (frontal operculum)		—
Perlstein et al. (2001)	17 patients Drug treated	13.9	fMRI during working memory task			Only examined r. dorsolateral prefrontal cortex

Potkin *et al.* (2002)	14 patients Drug free	16.7	FDG PET during vigilance task	l. + r. frontal pole l. medial prefrontal cortex l. anterior inferior frontal gyrus l. + r. posterior inferior frontal gyrus r. dorsolateral prefrontal cortex	—	Compared deficit and non-deficit patients Differences found in broad areas of the frontal lobe
Honey *et al.* (2003)	30 patients Drug treated	13.0	fMRI during working memory task	—	l. + r. lateral premotor l. + r. supplementary motor area r. posterior parietal cortex	—

were essentially linguistic in nature but which were not seen in neurological forms of aphasia. One of these was a disorder of word formation: a patient called a clock a 'time container', a brush a 'pluck container' and a law court a 'people container'; others referred to the fins of a fish as 'swimming wings'; a candle was described as a 'night illuminating object', a military insignia as 'service quality defined rank decoration'. Some patients used the same words over and over again, for example one used the word 'build' for any kind of useful activity. Also in this category was what Kleist called paragrammatism, where there was an incorrect use of auxiliary words, prefixes and suffixes, combined with an overproduction of word sequences, which resulted in confusing and monstrous language.

Kleist also noted that it was extraordinary that there was no comprehension deficit ('word deafness') in speech-confused schizophrenia, similar to that seen in Wernicke's aphasia. Some patients had difficulty finding words ('word amnesias'), but this played a minor role in comparison to its frequent occurrence in aphasia. (All known forms of fluent aphasia are characterised by some degree of impaired comprehension of speech and naming, hence the importance Kleist attached to the lack of these.)

Kleist's views provoked debate (e.g. Critchley, 1964; Benson, 1973), but gained no acceptance during his lifetime. It was a linguist, Chaika (1974) who re-awakened the controversy with an analysis of the speech of a 37-year-old chronically hospitalised schizophrenic woman who showed obvious incoherence. In the midst of this Chaika observed abnormalities which she argued could only be understood as being linguistic in nature. For example, after entering the room, spying a packet of cigarettes and picking it up, the patient said:

> Good mornin' everybody! (lower pitch, doubtfully) I don't know what that is. (laughs). The(re) sawendon saw turch faw jueri.

The string of neologisms (which Chaika referred to as gibberish) was uttered as if they were meaningful words, with no pause or stress before, during or after them. Each conformed to the stress and phonemic rules of English, and were produced according to the phonological rules of the patient's southern American uneducated dialect.

Generally, the patient showed little disturbance in her syntax. However, she did make one incontrovertible syntactic error at one point, using the article 'a' instead of 'the':

> In a month I've been upstairs, they've been taking my brains out a piece at a time or all together.

Chaika also argued that some of the more familiar features of formal thought disorder the patient showed betrayed a disruption of the ability to apply rules of language. She gave examples of clang associations and derailment, which she reconceptualised as production of sentences according to the phonological and semantic features of previously uttered words, rather than according to topic. She was also struck by the fact that the patient did not appear to notice anything odd in her speech and made no attempt to correct errors when they occurred.

Chaika concluded that these linguistic aberrations did in fact suggest that there is a disturbance in those areas of the brain concerned with language, although she stopped short of identifying thought disorder as a form of dysphasia. Her study led to a flurry of further case studies in which linguists exchanged views on whether linguistic mechanisms were disturbed and if so what were the similarities and differences to dysphasia (Fromkin, 1975; Lecours and Vanier-Clément, 1976; Herbert and Waltensperger, 1980; Hoffman and Sledge, 1984). However, in every case the arguments revolved around the fine points of linguistic theory and none of them decided the case either way.

Faber *et al.* (1983) sidestepped the theoretical debate altogether and attacked the problem pragmatically. They recorded interviews with 14 thought-disordered schizophrenic patients and 13 patients with dysphasia (which was fluent in 11 cases and non-fluent in the remaining two). They then made transcripts of the interviews, from which all references to age, psychiatric or neurological symptoms, drug treatment, and so on were removed, and presented these under blind conditions to two psychiatrists, two neurologists and a speech and language pathologist (equivalent to a speech therapist in the UK). Neither of the neurologists scored significantly above chance (both were correct in 18/27 cases). The psychiatrists performed somewhat better (correct in 20/27 and 22/27 cases respectively). The speech pathologist did best of all (correct in 25/27 cases), but even she was not completely successful. Her success was based on the facts that the schizophrenic patients were fluent, showed adequate auditory comprehension of questions, and used multisyllabic words, whereas the aphasic patients showed comprehension deficits, word finding problems, impaired naming, and used a reduced number of nouns.

The speech pathologist also blindly categorised the specific types of linguistic and thought abnormality she found in each transcript. The findings are shown in Table 9.5. It can be seen that the schizophrenic patients were frequently rated as showing paraphasias and the dysphasic patients were almost as frequently rated as showing poverty of content of speech.

Oh *et al.* (2002) explored this issue further in a study applying the single case study approach to six chronic schizophrenic patients with severe formal thought disorder and seven without the symptom. They found that all of the thought-disordered patients showed evidence of semantic errors that occurred within individual sentences, in contrast to only minimal evidence of this in the non-thought-disordered patients. These included paraphasias, for example: ' 'Cause it's [a boat] near the shore and it wouldn't *drown*'. Words were also used in a semantically unacceptable way: 'Oh it [life in a hospital] was superb, you know, the trains broke and the pond fell in the front doorway' – the

Table 9.5 Language abnormalities rated blindly in dysphasic patients and schizo-phrenic patients with formal thought disorder

	Dysphasic patients (N = 13)	Schizophrenic patients (N = 14)	p value
Paraphasias	8	9	NS
Agrammatism	2	0	NS
Impaired comprehension of speech	5	0	0.04
Anomia/word finding problems	7	0	0.01
Pronoun word problems	4	0	NS
Circumlocutions	1	0	NS
Neologisms	1	3	NS
Word approximations/ idiosyncratic use of words	0	8	0.01
Perseveration	1	4	NS
Incoherence	3	10	NS
Derailment/tangentiality	2	11	0.05
Poverty of content	8	1	0.04
Illogicality	1	5	NS
Clanging	0	3	NS

Source: Faber *et al.* (1983), Comparison of schizophrenic patients with formal thought disorder and neurologically impaired patients with aphasia. *American Journal of Psychiatry*, 140, 1348–1351. Copyright 1983, the American Psychiatric Association. Reprinted by permission.

propositional features of *pond* do not allow it fall in doorways. In some sentences, words were simply combined in a way that defied meaning: 'Seems to be like a white, like a white space deck hand, which is white all over and coloured like a white sort of dome-type hand.' Various categories of syntactic error were also found (see Chapter 8), but these were evenly distributed between the thought-disordered and non-thought-disordered patients. As Kleist originally noted, and was also evident in the study of Faber *et al.*, these errors occurred in the setting of largely preserved comprehension of speech, and naming. An important point was that within-sentence speech abnor-mality was relatively uncommon, with semantic errors occurring in less than 10 per cent of the thought-disordered patients' expressed speech.

Formal thought disorder as non-aphasic language disturbance

Kleist (1960) qualified his otherwise uncompromising views on formal thought disorder, stating that the only difference from neurological forms of aphasia was the involvement in schizophrenia of higher levels of speech 'responsible for word derivations, word constructions, the formation of sen-tences, and for the abstract meaning of speech conceptions – i.e. the thinking based on speech'. Chaika (1974) too expressed a not dissimilar view when she stated that the propositional content of individual sentences was usually understandable and the oddity of her patient's speech seemed mostly to be caused by aberrations in the structure of her discourse – in other words at the level of the connection between sentences, rather than the individual sentences themselves. She attributed some of the abnormality at this level to the patient's failure to use the discourse markers necessary to show connections and orient listeners to her topic. This can be seen in a further extract of the patient's speech:

> Nobody takes my word for what I wanna do. Not even God. I believe I'll try anyhow. (declaiming) I believe in the spirit of the mountains. Right now I'm thinking Pike's Peak for a rehaul of the Korean thing.

There is nothing in what the patient said in the preceding sentence (or any others) to clarify what Korean thing she was referring to.

Rochester and Martin (1979) also felt that much of what made schizophrenic speech difficult to follow lay in stretches of speech longer than the individual sentence. In particular they hypothesised that some of the abnormality might reflect a failure to abide by the devices speakers normally use to link sentences together into coherent 'texts'. Five such types of cohesive ties are recognised in English: reference, substitution, ellipsis, conjunction and lexical cohesion. Examples of these are shown in Box 9.1.

To test this hypothesis, Rochester and Martin obtained speech samples from two groups of 10 patients meeting an early set of diagnostic criteria for schizophrenia. One group was rated clinically as showing formal thought disorder, and the other showed no evidence of this; otherwise they were both relatively young, averagely educated, acutely ill patients. There was also a control group of 10 normal subjects. Transcripts of speech were analysed for the presence of various classes of cohesive ties. Both groups of schizophrenic speakers were found to use significantly fewer cohesive ties than the normal speakers; however, no significant difference between the thought-disordered and non-thought disordered patients was found for any of the four types of cohesive tie analysed (substitution accounted for less than 1 per cent of the ties and so was not examined).

While there was thus little to suggest that thought-disordered patients used quantitatively fewer cohesive ties, there were more grounds for believing that the way in which they used them was abnormal. Rochester and Martin went on to examine in more detail the patients' use of one particular class of cohesive tie, reference – where a personal pronoun (he, she, they, etc.), a demonstrative (e.g. this, that, etc.) or a comparative (smaller than, equal to, etc.) – is used to replace a noun or a proper noun. Their analysis was highly technical, but the main finding was that thought-disordered subjects showed more instances of unclear reference than both the non-thought-disordered patients and the normal controls.

Three further studies have also failed to find evidence that patients with formal thought disorder use fewer cohesive ties than those without the symptom (Harvey, 1983; Chaika and Lambe, 1989; McKenna and Oh, 2005). At

Box 9.1 Halliday and Hasan's five types of cohesive tie in English (from McKenna and Oh, 2005)

Reference
This can be seen as a direction for interpreting an element in terms of its environment. In the following example, *he* is interpreted to mean *John*, who has been mentioned previously.

John was my best friend at school. He taught me how to climb trees.

In English, personals (*he, she, they*, etc.), demonstratives (*this, that*, etc.) and comparatives (*smaller than, equal to, same*, etc.) make up reference items.

Substitution
This is the replacement of one item by another, as in:

I like your dress. Is it a new one?

Here, *one* is a substitute for *dress*. Only the items *one(s), same, do, so*, and *not* can occur as substitutes.

Ellipsis
Put simply, ellipsis can be defined as substitution by zero. It occurs when something that is structurally necessary is left unsaid, for example:

Do you have a light? Yes, I have . . .

Utterances that did not make use of ellipsis and substitution would appear stilted and unusually formal, or else signal to the listener that there was some significance in repeating what could have been left out.

Conjunction
There are four types of conjunctive relations, each expressing a different relationship: additive, adversative, causal and temporal. An example of each (underlined) is shown below.

She worked all day, almost without stopping.

And in all this time, no one offered her a drink. (additive)
Yet she was not aware of being tired. (adversative)
So by the time she finished, she was tired. (causal)
Then, when it got dark, she stopped. (temporal)

Lexical cohesion
Here the cohesive effect achieved is by the selection of vocabulary. This can be achieved in two ways, reiteration and collocations. Reiteration is a form of lexical cohesion that involves (at one end of the scale) the repetition of a lexical item, the use of a general word to refer back to a lexical item (at the

other end of the scale), and in between, the use of a synonym, near-synonym or superordinate. For example:

I turned to the ascent of the peak.

The <u>ascent</u> was perfectly easy. (same word)
The <u>climb</u> was perfectly easy. (synonym)
The <u>task</u> was perfectly easy. (superordinate)
The <u>thing</u> was perfectly easy. (general word)

Cohesion can also be achieved through collocation, or the association of pairs of words that regularly co-occur. The cohesive effect of such pairs is achieved more by their tendency to share the same lexical environment, i.e. to occur in collocation with each other. This category includes pairs of opposites such as complementaries (*boy – girl, stand up – sit down*), antonyms (*love – hate, wet – dry*) and converses (*order – obey*). It would also include pairs of words drawn from the same ordered series (*Tuesday – Thursday*), or unordered lexical sets (*road – rail, red – green*). There is also the possibility of cohesion between any pair of lexical items that are in some way associated with each other in the language, but whose meaning relation is not easy to classify in systematic semantic terms (e.g. *laugh – joke, blade – sharp*). Cohesion achieved through this sort of lexical relationship is not limited to pairs of words; it is possible also for long cohesive chains to occur (e.g. *poetry . . . literature . . . reader . . . writer . . . style*).

the same time, these and several other studies (Docherty *et al.*, 1988; Docherty and Gordinier, 1999; Docherty *et al.*, 2003) have been surprisingly consistent in finding unclear reference or other erroneous use of cohesive ties in association with formal thought disorder. Some examples of these abnormalities are shown in Table 9.6.

Beyond language: The dysexecutive hypothesis of formal thought disorder

Even Kleist did not believe that all the disordered speech seen in schizophrenia resulted from language abnormality. He (Kleist, 1930) identified two disorders of thought that were often but not necessarily seen in association with linguistic abnormalities. One of these was alogia, as described earlier. The other was paralogia, a breakdown in the conceptual processes underlying speech. Kleist described this even less clearly than alogia, but he seemed to be referring to a breakdown in the ability to make connections between concepts that led them to be replaced by loosely connected ideas or to emerge in incomplete or fragmentary fashion.

Kleist did not relate paralogia to the frontal lobes. However, when Liddle (1987b) drew parallels between disorganisation in schizophrenia and the

Table 9.6 Examples of erroneous use of cohesive ties by patients with formal thought disorder

Cohesive tie	Example	Comment
Reference	But uh . . . my father was not a machine, my father wasn't a machine | but . . . he got him from a . . . a little baby inside a capsule.	Referent is ambiguous and not in text.
Conjunction	It's a picture of a circus ring. | <u>But</u> the ring master is in it.	The semantic relation that conjunctive device is signifying is obviously wrong, i.e. should be 'and' instead of 'but'.
Ellipsis	I: What kind of work were you doing before you became ill? E: Portering. I: Can you tell me a bit more about that? E: . . . . . . Won't be nice. I: I'd like to hear about it. E: [ø] Rubbish. I: Can you explain a bit more? E: Very simple. Just clearing rubbish out of bins, I think.	[ø] signifies ellipsis in an inappropriate place. Here the use of ellipsis by the patient (E) results in an ambiguous response to the listener's (I) question.
Lexical cohesion	When people who come in here shouldn't try to get out, we ought to be locked up, and put into . . . a pair of hand<u>cuffs</u>! | Where do you get your <u>cuff</u> links from?	The second word of the same-word pair did not contribute to the cohesiveness, or appeared in a sentence that did not follow from the previous one.
Lexical cohesion	(Describing cookie theft picture) She has over-filled the <u>sink</u>. | She refused to pay the babies and <u>sink</u> which is what they do in these days.	Repetition of word in a way that does not contribute to lexical cohesion.

\| = sentence boundary
Source: McKenna and Oh (2005).

disinhibited form of the frontal lobe syndrome, he noted that more than one author had commented on garrulous speech as a feature of the latter. He cited one of Blumer and Benson's (1975) patients who replied to a question about whether his head injury had affected his thinking in the following way: 'Yeah – it's affected the way I think – it's affected my senses – the only things I can taste are sugar and salt – I can't detect a pungent odor – ha ha – to tell you the truth it's a blessing this way.' Other authors writing on the frontal lobe syndrome have made similar observations, for example: 'A tendency exists toward perseveration, confabulation and free association of ideas' (Novoa and Ardila, 1987); and 'Tangential, irrelevant comments are frequent and a vague rambling quality characterizes their verbal communication' (Alexander *et al.*, 1989). Kaczmarek (1984), in a study of patients with brain tumours in different locations, found that what he called digressions were almost exclusively seen in the frontal patients, where they were most pronounced in those with left orbitofrontal lesions. This group also showed an appreciable rate of misnamings.

At a theoretical level, authors like McGrath (1991) and Frith (1992), and also Chaika (1990, 1996) in her later work, have suggested how features of the dysexecutive syndrome, such as poor planning, monitoring and error correction, might give rise to some of the phenomena of formal thought disorder when they affected speech. Thus failure to establish a set, or in this case a focus for one's intended communication, could lead to the patient conveying little information and so result in the symptom of poverty of content of speech. Inability to plan, sequence and edit communications 'online' as they were being executed would render the speaker unable to organise his thoughts into the right linear sequence. Failure of monitoring could lead to speech being captured by irrelevant associations, which the speaker would also be unaware of and fail to correct. A further monitoring failure, this time the two-way interactions that take place in communication, might lead to the needs of the listener not being taken into consideration, a proposal that is discussed in more detail in the section on Frith's theory.

As indicated earlier in Table 9.2, there is no shortage of studies that have found significant correlations between the disorganisation syndrome in schizophrenia and impairment on executive tests. As in the case of negative symptoms, however, there have also been negative findings, and it is clear that the association is far from exclusive, as significant correlations have also been found with memory, other non-executive tests and general intellectual impairment. To date, there has been only one study that avoided the noise associated with use of a correlational design. Barrera *et al.* (2005) administered five executive tests to 15 schizophrenic patients with formal thought disorder and 16 with no evidence of the symptom. Seventeen normal controls were also tested. All patients were relatively generally intellectually intact, according to the criterion of having a current WAIS IQ of 85 (i.e. within one standard deviation of the normal population mean). The findings are shown in Table 9.7. The thought-disordered patients were found to perform

Table 9.7 Mean scores for schizophrenic patients with and without formal thought disorder and normal controls on tests of executive function

	FTD (N = 15)	NonFTD (N = 16)	Controls (N = 17)
Brixton Test	2.1*†	6.6	6.6
Hayling Test (errors)	2.1*†	6.2	6.1
Modified Six Elements Test	1.7*†	3.1	3.9
Cognitive Estimates Test (error score)	9.3*†	5.1	3.6
Verbal fluency (letter S)	14.5*	14.7*	20.2
Verbal fluency (animals)	17.0*	19.2*	24.7

* Significantly impaired compared to controls.
† Significantly impaired compared to non-thought-disordered patients.
Source: Barrera *et al.* (2005).

significantly more poorly than the non-thought-disordered patients on all the executive tests apart from verbal fluency. The non-thought-disordered patients also showed some degree of poorer performance than the normal controls on all the tasks, but the differences only reached significance on one of these, the Six Elements Test.

Barrera *et al.*, did not build non-executive control tasks into the design of their study. However, the study did include a test of naming and three other semantic tasks, as a test of a second hypothesis concerning the relationship of semantic memory impairment to formal thought disorder. Here the differences were considerably less marked: the patients with formal thought disorder differed significantly from those without on only one of the four tests.

Functional imaging of formal thought disorder

In Liddle *et al.*'s (1992) PET study of 30 stable chronic schizophrenic patients, disorganisation was significantly associated with reduced blood flow in Broca's area in the left frontal cortex, not strictly in the prefrontal cortex, and in a roughly similar but more anterior region on the right. This area did not overlap to any significant extent with that associated with negative symptoms. There was also an association with reduced flow in a posterior cortical region, the angular gyrus. The most marked association with increased flow was for the anterior cingulate cortex and adjacent areas of the medial prefrontal cortex. Temporal lobe abnormality did not figure prominently as a correlate of disorganisation, although an association was seen with overactivity in a circumscribed region of the left superior temporal sulcus. The findings are shown in Figure 9.2.

None of these findings were replicated in Kaplan *et al.*'s (1993) study carried out on 20 acute patients. This study found no correlations with increased activity, but there was an association with reduced activity in left superior temporal and adjacent parietal regions.

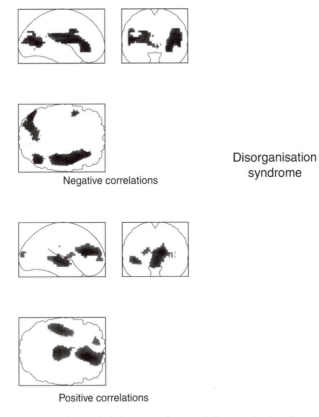

Disorganisation syndrome

Negative correlations

Positive correlations

Figure 9.2 Functional imaging correlates of disorganisation in schizophrenia (from Liddle *et al.* (1992), Patterns of cerebral blood flow in schizophrenia. *British Journal of Psychiatry*, 160, 179–186. Reproduced with permission from the Royal College of Psychiatrists).

Both these studies were carried out under resting conditions. Based on the assumption that the functional neuroanatomical correlates of formal thought disorder might be best revealed during the production of incoherent speech, McGuire *et al.* (1998) employed something akin to task activated functional imaging. They scanned six thought-disordered schizophrenic patients using PET while they described a series of deliberately ambiguous pictures from the Thematic Apperception Test. The patients' responses were recorded and rated for formal thought disorder by an investigator who was blind to the neuroimaging findings. In this way it was possible to establish areas where there were significant correlations between brain activity and production of thought-disordered speech (this analysis corrected for the number of words produced). Production of thought-disordered speech was associated with increased activity in a restricted area of the medial temporal lobe cortex adjacent to the hippocampus on the left, and to a smaller extent on the right. The areas where there was reduced activity in association with thought-disordered speech were more extensive and included the left inferior frontal cortex, the anterior insula, a left temporal region centred on the superior temporal gyrus, and the central area of the cingulate gyrus. The right inferior frontal cortex was also involved.

The finding of reduced activity in the left superior temporal gyrus in association with production of thought-disordered speech was again found in replication of this study by the same group (Kircher *et al.*, 2001). However, in this study there were no associations with underactivity in the prefrontal cortex.

Liddle *et al.*'s and McGuire *et al.*'s finding of an association between disorganisation and an area of reduced prefrontal cortex activity different from that associated with negative symptoms accords quite well with its alleged basis in a 'disinhibited' frontal lobe type picture, although it has to be borne in mind that it has not been found in all studies, and in Liddle *et al.*'s study it was more on the right, and so on the wrong side for verbal responses. A more consistent finding has been that formal thought disorder is associated with underactivity in areas of the temporal lobe cortex associated with language.

Positive symptoms (reality distortion)

One is hard pressed to find neurological diseases that feature delusions and hallucinations as characteristic symptoms. Phenomena like confabulation, reduplicative paramnesia and anosognosia can, with varying degrees of difficulty, be characterised as false beliefs, but whether they are delusions in any more than the technical sense is a matter of debate. Extremely few neurological disorders ever feature verbal auditory hallucinations, and it is fair to say that in none of these do they take the form of extended speech. The only author to propose any kind of cognitive neuropsychological account of these symptoms has been Frith (1992), who has attempted to explain certain classes of positive symptom in terms of a specialised form of executive dysfunction. In order to understand his approach to these symptoms, it is first necessary to briefly outline his general theory.

Frith's (1992) point of departure was an explanation of negative symptoms. In a similar way to other authors, he proposed that these were a consequence of frontal lobe dysfunction. However, he went further: first, he argued that the common denominator of these symptoms was lack of behaviour – of action, speech, emotional expression and social interactions – but, second, this did not apply to all actions. In his words: 'It is not the case, however, that the patient cannot or will not do anything when asked; patients are usually compliant and will perform complex psychological tests and answer difficult questions . . . The lack of behaviour in patients with negative features seems to occur specifically in situations in which actions have to be self-generated.' He therefore proposed that lack of volition and poverty of speech reflected a failure to form willed intentions, a proposal that fitted in well with failure in what was and still is the leading model of executive function, Shallice's (1988) supervisory attentional system. Direct consequences of failure in the supervisory attentional system would also be the occurrence other symptoms seen in schizophrenia, such as perseveration and certain forms of stereotyped behaviour.

With respect to formal thought disorder, Frith was rather dismissive of the dysphasia hypothesis and argued that the lack of a comprehension deficit pointed to abnormality at the level of language use rather than language competence. Like McGrath (1991), he proposed that an executive impairment would cause thought-disordered patients to fail to structure their discourse in such a way that the listener could understand how the various components linked together or what the purpose of the communication might be. This led on to a consideration of discourse and a disorder of cohesion, and then to the broader field of cooperative processes in communication and the proposal that schizophrenic thought disorder is caused in part by the patient's failure to make the appropriate inferences about the listener's knowledge, beliefs and intentions. As Frith (1992) put it, 'The normal speaker takes account of the listener's lack of knowledge, and thus the schizophrenic listener can understand. The schizophrenic speaker does *not* take account of the listener's lack of knowledge, and thus the listener has difficulty in understanding.'

Another type of monitoring played a key role in Frith's explanation of positive symptoms. His proposal here was that certain, characteristically schizophrenic, forms of delusion and hallucination – in other words some first rank symptoms – could be understood in terms of a failure in the self-monitoring of actions. Specifically, he implicated a rapid form of self-monitoring known as corollary discharge, efference copy or re-afference copy, which takes place as movements begin to be executed and before there has been time for any sensory feedback. The mechanism depends on a comparison being made centrally between the intention to move and a copy of the actual movement instructions. This is then used to correct the movement during its elaboration.

Frith used the example of eye movements to illustrate this (see Box 9.2). He also cited evidence for the existence of a similar control system for limb movements. Some of this was from studies of error correction in normal human subjects, where it has been shown that errors of movement can be detected and corrected in the absence of visual feedback, and too quickly for somatosensory information to have been used.

It is not difficult to envisage that the normal operation of such a monitoring system might contribute to a feeling that one's willed actions are self-generated. It is then a small step to imagine failure in such a system leading to a feeling that one's actions are no longer one's own. This could then plausibly lead onto a misattribution of one's willed actions to an external agent, by which time the experience would be one of passivity. This explanation is less easy to apply to another 'alien control' symptom, thought insertion, as there is no associated overt behaviour. However, Frith cited Feinberg (1978) who argued that monitoring mechanisms like corollary discharge could also apply

Box 9.2 Corollary discharge and its sensory consequences (from Frith, 1992)

Long ago, Helmholtz pointed out that each time we move our eyes, our image of the world moves across the retina. Yet the world stays still. Thus we are able to distinguish between movement on the retina due to movements in the world and movements on the retina due to our own movements. In order to achieve this, a 'corollary discharge' is sent to some monitor system at the same time as a message is sent to the eye muscles. On the basis of this message, movement of the image on the retina is expected. Compensation occurs and the image is perceived as stationary. Thus, a distinction is made between movements of images due to our own eye movements and movements that are independent of us. This distinction is achieved by monitoring intentions to make eye movements.

This mechanism depends upon a comparison between intentions to move and actual movements. Misleading discrepancies can be introduced into the system in at least two ways. Helmholtz observed that, if we move our eye by poking it with our finger, the image of the world appears to jerk. In this case no message has arrived indicating an intention to use the eye muscles. The opposite kind of disruption can be achieved by partially paralysing the eye muscles with curare. In this case a message is sent indicating an intention to move the eyes, but the expected movement does not occur. The world appears to move in the direction in which the movement would have occurred. In this example of eye movements, 'feed forward' of intentions is used to distinguish between events due to our own actions and independent events in the outside world. This mechanism (corollary discharge) applies to limb movements as well as eye movements and presumably to our own speech as well. There are, therefore, very good reasons for believing that a form of self-monitoring plays a vital role in modifying our perception of the world.

to covert actions such as thinking, based on the idea that thinking develops out of an internalisation of speaking to oneself. If so, failure would give rise to thoughts that were no longer labelled as self-generated.

The example in Box 9.2 concerning eye movements also indicates that the perceptual qualities of the experience produced by a mismatch between intended and actual motor acts can be compelling. Frith combined lack of self-monitoring with the inner speech theory of auditory hallucinations described in Chapter 8 to produce a tentative theory of auditory hallucinations: if the normal experience of inner speech were no longer labelled as self-generated, this would not only make it appear alien but would also give it perceptual qualities – the patient hears a voice and does not recognise it as his own.

Frith and Done (1989) tested whether alien control experiences in schizophrenia were associated with defective self-monitoring by means of an adaptation of the tasks used to demonstrate the existence of central control of movements in normal subjects. Ten of the patients they tested were currently experiencing one or more alien control symptoms, defined as delusions of control, thought insertion or thought block. The remaining four patients had no symptoms of this type. There were also nine patients with a diagnosis of psychotic affective disorder and six normal controls. All the patients were drug free at the time of testing in order to avoid the potential confounding effects of treatment on performance. The task began with presentation of a computer screen showing two men aiming guns, one on the upper left aiming right, and the one on the lower right aiming left. At intervals a bird would appear opposite one of the two men and the subject's task was to move a joystick left or right to make the appropriate man fire his gun, at which point a bullet would appear and slowly move across the screen, taking 2.8 seconds to reach the bird. If the subject fired the wrong gun, he could correct this at any time before it reached the bird by moving the joystick the other way, whereupon the first bullet would stop and a second bullet would appear from the other gun. In order to ensure that the subjects made many errors, the relationship between the left or right movement of the joystick and the man selected to shoot was periodically reversed. The subjects were given 80 trials of this type, and then 80 more trials where a wall was interposed across the middle of the screen. This had the effect of hiding the trajectory of the bullet for the first two seconds after it left the gun. On these trials, therefore, the subject could not use visual feedback to correct errors and had to rely on central error correction.

No significant differences were found between the groups in the numbers of errors made on the first version of the task. All the subjects made errors in approximately 25 per cent of the trials, and virtually all of these were corrected within two seconds, as expected given that the consequences of moving the joystick the wrong way were immediately visible. In the second version of the task there were again no major differences in the number of errors made, but the schizophrenic patients with alien control symptoms corrected significantly fewer of these within two seconds (i.e. without visual feedback) than those without, or the affective patients or the controls. The differences were marked: the schizophrenic patients with alien control symptoms only corrected a median of 8 per cent of their errors within two seconds, in contrast to 80 per cent, 40 per cent and 67 per cent in the other three groups.

The numbers of patients with and without alien control symptoms in this study were small, but Mlakar *et al.* (1994) found similar evidence of significantly poorer performance in 25 schizophrenic patients with and 14 without first rank symptoms when they had to copy and draw designs in the absence of visual feedback. Stirling *et al.* (1998) also found that poor performance on a number of tasks embodying similar principles to those used by Frith and Done and Mlakar *et al.* was significantly correlated with scores on delusions of control and thought insertion, and also with delusions and hallucinations in general on some of the measures of self-monitoring. There was also a significant association with formal thought disorder, but not with negative symptoms. In this study, interestingly, impairment on the measures of self-monitoring was not significantly correlated with measures of general intellectual impairment.

Functional imaging of delusions and hallucinations

In Liddle *et al.*'s (1992) study the main associations of reality distortion were with increased cerebral blood flow. This was seen in areas of the temporal lobe on the left, the parahippocampal gyrus, and the superior part of the temporal pole. There was also a significant positive association for the left lateral frontal cortex. The syndrome was characterised by relatively few associations with lower flow. These involved the right posterior cingulate cortex, the right posterior superior temporal gyrus and adjacent areas of the parietal lobe. The findings are shown in Figure 9.3.

Liddle *et al.*'s pattern of positive associations with the left temporal lobe cortex, but not that with the frontal cortex, was reproduced in the study by Kaplan *et al.* (1993). However, this was the only further study to examine the functional imaging correlates of reality distortion, and all other studies have restricted themselves to either delusions or auditory hallucinations. Auditory hallucinations, in particular, lend themselves to investigation using a technique where patients who experience these very frequently press a button or otherwise indicate when the voices start and stop, while being scanned. Eight studies of this type are summarised in Table 9.8. In all cases the temporal lobe neocortex was a major area of activation associated with auditory hallucinations, often bilaterally. Most of the studies also found other areas of activation. However, none of them found frontal or other areas of de-activation as would be predicted from Frith's theory.

It is not easy to conceive of an experimental design that would activate brain areas associated with delusions. However, there has been one study on the type of alien control delusion central to Frith's theory. Spence *et al.* (1997) compared seven schizophrenic patients who were actively experiencing passivity symptoms on the day of testing with six who had never reported having such symptoms, but were otherwise deluded and/or hallucinated. (Five of the former patients reported vivid experiences of passivity while they were performing the task in the scanner, for example 'feeling like an automaton'; 'guided by a female spirit who has entered me'; 'spirits moving my shoulder'.) Six normal controls were also scanned. Functional imaging (PET) was carried out while the subjects responded to a series of regularly spaced tones by moving a joystick in any direction they chose with their right hand. There were also two control conditions where they moved the joystick in a predetermined clockwise sequence or made no response at all. When performing freely selected joystick movements the normal subjects showed activation in the

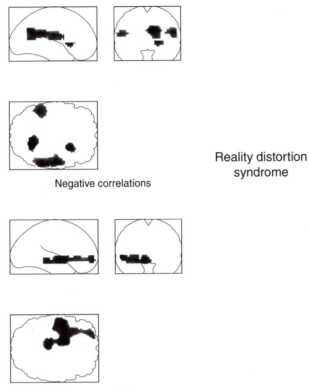

Reality distortion
syndrome

Negative correlations

Positive correlations

Figure 9.3 Functional imaging correlates of positive symptoms (reality distortion) in schizophrenia (from Liddle *et al.* (1992), Patterns of cerebral blood flow in schizophrenia. *British Journal of Psychiatry*, 160, 179–186. Reproduced with permission from the Royal College of Psychiatrists).

following areas: left prefrontal cortex, bilateral premotor cortex, contralateral sensorimotor cortex and bilateral parietal cortex, and also the left supplementary motor cortex and cerebellum. Compared to the patients without passivity symptoms, the passivity patients showed relatively greater activation of the inferior parietal cortex bilaterally (a region known to be concerned with spatial programming, spatial memory, and orientation within space, which is activated by movements in extrapersonal space), the cerebellum, and foci within the cingulate gyrus. The schizophrenic patients also failed to show significant prefrontal activation during performance of the task compared to the controls, but this affected those with and without passivity symptoms equally.

Table 9.8 Voxel-based functional imaging studies of auditory hallucinations

Study	N	Technique	Temporal lobe neocortex	Other
Silbersweig *et al.* (1995)	6	PET	✓	Thalamus Hippocampus/parahippocampal gyrus Ventral striatum Anterior cingulate cortex Orbitofrontal cortex
Dierks *et al.* (1999)	3		✓	Frontal operculum Amygdala Hippocampus
Lennox *et al.* (2000)	4	fMRI	✓	L. middle frontal gyrus L. inferior parietal cortex
Shergill *et al.* (2000)	6	fMRI	✓	Inferior frontal gyrus/insula Middle frontal gyrus Post parietal cortex
Shergill *et al.* (2001)	1	fMRI	✓ (r only)	Hippocampus/parahippocampal gyrus
Bentaleb *et al.* (2002)	1	fMRI	✓	—
Copolov *et al.* (2003)	8	PET	✓	Medial frontal Anterior cingulate and cingulum Lateral prefrontal cortex Hippocampus Post cingulate
Shergill *et al.* (2004)	2	fMRI	✓	Inferior frontal gyrus Insula

Conclusion

If the mainstream view is right and schizophrenia is a biological brain disease, then its symptoms have to be explainable in these terms. This is the task facing the cognitive neuropsychological approach, and one it has wrestled with for a considerable period of time now. Some ingenious theories have been developed and there has been plenty of time for experimental investigation, which has included highly sophisticated scanning studies. The question is, has the approach resulted in a convincing body of evidence?

Where the theory is at its simplest and clearest, in the frontal lobe hypothesis of negative symptoms, the picture is encouraging but is also one of unfulfilled promise. The clinical similarity between the negative syndrome and the apathetic form of the frontal lobe syndrome has face validity, has survived preliminary scrutiny, but has not been investigated any further. Where there has been far more research is on the association between negative symptoms and impaired executive function. There are clear indications of a relationship, but there is so much evidence of additional associations with impairment on non-executive tests that a specific relationship cannot be regarded as established. Functional imaging studies of negative symptoms got off to a strong start with Liddle *et al.*'s (1992) study. The disappointment here lies in the fact that there have been so few further studies that it is impossible to draw any conclusions from the pattern of replications and non-replications.

The simplest cognitive neuropsychological explanation of thought disorder – which is so simple that few have ever subscribed to it – is surprisingly well supported. Thought-disordered schizophrenic speech features genuine linguistic abnormalities and cannot always be distinguished from dyphasia. But at the same time, there are features such as intact comprehension and sparing of naming that make it different from any neurological form of fluent dysphasia. Nor is language disturbance the whole story. Studies of the neuropsychological correlates of formal thought disorder have also incriminated the prime suspect in all biological schizophrenia research, the frontal lobes. Functional imaging studies tend to favour temporal lobe abnormality, but do not rule out areas of the prefrontal cortex traditionally associated with the disinhibited form of the frontal lobe syndrome. There is of course no reason why language abnormalities should not combine with an executive impairment, especially in a disorder where the pathological process is reputed to involve both the temporal and frontal lobes, and McKenna and Oh (2005) have recently argued that this might be just what is needed to account for the multifaceted nature of formal thought disorder. This may or may not be correct, but it makes the point that the cognitive neuropsychological approach has moved beyond the stage of relying on clinical parallels with other disorders and is able to generate hypotheses of its own.

Frith's proposal that certain 'alien control' symptoms and perhaps also auditory hallucinations reflect impairment in a specialised aspect of executive function, receives consistent support at the psychological level, albeit from a very small number of studies. However, it is not supported at all by functional imaging studies, which instead have uniformly found that such symptoms are associated with increased rather than decreased brain activity, in areas that are not in the prefrontal cortex. The studies of hallucinations, in particular, are strikingly convergent in pointing to increased activity in the temporal lobe neocortex. But ultimately this may not matter, as the theory implicates a monitoring function so specialised that, if it is executive at all, it may not need to be housed in the frontal lobes.

A more serious problem for the theory is that in its original form it applied only to a circumscribed set of positive schizophrenic symptoms. To deal with this, Frith (1992, 1994) has broadened the approach with an argument that self-monitoring is a special case of a more general failure in the representation of mental states. This would encompass a failure to represent one's own mental states (previously failure of self-monitoring), and also, crucially, a failure to represent the mental states of others. Otherwise known as mentalising ability or theory of mind, in Frith's (1992, 1994) hands this has scope for explaining symptoms like persecutory and referential delusions and some of the features of auditory hallucinations not explained by the inner speech theory. A number of studies to date have found impairment on theory of mind tests in schizophrenia, and this, in stark contrast to most other cognitive tasks apart from the error correction tasks described earlier, does seem to be associated with presence of delusions and hallucinations (see McKenna and Oh, 2005; Brune, 2005). But this is where, for the moment, matters lie.

10 Neuroleptic drug treatment

As recounted by Caldwell (1970), the story of how schizophrenia became a treatable illness began with a French surgeon, Laborit. In the course of testing the usefulness of various compounds for combating the adverse autonomic and psychological consequences of surgery, he observed that an antihistamine, promethazine, tended to induce a state of calm, quiet, relaxation in volunteers. His attempts to maximise this effect by pharmacological manipulation resulted in the synthesis of chlorpromazine, a drug that reliably produced 'not any loss of consciousness, not any change in the patient's mentality, but a slight tendency to sleep and, above all, disinterest for all that goes on around him' (Laborit et al., 1952). Laborit immediately recognised the potential of this effect and managed to persuade some reluctant psychiatric colleagues to try it on psychotic patients. Successes in individual cases were quickly followed by the now classic report on a small series of patients by Delay et al. (1952).

This version of events does not tell quite the whole story. For centuries rauwolfia root had been used in India to treat severe psychiatric states. Reserpine, the active component of rauwolfia root was also isolated in 1952. A year later Hakim (1953) claimed cures of schizophrenia with this drug in India, and Kline (1954) in the USA described beneficial effects in various psychiatric disorders, though not specifically schizophrenia. It was soon noted that both chlorpromazine and reserpine commonly produced basal ganglia signs as side-effects (Steck, 1954), and this led Delay and Deniker (1955) to coin, somewhat obscurely, the term 'neuroleptic'. The use of chlorpromazine proceeded to spread explosively – within a year it was being used in several countries – and reserpine was relegated to a footnote in history.

Beginning with haloperidol, a range of drugs with similar effects to chlorpromazine was rapidly developed. The main chemical classes expanded to include the phenothiazines (e.g. chlorpromazine, thioridazine, trifluoperazine, fluphenazine), the butyrophenones (e.g. haloperidol, droperidol), the thioxanthines (e.g. flupenthixol, clopenthixol, thiothixene), the diphenylbutylpiperidines (e.g. pimozide, fluspirilene), and the substituted benzamides (e.g. sulpiride). Along the way, some drugs of miscellaneous other types were also found to have the same properties, including one called clozapine, which did not initially stand out as particularly unusual in any way, but was destined to become the first and most important of the so-called atypical neuroleptics.

Neuroleptic drugs are now the treatment of choice in schizophrenia, not to mention being its mainstay and the only treatment of universally accepted value. There is an immense body of literature on their preclinical effects, and the accumulated knowledge on their therapeutic benefits and side-effects is substantial. In this chapter an attempt is made to bring this clinical and preclinical information together, and integrate it where possible. This is worthwhile in its own right, but is also a prerequisite for understanding what it is that makes some drugs atypical.

The therapeutic effect of neuroleptic drugs

Within 10 years of the introduction of chlorpromazine, there was a consensus that neuroleptics had transformed the treatment of schizophrenia. As Freeman (1978) put it, while the outlook had not been entirely bleak before they were introduced, and it did not become entirely satisfactory afterwards, the drugs greatly mitigated the distress and suffering caused by the disorder. It was clear that neuroleptics provided an excellent means of controlling disturbed behaviour, and they also markedly decreased the need for hospitalisation. It was also widely believed that they had a specific therapeutic effect on schizophrenic symptoms, although this was less dramatic and could be individually quite variable.

It was, of course, necessary to demonstrate this effectiveness in properly controlled trials. Psychiatry was especially sensitive to this need because some time previously another physical treatment, insulin coma therapy, had also been hailed as a breakthrough. Like neuroleptics, its use had also spread worldwide, many leading psychiatrists supported its use, and numerous studies testified to its effectiveness. It was only after 20 years that the treatment was first questioned by Bourne (1953), and then exposed as worthless in the first study to use any proper controls and to be carried out under blind conditions (Ackner *et al.*, 1957).

The acute effects of neuroleptic treatment

By 1966 over 40 double blind, placebo controlled studies of neuroleptic treatment had been carried out (see Davis, 1985). Most of these showed that neuroleptics were significantly superior to placebo, and the minority that failed to do so invariably suffered from a combination of poor design, small sample sizes, low dosage, and short duration regimens.

One of the largest and most careful of these studies was carried out by the National Institute of Mental Health (NIMH, 1964; Goldberg *et al.*, 1965). In this, 380 newly admitted schizophrenic patients, recruited from nine centres, were randomly assigned to treatment with one of three neuroleptics (chlorpromazine, fluphenazine or thioridazine) or placebo under double blind conditions for six weeks. The findings are shown in Figure 10.1. It can be seen that, whereas the global improvement ratings for patients receiving placebo were fairly evenly distributed above and below 'no change' and 'minimally improved', less than 5 per cent of the neuroleptic-treated patients were rated as 'no change' and 75 per cent showed moderate or marked improvement. These differences between drug and placebo were in all probability an underestimate, since 36 of the 110 placebo-treated patients dropped out of the trial because of clinical deterioration.

This study also supported the clinical impression that the effect of neuroleptics went beyond mere sedation and tranquillisation. As shown in Table 10.1, the neuroleptic-treated group showed significant improvement in all the 21 aspects of psychopathology rated in the study, which was significantly greater than for the placebo group in 13 of these. Importantly, the effect sizes for the improvement in symptoms that might be anticipated to be most sensitive to a general tranquillising effect, like hostility, agitation and anxiety, were smaller than for symptoms such as delusions and hallucinations, and also for some symptoms like social participation and self-care, which a simple tranquillising effect would be anticipated, if anything, to worsen.

Even so, there was a strong clinical impression that neuroleptic drugs had differential effects on different schizophrenic symptoms. For example, in a

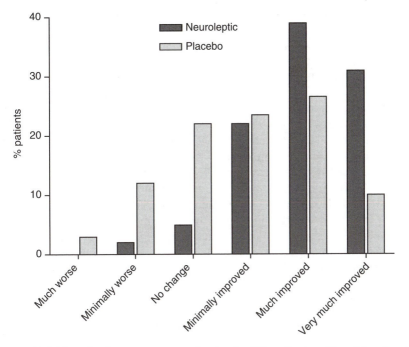

Figure 10.1 Neuroleptic treatment vs placebo in 380 patients with schizophrenia (from Goldberg *et al.*, 1965).

Table 10.1 Changes in symptoms and behaviour produced by neuroleptic treatment

Symptom/behaviour	Standardised change (treatment)	Standardised change (drug – placebo)
Resistiveness	.68**	.32
Hostility	.86**	.58**
Irritability	.86**	.79**
Pressure of speech	.87**	.46**
Agitation and tension	.96**	.68**
Delusions of grandeur	1.04**	.20
Ideas of persecution	1.13**	.57**
Auditory hallucinations	1.72**	.62**
Non-auditory hallucinations	1.66**	.19
Hebephrenic symptoms	1.44**	1.19**
Incoherent speech	1.47**	.87**
Slowed speech and movements	.85**	.73**
Indifference	1.24**	.89**
Self-care	1.28**	.93**
Social participation	1.78**	.99**
Observed sadness	.67**	.04
Guilt	.65**	.20
Confusion	1.69**	.98**
Feelings of unreality	1.68**	1.19
Memory deficit	1.90**	.60
Disorientation	2.06**	.34

$*p < 0.5, **p < .01$

Source: Goldberg *et al.* (1965).

frequently cited study of its day, Letemendia and Harris (1967) found an indifferent response to neuroleptics in previously untreated chronic schizophrenic patients with predominantly withdrawn, apathetic presentations. Goldberg *et al.* (1965) also found in their own study that certain symptoms such as indifference to the environment, slowed speech and movements, and poor self-care, which approximated to Bleuler's fundamental symptoms, appeared to improve less than 'accessory' symptoms such as excitement, ideas of persecution and incoherence of thought. However, this difference disappeared when placebo effects were taken into consideration. When Goldberg (1985) later reviewed the findings of his own and five other large placebo controlled studies of neuroleptic drugs with respect to this issue, he found that they all found some evidence of significant improvement on what were by now called 'negative symptoms', although this was less uniform for positive symptoms.

The pharmacological effects of neuroleptic drugs

For over a decade after their introduction, the basis of the therapeutic effect of neuroleptics remained unknown. Chlorpromazine was found to have numerous biochemical actions, but these seemed to reflect merely its high lipid solubility and consequent interactions with cell membrane systems (Iversen, 1978). It was not until Carlsson and Lindqvist (1963) discovered that chlorpromazine and haloperidol caused acute increases in catechol-amine turnover in rat brain that significant progress began to be made: they hypothesised that the likeliest cause of this was blockade of the post-synaptic receptors for these transmitters. For a further decade it remained unclear whether dopamine, noradrenaline or both catecholamine receptors were blocked. Then in 1974 direct evidence for preferential dopamine receptor blockade became available (Seeman *et al.*, 1974). As detailed in Chapter 6, the evidence that dopamine receptor blockade was the principal pharmaco-logical effect of neuroleptics, the one they all had in common, and the one that was responsible for their therapeutic effect went on to become incontrovertible.

The basis of neuroleptic antidopaminergic effects next become complicated by the evidence that there were two types of dopamine receptor (Kebabian and Calne, 1979; see also Joyce, 1983). D1 receptors, like many other types of receptor, are linked to an intracellular 'second messenger' system involving cyclic AMP, and stimulation of the receptor produces increased synthesis of this compound. Stimulation of D2 receptors by dopamine agonists, in con-trast, produces no increase in cyclic AMP. The circumstantial evidence at the time implicated D2 receptors in the therapeutic effects of neuroleptic drugs. These drugs were known to interact with D2 receptors at very low con-centrations, well within reach of their therapeutic dose ranges, whereas the concentrations necessary to block D1 receptors were found to be 100 times higher than the blood and cerebrospinal fluid that would be reached on therapeutic dosages. This hypothesis was elegantly confirmed by Creese *et al.* (1976) and Seeman *et al.* (1976) who both demonstrated that the clinical antipsychotic potency of different neuroleptic drugs correlated highly with their affinities at the D2 receptor; later it was shown that there was no correlation with their potency at the D1 receptor (see Seeman, 1987). These findings are shown in Figure 10.2.

In the years since the existence of D1 and D2 receptors was established, molecular genetic techniques have found evidence for at least three further types of dopamine receptor, D3, D4 and D5 (see Waddington *et al.*, 2003). Fortunately, these still seem to fall into two 'families' with D1-like (D1 and D5), and D2-like (D2, D3 and D4) pharmacological properties. Current evidence suggests that neuroleptics only bind to the D2 receptor family, and no known neuroleptics show more than a modest preference for D3 or D4 receptors over D2 receptors. For the time being, it therefore remains useful to talk of D1 and D2 dopamine receptors, but for how much longer this will be so is uncertain.

The main effect of neuroleptic drugs in animals is inhibition of spon-taneous motor activity without induction of drowsiness. In rats, lower doses produce a striking reduction in locomotor activity, especially the exploratory

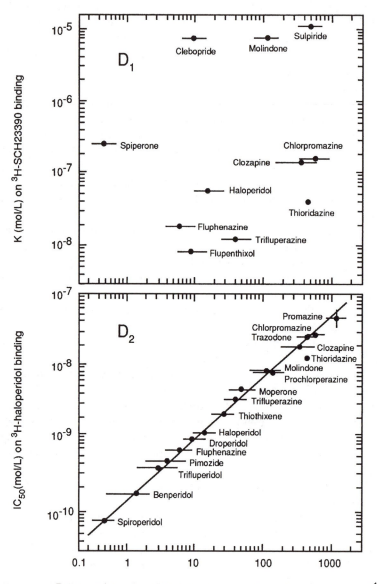

Figure 10.2 Correlations between clinical potencies of neuroleptic drugs and their affinities at dopamine D1 and D2 receptors (from Seeman (1987), Dopamine receptors and the dopamine hypothesis of schizophrenia. *Synapse*, 1, 133–152. Copyright © 1987 Alan R. Liss, Inc. Reprinted by permission of John Wiley and Sons, Inc.).

behaviour that takes place in a new environment (Kreiskott, 1980). Higher doses induce a state of profound immobility often refered to as catalepsy (Joyce, 1983; Mason, 1984); though conscious, the animal crouches in a hunched posture, making few movements and passive to all but the strongest external stimuli. If placed in an uncomfortable position, for instance with one hind leg raised on a platform, it will remain in it for many minutes before stepping down. The animal is not, however, paralysed: under intense adverse conditions (procedures employed have included immersing rats in freezing water or introducing a cat into the experimental area) motor activity temporarily reverts to normal, before it sinks back into motionlessness as soon as the danger is past.

A second, somewhat more esoteric, animal neuroleptic effect should be mentioned, since this has become the standard means of screening drugs for antipsychotic action. This is the hyperactivity/stereotypy model (Joyce, 1983: Mason, 1984). Acute administration of dopamine agonists like amphetamine or apomorphine to rats induces a state that is in many ways the reverse of catalepsy. An increase in locomotor activity is initially observed, which proceeds to give way to stereotyped movements. The range and unpredictability of the animal's behaviour becomes increasingly constrained until eventually it incessantly performs one or a few responses like sniffing and rearing. Neuroleptic drugs characteristically reverse both the hyperactivity and stereotypy components of this dopamine agonist response.

Based on various lines of evidence (see Costall and Naylor, 1981; Iversen and Fray, 1982), neuroleptic-induced catalepsy has been concluded to be essentially a basal ganglia phenomenon, due to blockade of dopamine receptors at this site. Accordingly, it is widely considered to be an animal model of human Parkinsonian side-effects. Other evidence has suggested that there is an anatomical dissociation between the hyperactivity and stereotypy components of the amphetamine/apomorphine response, with stereotypy reflecting mainly basal ganglia stimulation and hyperactivity being the consequence of similar activity in ventral striatal and mesolimbic regions. However, the partitioning of these responses, if there is any, is almost certainly considerably more complex than this (see Joyce, 1983; Mason, 1984).

Side-effects of neuroleptic drugs

Almost as soon as the success of neuroleptic drugs in treating schizophrenia was recognised, it was appreciated that a price had to be paid in serious side-effects. The most important and disabling of these side-effects were on voluntary movement, and they had in common the fact that they were also features of basal ganglia disease. They therefore became known as the extrapyramidal side-effects of neuroleptic drugs.

The four main types of extrapyramidal side-effect are, in order of the time course of their appearance, *acute dystonic reactions, akathisia, Parkinsonism,* and *tardive dyskinesia.* These have been described in numerous accounts, most recently and most authoritatively by Cunningham Owens (1999), which the following account principally draws on. This author did not include the uncommon *neuroleptic malignant syndrome*, but this is also probably best classed as at least partly extrapyramidal in nature.

Acute dystonic reactions

First clearly described by Delay *et al.* (1959) and Sigwald *et al.* (1959a), acute dystonic reactions are typically seen in the earliest stages of neuroleptic treatment: many occur within hours of its commencement and 90 per cent take place within the first four days (Ayd, 1961; Swett, 1975). A small number of cases develop later in the course of treatment, when they are typically seen as a recurrent phenomenon.

Ayd (1961), in a frequently cited early survey, reported a prevalence figure of 2–3 per cent in neuroleptic-treated patients. However, Cunningham Owens (1999) has pointed out that this rate was artefactually low because of a peculiarity of the rating system Ayd used, which rated acute dystonias as present only in patients who developed no other extrapyramidal side-effects. In a review of later studies Cunningham Owens (1999) concluded that a reasonable interpretation of the literature was that they can be seen in up to a quarter to a third of patients treated with conventional neuroleptics. According to the same author, acute dystonic reactions are most commonly seen in young patients. However, claims for an association with male sex have not been borne out.

The typical acute dystonic reaction (see Marsden *et al.*, 1975, 1986; Lees, 1985; Cunningham Owens, 1999) takes the form of remitting or sustained muscular spasms that begin abruptly or evolve stepwise. Attacks can last from seconds to hours and often wax and wane in intensity. The spasms are invariably painful and also, surprisingly, highly susceptible to external influences such as suggestion. Any muscle groups or even the entire body may be involved, but neck movements (especially retrocollis) and facial contractions are particularly common. Blepharospasm, perioral spasms and gaze fixations are said to be characteristic, and there may also be trismus (jaw closure due to masseter spasm), forced mouth opening and tongue protrusion. Acute dystonic reactions involving the torso cause lordosis, scoliosis, tortipelvis and opisthotonus. The Pisa syndrome (Ekbom *et al.*, 1972) is the name given to torsion movements of the trunk that became worse on walking, causing the patient to tilt to one side. Sometimes the limbs are held in distorted positions. A typical presentation is hyperpronation of the forearms accompanied by flexion at the wrists and metacarpophalangeal joints, and extension of the fingers; when unilateral this has been called the 'waiter's tip'. Laryngeal and pharyngeal dystonias causing dysphonia and dysphagia are rarely seen (and can be life-threatening).

Oculogyric crises (originally described in post-encephalitic Parkinsonism) are a complex form of acute dystonic reaction, which although well known, occur only in a small minority of cases (6 per cent according to a retrospective survey of clinicians by Swett, 1975). In the fully developed form of these, the patient's eyes become deviated upwards and often also laterally, the neck is hyperextended, the mouth is opened wide and the tongue is forced out.

An akathisia-like inner restlessness is commonly described as accompanying acute dystonic reactions, and there may be Parkinsonian signs like facial immobility, tremor and salivation. Autonomic signs, including hyperpyrexia, tachycardia and pallor occur in a few cases and can be severe. Occasionally, instead of being dystonic, the movements are more choreoathetoid in nature (Gerlach, 1979; Lees, 1985); the movements resemble those of tardive dyskinesia but are said to be somewhat more stereotyped and rhythmical.

Cunningham Owens has emphasised that acute dystonic reactions have a strong subjective component. There is often a prodromal period of anxiousness or foreboding, and during the attack itself the patient may become increasingly anxious and agitated. Oculogyric crises, as originally described in patients with the sequelae of encephalitis lethargica, could be associated with a wider range of mental state disturbances: fear (up to and including terror); stupor; speech disorders such as mutism, echolalia, palilalia and forced shouting, inhibition of thought, compulsive thinking, suspiciousness and persecutory beliefs. Latter-day neuroleptic induced oculogyric crises have been associated with worsening of auditory hallucinations and visual misperceptions (Chiu, 1989; Sachdev and Tang, 1992). Thornton and McKenna (1994) have described acute dystonic reactions that consisted predominantly of florid psychotic symptoms, with ocular deviation being only a minor and easily overlooked part of the picture. One of their cases is reproduced in Box 10.1.

Box 10.1 Acute dystonic reaction with marked psychotic symptoms (from Thornton and McKenna, 1994)

A 28-year-old woman had had admissions to hospital beginning at the age of 24. After the second of these, during which she showed definite schizophrenic symptoms, she was started on depot neuroleptic medication. Her psychotic symptoms improved but shortly after discharge she started experiencing attacks in which her eyes rolled up and her neck arched back; these were associated with a feeling of fear and autonomic accompaniments. During these attacks she also described a feeling as if she were having sexual intercourse and experienced a strong urge to jump out of windows.

The patient was re-admitted after these attacks had become an almost daily occurrence and she required continual supervision by friends to stop her acting on her urge to harm herself. At this time she was actively psychotic, showing delusions, auditory hallucinations, formal thought disorder and bizarre behaviour, e.g. walking round in circles and plucking objects out of the air. All these symptoms fluctuated markedly. Several times a week she also had attacks lasting from one to a few hours, which began with her looking upwards and were followed by disturbed behaviour. Several of these attacks were witnessed and one took the following form. The first sign was upward and lateral deviation of the eyes which the patient was able to reverse by an effort of will, but only briefly; at times only the whites of her eyes could be seen. This was accompanied by blepharoclonus. Slightly later she was found to be standing rigidly, bent forwards with her hand held a foot from her face. She had to be forced to sit down on the bed. At this point she showed marked persistence of postures, yawned repeatedly and repeated the phrase 'turn and back' over and over again with increasing volume. Her speech was incoherent and it was almost impossible to follow what she said. However she alluded to religious and referential delusions and said 'God is making me think things . . . when it happens thoughts are let into my head'. The gaze deviation and blepharoclonus remained noticeable throughout the attack.

The episode was terminated within five minutes by IV procyclidine.

The patient's depot medication was stopped and she was started on clozapine. She made a rapid and excellent clinical response, becoming essentially free of all psychotic symptoms within a month. The above attacks continued to occur, but with steadily decreasing frequency and intensity over the next four months. When they did occur motor abnormalities were subtle to the point of being scarcely detectable; however, the attacks still responded promptly to IV procyclidine.

The course of acute dystonic reactions is generally short and self-limiting. If neuroleptic treatment is withdrawn they remit, and even if it is continued they generally subside, with or without therapeutic intervention, not to recur. A few patients experience recurrent dystonic reactions over weeks or months; these are often but not always explicable on the basis of increases in the dose of neurolepic medication. Acute dystonic reactions almost always respond promptly to a single intravenous dose of an anticholinergic drug like procyclidine, which is the treatment of choice in the UK. From time to time other therapeutic strategies have been advocated, the most effective of which appears to be intravenous diazepam or clonazepam (see Lees, 1985).

The pathophysiology of acute dystonic reactions is unknown, but there are clues. As reviewed by Marsden and Jenner (1980) and Rupniak *et al.* (1986), circumstantial evidence from neurology links dystonias in general to alterations in basal ganglia dopamine function, but to both increases and decreases in this transmitter – for example dystonias are seen both in untreated Parkinson's disease and as a complication of its treatment with L-DOPA.

In the case of neuroleptic-induced dystonia, the evidence points to the former. Thus one species of baboon reliably develops dystonias after neuroleptic administration. Pretreatment with drugs that prevent dopamine synthesis and release attenuates or prevents these appearing. On the other hand, there is little evidence to suggest that they are ameliorated by dopamine agonist drugs. In order to explain how neuroleptic drugs, which are dopamine receptor blockers, might cause an initial functional dopamine excess, Marsden and Jenner (1980) speculatively but plausibly proposed that early in the course of neuroleptic treatment a preferential blockade of presynaptic dopamine autoreceptors occurs. As these are inhibitory to dopamine synthesis and release, a dopamine excess is produced. This then exerts agonistic effects on post-synaptic dopamine receptors whose blockade is not yet fully established.

In addition to the 'transient dopamine excess' hypothesis, Cunningham Owens (1999) has argued that the swift and complete response of acute dystonic reactions to anticholinergic treatment points to an increase in striatal anticholinergic activity as their immediate cause. In support of this hypothesis it has been found that acute administration of neuroleptics produces striatal acetylcholine release in animals, and that cholinergic agonists can induce dystonias in primates.

Akathisia

The peculiar phenomenon of mental and motor restlessness leading to an inability to remain seated was originally described in Parkinson's disease, in post-encephalitic Parkinsonism and as an idiopathic disorder. As a complication of neuroleptic treatment, it was first reported by Steck (1954). Although akathisia has been considered to have a relatively delayed onset, appearing between a few weeks and the first three months of treatment in 90 per cent of cases, a recent study has demonstrated that in just under a third of cases clinically significant symptoms are first reported within two weeks of starting treatment (Sachdev and Kruk, 1994).

Ayd (1961) found a prevalence of 21 per cent in his large sample of neuroleptic treated patients, and even this is probably an underestimate, for the reason described above. Based on further studies Cunningham Owens concluded that between 20 per cent and 45 per cent of patients on neuroleptic drugs will develop the full syndrome. Akathisia occurs at all ages and affects both sexes equally.

As described by Lees (1985), the core of the clinical syndrome is a subjective feeling of motor unease affecting the legs disproportionately but not exclusively, which leads to an irresistible urge to keep moving, and an inability to sit still. As a consequence, the patient continually taps his feet, moves his legs, or shifts his weight from foot to foot. In more severe forms, the patient treads on the spot, paces back and forth, breaks into a trot, or may dance, march, climb or rock. As well as the subjective feeling of restlessness, other mental accompaniments include inability to concentrate, malaise, depression, euphoria, rage or sexual arousal; claims for exacerbation of psychosis have also been made (Van Putten, 1975). Abnormal sensations in the legs are commonly reported, such as pins and needles, cramps, vibration, warmth or formication. Myoclonic jerks are a not infrequent associated symptom (Cunningham Owens, 1999).

Some patients complain of subjective inner restlessness on neuroleptic treatment without any objective signs of this being present. Cunningham Owens considered that the evidence was inconclusive as to whether this presentation could or should be regarded as mild akathisia. Other patients, particularly after the symptom has been present for a long time, lose the subjective component of the syndrome and exhibit only the objective motor restlessness. This is often referred to as pseudoakathisia or tardive akathisia (Barnes and Braude, 1985), although according to Cunningham Owens the terminology in this area is confused if not misleading.

If neuroleptic treatment is continued unchanged, akathisia may diminish or disappear over weeks to months. Alternatively, it may persist unchanged and distressing for years; or relapse or remit; or as mentioned above, lose some or all of its subjective component and/or shade into tardive dyskinesia (Lees, 1985; Barnes and Braude, 1985). No treatment, other than discontinuation of neuroleptic treatment, is of guaranteed effectiveness, and even if this is feasible resolution may be slow. According to Cunningham Owens, dose reduction or changing from a high-potency drug like haloperidol to a low-potency drug is a useful initial strategy. If this fails, anticholinergic drugs are the usual first line of treatment in the UK, but the evidence base supporting their effectiveness is extremely small, and even so only around half of patients respond. Propanolol has been claimed to be effective in a similar proportion of cases, but once again the studies are relatively few and have weaknesses (Sachdev, 1995). Benzodiazepines are often used, and are almost certainly effective, at least in the short term, but the evidence is largely anecdotal or from open studies.

The pathogenesis of akathisia is shrouded in mystery. It is widely suspected that dopamine deficiency is a factor: akathisia can complicate Parkinson's disease and post-encephalitic Parkinsonism, and it commonly co-exists with Parkinsonism in neuroleptic-treated patients; in addition, it can be produced by dopamine depleting drug treatment (Marsden and Jenner, 1980; Marsden *et al.*, 1986). Marsden and Jenner (1980) advanced the theory that an imbalance between striatal and cortical dopamine receptor blockade, with the latter being greater, might be the cause of the symptom. In support of this, they cited evidence that selective blockade of cortical dopamine receptors has been found to cause a paradoxical increase in locomotor activity in rats. Over 20 years later, it is apparent from Cunningham Owens' review of the literature that little further progress in understanding the pathophysiology of the symptom has been made.

Parkinsonism

This side-effect of neuroleptic drugs was also first described by Steck (1954), although according to Cunningham Owens it was common knowledge within a year of the introduction of chlorpromazine. The time course of its appearance roughly parallels, but slightly lags behind, that of akathisia. In Ayd's (1961) study, whose figures with regard to Parkinsonism are not regarded as an underestimate, it occasionally appears within days of starting treatment, half to three-quarters of cases develop within a month, and 90 per cent within 10 weeks.

Various prevalence surveys (see Marsden *et al.*, 1975, 1986) have concluded that 20–40 per cent of neuroleptic-treated patients show obvious Parkinsonian signs, and according to Marsden and Jenner (1980), a considerably higher percentage exhibit subtler but unmistakable akinesia. Cunningham Owens has suggested that a reasonable conclusion is that between one-fifth and one-third of patients exposed to standard neuroleptics will develop a clinically significant Parkinsonian syndrome. Paralleling idiopathic Parkinson's disease, it increases in frequency with age. A female to male ratio of 2:1 has been found in many but not all studies.

Every Parkinsonian sign can be seen in neuroleptic-induced Parkinsonism, including the classical akinesia, rigidity and tremor, as well as stooped posture, shuffling and festinant gait, sialorrhoea and seborrhoea (Marsden *et al.*, 1975, 1986; Cunningham Owens, 1999). In the clustering and sequence of progression of its signs, however, neuroleptic-induced Parkinsonism carries its own distinctive stamp. The earliest and most common finding is akinesia, which may appear as an entirely isolated phenomenon. Rigidity is less common and tends to develop later; cogwheeling is often conspicuous by its absence. The characteristic pill-rolling tremor is said to be even more uncommon and to occur later still. However, other forms of tremor are quite commonly seen. All degrees of the characteristic flexed posture are encountered. Sometimes, instead of this, patients show hyperextension, standing or walking bolt upright with a 'poker spine' or even leaning backwards slightly.

Once established, neuroleptic-induced Parkinsonism tends to resolve spontaneously over weeks or months despite continued treatment (Marsden and Jenner, 1980). If neuroleptics are withdrawn, the symptoms disappear, in most cases over a few weeks; sometimes over a longer period; and occasionally durations of up to 18 months have been recorded. According to Marsden and Jenner (1980), in about 1 per cent of cases, Parkinsonism persists indefinitely after drug withdrawal, a figure that they considered to be compatible with neuroleptic treatment revealing subclinical idiopathic Parkinson's disease. The responsiveness of neuroleptic-induced Parkinsonism to anticholinergic drugs has become so widely accepted that they form the standard method of treatment. Surprisingly though, the evidence for their effectiveness (exhaustively reviewed by Marsden *et al.*, 1986) is less convincing than might be expected. As Cunningham Owens put it, while patients may feel better on anticholinergics, signs of Parkinsonism often seem stubbornly to persist.

Unlike the other extrapyramidal side-effects, there is no uncertainty about the basis of neuroleptic-induced Parkinsonism, which is obviously a functional striatal dopamine deficiency. The most likely candidate for the cause of this is striatal dopamine D2 receptor blockade, but this has not been completely established and some inconsistencies are apparent (Marsden and Jenner, 1980; Marsden *et al.*, 1986). In the first place, there is the fact that not all patients taking neuroleptic drugs develop Parkinsonism. Second, there is the delay in its appearance as well as its tendency to spontaneous resolution. Early explanations that invoked individual variations in the degree of D2 receptor blockade achieved, or its gradual accumulation for pharmacokinetic reasons, have been contradicted by PET scan findings which demonstrate substantial striatal D2 receptor occupancy immediately after treatment is started (Farde *et al.*, 1989, 1992). However, these studies also support the view that patients with Parkinsonism have higher levels of D2 receptor occupancy than those without (Farde *et al.*, 1992; Scherer *et al.*, 1994; Kapur *et al.*, 2000).

Tardive dyskinesia

The first description of a lasting syndrome of involuntary movements developing late in the course of neuroleptic treatment was by Sigwald *et al.* (1959b), although two years previously Schonecker (1957) had reported persistent orofacial movements in three elderly patients that began after days or weeks of treatment. Tardive dyskinesia is the most important extrapyramidal side-effect of neuroleptic treatment (although, as described in Chapter 1, it can also occur in untreated patients), and, as the name suggests, develops latest in the course of treatment. There is no rigid time of onset criterion that can be applied to its onset, but in the words of Cunningham Owens, one should be circumspect about symptoms emerging before six months of exposure to neuroleptics.

Estimates of the frequency of tardive dyskinesia are very wide. Its prevalence has been found to range from 0.5 per cent to 41 per cent (Jus *et al.*, 1976) to as high as 72 per cent (Smith *et al.*, 1979). Kane and Smith (1982) pooled the data from a comprehensive set of studies available at the time and arrived at a mean figure of 20 per cent, and this has since been supported in two large and rigorous surveys (Woerner *et al.*, 1991; Muscettola *et al.*, 1993). Large-scale, well-designed studies have similarly narrowed down the incidence rate of tardive dyskinesia to around 5 per cent per year of treatment (Kane *et al.*, 1982; Morgenstern and Glazer, 1993; Chakos *et al.*, 1996).

Age is the only risk factor for tardive dyskinesia on which there is universal agreement, and this increases not only its frequency but also, in all probability, its severity (Cunningham Owens, 1999). Associations with female sex, prior brain damage, and duration and dosage of neuroleptics have been alleged but have not been found consistently across different studies (APA Task Force, 1979; Lees, 1985; Marsden *et al.*, 1986). There are, however, strong indications that the development of drug-induced Parkinsonism may predispose to later development of tardive dyskinesia (Crane, 1972; Gerlach, 1979; Kane *et al.*, 1985), although definitive evidence is lacking.

The most familiar form of tardive dyskinesia involves the lower third of the face and the tongue, but all parts of the body can be affected. Cunningham Owens' list of the main varieties of abnormal movement encountered is shown in Table 10.2. The disorder can to some extent be separated into a sub-syndromes, but it should be remembered that all of these overlap and may present in erratic combinations in individual patients.

Table 10.2 The major clinical features of tardive dyskinesia

Tongue
'Vermicular' movements (no displacement)
Displacement on one or more axes (rotation, lateral movement, 'tromboning')
Extension beyond dental margin
Irregular sweeping of buccal surface ('bon-bon' sign)
Irregular non-recurrent protrusion ('fly-catcher' sign)

Jaw
Mouth opening
Lateral deviation
Anterior protrusion
Chewing
Grinding

Lips
Pursing
Puckering
Sucking
Smacking
Retraction of lateral angles ('bridling')

Expression
Blepharoclonus
Blepharospasm (partial/complete–sustained/spasmodic)
Elevation/depression of eyebrows
Furrowing of forehead
Grimacing
Conjugate eye deviation (tardive oculogyrus)

Head/neck/trunk
Torti-/antero-/retro-/latero-collis
Lateral/anteroposterior displacement ('Pisa syndrome')
Shoulder elevation/shrugging
Axial hyperkinesis ('copulatory' movements)
(Tics)

Upper limbs
Hyperpronation

(Continued overleaf)

Table 10.2 Continued

Wrist/elbow flexion/extension
Metacarpo-pharyngeal flexion/extension ('piano playing')
Finger filliping
Lateral outsplaying
Exaggerated arm swing

Lower limbs
Adduction/abduction
Flexion/extension hips/knees/ankles
Ankle rotation
Inversion/eversion
Lateral 'outsplaying' of toes
Flexion/extension of toes

Internal musculature
Dysphagia
Irregular/audible respirations
'Dyspnoea'
Spontaneous vocalisations
   grunting
   moaning
Speech disorders
   dysarthria
   'nasal' speech
   irregular phrasing
   'staccato speech' (adductor spasm)
   'breathless whisper' (abductor spasm)

Source: Cunningham Owens (1999), *A guide to the extrapyramidal side-effects of neuroleptic drugs.* Cambridge University Press. Reproduced with permission.

Orofacial dyskinesias

Between 60 per cent and 80 per cent of patients show this form of tardive dyskinesia, and it is particularly common in patients over the age of 50, where it tends to present in relatively isolated form. The core of the syndrome is champing, chewing and lateral jaw movements. These may be accompanied by pursing, smacking and puckering of the lips, and tongue movements ranging from working and rolling to repetitive reptilian protrusions (the 'fly-catcher tongue'). In more severe cases there may also be puffing out of the cheeks, grimacing, frowning and periorbital contractions, gagging, retching, bruxism and neck movements. Very rarely respiration and swallowing are affected and the disorder can then be life-threatening. The movements tend to occur rhythmically, with a more or less fixed tempo (Mackay, 1982; Lees, 1985), and have a repetitive and stereotyped quality; while the sequence is never entirely predictable, a recurring theme is evident.

Trunk and limb dyskinesias

These are more common in younger patients and are especially characteristic of tardive dyskinesia in children. Irregular 'piano playing' or 'guitar playing' finger movements may be accompanied by dystonic posturing of the fingers, wrist movements, and pronating and supinating movements of the forearms (Lees, 1985; Marsden *et al.*, 1975, 1986). Analogous movements can involve the toes and feet. The trunk may be affected by rocking, torsion movements and pelvic thrusting ('axial hyperkinesia'). Some authors include more complex and integrated movements as dyskinetic, for instance, caressing and rubbing the face, hair or thighs, crossing and uncrossing the legs, and 'holokinetic' movements involving large parts of the body (Simpson *et al.*, 1979). The quality of the movements has variously been considered to be irregularly repetitive (Simpson *et al.*, 1979), nearly repetitive (Marsden *et al.*, 1986), indistinguishable from choreoathetosis (Lees, 1985), or perhaps most accurately, all of these and sometimes defying description.

Tardive dystonia

Here the movements have a predominantly sustained, dystonic quality. Unlike tardive dyskinesia they are distressing and often painful. The movements can also cause serious disability – blepharospasm can cause functional blindness and laryngeal dystonia can deprive the patient of virtually all speech. Generalised tardive dystonia can be fatal, often through exhaustion. While dystonias are the prominent symptoms, it is clear from the available descriptions that the presentation is not pure and elements of orofacial, trunk and limb dyskinesias are commonly also present (Lees, 1985). Tardive dystonia is an exception to the rule that at least six months of neuroleptic treatment are required before it can occur. It can start within weeks of treatment, and 50 per cent of cases have an onset within five years (Cunningham Owens, 1999).

Tardive Gilles de la Tourette's syndrome

In this form multiple tics and vocalisations are the leading feature. There may also be coprolalia and echolalia. Only a very small number of cases have been reported (Lieberman and Saltz, 1992), and it is clear that, while tics are the most prominent symptoms, they are not the only ones and more typical dyskinetic orofacial, trunk and limb movements are commonly also present (Sacks, 1982; Lees, 1985; Cunningham Owens, 1999).

As every psychiatrist knows, tardive dyskinesia tends to persist even if neuroleptics are withdrawn. At a conservative estimate up to 50 per cent of cases are irreversible in this sense (APA Task Force, 1979). Higher rates of remission may be seen in early cases and in younger patients – in children complete recovery is said to be the rule (Lees, 1985). When it does occur, improvement is slow and may continue for months or even years (Marsden *et al.*, 1986; Cunningham Owens, 1999). For the large majority of schizophrenic patients who require continued neuroleptic treatment, information on the course of tardive dyskinesia is less certain: it is clear that the condition is not commonly progressive and in the majority of cases it remains mild. Some patients improve even to the point of becoming symptom free despite continued treatment. In a small minority, in contrast, a slowly worsening course is followed (Lees, 1985).

The treatment of tardive dyskinesia is, or at least used to be, unsatisfactory. Of the many pharmacological strategies tried (reviewed by Jeste *et al.*, 1988; Marsden *et al.*, 1986; Cunningham Owens, 1999) success has been claimed for cholinergic drugs, dopamine depleting agents such as tetrabenazine, GABA agonists and beta-adrenergic drugs such as propanolol. Many of the studies have been methodologically flawed, however, and the improvements reported have not been great. Only one treatment provides any grounds for optimism, but these are genuine: the atypical neuroleptic, clozapine, which as well as not causing tardive dyskinesia to any significant extent (see below), has been found to bring about improvement in between a third and a half of established cases (Lieberman and Saltz, 1992; see also Wittenberg *et al.*, 1996).

A functional dopamine excess, presumptively affecting the basal ganglia, is widely considered to be the common denominator of choreoathetoid movements in a number of disease states (Klawans and Weiner, 1976). That this is also the case for tardive dyskinesia is supported by the powerful circumstantial evidence that the movements are suppressed and increased by dopamine antagonist and agonist drugs, respectively (Gerlach, 1979; Marsden and Jenner, 1980). The seeming paradox of how drugs whose action is to block dopamine receptors might cause a state of functional dopamine excess has been explained as being due to the development of post-synaptic D2 receptor supersensitivity; this is known to occur when animals are chronically treated with neuroleptics (see Lees, 1985; Marsden *et al.*, 1986), and has been found in post-mortem studies of schizophrenic patients, as described in Chapter 6. There are also, however, a number of difficulties associated with this proposal. Neuroleptic-induced dopamine receptor supersensitivity in rats reverses after a few months off treatment. Also, differences in dopamine D2 receptor numbers have not been found in the post-mortem brains of schizophrenic patients with and without tardive dyskinesia in life (Mackay *et al.*, 1982). Sadly, the conclusion reached by a committee of clinicians and scientists over 20 years ago (APA Task Force, 1979) remains appropriate:

> Although the aetiology of tardive dyskinesia remains unknown, there is considerable pharmacologic evidence to suggest that a functional over-activity of extrapyramidal mechanisms mediated by dopamine is an important aspect of pathophysiology. An explanation for the prolonged and even irreversible course of many cases of tardive dyskinesia awaits further research.

Neuroleptic malignant syndrome

This rare and potentially fatal complication of neuroleptic treatment was first described and named by Delay and Deniker (1968). A few years later Cohen and Cohen (1974) independently described what was almost certainly the same disorder, which they erroneously ascribed to combined treatment with halo-peridol and lithium. Since then there have been numerous accounts of the syndrome (e.g. Caroff, 1980; Levensen *et al.*, 1985; Shalev and Munitz, 1986). Like tardive dyskinesia, it is also increasingly recognised that a disorder show-ing at least some of the same features was seen in schizophrenic patients in the days before neuroleptic treatment, when it was known as lethal catatonia (see Mann *et al.*, 1986; Lohr and Wisniewski, 1987). Nevertheless the causal role of neuroleptic drugs in the vast majority of contemporary cases seems beyond dispute. All neuroleptic drugs can cause neuroleptic malignant syn-drome, including clozapine (Hasan and Buckley, 1998). Addonizio and Susman (1991) comprehensively reviewed the literature on the disorder and, except where otherwise stated, what follows is based on their account.

The incidence of neuroleptic malignant syndrome probably lies somewhere between 0.07 per cent and 1.4 per cent of treatment episodes and, contrary to some early views, affects both sexes equally and can occur at any age. It may develop after the institution of neuroleptic therapy, after switching to a dif-ferent drug, or after increasing the dosage of the same drug. While some cases may develop on small doses of neuroleptics, high or rapidly escalating dosage regimes are a risk factor for occurrence of the syndrome. Typically, symptoms appear within hours or days of the change in treatment; however, there is no doubt that a significant number of cases (up to a third) are seen after two weeks, and the interval has been claimed to be as long as six months.

The central clinical features of the syndrome are Parkinson-like rigidity, clouding of consciousness, and fever, tachycardia and other fluctuating autonomic disturbances. Sometimes after a period of acutely exacerbated psychosis (which often gives the impression of being particularly florid and accompanied by disturbed behaviour), a state of sluggish unresponsiveness supervenes over a period of hours to days. Akinesia, bradykinesia and rigid-ity appear; hypersalivation, dysarthria and dysphagia may also be present. Tremor is seen in about half of cases. Choreoathetoid or dystonic movements have also been described in some cases. It is also well documented that cata-tonic symptoms, especially mutism, posturing and waxy flexibility, can form part of the presentation (Caroff, 1980; Abbot and Loizou, 1986; see also Mann *et al.*, 1986; Lohr and Wisniewski, 1987) – hence the overlap with lethal catatonia. The altered consciousness in neuroleptic malignant syn-drome has eluded precise description, but it seems mostly to take the form of confusion and disorientation, often accompanied by drowsiness; sometimes there is a state of unresponsiveness or even coma. Stupor has also been described, and in some cases, conversely, agitation is a prominent feature. The temperature is usually elevated, sometimes though not always to hyperpyrexial levels. Tachycardia, tachypnoea, sweating and raised blood pressure are the main autonomic accompaniments and these characteristically fluctuate. Miscellaneous signs include increased tendon reflexes, upgoing plantars and seizures.

All of the above features may wax and wane unpredictably. Different classes of symptom may appear in erratic combinations, partial forms are seen, and there is no consistent order of progression.

The most consistent laboratory abnormality is raised creatine phosphokinase. This is elevated in over 90 per cent of patients, often massively so. This elevation is almost certainly related to muscular rigidity although the exact process underlying it is obscure. A related myoglobinaemia has been found in 75 per cent of patients. In about 70 per cent of cases, the white cell count is raised, with a polymorphonuclear leucocytosis of up to 40,000/mm³. Less consistently found are electrolyte imbalances and raised liver enzymes. Lumbar puncture and CT scan are usually unrevealing; the EEG remains normal or may show diffuse slowing or non-specific changes.

In the past neuroleptic malignant syndrome carried a mortality of 15–22 per cent, but there are now suggestions that this is decreasing, almost certainly reflecting better diagnosis and more vigorous treatment. Death is frequently due to the medical complications of dehydration, chest infection, and rhabdomyolysis leading to renal failure. Cerebral oedema has been found occasionally at post-mortem, and sometimes death is sudden and unexpected, possibly a consequence of cardiac arrest secondary to the autonomic dysfunction. In those who survive, the syndrome regresses after discontinuation of neuroleptics within a maximum of 40 days, the average duration being 1–2 weeks. This figure is approximately doubled if patients have been on depot neuroleptic medication.

The mainstay of treatment is supportive management with cooling and rehydration. Various drug treatments have also been tried: dopamine agonists of all types are commonly used and are usually reported to be beneficial, but decisive evidence that they are effective is lacking. ECT has been reported as bringing about rapid resolution or being without effect. It should be noted that a significant minority of the cases collected by Addonizio and Sussman died after receiving this treatment, mainly due to precipitation of cardiac arrythmias. Another therapeutic strategy is use of dantrolene, a peripherally acting muscle relaxant. Addonizio and Sussman found that studies reporting definite, possible or no therapeutic effect were roughly evenly divided.

The pathogenesis of neuroleptic malignant syndrome remains largely conjectural, and two main lines of speculation have been followed. The first of these implicates intense dopamine receptor blockade affecting the striatum and the hypothalamus (which receives dopamine innervation from two sources). Providing circumstantial support for this view are scattered case reports, for example of a patient with Huntington's chorea who developed neuroleptic malignant syndrome when treated with dopamine depleting agents, and several patients with Parkinson's disease who developed it on withdrawal of dopamine agonist drugs. The rigidity and other extrapyramidal features seen in neuroleptic malignant syndrome also strongly suggest that there is a hypodopaminergic state. Finally, neuroleptic drugs are known to affect thermal regulation and can produce hyperthermia when injected into the hypothalamus.

The second approach draws on similarities between neuroleptic malignant syndrome and malignant hyperthermia. In this rare, genetically mediated disorder, anaesthetic agents like halothane induce, via a direct effect on muscle fibres, sustained contractions that lead to rigidity, hyperpyrexia and rhabdomyolysis. While some evidence has suggested that patients with neuroleptic malignant syndrome show a malignant hyperthermia-like hypermetabolic response to both fluphenazine and halothane, subsequent work has not convincingly replicated this finding.

Finally, the unpredictable development of neuroleptic malignant syndrome suggests a possible role for host factors: an individual who had previously developed it on a particular neuroleptic may show no recurrence on treatment with the same drug. It may be that susceptibility to neuroleptic malignant syndrome varies at various times according to clinical condition; it may even be that the disorder will ultimately be best understood as an iatrogenic form of lethal catatonia (Mann *et al.*, 1986).

Atypical neuroleptics

As it became appreciated that the therapeutic effect of neuroleptics was limited, it also became clear that no drug had therapeutic advantages over any other; if a patient did not respond to one drug, switching to a different one would not be of any benefit. This was demonstrated in a particularly transparent way by Davis (1985), who examined the comparative efficacy of different neuroleptics simply by counting the number of studies that found them to be more effective, equally effective, or less effective than a standard drug such as chlorpromazine. Some of the results of this exercise are summarised in Table 10.3. It is depressingly clear that none of a quite long list of drugs has ever been found to be superior to chlorpromazine. Davis found exactly the same when haloperidol and thioridazine were used as the reference compounds.

In the absence of any conspicuous therapeutic differences, pharmacologists interested in the development of better neuroleptics had no option other than to focus on the remaining sources of variation between them – in other words their non-therapeutic properties discussed earlier in this chapter. Three drugs stood out in this way, by virtue of having an unusual profile of receptor blocking effects, animal behavioural effects, or human side-effects. The hope at this time was merely that close scrutiny of such 'atypical' neuroleptics, as they were sometimes designated, might lead to drugs with a more favourable side-effect profile in humans, and which in particular might not cause tardive dyskinesia.

Table 10.3 Studies comparing the effectiveness of different neuroleptics to chlorpromazine

	Compared to chlorpromazine, number of studies in which drug was		
	More effective	*As effective*	*Less effective*
Trifluoperazine	0	11	0
Perphenazine	0	6	0
Thioridazine	0	12	0
Fluphenazine	0	9	0
Haloperidol	0	4	0
Thiothixene	0	4	0
Prochlorperazine	0	10	0
Loxapine	0	14	1
Promazine	0	2	4
Molindone	0	6	0
Mesoridazine	0	7	0

Source: Adapted from Davis (1985).

The road that led to clozapine

The first neuroleptic to stand out as unusual in any of these respects was thioridazine. In animal behavioural studies this drug was found to be cataleptogenic to much the same extent as other neuroleptics, but some studies found that its ability to reverse the amphetamine/apomorphine response was restricted to the hyperactivity (putatively non-striatal) component of this (see Joyce, 1983). Although this was by no means a consistent finding, the failure to have an effect on the (putatively basal ganglia) stereotypy component of this response was hypothesised to account for the well-known clinical observation that thioridazine caused fewer extrapyramidal side-effects than other neuroleptics (Herman and Pleasure, 1963). This then led to a proposal that thioridazine might not cause tardive dyskinesia (Borison *et al.*, 1983), and this found its way into an advertisement for the drug. The result was immeditate: several leading American psychopharmacologists of the day wrote a letter to the journal concerned denouncing the claim, which lacked any prospective studies to support it (Ayd *et al.*, 1984).

Thioridazine was also known to have a pharmacological peculiarity, in that unlike other neuroleptics, it has strong cholinergic receptor blocking effects. This anticholinergic effect was a possible explanation for its unusual animal behavioural profile, and certainly seemed able to account for its relative lack of extrapyramidal side-effects, even if the evidence on these points was not clear-cut (see Crow *et al.*, 1977; Joyce, 1983). But otherwise its receptor blocking profile was unexceptional, and closely similar to its chemical relative, chlorpromazine.

The second drug to attract the designation of 'atypical' was sulpiride. This drug was developed in France in the late 1960s, and pharmacologically is characterised by a highly selective blockade of dopamine D2 receptors and very few interactions with other neurotransmitter receptors. It was also found that prolonged treatment with this drug did not lead to increased dopamine D2 receptor numbers in animals (Rupniak *et al.*, 1984). In animal behavioural models, the striking property of sulpiride was its weak cataleptogenic effect. More convincingly than with thioridazine, it was also found to preferentially reverse the hyperactivity rather than the stereotypy component of the ampthetamine/apomorphine response, a finding that could not be attributed to any intrinsic anticholinergic properties (see Joyce, 1983).

In man, sulpiride has a reputation for causing fewer extrapyramidal side-effects than other neuroleptics. One survey (Alberts *et al.*, 1985) found acute dystonic reactions, akathisia and Parkinsonism to be present in no more than 4 per cent of patients receiving treatment, but in other studies, however, the differences have been less impressive (Harnryd *et al.*, 1984; Soni and Freeman, 1985). Despite some early claims, no evidence has been produced to show that sulpiride does not cause tardive dyskinesia.

Whatever their unusual preclinical properties and lack of human side-effects, both thioridazine and sulpiride have never been considered anything other than unexceptional therapeutically. This was not the case for the third drug traditionally considered to be atypical by pharmacologists, clozapine. Like classical neuroleptics, clozapine blocks dopamine D2 receptors, and otherwise has a wide and unexceptional profile of receptor interactions. Additionally, like thioridazine it has very strong anticholinergic properties (Hyttel *et al.*, 1985). Like sulpiride, prolonged treatment with clozapine was also found not to produce dopamine D2 receptor supersensitivity in animals (Rupniak *et al.*, 1984).

The animal behavioural effects of clozapine are the most atypical of any neuroleptic. It is virtually devoid of cataleptogenic activity (e.g. see Coward, 1992), only causing this at extremely high doses or when given intrastriatally. It also reverses only the hyperactivity component of the response to amphetamine or apomorphine response, and even here its effect is weak (see Joyce, 1983).

Analogous atypical effects were soon noted in patients. Numerous studies found that the drug produced little or no Parkinsonism. Acute dystonic reactions were also not reported, and the drug was believed not to cause akathisia (although a more accurate view is now that it does so to a lesser extent than conventional neuroleptics). Of considerably more interest, none of a large number of patients treated with clozapine alone over periods of years in the USA (Davis, 1985) and Scandinavia (Povlsen *et al.*, 1985) appeared to have developed tardive dyskinesia (see also Casey, 1989).

The earliest studies of clozapine did not suggest that it was therapeutically superior to other drugs, but there were hints that it was unusual in other ways (see McKenna and Bailey, 1993; Crilly, 2007). For example it was considered to be particularly effective in the most severely ill schizophrenic patients, and it was noted that when the drug was stopped some patients underwent a marked worsening and could be difficult to manage even on large doses of other drugs. Later trials, in contrast, sometimes found clozapine to be therapeutically superior to other drugs. McKenna and Bailey (1993) carried out a similar exercise to Davis (1985) and found that it was reported to be superior to chlorpromazine in 6 out of 13 studies and superior to haloperidol in 4 out of 6 studies.

The Kane et al. study

Clozapine remained in routine clinical use until 1974, when in the wake of nine deaths in Finland, the unacceptably high rate of agranulocytosis it caused became clear. By this time, however, its lack of extrapyramidal side-effects and possible therapeutic superiority had become widely appreciated. From 1977, a number of carefully monitored investigations of clozapine were carried out, typically as a treatment of last resort in patients who were otherwise untreatable by reason of unresponsiveness or extrapyramidal side-effects. These culminated in the multicentre trial of Kane *et al.* (1988) on treatment-refractory schizophrenic patients.

Kane *et al.* recruited 268 patients meeting DSM III criteria for schizophrenia from 16 centres in America. Before entering the trial the patients had to fulfil retrospective, cross-sectional and prospective requirements for treatment resistance. Retrospective criteria revolved around documentation of poor response to multiple periods of treatment with different neuroleptics given in high doses. Cross-sectionally, patients had to show positive symptoms and have moderate or high ratings on an overall severity scale. Before entering the trial, all patients then had to demonstrate no more than minimal improvement on up to six weeks treatment with high-dose haloperidol.

The patients were then treated for six weeks with flexible dosages of either clozapine or chlorpromazine in double blind conditions. In order to avoid unblinding due to clozapine's lack of extrapyramidal side-effects, patients who were randomised to receive chlopromazine were also given anticholinergic medication, and those in the clozapine group were given placebo. The findings are shown in Figure 10.3. Improvement in the clozapine-treated group was greater than for the chlorpromazine-treated group, with the advantage being significant from the first week of treatment. The improvement in total symptom scores was approximately three times greater in the clozapine-treated patients, and was significant for both positive and negative symptoms. When a priori criteria for 'clinically significant improvement' were applied, 30 per cent of the clozapine-treated patients met these, as opposed to only 4 per cent of those receiving chlorpromazine.

Five further double blind randomised controlled studies of clozapine have continued to find significant superiority to what are now invariably referred to as 'conventional' neuroleptics (Kane *et al.*, 2001; Hong *et al.*, 1997; Buchanan *et al.*, 1998; Rosenheck *et al.*, 1997; Volavka *et al.*, 2002). One study also found that clozapine produced significantly faster remission in

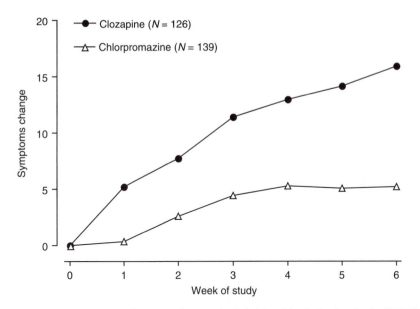

Figure 10.3 Mean change from baseline on the Brief Psychiatric Rating Scale (BPRS) in patients treated with clozapine or chlorpromazine ($p < .001$ for each week of the study (from Kane *et al.* (1988), Clozapine for the treatment resistant schizophrenic. *Archives of General Psychiatry*, 45, 789–796. Copyright © 1988 American Medical Association).

first episode schizophrenic patients compared to chlorpromazine, although there was no overall superiority at one year (Lieberman *et al.*, 2003). Most authors feel that the response rate of 30 per cent found in the Kane *et al.* study is an underestimate, and the true response rate is in the region of 50 per cent. Approximately 10 per cent of patients undergo dramatic improvement.

The evidence that clozapine causes little or no tardive dyskinesia also remains reasonably firm. Kane *et al.* (1993) followed up 28 patients who did not show definite evidence of tardive dyskinesia for an average of 6.2 years after their treatment was changed to clozapine. Only two developed tardive dyskinesia; in both cases this was in the 'mild' category, and both had had a 'questionable' rating at the time they started on treatment. Davé (1994) reported two patients who developed tardive dyskinesia while on treatment with clozapine. However, according to Cunningham Owens (1999), in one of these it appeared within a period of time where it could have been attributed to previous conventional neuroleptic treatment.

Other atypical neuroleptics

With clozapine, the concept of atypicality, that unusual preclinical pharmacology might translate into favourable clinical effects, paid off beyond its original modest aim of producing drugs with fewer extrapyramidal side-effects.

In the words of Crilly (2007), this prompted a scramble by other major drug companies to develop their own atypical antipsychotic medications. By the early 1990s, rival companies were developing their own atypical neuroleptics which, it was hoped, would be more effective than conventional neuroleptics, or if not would at least cause 'no more extrapyramidal side-effects than placebo'.

The main other atypical neuroleptics now in use are risperidone, olanzapine, amisulpride, and quetiapine, with aripiprazole recently being added to the list. These drugs form a heterogeneous group. Olanzapine and quetiapine have a broad profile of receptor blockade like clozapine (but also like chlorpromazine). Risperidone blocks mainly dopamine D2-like receptors and serotonin receptors. Amisulpride is a relatively pure D2/D3 receptor blocker. Aripiprazole is a partial agonist at D2-like receptors. Most have, or are claimed to have, unusual effects in the two animal systems used to screen drugs for antipsychotic potential, the catalepsy test and reversal of amphetamine and apomorphine-induced hyperactivity and stereotypy. However, it is clear that none of them show anything like the near-absolute failure to produce catalepsy and reverse amphetamine effects seen with clozapine, and the argument for what makes the drug atypical in these animal models often seems quite tortured.

Olanzapine, quetiapine and aripiprazole genuinely lack extrapyramidal side-effects. Risperidone and amisulpride, on the other hand do cause these. There is no doubt that risperidone and olanzapine can cause tardive dyskinesia (Llorca *et al.*, 2002), although the rate may be substantially lower with the latter drug (Beasley *et al.*, 1999). No data are as yet available for quetiapine or aripiprazole.

The more important question is whether these atypical neuroleptic drugs are therapeutically superior to conventional drugs. There have been several large-scale trials comparing risperidone and olanzapine to conventional neuroleptics, and these drugs have been marketed on the basis of findings of superior efficacy. There have been no such claims for quetiapine and aripiprazole. Amisulpride occupies an unusual position, having been available for some years in France before being relaunched as an atypical antipsychotic, and until recently it was supported only by trials with relatively small sample sizes.

Davis *et al.* (2003) meta-analysed trials comparing these (and several other) second-generation neuroleptics, and also clozapine, to standard drugs such as chlorpromazine or haloperidol. The results are summarised in Figure 10.4. As found in an earlier meta-analysis (Wahlbeck *et al.*, 1999), clozapine was superior to conventional neuroleptic treatment, and at 0.49 had a 'medium' effect size. Amisulpride, olanzapine and risperidone were all also found overall to be significantly superior to standard treatment, but for these drugs the effect size clustered around 0.25, in the 'small' range. The improvement was somewhat less than half that found for conventional neuroleptics over placebo. Quetiapine and aripiprazole were not significantly different from conventional drugs, in keeping with their lack of claims for superior efficacy.

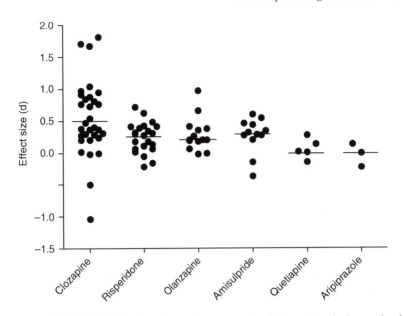

Figure 10.4 Individual effect sizes in studies comparing different atypical neuroleptics to conventional drugs. Horizontal lines are the pooled effect sizes for each drug (from Davis *et al.* (2003), A meta-analysis of the efficacy of second-generation antipsychotics. *Archives of General Psychiatry*, 60, 553–564. Copyright © 2003 American Medical Association).

The superiority of clozapine, amisulpride, olanzapine and risperidone was not attributable to various potential confounding factors, such as dose of the comparator drug, and the inclusion of small studies, open studies or studies that did not appear in peer-reviewed publications.

Why clozapine and certain other drugs are therapeutically superior remains, to date, unknown. The drugs concerned are very different from each other, in terms of both their receptor pharmacology and their animal behavioural effects. If nothing else, this has made a leading early hypothesis, that atypical drugs have in common marked serotonin receptor antagonism (Meltzer, 1991), untenable. Other hypotheses include preferential blockade of dopamine receptors in limbic and cortical areas (e.g. Kinon and Lieberman, 1996), and that atypical neuroleptics have a faster dissociation rate from (i.e. bind more loosely to) D2 receptors (Kapur and Seeman, 2001). Both these hypotheses face difficulties of their own (see Waddington *et al.*, 2003). Somewhat ironically, perhaps the only thing that seems clear is that the therapeutic superiority of atypical neuroleptics is not closely linked to lack of extrapyramidal side-effects, the phenomenon that to a large extent motivated their development in the first place.

11 The management of schizophrenia

Despite neuroleptic treatment, and the recent advances in this, the outlook for the average patient with schizophrenia is bleak. Over the course of what is likely to be a normal lifespan, he or she will be prone to flare-ups of active psychotic symptoms, may eventually come to experience these continuously, and may develop enduring deficits which will prevent him or her from being able to live without some degree of care and supervision. In the face of pessimism and sometimes despair, any and every therapeutic avenue has been explored in schizophrenia.

The treatments that have been tried in schizophrenia range from psychoanalysis to frontal lobotomy. Despite being enthusiastically advocated in some quarters, neither of these extreme modes of treatment has stood the test of time, and currently it is as uncommon for schizophrenic patients to be referred for psychosurgery as it is for them to be taken on for interpretative psychotherapy (although this does not mean that either practice has died out completely). Certain forms of drug treatment besides neuroleptics linger on, as does electro-convulsive therapy (ECT), neither discredited nor universally accepted but with the impression of having some limited usefulness. Often held in contempt by biologically oriented psychiatrists, there are also a number of psychological and social interventions, at least two of which have an evidence base that makes it difficult to dismiss them out of hand. Still other therapeutic approaches are not really forms of treatment at all, but merely measures designed to improve the quality of life for the sufferers of a chronic, incurable disease. Most of what is termed rehabilitation falls into this category.

This chapter takes the form of a critical review of the more practical, strategic aspects of the treatment of schizophrenia. These are approached in the way they tend to be approached in clinical practice, via a division into the treatment of acute schizophrenia when it does not respond to neuroleptics, prevention of relapse, and remediation of chronic disability or rehabilitation. Each of these areas has acquired its own literature, its own preoccupations, and in some cases its own idiosyncrasies.

Treatment-resistant schizophrenia

Because neuroleptics are of established effectiveness, and because they exert particular effects on positive symptoms, these drugs have become the mainstay of treatment for acute episodes. At the same time, however, their effectiveness is limited and treatment not infrequently fails. It is not uncommon to find schizophrenic patients in relapse whose symptoms cannot be controlled with conventional treatment, and in some of these patients the episode persists despite increases in dosage and switching to an atypical neuroleptic, including clozapine.

It follows that a large part of the management of acute schizophrenia involves the management of adjunctive physical treatments. A wide range of treatments have been advocated for this purpose and, in the way of clinical practice, tend to be used more often in the hope than the expectation that they will be of benefit. Only two such treatments, however, have ever been seriously considered to have genuine therapeutic value rather than just having non-specific, typically sedative or tranquillising effects. One of these is a drug, lithium. The other is electro-convulsive therapy which has fallen in and out of favour over the years.

Until recently nothing beyond physical treatment could be offered for patients with treatment-resistant acute schizophrenia. In the last 10 years or so, however, biological treatments have faced evidence-based competition in the shape of a psychological treatment, cognitive therapy.

Lithium

The story of how this drug became a routinely used treatment in psychiatry is rich in serendipity. In 1948, a psychiatrist working single-handedly in a laboratory attached to a provincial mental hospital in Australia decided to investigate mental illness in a way that was popular at the time, by injecting concentrated urine from patients into guinea pigs. The psychiatrist was Cade, and he chose to use urine from patients with mania (see Cade, 1970; Johnson and Cade, 1975). The procedure proved fatal to the guinea pigs in most cases, but it also became apparent that there was considerable variation in the toxicity of the urine. Cade suspected that this might be related to the amount of uric acid that was present. The next step was to inject mixtures of urea and uric acid into guinea pigs. Unfortunately he encountered a practical problem at this stage, in that uric acid is only slightly soluble in water. The solution was to use its least insoluble salt, which happened to be lithium urate. Injection of lithium urate was found to have the unexpected effect of making the guinea pigs placid and unresponsive to stimuli (which in retrospect probably reflected lithium toxicity).

After administering lithium to himself to ensure it was safe, Cade took the decision to try the drug on an excited psychotic patient. He selected a man who had been chronically hypomanic for five years. After a few days he wondered if he could see signs of improvement. After another few days there could be no doubt. The patient went on to make a full recovery, was subsequently discharged from hospital, and remained well. Cade went on to treat 10 manic patients, 6 patients with schizophrenia and 3 patients with chronic depression. While there was little effect in the schizophrenic and depressed patients, the results in the manic patients were little short of dramatic – all 10 showed rapid and marked improvement.

How lithium then made the transition from a little-noticed paper in the *Australian and New Zealand Journal of Psychiatry* to world-wide acceptance as first-line treatment for manic-depressive psychosis is another equally serendipitous and less well-known story, which owes almost everything to the Scandinavian psychiatrist Schou (see Johnson and Cade, 1975; King, 1985).

Despite, or perhaps because of, its success with manic-depressive psychosis, a distinctly unfavourable view developed of the usefulness of lithium in schizophrenia. The line taken in most contemporary textbooks and articles was that it was ineffective, except possibly to a minor extent when mood elevation formed a significant part of the picture. The evidence, however, severely limited as it was, was not completely in accordance with such a view. Delva and Letemendia (1982) found that all of seven uncontrolled studies – which were sometimes little more than anecdotal reports – reported improvement when lithium was given with or without concurrent neuroleptic medication. In some of the studies it was considered that only mood colourings of elation or depression were affected, but others noted a beneficial effect on a wider range of symptoms, occasionally to the point of their complete disappearance.

Leucht *et al.* (2004) meta-analysed these and further randomised controlled trials of lithium both as a sole treatment for schizophrenia and/or schizoaffective psychosis and as an adjunct to antipsychotic medication (see Box 11.1). Lithium as a sole treatment was found to be ineffective. By contrast, in 11 studies that compared lithium augmentation to treatment with neuroleptics alone, significantly more patients who received the combination were rated as improved. However, the effect became marginal when studies carried out on patients with schizoaffective disorders were excluded. The findings with respect to particular aspects of mental state were generally inconclusive, but there was little to suggest that the improvement found was due purely to effects on mood.

In summary, scanty though the available evidence is, it is reasonable to conclude that lithium is of some therapeutic usefulness in schizophrenia. Its benefits are almost certainly modest, but even so seem to have been underestimated. The question of whether the drug exerts its effects on mood disturbance or on a wider range of symptoms remains unresolved. This issue has been approached from a slightly different perspective in a large study by Johnstone *et al.* (1988), which is described in Chapter 13.

Box 11.1 The Cochrane collaboration meta-analysis of lithium for schizophrenia (from Leucht *et al.*, 2004)

The authors identified 20 randomised trials on a total of 611 patients with schizophrenia or schizoaffective disorder. These included trials both of lithium as sole treatment and of lithium as an adjunct to neuroleptic medication. Most of the studies were small and of short duration, but one had a sample size of 78. All but two studies were double blind. The studies commonly adjusted the dose of lithium to be within the therapeutic range by means of blood tests.

Three studies compared lithium as sole agent to placebo. The pooled results of these found no significant advantage for lithium on a variety of clinical measures. One large study also found no significant advantage for depressive and manic symptoms.

Eight studies compared lithium to neuroleptic treatment (chlorpromazine in all but one case in a range of 300–2000 mg/day). There was a tendency for lithium to be less effective than neuroleptics on several of the outcome measures, but the findings were difficult to summarise because of the variety of rating scales used.

Ten studies compared lithium to placebo as an augmentation treatment to neuroleptics. Significantly more patients who received lithium were rated as showing clinically significant improvement ($N = 244$, $RR = 0.8$, CI 0.7/0.96), and significantly more showed improvement as rated on the Clinical Global Impression Scale ($N = 115$, $RR = 0.6$, CI 0.5/0.9). There were numerical trends to better response in the lithium-treated patients on some but not all symptom-based measures. There were no differences in improvement in depression or mania ratings in these studies, although the relevant studies were few in number (three and one respectively).

Excluding patients with a diagnosis of schizoaffective disorder (155 with schizomania, 22 with schizophreniform psychosis, 7 with atypical psychosis, and 5 with delusional disorder) from the overall analysis resulted in loss of statistical superiority of lithium augmentation for the outcome of 'clinically significant improvement'. However, since the relative risk did not change, an alternative explanation for this could be the loss of statistical power.

Electro-convulsive therapy (ECT)

Although now firmly established in the treatment of depression, ECT was originally, and for quite long stretches of its subsequent history, a treatment for schizophrenia. How convulsive therapy was discovered has been recounted by Fink (1984). Based on the 'antagonism' theory of schizophrenia and epilepsy, and following unsuccessful attempts by others to treat epilepsy by injecting patients with the blood of schizophrenic patients, a Hungarian psychiatrist, von Meduna conceived the idea of inducing seizures to treat schizophrenia. He found a suitable trial subject in a patient who had been in a catatonic stupor for four years. After five seizure-inducing injections of camphor, the patient got out of bed, requested breakfast, and was interested in everything around him. Later he was discharged and remained well, apparently indefinitely. (Von Meduna's reward was to be hounded out of Hungary by his colleagues who at the time believed that schizophrenia was an incurable heredofamilial disease and not susceptible to treatment.)

After decades of indiscriminate, and at times gratuitous, use, the facts about ECT gradually became clear. According to Rollin (1981), its effective was recognised in depression where, particularly in severe cases with retardation and psychotic symptoms, it 'worked like a charm'. It also established a niche in the treatment of mania. Up until the 1950s ECT was the also most popular treatment for schizophrenia, and it was only after the introduction of neuroleptic drugs that the truth sank in that this was the condition for which it was least efficacious. Even then, the belief lingered on that ECT could be effective in states of acute catatonic stupor and excitement, and that it had its uses when neuroleptic treatment failed and there was ongoing grossly disturbed behaviour.

As expected, given the abundant case material, there has been no shortage of trials of ECT in schizophrenia. The best known, and also one of the largest of these was that of May (1968). This trial randomly assigned 228 clinically diagnosed patients (who were neither so acute that spontaneous recovery might affect results, nor so chronic that any improvement was unlikely) to treatment with ECT, neuroleptics, analytical psychotherapy or 'milieu therapy' (i.e. routine hospital care). Improvement rates, as measured by discharge from hospital and length of stay, were significantly better for the ECT-treated group than for the psychotherapy or milieu therapy groups, but not as good as for the neuroleptic-treated group.

This study made it clear that neuroleptic drugs were the preferred treatment for acute schizophrenia, but it left a case to answer about the use of ECT as an adjunctive treatment, especially in patients showing a slow or incomplete response to these drugs. Two more modern studies with rigorous designs have addressed this issue.

Taylor and Fleminger (1980; see also Taylor, 1981) selected a similar 'middle' group of schizophrenic patients to May, excluding those with a short history of illness (less than six months) or with clearly chronic illnesses (more than two years of continuous hospitalisation in the last five years, or more than six months in the last twelve months). If, after two weeks of neuroleptic treatment (or more in some cases), additional treatment was felt to be necessary, ECT was offered. From an initial sample of 55 patients, 20 entered the trial phase and were randomly assigned to real or simulated ECT under double blind conditions, given for between 8 and 12 treatments. Half of each group had high levels of depression. As shown in Figure 11.1, it was found that, while both groups showed improvement, this was significantly greater in the group that received real ECT; the difference was evident at two weeks (six treatments) and became more pronounced by four weeks. Depressive symptoms were better relieved by ECT than placebo, although the differences showed only a trend towards significance. Scores on a number of schizophrenic symptoms also improved differentially, reaching significance for four delusion and hallucination ratings, and also affective flattening. After the trial period the differences between the two groups diminished progressively until at three months they were minimal.

Brandon *et al.* (1985) reported on 17 patients with schizophrenia in a large-scale trial of ECT in all types of patient. The patients were randomly assigned to eight real or eight simulated treatments over four weeks under double blind conditions. The results were closely similar to those of Taylor and Fleminger: both groups improved, but after two and four weeks of treatment there was a significant advantage for those receiving real ECT. At the end of the trial differences in depression ratings between the two groups were marginal. As in Taylor and Fleminger's study, after the end of the trial, when a free choice of further treatment could be made, the advantage for the real ECT group progressively faded. Brandon *et al.*'s findings are also shown in Figure 11.1.

Although both Taylor and Fleminger and Brandon *et al.* found that the benefits were not sustained, and that the placebo-treated group subsequently 'caught up', different interpretations were given for this result: Taylor (1981) strongly implied that the main effect of ECT was to accelerate improvement that would have taken place with time and neuroleptic treatment anyway. Brandon *et al.*, on the other hand, merely contented themselves with pointing out that without adequate control of treatment during the follow-up period, it was not possible to comment on the duration of the effect of ECT.

Cognitive therapy

As long ago as 1952, Beck, the founding father of this currently ubiquitous form of psychological treatment, described its use in a schizophrenic patient, with encouraging results. Further case reports and reports of small series of cases followed (Watts *et al.*, 1973; Hole *et al.*, 1979; Chadwick and Lowe, 1990), and then a small-scale open trial (Tarrier *et al.*, 1993). These also found benefits, and collectively generated considerable optimism that key forms of psychotic symptom such as delusions and hallucinations might be susceptible to psychological treatment.

Nelson (1997) has described the way in which the principles of cognitive therapy (CBT) can be applied to delusions. The standard model used by cognitive therapists for the formation and maintenance of new beliefs in non-psychotic individuals is adapted by the addition of a 'psychotic activity' process, which is envisaged as a biological disturbance of brain function. This

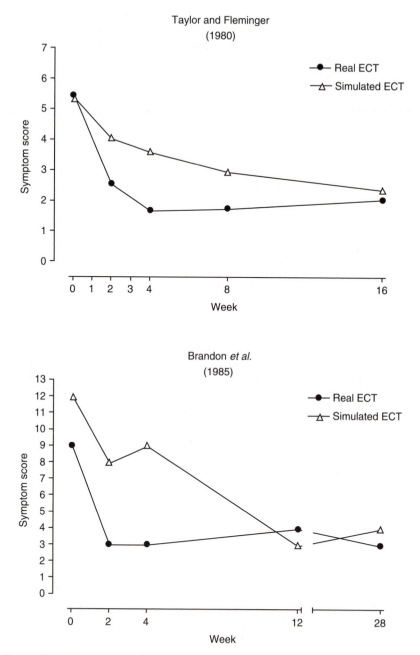

Figure 11.1 Two studies of real vs simulated ECT in schizophrenia (from Taylor and Fleminger (1980), ECT for schizophrenia. *Lancet*, i, 1380–1382. © by The Lancet Ltd 1980; Brandon *et al.* (1985), Leicester ECT trial: Results in schizophrenia. *British Journal of Psychiatry*, 146, 177–183. Reproduced with permission from the Royal college of Psychiatrists).

is proposed to affect conscious experience, principally by producing changes in emotion or mood state (defined broadly to include concepts of threat and self-esteem). Because this state is driven by biological disturbance rather than being a response to life experiences, it can trigger mood-congruent thoughts and then beliefs that may seem inappropriate or even inexplicable to others. Once acquired, these beliefs are maintained by the same irrational biases, simplifying heuristics and self-confirming circles of thought which, according to the cognitive therapy view, maintain dysfunctional beliefs in other pathological states such as depression, anxiety and obsessional disorder. The techniques of cognitive therapy can then be deployed to correct the delusional belief. Some of these techniques are summarised in Box 11.2.

Box 11.2 The cognitive therapy approach to delusions (from Nelson, 1997)

1. Cognitive behavioural therapy works by strengthening the reasoning/rational side of the person to argue against and thereby to influence the intuitional/feelings side.
2. It encourages the patient to make the split between 'I feel . . . but I know . . .'. This is particularly important when the psychosis is active because at this time the feelings will continue to some degree, however good the rational arguments against them might be.
3. It encourages the patient to act on the 'I know . . .' rather than on the 'I feel . . .'. In other words, it enables the patient to select a behaviour that will reduce rather than increase the strength of the delusional belief. For example, a young man who developed paranoid delusions about the nurses when unwell would isolate himself in his room, thereby providing more evidence that they were not concerned about him. Following CBT, he was able to detect and identify the re-emergence of these ideas as his psychosis fluctuated and, by using reason to counter the paranoid feelings while they were still mild, he was able to put into effect the previously discovered coping strategy of going to talk to the nurses. Their friendly response provided immediate feedback and evidence against the paranoid thoughts and thereby prevented the full-blown delusion from developing.
4. Having insight and being able to argue rationally against a delusional belief will lessen the impact that the delusional thoughts would otherwise have on emotions and behaviour. It will also help to prevent the development of secondary delusional beliefs. For example, in the case mentioned above, being able to produce evidence that the nursing staff felt kindly towards him prevented this paranoid patient developing a secondary delusional belief that the medication the nursing staff were giving him might be harming him.

5. CBT is more effective and progresses faster the less actively psychotic the patient, so when used as an adjunct to medication it is often appropriate to wait until the patient has settled down on his medication before starting the CBT.

The cognitive therapy approach to hallucinations is less clearly defined (it was not mentioned at all by Nelson). However, similar processes of insight promotion, logical reasoning, evidence evaluation, and development of coping strategies are brought to bear on the symptom.

The era of formal clinical evaluation began with a three-centre randomised controlled trial by Kuipers *et al.* (1997). They assigned 54 DSM-III-R schizophrenic patients with at least one treatment-resistant positive symptom to either cognitive therapy or routine care for nine months. By the end of this period the cognitive therapy group showed a 25 per cent reduction in symptoms, whereas there was hardly any change in those who received routine care. The difference was highly significant and was due mainly to reductions in scores for delusions and hallucinations in the treated group.

Kuiper *et al.*'s study was not free of weaknesses. It was carried out under non-blind conditions, and it did not employ a psychological intervention to control for the so-called Hawthorne effect, a psychological equivalent of the placebo effect. (The name derives from an electricity plant in the USA where a famous series of studies established that just about any intervention significantly increased the workers' productivity, by virtue of the special attention they received from the researchers.) Such criticisms do not apply to five further trials, which were carried out under blind conditions and compared cognitive therapy to a control intervention (supportive counselling or in one case befriending). These studies are summarised in Table 11.1. In the first such study, Tarrier *et al.* (1999) found greater improvement in a score based on delusions and hallucinations in the cognitive therapy group, but this was not significant. Two subsequent large studies (Sensky *et al.*, 2000; Lewis *et al.*, 2002) showed no significant advantage for cognitive therapy. Two more smaller studies both failed to show any significant advantage.

Some of the authors of these studies attempted to put a positive interpretation on their uniformly negative findings. Thus Tarrier *et al.* stated, on the strength of an overall significant difference among their cognitive therapy, supportive counselling and treatment-as-usual groups (but not between cognitive therapy and supportive counselling), that cognitive therapy was 'a potentially useful adjunct treatment in the management of patients with chronic schizophrenia'. Despite finding no advantage over befriending, Sensky *et al.* (2000) argued that cognitive therapy was effective in treating positive and negative schizophrenic symptoms; this claim was largely based on the finding that improvement was maintained in the CBT group over a subsequent nine month follow-up period, whereas the befriending group worsened. This finding has not since been replicated in two other studies (Tarrier

Table 11.1 Trials of cognitive therapy in schizophrenia employing blind evaluations and a control intervention

Study	Sample size	Duration of therapy	Finding	Comment
Tarrier *et al.* (1998, 1999)	23 CBT 21 SC	3 months	NSD	Mostly chronic patients
Sensky *et al.* (2000)	46 CBT 44 befriending	9 months	NSD	Mostly chronic patients Significant advantage for CBT emerged at 9-month follow-up
Lewis *et al.* (2002)	78 CBT 71 SC	5 weeks	NSD	First or second episode patients
Durham *et al.* (2003)	22 CBT 23 SC	9 months	NSD	All chronic patients
Valmaggia *et al.* (2005)	35 CBT 23 SC	5 months	NSD	Mostly chronic patients Medication held constant throughout trial Trend to superiority on positive symptom subscale

CBT – cognitive therapy, SC – supportive counselling

et al., 1999, 2004). Lewis *et al.* (2002) suggested that cognitive therapy speeded remission from acute symptoms in their patients with first or second episode schizophrenia, but this claim was based on differences in scores only on auditory hallucinations and not on other symptoms, that were was only present between the cognitive therapy group and the treatment-as-usual group. A more accurate summary of the state of the evidence is the recent statement by Tarrier and Wykes (2004) that, 'not one study has shown clear and significant overall differences between CBT and the non-specific control groups'.

Prevention of relapse

Schizophrenia is, particularly in the days of neuroleptic treatment, a disorder of exacerbations and improvements. If physical treatments are the mainstay of treatment of acute episodes, the management of patients after they have achieved their maximum degree of remission is a different and more complex matter. An important element remains maintenance neuroleptic drug treatment, whose efficacy has been examined in numerous well-designed clinical trials. For reasons to be discussed below, the suspicion also arose that social factors could play an important part in the precipitation of relapse, and this became the subject of a rigorous research initiative in the shape of expressed emotion.

Maintenance neuroleptic treatment

In the years after the introduction of neuroleptics, it became apparent that patients relapsed when they stopped taking their medication, although this could be delayed for weeks and months. At some point this recognition blurred into a realisation, in a number of uncontrolled reports, that neuroleptic drugs might have a genuine prophylactic effect, reducing the frequency of future relapses (see Davis, 1975). One of the first trials of maintenance treatment in schizophrenia was that of Leff and Wing (1971). They assigned 35 patients who had recently recovered from an acute schizophrenic episode to treatment with oral neuroleptic or placebo and followed their progress for a year. Only 33 per cent of the treated group relapsed, compared to 83 per cent of those receiving placebo.

Davis (1975) reviewed the findings from this and 34 further double blind studies comparing maintenance neuroleptic treatment to placebo. These all had a duration of more than six weeks, and they were carried out on both outpatients and inpatients. In all the studies fewer of the patients on placebo relapsed than those on active drugs, and the difference was significant in almost all cases. When the results of these studies were pooled, out of a total of 3609 patients, 20 per cent relapsed on active medication compared to 53 per cent on placebo.

These studies also revealed that schizophrenic patients do not necessarily relapse quickly after discontinuing neuroleptic medication. Davis (1975) reviewed the evidence from two large neuroleptic:placebo maintenance studies. He concluded that the rate of decline of patients who remained well on no medication followed an exponential function, indicating that patients tended to relapse at a constant rate over time – somewhere in the range of 8–15 per cent per month. This rate remained the same until up to 18 months. When the patients in these two studies who had been maintained on active medication for two years or more with no relapses had their medication stopped, they also began to relapse at much the same rate. The inference was that the whole population of schizophrenic patients maintained on prophylactic neuroleptic treatment are at risk of relapse; there was nothing to suggest the existence of a subgroup who do not need indefinite treatment.

Maintenance neuroleptic treatment has been shown to be of value in patients who have only had a single episode of schizophrenia. In a study with a conventional double blind, placebo controlled design, Crow *et al.* (1986) followed 120 first episode patients for two years or until relapse, and found 46 per cent of those on active medication relapsed, compared with 62 per cent on placebo, a highly significant difference. Robinson *et al.* (1999) found even more dramatic effects in a study of 104 first episode patients, who were given the option of discontinuing neuroleptic treatment after one year of stable remission. In this study the risk of relapse was almost five times higher in those who stopped taking medication.

Neuroleptic treatment also seems to be necessary even for patients who have remained in good remission for several years. Dencker *et al.* (1980) stopped the medication of 32 selected outpatients who were taking depot neuroleptic medication, had not had a relapse in the preceding two years, and showed no active psychotic symptoms. Seventeen of these patients relapsed in the next six months, a further nine relapsed in the next six months, and four of the remaining six had relapsed by the end of the second year without medication.

One study has also investigated the effectiveness of atypical neuroleptics in prevention of relapse. Csernansky *et al.* (2002) randomly assigned 365 clinically stable outpatients meeting DSM IV criteria for schizophrenia or schizoaffective disorder to treatment with either risperidone or haloperidol in flexible dosage under double blind conditions. They were then followed up until they relapsed (defined as hospitalisation, other increase in the level of psychiatric care, predefined increases in symptoms, self-harm, disturbed behaviour, etc.). At the end of the study period, 44 of 177 (25.4 per cent) patients on risperidone had relapsed compared to 75 of 188 (39.9 per cent) in the haloperidol group. This represented a 48 per cent reduction in risk and the difference was highly significant.

Social factors: The role of expressed emotion

The famous concept of expressed emotion (EE) had humble beginnings in a survey of the social adjustment of male patients who had been discharged from long-stay hospital care (Brown *et al.*, 1958; see also Brown, 1985). This found that schizophrenic patients, but not those with other diagnoses, were more likely to require readmission to hospital if they returned to live with their parents or wives than if they went to live in lodgings or with brothers or sisters. A second, more rigorous survey (Brown *et al.*, 1962) was therefore undertaken, with the aim of determining whether something about family relationships was influencing relapse. A series of acute and chronic patients and their relatives were interviewed together just after discharge from hospital and rated on a questionnaire developed to measure various aspects of their emotional interaction. It was found that high levels of emotional involvement in the relatives was a good predictor of subsequent deterioration in the patients' clinical state.

The third study (Brown *et al.*, 1972) was the first in which the term 'expressed emotion' was used. The patient sample consisted of 101 patients with a diagnosis of definite or possible schizophrenia, made according to the Present State Examination. An interview with the relatives (spouses or parents) was carried out before the patient was discharged from hospital, and the patient was then interviewed with his or her relatives about two weeks after discharge. Various aspects of the relatives' emotional response were assessed. The degree of expressed emotion was determined by combining ratings on three variables in the interview schedule: *critical comments* made by the relative about the patient and his or her illness; *hostility*, negative emotion or a clear statement of resentment, disapproval, dislike or rejection; and *over-involvement*, defined as excessive anxiety, overconcern, or overprotectiveness. Based on the combined expressed emotion scores, the sample was split so that approximately half the patients were assigned to high and low expressed emotion groups.

Relapse was defined in the same way as in the study of Brown and Birley (1968) (see Chapter 5), as either a re-emergence of psychotic symptoms or a marked exacerbation of persistent schizophrenic symptoms. Twenty-six of 45 patients (58 per cent) with high expressed emotion relatives relapsed during the 9-month follow-up period, compared to 9 of 56 (16 per cent) of those in the low expressed emotion group, a difference that was highly statistically significant. Further analyses suggested that the association between expressed emotion and relapse was not attributable to other factors like behavioural disturbance and poor compliance with neuroleptic treatment, which were independently associated with relapse.

Beginning with Vaughan and Leff (1976), essentially the same study has been repeated many times and in a number of different countries. Kavanagh (1992) summarised the results of these studies, and his findings are shown in Table 11.2. The finding of significantly higher rates of relapse in patients from high expressed emotion families has been substantially upheld. Only 7 out of 24 studies failed to replicate it.

Vaughan and Leff (1976) made the additional proposal that EE and maintenance medication interact in an additive way. By combining their data with those of the study by Brown *et al.* (1972), they were able to produce the

Table 11.2 Studies of expressed emotion in schizophrenia

Study	9–12 month relapse rate	
	Low EE% (N)	High EE% (N)
Vaughn and Leff (1976)	6 (16)	48 (21)**
Vaughn *et al.* (1984)	17 (18)	56 (36)*
Moline *et al.* (1985)	29 (7)	71 (17)
Dulz and Hand (1986)	65 (17)	48 (29)
MacMillan *et al.* (1986)	41 (34)	68 (38)*
Nuechterlein *et al.* (1986)	0 (7)	40 (20)*
Karno *et al.* (1987)	26 (27)	59 (17)*
Leff *et al.* (1987, 1990)	9 (54)	31 (16)*
McCreadie and Phillips (1988)	20 (35)	17 (24)
Parker *et al.* (1988)	60 (15)	48 (42)
Cazzullo *et al.* (1989)	27 (11)	63 (8)*
Gutierrez *et al.* (1988)	10 (21)	54 (11)*
Tarrier *et al.* (1988, 1989)	21 (19)	48 (29)*
Rostworowska *et al.* (1987)/Budzyna-Dawidowski *et al.* unpublished data	9 (11)	60 (25)**
Mozny *et al.* (1989)	29 (38)	60 (30)**
Montero *et al.* (1990)	19 (36)	33 (24)

Arevalo and Vizcarro (1989)	38 (13)	44 (18)
Ivanovic and Vuletic (1989)	7 (31)	66 (29)**
Buchkremer *et al.* (1991)	28 (40)	37 (59)
Barrelet *et al.* (1990)	0 (12)	33 (24)
Stirling *et al.* (1991)	47 (17)	31 (5)
Vaughan *et al.* (1992)	25 (40)	53 (47)**

* $p < .05$; ** $p < .01$

Source: Kavanagh (1992). Recent developments in expressed emotion and schizophrenia. *British Journal of Psychiatry*, 160, 601–620. Reproduced with permission from the Royal College of Psychiatrists.

diagram shown in Figure 11.2. This suggested that there was progressive increase in relapse rate from a low level in patients in low expressed emotion environments who were compliant with neuroleptic treatment, to a very high rate in those in high expressed emotion households who were not taking medication. MacMillan *et al.* (1986), however, failed to confirm this finding in a study of first episode patients who were randomly assigned to real or placebo medication under double blind conditions (this was as part of the study by Crow *et al.*, 1986, described earlier). Their findings are also shown in Figure 11.2.

Uncomfortable as it may be for some, the studies of expressed emotion provide compelling evidence that psychological factors contribute to exacerbations of schizophrenia. The important question from the point of view of management, however, is whether this has any practical usefulness. Barrowclough and Tarrier (1992) reviewed seven studies that examined the effect of family interventions on relapse in patients with schizophrenia living with high expressed emotion relatives. These studies varied considerably in factors such as sample size and choice of therapeutic intervention, and as a group they either included no control intervention or took an extremely complicated approach to this. Five found evidence for a therapeutic effect and two failed to do so. The results of a meta-analysis of a larger series of studies (Pilling *et al.*, 2002) are summarised in Box 11.3. This supported an effect of family intervention at one year, but not with longer periods of follow-up. Although the relevant numbers of studies are small, this meta-analysis also echoes the findings for cognitive therapy, providing no support for the superiority of family intervention over that seen with control interventions.

Rehabilitation

According to one of its key figures, Bennett (1978, 1983), the psychiatric rehabilitation movement began with humanitarian reforms of asylum care in the early and middle parts of the twentieth century. Three further factors seem to have been of particular relevance to schizophrenia. One was the introduction of neuroleptic drugs, which as well as producing a sharp

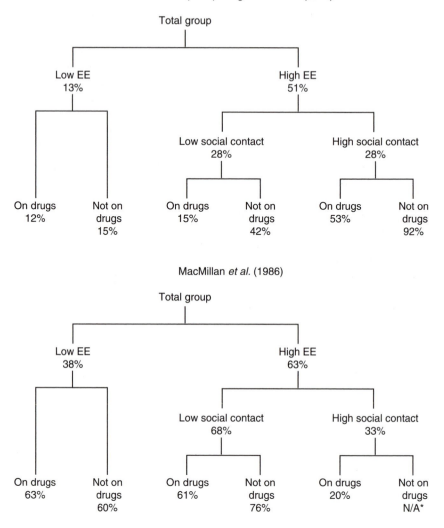

Brown *et al.* (1972)/Vaughan and Leff (1976)

*There was only one patient in this group (who relapsed)

Figure 11.2 Interactions between expressed emotion and neuroleptic treatment on
relapse rates in two studies (from Vaughn and Leff (1976), The influence
of family and social factors on the course of psychiatric illness. *British
Journal of Psychiatry*, 129, 125–137; MacMillan *et al.* (1986), The
Northwick Park study of first episodes of schizophrenia IV. Expressed
emotion and relapse. *British Journal of Psychiatry*, 148, 133–143. Reproduced with permission from the Royal College of Psychiatrists).

Box 11.3 Meta-analysis of family interventions in schizophrenia (from Pilling et al., 2002)

The authors identified 33 trials of family interventions for schizophrenia, but 15 had to be excluded because of inadequate randomisation, lack of a control group, lack of diagnostic specificity, or lack of usable data. The studies included those employing both intervention with single families and those where the primary component of treatment was a regular group session with more than one family. The authors also specified that the intervention comprised at least six sessions.

The 18 included trials involved a total of 1467 patients. Most patients had chronic illnesses with a mean number of 2.7 prior admissions.

In 11 studies the rate of relapse was significantly reduced in the first 12 months of follow-up. However, the difference was not maintained in 6 studies with assessments during a further 12-month period.

When the studies were broken down into those comparing family interventions (FI) with standard care alone (N = 6), and those employing a control intervention such as individual supportive therapy or a relatives' group and psycho-educational lectures (N = 5), it was found that the effect was only significant for standard care.

Follow-up	No. of studies	No. of patients	Odds ratio	Confidence interval
12 months				
FI vs all other treatment	11	729	0.63	0.46/0.86
FI vs standard care	6	355	0.37	0.23/0.59
FI vs other intervention	5	357	0.89	0.58/1.31
12–24 months				
FI vs all other treatment	6	264	0.74	0.44/1.25

Four studies also provided data on relapse from 4 to 15 months after the end of treatment. The pooled results from these studies found no benefit for family intervention over standard care (OR 0.79, CI 0.46/1.37).

increase in the number of patients who were potentially able to leave hospital, also created an atmosphere that emphasised treatment more than custodial care (Davis, 1985). Another was the development of behaviour modification techniques by psychologists, which suggested that quite simple strategies could have useful effects on the behaviour of mentally ill patients (Birchwood *et al.*, 1988). But probably the most important ingredient was a change that took place in the philosophy of psychiatric care, pioneered by Wing (e.g. 1963), Clark (1981) and Bennett himself, which advocated the de-institutionalisation of chronically hospitalised patients and their reintegration into the community.

Broadly speaking, rehabilitation in schizophrenia is targeted at patients with severe, chronic forms of illness. These are the ones who tend to fall into the worst two outcome groups in the follow-up studies described in Chapter 3, who are at risk of becoming permanently hospitalised, and who more often than not show both positive and negative symptoms. The changes that have taken place in the management of such patients has spawned a large literature, most of which takes the form of pseudo-scientific trials of different models of care and navel-gazing concerning the configuration of services. In these circumstances, it is not easy to unearth and expose to critical scrutiny the work that established the credentials of the field. What follows is a selection of three studies, each covering a different area of rehabilitation, and each of which is considered to have made a key contribution to the development of services in the post-war period.

Rehabilitation in the hospital setting

The study that is widely considered to have put the overall effectiveness of rehabilitation on a firm scientific footing was carried out by Wing and Brown (1970). They examined the adverse effects of long-term hospitalisation on schizophrenic patients, and investigated what happened when attempts were made to ameliorate these. They studied three mental hospitals, which differed markedly in their policies of care. From each, a random sample of 73–120 female inpatients was selected: these all had a clinical diagnosis of schizophrenia, were less than 60 years old, and had been continuously hospitalised for more than two years. Their positive and negative symptoms were rated (in fact, as described in Chapter 2, it was this study that first employed these terms in their modern sense), as was their behaviour on the ward. Nursing staff were also interviewed, and other more general observations were made, for example about the restrictiveness of the ward regime. Finally, an assessment of the patients' social circumstances was made, as measured in terms of the number of personal possessions (e.g. a toothbrush) they had, the number of hours they spent in activities each day, the time they spent off the ward, and the contact they had with the outside world.

A major finding of the study was that that the patients showed clinical differences reflecting the different milieus of the three hospitals. In one of the hospitals, where the patients received uniformly high ratings on a cluster of 'social impoverishment' ratings – little contact with the outside world, few personal possessions, little constructive occupation, spending much time doing nothing, and being regarded pessimistically by nursing staff – there were significantly more patients rated as moderately or severely ill than in another hospital where the level of social impoverishment was lower. Patients in the third hospital were intermediate in terms of social impoverishment, and were also intermediate in terms of their illness ratings. The clinical differences were most marked on ratings of negative symptoms and withdrawal.

The hospitals were then visited again four years later. By this time various administrative and social changes had been instituted in all three hospitals, particularly the one where there had been a lot of social impoverishment. Nearly a third of the patients who had been rated as severely impaired at the time of the original visit had improved by at least one category by the time of the second visit; sometimes the improvement was to the extent that they no longer fitted the stereotype of the 'back ward' patient. In contrast, fewer than 5 per cent had become worse. Most of the improvement was due to a decrease in social withdrawal, flatness of affect and other negative symptoms, although florid symptoms, particularly coherently expressed delusions, also improved somewhat. Further analysis indicated that clinical improvement was most closely related to an increase in the time spent in activities and occupational therapy, and a decrease in the time spent doing nothing. Other social changes, such as increased contact with the outside world, more optimism among nursing staff and an increased supply of personal belongings were less important. There was little to suggest that changes in drug treatment were responsible for the improvements seen.

Day care

Linn *et al.* (1979) carried out a study that is widely considered to have been instrumental in establishing the practice of day centre attendance for chronic schizophrenic patients discharged from hospital. They randomly assigned 162 chronic schizophrenic patients to either routine outpatient care or attendance at a day centre. Outpatient care consisted essentially of visits to a clinic where the emphasis was on monitoring of neuroleptic medication. The day centres were specialised for dealing with chronic patients, and their goals included maintaining or bringing about improvement in family and social interactions, providing a place for patients to socialise and engage in productive activities, and offering a sheltered environment outside hospital. Every six months for two years measures were made of symptoms, social functioning, time spent out of hospital (or prison), and also the patients' attitudes.

No differences were found in the the two groups' rates of relapse, measured in a variety of ways. Nor did any differences in their level of symptoms become apparent. Social functioning was, however, significantly better for the day centre attenders from a year onwards.

Intensive hostel care

Following informal findings that patients with chronic psychotic illness might be better cared for in a 'ward in a house' than in hospital, Hyde *et al.* (1987) carried out what remains the only study to formally evaluate the value of this type of unit. Their sample consisted of 22 patients who had been under inpatient care for longer than six months (the mean duration of the current hospitalisation was 3.5 years). The patients had resisted all attempts at resettlement outside hospital and were considered to need round the clock nursing care. In 14 the diagnosis was schizophrenia and the remainder had a variety of other functional and organic disorders. The patients were randomly chosen either to stay in hospital or to be transferred to a 24-hour staffed hostel in the community. The two groups were fairly well matched for age, sex, duration of illness, and in terms of their impairments and problem behaviours. In the hostel, the emphasis was on maintaining and/or improving self-care, and acquiring domestic skills such as cooking, cleaning, and shopping. Each patient had their own individual care plan in which problem behaviours were specifically targeted. Nursing was organised along behavioural lines under the supervision of a psychologist, and a reward system operated whereby points could be exchanged for money (now outlawed in the UK). The patients were encouraged to pursue leisure activities and they arranged group outings for themselves.

The control group remained in hospital, but had access to a comprehensive range of occupational and social therapies. They were able to use community facilities as they wished.

The patients were assessed six monthly or yearly on a variety of clinical and behavioural measures. For the 16 patients who remained in the study at the end of two years, those assigned to the intensive community hostel showed significantly fewer behavioural problems. The differences were most evident in ratings of indifference and non-assertiveness. Domestic skills showed a significant improvement, as did use of social facilities, and time spent on socially constructive behaviours like eating, working, and conversing with others. However, no differences were found between the groups in hygiene, self-care, and social and community skills. There were no differences between the groups on any of the clinical measures, although there was a trend towards fewer negative symptoms among the hostel patients.

Although not suitable for all patients – 3 of the original 11 had to be returned to hospital – Hyde *et al.* came to the conclusion that the patients who were able to survive in intensive hostel care fell into two groups. The first consisted of patients who did not show much improvement after the first six months, and who continued to require continuous nursing care. The second group progressively improved in psychosocial functioning and, rather to everyone's surprise, eventually became potentially able to move on to less dependent settings.

The three studies that have been described here are rather different in character from those in other sections of this chapter. All three studies face the criticism that they were carried out under non-blind conditions, and they could all be regarded as producing soft data that are open to interpretations in other ways. However, the message they convey most strongly is not in their findings – which were uniformly modest – but in the way they demonstrate that attempting to improve the quality of life of patients with severe, chronic schizophrenia, has a by-product in the form of useful clinical improvement. It is this, perhaps more than anything else, that captures the essential quality of rehabilitation.

12 Paraphrenia and paranoia

What terms like paranoia and paranoid should mean has exercised psychiatry for decades, if not centuries. As a noun, 'paranoia' denotes a disorder whose clinical features, course, boundaries with other disorders, and even existence are contentious. Used as an adjective, 'paranoid' has become attached to conditions ranging from paranoid schizophrenia, through paranoid depression to paranoid personality, not to mention a motley collection of 'reactions' and 'states' – and this is to restrict the discussion just to functional disorders. Even when abbreviated down to the prefix para-, it still manages to cause trouble as the stubbornly persistent concept of paraphrenia.

Part of the problem stems from the different meanings the term paranoid has acquired. In the European sense – which is traceable back to Kraepelin and beyond him to Kahlbaum – paranoid means, quite simply, delusional. This usage is exemplified by paranoid schizophrenia, where delusions – persecutory, grandiose, religious or hypochondriacal – are to the forefront of the clinical picture. In British and American psychiatry, in contrast, paranoid has come to be used more or less interchangeably with persecutory. This sense of the term is perhaps best illustrated by paranoid personality, a disorder characterised by touchiness, sensitiveness, suspiciousness and a tendency to misconstrue the intentions of others as hostile or contemptuous. In yet another usage, as seen, for example, in contemporary Scandinavian psychiatry, paranoid refers to any psychotic disorder where there are delusions and hallucinations.

After giving the concept of paranoia a thorough historical airing, Lewis (1970) concluded that the term paranoid should be applied to disorders where there are delusions, but not necessarily just those concerned with persecution, and that there should be no implications about presence of hallucinations, or of a relationship with schizophrenia. When defined in this way, the discussion narrows down to two disorders, paraphrenia and paranoia. After these have been tackled, there remain a few miscellaneous conditions that are traditionally discussed under the heading of 'paranoid disorders', more as a matter of custom and practice than for any compelling logical reasons.

Paraphrenia

The term 'paraphrenia' was introduced by Kahlbaum in 1863. He did not coin it to denote any particular clinical entity, but merely to draw attention to the tendency of certain psychiatric disorders to develop at certain periods in life – in his scheme, for example, *paraphrenia hebetica* was the insanity of adolesence and *paraphrenia senilis* was the insanity of the elderly (see Berrios, 1986). As with most of Kahlbaum's ideas, this classificatory scheme gained little acceptance and, within his own lifetime, came to be regarded as little more than a curiosity.

Kraepelinian paraphrenia

Fifty years later, Kraepelin (1913a) revived the term, if not the concept, to describe a comparatively small group of cases that he had concluded resembled schizophrenia, but which deviated from the typical picture in significant ways. He gave no reason for this choice of terminology, stating only that it seemed suitable. However, as he alluded to the marked delusional component that all paraphrenic states had in common, it might be inferred that he wished to emphasise the relationship of these cases to paranoid schizophrenia on the one hand and paranoia on the other. Beyond this, he may have been acknowledging his general indebtedness to Kahlbaum, who was the major formative influence on his views. What is less clear is whether Kraepelin had any particular age of onset in mind when he described these disorders.

The feature of paraphrenia that led Kraepelin to separate it from schizophrenia was first and foremost its course. This showed a 'far slighter development of the disorders of emotion and volition' that characterised schizophrenia. Despite persistent and remorselessly progressive florid symptoms, the more severe degrees of deterioration never supervened. The other conspicuous feature of paraphrenic states was the presence of a marked paranoid (in the European sense) colouring: the clinical picture was dominated by delusions, which were sometimes persecutory but sometimes of other kinds, accompanied by hallucinations, which were predominantly but not exclusively auditory. Formal thought disorder made at most a minor contribution to the clinical picture, and catatonic phenomena were hardly ever seen.

In his customary way, Kraepelin divided paraphrenia into a number of subgroups, although he considered that these were not sharply demarcated from one another. The largest of these was a slowly evolving form that he termed *paraphrenia systematica*. Next in frequency were two rather smaller, and possibly closely related groups, *paraphrenia expansiva* and *paraphrenia confabulans*. The last form was *paraphrenia phantastica*, which was exceptional, not only because of its rarity but also by virtue of its extraordinary clinical features.

Paraphrenia systematica was characterised by the insidious and continuously progressive development of persecutory and referential delusions, to which other delusions and hallucinations later become added. These illnesses began with the gradual development of delusions of reference, misinterpretation and misidentification – the patients started to believe they were being insulted, jeered at, followed, spied on, and so on – out of which delusions of persecution crystallised and then went on to become increasingly elaborate. Subsequently, sometimes only after many years, other delusions appeared, for example with a grandiose, religious or hypochondriacal content. At some point hallucinations crept into the picture; these were typically auditory, but could also be seen less commonly in other modalities. From Kraepelin's description, there is no doubt that first rank symptoms were also commonplace.

Paraphrenia expansiva took the form of a gradual or occasionally more abrupt development of grandiose delusions, which inclined to the fantastic and soon became accompanied by auditory and visual hallucinations. Often against a background of expansiveness or slight excitement, such patients began expressing grandiose delusions of exalted religious status, high descent, great wealth, and so on. In about half of the cases the presentation was one of erotomania – the belief that a highly placed person was in love with the patient. These ideas frequently went hand in hand with persecutory delusions, and they were invariably accompanied by multiple delusions of reference and misinterpretation. Hallucinations appeared early on, taking the form of voices and visions, often with a religious colouring. Delusional memories, first rank symptoms, and occasionally somatic hallucinations could also form part of the picture. In some cases the presentation eventually became very florid.

In *paraphrenia confabulans* the principal symptom was a proliferation of delusions and delusional memories. After a prodromal period of brooding and withdrawal, such patients would suddenly start voicing an enormous number of persecutory, grandiose and fantastic delusions. Also woven into the picture would be numerous delusional memories. These could be absolutely fixed and repeated again and again in almost exactly the same words, but more typically further details would be added on questioning, and the stories would undergo a progressive embroidering – the phenomenon of delusional confabulation. Although they tended to have an adventurous, story-like quality, these fictitious events would be related with complete conviction and precise details – one patient reported to the authorities that he had dug up a human arm and had then been compelled at gunpoint by his neighbour to keep silent about it, causing a police investigation. In the background were delusions of reference and misinterpretation and verbal auditory hallucinations.

Paraphrenia phantastica was the most extreme presentation of all, characterised by, in the words of Kraepelin, 'the luxuriant growth of highly extraordinary, disconnected, changing delusions'. Typically, the disorder set in with a period of listlessness, depression and withdrawal. This was slowly replaced by the appearance of delusions and auditory hallucinations, which even at this early stage were notably florid. The delusions then went on to acquire quite prodigious forms and seemed able to be produced in almost inexhaustible supply: patients would state that their bodies were being melted down and torn apart, that thousands or even millions of people were being murdered daily, that they were of multiple royal descent, infinitely rich, owned properties on different planets, and so on. Delusional memories and confabulations also loomed large in the picture. Hallucinations, for the most part auditory, might also be present, as could be a degree of formal thought disorder, although by and large this only became obvious when the patient was describing his delusions.

The age of onset of paraphrenia clustered between 30 and 50 in the majority of cases, although it could commence in the twenties and in one case it began at the age of 64. Both sexes were affected and overall there was if anything a slight male preponderance; however, almost all Kraepelin's cases of paraphrenia expansiva were female.

The course of Kraepelin's different types of paraphrenia showed more similarities than differences. In general, it was slowly progressive: while there could be fluctuations in the intensity of symptoms, marked improvement was unusual and recovery did not occur. As time went by the delusions tended to become more and more nonsensical and fragmented. In some cases a degree of formal thought disorder developed, expressing itself mainly in stilted or verbose speech, use of neologisms and peculiar turns of expression. Stereotypies or oddities of behaviour were a late feature in some patients, but these were usually of a more or less isolated kind. However, the most striking feature was the lack of serious evidence of deterioration: the patients remained lively, accessible and pleasant to outsiders; other than a certain superficiality of emotional expression, affective flattening was the exception rather than the rule. Many patients remained able to work. Typically, the terminal state was milder than even the mildest of those associated with schizophrenia.

The history of Kraepelinian paraphrenia was destined to be short. Even Kraepelin entertained doubts about its validity as a nosological entity: he wondered whether paraphrenia systematica might merely represent a mild form of paranoid schizophrenia; whether paraphrenia expansiva was really a variant of mania; and whether, in paraphrenia confabulans and paraphrenia phantastica, he was not just singling out cases of schizophrenia where the picture was dominated by a single, albeit unusual, symptom. Mayer (1921) then dealt what seemed to be a mortal blow to the whole diagnostic concept. He followed up 78 of Kraepelin's original patients between 15 years and several decades after they first became ill. By this time he considered that only just over a third could still be considered to show the characteristic features of paraphrenia. In approximately another third the picture had become unequivocally one of schizophrenia. The remaining patients had acquired a collection of revised or additional diagnoses – paranoia, manic-depressive psychosis, or dementia or other forms of organic brain disease – and in a small minority remissions had taken place. As can be seen from Table 12.1, a

Table 12.1 Results of Mayer's (1921) follow-up of Kraepelin's paraphrenic patients

Kraepelin's diagnosis	Diagnosis at follow-up	Comment
Paraphrenia systematica (N = 45)	Unchanged (17) Schizophrenia (11) Paranoia (2) Paranoia abortiva (3)* Paranoid personality (2) Cyclic psychosis (3) Senile dementia (2) Diagnosis unclear (2)	Patients who followed a typical paraphrenic course all had an onset at about age 50. This group considered to be closely related to schizophrenia genetically.
Paraphrenia expansiva (N = 13)	Diagnosis unchanged (5) Schizophrenia (5) Manic-depressive psychosis (1) Organic brain disease (1) Diagnosis unclear (1)	–
Paraphrenia confabulans (N = 11)	Diagnosis unchanged (5) Schizophrenia (5) Complete remission (1)	–
Paraphrenia phantastica (N = 9)	Schizophrenia (9)	All 9 patients showed a picture of paranoid schizophrenia with deterioration.

* According to Kraepelin, patients with this diagnosis were in reality suffering from manic-depressive psychosis.

Note: Numbers shown here are as in the original table.

Source: Mayer (1921).

substantial proportion of the systematic, expansive and confabulatory sub-groups retained their distinguishing characteristics. (Here, interestingly from the point of view of future developments, Mayer commented that all of the patients with paraphrenia systematica who followed such a course had an age of onset at around age 50.) However, all the cases of paraphrenia phantastica appeared to have evolved into schizophrenia.

Mayer's study lacked detail, and in some of the cases summarised in Table 12.1 the final diagnoses seemed contrived or even unsatisfactory. Nevertheless, his findings were fully endorsed by Kraepelin in a commentary he made on the study.

Perhaps, in the light of these findings, the best way to regard paraphrenia is as a fifth subtype of schizophrenia – a special variety whose features of delusions and lack of deterioration, and possibly also later age of onset, mark it out as quantitatively rather than qualitatively different from schizophrenia proper. While, as with the other classical subtypes, as the years go by it tends to merge into the amorphous pool of chronic schizophrenic presentations, there will always some cases that retain their characteristic features despite years of relentless illness. One possible such example is described in Box 12.1.

Box 12.1 Kraepelinian paraphrenia: The case of Richard Dadd (from Greysmith, 1973; Allderidge, 1974)

Richard Dadd (1817–1886) was a leading talent of the Royal Academy Schools where he was a student. While in his twenties he exhibited paintings which were well received, received commissions, and was considered to be on the threshold of a promising career. Two of his six siblings became permanently insane and a third 'required an attendant'. Before becoming ill the patient was described as gentle, affectionate, pleasant, and cheerful.

At the age of 25 he accompanied a patron on a journey around Europe and the Middle East. During this he began to feel that his companion was an emissary of the Devil and that people around him were spirits in disguise. After returning to England he was noted to be suspicious, hostile and at times bizarre in behaviour; at one point he cut out a birthmark believing it had been imprinted on him by the Devil. He came to believe he was subject to the will of the Eygptian god Osiris, and that he had a mission to destroy certain people who were possessed by evil spirits. 'Secret admonitions' (it is not clear whether or not these took the form of voices) urged him to carry out violent acts. Having been persuaded by these that his father was the Devil, he murdered him in a carefully planned way. He then fled to France where he was arrested after trying to murder a stranger in a carriage.

He was admitted to the State Criminal Lunatic Asylum and then to the Bethlem Hospital at the age of 27. He remained an inpatient for the rest of his life, later being transferred to the newly opened Broadmoor Hospital. His delusions remained fixed, but his intellectual capacity was said to have remained practically untouched. For several years he remained dangerous and was liable to attack others without any provocation, and then apologise. This was explained as arising from a belief that certain spirits possessed his body and compelled him to act in such a way. He also regarded himself as not being bound by social customs, and could be unpleasant in manner, for example gorging himself until he vomited. However, he could hold an intelligent and interesting conversation as long as his delusions were steered clear of. At the age of 37 he was described as a sensible and agreeable companion, who showed a well-educated mind in conversation and who was thoroughly informed in artistic matters. At the age of 43 he was said to associate very little with other patients but was generally civil and well behaved. At the age of 60 he was described by a journalist as simply dressed, courteous, with an unassuming manner. He remained obviously deluded.

He resumed painting some time after his admission to the Bethlem Hospital and continued to paint for the rest of his life. His two best-known works, *Contradiction: Oberon and Titania* and *The Fairy Feller's Master Stroke* were completed in 1858 and 1864, after 14 and 20 years of continuous illness.

> The quality of his work was of a consistently high standard, sometimes quite extraordinarily so, up to within three years of his death.
>
> Opinions have differed as to whether Dadd's art is great or pedestrian, although it is now widely acknowledged to be of outstanding quality. *Oberon and Titania* has been sold for £1,500,000, and the British Museum bought a recently discovered watercolour for £100,000.

Such a conclusion is quite close to that of Kraepelin in his comments on Mayer's follow-up of his cases and, while it failed to have much of an impact at the time (paraphrenia largely disappeared as a concept), it was to have important repercussions half a century later.

Late paraphrenia

By the middle of the twentieth century paraphrenia had been relegated to history, a minor nosological excursion that had not led anywhere very interesting. In Britain, and even more so in America, schizophrenia became regarded as a disorder of adolescence and early adult life, which rarely developed for the first time in middle age, and never later than this. When paranoid delusions developed in later life, the practice was to consider them as a manifestation of underlying organic brain disease, especially dementia (Fish, 1960), or of affective disorder, especially depression (Volavka, 1985).

Then, in the course of a survey of mental hospital admissions aged 60 or over, Roth and colleagues (Roth and Morrissey, 1952; Roth, 1955; Kay and Roth, 1961) observed a number of patients (approximately 10 per cent of all admissions) who presented with well-organised delusions accompanied or unaccompanied by auditory hallucinations. In all the cases the disorder had developed after the age of 45, and in many after the age of 60. The patients did not seem to be diagnosable as having affective psychosis, and in the majority of cases there was no evidence of intellectual impairment on examination, or underlying brain disease on investigation. Because they showed predominantly persecutory delusions with a striking preservation of personality and affect, the authors resurrected Kraepelin's term to describe the disorder, naming it late paraphrenia.

The clinical features of this newly discovered (or rediscovered) clinical entity were subjected to close scrutiny in two more or less contemporary studies, both of which came to substantially similar conclusions. The first of these was a series of 99 cases from two centres investigated by Kay and Roth (1961). The second study was carried out by Post (1966), who examined a total of 93 patients from his own unit. In both series, patients were excluded whose onset of symptoms occurred before middle or late life (the age cut-offs were 55 and 50 respectively), or where the paranoid symptoms were clearly part of a depressive illness. Kay and Roth excluded all patients who showed unequivocal evidence of cognitive impairment. Post took a different approach and included such patients, but subdivided his sample into those showing no, doubtful and definite organic impairment.

In both studies the mean age at admission was 70. Kay and Roth found a large excess of women in their series (93 per cent and 84 per cent in the two centres). Eighty-six per cent of the patients in Post's study were also female. Physical health tended to be good, and in many cases adjectives like 'vigorous' and 'sturdy' were employed. Kay and Roth found that 40 per cent of their patients showed some degree of hearing impairment, a higher frequency than in other diagnostic groups of comparable age; in Post's study the corresponding figure was 31 per cent. Visual defects were present in a further 15 per cent of Kay and Roth's series, but this rate was not greatly different from other patient groups in the same age range. Absence of generalised organic brain disease was a prerequisite of Kay and Roth's study, but they noted that a small proportion showed minor or longstanding neurological abnormalities, such as epilepsy, tremor and mono- or hemiparesis, which were not obviously related to the onset of psychosis.

As a group, Kay and Roth's patients were also distinguished by a high rate of abnormal personality traits before they became ill. They were often unmarried, tended to live in isolation, and several belonged to obscure religious sects. Their relatives frequently described them as always having been narrow, quarrelsome, religious, unsociable, sensitive or cold-hearted. On questioning, evidence of schizoid or paranoid traits was frequently found, but Kay and Roth made the point that any simplistic statements did not fully capture the quality of the personalities of many of their late paraphrenic patients, which had positive as well as negative attributes, strengths as well as vulnerabilities.

Kay and Roth noted that the first discernible sign of illness was often an accentuation of these personality traits; the patient became more irritable, bad-tempered, hostile, suspicious, hypochondriacal or morose than previously; their relatives made statements such as '[she is] not ill but exaggeratedly herself' or 'I always expected this to happen'. Other changes then began to appear: the patient would become seclusive, refuse to see callers, then begin to pester the police with complaints, write anonymous letters, and so on. The second stage was initiated, often abruptly or dramatically, with the onset of auditory hallucinations and florid delusions, which typically led to disturbed behaviour and brought about admission to hospital.

Both Kay and Roth and Post found essentially similar clinical characteristics among their patients. Delusions were invariable, and usually persecutory; however, there could also be grandiose, depressive, hypochondriacal and erotic beliefs. The delusions were frequently fantastic, but they also tended to be systematised and were often intimately bound up with hallucinations – for example, a patient might hear a voice making threats and therefore believe that someone was intent on murdering her, or smell an odour and believe that gas was being pumped into the room. Another notable feature was the tendency for the delusions to revolve around the daily life, anxieties and unfulfilled wishes of elderly people: they were focused on the bed, the room, the house, neighbours, and those with whom the patient was in daily contact; their themes revolved around theft, interference with the gas, water and electricity supplies, and the like. Hallucinations were present in 80–90 per cent of cases. Auditory hallucinations were by far the most common type; these were usually verbal, but elementary hallucinations were also frequent. Visual, olfactory, gustatory and somatic hallucinations, all of the familiar schizophrenic kind, were also encountered. First rank symptoms were evident in the descriptions of some of Kay and Roth's cases, and were explicitly recorded by Post in about a third of cases.

Other symptoms figured much less prominently. Although Kay and Roth alluded to verbosity, circumstantiality and irrelevance in 30 per cent of their cases, more definite formal thought disorder was considered unusual. According to Post, this symptom was never recognised with certainty. Catatonic phenomena were also conspicuous by their absence: stupor was rare in Kay and Roth's series, and Post noted only occasional isolated stereotypies and mannerisms. Kay and Roth stated that, while a degree of flattening or incongruity was quite common, gross affective abnormalities were not seen. Mood colourings, of fear, anger, euphoria and depression and occasionally excitement, were, however, commonplace. Post drew attention to the frequency of subjective depression, which he found in over half his cases – not infrequently there was a depressive syndrome complete enough to raise the possibility of an alternative diagnosis of major depression.

According to both sets of investigators, late paraphrenia typically followed a chronic course. In Kay and Roth's series, temporary remissions occurred spontaneously or were achieved with treatment in about a quarter of cases, and in the rest there was no great improvement. Post, in contrast, was more optimistic about the outcome, especially with neuroleptic treatment (see below). The clinical changes that took place with time resembled to some extent those described by Kraepelin and Mayer for paraphrenia: after years of illness many patients remained clean, tidy, normally motivated, and showed no pronounced deterioration in personality. Some, however, developed increasing affective flattening or incongruity, and others ended up mute, inaccessible, withdrawn and preoccupied, or alternatively periodically incoherent, hostile and negativistic. In a few the disorder eventually seemed to 'burn out', leaving a simple defect state similar to that of schizophrenia.

Kay and Roth argued that the incidence of dementia in late paraphrenia was no higher than in the corresponding age group of the general population – about 20 per cent of both their late paraphrenic patients and those in other psychiatric groups went on to develop either dementia or signs of focal brain disease. Only 2 of the 44 patients in Post's study who showed no evidence of organic brain disease at the time of diagnosis developed evidence of intellectual impairment within his 3-year follow-up period (two further patients died, one of bronchopneumonia and the other in a road traffic accident). At the same time, Kay and Roth observed that as time went on memory tended to fail in a proportion of cases, and episodes of disorientation sometimes occurred for which a cause could not always be established.

These studies leave no room for doubt that patients exist who develop something closely similar to Kraepelin's paraphrenia in later life, and who are not suffering from depression or dementia at the time of initial presentation. A good example is the artist and illustrator Louis Wain who became permanently psychotic in his late fifties but showed little in the way of deterioration and continued to be artistically productive until very near the end of his life. His case is summarised in Box 12.2. As with Kraepelinian paraphrenia, it is

---

Box 12.2 Late paraphrenia: The case of Louis Wain (from Dale, 1991)

For much of his adult life, Louis Wain (1860–1939) was famous in Britain for his cartoons, drawings and paintings of cats. However, demand for his work fell off in his later years.

He was an imaginative solitary child, who did poorly academically and truanted from school. As an adult he was regarded as a social oddity. He held cranky ideas about science, and tried to patent several unlikely mechanical devices; one contemporary described him as being 'as eccentric as they come'. At the age of 54 he fell off a bus and was unconscious or semi-conscious for several days; however he made a full recovery and returned to work ignoring doctors' advice to take six months off. One sister suffered from what was almost certainly schizophrenia, which developed in early adult life.

From around the age of 58, he became more and more hostile to his sisters, although to outsiders he appeared normal. By the age of 61 he was writing at great length about various theories, in the course of which he alluded to ideas about being full of electricity and being influenced by spirits. He came to believe that his living sisters were responsible for another sister's death from influenza, and that they were stealing cheques and personal effects from him. He also became preoccupied with the idea of breeding spotted cats.

He was admitted to the Bethlem Hospital at the age of 64. This was after he had become obviously behaviourally disturbed, endlessly re-arranging furniture, wandering the streets in the middle of the night, writing abusive letters about his sisters and being violent towards them. On examination he was found to be floridly deluded, believing that his sisters were maltreating him and claiming to have powers of healing by virtue of electricity imprisoned inside him. He believed that ether was the source of all evil and was present in his food. Later, he also came to believe that he was influenced by icicles. He appeared quaint and eccentric in manner, as he always had, but was quiet, cooperative and courteous.

He continued to draw and paint in hospital, giving the impression of working at close to his earlier standards. However, particularly in later years, his work was sometimes crude. Although somewhat reclusive, he was described as reasonable, responsive to questions, and retaining his sense of humour. A letter written in 1929, five years after admission, was stilted and showed evidence of poverty of content of speech.

In 1930, at the age of 70, he was transferred to Napsbury Hospital. By this time his behaviour had become obviously bizarre. He insisted on wearing many layers of clothes, even in summer, and avoided washing, bathing, shaving and undressing. He was inordinately fond of drinking liquid paraffin, and also took to rubbing this in his hair. He spoke in a rambling, incoherent way. He was also noted to be physically feeble and may have shown some signs of intellectual impairment. Even so, he was able to appreciate his pleasant surroundings and his art was reported as having lost none of its skill. Over the next few years he developed signs of arteriosclerosis and at the age of 76 he suffered a stroke. After this he became increasingly withdrawn and incoherent, and was hostile when approached. He died at the age of 78 of renal failure.

also clear that the disorder is a type, a variant, or at the very least a close affiliate of schizophrenia: all the cardinal features of schizophrenia are either seen at presentation or can turn up at a later stage, if only as minor elements of the clinical picture. The natural history of late paraphrenia, however, differs from schizophrenia in that dementia supervenes in a proportion of cases. It may be that this happens no more frequently than in the general population of the same age, but there are hints that the relationship with cognitive impairment is more complicated than the authors who gave the original descriptions of the disorder cared to admit.

Aetiological factors in paraphrenia

In the absence of any firm knowledge about the cause of schizophrenia, it is only possible to examine whether and to what extent some of the aetiological factors identified in Chapter 5, namely genetic factors and structural and functional brain abnormality, are also operative in paraphrenia. Its apparent later age of onset, the female sex preponderance, and the relationship with deafness also require comment. Also needing close scrutiny is the question of the relationship of late paraphrenia to dementia.

Hereditary predisposition

Roth and co-workers (Kay, 1959; Kay and Roth, 1961) reported a rate of 3.4 per cent for schizophrenia among the siblings and children of patients with late paraphrenia. Two other early studies (Funding, 1961; Herbert and Jacobson, 1967) also found rates which suggested that the risk was higher than that for the general population but less than the 10 per cent rate in the first-degree relatives of patients with schizophrenia.

Howard *et al.* (1997) have recently carried out what can be regarded as a fairly definitive family study. Their sample consisted of 42 patients who met their own criteria for late paraphrenia. These required presence of delusions, with or without hallucinations, with an age of onset over 60, absence of a primary affective disorder, and no evidence of dementia or history of stroke or other neurological conditions. The patients were interviewed using family history interviews and 115 of the 269 relatives were contacted to corroborate and supplement the information obtained. Using a narrow age range of risk of 15 to 50 years, 3 of the 269 (1.1 per cent) relatives of the paraphrenic patients were given an RDC diagnosis of schizophrenia. This is not obviously elevated above the general population rate and no different from the rate of 3/272 in the first-degree relatives of age-matched normal controls. The risk of depression, in contrast, was over three times higher – 21/269 (7.8 per cent) versus 6/272 (2.2 per cent).

Lateral ventricular enlargement

Two CT scan studies have been carried out on late paraphrenic patients. Rabins *et al.* (1987) scanned 29 patients with an average age of 73 who met DSM III criteria for schizophrenia except that their age of onset was 45 or older. These were compared with 23 age-matched normal volunteers. The mean ventricle:brain ratio (VBR) was nearly twice as great in the patients as in the controls (13.3 vs 8.6). Naguib and Levy (1987) compared 43 patients with a mean age of 75 who had developed typical paraphrenic symptoms for the first time from the age of 60, with 40 age-matched normal volunteers. They also found evidence of significant lateral ventricular enlargement, with the mean VBR being 13.1 for the patients and 9.7 for the controls. The degree of enlargement was considered to be much less than that reported in patients with dementia, but comparable to that found in schizophrenia.

The late age of onset and the preponderance of females

Bleuler (1911) regarded it as well accepted that individuals who developed schizophrenia in adolesence or early adult life were for the most part hebephrenics and catatonics, whereas those becoming ill later more often showed the paranoid form of the disorder. This was supported by Fish (Fish, 1962/Hamilton, 1984) who produced a table showing that paranoid schizophrenia became more common with increasing age at the expense of hebephrenic and catatonic presentations (see Table 12.2). Paraphrenia can easily be viewed as a continuation of this trend, with, on the one hand, catatonic phenomena, affective flattening and formal thought disorder dropping out as

Table 12.2 Age of onset of classical subtypes in 110 chronic schizophrenic patients

Age group (years)	Hebephrenic	Catatonic	Paranoid
up to 19	4	7	–
20–24	2	7	8
25–29	7	8	10
30–34	4	7	7
35–39	–	5	11
40–44	–	1	7
45–49	1	–	4
50–54	–	–	6
55–59	–	–	3
over 60	–	–	1

Source: Hamilton (1984), *Fish's schizophrenia*, 3rd edition. John Wright and Sons. Reproduced with permission.

delusions and hallucinations come to occupy more and more of the clinical picture; and on the other, the severity of the deterioration being progressively attenuated.

The marked female sex preponderance in both Kay and Roth's and Post's studies has been found in all subsequent series of late paraphrenic patients. This key feature of paraphrenia may also be recognisable as the continuation of a trend that is discernible in schizophrenia. Once again, the relevant observation was first made by Bleuler (1911). Quoting figures from his own hospital, he found that there was a slight male predominance at the youngest ages of onset. The sex ratio equalised at a point between the ages of 30 and 40. After this an excess of female cases became progressively more evident until all of the small number of cases beginning the age of 50 were women. This finding has been amply confirmed in later studies (e.g. Lewine, 1980; Gold, 1984).

The association with deafness

The high rate of deafness among late paraphrenic patients noted by both Kay and Roth and Post has also been confirmed in all subsequent studies (see Grahame, 1982; Hassett *et al.*, 1992). Cooper *et al.* (1974) examined this association further. They compared 54 patients with paranoid psychoses (the diagnosis was not further specified) with 57 age- and sex-matched patients with manic-depressive psychosis; in both groups the age of onset of illness was 50 or older. The paranoid patients showed greater hearing loss than the affective patients. In the former the rate of deafness was three times greater than the general population rates, whereas that for the affective patients was only marginally higher. Other analyses suggested that the deafness antedated the onset of illness in a high proportion of the paranoid patients, but not the affective patients.

The lack of progression to dementia

While Kay and Roth's view was that dementia supervened in late paraphrenia no more frequently than in the general population, later studies have suggested that this is not the case. On the one hand, it has been established that patients with the disorder show neuropsychological deficits which are broadly similar in pattern to that seen in schizophrenia (Almeida *et al.*, 1995), and these appear to be no worse than in schizophrenic patients of the same age with an onset of illness earlier in adult life (Jeste *et al.*, 1995). On the other hand, two follow-up studies have found evidence that, unlike in adult-onset schizophrenia, these deficits tend to progress. Holden (1987) traced 37 patients who met both Kay and Roth's and Post's definitions of late paraphrenia, in whom cognitive impairment was not present at the time of initial presentation. Based on all sources of information (including personal interviews and supplementary information from surviving relatives and medical records), 13 (35 per cent) appeared to have progressed to dementia within 3 years of diagnosis, and two more were found to be demented at 10 years. Hymas *et al.* (1989) followed up a group of 42 prospectively identified late paraphrenic patients 3 to 5 years later. Of the 31 who were still alive, only two had developed a global intellectual decline suggestive of dementia clinically. However, a further nine (32.5 per cent) showed cognitive impairment falling short of dementia: they showed serious difficulties in recall of a name and address in all cases and some of them had obvious difficulties in time and place orientation. The findings were much worse than in a control group of age- and sex-matched normal individuals, only one of whom had developed any degree of intellectual deterioration.

These findings recall Kay and Roth's own observations of memory failures and disorientation in some late paraphrenic patients as time went on. Whether they point to an association between the disorder and standard causes of dementia like Alzheimer's disease and cerebral arteriosclerosis, or whether late paraphrenics merely follow an accelerated route to a state resembling the 'schizophrenic dementia' described in Chapter 8, is an unanswered question.

Treatment of paraphrenia

There is complete agreement that late paraphrenia responds to neuroleptic drugs. This was convincingly, if rather informally, demonstrated by Post. His study spanned the introduction of neuroleptic drugs, allowing him to compare a group of 20 patients who were not treated with a later group of 71 patients who were. None of the first group lost their symptoms, in contrast to 40 (56 per cent) of the second group who showed partial remission and 22 (31 per cent) complete remission of active symptoms. The vast majority of patients did not gain insight, however.

According to Post, the dosage of neuroleptics required to control symptoms was unexceptional or even low (thioridazine 75–600 mg/day or trifluopeazine

15–30 mg/day). Roth and co-workers (see Mayer-Gross *et al.*, 1969) took a different view, commenting that sometimes very high doses were needed. Clozapine and other atypical neuroleptic drugs have also successfully been used (Jeste *et al.*, 1996).

Paranoia

Lewis (1970) noted that the history of paranoia was long and troubled. In the eighteenth century when the term was first used in anything like its modern sense, it initially had a strict connotation of dementia, but its usage rapidly widened to include virtually any abnormal mental state. It was then re-introduced twice more in the nineteenth century, first by Heinroth, and later and more successfully by Kahlbaum, both times to refer to states characterised largely or solely by delusions. Kahlbaum's particular contribution was to identify paranoia as an essentially stable disorder in contrast to most other major psychiatric disorders, which he viewed as passing through various stages culminating in deterioration or dementia. Once again the term became debased over the next 50 years; although the core meaning of 'delusional' remained, its application became so wide that by the end of this period as many as half of all mental hospital patients were diagnosed as suffering from some form of paranoid state.

Kraepelinian paranoia

Once again it was Kraepelin (1913b) who delimited the modern concept of paranoia. He came to the conclusion that no matter how disorders presenting with delusions were classified – into those with and without hallucinations, those with or without an identifiable organic basis, or those pursuing a schizophrenic or a paraphrenic course – there remained a small group of awkward exceptions. The essential feature of these cases was the insidious development of a system of delusions that were logical, well integrated and without gross internal contradictions. The disorder was chronic, remaining essentially unchanged for years or decades. Finally, large areas of mental life were left untouched, or nearly so: thinking was sensible, behaviour was reasonable, and the personality remained perfectly preserved.

In the Kraepelinian sense paranoia was a rare disorder: it accounted for less than 1 per cent of hospital admissions, although this undoubtedly under-estimated the true frequency, as many cases did not come to hospital care. From the limited figures Kraepelin had available, the onset was most frequently between the ages of 30 and 40. Sometimes it was later than this, and occasionally the beginning of the symptoms could be traced back to early adult life or adolescence. The male to female ratio was just over two to one.

The disorder developed mostly, but not always, very gradually, so that as a rule the onset could be dated only approximately. Sometimes there was a prodromal period in which abnormal ideas emerged in partial form and then disappeared or were forgotten about. Typically, the first sign was the development of delusions of reference, misinterpretation and misidentification which became increasingly pervasive and were related to each other in intricate ways: a movement of the hand, a shrug of the shoulders, the glances of passers-by all seemed to have mysterious meanings; remarks at a neighbouring table contained hidden allusions or pointed to some dimly perceived secret; references would be made to the patient in plays, books and newspapers; his clothes were being copied by numerous people; he would keep meeting the same individuals, who must be watching him. Often the beliefs included delusional memories. Sometimes this was merely a case of false constructions being placed on real past events, as in patients who recalled that clear intimations of their future destiny had been given to them in childhood, or traced back suspicious observations to many years previously. But other patients described events that were clearly wholly fictitious, such as meetings with prominent people.

Eventually – sometimes suddenly, sometimes taking years to mature – an explanation of all that had been happening would form in the patient's mind and crystallise into a central unshakeable delusion, usually one that was persecutory or grandiose. Although this explanation would be inherently extremely unlikely and have the only flimsiest justification, characteristically it would not contain any absolute impossibilities. To a certain extent it could even be considered to be an understandable, if pathological, realisation of the fears, wishes and hopes that many people harbour. (This feature of paranoia was later to become important as the 'non-bizarre' quality of the delusions.) Thereafter, a tightly knit delusional system developed where the central belief and surrounding referential delusions supported and reinforced each other; contradictions and unclear points would be thought through laboriously until they were resolved.

Other symptoms were conspicuous by their absence. In particular, auditory hallucinations never occurred. Abnormal visual perceptions, on the other hand, were not uncommon. Typically, these took the form of isolated visionary experiences, of stars, shining figures, divine apparitions, often occurring at night. In some cases these could be construed as illusions (e.g. a cloud taking on the form of an apocalyptic animal), or as having taken place during a dream-like state; in others the experience could not be disentangled from delusional memories (e.g. a patient who stated that she saw Heaven open at the age of 4). Affect was objectively normal, although there could be mood colourings in keeping with the content of the central delusion, for example suspiciousness or exaggerated self-confidence. Some patients became withdrawn, or took to writing obscure documents, or moved around from place to place, but in general behaviour remained surprisingly normal and many patients continued to work.

At some point the clinical development would reach a standstill. The central delusion would be elaborated no further and the referential delusions that nourished it would to a greater or lesser extent abate. After this, the abnormal ideas might be observed to be less preoccupying, or no longer seem to have the emotional investment they once had. Often, the delusions themselves and what they were believed to be founded on became indistinct. But beyond this, deterioration to even the mildest degree did not occur.

Kraepelin subdivided paranoia into four subtypes based on the content of the central delusion. The persecutory form was the most common type. Here, in the face of continual observation and hounding, the patient came to believe that he was being conspired against by a person or organisation, a sister-in-law, a colleague, the mayor, the freemasons, and so on. In the jealous form, the same kinds of goings on were seized on as evidence of a partner's infidelity. The grandiose form included cases where patients believed they had invented things – typically useless and sometimes already in existence – and the supporting referential delusions often revolved around machinations to suppress or steal the device. Also in this category were ideas of high descent, where the patient found that he was continually being subjected to tests of his worthiness for his future position, conspired against by the rest of the aristocracy, and so on, religious delusions of being a prophet or saint, and finally erotomania. The final subtype was a hypochondriacal form of paranoia which Kraepelin acknowledged, but had never seen a case of.

Kraepelin was more ambivalent about the inclusion of a fifth disorder under the heading of paranoia. This was the querulous paranoid state, where the patient became preoccupied by a real or supposed wrong and pursued his case vigorously and determinedly, usually dragging it through a succession of courts. This departed significantly from the general account given above, not least in the way that the central belief was not surrounded by multiple, clear-cut delusions of reference, misinterpretation and misidentification. Originally, Kraepelin (1905), classified this as a 'secondary form' of paranoia, but by 1913 he had decided that it was more closely allied to other disorders. This form of paranoia is discussed further below.

There is no doubt that Kraepelin was never entirely happy with the concept of paranoia. He conceded that a number of illnesses could exhibit a similar picture, particularly in their early stages, and so it was a disorder to be diagnosed reluctantly, after everything else had been excluded. Later, he debated whether paranoia was in reality a form of schizophrenia running a particularly slow and mild course, but ultimately decided that this was not the case. This latter difficulty, in particular, refused to go away and was widely discussed as 'the paranoia question'. Bleuler (1911) put the central clinical uncertainty succinctly: 'it may be possible that paranoia is an entirely chronic schizophrenia which is so mild that it could just about lead to delusional ideas; its less striking symptoms, however, are so lacking in prominence that we cannot demonstrate them', before going on to state:

> I would consider this extremely probable if it were more common that an originally pure paranoia at a later stage also develops schizophrenic

symptoms. Only in a very few cases have we been forced to change our diagnosis from paranoia to schizophrenia and among these there were none that were not right from the start suspected of being schizophrenic. Unfortunately, such experiences are not sufficient proof for the basic difference between the two diseases since paranoia is very rare among hospital patients.

Clearly, what was needed was a follow-up study of the kind Mayer (1921) carried out in paraphrenia. This eventually appeared when Kolle (1931) followed up (or rather re-examined the case-notes of) the 19 patients diagnosed as suffering from paranoia by Kraepelin or his colleagues 4 to 22 years after the diagnosis was originally made. Kolle excluded from consideration two cases in which Kraepelin had added 'manic predisposition' or 'possible manic-depressive psychosis' to the diagnosis. Of the remaining 17 cases, seven more were excluded on various grounds: one had experienced ecstatic visionary experiences and later in the course of her illness was prone to talk incoherently about Hitler and other topics. Another developed bizarre delusions of being affected by radiation and had felt blows to his chest. Another had a history of alcoholism and his paranoid delusion followed in the wake of an admission for delirium tremens. Another ultimately became withdrawn and lived a hermit-like existence. The reasons for exclusion were not specified in the other three.

The remaining 10 cases fitted without difficulty into the category of paranoia as defined by Kraepelin. However, Kolle argued that in all these cases the delusion showed some of the phenomenological characteristics of true, primary or schizophrenic delusions. It is possible to infer from his lengthy discussion that he considered the patients' delusions to lack the systematisation, logical development and not completely impossible nature specified by Kraepelin. This would be, however, to oversimplify a tortuous and largely impenetrable foray into the minutiae of German psychopathology. In any event, Kolle's conclusion was that primary delusions were diagnostic of schizophrenia and therefore paranoia was a subtype of schizophrenia.

Apart from its relationship to schizophrenia, the concept of paranoia faced another difficulty. This was exemplified by the querulous paranoid state mentioned above. Having originally classed this with paranoia, Kraepelin came to feel that it was different, being struck by its precipitation by external causes rather than arising gradually through an internal change, and by the fact that it did not seem to have such far-reaching effects as other forms of paranoia. However, it was not at all clear that querulous paranoid patients adhered to either Kraepelin's first or second classifications. As Bleuler (1911) once again put it: 'We find numerous transitions from simply unbearable people to the paranoid litigants with marked delusions. The best solution perhaps is to draw a line somewhere in the middle of the scale and place the half that do not have real delusions there and count the others as paranoid.'

The scope of the problem was widened by Jaspers (1959), who argued that exactly the same point could be made about individuals with morbid jealousy, as well as about some cranky inventors and world reformers. It almost seemed that any definition of paranoia would inevitably end up encompassing some individuals who were not psychotic, and possibly not even ill in any meaningful sense of the term.

Yet, despite Kolle's attack on its separation from schizophrenia and other serious nosological uncertainties, at the end of the classical period there were many who believed that paranoia was a genuine clinical entity (see Fish, 1962/ Hamilton, 1984). This undoubtedly to some extent reflected the fact that, in spite of its rarity, cases that were absolutely characteristic of paranoia in the Kraepelinian sense were encountered from time to time. One such case, where there were also important medico-legal implications, is described in Box 12.3.

Box 12.3 Paranoia: The case of Ernst Wagner (from Gaupp, 1914)

Ernst Wagner was a teacher who, in 1913, committed what was at the time a sensational mass-murder. Two of his mother's brothers were mentally ill, one with delusions of persecution. A brother drank heavily. His mother was impulsive and unstable, and also litigious. The patient was described as lively and somewhat self-conscious, imaginative but with a tendency to arrogance and cynicism. He was also said to have a fanatical regard for the truth.

At the age of 27, while working as a teacher and at a time of sexual frustration, he committed some form of sexual act with animals (he never revealed the precise details). The next day he believed that others could tell what he had done by looking at him. Before long, he noticed that people were making remarks about him and pointing at him behind his back. He came to believe that groups of people standing together were laughing and jeering at him, that obscene remarks were being passed about him, and that he was an object of general derision. He took to carrying a loaded gun with him at all times so that he could shoot himself in case the police came for him.

After he married and moved to another village, his ideas did not develop further, although when he returned to his previous place of residence he still noticed all the previous mockery. Eventually, however, he began to notice friends and colleagues making remarks which showed that they knew about his abnormal sexual practices. He requested a transfer, but after this the same thing happened. By the age of 35 he had worked out a plan to murder the residents of the places he had lived in and then to kill himself. He also came to the conclusion that he should kill his family, as his children might carry the germ of the same or even worse sexual deviations. This caused him to postpone carrying out his plan.

At the age of 41 he cut the throats of his wife and children while they slept and then travelled to the village of his birth where he set fire to houses, shot dead eight men and severely wounded 16 others. It was clear from letters that he had posted just before the event that he intended to kill himself as well, but he was apprehended before he could do so.

When examined in custody, he was temporarily shaken that no one knew anything about his sexual misdemeanours, but soon returned to his belief that he had been persecuted for years. He tried unsuccessfully to have his case re-opened so that he could be proved mentally healthy and be sentenced to death. Apart from the above delusion, and a belief that bestiality was a worse crime than murder, he remained an intelligent individual whose judgement in many matters was shrewd and accurate. His delusion fluctuated, subsiding only to flare up again – for instance when a patient who made animal noises to himself was admitted. In later years he wrote poems and several plays. He developed the belief that one of his plays was plagiarised and conducted an extended legal action about this, which he lost.

In 1932, over 30 years after the onset of his illness, the patient was presented at a meeting of psychiatrists and he spoke for two hours. According to Gaupp, it was concluded at this meeting that he showed no signs of schizophrenia. He remained interested in current affairs, which he followed attentively through newspapers and the radio. A year before his death at the age of 64 he was reported to be well-informed about everything and to show excellent judgement. However he still believed that everyone in the asylum was talking about his bestiality.

Half a century later, Wagner's brain was discovered in the Vogt post-mortem collection (see Bogerts, 1997), where it had never been examined. It looked normal and there was no evidence of ventricular enlargement or cortical atrophy. However, there was a distinct invagination in the left posterior hippocampal cortex, clearly indicative of a developmental abnormality.

Contemporary paranoia

In the years leading up to the introduction of criterion-based approaches to psychiatric diagnosis, paranoia languished in the same kind of nosological uncertainty that had marked most of its earlier history. As described by Lewis (1970) and Kendler and Tsuang (1981), in Europe there continued to be controversy over whether paranoia was part of schizophrenia, or whether some cases at least were an independent entity. The lingering question of how far the concept of paranoia should include forms that were understandable as the response of a predisposed personality to adverse events led, in America, to a very loose usage of the diagnosis indeed. British psychiatrists accepted that a series of paranoid 'states' existed which, if they had to commit themselves, they probably considered were more closely related to each other than to schizophrenia.

The relationship of paranoia to schizophrenia was thoroughly examined by Kendler (1980). He renamed paranoia as 'simple delusional disorder' (later just delusional disorder) and established a set of criteria for it, so that it could be included in DSM III. These are shown in Table 12.3. The central requirements were presence of persecutory, grandiose, hypochondriacal, jealous or other delusions, or pervasive delusions of reference (Kendler actually used the term ideas of reference). Required to be absent were hallucinations, a full affective syndrome or symptoms suggestive of schizophrenia. It was also stipulated that the delusions should be 'non-bizarre', an acknowledgement of Kraepelin's insistence on the logical construction and not utterly impossible nature of the beliefs in paranoia. He then proceeded to subject the various follow-up studies of paranoid disorders that had been undertaken over the years to a critical, patient (and to anyone familiar with the stultifying effects of such an endeavour, even Herculean) review.

After sifting through the literature, Kendler was able to identify four follow-up studies of paranoia that met his inclusion criteria. The findings of these are shown in Table 12.4. The proportion of patients who developed schizophrenia over follow-up periods ranging from a few months to 20 years ranged from 3 per cent to 13 per cent; one study suggested a higher proportion, but this was based on a sample of nine patients, two of whom became schizophrenic. Somewhat surprisingly, two of the studies also indicated that a small minority of patients with paranoia (3 per cent and 6 per cent) developed affective psychoses over time; one of these studies, however, did not rigorously exclude affective symptoms at initial presentation. The majority of patients meeting Kendler's criteria for paranoia thus showed diagnostic consistency over time.

With respect to social and occupational outcome, around three-quarters of

---

Table 12.3 Kendler's criteria for delusional disorder (paranoia)

1. Onset of illness before age 60.
2. Non-bizarre delusions of any type (i.e. persecutory, grandiose, somatic, jealousy, etc.) and/or persistent, pervasive ideas of reference are present. These delusions are usually of a fairly systematised kind.
3. These symptoms have been present for a minimum of two weeks.
4. Persistent hallucinations of any kind are absent.
5. A full affective syndrome, either depressive or manic, is absent when the patient is delusional.
6. There are no symptoms suggestive of schizophrenia, including prominent thought disorder, inappropriate affect, patently bizarre delusions, and first rank symptoms.
7. Symptoms suggestive of an acute or chronic brain syndrome are absent.

Source: Kendler (1980), The nosologic validity of paranoia (simple delusional disorder). *Archives of General Psychiatry*, 37, 699–706. © 1980, American Medical Association.

Table 12.4 Outcome studies of paranoia/delusional disorder

Study	Numbers of patients	Follow-up period	Diagnosis unchanged	Diagnosis changed	Comment
Faergeman (1963)	9	5 years	7 (78%)	2 (22%) schizophrenia	Uncertain cases and cases presenting with bizarre delusions excluded by Kendler.
Johanson (1964)	52	Few months to 4½ years	46 (88%)	6 (12%) schizophrenia	No systematic follow-up. No follow-up diagnoses other than schizophrenia found.
Retterstol (1966, 1970)	163	5–15 years	132 (81%)	21 (13%) schizophrenia 10 (6%) ?manic-depressive	Good systematic follow-up. Some evidence that 6% of patients had affective disorder at follow-up.
Winokur (1977)	25	Few months to 20 years	23 (93%)	1 (4%) schizophrenia 1 (4%) ?manic-depressive	For 86% follow-up was longer than 6 months, for 34% longer than 2 years.

Source: Kendler (1980), The nosologic validity of paranoia (simple delusional disorder). *Archives of General Psychiatry*, 37, 699–706. © 1980, American Medical Association.

the patients in the above studies were found to be out of hospital at follow-up. Two-thirds had been in employment much of the time since their index admission. Approximately a third had no further hospitalisations, and some of this last group showed improvement that could amount to social recovery. In this respect the outcome of paranoia was very different from that of schizophrenia.

Kendler concluded that the majority of patients who develop states characterised purely by delusions go on to follow a course similar to that outlined by Kraepelin for paranoia – they do not go on to develop a wider range of schizophrenic symptoms, or deterioration, or other psychiatric disorders. A small number of cases do evolve into schizophrenia, and some turn out to have what later appears to be an affective disorder. Neither of these findings are irreconcilable with a disorder where Kraepelin considered that the diagnosis was essentially impossible to make cross-sectionally.

The question of the demarcation of paranoia from certain conditions that can only uncomfortably be regarded as psychotic has not been answered nearly as clearly. There are undoubtedly patients who develop circumscribed, persistent abnormal beliefs which are often, but by no means always, persecutory. The course these illnesses take is typically chronic and the outcome is often unfavourable. The prototypical example is, as mentioned above, the querulous paranoid state. Kraepelin's (1905) description of such a case is reproduced in Box 12.4, and other English-language accounts of this rare

---

Box 12.4 The querulous paranoid state (from Kraepelin, 1905)

A 38-year-old master tailor had previously become insolvent and at that time had fought out a fierce lawsuit with a creditor. Three years later he again fell into debt and, in the course of trying to prevent a creditor and a bailiff removing his furniture, he locked both of them up in his house while he lodged a complaint in court. The patient was tried for this and found guilty of false imprisonment.

A short, humorously treated account of the affair, which contained inaccuracies, appeared in a newspaper. The patient became angry and wrote a correction, only part of which was printed. A further enraged letter to the editor was responded to by publication of a full report of the proceedings. In this, the words 'master tailor' were printed in large type; the patient took offence at this and brought three legal actions against the newspaper. These actions were all rejected in the courts. The patient was not satisfied and gradually set in motion a series of appeals through higher and higher courts, eventually petitioning the Ministry of Justice, the Ministry of State, the Grand Duke and the Emperor. After these failed the patient tried the experiment of complaining to the heads of the courts, appealed to the public, and was considering proposing disciplinary proceedings against the Public Prosecutor.

On examination, the patient was coherent and able to give a clear account of the history of events. On the subject of his court actions he expressed himself volubly and showed increased self-confidence and superiority, a certain satisfaction and readiness for battle. He was also exceedingly touchy – if pressed on whether he might have been mistaken in his interpretation of events, he immediately became mistrustful and raised the suspicion that the interviewer supported his opponents. He was never at a loss for an answer to objections, which he justified by quoting minutiae of the law. In prolonged conversation a wearisome diffuseness crept into his narrative. The patient believed that an attorney involved for the plaintiff in his original bankruptcy proceedings was the real source of his misfortunes. This was because, when he first wanted to bring an action against the editor of the newspaper, the clerk of the court dissuaded him from doing so, referring to these earlier proceedings – he believed that this attorney had prejudiced the clerk of the court against him, and also wished to ruin him. As a result, the clerk did not draw up the accusation properly; the Public Prosecutor gained an erroneous impression from it; the judges of several courts did not want to reverse verdicts once agreed to; and they were as a body prejudiced. He believed that the whole system of law had been obstructed via a conspiracy involving Freemasonry. He also believed that Jewish financiers played a part in the conspiracy as the newspaper which wrote about him was supported by them; and that the press was associated with the attorney in question. He believed that a whole series of individuals were working together secretly to bring about his ruin.

As a consequence of his incessant pestering of the authorities, the patient was eventually pronounced to be mentally deranged, against which opinion he adopted every possible legal means of redress. Meanwhile he continued to carry on his business, and apart from writing innumerable petitions, did not appear strange or troublesome. Because of his course of action he had brought his family deeper and deeper into misfortune. Nevertheless, in spite of every failure, he remained optimistic about the outcome of his case.

disorder have been provided by Rowlands (1988) and Ungvari and Hollokoi (1993). The essential problem is that these states fulfil the criteria for delu-sional disorder in many or all respects, but they do not show the multiple delusions of reference, misinterpretation and misidentification which, given the non-bizarre nature of the central belief, go a long way to defining the disorder as psychotic.

There has been no empirical investigation of this issue, but there have been two attempts to deal with it at a conceptual level. The first is in the work of Jaspers (1959) who, originally in connection with morbid jealousy, drew a distinction between abnormal beliefs that were due to 'process' and to 'personality development'. In the former case, a belief appears which is essentially the first sign of an evolving psychosis (usually schizophrenia). The belief cannot be seen as arising comprehensibly from the individual's personality and experience; its nature is ultimately 'un-understandable'. The psychosis may eventually become manifest in more florid symptoms, but there is no absolute necessity for this to happen – the process may arrest or spontaneously remit. The latter form of abnormal belief is the outcome of an interaction between the individual and his environment which brings a focus to his life and results in the development of an idea which is certainly pathological, but is also understandable – it is a 'hypertrophy' of an already abnormal personality in reaction to adverse events. The contrasting features of processes and personality developments as summarised by Fish (Fish, 1962/Hamilton, 1984) are illustrated in Table 12.5.

The shortcoming of this approach is its fallibility in practice. While as a general principle the distinction has a great deal of intuitive appeal and is backed by the intellectual weight of Jaspers, when it is applied to any particular patient it depends ultimately on an evaluation of what is understandable given the personality, background, life experiences and current situation of the individual concerned. This judgement is inevitably subjective and, as Fish (Fish, 1962/Hamilton, 1984) pointed out, clinicians vary considerably in what they will accept as understandable: some psychiatrists are always ready to go to extraordinary lengths to construe obviously bizarre experiences as comprehensible, whereas others take a distinctly narrow view of what is normal and abnormal, confidently diagnose early schizophrenia, and then find themselves waiting a very long time for the full blown syndrome to appear.

Table 12.5 Summary of differences between Jaspers' concepts of process and personality development

Personality development	Psychic process
Slow, gradual change analogous to the development of a child.	A new development that begins at a definite point in time.
Acute events do not signify a lasting change. The *status quo ante* is restored again.	Acute events signify a change which is not reversible (although the process can arrest).
The whole course of life can be understood from the predispositiion of the personality.	When an attempt is made to derive the changes from the personality, a limit is found at a given point in time where something new appeared.
	There is a definite regularity of development and course of the changed personality, which can be understood in the same way as the normal events of psychic life and which possesses a new unity.

Source: Hamilton (1984), *Fish's schizophrenia*, 3rd edition. John Wright and Sons. Reproduced with permission.

The second approach, which also owes much to Jaspers, focuses not on the characteristics of the individual with the abnormal belief, but on the characteristics of the belief itself. The proposal is that two quite different types of belief can be distinguished. The first of these, seen in schizophrenia and Kraepelinian paranoia, is delusion proper. As described briefly in Chapter 1, and discussed more fully by Jaspers (1959), Walker (1991) and Sims (2002), these are essentially qualitatively different from normal beliefs. They are held with an incomparable subjective certainty, in a way that seems uncanny and alien, and are justified by the patient in a characteristic, self-evidently illogical fashion. It may be added that a delusion proper is rarely encountered as a solitary phenomenon but is generally accompanied by other psychotic symptoms, even if these are only delusions of reference and misinterpretation. In paranoia, the central delusion is not particularly bizarre and the network of referential delusions tend to be intricate and almost logical, but the difference from the more florid delusions seen in schizophrenia is a only matter of degree.

The second form of abnormal belief is the overvalued idea, a concept that was introduced by Wernicke, elaborated on by Jaspers, but has since been largely neglected. As reviewed by McKenna (1984), the overvalued idea often appears following a key adverse event in an individual's life, comes to single-mindedly preoccupy him or her, and is acted on, determinedly and repeatedly. The idea is solitary; that is, it is not accompanied by delusions of reference and misinterpretation. Phenomenologically, it is simply an exaggeration of the passionate political, religious, and ethical beliefs of many normal individuals, rather than showing the qualitatively different un-understandable form of conviction that lies at the heart of delusions. The disorder in which the concept of the overvalued idea is usually described is, in fact, the querulous paranoid state. The term has also been considered to be applicable to morbid jealousy, hypochondriasis and dysmorphophobia, and, according to McKenna, to anorexia nervosa.

The phenomenological concept of the overvalued idea places the debate about the scope of the concept of paranoia on a clinical footing and avoids dragging in arguments about understandability and speculation about aetiological factors in the development of a belief. It also has the advantage of a certain objectivity – a good rule of thumb is that beliefs which are delusions will always be accompanied by delusions of reference and misinterpretation (or other obviously psychotic symptoms), whereas if it is entirely isolated it is likely to be an overvalued idea. The difficulty with this approach to the partitioning of paranoia is that its simplicity is more apparent than real: sometimes patients with established schizophrenia show delusions that are overwhelmingly preoccupying and solitary. In other cases the evolution of an abnormal belief does not seem to follow any simple rules, with abnormal personality, earlier periods of psychosis and perhaps even organic factors all having to be taken into consideration.

Aetiological factors in paranoia

The discussion here concerns paranoia in its main, psychotic, 'Kraepelinian' sense. The findings are mainly taken from Kendler's (1980) review, since which there has in fact been very little further work.

Family history

Kendler considered three studies suitable for inclusion (Kolle, 1931; Debray, 1975; Winokur, 1977). These found frequencies of schizophrenia in first-degree relatives of between 2.4 per cent and 3.2 per cent; these rates included some cases where the presentation was paranoia-like; that is, one of delusions alone or delusions plus hallucinations. This risk is clearly higher than that for the general population of 0.8 per cent, but much lower than that of around 10 per cent for the first-degree relatives of schizophrenics. All three studies also found appreciable rates of affective disorders of 1.1 per cent, 2.4 per cent and 5 per cent (however, in the last study the frequency was no higher than in a control group of normal individuals). Two of the three studies also found a clustering of 'pathological personalities' (5.7 per cent) or 'soft paranoid syndromes' (2.4 per cent) in the relatives of patients with paranoia.

Premorbid personality

Kendler found three studies which provided worthwhile information, all comparing patients with paranoia with those with schizophrenia (Bonner, 1951; Johanson, 1964; Retterstol, 1966). These all found that patients with paranoia were less likely to be schizoid, introverted or submissive than schizophrenic patients; two (Bonner, 1951; Retterstol, 1966) also suggested an increased frequency of extraverted, dominant or oversensitive traits.

Other aetiological factors

The slight sex preponderance of males found by Kraepelin was not borne out in two substantial series (Kolle, 1931; Retterstol, 1966). Four studies, however, did suggest, in line with Kraepelin, that paranoia had a significantly later age of onset than schizophrenia. Two of these (Bonner, 1951; Rimon *et al.*, 1965) recorded a mean age of onset of 46; two other studies (Kolle, 1931; Retterstol, 1966) pointed towards a peak age of onset of between 35 and 50.

Treatment of paranoia

Surprisingly little has been written on this topic, which is probably to some extent a reflection of the lack of clarity about the boundaries of the disorder. Once again, the best evidence comes from Kendler's (1980) review. He considered the relevant studies to be generally poor (for instance, lacking controls), but it could be concluded that at least a subgroup of patients show a response to neuroleptics. One open trial of ECT in a small group of patients with paranoia found that the response was comparatively poor (Huston and Locher, 1948).

Other paranoid disorders

Paranoid depression

Among a number of subtypes of manic-depressive psychosis (see Chapter 13), Kraepelin (1913b) included a form which he called paranoid melancholia. Such patients showed obvious evidence of depression, which was often associated with retardation, agitation, ideas or delusions of hopelessness, and guilt. At the same time they exhibited persecutory and referential delusions, that they were being watched, spied on or threatened with murder. In some cases these beliefs were accompanied by auditory hallucinations of a derogatory kind.

The definitive investigation of paranoia in depression was carried out by Lewis (1934) as part of a survey of 61 cases of melancholia (as described in Chapter 13, his definition conformed closely to the modern concept of major depression). Persecutory and referential ideas, ranging from mere impressions of contempt, jeering, or hostility on the part of others, to full delusions of being poisoned, followed about, shot at, tormented, and so on, were common, being found in 43 out of the 61 patients. Lewis then went on to consider the received wisdom that such beliefs were not truly persecutory, but were an elaboration of depressive self-depreciation and self-blame, according to the formula, 'I'm worthless; others know it; they treat me accordingly; they put slights on me, they persecute me.' He found that 17 of his patients thought they were getting their just desserts, although this conclusion had to be qualified in some cases. Seven patients expressed resentment or hostility about their persecution in their words or behaviour. Another eight, while conceding their sinfulness or wrongdoing, also described persecution that they could not account for. Finally, 11 patients felt they should take no blame whatsoever for what they were experiencing. Lewis concluded that the view that the paranoid ideas and delusions seen in depression were understandable in terms of the mood disturbance was 'to make the matter very simple, simpler than the data permit'.

Since Lewis' survey, there has been an almost total silence on the topic of paranoid depression in the English-language literature. Just about the only contemporary author to discuss the matter has been Fish (Fish, 1962/Hamilton, 1984). He proposed that some persecutory delusions in depression were an exaggerated form of lifelong paranoid personality traits, obsessionality or anxiety. But he agreed that persecutory and referential delusions that are not mood-congruent can be seen in major depression.

Such patients are not easily understood as suffering from schizoaffective disorder, since their illnesses can otherwise be entirely typical of affective disorder – it is not uncommon to encounter patients who have had a number of previous episodes of major depression and sometimes mania, who then have an episode where the major symptoms are paranoid and referential delusions, with the depression being quite far in the background, who then recover and go on to have further typical episodes of depression or mania.

The sensitive delusion of reference

This term was coined by Kretschmer (1927) and has become enshrined in British and European psychiatry (e.g. Sims, 2002). It is usually considered to describe individuals who have a particular form of shy and inhibited personality and who, in the face of a stigma such as illegitimacy or physical deformity, or following some humiliating experience, develop self-torturing ruminations which eventually come to be held with a delusion-like intensity and fixity. The important point is that the belief is not a delusion proper and that the resultant state is not psychotic in the strict sense of the term. In contrast to true paranoia, there are reasonable prospects for recovery.

It is instructive to read Kretschmer's (1927) original account, parts of which are available in English translation (Hirsch and Shepherd, 1974). As part of his own, quite idiosyncratic classification of personality (see Chapter 16), he described a 'sensitive' type. This referred to individuals with gentle, insecure natures who were ethically or spiritually inclined, and who, while appearing quiet and reserved, felt experiences deeply to the extent of being consumed by them. When the delicate emotional life of these individuals was subjected to particular forms of conflict that they could not cope with, the sensitive delusion of reference was liable to develop. He described a number of examples, of which two were translated.

The first was the case of a 29-year-old woman who had previously experienced a prolonged grief reaction following the death of her mother. She became sexually attracted to a fellow worker, but at the same time tried to suppress her feelings, until this developed into a continual struggle. Eventually she confided in a relative who became exasperated with her and shouted about the matter by an open window. After this the patient began to believe that remarks were being passed about her, heard allusions to herself in conversations, and started to notice items in the newspapers which indicated that the police were coming to arrest her. Over the next 2 to 3 years she became floridly psychotic, displaying persecutory and referential delusions, auditory and possibly also visual hallucinations, all in the setting of depression, anxiety and self-reproach. After another 5 to 7 years she improved and was discharged from hospital. A few years later she relapsed and was re-admitted. After a further 12 years she made a full recovery, returned to work and on follow-up showed no sign of schizophrenic deterioration.

The second case was a middle-aged man who developed fluctuating feelings of listlessness and restlessness shortly after being passed over for promotion at work. These evolved into a state characterised by nervousness, excitability and constant movement, accompanied by sleep disturbance, loss of appetite and constipation. At a later point he became suspicious, believed that he had stared too long at the wife of the colleague who had been promoted over him, and elaborated this idea until he believed that she was at the centre of a conspiracy to drive him from his job and destroy him; the police and a whole army of adversaries, including his own wife, were involved in this. His illness improved over several weeks. He returned to work but the same symptoms recurred, first after several months and then again 2 years later. Afterwards he remained well until his death a few years later.

Neither of these cases conforms to the present day stereotype of an isolated, easily understandable persecutory belief developing in a thin-skinned individual. In fact, neither of them would necessarily be considered particularly unusual – the first case had a florid, relapsing illness in which there were both schizophrenic symptoms and a full affective syndrome. The second would seem to represent a fairly unexceptional case of paranoid depression.

Etats passionnels

As mentioned in Chapter 4, French psychiatry has traditionally recognised a large number of paranoid disorders. One reason for this was the sway that Magnan, a contemporary of Kraepelin's, and his followers Capgras and Serieux, held (and seemingly continue to hold) in this country. They insisted on a much narrower definition of schizophrenia than elsewhere, and correspondingly developed a wider and more detailed classification of paraphrenia-like and purely delusional states (see Pichot, 1982).

The other reason was the somewhat maverick influence of de Clérambault, who postulated the existence of what he called *états passionels*. He distinguished three types of presentation of this disorder: the querulous paranoid state, morbid jealousy, and erotomania, with which his name has become synonymous. In all three conditions, but most strenuously in the last (see de Clérambault, 1942; Baruk, 1959), he argued that the nature of the belief was isolated, preoccupying and, as his name for them implied, had a passionate quality phenomenologically distinct from the delusions of paranoia and schizophrenia. In his words, the patient with an *état passionnel* was in a state of constant striving and advanced to his goal consciously and determinedly; there was a 'hypersthenic' quality that extended to the point of hypomania. He acknowledged that some cases eventually gave way to schizophrenia, but pointed out that when this happened the quality of the belief also changed to one that was more obviously delusional.

While the points de Clérambault made about the querulous paranoid state have since been regularly rehearsed in the literature, and would not be out of place in contemporary accounts of morbid jealousy (see Cobb, 1979), ironically, as applied to erotomania, they have been largely forgotten. The existence of erotomania as a pure, not frankly psychotic form is currently regarded as, at best, controversial (e.g. Enoch and Ball, 2001) – almost certainly wrongly, as witnessed by the contemporary phenomenon of stalking, where many of the perpetrators are manifestly not psychotic (e.g. Mullen *et al.*, 1999; Kamphuis and Emmelkamp, 2000).

The concept of the *état passionnel* is clearly closely similar to that of the overvalued idea, and the clinical forms they are alleged to take obviously overlap. It is also noteworthy that both concepts embody elements of the process: personality development distinction advocated by Jaspers and Fish. It seems that wherever a classification of paranoid disorders is attempted, similar problems arise, and similar, not entirely satisfactory solutions are proposed.

Hypochondriacal paranoia?

Kraepelin (1913b) stated that he had not been able to find an unequivocal case of paranoia which was characterised only, or at least predominantly, by a hypochondriacal delusion. When Kolle (1931, cited by Lewis, 1970) later enumerated the different forms that the delusions of paranoia could take, he included persecution, grandeur, litigation, jealousy, love, envy, hate, honour, and the supernatural; bodily illness was noticeably absent from the list. More recent studies have done little to change this view: for example, Winokur (1977) found hypochondriasis to be the major theme in none of his 29 cases, and subsidiary hypochondriacal beliefs were found in only three.

The concept of hypochondriacal paranoia, renamed 'monosymptomatic hypochondriacal psychosis', was revived by Munro (1980, 1999). He defined this as a rare disorder characterised by a single hypochondriacal delusion that is sustained over a considerable period, sometimes for many years. As in other forms of paranoia, the state is not secondary to another disorder, and the personality remains otherwise well preserved. According to Munro, the hypochondriacal belief is fundamentally delusional in character, and the disorder is thus only superficially similar to hypochondriasis of a neurotic type. Such patients seek out a succession of medical opinions and are insistent that there is a physical cause for their symptoms. They become angry and disdainful if this is not accepted. Although the patients may give the impression of being hallucinated – for example, reporting seeing insects or being able to smell the odour they believe they emit – in most cases the apparent abnormal perception is in reality a delusional misinterpretation. In Munro's own series of patients around half were claimed to show ideas of reference.

Munro included a number of different syndromes under the heading of monosymptomatic hypochondriacal psychosis: delusions of infestation; dysmorphic delusions of ugliness, misshapeness, or overprominence of a feature; the olfactory paranoid syndrome where an individual believes he gives off a foul smell; and also some instances of chronic pain syndromes and anorexia nervosa where the symptom has a recognisably delusional quality. The prognosis is poor. Some patients eventually progress to clear-cut schizophrenia. Treatment is usually considered unsatisfactory, but Munro has claimed that the neuroleptic pimozide (now no longer in use) produced a response varying from fair to excellent in nearly two-thirds of patients.

The concept of hypochondriacal paranoia or monosymptomatic hypochondriacal psychosis provides an exceptionally clear illustration of the difficulties that are run into when attempts are made to separate psychotic and non-psychotic forms of paranoia. Hypochondriacal delusions are commonly encountered in schizophrenia. Hypochondriacal beliefs that qualify as delusions on all counts except for that of being bizarre or fantastic are also seen in major depression. Finally, as hypochondriasis (Merskey, 1995), dysmorphophobia (Hay, 1970; Andreasen and Bardach, 1977), and parasitophobia (Hopkinson, 1973), isolated beliefs have been described which are similar, if not identical, to those identified by Munro, except that the authors concerned were deeply unsure whether they should be regarded as delusional in nature.

Conclusion

In 1912 Kraepelin (cited by Lewis, 1970) considered whether, in view of its shabby record, paranoia should be dropped altogether as a concept. Over 50 years later, Lewis concluded that the term should only be retained in psychiatric usage in its descriptive sense and not as a diagnostic category. For him, a paranoid syndrome was one in which there were delusions that could not be immediately derived from a prevailing abnormal mood state. Its recognition was a preliminary to diagnosis, and this would invariably turn out to be one of the major known categories of mental disorder.

The conclusion of this chapter is different. It is that, in the clinical sense at least, both paraphrenia and paranoia do genuinely exist. Patients showing the kinds of presentation first described by Kraepelin continue to be encountered, and many, though not all, go on to pursue a course that is not at all typical of schizophrenia. For paraphrenia, it seems clear that the cross-sectional and longitudinal differences from schizophrenia are merely quantitative. In paranoia, however, the differences in clinical picture, course and outcome edge towards, or even over into, the qualitative.

Aetiologically, the picture is undoubtedly more muddy. While a case can be made that neither disorder is entirely separable from schizophrenia, a more honest conclusion would have to be that in paraphrenia some modification of the underlying pathological process appears to be likely. In paranoia, the weight of the admittedly scanty evidence points to a different genetic basis from schizophrenia altogether.

13 Schizoaffective and other atypical psychoses

While everyone accepts that the boundaries of schizophrenia are not well defined, its particular relationship with the other main variety of functional psychosis has been the subject of a long-running border dispute. The orthodox view, still held by many, is that schizophrenia and manic-depressive psychosis are separate disorders. On the other hand, there have always been some who, as described in Chapter 4, have regarded the two presentations merely as points along a continuum of psychosis, and this is currently a respectable, even fashionable position. What both sides in the argument would accept is that patients exist who show combinations of schizophrenic and affective symptomatology, sometimes simultaneously, sometimes at different points in the same episode of illness, and sometimes at widely separated points in time.

Kendell (1986) drew up a list of what it might mean when a patient presents with a combination of schizophrenic and affective symptoms. It could be that the patient is suffering from schizophrenia with some incidental affective symptoms – in other words the mood colourings described in Chapter 1. Alternatively, he or she might be sufferering from manic-depressive psychosis with incidental psychotic symptoms – for example the well-known mood congruent delusions and hallucinations of the disorder. Or the patient could have been unlucky enough to have developed both schizophrenia and affective psychosis; there is no reason to suppose that this should not sometimes occur by chance. Another possibility is that there exists a third psychosis, unrelated to schizophrenia or manic-depressive psychosis, which shows combinations of schizophrenic and affective symptoms. Conversely, it might be that the presentation is some kind of genuine 'interform', reflecting unknown aetiological interactions between schizophrenia and manic-depressive psychosis. Finally, it is quite possible that some combination of the preceding five factors might be operating; the answer does not have to be simple.

Historically, the concept of schizoaffective psychosis, the term normally applied to patients who present with both schizophrenic and affective symptoms, has had two main themes. On the one hand it has been used to describe a disorder that has gone by many different names but is most frequently referred to as 'cycloid psychosis', in which there are fluctuating schizophrenic and affective symptoms, plus other distinguishing features. It also embraces what might be termed schizoaffective psychosis proper, a disorder characterised purely and simply by a combination of both schizophrenic and affective symptoms, occurring either simultaneously or at different times. There are also a number of other atypical psychoses that tend to be discussed under the heading of 'schizoaffective'. But before the status of these disorders can be subjected to any kind of critical evaluation, the discussion has to be informed by some understanding of the limits of the two main psychoses – how far schizophrenia can be complicated by affective symptoms and still be regarded as unquestionably schizophrenia, and vice versa for manic-depressive psychosis.

The limits of schizophrenia and manic-depressive psychosis

The natural starting point for this exercise is, as usual, the writings of Kraepelin and Bleuler. As the architects of the concepts of schizophrenia and manic-depressive psychosis, not only did these authors give the relevant issues careful consideration, but they also sharpened and refined their views with years of patient observation.

Affective symptoms in schizophrenia

By 1913, as described in Chapter 2, Kraepelin (1913a) had come to the conclusion that his earlier division of schizophrenia into paranoid, hebephrenic and catatonic subtypes was inadequate. One reason for this was the incorporation of simple schizophrenia; another was his separation of paranoid schizophrenia into mild and severe forms of paranoid schizophrenia and the distinction of a form characterised principally by confusion of speech. But the most important change was the introduction of five new subtypes in which there were pronounced intercurrent affective symptoms. These included two depressive forms (*simple depressive* and *delusional depressive dementia praecox*) and three that featured states of excitement as well (*circular*, *agitated* and *periodic dementia praecox*).

In the depressive forms, anxiety, tearfulness, lack of interest and dejection formed a long introductory phase. These symptoms could be accompanied by poor appetite and disorders of sleep, as well as hypochondriasis, suicide attempts, and delusions of sin, guilt and worthlessness. However, many other delusions and hallucinations were invariably also present that were unrelated to the depressed mood, and the patient's emotional attitude and behaviour were out of keeping with the usual picture of depression. Sometimes there were periods of stupor but there could occasionally be brief periods of excitement as well. The common feature of the three excited forms was a progression through one or more phases of elation and overactivity. As with the depressive forms, the mood change could be distinguished from that of manic-depressive psychosis by the presence of many florid delusions and hallucinations, speech that was completely incoherent rather than showing distractibility and flight of ideas, and behaviour that was bizarre, divorced from the surroundings and in which catatonic phenomena abounded. Both the depressive and excited forms ran a notably periodic course, sometimes with one or more periods of good remission; nevertheless, a characteristic impoverishment of thought could be discerned from an early stage, and ultimately a typical state of schizophrenic deterioration supervened.

Under the headings of 'melancholic' and 'manic' conditions, Bleuler (1911) gave a definitive phenomemological analysis of depression and elation in schizophrenia. Depression, he stated, was one of the most frequent symptoms of acute schizophrenia. In many cases, this was an essentially normal reaction in the face of distressing experiences, or a painful subjective awareness of the effects of deterioration. He also considered that there were depressive states that stemmed from the disease process itself. Sometimes these were easily identifiable as 'the usual schizophrenic melancholias' – that is, schizophrenic mood colourings – but in other cases they showed all the features of depression as seen in other disorders. But even in these cases, schizophrenic depression was characterised by a strange lack of pervasiveness, a failure of the whole personality to be engaged: some patients criticised or laughed about their own depressive thoughts and behaviour; others, despite being extremely distraught, carried on activities that were incompatible with depression: smearing faeces, interfering with the care of other patients, or engaging in indiscriminate sexual intercourse. Even when the depressive affect seemed overwhelming it still had something of the typical schizophrenic stiffness, superficiality and exaggeratedness about it; one could not quite believe that deep painful feelings were present. Florid delusions and hallucinations, as accompaniments, were rarely absent. Sometimes depression and depressive delusions existed side by side with grandiose delusions, the patient being unhampered by the logical contradictions.

Bleuler's manic conditions in schizophrenia could appear alone, or alternate with melancholic conditions, or be seen in combination with mild catatonic features. In many cases, rather than elation, the mood was one of hebephrenic-like capriciousness, with patients teasing, engaging in silly pranks, and making stupid puns and jokes. Often the mood was stilted, the patient was 'cheerful in a mechanical way'. Sometimes little real euphoria was seen. But there were nevertheless some patients who, often when they were in transition to full-blown catatonic excitement, showed elated mood, flight of ideas, and made unrealistic plans. However, these patients did little and showed a striking tendency to ignore their surroundings.

Beyond Kraepelin's and Bleuler's accounts, little further thought has been given to the nature and extent of depressive and manic mood changes in established schizophrenia. The nearest thing to a contemporary authoritative statement are the views expressed by Fish (Fish, 1962/Hamilton, 1984), which are reproduced in Box 13.1. In stating that depression was common in the early stages of schizophrenia, but that true depression and elation were

---

Box 13.1 Fish's view on the presence of manic and depressive symptoms in schizophrenia (from Hamilton, 1984)

Elevated mood of the hypomanic variety is not common in schizophrenia, although some chronic fantastic schizophrenics have a hypomanic mood. These patients are cheerful, with marked pressure of talk, but the fantastic content of their speech makes the diagnosis obvious. The elevated mood in schizophrenia usually has none of the infectious gaiety of true mania, but is one of exaltation and ecstasy. The patient has an ecstatic transfigured look and the examiner is impressed by the lack of rapport. Often the patient is not willing to talk about his feelings, but if he does so he will talk about being in a state of grace, of an indescribable happiness, or even use the word 'ecstasy'. Usually he believes tht he has been in a special type of relationship with the Almighty and may express this by saying that God has spoken to him.

Depression is extremely common in the early stages of schizophrenia. Sometimes a classical melancholia ushers in the illness and this is not uncommon in the so-called paraphrenias in middle age . . . Sometimes the depression seems to be a natural reaction to the distress caused by schizophrenic symptoms. Since some intelligent young schizophrenics have a painful realisation of the inner change which is taking place, they may justifiably be afraid that they are going mad, and may attempt suicide. In other patients the sudden onset of auditory hallucinations seems to produce marked depression and anxiety. Although disorders of emotional expression rather than disorders of mood are prominent in chronic schizophrenics, nevertheless depressive moods are met with in chronic schizophrenia, so that some hebephrenics appear to be depressed and patients with marked bodily hallucinations are usually depressed and morose.

---

uncommon in chronic patients, he echoed the views of Kraepelin and Bleuler. However, he also made the point that an apparently typical depressive state could be the beginning of a schizophrenic illness, particularly in later life.

In summary, the orthodox view has consistently been that mood changes – sometimes striking and in both directions – do form part of the clinical picture of otherwise unexceptional schizophrenia. At the same time they have been considered to be distinguishable from manic-depressive mood changes, by virtue of being incomplete, bizarre, distorted in form, and having a superficial quality. Put in contemporary terminology, the depression and elation seen in schizophrenia does not amount to a full affective syndrome: depression is not accompanied by the biological and other accessory symptoms that define major depression; mania is stripped of its richness, and the hallmark features of distractibility, overactivity and overspending are not seen.

Schizophrenic symptoms in manic-depressive psychosis

Here, Kraepelin had a great deal to say, whereas Bleuler, not having written an account of manic-depressive psychosis comparable to his work on schizophrenia, was virtually silent. In his account of manic-depressive psychosis, Kraepelin (1913b) distinguished four increasingly severe subtypes of mania, hypomania, acute mania, delusional mania and delirious mania, and four corresponding subtypes of depression; he also included two more depressive presentations which had no counterparts in mania, *stupor* and *paranoid melancholia*. The features of these are summarised in Box 13.2, but the important point is that with the exception of *hypomania* and *melancholia simplex*, all types were accompanied by delusions and hallucinations, and to a lesser extent disturbances of speech and behaviour.

Box 13.2 Kraepelin's subtypes of mania and depression (from Kraepelin, 1913b)

Mania

Hypomania: Characterised by increased liveliness, busyness and restlessness. Mood is predominantly cheerful with jocularity and subjective feelings of heightened capabilities. There is garrulousness, overactivity and increased sexual drive. Flight of ideas is slight.

Acute mania: All the symptoms seen in hypomania are present in increased severity. The patient cannot sit or lie still, and behaviour is unrestrained, disturbed and occasionally destructive. Speech is distractible and disconnected. Mood is merry or exultant, but fluctuates to irritability or tearfulness. Delusions, generally of a grandiose nature, may be present fleetingly, and there may be isolated hallucinations.

Delusional mania: The patient is restless and interfering, sings and preaches. Excitement is not usually very marked, and the patient may appear to be relatively well ordered in behaviour. However, there are florid and often relatively fixed grandiose delusions: these are often of a religious nature, or concern immense wealth, being of royal descent, etc. Auditory, visual and somatic hallucinations may be present.

Delirious mania: The patient shows marked excitement and senseless raving. Mood fluctuates between unrestrained merriment, tearfulness and erotic or ecstatic states, occasionally with brief periods of stupor. Consciousness is dreamy or clouded and the patients often show an almost complete amnesia for the episode. There are many confused delusions and hallucinations: the patients think they are in a palace, see angels and spirits, have revelations, see heaven open, hear the voice of God announce the day of judgement, believe that a great battle with the antichrist is being fought. Catatonic phenomena may be present.

Depression

Melancholia simplex: A state of simple depression without hallucinations and with no marked delusions. Obvious lowering of mood is accompanied by anxiousness, hopelessness, and gloominess. Everything is disagreeable, and the patient lacks all energy and enthusiasm. There may be obsessions and ideas of guilt and unworthiness which border on the delusional.

Stupor: The patient is deeply apathetic, and lies in bed, mute or nearly mute with a peculiar vacant strained expression. Depressive delusions may be alluded to in occasional detached utterances.

Melancholia gravis: Similar to simple melancholia but complicated by delusions and hallucinations. Patients see figures, spirits, corpses and hear abusive language, or voices inviting them to commit suicide; there may also be olfactory, gusatory, and somatic hallucinations. Nihilistic delusions are invariably present.

Paranoid melancholia: Persecutory delusions and auditory hallucinations are to the foreground of the picture. At the same time mood is gloomy and despondent; occasionally the patients appear good humoured and even cheerful in regard to their delusions. Anxiousness and restlessness may also be seen. Depressive delusions can be present.

Fantastic melancholia: Hallucinations are abundant, the patient sees evil spirits, crowds of monsters, hears his tortured relatives screaming. There are many extraordinary depressive delusions, the patient believes he has caused an epidemic, laid waste to cities, his family are being crucified by a mob, his head is as large as Palestine. Mood is characterised by a dull despondency. Consciousness may be impaired.

Delirious melancholia: Characterised by a profound visionary clouding of consciousness. Patients see the room stretch out into infinity, feel they are in prison or purgatory. They appear perplexed and confused and are hardly capable of saying a word. Catatonic phenomena are evident.

According to Kraepelin, the delusions of mania were, for the most part, grandiose and those of depression were the familiar ones of sin, guilt and bodily illness. He only described persecutory delusions in paranoid depression, where, however, they could be quite florid. Hallucinations on the other hand, were considered to be frequent in both mania and depression. Verbal auditory hallucinations, in particular, could be quite extensive and sometimes had a bizarre quality, for example emanating from the patient's own body. In delirious mania and delirious melancholia they could take on truly spectacular, apocalyptic or revelatory qualities. Invariably, though, the voices had a close connection to mood: in depression they were unpleasant; and in mania they praised, took the form of communication of sacred knowlege, and so on.

The next historically important account was Lewis' (1934) authoritative study of the clinical features in 61 cases of melancholia. In his hands this term conformed closely to the modern concept of major depression: he excluded cases where the mood change was secondary to other symptoms of ill health or organic brain disease, and none of them showed any evidence of schizophrenia beyond the 'slight or subordinate'. The diagnosis was made after final discharge of the patient and usually represented the consensus view of several psychiatrists. He found that persecutory and referential ideas ranging from mere attitudes to full-blown delusions were present in 70 per cent of the patients. Disorders of perception, including in some cases second and third person verbal auditory hallucinations, were present in 34 per cent. 'Schizophrenic features' were present in 38 per cent – these were as a rule isolated, and included patients showing delusions of reference and misinterpretation, bizarre delusions with or without auditory hallucinations, mystical ideas, odd, impulsive behaviour and in one case grimacing.

Winokur *et al.* (1969) carried out a corresponding phenomenological analysis of mania. From a group of 61 patients with manic-depressive psychosis diagnosed according to strict criteria (later to become the Feighner criteria), they obtained detailed descriptions of 36 manic episodes. Grandiose delusions (religious, political or of wealth) were present in 64 per cent. Other delusions, with sexual and other themes, were present in 26 per cent, and what were described as delusions of control in 22 per cent (it is not clear how many of these represented true passivity experiences). Usually, these other delusions also had a grandiose flavour. However, 19 per cent showed persecutory delusions and 28 per cent delusions of reference and misinterpretation, and these were typically not grandiose in quality. In all cases the delusions tended to be evanescent, often appearing and disappearing during the course of a single day. At times the patients could be talked out of their delusions, and in some cases they gave the impression of holding the ideas playfully rather than being truly deluded.

Auditory hallucinations were present in 21 per cent and visual hallucinations in 9 per cent. Once again these tended to be closely related to the elated mood, taking the form of hearing choirs of angels, hearing God's voice, seeing heaven in all its glory, and so on. Visual hallucinations, in particular, tended to be fragmented and fleeting.

The last word on schizophrenic symptoms in manic-depressive psychosis was provided by Pope and Lipinski (1978). In a review article which became highly influential in America, they subjected Kraepelin's, Lewis', Winokur *et al.*'s and a number of other studies of the phenomenology of manic-depressive psychosis to a searching examination. As shown in Table 13.1, it was clear that, even after exclusion of all cases where the clinical features, outcome, family history or response to treatment was equivocal, delusions and hallucinations were recorded in 20–50 per cent of patients. Certainly, some of the delusions reported could be seen as mood-congruent, but several studies gave detailed examples of beliefs that were difficult to understand as

Table 13.1 Studies of schizophrenic symptoms in manic-depressive psychosis

Study	Sample	Findings
Lange (1922)	700 cases of manic-depressive psychosis	Formal thought disorder in 7.5%, hallucinations in 6.6%, other symptoms including catalepsy, stereotypy, passivity, extreme regression in 27%
Bowman and Raymond (1931)	1009 cases of manic-depressive psychosis	Delusions of persecution in 20%
Lewis (1934)	61 cases of melancholia	'Schizophrenic' symptoms in 20%
Rennie (1942)	208 cases of manic-depressive psychosis. Excluded 99 cases because 'wished to include only clear-cut manic-depressive reactions'	24% of 66 manics had persecutory or passivity delusions; 22% had hallucinations. Depth of psychosis unrelated to status follow-up
Astrup et al. (1959)	96 cases of manic-depressive psychosis with 7–19 years of follow-up	Auditory hallucinations in 24%, delusions of passivity in 9%, of persecution in 13%, ideas of reference in 5%. None of these symptoms significantly differentiated patients who recovered completely from those with a chronic course
Clayton et al. (1965)	31 manics diagnosed by structured interview; prior good social functioning required; most had past history and family history of manic-depressive psychosis	Delusions recorded in 73%, ideas of reference in 77%, passivity in 47%. Two-year follow-up in the 7 cases with unequivocal passivity and other 'schizophrenic' symptoms revealed no differences from remaining 24 'typical' manics
Winokur et al. (1969)	100 manic episodes, 14 mixed episodes and 33 depressive episodes in 61 rigorously diagnosed cases of manic-depressive psychosis	Passivity in 22%, delusions of persecution in 19%, and auditory hallucinations in 21% of manic episodes; also auditory hallucinations in 6% of depressive episodes and 14% of mixed episodes
Beigel and Murphy (1971)	12 patients with 'unequivocal diagnosis of manic-depressive illness' on two research wards	'Paranoid-destructive' subtype of mania in 33% of cases, all with paranoid delusions

Continued overleaf

Table 13.1 Continued

Study	Sample	Findings
Mendlewicz *et al.* (1972)	60 bipolar patients at lithium clinic; 30 with family history, 30 without this	'Psychotic symptoms' in 70% of patients, appearing in mania or depression, and equally in patients with and without a family history
Carlson and Goodwin (1973)	20 bipolar patients on two research wards, screened on admission to exclude equivocal cases	'Schizophrenic' symptoms in 70% of cases
Ianzito *et al.* (1974)	47 unipolar depressed patients with diagnosis confirmed by 1½ to 2-year follow-up and by prior exclusion of cases contaminated by a second diagnosis	Formal thought disorder in 19% of cases; thought broadcasting, thought control, hallucinations or systematised delusions in 45% of cases
Murphy and Beigel (1974)	30 highly screened manic-depressive patients on two research wards	Expanded on 1971 paper to demonstrate again 'paranoid-destructive' subtype of mania in 23% of cases
Guze *et al.* (1975)	139 unipolar and 19 bipolar patients diagnosed by research criteria	'Psychotic symptoms' (delusions, hallucinations, ideas of reference) in 53% of bipolars and 31% of unipolars. None of 37 demographic, family history, premorbid function, or parental home variables distinguished patients with psychotic symptoms from those without

Source: Pope and Lipinski (1978), Diagnosis in schizophrenia and manic-depressive illness: A re-assessment of the specificity of 'schizophrenic' symptoms in the light of current research. *Archives of General Psychiatry*, 35, 811–828. Copyright © 1978, American Medical Association.

related to the prevailing mood. This also applied to auditory and visual hallucinations which, without obvious mood-congruence, were reported in at least three studies. The largest and most rigorous studies suggested that more characteristically schizophrenic delusions and hallucinations were relatively uncommon, occurring in around a fifth to a quarter of cases. The frequency of formal thought disorder and catatonic phenomena was not clear from these studies, but the impression is that they were also uncommon. Some of the studies suggested that schizophrenic symptoms formed a relatively inconspicuous part of the overall clinical picture, and others found that they tended to be transient.

Pope and Lipinski also considered the question of whether first rank symptoms could be seen in otherwise typical mania and depression, based on some of the studies described in Chapter 4. Like other authors, they concluded that they were.

This work leaves no room for doubt that delusions and hallucinations which go considerably beyond what is understandable as mood-congruent are seen in both phases of manic-depressive psychosis. At the same time there is reason to suppose that such symptoms tend be relatively uncommon, transitory or in the background. In short, something approximating to the same overall conclusion reached for affective symptoms in schizophrenia seems to be justified: while individual schizophrenic symptoms occur in manic-depressive psychosis, a florid syndrome with multiple symptoms that are to the forefront of the clinical picture for long periods is not usually seen.

Armed with the information that typical schizophrenia is not associated with a full affective syndrome, and that it is unusual for there to be a full – or rather florid and sustained – schizophrenic syndrome in patients with manic-depressive psychosis, the minimal requirements for schizoaffective states can be defined, as presentations where there is a roughly equal admixture of the two sets of symptoms.

Cycloid psychosis (acute polymorphic psychotic disorder)

The curious tradition which culminated in the contemporary concept of cycloid psychosis goes back a long way (see Leonhard, 1961; Fish, 1964; Brockington *et al.*, 1982a; Perris, 1974, 1986). Its clearest point of origin was the classification of psychosis developed by Wernicke. He rejected the Kraepelinian dichotomy, and, drawing on an earlier French tradition of degeneration psychoses – disorders that ran in families and were prone to evolve through a succession of forms – proposed a more finely differentiated scheme. Wernicke died in 1905, but his ideas were kept alive in the work of Kleist, who postulated the existence of more than 10 discrete psychotic disorders which were neither schizophrenic nor manic-depressive, and which he considered to be the manifestations of different focal brain dysfunctions. Some of these were grouped together as 'cycloid marginal psychoses'.

Kleist's follower Leonhard was sceptical about the neuropathological basis of cycloid psychoses, but considered the clinical distinction to be valid in itself. Over time, he elaborated Kleist's classification into three bipolar psychoses. The core of each of these was an alternation between two opposing sets of symptoms. The *anxiety – elation* psychosis had poles in an all-pervasive anxiousness (angst) and ecstatic happiness. The manifestations of the *motility* psychosis were hypo- and hyperkinesia. The *confusion* psychosis had its extremes in inhibition and acceleration of thought. In addition to these features, it was clearly evident from Leonhard's description that manic-depressive type mood disturbance, delusions and hallucinations, and something resembling catatonic phenomena could be present in the background. Cycloid psychoses also had other distinctive features, including sudden onset, a tendency for there to be fluctuations and oscillations between the two poles within a single episode, and a full recovery between episodes.

Perris took the bold step of synthesising Leonhard's three forms of cycloid psychosis into a single disorder. He felt justified in doing this on two grounds. In the first place, he noted that Leonhard accepted that each of the three forms was not sharply delimited from the other two: in any one form minor symptoms of one or both of the other two were sometimes seen, and occasionally there was a combination of the symptomatology of all three. Second, he argued that states showing just such a combined clinical picture had been described again and again under different names for nearly a century. These are shown in Table 13.2. Noteworthy inclusions are the French *bouffée délirante*; Kasanin's schizoaffective psychosis (although this was the first use of the term schizoaffective, it was clearly a cycloid-like state that was described); oneirophrenia, a dream-like psychotic state described by von Meduna the discoverer of convulsive therapy; and not least, that culture-bound American syndrome of homosexual panic – in its original description by Kempf this described a sudden-onset state of feverish agitation or rage sometimes amounting to temporary insanity (see Chuang and Addington, 1988). Although Perris did not include them, it is evident that Kraepelin's delirious mania and delirious melancholia could also be included in the list.

The salient feature of Perris' reconceptualisation of cycloid psychosis was a clinical presentation marked, above all, by its polymorphousness and kaleidoscopic shifts from one set of symptoms to another. Delusions, hallucinations, first rank symptoms, pan-anxiety, happiness or ecstasy, motility disturbances, catatonia-like symptoms and confusion were all jumbled together and phased in and out of the picture without any discernible pattern. The picture could shift between affective-like, schizophrenia-like and delirium-like symptoms from day to day, or even hour to hour, with no theme being persistent or dominant. The intensity of symptoms could also fluctuate wildly. In Perris' own series of patients confusion was the most common symptom; this varied from perplexity, through dream-like states, to disorientation that could at times be gross. Anxiety was typically bound up with ideas about death or catastrophe, and was prone to be accompanied by depersonalisation and derealisation. The ecstasy seen in cycloid psychosis was generally

Table 13.2 Some of the different names proposed for psychotic syndromes quite similar to cycloid psychosis

America and Canada	
Bell's mania	(Bell)
Homosexual panic	(Kempf)
Schizoaffective psychosis	(Kasanin)
Benign stupor	(Hoch)
Oneirophrenia	(Meduna)
Scandinavia	
Schizophreniform psychosis	(Langfeldt)
Psychogenic psychosis	(Faergeman, Stromgren)
France	
Degeneration psychoses	(Magnan)
Schizomania	(Claude)
Bouffée délirante	(Magnan, Ey)
Japan	
Atypical psychosis	(Mitsuda, Asano, Kaij)
Germany	
Expansive psychosis with autochthonous ideas	(Wernicke)
Motility psychosis	(Wernicke)
Mixed psychoses	(Gaupp)
Metabolic psychosis	(Schroeder)
Phasophrenia	(Kleist)
Acute exhaustive psychosis	(Adland)
Russia	
Periodic (recurrent) schizophrenia	(Schnevnesky)

Source: Perris (1974), A study of cycloid psychosis. *Acta Psychiatrica Scandinavica*, Supplement 253, 1–76. © 1974 Munksgaard International Publishers Ltd, Copenhagen, Denmark. Reproduced with permission.

distinguishable from the elation of mania, in that it tended to occur in a setting of unassertive calmness and tranquillity, often with religious or mystical overtones. Depressive moods occurred, but generally were not severe and did not last any length of time. Motor disorder consisted mainly of overactivity or retardation; the former was considered to have a characteristic fluid and 'pseudoexpressive' quality that distinguished it from catatonia as seen in schizophrenia.

Perris' cycloid psychosis had other distinguishing features. The onset of the disorder was typically abrupt: there could a rapid change from a state of complete health to full-blown psychosis within hours or a few days. A small minority of cases had a less acute onset and in some there was a prodromal period of non-specific symptoms like irritability or poor sleep. The duration of the episode could also sometimes be short. Perris knew of cases that remitted after a few days; however, the average length was two to four months. There was a strong tendency for the illness to recur, but even after many attacks schizophrenia-like deterioration did not supervene – some of his patients had experienced more than 30 episodes with complete recovery every time. Between episodes, most patients showed no abnormalities, but in some, minor residual symptoms could be detected, such as anxiety, depression, emotional lability or increased vulnerability to stress.

The existence of cycloid psychosis has not been universally accepted. For example, it is recognized in ICD 10 where it is referred to as acute polymorphic psychotic disorder, but there is no corresponding category in DSM IV. Since it is a purely clinical concept, its validity would seem to depend on establishing whether: (a) patients exist in whom there is a clinical picture dominated by unstable, pleomorphic symptoms; (b) they follow a short-term course characterised by full recovery but a risk of further similar episodes; and (c) despite showing symptoms that go considerably beyond what could be considered manic-depressive, they have an outcome which is better than that seen in schizophrenia. Each of these questions has been addressed in different studies.

Cutting *et al.* (1978) carried out the first study that examined the cross-sectional bona fides of cycloid psychosis. They searched the case-notes of all first admissions to a psychiatric hospital over 10 years for patients fitting Perris' description of cycloid psychosis. For this they used a set of criteria for the disorder developed by Perris and Brockington (Brockington *et al.*, 1982a), which are shown in Box 13.3. They were able to find 73 patients (around 8 per cent of psychotic admissions) who fulfilled the criteria. Twenty-nine of these had been given a case-note diagnosis of schizoaffective or atypical psychosis, and the rest had been diagnosed as either schizophrenic or affectively ill. In these latter cases, however, hints of clinical uncertainty were often betrayed in the use of terms like 'schizophrenia with depressive features', or 'mixed affective state'. While acute onset was common in these patients – 44 per cent appeared to have had symptoms for less than a month

---

Box 13.3 Perris' criteria for cycloid psychosis (from Brockington et al., 1982a)

The patient must have affective symptoms (mood swings) and two of the following five symptoms:

(i)   confusion (ranging from slight perplexity to gross disorientation) together with agitation or retardation;
(ii)   delusions of reference, influence or persecution and/or mood-incongruent delusions;
(iii) motility disturbances of the type described by Leonhard;
(iv)   ecstasy as described by Leonhard and others;
(v)   pan-anxiety, i.e. anxiety associated with ideas of self-reference and persecution.

prior to admission – this was not an invariable finding. Ninety per cent were described as either having made a full recovery or having a good outcome – the latter being free of psychotic symptoms but showing some lowering of mood.

Three further studies using prospective designs rather than review of case-notes have also supported the existence of cases with a cycloid cross-sectional presentation. Van der Heijden *et al.* (2004) found that 18 per cent of consecutively admitted non-organic psychotic patients met the Perris/Brockington criteria for cycloid psychosis. Peralta and Cuesta (2003) found a rate of 10.3 per cent in a series of 660 patients who showed at least one psychotic symptom or severe negative symptoms. Marneros and Pillman (2004) found a lower rate: only 2.7 per cent of 1036 psychotic admissions over five years met ICD 10 criteria for acute polymorphic psychotic disorder. However, they only included patients with a duration of up to a month.

Information on the course of patients identified as cycloid was obtained by Maj (1988). He prospectively followed up 18 patients meeting Perris/ Brockington criteria three years after initial diagnosis, and compared their course with that of 22 patients meeting research diagnostic criteria (RDC) for depression and 21 meeting RDC criteria for mania. The cycloid group showed between zero and five further episodes during the 3-year follow-up, slightly, but not significantly higher than the manics and depressives. In 50 per cent of patients, criteria for cycloid psychosis were met in further episodes, with the remainder meeting criteria for major depression or schizoaffective (depressed) disorder. In contrast none of the manic or depressed patients experienced subsequent episodes diagnosable as cycloid (or schizoaffective for that matter). Interestingly, Maj also included in his follow-up a group of 41 patients meeting the RDC for schizoaffective disorder. Fifteen of these were found to have episodes meeting criteria for cycloid psychosis.

The long-term outcome of cycloid psychosis was examined by Brockington *et al.* (1982b). This study utilised a series of 242 psychotic patients including those with schizophrenic, affective and schizoaffective diagnoses. Very detailed history and mental state information was available on these patients, and they had all been subjected to a follow-up examination several years later. Out of these patients, Perris personally selected 30 cases he considered met his criteria for cycloid psychosis, and compared their course and various measures of outcome with the remainder of the group. The cycloid patients had as many subsequent admissions as the rest of the group, but their status at follow-up was significantly better – 27/30 (90 per cent) were considered to be completely well at the time of follow-up, compared to 137/203 (67 per cent) with a non-cycloid diagnosis. When the comparison group was broken down into those with schizophrenia and those with manic-depressive psychosis, the cycloid patients' outcome was much better than for the former, and comparable to those with the latter diagnosis.

Marneros and Pillman (2004) also found a significantly better 5-year outcome in 25 patients with acute polymorphic psychotic disorder compared to that of 34 patients with schizophrenia. However, it is noteworthy in this study that 5 of the 25 patients showed what the authors called persisting alterations or residual syndromes. These included apathy, affective flattening, reduced concentration, increased distractibility, lack of awareness of disturbances, personality change, persisting delusions and/or hallucinations, or chronic depressive or hyperthymic symptoms.

Cycloid psychosis thus appears to stand up to quite close clinical scrutiny. A small minority of acutely psychotic patients do present with the requisite polymorphous clinical picture and go on to show full or nearly full recovery after attacks. The polymorphousness also extends to the course the disorder follows – patients may have further episodes of cycloid psychosis, or uncomplicated mania and depression, or schizoaffective presentations without fluctuations and emotional turmoil; only schizophrenic episodes seem to be proscribed. The concept does, however, show signs of strain with respect to its alleged acute or hyperacute onset, which was found in less than half of the cases in Cutting *et al.*'s study. There is also the suspicion that the alleged lack of progression to a state of schizophrenia-like deterioration is relative rather than absolute. Marneros and Pillman's study makes it clear that a small number of cycloid patients are or eventually become symptomatic between episodes, and that sometimes these symptoms are schizophrenic in nature.

Aetiological factors in cycloid psychosis

The information here is meagre and most of the investigation has been devoted to the time-honoured question of family history. There is an additional unique aetiological tradition in cycloid psychosis, in the form of claims for a relationship with epilepsy, which shows itself in a high prevalence of epileptiform EEG abormalities in the disorder.

With respect to family history, Perris (1974) found that 7.2 per cent of the first-degree relatives of his 60 patients with cycloid psychosis also suffered from cycloid psychosis, 0.6 per cent from schizophrenia, and 3.4 per cent from affective disorders. He concluded that cycloid psychosis 'bred true', and represented a third psychosis genetically independent from schizophrenia and manic-depressive psychosis.

The only study to date to employ diagnostic criteria for cycloid psychosis had somewhat different findings. Peralta and Cuesta (2003) found a morbid risk for schizophrenia of 1.2 per cent in the first-degree relatives of 68 patients meeting Perris/Brockington criteria, and a morbidity risk of 5.2 per cent of mood disorder. The risk of schizophrenia was significantly lower than that of 5.4 per cent in the first-degree relatives of 69 patients with schizophrenia. In contrast, the risk of mood disorder was not significantly different from that found in the first-degree relatives of 69 patients with mood disorders. This study did not investigate whether any of the relatives showed cycloid psychosis.

Perris included in his list of disorders quite similar to cycloid psychosis the Japanese concept of atypical psychosis. In this country psychotic states showing unusual clinical features such as visual and olfactory hallucinations and running a fluctuating and episodic course are widely believed to have a basis in an epilepsy-like disturbance of brain function. (In fact, it was this, along with the observation that carbamazepine often had positive effects on mood in epileptic patients (see Dalby, 1975), that led to the introduction of carbamazepine and subsequently other anticonvulsants in psychiatry.) Mitsuda and co-workers (see Mitsuda, 1967) compared the EEGs of patients with such presentations with those of patients with typical schizophrenia and manic-depressive psychosis and found that all types of EEG abnormality were over-represented in the atypical patients. When the EEG was activated with an analeptic agent such as bemegride, the disturbance in the atypical patients tended to become enhanced – often to the point of appearance of clear-cut spike discharges. Monroe (1982) and Tucker *et al.* (1986) reported roughly comparable findings in America.

In Perris' own study, 19 of his 60 patients with cycloid psychosis showed runs or paroxysms of slow (theta) activity on EEG. In contrast, Marneros and Pillman (2004) rated under blind conditions the EEGs of 39 patients meeting ICD 10 criteria for acute and transient psychosis, 28 of whom also met criteria for acute polymorphic psychosis. None of the patients were found to show epileptiform discharges, and borderline evidence of cerebral hyperexcitability was only present in three (7.7 per cent). These rates were not significantly different from those found in 40 patients with schizophrenia and 40 with schizaffective disorder. Intermittent slowing was somewhat more common but still failed to distinguish the acute and transient patients from the remaining groups.

Treatment of cycloid psychosis

No treatment studies, controlled or otherwise, have been carried out in cycloid psychosis. In these circumstances, it is not possible to do more than reiterate Perris' (1974, 1986; Brockington *et al.*, 1982a) views. His treatment of choice was neuroleptics, and he found that this brought about complete remission within a few weeks in most cases. He tended to combine these drugs with lithium, but was uncertain whether or not this made a significant contribution to shortening of the episode. He also considered that ECT was useful, consistently producing a dramatic improvement after only a few applications. Relapse, however, was frequent and treatment needed to be continued for a minimum of 6–8 applications.

Perris had the impression that long-term treatment with lithium reduced the rate of relapses by about half. Usually it was effective alone, but exceptionally combined therapy with neuroleptics needed be undertaken. Neuroleptic treatment alone, however, was not found to be effective as a prophylactic treatment.

Schizoaffective psychosis proper

The term 'schizoaffective' was coined by the American psychiatrist Kasanin in 1933, although, as noted above, the state he was describing was one of cycloid psychosis. His term persisted in American psychiatry, where it transformed into the modern concept of a disorder marked simply by combined schizophrenic and affective symptoms without the sudden fluctuations, confusion, hyper- and hypokinetic motor phenomena of cycloid psychosis. Pichot (1986) charted its course through successive editions of the *Diagnostic and Statistical Manual*, culminating in DSM III.

The first edition of the manual in 1952 included a schizoaffective type of schizophrenia. This specified cases showing admixtures of schizophrenic and affective symptomatology. The mental content could be predominantly schizophrenic, with pronounced depression or elation, or alternatively predominantly affective, but with pronounced schizophrenic-like thinking or bizarre behaviour. It was noted that the premorbid personality might be at variance with expectations, and also that on prolonged observation such cases usually proved to be basically schizophrenic in nature.

By the second edition, DSM II, published in 1968, the definition had become considerably more terse. Schizophrenia, schizoaffective type was described as referring to 'patients showing a mixture of schizophrenic symptoms and pronounced elation or depression'. Although by this time it was widely appreciated that American psychiatry was adopting a wayward concept of schizophrenia (see Chapter 4), a schizoaffective subtype of schizophrenia was nevertheless incorporated into the eighth and ninth editions of the *International Classification of Diseases* (ICD). According to Pichot, this was probably because there were a number of American psychiatrists on the relevant expert committees of the World Health Organization.

In 1978 Spitzer and his co-workers noted in a draft version of DSM III that the term schizoaffective had been used in many different ways, and it was uncertain whether the disorder represented a variant of affective disorder or schizophrenia, or was a third independent nosological entity, or formed part of a continuum between pure forms of the two functional psychoses. Accordingly, a special category was created for schizoaffective disorders, which were defined as states in which a depressive or manic syndrome preceded or developed concurrently with certain psychotic symptoms thought to be incompatible with a purely affective diagnosis. Two years later, in the final published version of DSM III, the category had practically disappeared (it lingered on, but as the only major disorder without any diagnostic criteria). History does not record why the members of the task force made this decision, but it is possible that the review of Pope and Lipinski (1978) described earlier in this chapter, which argued that the presence of schizophrenic symptoms in otherwise affective presentations was of little significance for diagnosis, prognosis and response to treatment, influenced their decision.

Criteria have been reinstated in DSM-III-R and DSM IV, but only in a cursory way. There are no criteria in the usual meaning of the term in ICD 10.

Fortunately, Spitzer and co-workers' original operational criteria for schizoaffective disorder entered the public domain in the Research Diagnostic Criteria (Spitzer *et al.*, 1978). These criteria are shown in Box 13.4. These criteria are sophisticated. The presence of both full affective and schizophrenic symptoms over and above what can be reasonably regarded as

---

Box 13.4 Research Diagnostic Criteria for schizoaffective disorder (from Spitzer *et al.* (1978), *Research diagnostic criteria for a selected group of functional disorders*. Biometric Research, New York State Psychiatric Institute. Reproduced with permission)

(a) Criteria for schizoaffective mania
(A through E are required)

A. One or more distinct periods with a predominantly elevated, expansive, or irritable mood. The elevated, expansive, or irritable mood must be relatively persistent and prominent during some part of the illness or occur frequently. It may alternate with depressive mood. If the disturbance in mood occurs only during periods of alcohol or drug intake or withdrawal from them, it should not be considered here.

B. If mood is elevated or expansive, at least three of the following symptoms must be definitely present to a significant degree, four if mood is only irritable.

1. More active than usual – either socially, at work, at home, sexually or physically restless.
2. More talkative than usual or feeling a pressure to keep on talking.
3. Flight of ideas or subjective experience that thoughts are racing.
4. Inflated self-esteem (grandiosity, which may be delusional).
5. Decreased need for sleep.
6. Distractibility, i.e. attention is too easily drawn to unimportant or irrelevant external stimuli.
7. Excessive involvement in activities without recognising the high potential for painful consequences, e.g. buying sprees, sexual indiscretions, foolish business investments, reckless driving.

C. At least one of the following symptoms suggestive of schizophrenia is present during the active phase of the illness.

1. Delusions of being controlled (or influenced) or of thought broadcasting, insertion or withdrawal (as defined in this manual).
2. Non-affective hallucinations of any type throughout the day for several days or intermittently throughout a 1-week period.
3. Auditory hallucinations in which either a voice keeps up a running commentary on the subject's behaviours or thoughts as they occur, or two or more voices converse with each other.

4. At some time during the period of illness had more than 1 week when he exhibited no prominent depressive or manic symptoms but had delusions or hallucinations.

5. At some time during the period of illness had more than 1 week when he exhibited no prominent manic symptoms but had several instances of marked formal thought disorder, accompanied by either blunted or inappropriate affect, delusions or hallucinations of any type, or grossly disorganised behaviour.

D. Signs of the illness have lasted at least 1 week from the onset of a noticeable change in the patient's usual condition (current signs of the illness may not now meet criteria A, B or C and may be residual affective or residual schizophrenic symptoms only, such as mood disturbance, blunted or inappropriate affect, extreme social withdrawal, mild formal thought disorder, or unusual thoughts or perceptual experiences).

E. Affective syndrome overlaps temporally to some degree with an active period of schizophrenic-like symptoms (delusions, hallucinations, marked formal thought disorder, bizarre behaviour, etc.).

(b) Criteria for schizoaffective depression
(A through E are required)

A. One or more distinctive periods with dysphoric mood or pervasive loss of interest or pleasure. The disturbance is characterised by symptoms such as the following: depressed, sad, blue, hopeless, low, down in the dumps, 'don't care anymore', or irritable. The disturbance must be a major part of the clinical picture during some part of the illness and relatively persistent or occur frequently. It may not necessarily be the most dominant symptom. It does not include momentary shifts from one dysphoric mood to another dysphoric mood, e.g. anxiety to depression to anger, such as are seen in states of acute psychotic turmoil. If the symptoms in C occur only during periods of alcohol or drug use or withdrawal from them, the diagnosis should be unspecified functional psychosis.

B. At least five of the following symptoms are required for definite and four for probable.

1. Poor appetite or weight loss or increased appetite or weight gain (change of 1 lb per week over several weeks or 10 lb per year when not dieting).

2. Sleep difficulty or sleeping too much.

3. Loss of energy, fatiguability, or tiredness.

4. Psychomotor retardation or agitation (but not mere subjective feeling of restlessness or being slowed down).

5. Loss of interest or pleasure in usual activities, including social contact or sex (do not include if limited to a period when delusional or hallucinating). (The loss may or may not be pervasive.)

6. Feelings of self-reproach or excessive inappropriate guilt (either may be delusional).

7. Complaints or evidence of diminished ability to think or concentrate, such as slowed thinking, or indecisiveness (do not include if associated with obvious formal thought disorder, or preoccupation with delusions or hallucinations).

8. Recurrent thoughts of death or suicide, or any suicidal behaviour.

C. At least one of the following is present:

1. Delusions of being controlled (or influenced) or of thought broadcasting, insertion, or withdrawal.

2. Non-affective hallucinations of any type throughout the day for several days or intermittently throughout a 1-week period.

3. Auditory hallucinations in which either a voice keeps up a running commentary on the subject's behaviours or thoughts as they occur, or two or more voices converse with each other.

4. At some time during the period of illness had more than 1 month when he exhibited no prominent depressive or manic symptoms but had delusions or hallucinations (although not typical depressive delusions such as delusions of guilt, sin, poverty, nihilism, or self-deprecation, or hallucinations of similar content).

5. Define instances of marked formal thought disorder accompanied by either blunted or inappropriate affect, delusions or hallucinations of any type, or grossly disorganised behaviour.

D. Signs of the illness have lasted at least 1 week from the onset of a noticeable change in the patient's usual condition (current signs of the illness may not now meet criteria A, B or C and may be residual affective or residual schizophrenic symptoms only, such as mood disturbance, blunted or inappropriate affect, extreme social withdrawal, mild formal thought disorder, or unusual thoughts or perceptual experiences).

E. Affective syndrome overlaps temporally to some degree with the active period of schizophrenic-like symptoms (delusions, hallucinations, thought disorder, bizarre behaviour).

---

mood-congruent symptoms are required, or that schizophrenic symptoms are present for some time during the episode without any evidence of mood disturbance. There must be some temporal overlap between the two sets of symptoms. Loss of interest or pleasure in usual activities is excluded if it is limited to periods when the patient is deluded or hallucinated.

Between the bald statement that schizoaffective psychosis is characterised by combinations of schizophrenic and affective symptoms, and the operational criteria of Spitzer *et al.* (1978), there has been very little actual description of the clinical features of the disorder. One of the very few authors to undertake this task has been Guze (1980) whose description, with a few minor additions, went as follows.

Schizoaffective psychoses typically begin abruptly. The affective and schizophrenic symptoms may appear more or less simultaneously or after an affective syndrome has been evident for some days or weeks. Although this acute onset is the rule, other presentations are possible; for example patients can be encountered where the initial presentation is one of delusions without any obvious mood disturbance who then, sometimes after a quite lengthy period, flare up into a predominantly depressed or manic state.

All patients present with a mixture of affective features amounting to a more or less fully formed affective syndrome, together with clearly evident delusions and/or hallucinations which are either characteristic of schizophrenia (e.g. first rank symptoms), or are unusual for affective disorder in that they bear no apparent relation to the abnormal mood. The overall presentation tends to be dramatic, with considerable social and behavioural disturbance. The affective and schizophrenic symptoms may parallel each other in intensity, or fluctuate independently, or one may wax and wane while the other holds steady. A common sequence is for both sets of symptoms to begin more or less coincidentally, then the schizophrenic symptoms subside, leaving the patient with a typical depression or mania. Individual catatonic symptoms may be present and there may be brief episodes of catatonic stupor or excitement. Suicidal thinking and attempts (which may be serious) are also common.

The duration of an episode may be short, but more usually it lasts weeks to months. The course the illness follows tends to be episodic. Some patients experience subsequent schizoaffective episodes, sometimes separated by months or years of full remission. In others the picture of mixed schizophrenic and affective symptoms is followed, after several attacks, by simple manic or depressive episodes. In yet others, periods of acute illness are eventually supplanted by a state that is indistinguishable from chronic schizophrenia, against the background of which mood disturbance may re-emerge from time to time. The outcome is variable but on average is better than for schizophrenia.

It is widely believed that the term schizoaffective encompasses a range of presentations that quite possibly reflect more than one kind of disorder. At one 'mainly affective' end of the spectrum are pictures that can be considered as schizoaffective only in a technical sense. Such cases show an unexceptional manic or depressive picture, but in addition one or two first rank symptoms are elicited on questioning. At the other 'mainly schizophrenic' extreme are patients who, in the course of a hitherto typical schizophrenic illness with deterioration, start to show a degree of depression or mood elevation (or alternations between the two) that seems to go considerably beyond what is acceptable as mood colouring. A final variety of schizoaffective psychosis is where patients present with purely schizophrenic and purely affective syndromes in different episodes. Cases have been described where an initial schizophrenic illness subsequently becomes manic-depressive (Sheldrick *et al.*, 1977). According to Fish (Fish, 1962/Hamilton, 1984), depression with typical associated features including mood-congruent delusions and hallucinations is also not uncommon as the initial presentation of an illness which subsequently becomes schizophrenic.

To many British psychiatrists, the diagnosis of schizoaffective psychosis is to be frowned on, a faintly distasteful label that should only be applied provisionally until the true nature of a psychosis declares itself with the passage of time. In America, on the other hand, it is a routinely made clinical diagnosis. Clearly, the validity of the concept needs to be established and it is equally clear this can only be done clinically, in the same ways as for cycloid psychosis. Specifically, it needs to be demonstrated (a) that patients exist in whom there is a genuine combination of schizophrenic and affective symptoms, avoiding the pitfalls of schizophrenic mood colourings, reactive depression, mood-congruent psychotic symptoms, and so on; (b) that such patients follow a distinctive course, in the sense of having further schizoaffective episodes; and (c) that they have an outcome which is different from that of either schizophrenia or manic-depressive psychosis. This last requirement is the most challenging since, in order to be distinguishable from both disorders, schizoaffective psychosis is constrained to show an outcome intermediate between the wide limits of both of them. It hardly has to be added that a strict and sophisticated set of diagnostic criteria for schizoaffective psychosis needs to be employed, and the gold standard here is the RDC.

The definitive cross-sectional examination of schizoaffective psychosis was carried out by Brockington *et al.* (1980a, b). They screened the case-notes of nearly 4000 admissions to four psychiatric hospitals for patients who showed any apparent combination of schizophrenic and affective features. Any such patients were then interviewed and a preliminary, deliberately broad definition of schizoaffective psychosis was applied. This required signs of mania or depression that approximated to a full affective syndrome, plus one or more schizophrenic symptoms from a checklist that included persecutory delusions, first rank symptoms, catatonic phenomena, affective flattening or incongruity, and formal thought disorder. Around six hundred patients were interviewed and 76 'schizodepressive' and 32 'schizomanic' patients were identified in this way (approximately 10 per cent and 4 per cent of all psychotic admissions respectively). These patients were then subjected to a more intensive mental state examination using the Present State Examination. Sixty of the 76 schizodepressive patients met RDC for schizoaffective disorder, depressed type. Among the 32 broadly defined schizomanic patients, however, only 8 met these criteria.

Kendell (1986) re-assessed 106 of Brockington *et al.*'s 108 broadly defined 'schizomanic' and 'schizodepressed' patients 1–4 years after their index admission. The patients were interviewed where possible, and information was collected from other sources about episodes of illness before and after the index admission. All episodes were then diagnosed blindly over an average of four years for the 31 schizomanics, and six years for the 75 schizodepressives. The results are shown in Table 13.3, and indicate that both sets of patients experienced schizophrenic, affective and schizoaffective episodes. The commonest presentation in the schizomanic group consisted of simple depressive episodes or further episodes of schizomania. One patient had a subsequent episode with only schizophrenic symptoms. Among the schizodepressive patients, there were three main patterns: further schizodepressive episodes, further episodes with schizophrenic symptoms alone, and further episodes with depressive symptoms alone. Manic or schizomanic episodes were uncommon in this group of patients. A minority of patients in both groups had complex sequences featuring two or more different types of presentation. One patient, for example, had four manic episodes, three depressive episodes, three schizodepressive episodes and one episode with schizophrenic symptoms alone.

The patients in this study met a broad definition of schizoaffective psychosis. However, Maj (1988) found closely similar results in a smaller study of 23 schizomanic and 24 schizodepressive patients which employed RDC criteria.

There have been any number of long-term outcome studies of patients diagnosed as schizoaffective. These have variously found the outcome to be intermediate between that of schizophrenia and manic-depressive psychosis (Tsuang and Dempsey, 1979; Jager *et al.*, 2004), similar to schizophrenia (Welner *et al.*, 1977; Himmelhoch *et al.*, 1981; Tsuang and Coryell, 1993), similar to manic-depressive psychosis (Pope *et al.*, 1980; Marneros *et al.*, 1990); or to be heterogeneous (Brockington *et al.*, 1980a, b; Berg *et al.*, 1983). However, these studies either diagnosed schizoaffective disorder clinically, or used DSM or ICD 10 criteria which, as mentioned above, are barely more rigorous. Only three studies have employed RDC criteria (Coryell *et al.*, 1984; Grossman *et al.*, 1984; Maj, 1985), and of these the 1-year follow-up study of Grossman and co-workers stands out as the largest, and the only one to

Table 13.3 Other episodes in schizoaffective patients

Schizodepressive (N = 75)	No.	Schizomanic (N = 31)	No.
Schizodepressive	13	Schizomanic	6
Schizophrenic	15	Schizodepressive	2
Depressive	14	Depressive	7
Schizomanic	1	Schizophrenic	1
Manic	1	Chronic schizophrenia previously	4
Complex sequences	11	Complex sequences	2
No other episode	20	No other episode	9

Source: Kendell (1986), The relationship of schizoaffective illness to schizophrenic and affective disorders, Tables 1 and 3. In A. Marneros and M.T. Tsuang (Eds.), *Schizoaffective psychoses*, pp. 18–30. Springer. © 1986 Springer Verlag. With kind permission of Springer Science and Business Media.

compare schizoaffective patients with both schizophrenic and affective patients. This study also has the advantage that the follow-up period was subsequently extended to 10 years (Harrow *et al.*, 2000).

Grossman *et al.* identified 39 acute admissions meeting RDC for schizoaffective disorder, plus 47 meeting the same criteria for schizophrenia, and 81 meeting criteria for affective disorder (33 with mania and 48 with major depression). All the patients were followed up by means of personal interview a year later. No attempt was made to control the treatment received during the follow-up period. A battery of clinical and social interview schedules was administered, from which a measure of overall outcome was derived. The schizoaffective patients were found not to differ significantly from the schizophrenics in terms of overall outcome, and to have a significantly less favourable outcome than the affective patients. A more detailed breakdown of the findings revealed that there were more schizophrenic patients in the poor outcome category than schizoaffective patients (51 per cent vs 31 per cent), and this difference was significant at trend level. The schizoaffective patients also had a significantly better work performance than the schizophrenics. No differences were found between schizoaffective patients classified as 'mainly affective' or 'mainly schizophrenic' at the time of initial assessment.

Harrow *et al.* (2000) continued to follow 36 of the original group of 39 schizoaffective patients, assessing them at 2, 4.5, 7.5 and 10 years using the same scales. In this phase of the study their overall functioning was compared to an enlarged group of 70 patients with schizophrenia, 44 patients with psychotic forms of affective disorder (26 with bipolar and 18 unipolar depressed), and 60 patients with unipolar, non-psychotic major depression, all diagnosed according to RDC. The results are shown in Figure 13.1. Across the whole follow-up period the schizoaffective patients were found to occupy an intermediate position between those with schizophrenia and those with affective disorder. At some points their outcome was not significantly better than schizophrenia (2 years and 4.5 years) but at others it was (7.5 years and 10 years). The schizoaffective patients showed a significantly poorer outcome than patients with unipolar major depression at all time points, but their outcome was not significantly worse than the psychotic affective group except at 4.5 year follow-up.

Rather than trying to demonstrate quantitative differences in outcome, Kendell and co-workers (Brockington *et al.*, 1979; Kendell, 1986) attempted to determine whether schizoaffective patients remained homogeneous in the long term or tended to split into those with more schizophrenia-like and affective-like pictures. They applied discriminant function analysis to symptoms and course variables at a 1–4 year follow-up of 104 patients in their group of broadly defined schizomanic and schizodepressive patients. The discriminant function was made up of eight variables that they had previously established as giving the best discrimination between schizophrenic and affective patients (see Chapter 4); this gave a convenient measure of how far each patient's symptomatology and course during the follow-up period had been

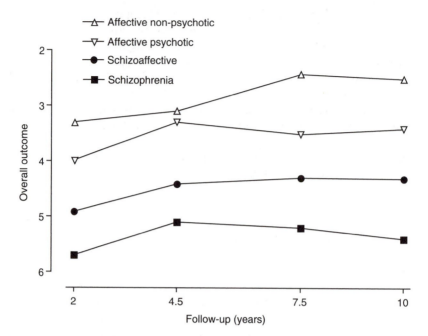

Figure 13.1 Outcome for 36 RDC schizoaffective patients over 10 years compared to patients with schizophrenia and affective disorder (lower score on outcome scale = better outcome) (from Harrow *et al.* (2000), Ten-year outcome: Patients with schizoaffective disorders, schizophrenia, affective disorders and mood-incongruent psychotic symptoms. *British Journal of Psychiatry*, 177, 421–426. Reproduced with permission from the Royal College of Psychiatrists).

schizophrenic or affective in character. When the distributions of the schizoaffective patients were plotted on this function, no suggestion of bimodality was found, either for the group as a whole or for the schizomanics and schizodepressives taken separately. The findings are shown in Figure 13.2.

These studies clearly establish the existence of schizoaffective psychosis in the cross-sectional sense. Around 15 per cent of cases of functional psychosis show both schizophrenic and affective symptoms, and something over half of these – by virtue of meeting RDC criteria – exhibit combinations which go beyond what can be attributed to the mood colourings of schizophrenia or the psychotic features of manic-depressive psychosis. Longitudinally, the issues are possibly more complicated. Schizoaffective patients have further episodes that can be schizophrenic, affective and schizoaffective in character, rather than just schizoaffective. According to the single methodologically rigorous and reasonably large study to date, the outcome does seem to be intermediate between schizophrenia and manic-depressive psychosis, as required, but statistical significance remains sadly elusive. Discriminant func-

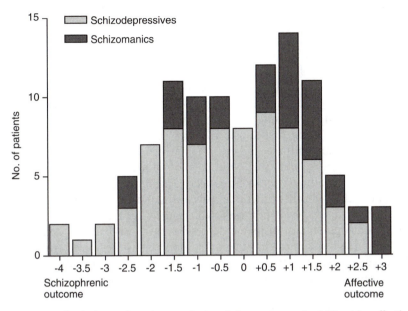

Figure 13.2 Discriminant function analysis of the outcome in 104 schizoaffective
patients (from Kendell (1986), The relationship of schizoaffective illness
to schizophrenic and affective disorders, Fig. 1. In A. Marneros and M.T.
Tsuang (Eds.), *Schizoaffective psychoses*, pp. 18–30. Springer. Copyright
© 1986 Springer-Verlag GmbH and Co., KG).

tion analysis provides an elegant way round the difficulties inherent in these
studies, but not perhaps one that can be regarded as conclusive.

Aetiological factors in schizoaffective psychosis

The only aetiological factor that has been examined in schizoaffective psychosis is its pattern of heredity. The investigation has, however, been substantial: Coryell (1986) was able to find 14 studies of the first-degree relatives of
patients with schizoaffective psychosis carried out between 1973 and 1983.
These found rates of schizophrenia ranging from zero to nearly 11 per cent;
and rates of manic-depressive psychosis that approached or sometimes
exceeded those seen in the relatives of affective patients. The five studies that
assessed for the diagnosis of schizoaffective disorder in relatives found rates
of 1.0 per cent, 2.2 per cent, 2.5 per cent, 3.8 per cent and 6.1 per cent –
frequencies that appear to be appreciable, given that this is an uncommon
form of psychosis.

Some of these studies conceptualised the schizoaffective category very
loosely indeed, including schizophreniform psychoses, manic-depressive
psychosis with mood-incongruent delusions, or atypical psychosis, not
otherwise specified. However, eight of the studies employed RDC criteria and

the findings of these are summarised in Table 13.4, together with another more recent study by Maier *et al.* (1993). These studies uniformly found high, sometimes exceptionally high, rates of affective disorder in the relatives. Three of the six studies found no schizophrenia in the relatives; one found a rate of 1.4 per cent; but the remaining three found the rates for schizophrenia to be increased two to three times over the general population rate of 1 per cent – or more given that the rate of schizophrenia is lower when diagnostic criteria are used (see Chapter 5). The original appreciable rate of schizoaffective psychosis among first-degree relatives of schizoaffective patients continued to be found in these studies.

It is easier to say what these findings do *not* mean rather than what they mean. The hypothesis that schizoaffective disorder is genetically separate from both the two other functional psychoses and 'breeds true' can be ruled out with certainty. The hypotheses that the disorder is simply a genetic variant of schizophrenia or of manic-depressive psychosis can also be excluded, but only if it is assumed that these disorders themselves breed true; that is, there is no overlap in their own genetic risks. This appears to hold true broadly, apart from an increased risk of unipolar major depression in the relatives of schizophrenic patients (e.g. see Berrettini, 2003). The only other credible hypothesis is the fifth of the six outlined by Kendell at the beginning of the chapter – that schizoaffective psychosis is the manifestation of an unknown aetiological interaction between schizophrenia and manic-depressive psychosis.

Treatment of schizoaffective psychosis

In treatment studies, the term schizoaffective loses all diagnostic precision. Treatment of schizoaffective psychosis tends to be the treatment of schizoaffective psychosis proper, cycloid psychosis, schizophreniform psychosis, atypical manic-depression and no doubt other types of psychotic illness as well.

Of a handful of controlled trials of neuroleptic versus other treatments, the largest was that of Prien *et al.* (1972). They randomly assigned 83 patients with clinically diagnosed schizoaffective disorder, excited type, to treatment with lithium (in dosages determined by serum levels) or chlorpromazine (up to 3000 mg/day) for three weeks. At the start of the study the patients were divided into two subgroups, 'highly active' and 'mildly active', on the basis of psychomotor symptoms. Both drugs were found to be equally effective in the mildly active patients, but chlorpromazine was significantly superior for those in the highly active group. However, this latter finding was due almost entirely to patients on lithium who dropped out of the study because of poor control of symptoms like hostility and overactivity. When these patients were excluded from the analysis the differences between the two treatments became insignificant. Lithium- and neuroleptic-treated patients showed significant improvement in both schizophrenic and affective symptoms.

Table 13.4 Studies of psychosis in the first-degree relatives of patients meeting RDC criteria for schizoaffective disorder

Study	Sample size	% affected relatives			Comment
		Schizophrenia	Affective psychosis	Schizoaffective psychosis	
Abrams and Taylor (1976a)	7	0	13.9	—	No details given of method of assessing relatives
Rosenthal et al. (1980)	25	0	24.6 (MR)	—	Diagnoses in relatives made using criteria that did not include schizoaffective psychosis
Pope et al. (1980)	52	0	40.4	—	Diagnoses in relatives made using criteria that did not include schizoaffective psychosis 9.6% of relatives had psychotic disorders that could not be specified
Baron et al. (1982)	50	2.2 (MR)	18.9 (MR)	2.2 (MR)	'Mainly schizophrenic' and 'mainly affective' subgroups had higher rates of schizophrenia and affective disorder respectively in relatives
Gershon et al. (1982)	11	3.6 (MR)	31.0 (MR)	6.1 (MR)	—
Andreasen et al. (1987)	55	1.4	22.9	0.7	—
Endicott et al. (1986)	23	3.0	25.2	1.0	Index group were only schizoaffective depressed
Maier et al. (1993)	115	3.1	15.3	3.3	—

MR – Morbid risk
Source: Adapted from Coryell (1986).

Beyond this, the study of Johnstone *et al.* (1988) mentioned in Chapter 11 is of relevance. They examined the response of patients with any form of functional psychosis to neuroleptics, lithium or the combination of the two drugs. The sample consisted of 105 patients who showed one or more definite psychotic symptom (as rated using the Present State Examination) in the absence of organic brain disease. Nearly all the patients showed delusions and hallucinations. DSM III diagnoses included schizophrenia, mania, major depression, schizoaffective disorder, atypical psychosis and paranoid disorder. Twenty-six were rated as having predominant elevation of mood, 34 predominant depression, and 60 no predominant mood disturbance (these judgements were made clinically – however, reclassifying patients as schizophrenic, schizoaffective or affective according to two systems (CATEGO and DSM III) made no difference to the results of the analysis).

All patients were randomly assigned to treatment for four weeks with either neuroleptic (pimozide), lithium, both, or placebo under double blind conditions. Analysis revealed that neuroleptic treatment had a highly significant beneficial effect on psychotic symptoms (i.e. summed scores on delusions, hallucinations and formal thought disorder), and also on incongruity of affect, irrespective of whether these symptoms were associated with elevation or depression of mood. At the same time, neuroleptic treatment had no demonstrable effect on elevation or depression of mood. Lithium showed the reverse pattern of effects. It had no significant effect on delusions, hallucinations and formal thought disorder, but a significant effect on reducing elevation of mood; it did not show a significant effect on depression. There was no evidence of any interactive effect between lithium and neuroleptic treatment.

Miscellaneous atypical psychoses

Puerperal psychosis

Marcé (1858) is generally acknowledged as founding the study of psychoses that developed in the weeks or months following childbirth. He considered these states to be important for two reasons: first, because of the frequency with which they seemed to occur, and second, because of their clinical features, which he felt marked them out from psychoses occurring at any other time of life. For Marcé and a succession of later authors culminating in Hamilton (1962), puerperal psychosis was characterised by dreaminess, perplexity, confusion or delirium, superimposed on which could be panic, nightmarish hallucinations, delusional misidentifications and also stupor and excitement. Variability of symptoms was the rule, with patients rarely conforming to simple textbook patterns, but instead moving unpredictably from one syndrome to another, and relapsing and remitting unpredictably.

Contemporary work has supported Marcé's first contention: it is now firmly established that the incidence of functional psychosis is greater following childbirth than at any other time of life (e.g. Pugh *et al.*, 1963; Kendell *et al.*, 1976). However, the view that puerperal psychotic states have their own set of distinctive features has not fared so well. To a considerable extent this is due to the work of Kendell and co-workers (Kendell *et al.*, 1987; Platz and Kendell, 1988), who convincingly demonstrated that the vast majority of cases of psychosis admitted within three months of childbirth met RDC criteria for some form of affective disorder and went on to follow a course similar to that of affective disorder. As a result, it is now widely accepted that many, probably the overwhelming majority of, puerperal states are affective in nature. Brockington (1996) noted that there was a category for puerperal psychosis in ICD 10, but this came with a recommendation that it only be used when unavoidable, and that most experts in the field were of the opinion that a special category was not justified.

In spite of such efforts to persuade them to the contrary, some psychiatrists continue to maintain that puerperal psychotic states tend to be marked by their similarities to each other (e.g. Snaith, 1983), or reveal atypical features when attempts are made to classify them according to the conventional scheme (Brockington, 1996). A handful of studies lend some credence to this view.

Brockington *et al.* (1981) examined the clinical features of 58 episodes of psychosis in 56 women whose psychoses began within two weeks of childbirth. Their symptoms were compared with those of 52 female patients of childbearing age with a variety of non-puerperal psychotic disorders, including those with diagnoses of schizophrenia, schizoaffective psychosis, mania and depression. All the patients were subjected to a detailed mental state assessment using a structured psychiatric interview, video recording and interviews with relatives where possible. The main symptomatic difference between the two groups concerned the presence of confusion, ratings of which were nearly twice as high in the puerperal group. Ratings related to behavioural incompetence were also more common in the puerperal group. Manic symptoms were more common in the puerperal group, and characteristic symptoms of schizophrenia (odd affect, bizarre delusions, social withdrawal, auditory hallucinations, etc.) were less common.

Dean and Kendell (1981) compared 33 patients meeting Research Diagnostic Criteria for major depression whose illnesses developed within three months of childbirth, to 33 age-matched patients with the same diagnosis unrelated to childbirth. Nearly half of the puerperal depressives were deluded or hallucinated, a similar proportion were agitated or retarded, and over two-thirds were perplexed; in all cases these rates were two or three times higher than in the non-puerperal group. Also, 18 per cent were disoriented, compared to none of the controls. Other features shown significantly more frequently by the puerperal depressives included lability of mood, other organic signs and miscellaneous psychotic symptoms such as delusional mood, minor auditory and visual hallucinations and perceptual distortions.

Pfuhlman *et al.* (1998) examined the case-notes of 48 women who were hospitalised with a psychiatric disorder developing within six months of childbirth, and assigned diagnoses according to ICD 10. The most frequent diagnosis was unipolar depressive disorder, found in 28 per cent. Next most frequent was acute polymorphic psychotic disorder, found in 21 per cent; 13 per cent met criteria for bipolar disorder and 13 per cent for schizoaffective disorder. Schizophrenia was diagnosed in only five cases, and in four of these the presentation was accompanied by marked catatonic symptoms.

From these studies, especially the last, what makes puerperal psychoses sometimes difficult to classify in conventional ways hardly needs to be spelled out. As Brockington (1996) put it, 'it is obvious that puerperal psychosis, with its strikingly acute onset, prominent "confusion" and motility disturbances, and frequent schizoaffective features, resembles cycloid psychosis, and this has been remarked on from time to time by those who use the concept'.

Benign/periodic catatonia

No sooner had Kraepelin incorporated catatonia into the diagnostic category of schizophrenia, than some authors began to suggest that it was not always correct to do so. Kirby (1913) described five patients who developed stuporose states that were unequivocally catatonic in nature, but who then recovered spontaneously after several months (or in one case 6 years) and went on to remain well for up to 7 years. He noted that the attacks were not preceded by the typical prodromal symptoms of schizophrenia and that some of the patients also had an earlier history of depression. In some cases the period of stupor was followed or interrupted by episodes of excitement which were more manic than catatonic in character. He concluded that the course of these illnesses, as well as certain of their clinical features, betrayed their essentially manic-depressive nature.

Later, Hoch (1921) collected a series of 19 similar patients (in fact the patients were drawn from the same hospital and at least one of the patients was the same as Kirby's). He introduced the term 'benign stupor' to describe them, and this soon became part of the lore of atypical psychosis, finding its way, for example, into Perris' list of disorders resembling cycloid psychosis. Later, Gjessing (1938; see also Fish 1962/Hamilton, 1984) described a series of patients in whom catatonic states developed and remitted abruptly; periodic catatonia, as he called it, also became absorbed into the same tradition.

What these authors seemed to forget was a point made by Kraepelin (1913a) about the sometimes markedly episodic course of catatonic schizophrenia itself. He observed that about a third of catatonic schizophrenics initially showed improvement 'sometimes resembling complete recovery or coming very near it'. These remissions frequently lasted 2 or 3 years, sometimes a decade or more, and in one case 29 years. Nevertheless, sooner or later in all cases deterioration – often of a particularly malignant type – supervened. An ultimately schizophrenic outcome was certainly evident in Gjessing's cases of periodic catatonia: he described his patients as being dull, apathetic and showing no insight between episodes, and eventually a state characterised by poverty of ideation, lack of critical faculty, emotional flattening and mannerisms was reached.

Partly for this reason, Rachlin (1935) undertook a long-term follow-up of Kirby's and Hoch's cases. Of the 12 patients he was able to obtain reasonable information on, 6 were chronically hospitalised and showed severe schizophrenic deterioration. Three were alive and out of hospital; two of these, however, were chronically psychotic. The third showed residual catatonic symptoms but was otherwise well. Two patients had had long-term full remissions lasting 9 and 11 years respectively, but had then died (one possibly of malignant catatonia). Only one living patient had had a sustained full remission, in whom it had lasted 20 years.

While in their strong form Kirby and Hoch's claims turned out not to rest on firm foundations, the weaker question of whether catatonia can be seen in manic-depressive psychosis has refused to go away. Several early surveys of manic-depressive patients found that up to a third showed grimacing, posturing, mannerisms and other catatonic symptoms (Lange, 1922; Bonner and Kent, 1936; Rennie, 1942). However, in these studies the diagnosis was made clinically and often simply taken from the case records. Criticisms concerning retrospective design and reliance on case-notes also apply to the study of Morrison (1973), who screened the case-notes of 250 patients with diagnoses of catatonia or catatonic schizophrenia and found that 10 per cent of the retarded and 28 per cent of the excited patients met Feighner criteria for affective psychosis.

Taylor and Abrams (1977) found a substantial frequency of catatonic phenomena in a more rigorous prospective study. They examined 123 acute admissions meeting their own diagnostic criteria for mania and found that 28 per cent exhibited two or more catatonic phenomena at some point. Even this study is not beyond reproach, since it is widely acknowledged that Taylor and Abram's criteria for mania are easy to meet and would tend to include cases that would be classified as schizoaffective by other schemes (in fact, 21 per cent of their patients showing catatonic symptoms also showed first rank schizophrenic symptoms). The findings of another rigorous study, the International Pilot Study of Schizophrenia (WHO, 1973), were less impressive: only 1 of 99 patients who received a final clinical diagnosis of psychotic depression was found to score in the category 'qualititative psychomotor disorder', which rates catatonic phenomena other than stupor or excitement.

Nevertheless, for better or worse, catatonia is now accepted as a feature of affective disorder (see Rogers, 1992; Fink and Taylor, 2003). It is certainly true that convincing cases are occasionally encountered, and one of these is summarised in Box 13.5.

Box 13.5 Catatonia in a manic-depressive patient (from McKenna *et al.*, 1999)

The patient was a 58-year-old woman with a history of episodes of mania and depression from the age of 19. These were apparently unexceptional in nature and she made a full recovery between episodes. She was said to have been briefly 'catatonic' in one previous episode.

The current episode began two months previously with her becoming increasingly overactive and disinhibited. She was admitted to hospital and initially improved on treatment with neuroleptics. After five weeks she started to appear tense and expressed ideas about being scared of other patients. She started speaking in non-sequiturs and became incontinent of urine and faeces. Over the next one to two weeks she deteriorated, speaking less and less and appearing depressed. Ultimately she became mute and stuporose and required intravenous fluids.

On examination she showed continual slow, sustained facial movements. She continually clenched her jaws with her lips pulled back in a grimace, screwed her eyes up and wrinkled her forehead. She often held her breath for up to a minute and then exhaled with a loud gasp. She was nearly mute, but answered some questions with a few words and occasionally mumbled incoherently to herself; when she spoke her voice was strained and croaky. She exhibited psychological pillow and waxy flexibility in her arms. She was rigid in her upper body and showed gegenhalten in her wrists, arms and neck. Tone was normal in her lower limbs, but gegenhalten was still present. At this time her mood was not obviously depressed and at times she appeared almost jocular.

All organic investigations were normal, and the possibility of neuroleptic malignant syndrome seemed unlikely in view of repeatedly normal or only mildly raised creatine phosphokinase levels. She improved slowly on treatment with ECT. After four weeks she was free of most of the above phenomena but still moved abnormally slowly. Examined at home six months later she was well, free of all affective symptoms and showed no catatonic phenomena. However, she had developed moderately severe tardive dyskinesia.

Tropical schizophrenia?

A number of authors, notably German (1972) and Stevens (1987), have drawn attention to the frequent occurrence of short-lived self-limiting episodes of psychosis in Africa. These were considered to be distinguishable from acute confusional states and accounted for up to 30 per cent of admissions to hospital in Senegal. Such brief psychoses could occur at any age but predominantly affected young men and women. They appeared to be uncommon or rare in the better-off, literate classes, but were endemic in rural settings where there was poverty, poor nourishment and disease.

The psychoses were commonly preceded by a definite environmental stress. The onset was typically abrupt, but there could be a prodromal period of up to several weeks, in which there were, for instance, delusions. Most commonly, the picture was one of extreme restlessness, insomnia, confusion, auditory and visual hallucinations, delusions of being controlled, incoherent, rambling, pressured speech, and disturbed behaviour including undressing, tearing or burning clothes, destroying property or attacking relatives. Less commonly, the predominant symptoms were extreme withdrawal, mutism and negativism, or dreaminess. Without treatment, spontaneous remission took place in one to four weeks. Use of neuroleptics and ECT halved the length of the episode. With or without treatment, recovery was usually complete. However, the patient usually claimed amnesia for the episode.

German favoured causative factors such as perinatal trauma, brain-damaging illnesses in infancy and chronic poor nutrition. He speculated that there was a large reservoir of subclinical cerebral dysfunction in Africa which facilitated the appearance of psychosis in response to physical or mental stress. Stevens was impressed by the fact that investigations for underlying physical disease were generally negative, and that the disorder typically followed in the wake of some definable life stress.

If these descriptions are to believed, something very similar to cycloid psychosis seems to be extremely common in some tropical countries. Stevens suggested that these presentations might account for the difference in prevalence of schizophrenia found in the International Pilot Study of Schizophrenia, in which there was an obvious excess of psychoses that were functional and not affective in nature in most of the tropical countries that took part (see Jablensky, 1987).

Conclusion

There are reasonable grounds for accepting that cycloid psychosis and schizoaffective psychosis proper are both genuine clinical entities. They are discernibly different in terms of their cross-sectional clinical picture from schizophrenia and manic-depressive psychosis (and also from each other). They also retain features in the long term that distinguish them from schizophrenia and manic-depressive psychosis, even if this distinctiveness lies in the variety of further episodes more than in clear differences in outcome. This conclusion does not necessarily have any implications for the classification of functional psychosis, other than it is more complicated than one might wish. But some contemporary authors, notably Kendell and Crow, have taken it to mean that the separation of schizophrenia and manic-depressive psychosis is invalid, and that a continuum view of functional psychosis needs to be accepted – a revival of the concept of unitary psychosis (Berrios, 1987; Beer, 1996).

In the hands of Kendell (1987, 1991), the continuum of psychosis is purely clinical. The fact that there are functional psychotic states that share the features of the two major syndromes means that neither schizophrenia nor manic-depressive psychosis – whose existence has anyway never been more than provisional in the absence of firm aetiological knowledge – can be properly regarded as disease entities, and clinicians will sooner or later have to reject this outdated view. Unfortunately for this argument, it is not clear that schizoaffective psychosis – with a maximum frequency of 15 per cent of psychotic admissions – provides a large enough conduit for schizophrenia to merge by degrees into manic-depressive psychosis. In addition, cycloid psychosis fits no better into a continuum view than it does into a binary concept of psychosis.

For Crow (1986, 1991), the implications are aetiological; he argues that it is the genetics of manic-depressive psychosis and schizophrenia that lie on a continuum. The studies reviewed in this chapter do not particularly strengthen his case. It is true that the relatives of patients with schizoaffective psychosis show an excess of cases of both schizophrenia and affective disorder. But the association with the former is not a consistent finding, and the skew is clearly towards the latter, where the rates are sometimes very high indeed. In cycloid psychosis, the evidence, such as it is, points to it being related to affective disorder.

14 Schizophrenia and organic brain disease

States bearing at least a passing resemblance to schizophrenia develop with some regularity in patients who have a wide range of diseases affecting brain function. When this happens, the presentation is customarily referred to as 'organic schizophrenia' or 'organic schizophrenia-like state', slightly confusingly in view of the presumptive biological aetiology of schizophrenia itself. A further layer of complexity is added by the fact that the term 'organic' itself has two meanings in psychiatry. The first is organic as symptomatic of underlying brain disease, and the second is organic as opposed to functional in the classification of psychotic states.

Symptomatic schizophrenia refers to – or at least will be used to refer to here – the development of states diagnosable as schizophrenia in patients with known forms of neurological disease. This sense of organic schizophrenia is exemplified by Lishman's (1998) well-known textbook *Organic Psychiatry*, in which he authoritatively reviewed the extent to which different psychiatric syndromes could be seen as a complication of a large number of central nervous system diseases. While the sheer weight of claims for schizophrenia in this book makes the existence of some kind of association highly probable, its exact nature is a subject of dispute. As Mayer-Gross *et al.* (1969) noted quite a long time ago, although some would consider such cases to be genuine examples of what is in all probability an aetiologically heterogeneous disorder, others would regard them as distinguishable from true schizophrenia and merely offering a temporary illusion of the disorder. Another view, endorsed by Lishman, is that some such presentations are examples of regular schizophrenia triggered off in a genetically predisposed individual.

Although the distinction between organic and functional is fundamental to the classification of mental disorders, what the terms actually mean – especially the latter – has never been entirely clear (see Trimble, 1982; Berrios, 1996; Beer, 1996). In what is probably the most typical usage, 'organic' refers to two main disorders, the common denominator of which is obvious cognitive impairment: dementia and the acute confusional state. The definition of functional is by exclusion: if there is no evidence of cognitive impairment, and also if there is no other 'organicity' in the sense of evidence of underlying neurological disease (i.e. the presentation is not symptomatic as defined above), then the disorder is functional, or primary or idiopathic. It is import-ant to note that this does not mean that there is no underlying biological cause, but merely that any pathological lesion is subtle to the point that it cannot be detected by current methods.

Unanswered questions still surround both the terms organic and schizophrenia-like states. Can a psychosis be functional in the presence of organic brain disorder? Does it have to occur in clear consciousness? Does the full syndrome need to be present, or will, say, isolated delusions or hal-lucinations suffice to qualify for the diagnosis? How should one classify states where there is full-blown schizophrenia-like psychosis but also obvious cogni-tive impairment? Should the accompanying brain disease always be identifi-able? Some of these questions are easy to answer, others raise questions that go to the heart of what is meant by schizophrenia. In this chapter the evidence that symptomatic schizophrenia-like states can complicate certain key forms of brain disease is first reviewed. Following this an attempt will be made to try to disentangle some aspects of the considerably more knotty problem of what the occurrence of schizophrenic symptoms in dementia and in acute confu-sional states means. This still leaves a small number of disorders in which neurological and psychiatric symptoms are even more closely intertwined, one of which, encephalitis lethargica, seems especially intimately related to schizophrenia.

Symptomatic schizophrenia

To make explicit what has almost always been left implicit in the literature, symptomatic schizophrenia refers to the occurrence, in a patient with brain disease or systemic disease that can affect brain function, of symptoms that in other circumstances would lead to a diagnosis of schizophrenia being made. The clinical picture is quasi-functional; that is, there should be no evidence of cognitive impairment either in the form of clouding of consciousness, subtle or otherwise, or in the form of dementia, early or otherwise. Although the presentation needs to resemble schizophrenia, it only has to do this qualita-tively – that is, be diagnosable as this rather than any other form of psychosis – and not quantitatively – there is no particular need for the clinical picture to conform to the stereotype of acute schizophrenia, or for a course to be followed that leads to deterioration.

Symptomatic schizophrenic states meeting none, some or all of these requirements have been documented for a large number of different brain diseases in a steady stream of case reports, series and large-scale surveys from the end of the nineteenth century. To review these with a view to determining whether the associations were more than coincidental would be an enormous task, one that would probably be considered impossible, were it not for the fact that it has already been done. Davison and Bagley (1969), in a 71-page, 782-reference review critically examined the entire English and European language literature on the occurrence of what they termed schizophrenia-like psychosis in 13 classes of organic disease of the central nervous system. They used diagnostic criteria for schizophrenia which were, for the time, commendable; these are shown in Box 14.1. They took pains to exclude the presence of significant concurrent cognitive impairment, in the form of either acute confusion or dementia. They considered whether there was an association with schizophrenia principally from a statistical standpoint, relying on figures for the annual incidence of schizophrenia of 0.01–0.05 per cent, lifetime risk of 0.8–1.2 per cent and prevalence of 0.2–0.5 per cent. However, where possible they also considered the question from the viewpoint of predisposition to schizophrenia, as gauged by presence of a schizoid premorbid personality or a family history of schizophrenia.

Davison and Bagley's monumental work is not easy to precis. Some sections went beyond strict clinical considerations, for instance into a discussion of abnormal EEG findings in schizophrenia in the section on epilepsy. In others, they were only able to mount an informal review of mainly anecdotal findings, for example with regard to psychosis in association with motor neuron disease and Friedrich's ataxia. At times they strayed into poorly charted territory like metabolic brain diseases and sleep disorders. Accordingly, an approach is taken that preserves the spirit and contains the highlights of their review. First, their findings in four principal categories of brain disease are summarised, presenting an illustrative study in each case. This is followed by a review of more recent findings where these have since become available.

Epilepsy

As befitting a disorder whose relationship with schizophrenia has aroused so much controversy, and incidentally provided psychiatry with one of its most

---

Box 14.1 Davison and Bagley's criteria for symptomatic schizophrenia (from Davison and Bagley, 1969)

1. The presence of an unequivocal disorder of the central nervous system.
2. The presence, at some stage, of at least one of the following characteristic features of schizophrenia:
   Thought disorder, defined as bizarre statements, abnormal syntactical, grammatical or other linguistic usages; incapacity to pursue a sustained train of thought; use of private symbols.
   Shallow or incongruous affect.
   Hallucinations and delusions.
3. The absence, at the stage when these psychotic features are displayed, of features that would reasonably lead to a diagnosis of affective psychosis, dysmnesic syndrome, delirium or significant dementia.

effective treatments, Davison and Bagley gave epilepsy pride of place in their review. They noted that the occurrence of paranoid-hallucinatory psychoses in epileptic patients was increasingly reported in the latter half of the nineteenth century. The early years of the twentieth century saw this 'affinity' view become widely accepted (among others, Kraepelin, 1909 commented on the association). A little later, however, another view that also dated from the nineteenth century became dominant; this was the 'antagonism' hypothesis, that epilepsy and schizophrenia were biological opposites. As described in Chapter 11, it was this that led to the introduction of convulsive therapy into psychiatry.

A number of studies carried out between 1925 and 1958 examined the rate of schizophrenia in patients with a diagnosis of epilepsy. These studies had large numbers (between 487 and 2000 patients), and they produced a measure of agreement, with the figures clustering around 0.7 per cent. They thus did little to support the view that the two disorders might be related. However, as a group these studies contained so many methodological shortcomings – in most the examination was clearly superficial – and there were so many factors that were not controlled for that Davison and Bagley concluded that little weight could be attached to their findings.

Against this background, one study virtually singlehandedly established the modern view that epilepsy and schizophrenia are clinically associated. Over an 11-year period, Slater *et al.* (1963) collected and meticulously analysed a series of 69 patients who suffered from a combination of both disorders. In all patients the diagnosis of epilepsy was based on unequivocal evidence of seizures with or without EEG confirmation. A large majority of the patients (55 of the 69) had temporal lobe epilepsy or evidence of a temporal lobe EEG focus. The diagnosis of schizophrenia was made clinically, but easily satisfied Davison and Bagley's criteria: all but two cases showed delusions with or without hallucinations, and in these two there was formal thought disorder plus other symptoms. In all cases the psychotic symptoms had lasted for weeks or months in the absence of any cognitive impairment.

All the cases came from two hospitals in London. Based on lifetime expectancy rates of 0.8 per cent for schizophrenia and 0.5 per cent for epilepsy, Slater *et al.* calculated that chance association of the two disorders could give rise to at most 33–55 cases in the areas covered by the hospitals over the 11-year study period. They therefore concluded that a significant association existed between the two disorders. They acknowledged that the two hospitals concerned were both prestigious national referral centres and contained neuropsychiatric units, but they argued that even allowing for selective referral it was inconceivable that they could have easily ascertained so many cases, given the many other general and psychiatric hospitals scattered throughout the area.

Slater *et al.*'s patients exhibited all the cardinal symptoms of schizophrenia. As well as delusions and auditory hallucinations in the vast majority of patients, visual somatic, olfactory and gustatory hallucinations were found in descending order of frequency. Formal thought disorder was present in 31 of the patients, and affective flattening or inappropriateness in 28. Catatonic symptoms were surprisingly prevalent; one or more of these were seen in 40 patients, most commonly mannerisms. Various first rank symptoms were also evident in the case descriptions.

The outcome of the psychosis was variable. Most typically, it ran a stormy course. A third of the series underwent remission of florid symptoms, and a further third showed improvement in these. Almost all patients showed negative symptoms to some degree, but these were mild in many cases. Slater *et al.* remarked that 'loss of affective response did not occur so early or become so marked in the great majority of these patients, as in the typical schizophrenic ... The psychosis from which they suffered tended to leave them preoccupied with old delusional ideas or with the remnants of thought disorder, but not with bleached, washed out or vacuous personalities.' At follow-up, nearly half the patients were in full- or part-time work. Twenty-nine of the patients did, however, develop impairments of a more organic type, showing perseverativeness, dullness, circumstantiality or loss of memory, which were similar to changes seen in the late stages of severe epilepsy. However, the state did not amount to dementia.

Family history was examined, with a relative being interviewed in 62 of the 69 patients. Only one first-degree relative had a definite diagnosis of schizophrenia. Another had been given a diagnosis of paranoid psychosis. One suffered from the combination of epilepsy and psychosis, and one more had an unspecified psychiatric illness. Based on the first two cases, the familial risk for schizophrenia was calculated to be 0.7 per cent, not obviously different from that of the general population.

Davison and Bagley accepted Slater *et al.*'s findings, but they also expressed reservations about whether the question was fully settled. In the years following their review, several more studies have appeared. As reviewed by McKenna *et al.* (1985) and Toone (2000), these have yielded a prevalence of schizophrenia that varies between 3 per cent and 7 per cent. Most of these studies were not epidemiologically satisfactory and/or failed to use diagnostic criteria for schizophrenia; however two recent studies, one that was epidemiologically based (Bredkjaer *et al.*, 1998) but did not use diagnostic criteria, and one that was not epidemiological but did use diagnostic criteria (Mendez *et al.*, 1993), both supported the association. Most studies continue to find a particular relationship with temporal lobe epilepsy.

Cerebral trauma

According to Davison and Bagley, the view that schizophrenia could be a complication of head injury first gained authority from a review of the literature between 1900 and 1921 by the German psychiatrist Wilmans. However, neither Kraepelin (1913a) nor Bleuler (1911) considered this to be the case.

Some decades later, a further review by Elsasser and Grunewald (1953) also cast doubt on the association.

Determination of whether or not an association exists between head injury and schizophrenia faces a number of methodological difficulties. One of these is the wide range of severity of head injury and its sequelae, from mild concussion with full recovery to states of dementia and/or severe neurological disability. Another difficulty concerns the interval between the trauma and the onset of psychosis – how long can this be before the head injury is no longer regarded as aetiologically relevant? A further complicating factor is the frequent development of post-traumatic epilepsy following head injury, which the previous section indicates is independently associated with the development of schizophrenia-like psychoses. Davison and Bagley adopted a policy of reviewing studies that followed patients who were unselected for severity over a long period. Their findings are reproduced in Table 14.1.

It can be seen that, in six studies that had follow-up periods of 10 to 20 years, the risk of developing schizophrenia ranged from 0.7 per cent to 9.8 per cent. Compared to a risk of 0.8 per cent in the general population over 25 years, on average the rate was increased two to three times. One study that found no increase (Liberman, 1964), included only cases with a diagnosis of concussion. Two further studies (Aita and Reitan, 1948; Poppelreuter, 1917) found low rates of development of schizophrenia, but their findings are difficult to interpret as the follow-up period was very short.

Probably the best study was that of Hillbom (1960). He reviewed clinical case material on 415 individuals randomly selected from 3552 Finnish men who had received brain injuries during military service, where this was not complicated by other injuries, such as to the eyes or spinal cord. Severity of injury was rated as mild, moderate or severe based on the degree of permanent work disability. The follow-up period was long, on average 20 years. Psychiatric disturbances of various types were common, and there were 11 cases of psychosis 'more or less reminiscent of schizophrenia'. This was

Table 14.1 Frequency of schizophrenia in patients with head injury

Study	Number of patients	Mean observation period	% developing schizophrenia
Poppelreuter (1917)	3000	2 years	0.07
Feuchtwanger and Mayer-Gross (1938)	1564	15 years	1.7
Aita and Reitan (1948)	500	3 months	0.4
Hillbom (1951)	1821	10 years	1.2
Meinertz (1957)	1110	15 years	1.5
Lobova (1960)	1168	15 years	9.8
Hillbom (1960)	415	20 years	2.6
Liberman (1964)	4807	15 years	0.7

Source: Davison and Bagley (1969).

distributed among patients with mild, moderate and severe head injuries, but was most common in the last group. The 11 cases were all described, and in 9 the diagnosis was fairly clear, with presence of delusions and/or auditory hallucinations sometimes with other symptoms in 8, and (probable) formal thought disorder and affective flattening in the ninth. The tenth case developed a clear-cut psychosis characterised by multiple persecutory delusions, and the eleventh case was stated to suffer from an episodic paranoid disorder, but decisive evidence of psychosis was not presented. Only one of the core group of nine cases definitely also suffered from epilepsy, with two more showing uncertain evidence of this. Four further cases were diagnosed as suffering from psychosis, of which two might possibly have been schizophrenic. Three of these four cases also suffered from epilepsy. The incidence of schizophrenia following head injury could thus be estimated as ranging from 1.9 per cent (defined narrowly in patients without definite epilepsy) to 3.1 per cent (defined broadly and including cases with epilepsy).

Several authors in these and the other studies reviewed by Davison and Bagley commented on the rarity of a family history of schizophrenia. The clinical features of schizophrenia following head injury also attracted comment in these studies. The general tenor of the relevant statements was that, while all the symptoms of schizophrenia could be encountered and the disorder could be indistinguishable from 'true' schizophrenia, there was a tendency to paranoid forms, hallucinations were often the most conspicuous feature, formal thought disorder tended to be absent, and there was a relative preservation of affect.

David and Prince (2005) critically reviewed three further studies that appeared after Davison and Bagley's review. Achte *et al.* (1969) extended Hillbom's study to the whole sample of 3552 men and followed them up 22–26 years later. The proportion who developed schizophrenia, once again diagnosed clinically, was found to be much the same at 2.1 per cent; a further 2 per cent, however, were diagnosed as having paranoid psychoses. In this extended sample, schizophrenic psychoses were found to be more frequent among those with mild injuries than those with severe ones. Roberts (1979) diagnosed 3.1 per cent of 291 civilian cases who were followed up for 10–24 years as either schizophrenia or 'paranoid dementia'; again all diagnoses were made clinically. De Mol *et al.* (1987) found that 2.3 per cent of 530 civilian cases followed up for 10 years met DSM III criteria for schizophrenia or paranoid disorders. In this study it was claimed that 83 per cent of the psychoses developed within six months of the head injury, being apparent in many cases from the time of recovery. David and Prince concluded that collectively the long-term follow-up studies supported an increased incidence of schizophrenia in head injury. They were critical, however, first of the lack of use of diagnostic criteria in all but one of the studies, and second, of the fact that the majority of studies were based on penetrating injuries in servicemen, which might have different effects from the mainly closed head injuries seen in peacetime. Also evident in the studies was a lack of consensus about the relationship with severity of the injury and the duration between the injury and the onset of psychosis.

Multiple sclerosis

Early authors such as Gowers considered that psychosis was rare in multiple sclerosis. By the early part of the twentieth century, however, case reports had begun to appear that described psychosis as a complication, often as an early symptom or even heralding the onset of the disease. Altogether, Davison and Bagley were able to collect 39 such reports in which the associated psychosis satisfied their criteria. These confirmed the impression that the psychosis usually presented early in the course of the disorder, although in 10 cases it developed five years or more after the neurological diagnosis had been made. They also found eight case reports where the psychosis preceded the onset of neurological symptoms by up to five years. The clinical picture was invariably felt to resemble schizophrenia very closely: paranoid, hebephrenic and cata-tonic forms were described, and as far as could be determined the course was unexceptional, with some cases progressing to deterioration (although the term dementia was often used). There was little to suggest a family history of schizophrenia in the cases.

Davison and Bagley also found three larger studies that investigated the psychiatric aspects of multiple sclerosis. These had sample sizes of 544, 63, and 330, and only one case of schizophrenia was found in each.

On the one hand, Davison and Bagley were inclined to accept that the latter evidence, which clearly suggested there was a no greater than chance association between the two conditions. On the other, they speculated that the high rate of other mental disorders, especially dementia, might have reduced the opportunity to observe schizophrenia in a recognisable form. They were also impressed by the tendency of psychosis, when it was seen, to have its onset at around the same time as neurological symptoms first appeared.

Subsequent to Davison and Bagley's review, Surridge (1969) found only one case of schizophrenia (diagnosed clinically) in a generally thorough survey of 108 cases of multiple sclerosis. More recently still, Ron and Logsdail (1989) took lifetime psychiatric histories and assigned DSM-III-R criteria to 116 consecutive attenders at a neurological hospital who had a well-founded diagnosis of multiple sclerosis. Their findings are shown in Table 14.2. Six patients (0.5 per cent) were found to have developed a non-affective functional psychosis after the disease had become established, none of which met criteria for schizophrenia. The diagnosis was delusional disorder in four cases, and the remaining two only qualified for a diagnosis of atypical psychosis. One further patient was also given a diagnosis of atypical psychosis, but had experienced a previous episode more than three years prior to the onset of the neurological disorder. Organic, affective psychotic (depressive and bipolar), and a variety of neurotic disorders were also found, in all cases considerably more frequently than the delusional and atypical psychoses.

Table 14.2 DSM-III-R diagnoses in 116 patients with multiple sclerosis

Diagnosis	Relationship to onset of physical illness		
	Before	*After*	*At interview*
Adjustment disorder	11	22	17
Bipolar disorder	1	5	2
Depressive disorder	4	12	18
Somatoform disorder	1	1	1
Anxiety disorder	4	1	0
Delusional disorder	0	4	4
Atypical psychosis	1	3	1
Organic disorders*	0	1	7

* At interview three patients were markedly elated in the presence of cognitive impairment, three were demented, and one had a hypomanic episode related to steroid treatment.

Source: Ron and Logsdail (1989), Psychiatric morbidity in multiple sclerosis: A clinical and MRI study. *Psychological Medicine*, 19, 887–896. Reproduced with permission from Cambridge University Press.

Multiple sclerosis may or may not be associated with an increased rate of psychosis when this is defined broadly to include psychotic forms of affective disorder, and to find four cases of delusional disorder in a sample of 116 subjects has to be regarded as unusual. However, the findings with respect to schizophrenia appear unequivocal – it is not a significant complication of the disorder.

Basal ganglia disorders

Davison and Bagley introduced this section by noting that the points of contact and areas of overlap between schizophrenia and basal ganglia disorders were many and varied. Psychosis was accepted as an important sequel of encephalitis lethargica, and there were longstanding traditions of schizophrenia-like psychoses occurring in other basal ganglia disorders, including torsion dystonia, Wilson's disease and Huntington's disease. In addition, they stated that the similarity between the catatonic symptoms of schizophrenia and the hyper- and hypo-kinetic phenomena of basal ganglia disease had been noted many times. They went on to examine the rate of occurrence of schizophrenia in three disorders, Parkinson's disease, Wilson's disease and Huntington's disease (and also a fourth, encephalitis lethargica, discussion of which is postponed until later in the chapter).

Parkinson's disease

Davison and Bagley found that case reports documenting the combination of schizophrenia and idiopathic or arteriosclerotic Parkinsonism were extremely sparse (in contrast to the rich literature on post-encephalitic Parkinsonism, discussed below). Two series of 146 patients (Patrick and Levy, 1922) and 200 patients (Schwab *et al.*, 1951) also failed to turn up any cases of schizophrenia.

A third series, the most detailed from the psychiatric point of view, was carried out by Mjones (1949). He collected 250 patients with a diagnosis of idiopathic Parkinson's disease (194 cases) or arteriosclerotic Parkinsonism (32 cases); he also included 24 patients with unclassifiable Parkinsonian symptoms. Patients with a history of encephalitis or who showed typical sequelae of post-encephalitic Parkinsonism such as oculogyric crises were excluded. All patients were then interviewed personally and examined physically and psychiatrically. Among the 194 patients with idiopathic Parkinson's disease he found 4 (2.1 per cent) cases of schizophrenia, paranoid psychosis or psychosis not otherwise specified (data on the other two groups were not presented). Although these findings could be considered suggestive, Davison and Bagley felt that it was just not possible to come to any conclusion about whether the risk of schizophrenia was increased in Parkinson's disease.

Wilson's disease

Two of Wilson's original cases (who were siblings) developed psychosis; one showed auditory hallucinations and passivity 18 months before neurological symptoms appeared. This association was reported several more times, and it became dogma that schizophrenia could be the presenting feature of Wilson's disease – so much so that to this day psychotic patients who develop early or severe involuntary movement disorders are routinely tested to exclude the disorder.

When Davison and Bagley reviewed the 520 case reports of Wilson's disease in the literature up to 1959, they found 8 cases of schizophrenia that were acceptable according to their criteria, plus 11 doubtful ones. In most cases the psychosis and the neurological abnormalities appeared at around the same time, but in two cases the psychiatric symptoms preceded development of organic signs by 8 years and 20 years respectively. On the strength of this – and no other sources of information were available – Davison and Bagley decided that the evidence pointed to an association between the two disorders.

The absence of any formal survey of psychiatric disorder in Wilson's disease has since been rectified by Dening and Berrios (1989). They examined the detailed case material that existed on 195 patients under the care of a neurologist who had a special interest in the disorder. Although psychiatric disturbance was found to be common, with 20 per cent of the sample having seen a psychiatrist before the diagnosis of Wilson's disease was made, psychotic symptoms were unusual. At most three patients showed delusions (two definite and one possible) and only two (one definite and one probable) were reported as experiencing hallucinations. The authors therefore calculated that only of the order of 1 per cent of the sample could have been psychotic. It is possible that the retrospective nature of the study meant that this figure could have been an underestimate, but it seems unlikely that the frequency of schizophrenia is greatly increased in Wilson's disease.

Huntington's disease

Psychosis, sometimes schizophrenic and sometimes not specified, was repeatedly described in Huntington's disease in four series reviewed by Davison and Bagley. The frequency ranged from 5 per cent to 11 per cent, and psychosis presented as the initial feature in at least a third of cases. Although these rates are many times higher than chance would predict, the relevant studies were generally lacking in psychiatric detail and the cases did not meet Davison and Bagley's criteria for schizophrenia. Overall, however, they concluded that it seemed reasonable to include schizophrenia among the many psychiatric manifestations of Huntington's disease.

There has since been little to alter or add to Davison and Bagley's conclusion. Caine and Shoulson (1983) carried out a detailed psychopathological evaluation on a group of 30 patients with Huntington's disease and found that three met DSM III criteria for schizophrenia, one more had experienced a brief schizophrenic episode, and one was diagnosed as suffering from paranoid disorder. Folstein (1989) found 10 cases of schizophrenia meeting DSM-III-R criteria for schizophrenia in a larger sample of approximately 200 patients (the exact number was not given). Watt and Seller (1993) interviewed a representative sample of 65 patients with Huntington's disease from 34 families who had been assessed by a regional medical genetics department. Eight (12.3 per cent) were diagnosed as having schizophrenia. However, in this study the diagnosis of schizophrenia was broad and included patients with just persecutory or referential delusions. In three cases schizophrenic symptoms preceded the onset of the disorder by 4–20 years. In two they developed in the first four years of illness and in two more up to 12 years after onset.

The conclusions of this updated and compressed account of Davison and Bagley's work can be summarised as follows. Schizophrenia is overrepresented in some central nervous system disorders, but not in all of them. In temporal lobe epilepsy, the risk appears to be increased several-fold; after cerebral trauma it is approximately doubled; in other disorders including disseminated sclerosis, Wilson's disease and Parkinson's disease, notwithstanding numerous anecdotal reports, the balance of evidence is that the risk is no greater than in the general population. Where the risk is increased, there is generally little support for the widely perpetuated view that the cerebral disorder has merely precipitated schizophrenia in a genetically predisposed individual. Finally, a recurring theme is that the clinical picture of schizophrenia as seen in organic brain disease shows differences from 'true' schizophrenia: the presentation is commonly of a paranoid-hallucinatory syndrome, there is a lack of affective flattening and retention of warmth and rapport, and the disorder may run a relatively benign course.

Schizophrenic symptoms in dementia and acute confusional states

Symptomatic schizophrenia, as defined in the previous section, refers to schizophrenia-like states that develop in clear consciousness, in other words in the absence of any impairment of cognitive function. This definition precludes consideration of two important and common classes of brain disorder, dementia and the acute confusional state. There is no question that isolated, or sometimes not so isolated, psychotic symptoms are commonly seen in these disorders. There are also grounds for suspecting that they can both be complicated by something approximating to a full-blown picture of schizophrenia – if nothing else, dementia figures in the differential diagnosis of any psychiatric disorder occurring in old age, and there are undoubted instances where acute confusional states have been misdiagnosed as schizophrenia.

Dementia

In the classical picture of dementia there is little that could be mistaken for the symptoms and signs of psychosis. According to Lishman (1998), perception is not affected to any great extent, and not in the direction of hallucinations. In the later stages speech may become grossly disorganised and fragmented, but this is very different in nature from formal thought disorder. Disorders in the content of thought are seen, but these typically take the form of mistaken ideas and paranoid attitudes more than delusions. The only seeming exception is the occurrence of stereotypies and mannerisms in advanced dementia, usually as an accompaniment to the grossly deteriorated behaviour seen in this stage of the disorder.

Going beyond this, most authors accept that delusion-like ideas can be seen in some cases, where they are usually a minor part of the clinical picture. Typically, these are considered to be crude, transient and poorly systematised – 'paranoid ideas', 'false ideas', 'beliefs that are only delusional in the technical sense' (e.g. Mayer-Gross *et al.*, 1969; Raskind and Storrie, 1980; Lishman, 1998). In one study (Rubin *et al.*, 1988) such ideas were found in a quarter of patients with Alzheimer's disease. Closely related to these are abnormal ideas dementing patients entertain about the presence or identity of individuals in the house. These may involve the belief that people are in the house, or that people on television are really in the room. Alternatively the patient may fail to recognise his or her own reflection in the mirror and converse with the alleged other person. These were seen in nearly a quarter of Rubin *et al.*'s sample of Alzheimer's disease patients. Some examples of these phenomena are described in Box 14.2.

Box 14.2 Descriptions of typical abnormal ideas in dementia

Judgement is impaired early as a result of these various changes [loss of intellectual flexibility, becoming tied to the immediate aspects of situations, and loss of ability to make abstract interpretations]. The patient's insight into his defects is characteristically poor and sometimes there is little awareness of illness at all. False ideas readily gain ground and paranoid ideation is particularly common. Ideas of reference may partly reflect an exaggeration of premorbid tendencies, likewise the specific form which delusions may take. Characteristically the delusions are poorly systematised and evanescent, though occasionally they become entrenched and unshakeable . . . They may be delusions in the technical sense, in that the beliefs are held in the face of evidence of their falsehood, but this is largely because the evidence fails to be understood, not because it is rejected. Delusional themes are often crude and bizarre, typically of being robbed, poisoned, threatened or deprived. Delusions of influence and other frankly schizophrenic phenomena may appear, perhaps by virtue of special premorbid vulnerability in this respect.

(Lishman, 1998)

Some paranoid phenomena are closely related to memory loss. The patient will forget the location of some object or forget having eaten a meal. When the misplaced object is perceived as missing or the food eaten is discovered to be absent from the refrigerator, accusations of theft result. Such delusions of theft are quite common and are a frequent cause of interpersonal turmoil.

(Raskind and Storrie, 1980)

The imagined people could be either relatives or strangers. A subject might imagine that a stranger had entered the house and hidden in the closet or that an unknown person was hiding in the bedroom with the subject's wife . . . [Other] subjects were unable to recognise their faces in a mirror. These subjects would converse with the person in the mirror and might try to open the door to which the mirror was attached to invite the person in. The subject would ask others why a person was being kept in a mirror. One subject became agitated because the person in the mirror was always following him . . . The final subgroup is characterised by the inability to recognise that people on television were not real . . . One subject did not want the people on television watching her undress and left the room to change. Another was frightened by television violence and thought that 'they' were shooting at him. While watching a ballgame one subject was convinced that the players were in the room with him.

(Rubin *et al.*, 1988)

It is also accepted, if mostly only tacitly, that a florid schizophrenic syndrome can develop in the context of evolving dementia. For example, Lishman (1998) stated that dementia could rarely initially present with the picture of a functional psychotic illness, in which the underlying intellectual deterioration was inconspicuous. The occurrence of delusions and hallucinations with a bizarre quality and revolving around plots to molest or harm the patient was also mentioned by Raskind and Storrie (1980). The author whose name is most associated with this view, however, is Post (1966, 1982): as described in Chapter 12, in his sample of 93 patients with late paraphrenia, he found 16 cases who had what turned out to be definite dementing illnesses. He considered that these patients were indistinguishable from the non-cognitively impaired patients in terms of the symptoms they showed, and concluded that 'some patients suffering from dementing illnesses of late life exhibit well structured and persistent paranoid pictures which are only later erased by the increasing dementia'.

Studies of the frequency of psychotic symptoms in dementia – invariably Alzheimer's disease – tend to bear out this conclusion. Reviewing some of the earlier studies, Wragg and Jeste (1989) found that delusions were reported found in 10–73 per cent, but in most studies the rates clustered around 33 per cent. These studies also found appreciable rates of hallucinations, the median frequency of these being 28 per cent. Burns *et al.* (1990) found rather lower rates of delusions (16 per cent) and hallucinations (visual 13 per cent and auditory 10 per cent) in 178 patients with Alzheimer's disease. Delusions commonly took a simple 'organic' form, but about a quarter of the time they were complex and/or bizarre: one patient believed that people were cutting his throat at night, and another that a tape machine was giving him messages. Delusions and hallucinations have also been found to co-occur in many cases (Drevets and Rubin, 1989; Rosen and Zubenko, 1991).

In short, there is no doubt that individual schizophrenic symptoms in the shape of delusions and hallucinations are seen in dementia. These may also occur in combination and something similar to and diagnosable as schizophrenia will be present in a proportion of such cases. While the former are fairly common, the latter is less frequently seen, and there are no reliable estimates of its rate of occurrence.

Acute confusional states

As with dementia, while acute confusional states need not and frequently do not feature anything that could be mistaken for psychosis, they are often complicated by abnormalities in thought, perception, affect and behaviour. When this happens the state is called delirium in Britain, whereas in the USA this term is used to refer to the syndrome as a whole. These 'psychotic' symptoms always occur against a background of impaired consciousness, which varies from the barely perceptible ('clouding of consciousness'), through more obvious degrees of muddling and disorientation ('confusion') to a state of torpidity or somnolence. Occasionally there is a state of hyper-arousal or hyper-alertness, although the defective grasp of the environment is still evident.

One prominent symptom in delirium is visual hallucinations. These range from misinterpretations or illusions (e.g. of window panes as bars on a cell, a table as a coffin), to flashes of light and geometrical patterns, to fully-formed animals, people, and whole scenes, sometimes depicting bizarre or apocalyptic events. One of Lishman's (1998) patients with delirium tremens followed intently and with excited comments a football game performed for half an hour by two teams of normal-coloured miniature elephants in a corner of his room. A particularly common variant in the elderly is 'silent boarders' – full-sized figures seen in various places around the house who do not speak.

Another characteristic feature of delirium is incoherence of speech: the train of thought is disjointed, chaotic and fragmented, and in severe cases there may be no more than incoherent muttering. Distractibility may be present, but underneath thinking is concrete, banal and impoverished. Many emotional changes are seen, from depression, anxiety or irritability, to perplexity, lability, elation, anger and fear. Typically, affect is shallow, and indifference and withdrawal are common accompaniments of severe states. Usually, the overall level of activity is reduced in acute confusional states. When left alone the patient does little and when asked to do things is slow, hesitant and often perseverative. In some cases, however, the reverse is seen with restless hyperactivity and noisy disturbed behaviour.

Such symptoms may be florid, but by and large are not easy to confuse with the symptoms of schizophrenia. However, the distinction is not always quite so easy. According to Lishman (1998), as well as the classical delirious visual hallucinations, auditory hallucinations may be seen, and also bizarre somatic sensations of body parts feeling shrunken, enlarged, misplaced or disconnected. Lishman also described clear-cut persecutory, grandiose, referential, or hypochondriacal delusions that welled up suddenly and were expressed with full conviction. Usually such beliefs betrayed their organic origin by being vague, shallow, poorly elaborated, transient and inconsistent. When consciousness was relatively clear, however, they could be coherent and systematised. Such beliefs have even been known to persist after recovery: Mayer-Gross *et al.* (1969) gave the example of a soldier who became delirious after being wounded in battle, during the course of which he formed the belief that he had received a decoration. He obstinately continued to cling to this belief even after all his other symptoms had cleared up.

Cutting (1980, 1987) carried out the only study to examine the phenomenology of delirium in detail and with particular reference to its relationship to the symptoms of schizophrenia. He administered the Present State Examination and Andreasen's scale for formal thought disorder to 74 patients who showed one or more psychotic symptoms that were secondary to some clearly identifiable organic cause. In 62 of the 74 (84 per cent) there was clinical evidence of clouding of consciousness, and most showed some evidence of cognitive impairment at times. Thirty-five of the 74 patients showed delusions. In eight, these were simple and similar to the 'organic' delusions described above in dementia. In 18, however, the beliefs were complex or bizarre; Cutting's examples are shown in Table 14.3. Nine patients also showed delusions that were congruent with an elated, depressed or mixed mood-state. Even so the beliefs showed qualities that set them apart from schizophrenia. Thus in half the deluded patients, the content of the beliefs revolved around imminent misadventure to others or bizarre happenings in the immediate vicinity, whereas such themes were only apparent in 6 out of a comparison group of 67 schizophrenic patients.

Visual hallucinations were present in 25 patients, and verbal auditory hallucinations were found in 9 (including third-person hallucinations in two cases). First rank symptoms were not seen, apart from possible passivity (thoughts controlled) in one case. Formal thought disorder was present in 33 of the 74 patients, who were rated on illogicality (15 patients), tangentiality (6 patients), circumstantiality (4 patients), distractibility (2 patients), pressure of speech (2 patients), word approximations (2 patients), incoherence (1 patient) and poverty of content of speech (1 patient). Here again, Cutting noted a difference from formal thought disorder as seen in schizophrenia: typical schizophrenic phenomena like derailment, neologisms and poverty of content of speech were uncommon, and the most commonly rated abnormality was illogicality, which was not seen in any of the comparison group of schizophrenic patients. Even the term 'illogicality' did not fully capture the quality of the abnormality, which always took the form of giving absurd answers to questions about orientation, and facile and inconsequential explanations for these (he suggested the term 'fantastic disorientation' instead). For example, one patient claimed that it must be the 20th of May because her sister had died then, without explaining why the date of her sister's death should determine today's date. Other patients gave answers to questions about orientation in place that included East Finchley airport (where there is no airport), waiting at a bus-stop, on a boat, in Wales (and then a minute later in London), and justified these with statements such as, 'Well, it looks a bit like an airport' or 'It's a boat because all my friends are here'.

Drawing the findings on schizophrenic symptoms in dementia and acute confusional states together, the conclusions that emerge seem to be as follows. First, both disorders are quite commonly accompanied by psychotic symptoms that are simple, isolated and carry a distinctive 'organic' stamp. Second, in some cases there can instead be a more florid syndrome where the psychotic symptoms are comparable in form and complexity to those seen in schizophrenia, and not infrequently occur in combination. Details of these latter states are sketchy, but it seems clear that any alleged differences – such as in the content of the delusions – are relative rather than absolute. Finally, it seems probable that there is no hard and fast dividing line between the two

Table 14.3 Complex, bizarre or multiple delusions in patients with acute confusional states

Case	Cause	Content of delusion
Female, age 70	Right parietal CVA	When people washed in sink they scrubbed her back; things shown to her became muddled up in pillow; carrot in windpipe
Female, age 69	Drugs	Thoughts controlled; something funny going on; she was dying; woman in next bed being harmed
Male, age 58	Cardiac failure	Irish Catholics from Streatham driving to Brixton and harming locals by transmitting decomposed matter into their and his own necks by affecting circulatory system parallel to bloodstream called 'man's money'
Male, age 76	Respiratory failure	Wife had left him
Male, age 59	Drugs	X-ray girls involved in sexual misdemeanours; wife outside curtain; something in head turning to dust
Female, age 40	Carcinoma	Mother, sister and herself dying; relatives in ward; nurses going to kill her
Female, age 76	Myxoedema	Relatives and herself had died; doctor on ward going to marry a beautiful person
Female, age 69	Electrolyte imbalance	Husband eaten by cannibal; drunken nurses obtaining money from patients by doing unspeakable things; she had VD
Female, age 48	Electrolyte imbalance	Fire in hospital; children coming to Casualty choking; husband and friend underneath bed, moving it; psychologist testing her
Male, age 68	Carcinoma	Unpleasant incidents on ward blamed on him; all the excrement in ward is his; hospital floating on water; daughter to be shot
Female, age 27	Alcohol	Doctor taking blood out of her and putting it back into her neck; brother out to kill her, her dog and old ladies
Male, age 81	Respiratory failure	People exporting illicit material, giving dummy drugs; he was substitute patient for someone else
Male, age 62	Cardiac failure	About to die; nurse moving things around in bags, possibly dynamite and involving IRA; doctors not real doctors
Male, age 27	Epilepsy	About to die; people changing things to test him; discrepancy between his thoughts and what he expected to think
Female, age 28	SLE	Something bad going to happen; mother dying
Male, age 63	Cardiac failure	Building bombarded; police all around

Continued overleaf

Table 14.3 Continued

Case	Cause	Content of delusion
Female, age 57	Drugs	Son down road taking drugs; men out to kill husband
Female, age 37	Carcinoma	Baby taken away; nurses met daily to decide who was worst patient on the ward

Source: Cutting (1987), The phenomenology of acute organic psychoses: Comparison with acute schizophrenia. *British Journal of Psychiatry*, 151, 324–332. Reproduced with permission from the Royal College of Psychiatrists.

types of presentation: some patients have one or two crude 'organic' delusions; others show delusions that are more schizophrenia-like but are still relatively isolated; others still develop a combination of delusions and hallucinations; and a few patients with dementia present with a florid paraphrenia-like picture whose organic basis may not declare itself for some time.

Encephalitis lethargica

Having established that schizophrenia or something very similar to it can complicate certain brain diseases, and reviewing the altogether more complicated relationship between psychotic symptoms and dementia and acute confusional states, the links with organic brain disease are not quite exhausted. There remain a number of brain diseases where the combined presentation of neurological and psychiatric symptoms is so routine that they are, in fact, generally referred to as neuropsychiatric disorders. These disorders include epilepsy, particularly temporal lobe epilepsy, which is associated with so many psychotic and non-psychotic forms of psychiatric disorder that it has been said, 'understand temporal lobe epilepsy and you understand psychiatry'; and Gilles de la Tourette's syndrome where there are many colourful behavioural symptoms beyond simply tics and vocalizations (Lees, 1985; Comings, 1991). There is, however, one disorder that has affiliations with schizophrenic symptoms above all others, and where the relationship is so close that it can almost be regarded as schizophrenia's organic next of kin; this is encephalitis lethargica.

Von Economo (1931) was, as he pointed out in the foreword to his book, the first author to describe encephalitis lethargica, giving an account of a small local epidemic of cases in Austria in 1917. Initially met with some scepticism, his claim to have discovered a new illness was soon verified by an outbreak that started in London a year later and spread through Europe over the next two years. As recounted by Sacks (1982) this pandemic went on to attack nearly five million people worldwide, killing a third of them and sooner or later disabling the majority of the rest before it disappeared as mysteriously as it appeared in 1927. Earlier epidemics were subsequently recognised to have occurred from the sixteenth century onwards, and cases continued to occur throughout the 1930s. Since then there have been no further outbreaks. However, sporadic cases still undoubtedly occur and it is uncertain whether the disorder can now be consigned to history.

The acute phase of encephalitis lethargica

According to von Economo, the vast majority of cases were ushered in by a short prodromal period of fever and sore throat, which could be slight. This subsided after a few days or occasionally a few weeks but was then replaced by a series of neurological (and psychiatric) symptoms, which though very diverse and haphazard, tended to be classifiable into one of three main forms.

The most common form was a *somnolent-ophthalmoplegic* presentation. This set in with a deceptively normal appearing sleepiness, which progressed to the patient falling asleep while sitting, standing, eating or even walking. This could resolve, or progress to more or less permanent sleep, from which the patient could only be roused with difficulty, or to coma. In the *hyperkinetic* form the prodromal malaise and fever gave way to general mental unrest and ceaseless motor activity, and then to chorea. The involuntary movements could be extremely severe, more severe than in any other form of chorea, with patients rolling about continuously, jerking themselves up, throwing themselves down and often requiring restraint. Typically, there would also be severe and treatment-resistant insomnia, or alternatively reversal of the sleep–wake cycle. The least common, *Parkinsonian* form (called the amyo-static-akinetic form by von Economo) began with the usual prodromal signs, which tended to be mild, after which a state of general weakness supervened: the patient would lie in bed with closed eyes but not really asleep, and a slowness and paucity of all movements and speech would become increasingly obvious. All the signs of Parkinsonism could be seen, but the akinesia could be marked in the presence of very little rigidity. The symptoms often showed marked diurnal variation and patients could become normal or even exhibit a little psychomotor excitement as the day wore on, only to revert to immobility the next morning.

The three basic forms could occur in any combination, shade into each other, or follow one another in successive phases. All the forms developed against a background of a much wider set of neurological signs. These included particularly ophthalmic signs: one or more of ptosis, ophthalmoplegia, absent pupillary responses, or nystagmus were 'almost regularly present'. Other signs seen included trismus, hiccuping, headache, other cranial nerve palsies, seizures, cerebellar signs, neuralgias and aphasias. Sensory disturbances, however, were uncommon. Such signs tended to be mild and fleeting, although not always so.

All three varieties of acute encephalitis lethargica were apt to be complicated by psychotic phenomena. The most striking group of symptoms were openly referred to by von Economo as catatonic: in the Parkinsonian form, patients were reported as showing blocking, psychological pillow, and persistence of postures sometimes amounting to full waxy flexibility; sometimes there was an apathy and failure to take nourishment that reminded him of catatonic stupor. In the hyperkinetic form, the motor unrest was sometimes expressed mainly or wholly as 'a general, curious restlessness of an anxious or hypomanic type, which may occasionally reach a state bordering on frenzy . . . the patient tosses about in bed, pushes the blankets back, pulls them up again, sits up, throws himself back again in a wild sort of haste, jumps out of bed, strikes out aimlessly, talks incoherently, clucks his tongue, and whistles' – surely a description of catatonic excitement.

Von Economo also described, in decreasing order of frequency, delirium, hypomania-like excitement, dream-like states and apathetic depression, which occasionally dominated the presentation throughout with neurological signs being subtle or absent. He did not recognise schizophrenia-like states, but later authors such as Hall (1924) and Wilson (1940) considered that euphoria, hypomania, depression, stupor, hallucinations, and paranoia could all be prominent features. As noted by Lishman (1998) the possibility that the whole course of encephalitis lethargica could be played out as a psychiatric disturbance is attested to by the fact that many patients admitted to mental hospitals with diagnoses of non-specific confusional, delusional or hallucinatory states later developed typical post-encephalitic symptoms. An example of such a case is shown in Box 14.3.

The chronic sequelae of encephalitis lethargica

If schizophrenic symptoms were not especially conspicuous in the acute phase of encephalitis lethargica, they certainly became so as part of the later manifestations of the disorder which, in the words of Sacks (1982), rolled in from the 1930s in a great sluggish torpid tide. These developed in the majority of those who survived, sometimes immediately and sometimes after a delay of years, and comprised Parkinsonism, oculogyric crises and psychiatric changes.

Parkinsonism

This constituted the most frequent and serious sequel. In general, the syndrome resembled idiopathic Parkinsonism both in its onset and its constellation of symptoms. However, it also showed differences, mainly in that it could progress to extremely severe states of immobility, with some patients making no movements at all for decades. Post-encephalitic Parkinsonism also differed from the idiopathic form of the disorder in another important respect, in that it was frequently complicated by repetitive motor phenomena. These took the form of masticatory movements, blepharospasm, torticollis, other dystonic and athetoid movements, and also tics of various kinds, including vocal tics.

Box 14.3 Acute encephalitis lethargica dominated by schizophrenic symptoms (from Sands, 1928)

FM, 30, white, married, and has two healthy children. Family history is negative except for the fact that one brother died from encephalitis at the age of 30, two years ago. Personal history is normal. Present illness dates back to February 1st, 1927, when the patient complained of general weakness and intense headache. From February 5th there was persistent insomnia. She commenced to act rather strangely, became suspicious and irritable, and complained that people were talking about her. On February 7th, she had a generalised convulsion and this was repeated on the following day. On February 11th she was admitted to hospital complaining of intense headache, restlessness and irritability, and of hearing all sorts of voices.

On examination the patient showed definite cervical rigidity and a moderate Kernig sign. Pupils were decidedly irregular and both reacted sluggishly. There was bilateral weakness of the external rectus muscles. There were active abdominal reflexes, generalised hyperreflexia, and bilateral spontaneous extensor toe phenomena. There was marked vasomotor instability. Her temperature was 99 °F, pulse 104 and respirations 24. Blood count showed a white cell count of 7800, 68 % polymorphs. Clear spinal fluid was obtained under three plus pressure and showed a trace of globulin, ten cells and no colloidal gold curve reduction. The blood and spinal fluid Wassermann were negative.

The patient remained in a more or less confused state and was very evasive and suspicious. She would not permit examination at times. She asked the nurse repeatedly if someone was going to kill her. She would not sleep nights. Her temperature remained at 99 °F, pulse varied between 88 and 100, and respirations between 16 and 24. She was finally discharged from the hospital on March 3rd, 1927. I saw her again on April 4th, 1927. She then showed decided masking of her face with diminution in her winking reflex. Her gait was decidedly of Parkinson type. There was impairment of voluntary associative movements. There was decided left internal rectus weakness. The pupils were equal, somewhat irregular in outline but very sluggish, both to light and accommodation. Mentally she admitted auditory hallucinations and persecutory delusions. She said: 'I hear ear phones telling me that everything is OK and my husband, my home and my children are well. I remember you in the hospital. Tell me the truth, didn't you try to kill me? You wanted to poison me, didn't you? I still hear peculiar voices in my ears. These voices guide me and tell me what to do. They are human voices. They advise me what to feed my children and what to do.'

In addition, it seems clear that post-encephalitic Parkinsonism was shot through with catatonic phenomena. Blocking and freezing were regularly seen, according to von Economo and other authors. Waxy flexibility, or something closely similar to it, was also described. There could also be a psychic torpor reminiscent of catatonia. The repetitive movements accompanying the Parkinsonism sometimes, perhaps characteristically, took complex and intricate forms. Von Economo described patients whose tics gradually evolved towards repetitions, iterations and stereotypies. In others, passive movements were repeated for a long time. Bellowing, echolalia and palilalia could also be seen. Psychological elements could associate themselves with the movements, leading the patients to perform often grotesque compulsive actions. One patient repeated the question 'when will I be well again?' over and over again for hours, always accompanied by identical compulsive movements.

Oculogyric crises

Nearly half the survivors of the 1918–1927 epidemic became subject to these complex forms of acute dystonic reaction. They could develop as an isolated phenomenon or in association with Parkinsonism; perhaps most typically they heralded the onset of post-encephalitic Parkinsonism, sometimes preceding its onset by years. The motor aspects were in themselves unexceptional: the attacks consist of abrupt onset of gaze deviation, usually upwards and often to one side, but occasionally downwards or sideways. This could be the only motor manifestation, but it was frequently accompanied by blepharospasm or blepharoclonus, and dystonic spasms of the neck, trunk or limbs – the classical presentation was of a patient with his or her head flung back and eyes staring upward.

Von Economo noted that in many patients undergoing oculogyric crises there was a peculiar state of consciousness, reminiscent of a fugue, and that other patients always experienced the same compulsive thoughts. Later accounts have made it clear that the dystonic muscle spasms were often only one component of what tended to be a complex neuropsychiatric disturbance. Affective changes, such as fear, autonomic arousal, malaise, restlessness and depression, were common (Jelliffe, 1929, 1932); one patient was so tormented by murderous and suicidal thoughts that he attempted to jump through a window. Complex ritualistic behaviour has been noted, as has echolalia, palilalia, mutism and many other speech disturbances (see Lishman, 1998; Owens, 1990). In some cases there were visual misperceptions or hallucinations (Sacks, 1982). Steck (1931) (cited by Ward, 1986) gave the clearest account of schizophrenic symptoms: 'A young man with severe parkinsonism . . . had oculogyric crises during which he said he was controlled by . . . evil spirits . . . which spoke ill of God and Jesus Christ, saying, for example, that He was a German. . . . He said that the voices were "on me, in me, in my body, in my mouth".'

Psychiatric disorders

Personality changes were widely recognised to follow encephalitis lethargica (von Economo, 1931; Lishman, 1998). These often took the form of disinhibition and antisocial behaviour. Children, in particular, often underwent a marked change, becoming wilful, disobedient, lying, stealing, and showing gross swings of mood; sometimes they became so disturbed, violent and destructive, particularly at night, that they had to be kept in caged cots (Ward, 1986). Although felt to be rare by von Economo, depression and mania subsequently came to be considered to be relatively common (Lishman, 1998).

Davison and Bagley (1969) reviewed the evidence that schizophrenia occurred at a higher than chance frequency. They noted that reports abounded of schizophrenia developing before, simultaneously with or after the onset of post-encephalitic Parkinsonism, in marked contrast to the idiopathic and arteriosclerotic forms of the disorder. A number of studies of post-encephalitic patients found rates for schizophrenia in the range of 10–30 per cent. However, these were undoubtedly overestimates of the true rate as they all consisted of patients who were preselected on the basis of showing psychiatric disorder. Even so, Davison and Bagley felt that schizophrenia should probably be considered as one of the sequelae of encephalitis lethargica, a view that was later endorsed by Sacks (1982).

An extraordinary postscript was added to the history of encephalitis lethargica by Sacks (1983). In 1969, he began treating a group of patients with severe post-encephalitic Parkinsonism with the then experimental and restricted drug, L-DOPA. The dramatic improvements this treatment produced have been documented in his book *Awakenings*, and subsequently in several documentaries, a play and a Hollywood film. Tragically, this improvement was cut short in the vast majority of cases by the appearance of drastic side-effects. While the most disabling of these took the form of involuntary movements and oculogyric crises, once again psychiatric and psychotic symptoms formed an integral part of the clinical picture. Many of the patients developed catatonic phenomena up to and including excitement, as well as florid delusions and hallucinations. In some of the cases at least the episodes took place in apparently clear consciousness.

Conclusion

The over-representation of schizophrenia in a variety of brain diseases, often cited as evidence of its biological aetiology, seems to be vindicated, but with a few surprises and complexities along the way. The main surprise is that the association is not uniform; some central nervous system disorders, such as head injury and epilepsy, confer an increased risk of schizophrenia; others, it seems, particularly multiple sclerosis, do not. Sometimes the pattern of association seems to make sense – it is logical for Parkinson's disease not to be associated with schizophrenia, if the latter disorder involves a functional dopamine excess. But at other times it does not – both head injury and disseminated sclerosis produce widespread and variable brain damage, but one seems clearly to confer an increased risk of schizophrenia and the other seems equally clearly not to.

The statement that schizophrenia is associated with organic brain disease also turns out to be something of a phenemonological oversimplication. The concept of symptomatic schizophrenia holds up well enough so far as its relationship to a variety of discrete central nervous system disorders is concerned. The simple idea of clinical association, however, starts to show signs of strain when the generalised brain disorders of dementia and delirium are brought into consideration. Seen here are a complicated range of psychotic symptoms, from isolated, crude organic delusions and hallucinations, to (in dementia at least) something that is indistinguishable from a full schizophrenic syndrome – and probably everything in between as well. When it comes to a neuropsychiatric disorder like encephalitis lethargica even this does not do justice to the clinical facts. Different areas of schizophrenic psychopathology enter the clinical picture – sometimes expressed in a very distorted fashion – in a way that seems to ignore any rules. At this point, 'organic' and 'functional' perhaps become outmoded terms.

15 Childhood schizophrenia, autism and Asperger's syndrome

Until recently, childhood schizophrenia was barely acknowledged as a legitimate topic of psychiatric interest. It tended to arouse defensiveness in child psychiatrists, and adult psychiatrists could be relied on to be vague about whether schizophrenia could have an onset before early adult life. The subject was (and still is) scarcely alluded to in either child or adult psychiatry textbooks, and the research literature was exceedingly small – not too long ago a leading journal in the field felt the need to change its name from the *Journal of Autism and Childhood Schizophrenia* to the *Journal of Autism and Developmental Disorders*.

The reasons for this unmentionability are not hard to find. In the first half of the twentieth century, the term 'childhood schizophrenia' was used, as Rutter (1972) put it, to cover an astonishingly heterogeneous mixture of disorders that had little in common other than their severity, chronicity and occurrence in childhood. Then, in 1943, Kanner described a new syndrome, which he first referred to as autistic disturbances of affective contact, then as early infantile autism, and finally simply as autism. A year later, working completely independently of Kanner, Asperger (1944) described another disorder with similar, though generally milder features, and gave it an uncannily similar name, autistic psychopathy of childhood. Almost overnight (or more accurately after a lag of several years), it was realised the many children who had previously been called schizophrenic were in fact suffering from one of these quite different forms of disorder.

The concept of autism has gone from strength to strength, and that of Asperger's syndrome has also belatedly begun to flourish. Meanwhile, interest in childhood schizophrenia languished. In the last 10 years research has revived, but even now, the relationship of schizophrenia, whatever its age of onset, to autism and Asperger's syndrome is not at all clear: while adult psychiatrists may be impressed by certain points of resemblance, their child psychiatric colleagues, having previously been guilty of much phenomenological lack of precision, have become entrenched in the view that the disorders are completely different. The aims of this chapter are therefore first, to attempt to establish the truth about whether schizophrenia can develop in childhood, and second, to try to settle some of the questions about the relationship – if any – of schizophrenia to autism and Asperger's syndrome.

Schizophrenia in childhood

The first claim that something recognisable as schizophrenia could begin in childhood was made by de Sanctis, who called the disorder 'dementia praecosissima'. In a series of case reports between 1906 and 1909 (cited by Lay, 1938) he described a number of young children, who, following a period of normal or relatively normal development (one showed some delay), underwent a marked change. The onset of this change could be abrupt or insidious. Catatonic symptoms, including mannerisms, stereotypies, posturing, echolalia and negativism were the outstanding features, accompanied by emotional blunting and other features such as outbursts of anger. Some cases recovered, but most progressed to a state of deterioration. Having observed similar cases himself, Kraepelin (1913a) was inclined to accept that they belonged with schizophrenia, stating that 'the clinical agreement of some morbid states, which develop in the first or at the beginning of the second decade, with the dementia praecox of adults, in phenomena, course and issue is so apparent, that there can be no reasonable doubt about the relationship'.

With Kraepelin's endorsement, childhood schizophrenia became firmly lodged in psychiatric thinking. The concept quickly became overinclusive, with children showing obvious dissimilarities in symptoms and age of onset being lumped together. A few authors, however, continued to adhere to a relatively narrow definition of childhood schizophrenia that required the presence of symptoms similar to those seen in the adult form of the disorder. By far the most phenomenologically minded of these were Potter (1933) and Despert (1968), who described a series of children admitted to a New York hospital in the 1930s. These children all presented with severe symptoms that began after a period of normal or relatively normal early development. The following account is synthesised from their detailed descriptions. One of their case histories is also reproduced in Box 15.1.

Box 15.1 Schizophrenia in childhood (from Potter, 1933; Despert, 1968)

The patient was the eldest of four children. A maternal cousin developed a puerperal psychosis which led to life commitment. Before her marriage the patient's mother suffered from depression.

The patient was born after a prolonged labour but there were no indications of intracranial damage. He was a well nourished infant who walked and talked at the usual ages. He suffered no serious illnesses. He was restless, fretful and and cried a great deal as a baby. At the age of three it was noted that, although he spoke freely, his 'thoughts were not related'. He never appeared to be of a sunny, happy, cheerful disposition but was always a morose irritable child who put on temper tantrums, usually with head banging. He rarely, if ever, displayed the usual amount of affection for his parents. He tended to be indifferent to his brothers and sister, except to one brother who was six years his junior, for whom he showed some affection. His whole life was marked by a generalised indifference. From early childhood he would have periods of marked sullenness and obstinacy.

He started school and made regular progress until about the age of nine when he began to lose all interest in school work and seemed absorbed in his own thoughts. At about the same time his sullenness and irritability increased. At times his talk became so incoherent that it was not possible to understand him. He would have outbursts of anger, laughter and grimacing. At times he would refuse to eat. He began claiming that things were crawling on his body and that other children made fun of him. He called his mother vile names, would stand for hours before the mirror, stayed in the bathroom for prolonged periods, sat by himself in the dark, and sometimes disappeared from home to be found at a nearby movie. In the two months prior to admission his symptoms increased: he was very antagonistic to his mother, was exceedingly irritable, threatened suicide, and masturbated frequently.

He was hospitalised at the age of 11. During the first 12 months of his stay, he spent the major part of the time gazing fixedly out of the window with a perplexed frown on his face, and at times could be found under the bed or crouched in a corner behind a piece of furniture. At times he would become quite excited and attack the other children. His speech was voluble at times but irrelevant, disconnected and full of neologisms. His replies to most questions were a stereotyped, colourless 'I don't know'. There was no outstanding mood deviation and his affect was characterised by a combination of disinterest, detachment and perplexity. He sometimes laughed long and loudly for no reason. He showed somatic delusions, making statements like, 'Do you see the bone,' (indicating left shoulder) 'I slept on it and now my bowels moved out through it', 'I never breathe', 'I have red pulse sores', and 'the inside of my skin is bitten'. He spontaneously referred to voices at times but one could not learn their content.

After approximately a year, he began to show improvement, becoming interested in occupational therapy, and then in people around him, especially the nurses. He became more communicative and went to a summer camp where he made a reasonably good adjustment in a negative, colourless fashion. He returned home and re-entered school where he made mediocre progress. He had to be re-admitted a year later, after which time he went downhill rapidly. When followed up at the age of 18, he showed obvious deterioration and was chronically hospitalised in a state institution.

The age of onset in their cases ranged from around 3 years to over 10 years. Prior to becoming ill the children appeared normal or at least reasonably well adjusted, but in some cases there was a tendency to daydreaming, poor socialisation, or minor abnormalities in language development. The disorder could either begin acutely, occasionally over a matter of days, or insidiously over months or as long as two years; in a few instances the onset was so gradual that the beginning was impossible to date. In a small number of cases there had been what in retrospect were clear previous episodes that had improved spontaneously after a few weeks or months.

Acute onset cases were commonly preceded by a short prodromal period characterised, for example, by inability to concentrate, a fall-off in school performance, or vague physical complaints. In the group of insidious onset cases, the earliest signs were withdrawal, quietness and a progressive loss of interest in activities such as play; or alternatively brooding, sullenness, or hatred towards a parent. These features subsequently gave way to a psychotic state whose features tended to be different in children of different ages.

Cases beginning before the age of 7 tended to present principally with disturbances of behaviour and speech. Examples included staring into space, wandering aimlessly, masturbating continuously, hoarding, spending hours staring into mirrors, crouching under the bed or peering into empty windows and doorways. Many children were violent or destructive, and some tried to harm themselves: one patient repeatedly beat himself on the head, another tried to choke himself. Catatonic phenomena were also evident: examples noted by Potter and Despert included facial grimacing, posturing, marked underactivity, freezing, waxy flexibility, stiff gaits, mutism, playing with fingers, picking up bits of paper and arranging them in rows, walking taking one step forward and two back, closing drawers, and saying the word 'park' over and over again. In a few cases, simple motor phenomena in the form of blinking and choreiform movements were also seen. Speech sometimes became inarticulate or unintelligible, or took the form of an uninterrupted flow of disconnected utterances, with answers to questions being totally irrelevant; neologisms could also be observed. One child, who was observed running hot water onto a cut-out picture of a cake said, 'to make it hurt, so I should throw it away, so I couldn't make it real, so I couldn't make it a picture. I wouldn't do that to a hungry picture.'

In this age group, full fledged delusions were not usually present, but abnormal ideas were certainly alluded to: one child spoke of herself as the girl princess, another seemed to believe that she was an adult and had magical powers. Hallucinations were more clearly evident. One girl stated that she saw 'water balls with keys for eyes' and heard people in magazines 'talking sassy' to her. Another stopped in the midst of activity and addressed fairies. Affect was invariably abnormal, with perplexity, flattening, inappropriateness, or causeless laughing.

Cases beginning from the age of 7 onwards tended to be characterised by delusions and auditory hallucinations. There could also be disturbed behaviour, but as a rule catatonic phenomena were not prominent. At the younger end of this age group, the delusions had a naive quality. Children identified themselves with animals: one patient believed himself at different times to be a rhinoceros, a dog and a woodpecker; others felt they were frightening characters from films, cartoons or fairy tales. After the age of 10 or 11, the delusions became similar to those of adults except that they tended to be simpler and to show a lack of systematisation. Several patients first presented with complaints that other children were talking about them. One boy believed he was a philosopher and a genius. A girl gradually came to believe that a 'rip breast team' of 68 men were spying on her and planned to mutilate her. Auditory hallucinations also took familiar forms in this age group: hearing the voices of children or imagined persecutors talking about the patients, or their parents accusing them of horrible deeds. Visual hallucinations were also described, such as seeing spooks, and things crawling on the body. Formal thought disorder, sometimes with neologisms, and inappropriate affect were commonly noted, as were withdrawal and states of dreamy abstraction.

As in the adult form of the disorder, acute episodes often improved but left behind greater or lesser degrees of impairment. Further attacks could follow, leading to increasing degrees of deterioration. Occasionally there was no real improvement and permanent hospitalisation became necessary.

Potter and Klein (1937) carried out a 5-year follow-up of 14 of their children. They found that only one had made a reasonable social adjustment and the rest had become progressively worse. Thirty years later Bennett and Klein (1966) followed up 10 of them in adult life (four had died). One patient was living outside hospital; he worked as a dishwasher, was socially isolated, and showed emotional flattening and impoverishment of thought. Two patients were in hospital but showed no evidence of deterioration beyond that noted in the early stages of their illness. One of these was described as shy and anxious but followed an active (and consistently successful) pursuit of betting on horses. The other showed intact self-care, but was laconic and extremely passive. The remaining seven patients were all on long-stay wards, where they did not stand out in any way from their fellow patients with adult-onset schizophrenia.

Potter and Despert's findings have been on the whole confirmed in the small number of contemporary studies that have been carried out. Kolvin *et al.* (1971) examined 33 children in the age range of 5 to 15 with a diagnosis of schizophrenia based on the presence of first rank symptoms. Of these, 19 (57 per cent) showed delusions; 27 (81 per cent) showed auditory hallucinations; 10 (30 per cent) and 9 (27 per cent) showed visual or somatic hallucinations, respectively; 20 (61 per cent) showed at least one element of formal thought disorder. Flattening and incongruity of affect were described in many cases. Nearly all the sample showed one or more catatonic phenomena: mannerisms were most common, and grimacing, ambitendence and abnormal jerkiness of movement were also frequent. In two similar studies, Green *et al.*

(1984) and Russell *et al.* (1989) examined groups of 24 and 35 children who met DSM III criteria for schizophrenia. Their ages of onset ranged from 3 to 11 and 5 to 13 respectively. Delusions, auditory hallucinations and formal thought disorder were present in the majority of cases, regardless of age. In Russell *et al.*'s series, first rank symptoms were also commonly noted: between a quarter and a third showed third person auditory hallucinations, 11 per cent had thought insertion, 6 per cent showed passivity and 6 per cent thought broadcasting. Catatonic phenomena were recorded in a quarter of Green *et al.*'s patients, but were not commented on by Russell *et al.*

Eggers (1978) carried out a follow-up study on 57 children who had been diagnosed as schizophrenic on average 15 years (6–40 years) earlier. He excluded cases with an onset of symptoms before the age of 5, and required the presence of clear schizophrenic symptoms as found in 'conservatively diagnosed adult schizophrenia'. Rather differently to Potter and Despert, he found that 15 of the 57 (26.3 per cent) were in good or excellent remission, sometimes after multiple episodes of illness; however, in at least 4 of these patients there were personality changes which were 'so slight that they can hardly be called defects'. In the remainder there was deterioration which was mild in 9 cases (15.8 per cent) and severe in 33 (57.9 per cent). Poor outcome was frequent when there had been an age of onset before age 10, but was not obviously associated with any particular clinical features. Three patients committed suicide.

Altogether, it is reasonable to conclude, as Rutter (1972) did, that a disorder bearing an unmistakeable resemblance to adult schizophrenia in clinical picture, course and outcome can begin in childhood. Although reliable incidence and prevalence figures are not available, it is clear that presentation in the pre-adolescent period is uncommon or rare, and becomes rarer still in young children.

Aetiological factors in childhood schizophrenia

For a long time, only the sketchiest information was available on the hereditary and other aetiological factors cited in connection with the adult form of the disorder. This has now been remedied, due principally to the ongoing studies of Rapoport and her colleagues (e.g. see Jacobsen and Rapoport, 1998) on a series of cases collected from all over America that now stands at around 75 in number.

Sex ratio

Among Despert's (1968) series of cases, there were eight boys and one girl who were aged 7 or less on admission, and 15 boys and 5 girls whose first admission was between 7 and 13 years of age. An excess of male cases has been found in all subsequent series (e.g. Green *et al.*, 1984; Russell *et al.*, 1989; Spencer and Campbell, 1994; Hollis, 1995; Asarnow *et al.*, 2001), except in the study by Eggers (1978). In most of these studies the ratio has clustered around 2:1. In the large sample of Rapoport and co-workers it is currently 1.5:1 (Sporn *et al.*, 2003).

Hereditary predisposition

In an early study, Kallman and Roth (1956) collected a sample of 102 children with a diagnosis of schizophrenia, 52 of whom were members of a twin pair. The diagnosis was made by one of the investigators and relied heavily on diminished interest in the environment, blunted or distorted affect, peculiar motor behaviour, hallucinations, and bizarre thinking with a tendency towards exaggerated fantasies. Among the 17 monozygotic twins, 12 (71 per cent) of the co-twins were also diagnosed as schizophrenic before adolescence, with a further 2 (12 per cent) acquiring the diagnosis in adulthood. Eight (23 per cent) co-twins of 35 dizygotic twins were diagnosed as schizophrenic. Kallman and Roth also found a 9–14 per cent rate of schizophrenia among the first-degree relatives of the patients.

Two contemporary studies using diagnostic criteria have had contradictory findings. Asarnow *et al.* (2001) examined 102 first-degree relatives of 51 children who met DSM-III-R criteria for schizophrenia, and who had a first onset of illness before the age of 13. Children who had an IQ of less than 70 or showed evidence of central nervous system disease (including temporal lobe epilepsy) were excluded. There were five cases of schizophrenia (4.9 per cent) and one of schizoaffective psychosis (1.0 per cent) among the parents. There were no cases of schizophrenia or schizoaffective disorder among the siblings of the childhood schizophrenic patients, but as the authors pointed out the vast majority of these had not entered the typical age of risk for schizophrenia. In contrast, Nicholson *et al.* (2003) interviewed 97 parents of 54 patients with childhood-onset schizophrenia in the cohort collected by Rapoport and co-workers. In this study only 1 of the 97 patients was given a DSM IV diagnosis of schizophrenia and none had schizoaffective psychosis or other non-affective psychosis.

Premorbid personality

It is of course hazardous to try to decide what personality traits are present or absent in children, particularly young children. Even so, Potter and Despert noted that various oddities had been recorded by the parents of their schizophrenic children. These included shyness, unsociability, being a loner, living in a world of their own, being an avid reader with interests in archaeology and astrology – traits clearly suspicious of a schizoid personality type. Other children were described as morose, irritable, aggressive, hyperactive, fearful, or showing indifference and lack of affection. Several studies since then have confirmed a high prevalence of similar traits. Kolvin *et al.* (1971) found that 29 (87 per cent) of their 33 children with an onset of psychosis after 5 years of age had been reported as being odd by their parents, or had been noted to show unusual features at medical or psychiatric clinics they attended before overt schizophrenic symptoms developed. The most frequent traits were shyness, withdrawal, timidity and sensitivity, found in just over half the group.

Structural brain abnormality

All the findings here are from Rapoport and her co-workers. Kumra *et al.* (2000) measured brain volume using MRI in 44 children meeting DSM-III-R or DSM IV criteria for schizophrenia and 64 normal controls matched for age, sex, height and handedness. Lateral ventricular volume was significantly increased in the patients, and at 56.1 per cent the magnitude of the increase was double that found in adult patients (see Chapter 5). The schizophrenic patients also showed a significantly smaller cerebral volume, with a mean reduction of 4.2 per cent, once again larger than in adult patients. There were no differences in anterior frontal lobe, temporal lobe, hippocampal or amygdala volumes between the groups after total brain volume was adjusted for.

Rapoport's group has also found evidence that the brain changes in childhood-onset schizophrenia, in contrast to those in adult-onset schizophrenia, are progressive. Thirty-nine of their childhood-onset schizophrenic patients and 43 matched normal controls underwent repeated scanning at approximately 2-year intervals for up to 6 years (Sporn *et al.*, 2003). Both groups showed increases in lateral ventricular volume over time (2–4 years in most cases), but these were significantly greater in the patients (10.8 per cent vs 3.2 per cent). Both groups also showed decreases in cortical grey matter volume, and these were also greater in the patients (−5.2 per cent vs −2.2 per cent).

Treatment of schizophrenia in childhood

Despite occasional statements to the contrary, the views of most early authors were exemplified by Kolvin (1972), who stated that neuroleptic drugs often led to the rapid disappearance of florid symptoms, and might even arrest the progression of the illness. Spencer and Campbell (1994) later reviewed their own and five other trials of neuroleptic drugs, two of which were placebo controlled studies and the rest of which had open or retrospective designs. These all supported the effectiveness of these drugs.

There has also been one controlled trial of clozapine. Kumra *et al.* (1996) randomly assigned 21 children meeting DSM-III-R criteria for schizophrenia who were non-responsive to typical neuroleptics to treatment with either clozapine up to 525 mg/day or haloperidol up to 27 mg/day. Despite the small numbers, at the end of the six-week study period, clozapine resulted in significantly more global improvement and significantly greater reduction in symptom scores.

Schizophrenia in infancy?

In 1908, Heller (see Hulse, 1954) described a series of children between the ages of 3 and 4 who, after a period of normal development, began to show signs of personality change, then lost their speech, and ultimately deteriorated to a state of extreme regression. He called this disorder 'dementia infantilism'. Subsequently it has become known as disintegrative psychosis or Heller's syndrome.

According to Heller, the illness most commonly began with changes in mood and character. Having been previously lively or placid, the children became moody, negativistic, disobedient, whining and prone to attacks of rage and destructiveness. In many cases anxiety symptoms were a prominent symptom, and these sometimes had 'a hallucinatory character' – the only allusion to anything approaching psychotic symptoms in Heller's account. Over a period of around nine months, the children then underwent a catastrophic mental decline. Speech became progressively impoverished, words were distorted, sentences could no longer be repeated, and finally language was lost altogether. The capacity to understand speech was also lost except for some primitive remnants. At the same time, motor abnormalities frequently appeared: the children developed tic-like movements, grimaced, or posed in peculiar positions.

From then on, the children remained in a state of complete idiocy, which, however, was stationary. Many were incontinent and required to be fed, but with intensive nursing some could be trained to eat and keep themselves clean. Notable features of the state were a severe motor restlessness accompanied by stereotypies and tic-like movements, and also the retention of an intelligent facial expression, a clear-eyed look, and a deceptive attentiveness to the environment.

By 1930 Heller had collected 28 such cases in whom physical diseases – including especially encephalitis lethargica – had allegedly been carefully excluded. Other authors described similar cases and added their own observations, for example that motor function was preserved and that there was an absence of focal neurological signs. Even after speech was lost, it was noted that the ability to sing or hum melodies could be retained. Some of the children were followed up after several years, and occasionally into adult life. They continued to show restlessness, rocking, tics and stereotypies, but none seemed to undergo further deterioration or die from the disorder. A typical example of such a patient is shown in Box 15.2.

Almost immediately thereafter, however, the status of the disorder became controversial. The conflict was ushered in by Corberi (cited by Lay, 1938) who found evidence of degenerative brain changes resembling those seen in lipid storage diseases in brain biopsies carried out on three affected children, two of whom were siblings. Subsequently, other authors described cases that at post-mortem revealed evidence of one or another form of organic neuropathology. In one of the most widely quoted studies of this type, Malamud

Box 15.2 Schizophrenia in infancy? A case of Heller's syndrome (from Lay, 1938)

The patient was an only child. Pregnancy and birth were normal. He was a healthy baby, who sat up at nine months, and began to talk at about 12 months of age. Although heavy he could walk at 15 months. He was difficult to wean on to solid foods; later he was 'finicky' and disliked meat, and on the whole was a fretful child. Thumb-sucking was noticed. Toilet training was achieved early, but there was a temporary relapse at the age of about 18 months. In early life there were no illnesses of importance, and none on which a suspicion of encephalitis might rest.

At the age of three he was taken to see a film, during which he was terrified by the accompanying animal noises, and for some time afterwards repeated the phrase 'noises of animals' as if he were remembering them. He also disliked dogs; after seeing a dog at a friend's house, he woke up from sleep in a great fear, screaming that there were dogs on the ceiling. He never played much with other children, partly as a result of parental regime.

The patient was first seen psychiatrically at the age of 4½ years because of inability to talk. At the age of four he had had an illness in which he was delirious for one night and spent two days in bed. After this there occurred fits of temper, in which he screamed and threw himself on the ground, and also delusions that this mother was cutting him. About this time he was said to have acquired quite a large vocabulary, but deterioration had occurred in his speech. At the time of coming to hospital he used only single words, and then only if he could not make his wants attended to by other means. Physically he was normal, but his gait was a little uncertain.

At the age of six, he talked in an unintelligible way, uttered cries at intervals, fell on the floor and did not get up for several minutes. He laughed occasionally for no apparent reason. His attacks of violent screaming and crying continued. At home, he took knives from the table and thrust them into the jam dish. He stood in front of a visiting social worker making curious stiff clutching movements with his raised arms, and giving high squeaking cries; he also tried to cram paper into her mouth. Usually he slept well in a bed to himself in the parents' room. About fortnightly, however, there would be nights of frequent screaming.

Between the ages of six and seven, he was described as a tall well-built boy, who entered the consulting-room reluctantly. He played quietly at first, but later cried loudly. He behaved very much as a child of 18 months, turning the pages of a book quickly, and speaking only odd words. His glance was restless, his movements uncontrolled, and constant except when interested. Occasionally he would follow one occupation for as long as 35 minutes. He hummed to himself and rocked to and fro when only partly occupied, and jumped and shouted from time to time. Often he would stare into the fire, humming and repeating short rhymes, and singing a few words from popular songs. His curiosity was marked and easily stimulated.

Seen again at the age of eight he was well grown and healthy, giving the impression that his real age was 11. In the playroom he was neat with his fingers. He turned over the pages of a book without looking at them; later he tore the book and, when prevented from doing this, took to biting plasticine and spitting bits from his mouth. There were frequent screams which stopped when he was ignored.

The patient was seen again by a social worker at the age of 12. On the whole he was reported to be unchanged. It was noticed that he made no response to anything that was said. He once put his face close to the social worker's and laughed in an inane way. His mother said that he was prone to periods of violence, but was in general somewhat easier to manage.

(1959) described post-mortem findings in four patients whose diagnosis in life was dementia infantilis; two of these were brother and sister and the other two had affected siblings. Two were found to have been suffering from a neurolipidosis (amaurotic family idiocy) and the two related patients both showed marked but unclassifiable subcortical degenerative disease. In this study, however, the presentation was not typical of Heller's syndrome, starting at a later age, being accompanied by obvious neurological signs, and showing a continuously progressive course.

The view that all cases of disintegrative psychosis are due to misdiagnosed neurological disease is, however, difficult to sustain. Darby (1976) reviewed 17 cases conforming clinically to Heller's syndrome in which biopsy or necropsy findings were available. Some showed obvious pathologies suggesting neurolipidoses, Pick's disease, metachromatic leucodystrophy, tuberose sclerosis or other, often undiagnosable neurological disease. Four showed only gliosis or other non-specific changes. In another four there were no significant findings. Evans-Jones and Rosenbloom (1978) described 10 living patients at least 9 of whom showed the typical features of syndrome (one could possibly have had regressive autism – see below). All neurological investigations were normal apart from the finding of marked EEG abnormalities in three cases. They considered that the consistency of the clinical features in their cases suggested that they represented a homogeneous clinical grouping.

By 1930 Heller had decided that dementia infantilis and schizophrenia were entirely different disorders. There is, however, an argument that some cases of the disorder (i.e. those where there is no organic pathology) are a consequence of the same disease process that gives rise to schizophrenia when it presents in later childhood and adult life. This argument rests on the presence of catatonic phenomena and the development of a distinctive form of deterioration that is not progressive and not accompanied by neurological signs. The loss of speech is not typical of schizophrenia, but a developmental explanation could conceivably be invoked to account for this. Less easy to deal with is the absence of episodicity and lack of variability in outcome, both of which are features of childhood as well as adult schizophrenia. On balance the similarities are intriguing and the differences can just about be explained away, but a definitive answer is impossible.

Autism

Out of the nosological morass of what at that time constituted early child-hood psychosis, Kanner (1943) extracted and brilliantly described a new and distinctive syndrome. He gave a detailed account of 11 children whose common characteristic was what he termed 'extreme autistic aloneness', an inability to relate to people and situations. This could be seen at as early as four months of age when the children failed to assume the normal anticipa-tory posture preparatory to being picked up. Later, the parents described them using terms like 'self-sufficient', 'in a shell', 'acting as if people weren't there' and 'perfectly oblivious to everything about him'. Other features Kanner noted (Kanner, 1943; Kanner and Eisenberg, 1956) included an obsessive desire for the preservation of sameness, as manifested by monotonously repetitive activities and distress on changes in routine; a fascination with objects which were handled with dexterity; mutism or abnormal language with echolalia, pronoun reversal and several other characteristics; and finally an intelligent physiognomy with latent cognitive potential being manifested in unusual feats of memory or skill.

All Kanner's observations went on to be incorporated into the modern concept of autism with very little modification. Modern diagnostic approaches emphasise the presence of three core features: (1) absent or severely impaired two-way social interaction; (2) qualitative impairment of verbal and non-verbal communiciation; and (3) a markedly restricted repertoire of activities and interests with behaviour that is dominated by repetitive, stereotyped rou-tines. The following summary of these and other features of the syndrome is taken from the accounts of Wing (Wing 1980; Wing and Attwood, 1987) and Frith (2003).

The abnormal social interactions in autism are now recognised to take multiple forms. Children with the classical *aloof* form reject physical and social contact, become distressed when in close proximity to others, especially other children, and lack most or all of the normal attachment behaviours displayed by young children, such as following their parents, running to greet them, and seeking comfort from them when in pain. Other children show the *passive* form of the disorder: they do not make spontaneous social approaches, except to obtain needs, but accept the approaches of others with-out protest and even with some appearance of enjoyment. The *active-but-odd* subgroup do make spontaneous approaches to others but these are peculiar and even embarrassing in their one-sidedness and persistence. In all types non-verbal communication in the form of eye contact, bodily movements and gestures is absent or obviously abnormal. Pretend play is not seen.

Half of all autistic children are mute, or nearly so. In most of the remainder speech is abnormal: there may be echolalia, or a peculiar variant of this in which words, phrases or whole texts (e.g. of television adverts) are reproduced verbatim, sometimes in the original intonation. Reversal of pronouns, and stereotyped and idiosyncratic use of words and phrases are particularly characteristic. Sometimes speech is – or becomes – grammatically correct but is still noticeably odd, pedantic or stilted. Literalness, concreteness, and an inability to handle nuances of language are ubiquitous. Even when relatively normal in form, speech is not used as a means of social interaction or to exchange knowledge, but rather as a vehicle for the patient to obtain his or her wants or describe his or her circumscribed interests.

The restricted repertoire of activities and repetitive routines of autism – Kanner's 'insistence on sameness' – encompasses on the one hand, a range of stereotyped behaviours. Some of these are simple and self-directed: rocking, eye-poking, flicking fingers, flapping hands, and twirling around. Others involve objects, such as flicking pieces of string, tapping or shaking objects, turning wheels of toy cars, or dextrously spinning toys and other objects. Equally characteristic are more elaborate routines, which the child insists on following: making repetitive patterns from leaves, stones, kitchen utensils, and so on; insisting on taking particular routes around the house or on walks, making everyone in a room sit with their right leg crossed over their left, demanding to have certain foods presented in certain ways, or that they be eaten in a ritualistic fashion; showing a fascination with and collecting objects like empty detergent packets, tin lids, shoes, umbrella handles and all manner of peculiar and useless things. On the other hand are single-minded interests, in having a bath, in rooms with yellow curtains, or in books, but only those with red covers. In the most able children these may blur into academic interests in esoteric subjects, large numbers of facts about which are learnt by rote with little regard for their significance.

Other symptoms are not seen in all cases and include abnormal responsiveness to sensory stimuli – the child may ignore some sounds (often he or she first comes to medical attention because of the suspicion of deafness), while being distressed or delighted by others. There may be fascination with bright lights, shiny objects, particular textures, or the smells and tastes of things. Gait is often abnormal, with walking on tip-toe, lack of arm swing, or other oddities. Some movements are clumsy while others are graceful and finely executed. Around 70–90 per cent of autistic children show some degree of mental handicap and only 10 per cent are of average or above average intelligence (Gillberg and Coleman, 1992). Despite this, many autistic children show the phenomenon of savantism: often against a background of low IQ, particular abilities, mathematical, musical or artistic, stand out as normal or even exceptional by any standards.

Autism was originally considered by Kanner to be present from birth, but he later accepted that the typical patterns of behaviour could begin after up to 20 months of apparently normal development (Kanner and Eisenberg, 1956). Later authors have documented ages of onset of up to 3 years, and occasionally later, sometimes following viral infection or other cerebral insults – so-called regressive autism (Wing and Attwood, 1987; Frith, 2003). There is a well-accepted excess of cases among boys, of the order of 2–3 : 1.

The essential point about the course of autism is that it follows a developmental trajectory. As Frith (2003) put it, while they remain discernibly different as adults and their intellectual attainments never catch up, autistic children are perhaps no more like autistic adults than normal children are like normal adults. They tend to speak more as they grow older, have better contact with people, and become more disciplined in behaviour. They acquire intellectual skills like reading and writing, and even some social skills. Some autistic adults have a large vocabulary, but speech is not used as a means of social interaction, only as a vehicle to obtain their wants or describe their specific interests. But almost all autistic adults remain obviously handicapped, completely naive, and show obvious peculiarities in speech and behaviour. A few are able to work, but many more live uncomplicated lives at home, doing odd jobs and helping out their parents in small ways. A substantial proportion end up in sheltered accommodation or institutional care.

Is there a relationship between autism and schizophrenia?

It is clear from the above description that autism and schizophrenia are quite different conditions. But it is also apparent that their clinical pictures sometimes strike similar chords. These points of apparent resemblance have not been widely discussed in the literature, and when they have, the debate has not been sober. In what seems to be a reaction against the position before Kanner, where all severe, chronic disorders of childhood were lumped together, the differences between the two disorders are emphasised whereas any similarities are glossed over or dismissed out of hand. Sometimes it almost seems as if authors have gone out of their way to avoid describing phenomena in autism in the most natural way, because doing so would involve using terms that have already been applied to schizophrenic symptoms.

In trying to take a more even-handed approach, three possible areas of overlap between schizophrenia and autism can be distinguished. These concern the aetiology of the two disorders, specifically their genetics; the apparent points of similarity in their symptoms; and finally whether there is any overlap in their course and outcome, or not to put too fine a point on it, do children with autism ever become schizophrenic?

Overlap in aetiology

It is accepted that there is a genetic contribution to autism. Reviewing the relatively small literature, Lauritsen and Ewald (2001) found autism in 2.8–5.9 per cent of the first-degree relatives (siblings) of autistic patients. Although this rate seems low, it is 30–100 times more common than the general population rate. Four studies also found concordance rates in monozygotic twins of between 36.3 per cent and 95.9 per cent, with the lower figures being considered to be a more accurate reflection of the true concordance.

Hanson and Gottesman (1976) reviewed five studies that examined the prevalence of schizophrenia among the parents of children with a diagnosis of childhood psychosis beginning before the age of five. Leaving aside one study which was obviously flawed, the mean rate for schizophrenia was 0.5 per cent, a value not significantly different from the general population risk.

A more recent study was only slightly less unequivocal. Gillberg *et al.* (1992) examined the parents and siblings of 35 children with a DSM III diagnosis of autism; 12 of these also had additional diagnoses ranging from fragile-X syndrome to congenital hydrocephalus. There were no cases of schizophrenia among the relatives. Three mothers had a diagnosis of schizoaffective psychosis; however, two of these were mothers of children with autism in association with fragile-X syndrome. This study did, however, reveal an unexpectedly high rate of affective disorder in the mothers: major depression (three cases) and bipolar disorder (one case).

Overlap in clinical picture

The similarities between the core affective disorder of autism and affective flattening in schizophrenia certainly impressed Kanner, to the extent that he named the disorder after one of Bleuler's fundamental symptoms. Rumsey *et al.* (1986) explored this potential point of similarity further by rating affective flattening in 14 adults meeting DSM III criteria for the disorder (six of whom had originally been diagnosed by Kanner). None of the autistic patients were taking medication at the time of the study. Ratings of affect were made by Andreasen, using a forerunner of her rating scale for the assessment of negative symptoms. The findings are shown in Table 15.1. Eight of the patients were given a global rating of at least mild affective flattening compared to only one of a control group of normal adults. Ratings were particularly frequent on the motor and behavioural expressions of affective flattening, and a somewhat smaller proportion showed evidence of the corresponding syndrome in speech (i.e. lack of inflection, slowed speech and increased latency of responding). Three showed clear instances of inappropriate affect.

A second area where autism might be anticipated to share some common ground with schizophrenia is that of speech. As mentioned above, even when autistic patients acquire speech, this is almost always abnormal to some extent. As well as the characteristic pronoun reversal, echolalia, and

Table 15.1 Affective flattening and inappropriateness in adult autistic patients

	Number showing abnormality*	
	Autistic patients *(N = 14)*	*Normal controls* *(N = 14)*
Unchanging facial expression	9	1
Decreased spontaneous movements	4	0
Paucity of expressive gestures	6	0
Poor eye contact	2	3
Affective non-responsivity	4	0
Inappropriate affect	3	0
Lack of vocal inflections	6	0
Slowed speech	1	0
Increased latency of response	2	0
Global rating of affective flattening	8	1

* Scores of >2 (mild) were required for the abnormality to be considered present.

Source: Rumsey *et al.* (1986), Thought, language, communication, and affective flattening in autistic adults. *Archives of General Psychiatry*, 43, 771–777. Copyright © 1986, American Medical Association.

stereotyped and inflexible use of words and phrases, there are many descriptions in the autism literature of abnormalities like long-windedness, over-literalness of meaning, repetitiveness, neologisms and idiosyncratic word usage (see McKenna and Oh, 2005 for a more detailed discussion of this).

Rumsey *et al.* (1986) also assessed formal thought disorder in their study of 14 adult autistic patients. Once again, the ratings were made by Andreasen, using her own scale for thought, language and communication disorders (see Chapter 1). This time the similarities to schizophrenia were not marked. The most commonly rated abnormality was poverty of speech, which was shown by 10 of the patients, including 1 who was mute, another who had minimal speech and another who showed telegraphic speech. Eight patients were rated on perseveration, and seven were rated as showing poverty of content of speech. These were the only items where ratings were significantly more frequent than in the controls. Rumsey *et al.* commented that the high ratings on perseveration were likely to have reflected autistic single-mindedness and rigidity. Similarly, it is also possible that some of what was rated as poverty of content of speech simply reflected repetitiveness.

Every account of autism makes reference to the repetitive, stereotyped routines of behaviour seen in the disorder, and some have described other abnormalities that also seem on the face of it to be strikingly similar to the catatonic symptoms of schizophrenia. Victor (1984) gave one of the most detailed tabulations of the wide spectrum phenomena that could be encountered, and this is reproduced, using the author's original terminology, in Table 15.2. It is clear that the list includes virtually every motor, volitional and behavioural abnormality described in schizophrenia, even down to a

Table 15.2 Motor, volitional and behavioural disorders described in autism

Whirling
Whirling when given a turn of the head
Running to and fro
Bouncing
Walking on toes or in other peculiar ways
Banging or rolling head
Grinding teeth
Mouthing and licking things
Blinking
Wiggling fingers near eyes
Grimacing
Allowing moulding by others (waxy catalepsy)
Moving fingers as if double-jointed or made of dough
Moving constantly
Sitting or standing in one place for hours
Dancing round an object
Making strange repetitive dance steps
Making body gyrations
Making intricate hand movements

Source: Victor (1984).

description of what appears to be mitgehen, and simple movements and finger play reminiscent of parakinesia.

From Kanner onwards the approach taken to such autistic phenomena has been to categorise them under blatantly interpretative headings like 'insistence on sameness' or 'fascination with objects', a tendency that continues to be discernible in the contemporary diagnostic criterion of 'markedly restricted repertoire of activities and interests with behaviour that is dominated by repetitive, stereotyped routines'. Recently, though, authors such as Rumsey *et al.* (1985, 1986), Realmuto and August (1991), and Wing and Attwood (1987) have begun to take a firmer phenomenological hand. Wing and Attwood, in particular, have explictly endorsed the view that '[t]he phenomena of catatonia, including hand postures, interruption and freezing of ongoing movements, difficulty in completing actions, and catatonic excitement can be seen in minor or marked form in association with the autistic spectrum.'

Wing and Shah (2000) subsequently screened referrals to a specialist centre who met criteria for autistic spectrum disorders for presence of catatonia. They found 30 of 506 (6 per cent) who met their criteria for catatonia, which required the appearance or worsening of slowness, difficulty initiating and completing movements, and passivity and reliance on physical or verbal prompting sufficient to interfere with movement and everyday functions. The age of onset of these symptoms was almost always between 10 and 19 years, but five individuals had had brief episodes of slowness and freezing prior to age 10. Their descriptions of the kinds of abnormalities seen are summarised in Box 15.3.

Box 15.3 Catatonia in 30 patients with autistic spectrum disorders (from Wing and Shah (2000), Catatonia in autistic spectrum disorders. *British Journal of Psychiatry*, 176, 357–362. Reproduced with permission from the Royal College of Psychiatrists)

Most of the manifestations of catatonic behaviour seen in the group resulted in slowing or stopping activities, but episodes of excitement and sudden impulsive actions also occurred.

The most common abnormalities of movement were odd gait (present in 27), odd, stiff postures (19), freezing (17), impulsive acts (16), and difficulty crossing lines and thresholds (16). Incontinence resulted when the individual concerned did not initiate the movement needed to reach the toilet. Seven were unable to stop actions once started. Seven had phases of excitement.

Twelve patients showed bizarre behaviour that was difficult to classify. For example, two individuals would never use one arm and hand (the left in one case and the right in the other), although no physical reason could be found. One man walked the same route to the same destination each day in order to stand motionless, staring for two hours at a spot where a building used to be before it was pulled down.

Speech was absent or markedly reduced in quantity in all cases when catatonia was present.

There was considerable variation in the degree to which catatonia interfered with daily activities. Twelve with the least severe symptoms were mobile but were very slow in carrying out all self-care activities, often freezing during an activity and needing prompting to begin moving again. They had difficulty crossing thresholds or demarcation lines, but were able to take part in everyday activities with assistance. Fourteen were more severely affected. They were so slow, or so unable to cross thresholds, or so locked into one repetitive activity, that their daily programme was severely impoverished. The lives of four individuals were completely disrupted by their symptoms. One stayed in one room, rocking in a chair, and could not leave the house unless carried out, as stiff as a statue, completely covered by a blanket. One had to be half-lifted by two caregivers to enable him to cross any demarcation lines, including cracks in pavements. One sat immobile unless physically prompted, not even moving to empty her bladder. However, when taken out and started on a route, she would walk for miles without a pause until prompted to stop. The fourth was permanently confined to a wheelchair, apart from one occasion when his elderly father stumbled and nearly fell. Seeing this, the son leapt from his wheelchair, helped his father to sit down and then returned to immobility.

Eight patients developed obsessive-compulsive symptoms before they became catatonic. In 15 the onset was immediately preceded by a period of very disturbed, often aggressive behaviour. In 17 of the patients, the catatonia remained static once it was established. Three of the patients had experienced a slow progressive deterioration in mobility and practical skills. The remaining 10 patients showed major or minor fluctuations in severity. A number of the patients experienced occasional visual hallucinations or paranoid ideas that did not fit any particular diagnosis. None had ever showed first rank symptoms of schizophrenia. All the patients showed speech abnormalities, but these were typical of those found in autistic disorders.

In 17 of the patients the catatonia remained stable once it became established. Three showed a slow but steady deterioration, and the remaining 10 patients showed minor or major fluctuations in severity.

Overlap in course and outcome

The orthodox view of autism, that it follows a strictly developmental trajectory, may be an oversimplification. Rutter (1970), Wing and Attwood (1987) and particularly Gillberg (1991) have documented that a small proportion of patients undergo a temporary or permanent deterioration around the time of adolescence. Hyperactivity, aggressiveness and destructive behaviour give way, in cases where permanent deterioration takes place, to inertia, loss of language skills and slow intellectual decline. According to Gillberg, some of these cases show repetitive behaviours, and so may be examples of autistic catatonia; in others the change coincides with the onset of epilepsy.

Rutter (1970) commented that very few autistic children developed delusions and hallucinations in adult life, and Wing and Attwood stated that they had never seen a convincing case of autism in which schizophrenia developed. This may also be something of an oversimplification. Petty *et al.* (1984) described three patients who clearly had autistic symptoms prior to 30 months of age, and who all met DSM III criteria for autism. By school age or early adolescence, all three had also developed symptoms which led to an additional diagnosis of schizophrenia. The first described hearing 'parrot-like voices' at the age of 9. By the age of 12 he was experiencing auditory hallucinations giving commands and keeping up a running commentary, delusions of control, and marked formal thought disorder. The second patient held the apparently literal belief that he was a car from the age of 5, and also expressed the idea that his thoughts were falling out of his head. At the age of 13 he started to believe that other children were talking about him and persecuting him. He described hearing a voice which said things that 'piled up' in his head. The third patient developed increasing evidence of formal thought disorder from the age of 7, and this was associated with probable delusions and auditory hallucinations. None of the patients suffered from epilepsy. All three patients showed some improvement with neuroleptic treatment.

A further example of a patient who was convincingly autistic and developed equally convincing schizophrenia is described in Box 15.4. The theme of an association between the two disorders also continues in the section on Asperger's syndrome, below.

Rapoport and co-workers have also found evidence to suggest that childhood schizophrenia might not be as completely divorced from autism as is thought. Noting that a high rate of premorbid social impairment and delayed language and motor development has been a regular finding in such children (e.g. Kolvin *et al.*, 1971; Watkins *et al.*, 1988; Hollis, 1995), and that the diagnosis of autism or pervasive developmental disorder had frequently earlier been queried in their own patients, Sporn *et al.* (2004) examined how many of them met diagnostic criteria for autism before they developed schizophrenia. Out of a total sample of 75 patients, 3 met DSM IV criteria for pervasive developmental disorder, either autistic-type (1) or Asperger syndrome (2). A further 16 met criteria for pervasive developmental disorder not otherwise specified. In most cases the autistic symptoms had been present before the age of 3, but in four they appeared between the ages of 4 and 6.

Asperger's syndrome

The syndrome Asperger (1944) called autistic psychopathy of childhood, but has since become universally known by his name, occupies an uncertain nosological position. In the past it has been argued to be distinct from autism and more closely related to schizoid personality disorder (Van Krevelen, 1971; Wolff and Chick, 1980). More recently there has been a tendency to subsume it partly or wholly under the active-but-odd variety of autism (Wing and Attwood, 1987). The currently favoured view (e.g. Wing, 1991; Frith, 2003) is that Asperger's syndrome and autism are mild and severe variants of the same disorder. Asperger's syndrome, in particular, is associated with much less intellectual disability and there is little or no language delay.

The clinical features of Asperger's syndrome have once again been described by Wing (1981). The disorder is very much more common in boys than in girls, and is not usually recognised before the third year of life. Speech develops at the normal time, or is at worst somewhat delayed. Pronoun reversal and other autistic-like disturbances may be present in a minor form, but a full command of language is generally developed. Nevertheless, speech is abnormal, being long-winded and pedantic, impoverished, and featuring stereotyped repetitions of words and phrases, and sometimes also neologisms. The non-verbal accompaniments of speech are also abnormal: intonation is monotonous, exaggerated or otherwise aprosodic; gestures are reduced, or

Box 15.4 Autism complicated by the development of schizophrenia (author's own case)

The patient was the illegitimate child of an African prostitute who was adopted by English parents at the age of 6 weeks. As a baby he was healthy, but behavioural difficulties were noted from the time of adoption. He typically slept all day and was awake most of the night, and he could not bear to be handled, screaming and shuddering when touched. He acquired toilet training at the normal times. Between the ages of 2 and 3 he fell into the habit of refusing to defecate until he could hardly walk. He began to speak at the age of 2½, but for the first 6–8 months spoke only in a self-invented language: this had no grammar and consisted of nouns which referred only to objects and not people. At the age of 3 he suddenly started using English, understanding it well, but not always expressing himself properly. He was described as having some echolalia and his tone of voice was very flat.

During childhood, he rarely asked questions, and showed very little natural curiosity. He was described by his parents as 'obsessive': his play centred almost exclusively on toy farmyard animals which he would place in particular positions, becoming distressed if they were moved. Between the ages of 5 and 14 he wrote single words or phrases up to hundreds of times on any available scraps of paper. Later, he became obsessed with football, watching games and collecting cards. He never cried except sometimes when in pain. He continued to try to avoid being touched, withdrawing if someone accidentally touched him. He disliked women, to the extent that he would not sit in a chair that a woman had been sitting in or had put her coat on. He spoke little to his parents, and was completely socially isolated.

Other features of the patient during childhood were laughing and talking to himself, and to inanimate objects, e.g. hedges – if confronted with this he would deny that he had been doing it. He also clicked his teeth. He was unusually good at sports like table tennis, and had excellent hand–eye coordination. However, he was completely unable to play as part of a team. He taught himself Swahili, acquiring a several hundred word vocabulary. However, he never spoke this language.

From the age of 11 the patient improved intellectually, being described as starting to 'shine' and 'flourish' at school. His social isolation became less of a problem, but he remained odd. For example, for several months after a teacher jokingly threatened to 'bounce a wall off his head', the patient repeatedly asked his parents which wall he was going to be hit with.

At the age of 13, around the time of puberty, the patient began to undergo a gradual change. He spoke less, and laughed and talked to himself more. His educational performance fell off dramatically, and his ability to relate to others disappeared. He became lazy, unkempt and stopped changing his clothes. He spent more and more time by himself, much of it in bed. His parents became unable to cope and at the age of 17 he was transferred to a residential facility for mentally handicapped adults. Around this time he started expressing the ideas that everyone hated him because he was 'rude', and that his feet were making a noise and getting him into trouble. He told his parents that he could hear the voice of a staff member shouting at him, even though he was on leave at home at the time. He also heard the wife of a staff member shouting at him and telling him she loved him. Later he stated he could hear people shouting in Bradford, Edinburgh and London, and repeatedly heard Leeds football fans saying they were going to kill him. After innumerable instances of antisocial behaviour including entering other residents' bedrooms, urinating in public, stealing and making unprovoked attacks on people, he was admitted to hospital at the age of 21.

Mental state examination revealed an unkempt appearance with torn clothes, marked poverty of speech, and obvious flattening and shallowness of affect, accompanied by inappropriate laughter. In addition to experiencing auditory hallucinations, he stated that someone was pulling his neck round. Cognitive status was difficult to test but the patient was more or less oriented and knew recent facts, both concerning his family and world events. Full scale IQ at age 15 (WISC-R) was 80 (verbal IQ 96, performance IQ 67). All investigations, including chromosomal analysis and screening for inherited disorders of metabolism have been normal. CT scan revealed an empty sella turcica; this was not associated with endocrine abnormality.

The patient remains in hospital. His mother commented that there was 'almost nothing of the child I once knew'.

alternatively excessive but clumsy; and there is often a lack of facial expression. Although there is no aloofness or desire to avoid others, two-way interaction is handicapped by a marked inability to grasp the rules governing social behaviour: patients stare, stand too close, wear inappropriate clothes, and attempt to touch or kiss strangers. Posture is odd and movements are ill-coordinated; the vast majority of patients are poor at games and show impairments in other activities requiring motor skills, such as writing and drawing. Many patients show the stereotypies and rituals typical of autism but to a less marked extent. They tend to become intensely attached to particular personal possessions and are often very unhappy when away from their familiar surroundings. Intelligence is normal or sometimes high, and many patients show savant-type skills, having exceptional memories, developing absorbing interests in narrowly defined fields, having musical ability, and so on.

Wing did not share the view expressed by Asperger in his original paper that some patients showed particular originality of thought, but it is now increasingly accepted that many exceptional scientists, mathematicians, and even some writers, poets and politicians have shown the typical features of the disorder (James, 2003; Fitzgerald, 2004).

One of the main points of interest of Asperger's syndrome is the frequency with which it appears to be complicated by development of psychiatric disorders. Anxiety and depression are frequently reported (e.g. Wing, 1981), and suicidal attempts are common. Whereas Asperger (1944) reported that only 1 of his 200 cases developed schizophrenia, the occurrence of states to a greater or lesser extent resembling schizophrenia has been documented in virtually all subsequent series of cases. One of Wolff and Chick's (1980) 19 patients developed florid schizophrenia and one more was chronically hospitalised with a diagnosis of simple schizophrenia. Wing (1981) noted that out of 18 patients seen in adult life, 1 had a psychosis with delusions and hallucinations, 1 had had an episode of catatonic stupor, 3 had bizarre behaviour but with no clear psychiatric diagnosis, and 4 had become increasingly odd and withdrawn perhaps related to underlying depression.

The most detailed information on the prevalence of schizophrenia and other non-developmental psychiatric disorder in Asperger's syndrome is to be found in Tantam's study (1988, 1991). He built up a sample of 85 patients who met a combination of his own and other criteria for the disorder. Thirty (35 per cent) were diagnosed as having a secondary psychiatric diagnosis. The diagnostic breakdown is shown in Table 15.3. Three had a diagnosis of schizophrenia, four had isolated hallucinosis (not further specified) and one was considered to have a psychosis associated with epilepsy. Two more held complex and extremely bizarre beliefs: one believed that he was really asleep (in a 'missage') between two periods of existence ('boating lines'), and that he was only conscious because a witch had made him have a bad dream. The other believed that he had been abducted from a heavenly home by the people who called themselves his parents, was afraid that he might turn into a skeleton, and may have believed he was in contact with the Holy Ghost. These

Table 15.3 Psychiatric diagnoses in 85 adults with Asperger's syndrome

Schizophrenia	3 (3.5%)
Hallucinosis	4 (4.7%)
Epileptic psychosis	1 (1.1%)
Mania	4 (4.7%)
Mania alternating with depression	4 (4.7%)
Depressive psychosis	2 (2.4%)
Depression	5 (5.9%)
Depression and anxiety	2 (2.4%)
Anxiety	4 (4.7%)
Obsessive-compulsive disorder	2 (2.4%)

Note: All diagnoses were made according to ICD 9.

Source: Tantam (1991), Asperger syndrome in adulthood. In U. Frith (Ed.), *Autism and Asperger syndrome*, pp. 147–183. Cambridge University Press. Reproduced with permission from Cambridge University Press.

two patients' symptoms were not considered to be evidence of psychosis, but rather attempts to rationalise their differences from other people.

As Tantam noted, this proportion was likely to be higher than in an unselected community sample, since the superimposed psychiatric disorder may have predisposed to the original psychiatric referral. Even so, after excluding the last two cases, 9.4 per cent suffered from a psychosis broadly resembling schizophrenia, a rate approaching 10 times the general population rate.

Tantam diagnosed schizophrenia clinically in his study, but similar results were obtained by Stahlberg *et al.* (2004) in a study using diagnostic criteria. They found that only 1 of 49 (2.0 per cent) adult patients who met DSM IV criteria for Asperger's syndrome also had a DSM IV diagnosis of schizophrenia, but that 5 more (10 per cent) had other psychotic disorders, a category which included delusional disorder, brief psychotic disorder, substance-induced psychotic disorder and psychotic disorder not otherwise specified. In this study, three patients (6.1 per cent) also had a diagnosis of bipolar disorder.

Conclusion

Having endured both severe overdiagnosis and severe underdiagnosis, there is no longer any dispute that something which resembles schizophrenia in clinical features, course and outcome can develop in childhood. When it begins in later childhood its identification as schizophrenia is unquestionable. Even when it begins earlier it is surprisingly recognisable, given the widely held view that children cannot verbalise their feelings, hold complicated beliefs, or engage in sophisticated symbolisation. It is not impossible that it can even develop in infancy. As far as the evidence permits any conclusions to be drawn, the same aetiological factors appear to be operative.

Where controversy remains rife is in the relationship between childhood schizophrenia and the main disorder it was confused with in the past, autism. The belief that the two disorders are entirely different has acquired the status of dogma, and like all dogmas is a simplistic version of a more complicated and also more interesting reality. It is true that the two disorders are, on present evidence, genetically distinct. But it is also true that the phenomena of autism and schizophrenia overlap to a greater extent than child psychiatrists have been prepared to admit. This applies particularly to catatonic symptoms, the pointed ignoring of which prior to the recent work of Wing and others is a somewhat shameful chapter in the recent history of autism research. There is also some evidence for overlap in the abnormalities of affect seen in the two disorders, and in one aspect of speech, poverty of speech.

There is also increasing evidence that autism can be associated with the development of schizophrenia. The proportion of cases where this occurs is almost certainly small, at least in the classically defined form of the disorder. However, if it is accepted that Asperger's syndrome is a subtype of autism, then it is difficult to resist the conclusion that schizophrenia – or at least non-affective functional psychosis – develops at several times the general population rate. This should not raise fears that autism and schizophrenia are in imminent danger of being combined back into a single disorder. In the first place, it is clear that the relationship is not exclusive to schizophrenia. In the second, it would be slightly surprising if autism was different to the quite wide variety of other neuropsychiatric syndromes where psychosis is recognised as a complication.

16 Schizophrenia and personality

On the scale of unknowns and unresolved issues facing schizophrenia, its relationship to certain features of personality has not ranked particularly highly. That there is some kind of link is undeniable – if nothing else personality has been mentioned too many times in too many contexts throughout this book for this not to be the case. But to venture further produces an uneasy feeling that one is stepping into a field where concepts are far less well defined than in the rest of schizophrenia research.

It might be anticipated that part of the problem would be the lack of consensus about the nature of personality itself in psychology. But this is not the case: the debate has revolved almost exclusively around narrow psychiatric concepts of abnormal personality, and questions about the underlying dimensions of normal personality rarely, if ever, raise their head. In a recent review of the field, Claridge and Davis (2003) began by noting that psychiatry has developed its own taxonomy of abnormal personality types, an important organising principle of which has been that these have some form of continuity with different forms of mental illness. One of these alleged continuities is between schizoid personality and schizophrenia. They then touched briefly on Freud's views about the development of personality through oral, anal and genital stages, before drily commenting that his explanation of how this resulted in different psychological disorders has found little support from empirical study. Despite this, the psychodynamic approach to personality currently enjoys acceptance and respectability in the concept of borderline personality disorder, where the border is (or at least has been in the past) with schizophrenia. Almost all theories of personality attempt to relate personality to underlying biological variables, including particularly genetics. One of Claridge and Davis' main clinical examples of this type of relationship again concerned schizophrenia, in the shape of schizotypal personality disorder.

The net result is that schizophrenia has been considered to be associated with three different forms of personality disorder in three different ways. One of the classically recognised psychiatric forms of personality disorder, schizoid personality, is said to predispose to the development of schizophrenia. For schizotypal personality the emphasis is on a genetic relationship – individuals with this type of personality are claimed to be over-represented among the relatives of patients with schizophrenia. As befitting a largely unreconstructed psychoanalytic concept, borderline personality is linked to schizophrenia by illustrating how psychotic symptoms can be caused by psychological mechanisms. Such individuals, by virtue of their unique form of personality organisation, tend to develop short-lived psychotic symptoms under conditions of stress and conflict.

Schizoid personality

Almost from time immemorial, it was recognised that patients with schizophrenia often showed certain characteristic traits before they became ill. Kraepelin (1907, 1913a) considered that at least 20 per cent of patients who developed schizophrenia, especially males, had exhibited 'mental peculiarities' from early youth, including affectation and eccentricity, but particularly a quiet, shy, docile, retiring disposition with no ability to make friendships. Bleuler (1911) considered that that anomalies of character could be uncovered by careful enquiry in more than half of all individuals who later became schizophrenic. There was a tendency to seclusion and withdrawal, together with moderate or severe degrees of irritability. Even as children they stood out by virtue of an inability to play with others – all 10 of Bleuler's own schoolmates who later became schizophrenic 'were quite different from the other boys'. It was Bleuler's students who, according to his son (M. Bleuler, 1978), started using the term 'schizoid' to describe such individuals.

In this era, the concept of personality disorder was primitive, with the emphasis being on liars, swindlers, impulsive and shiftless types and sexual deviants. The modern psychiatric approach to personality disorder was shaped by Schneider (1950) over successive editions of his influential book, *Psychopathic personalities*. In often memorable descriptions, he distinguished 10 different types of abnormal personality, many of which survive essentially unchanged in present-day classifications. Strangely enough, schizoid personality was not among them, and Schneider's comments on this personality type were confined to a critique of Kretschmer's theory linking body-build, heredity and temperament, which he did not agree with. These comments are reproduced in Box 16.1. (Kretschmer's theory is discussed further in the section on schizotypal personality.)

For all authors, even Schneider, the raison d'être of schizoid personality was its association with schizophrenia. Some were content with it simply playing a predisposing role. Most, though, considered that the similarity of features like coldness and aloofness, withdrawal, suspiciousness and preference for introspective fantasy, to symptoms of schizophrenia could not be overlooked and pointed to a closer aetiological relationship. It seemed probable to Bleuler (1911) that 'autistic character anomalies' constituted the first symptoms of the disease and were not merely expressions of a predisposition to the disease. Kraepelin (1913a) wondered whether such traits might even be a product of schizophrenia occurring in the earliest childhood, and then

Box 16.1 Schneider on schizoid personality (from Schneider, 1950)

It has been recognised for a long time now that the premorbid personality in schizophrenia tends to be an abnormal one. It commonly has a queer, hypersensitive, shut-in, cold, bizarre quality . . . However, it was Kretschmer who tried to prove there were gradual changes between abnormal personality and schizophrenic processes and between normal personality and schizophrenia.

Schizoids [in Kretschmer's classification] have hidden depths. The presenting surface may be most misleading. There may be little or there may be much behind the uncommunicative facade. One can never be sure what schizoids are feeling. They are like cool Italian houses that keep their shutters fast against the heat while life goes on festively within their dim interiors. Outwardly schizoids are uncompanionable, withdrawn, humourless, rather odd folk; shy, timid, sensitive, emotional and nervously excitable. They may be docile, inoffensive, upright and not quarrelsome, unresponsive and dull. Their opposite poles are irritability and unresponsiveness. Little notice has been taken so far of their excessive irritability, but the majority of schizoids are prickly and cold at the same time. The admixture in which the oversensitive and undersensitive elements are combined has been termed the psychaesthetic ratio. The schizoid is either wholly uncompanionable or extremely selective of his companions, shy, wary. Exclusiveness is often self-protection and glossy formality of manner covers lack of genuine warmth. Some incongruity is evident between stimulus and motor response. The behaviour tends to have something inhibited about it, the manner is stilted, the general psychic tempo is abrupt and irregular, there is no curving swing of mood but sudden leaps and starts. The oversensitive group have touchy, unsympathetic temperaments and include personalities such as ruthless idealists and imperturbable aristocrats. The colder, blanker aspect of schizoid temperament provides its quota of despots, bad tempered dullards and deteriorated ne'er-do-wells, any of whom may be the product of a pre- or post-psychotic state (schizophrenic).

An opposite view to Kretschmer's is that which, while it allows for specific interrelations between mental and bodily constitution in schizophrenia, maintains a firm boundary between abnormal personality and schizophrenia itself. To allow for a specific bodily constitution and type of personality as predisposing elements in schizophrenia is one thing; it is quite another to make the whole development a matter of degree . . . There need be no reluctance to accept such transitions in theory but we must admit that we have not found such transitions in actual clinical experience. Cases are very rare indeed in which there is ever any doubt as to whether abnormal personality or schizophrenia is present.

brought to a standstill. More fancifully still, Kretschmer (1925) talked of 'schizoids who look just as if they had already been through a schizophrenic psychosis before they were born' (quoted by Planansky, 1966). But all speculation aside, while it was accepted that not all individuals with a schizoid personality became schizophrenic, and that patients with schizophrenia did not necessarily show any evidence of schizoid traits before they became ill, there was no doubting the importance of the association.

Cutting (1985) reviewed five studies carried out between 1912 and 1978 directed to quantifying this association. These studies respectively found that 10 of 34 (29 per cent) schizophrenic patients had a 'shut in' personality; 36 of 139 (26 per cent) were 'shy and solitary'; 130 of 500 (26 per cent) were 'schizoid'; and 50 of 208 (24 per cent) were 'schizoid-pathological', with a further 58 (28 per cent) being 'schizoid aberrant within the norm'. However, the way in which schizoid personality was defined was neither very rigorous nor very consistent in these studies. The last set of figures was from Manfred Bleuler's (1978) own study described in Chapter 3, and he gave two detailed examples, neither of whom showed any clear evidence of the core traits. The personality of a female patient who was classified as 'schizoid-pathological' was described as a peculiar combination of hurry, inquisitive curiosity, cheeky flippancy, general aimlessness, and restlessness, and she never kept company with boys. The only relevant statement concerning the other patient, who was considered to be 'schizoid aberrant within the norm', was that she had never fostered friendships, although she had had one rather close girl-friend for a number of years, where despite their friendship they seemed always to be competing against each other as rivals.

There has been only one contemporary study, but fortunately this can be regarded as reasonably definitive. Tyrer *et al.* (1988) administered the Personality Assessment Schedule (PAS) (Tyrer and Alexander, 1988), to 109 patients meeting DSM III criteria for schizophrenia, and to 200 normal subjects. Most of the interviews were carried out with a relative or other informant, but in a minority of cases it was only with the patients themselves. The PAS contains multiple questions directed to each of 24 different traits, and the ratings are combined into personality groupings using an 'agnostic' method of classification based on factor and cluster analysis. There are four broad groupings: sociopathic, passive-dependent, anankastic (obsessional) and schizoid, divided into 13 individual subtypes: sociopathic, explosive, sensitive-aggressive, passive-dependent, histrionic, asthenic, anankastic, anxious, hypochondriacal, dysthymic, schizoid, avoidant and paranoid. The scoring system separates different levels of severity, from personality difficulty, to personality disorder, to severe personality disorder.

The results are shown in Figure 16.1 and Table 16.1. The schizophrenic patients had significantly higher ratings than the controls on 19 of all 24 traits. These included characteristic schizoid traits such as suspiciousness, introspection, shyness, aloofness, sensitivity, and eccentricity (and perhaps also irritability), but also numerous others not ordinarily associated with this

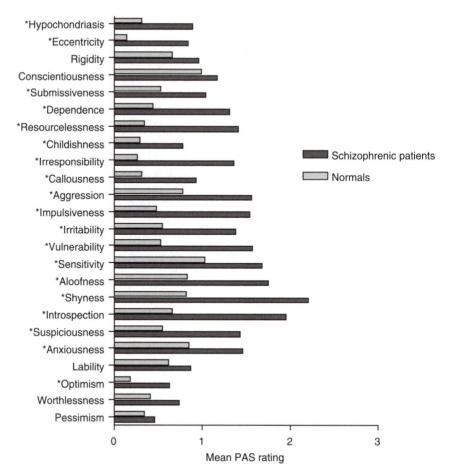

Figure 16.1 Ratings on individual traits in the Personality Assessment Schedule (PAS) for 109 schizophrenic patients and 200 normal controls (asterisks indicate significant differences) (from Tyrer *et al.* (1988), Personality disorder and mental illness. In P. Tyrer (Ed.), *Personality disorders: Diagnosis, management and course*, pp. 93–104. London: Wright).

personality type, such as impulsiveness, aggression, callousness, irresponsibility, childishness and optimism. Twenty-five of the 109 patients (22.9 per cent) showed personality traits in the schizoid cluster (schizoid, paranoid and avoidant personalities), of whom 14 (12.8 per cent) showed classical schizoid traits ranging from personality difficulty to severe personality disorder, alone or in combination with other traits. Another 19 (17.4 per cent) had a personality abnormality that fell in the antisocial cluster.

Tyrer *et al.* commented that although schizoid personality was over-represented in patients with schizophrenia, the co-occurrence was not nearly as high as might be expected from clinical impression, and that the

Table 16.1 Personality Assessment Schedule classification of 109 schizophrenic patients

Personality type	Schizophrenic pts (%)
Normal	38 (34.9)
Sociopathic	4 (3.7)
Explosive	12 (11.0)
Sensitive-aggressive	3 (2.8)
Passive-dependent	6 (5.5)
Histrionic (hysterical)	5 (4.6)
Asthenic	2 (1.8)
Anankastic (obsessional)	3 (2.8)
Anxious	5 (4.6)
Hypochondriacal	1 (0.9)
Dysthymic	5 (4.6)
Schizoid	14 (12.8)
Avoidant	9 (8.3)
Paranoid	2 (1.8)

Note: Rates include personality difficulty, personality disorder and severe personality. Rates also include individuals with combined forms of personality disorder.

Source: Tyrer *et al.* (1988).

abnormality extended beyond the schizoid category. It should also be noted that Tyrer *et al.*'s findings indicate that in a third of cases of schizophrenia, the premorbid personality shows no abnormalities, and that in another substantial proportion the abnormalities found are those which are minor and commonplace in the normal population.

Schizotypal personality disorder

One of the early themes in the history of schizoid personality, as described above, was that its features seemed to correspond in some ways to a mild form of schizophrenia. At some point this idea branched away, first into borderline schizophrenia and then into what ultimately became schizotypal personality disorder in DSM III. The complicated and at times quite unexpected story of how this happened has been reconstructed by Kendler (1985). He identified two major 'familial' and 'clinical' historical trends, although these proceeded in far from complete isolation from each other and their paths crossed at a number of points.

The familial trend: Abnormal traits in the relatives of schizophrenics

This trend was represented by an extensive literature that could be traced back to some rather casual observations by Kraepelin and Bleuler. Kraepelin (1913a) wrote that not infrequently among the relatives of schizophrenic patients there were found 'striking personalities, criminals, queer individuals, prostitutes, suicides, vagrants, [and] wrecked and ruined human beings'. Describing what he called latent schizophrenia, Bleuler (1911) remarked on the 'irritable, odd, moody, withdrawn or exaggeratedly punctual people' who aroused the suspicion of being schizophrenic and showed in nuce all the symptoms and combinations of symptoms seen in the manifest forms of the disorder.

Several later authors added their own contributions, and extended the traits to suspiciousness, stubbornness, pedantry and avariciousness, as well as including individuals who were feckless, subservient, out of touch with reality, literal minded, rambling, vague, daydreamers or fanatics, and who believed in spiritualism or self-cure by hypnotism. Some of these descriptions seemed, as Kendler put it, as much in the province of the novelist as the nosologist, but when he tabulated the most frequently recorded traits by 10 leading authors of the day, a somewhat more consistent pattern emerged. Eccentricity or oddness was noted by 9, irritability or unreasonableness by 7, social isolation by 6, an aloof, cold demeanour by 6, and suspiciousness by 5. Superstitiousness, poor psychosocial functioning, nervousness, odd speech and hypersensitivity were also mentioned by two or three authors.

One of these 10 authors was Kretschmer (1925). He had developed a complicated theory that related physique to character, and character to mental illness. In his scheme there were three forms of physique: leptosomic or asthenic, pyknic, and athletic (which correspond closely to the more familiar terminology of ectomorphs, endomorphs and mesomorphs). The first two of these were associated with schizothymic and cyclothymic temperaments, respectively. Later he added a 'viscous' or 'massive' temperament said to be associated with the athletic type. While these temperaments were part of the normal range of variation in personality, there was a continuum between the normal schizothymic personality, through a pathological exaggeration of this, which Kretschmer called schizoid personality, to full schizophrenia. This was also the case for cyclothymia and manic-depressive psychosis. An important point for Kretschmer was that the close relatives of schizophrenic patients often showed a schizoid/schizothymic temperament, which was sometimes more apparent in them than in the patients themselves.

Kretschmer's concept of the pathological exaggeration of schizothymia certainly embodied elements of the evolving view of schizoid personality. He described such individuals as unsociable, quiet, reserved, serious, eccentric, timid, shy, fond of nature and books, and lacking the normal range of intimate human relations. However, he went further with a great deal of literary-style conjecture about their sensitivity and inner conflicts, and how this might, for example, give rise on the one hand to creativity or on the other to sullen eccentricity. At times he was frankly contradictory – the patients were both insensitive and oversensitive, they tended to be pliable, kindly and honest people, but also capable of extreme cruelty.

Kendler cited several later authors, including well-known genetic researchers like Kallman (1938) and Slater (1953), who went on to describe abnormalities in the relatives of schizophrenic patients that were beyond any narrow concept of schizoid personality. This tradition, however, reached what must have been its apogee in a study that he did not refer to. In Heston's (1966) study of the adopted-away offspring of schizophrenic mothers, described in Chapter 5, 21 of the 47 who exhibited no significant psychosocial impairment were described as giving a strong impression of much more variability of personality and behaviour than normal. They were not only successful adults, but in comparison to the control group were more spontaneous when interviewed and had more colourful life histories. They held more creative jobs: musician, teacher, home-designer; and followed the more imaginative hobbies: oil painting, music, antique aircraft. Heston (1970) went on to propose that there was a genetic trait of 'schizoidia', which could be expressed in a very wide range of behaviour, covering social isolation, antisocial behaviour, illogical poorly planned and impulsive crime, social isolation, heavy drinking and sexual deviance, as well as many traits that were later to figure in the concept of schizotypal personality. He also made the statement that some of these individuals' behavioural lapses could be bizarre enough to suggest 'micropsychotic episodes'.

The clinical trend: Non-psychotic patients presenting with schizophrenia-like symptomatology

This second major tradition can also been seen as a development of Bleuler's concept of latent schizophrenia, perhaps influenced by Kretschmer's concept of a continuum between normality and schizophrenia. However, it developed exclusively in American psychiatry, often but not always within this country's psychodynamic framework.

One of the early figures Kendler singled out was the analyst Zilboorg (1941). He coined the term 'ambulatory schizophrenia' to describe individuals who could appear superficially normal, but who had a tendency to confuse the real world with fantasy, who were taciturn and emotionally tense, and who had perverse sexual interests and bizarre and sometimes violent fantasies. Three of the patients he described were brutal murderers and a fourth was a woman who spent many hours acting various Shakespearian roles in front of a mirror. Another important author was the psychologist Meehl (1962), who argued that one of the key features such individuals displayed was anhedonia (which he also believed was part of the inherited predisposition to schizophrenia). Deutsch (1942) also described passive individuals with a striking absence of feelings, for whom he coined the term the 'as if' personality. But by far the most important influence on the future DSM III concept of schizotypal personality disorder was Hoch and Polatin's (1949) paper on pseudoneurotic schizophrenia.

Hoch and Polatin used this term to describe a by no means small group of patients who were often diagnosed and treated as neurotic, but who they felt justified in classifying with the schizophrenic reactions, 'because many of the mechanisms in these cases are very similar to those commonly known in schizophrenia'. Some of these mechanisms were subtle forms of Bleuler's fundamental symptoms. All patients showed an 'autistic and dereistic life approach', with a withdrawal from reality that was usually much more general than that seen in the neuroses. While appraisal of this could be very much a subjective issue for the clinician, ambivalence, on the other hand, was obvious. This was diffuse and widespread, involving the patient's aims, his social adaptation and (inevitably) his sexual adjustment – polymorphous sexual preoccupations were a feature of all their cases. With respect to affect, the patients only rarely showed an impoverished, rigid or inflexible affect. Instead they showed a lack of modulation and flexibility in emotional display. Many of the patients showed a cold, controlled and at the same time hypersensitive reaction to emotional situations, characteristically overemphasising trivial frustrations and not responding to major ones. Lack of inhibition in displaying certain emotions could be striking, especially in otherwise markedly inhibited persons. Association disturbance was not present in a gross form as seen in schizophrenia, but 'condensations and concept disorganisations' were nevertheless apparent in some. Much more conspicuous was a feeling of omnipotence and magical thinking.

Other features were not quite what Bleuler had in mind. The most important symptom from the diagnostic point of view was what Hoch and Polatin called pan-anxiety or pan-neurosis. Anxiety and tension was an all-pervading feature of the patient's life; the patients usually did not have one or two neurotic illnesses, but showed symptoms of all them – free-floating anxiety, phobias, and obsessive-compulsive symptoms, which were simultaneously present, constantly shifting, but never absent. In a good many patients depression was also present, or an anhedonic state where the patient did not derive pleasure from anything.

Fatefully for the future direction of schizotypal personality (and even more so for borderline personality – see below), Hoch and Polatin also stated that quite a number of patients with pseudoneurotic schizophrenia developed psychotic episodes that were often of short duration and followed by recovery which was so complete that 'if one does not see them in the psychotic episode one does not believe that they were psychotic'. In these cases a daydream could merge into a hallucination, or a vague hypochondriacal idea became a somatic delusion, or ideas on relationships with other people in the framework of social anxiety developed into ideas of reference. Many of these patients zig-zagged repeatedly over the reality line. Depersonalisation was considered to be very significant in this context.

The five case histories Hoch and Polatin described certainly showed the pan-anxiety, pan-neurosis and pan-sexuality that came to be the shorthand for the syndrome. Two of the patients also seem to have developed delusions and hallucinations. But most of the time it is impossible to be sure what was going on with them, as the normal conventions of history and mental state examination were largely dispensed with in favour of associations, dreams, Rorschach test findings and the results of amytal interviews. More than anything else the case histories provide a graphic portrayal of American psychoanalytic psychiatry at the height of its power and showing the excesses that were to lead to its downfall. The five cases were all very different, but the one that is most accessible is summarised in Box 16.2.

Box 16.2 One of Hoch and Polatin's cases of pseudoneurotic schizophrenia (from Hoch and Polatin, 1949)

P.C. is a 29-year-old married woman who, following an automobile accident, in which her oldest male child was severely injured, has suffered from marked self-recriminatory ideas, a feeling that she is two persons, a desire to kill members of her family and a fear that her husband might kill her. She has been married twice; there are no children by the first union, but three by the second.

There is no history of mental illness on either side of the family. The mother and father came to this country just after the First World War and were almost immediately married. They had at this time and still have marked language difficulties, not only concerning English, but with each other's languages. The mother was markedly overprotective of the daughter. The father was very strict, alcoholic and somewhat improvident.

P.C's birth and early development were normal. She experienced marked difficulties in speaking, however, because of the general language confusion at home; and the father was very strict, not permitting the child to speak at the table. The mother was very overprotective, restricting the patient's play activity to girls, and only girls could come to the house. The mother and father were often separated because of their diverse jobs. The patient usually went with her mother from one domestic situation to another. She felt very insecure and lonely as a child and became seclusive and moody. The father and mother constantly quarrelled with each other. P.C. preferred her father even though he was abusive to the mother on many occasions. Her attitude toward the mother is now one of frank hostility, and she is rather ambivalent toward the father. The patient completed public school and went to trade school for a year. She did some sewing and designing. Later on, however, she became a model. She received no sex education. She denies having masturbated. Her first heterosexual experience was at 19. Soon after that, she married. This marriage ended five months later by a divorce. She gave up her first husband because he was cruel, unreliable and mysterious, although she enjoyed him sexually.

P.C. was well until October 1946 when her illness was precipitated by an accident to her oldest boy. He fell out of the back seat of a car which she was driving. Similar accidents had happened to the same child twice before. On these occasions, however, she was not alone with him in the car. The patient did not mention the last accident to her husband, who was away working. She asked him to send money because the child was sick. It was established later that the patient actually did not become ill after the accident but 40 days later, when the child was practically recovered. She then began to cry, expressed self-accusatory ideas, said that she was a bad mother and an inefficient housewife. She began to feel hopeless and had no desire to live. Phobic manifestations appeared and she was afraid that she would kill her three children and be killed by her husband. She played with the idea of suicide, but made no overt attempt at it. She also complained about hearing motors roaring in her ears; began to think of herself at times very objectively; and she would smile at her own activities and reactions. She also could hear herself talk to herself as if there were two persons. At times she would laugh at her own feelings. She had a sensation of voices inside her head repeating things which she had previously thought of, or reminding her of what she had done. She realised that these voices were products of her own thinking, nevertheless she could not control them; she felt obsessed by them.

The woman was seen in a psychiatric clinic and treated unsuccessfully for depression. Later she was sent to the Psychiatric Institute. Here she was cooperative, attentive and did not exhibit anxiety, sadness or tension. She expressed the ideas already mentioned and added that she felt two different voices inside herself. At times she stated that she would smile at herself as though she were a person looking down from a distance at her own self and her own actions. It was found that this patient had a mystical, ritualistic type of thinking.

Under sodium amytal, she talked in abstractions and in a very detached manner. She brought forth the following dream, which occurred several times. It has a definite religious, cosmic significance for her. 'I was in labour in a barn, in a cradle, part of the time I was in the cradle and part of the time I was in the straw, but the straw was very soft. I could see the little cradle like an old American antique. There was a gold life-like light. The baby that was born was two years old. He had little yellow ringlets. He got up and walked away and the Wise Men followed him. I sat, and the labour pains continued uneventfully. The crowds outside wanted to see him.' This dream she did not treat as an ordinary dream. It was considered a vision and for three or four months following it, while she was 16, she considered very seriously becoming a nun. She says, 'With these dreams I used to get the feeling of being holy. It was like sunshine radiating from within. I thought it might be a feeling of ambition or a feeling to get ahead.' She believes that all her dreams have a significance but not similar to this. She is markedly catathymic. She believes that she may attain anything by wishing. Her thoughts are, in fact, constantly wish desires, wish fulfilments. She believes that by wishing she can control, she believes in thought magic, she can kill by ideas.

P.C. related in another interview that she feels torn between two conflicting emotions concerning her husband and children. She wants to be a good wife and mother. At the same time, she resents very much that she is 'tied down'; that she is not free to live her own life. She would like to become a writer. Sexually, the husband is repulsive to her, and she is frigid to him. With the first husband, she had sexual satisfaction, mainly obtained by oral activity.

The Rorschach examination revealed several 'contaminated' responses which were considered pathognomonic of schizophrenia.

Summary of salient features: The central theme here is aggressive reaction formation around which a great deal of guilt feeling is generated. Aggression is partly outward (killing the husband and children, or the frustrating environment), partly inward (suicidal ideas, ideas of unworthiness).

Some projection is present, which is unusual: she fears being killed by her husband. The patient's mental disturbance showed three levels – neurotic, depressive and schizophrenic. On the neurotic level, P.C. displays symptoms of anxiety hysteria, phobic and obsessive manifestations. On the depressive level, there is a marked introjection; deep hostility towards the mother; marked ambivalence toward the father: a rigid conscience with a tendency to rebel; strong oral drives; the seeking of expiation of guilt. This is not on an unconscious but practically on a conscious or preconscious level. On the schizophrenic level, this woman is introverted, loosely connected with the environment, replacing reality with day-dreaming, always anxious, catathymic. In her paintings, the patient shows symbolic condensations and fragmentations. She believes in thought magic, projects her ideas into utterances and performances. She animates things. Boundaries between the ego and the world are hazy. A tendency to cosmic fusion is present. Sexually, P.C. shows a strong narcissistic, exhibitionistic trend, with sado-masochistic behaviour. The male–female differentiation is unclear. This patient fights disintegration vigorously and tries to hold onto reality.

DSM III and the emergence of schizotypal personality disorder

The process that fused Kendler's 'familial' and 'clinical' traditions into the modern concept of schizotypal personality disorder (and incidentally also borderline personality disorder) began with a single study. This was a companion study to Rosenthal *et al.*'s (1968, 1971) study of the adopted-away children of schizophrenic and manic-depressive parents, described in

Chapter 5, which was later (justifiably) attacked by Lidz (Lidz *et al.*, 1981, Lidz and Blatt, 1983). In the Danish adoption study, as the companion study came to be called, Kety *et al.* (1968, 1971) identified 33 adoptees with schizophrenia and 33 control adoptees, traced their biological relatives, and determined the rates of schizophrenia and related disorders that they showed. The findings were in the expected direction: 13 of 150 of the biological relatives of the schizophrenic adoptees had a diagnosis in the schizophrenia spectrum, compared to only 3 of 156 biological relatives of the controls. However, the important feature of the study was not its findings, but the way in which schizophrenia was diagnosed. As in the study by Rosenthal, cases were categorised as chronic schizophrenia, acute schizophrenic reaction, or borderline schizophrenia 'as these terms are commonly used in the United States'. (They also included a fourth subcategory of milder than borderline schizophrenia, which they termed possible schizophrenia or inadequate personality.)

Kety *et al.*'s criteria for borderline schizophrenia are shown in Table 16.2. As Kendler pointed out, it is apparent that, despite the study being firmly in the 'familial' tradition, most of the features – unusual mentation, micropsychosis, chaotic sexual adjustment, multiple neurotic symptoms and pan-anxiety – were drawn from the psychodynamically influenced 'clinical' tradition, especially Hoch's pseudoneurotic schizophrenia. Many of the features emphasised by familial writers, such as eccentricity, aloofness, social isolation and suspiciousness, barely rated a mention.

Approximately 10 years later the decision regarding whether to include borderline schizophrenia in DSM III was proving to be difficult. According to Spitzer *et al.* (1979), the chairman of the APA Task Force on Nomenclature and Statistics, on the one hand some members believed that the borderline

---

Table 16.2 The Danish adoption study's definition of borderline schizophrenia

---

1. *Thinking:* Strange or atypical mentation; thought shows tendency to ignore reality, logic and experience (to an excessive degree) resulting in poor adaptation to life experience (despite the presence of a normal IQ); fuzzy, murky, vague speech.

2. *Experience:* Brief episodes of cognitive distortion (the patient can, and does, snap back but during the episode the idea has more the character of a delusion than an ego-alien obsessive thought); feelings of depersonalisation, of strangeness or unfamiliarity with or toward the familiar; micropsychosis.

3. *Affective:* Anhedonia – never experiences intense pleasure – never happy; no deep or intense involvement with anyone or anybody.

4. *Interpersonal behaviour:* May appear poised, but lacking in depth ('as if' personality); sexual adjustment: chaotic fluctuation, mixture of hetero- and homosexuality.

5. *Psychopathology:* Multiple neurotic manifestations which shift frequently (obsessive concerns, phobias, conversion, psychosomatic symptoms, etc.); severe widespread anxiety.

Source: Kety *et al.* (1968).

concept represented everything that was wrong with American psychiatry, whereas on the other, one of the guiding principles in the development of DSM III was to include all conditions that clinicians felt were important, providing they could be reliably defined. They therefore turned to Kety and his co-workers, and in consultation with them drew up a list of 24 behavioural items that seemed to capture what these authors used to make the diagnosis of borderline schizophrenia in their study. These items had to be modified when they first tried to apply them to 36 cases from the Danish adoption study that Kety and co-workers considered to show evidence of borderline schizophrenia – it was found that many of them were not seen at all, and also that some important features, such as signs of odd communication falling short of gross formal thought disorder, were being missed. Eventually, after systematically reviewing the 36 case records and eliminating rare behaviours and combining others that seemed related to the same clinical concept, Spitzer *et al.* arrived at a set of 17 items that seemed to adequately represent the concept. They found that presence of three or more of the eight most frequently observed of these items correctly identified 30 of the 36 borderline cases, and misidentified only 2 of 43 cases considered by Kety *et al.* not to fall within the schizophrenia spectrum. This sensitivity of 86 per cent and specificity of 95 per cent was considered acceptable and the eight items formed the basis of the DSM III criteria for borderline schizophrenia, which they renamed schizotypal personality. The eight features are shown in Table 16.3.

Table 16.3 Features of schizotypal personality disorder developed by the APA Task Force

Odd communication (not gross formal thought disorder), e.g., speech that is tangential, digressive, vague, overelaborate, circumstantial, metaphorical
Ideas of reference, self-referential thinking
Suspiciousness or paranoid ideation
Recurrent illusions, sensing the presence of a force or person not actually present (e.g., 'I felt as if my dead mother were in the room with me'), depersonalisation or derealisation, not associated with panic attacks
Magical thinking, e.g., superstitiousness, clairvoyance, telepathy, 'sixth sense', 'others can feel my feelings'
Inadequate rapport in face-to-face interaction due to constricted or inappropriate affect, e.g., aloof, distant, cold, superficial, histrionic, effusive
Undue social anxiety or hypersensitivity to real or imagined criticism
Social isolation, e.g., no close friends or confidants, social contacts limited to essential everyday tasks

Note: DSM-III-R removed depersonalisation and derealisation as criteria for schizotypal personality disorder, on the grounds that most patients did not exhibit these symptoms. A criterion of eccentric and peculiar behaviours was also added.

Source: Spitzer *et al.* (1979).

The validity of schizotypal personality disorder

Reliability may have been achieved, but there remains something oddly intangible about the DSM III concept of schizotypal personality disorder. The picture does not seem to hang together in quite the same way as, say, the personality types described by Schneider, whose accounts still trigger off an immediate sense of recognition when they are read. One way of further establishing the validity of schizotypal personality disorder is simply to demonstrate that individuals showing the required traits do actually exist. Another way, which reflects the unique 'familial' origins of the concept, is to show that there is an excess of such traits in the relatives of patients with schizophrenia.

In contrast to all other forms of psychiatric disorder, descriptions of patients with schizotypical personality disorder are curiously elusive. The *DSM III case book* (Spitzer *et al.*, 1981) gave two examples. One, 'Clairvoyant', described a 23-year-old single unemployed woman who complained of feeling 'spacey', and for many hours each day felt as if she were watching herself move through life and that the world around her seemed unreal. For many years she had felt able to read people's minds by 'a kind of clairvoyance that I don't understand'. She was also preoccupied by the thought that she had some special mission in life, but she was not sure what it was. She was self-conscious in public, and often felt that people were paying special attention to her, or that strangers crossed the street to avoid her. She had no friends and spent much of her day lost in fantasies or watching soap operas on TV. She had had occasional jobs but had drifted away from them because of lack of interest. She spoke in a vague digressive way but was not considered to be incoherent. There were no delusions or hallucinations.

The second case, 'Wash before wearing', was quite different. A 41-year-old-man was described who had a lifelong pattern of social isolation and spent long hours worrying that his angry thoughts about his older brother would cause the brother harm. He had previously worked as a civil servant but had lost his job because of poor attendance and low productivity. On interview the patient was distant and somewhat distrustful. He described in elaborate and often irrelevant detail his rather uneventful and routine daily life. He told the interviewer that he had spent an hour and a half in a pet store deciding which of two brands of fish food to buy, and explained their relative merits. For two days he had studied the washing instructions on a new pair of jeans – Did 'Wash before wearing' mean that the jeans were to be washed before wearing the first time, or did they need, for some reason, to be washed each time before they were worn? He did not regard concerns such as these as senseless, though he acknowledged that the amount of time spent thinking about them might be excessive. When asked about his finances, he could recite from memory his most recent monthly bank statement, including the amount of every cheque, his balance on any particular day, and the running balance as each cheque was written. He was anxious about whether, if he joined the treatment programme, he would be required to participate in groups, as groups made him very nervous.

Two more cases were added in the *DSM-III-R case book* (Spitzer *et al.*, 1989). One of these was 'Sitting by the fire', the case of simple schizophrenia described in Chapter 2. In this patient the diagnosis of schizotypal personality was made reluctantly because it was the only one permissible in DSM-III-R. The other case, 'Alexei' from the Soviet Union, underwent a similar deterioration in function beginning in early adolescence, but in addition had been described as a perfect infant and then as a loner in his childhood. He had also been given a diagnosis of simple schizophrenia in his home country.

Only the first of these four cases is at all reminiscent of the DSM III concept of schizotypal personality, and even then it is hard to avoid thinking that a more searching history and a mental state examination might have led to another diagnosis. Most psychiatrists would consider the second patient to be suffering from schizoid personality or Asperger's syndrome. The third and probably also the fourth are cases of what DSM IV now recognises as simple deteriorative disorder (although only provisionally).

An initial attempt to validate schizotypal disorder by means of its frequency in the relatives of schizophrenic patients was made by Kendler *et al.* (1981) in a re-analysis of the Danish adoption study. They found that 11 of 105 (10.5 per cent) biological relatives of the schizophrenic adoptees met DSM III criteria for schizotypal personality, compared to 3 of 224 (1.5 per cent) for all other relatives. Since this was the study from which the modern definition of schizotypal personality was established in the first place, and also since the index cases were the same clinically diagnosed chronic, acute and borderline patients identified by Kety *et al.*, its findings are somewhat open to question.

The four further studies employing diagnostic criteria and blind evaluations are shown in Table 16.4. Two studies have been excluded because they gave only combined rates for schizotypal and other forms of personality disorder (Kendler *et al.*, 1984; Silverman *et al.*, 1993). The large and methodologically rigorous epidemiologically based study of Kendler *et al.* (1993b) has also been excluded on the grounds that the index group of schizophrenic cases used in this particular part of the study consisted of 319 patients diagnosed as schizophrenic 'with any level of certainty' rather than the 123 who met DSM-III-R criteria. Two of the studies found a significantly increased rate of schizotypal personality disorder and two did not. In one of the negative studies, however (Frangos *et al.*, 1985), the rate was nearly three times higher in the relatives of schizophrenic patients, although it was extremely low in both groups. In fact, given that the studies all used essentially the same (DSM III or DSM-III-R) criteria, it is surprising how much the rates varied across the studies, from just over 1 per cent in that of Frangos *et al.*, to nearly 15 per cent in that of Baron *et al.* (1985) – a rate that rose to over a quarter of the sample when probable schizotypal disorder was also included!

Table 16.4 Studies of schizotypal personality disorder, diagnosed according to DSM III/DSM-III-R criteria, in relatives of schizophrenic patients

| Study | Sample size | Means of assessment | Percentage with schizotypal personality disorder | | Comment |
			Relatives of patients	Relatives of controls	
Baron et al. (1985)	90 patients/376 relatives 90 controls/374 relatives	Blind Personal interview where possible	14.6 (MR)	2.1 (MR)	Rates are for definite schizotypal personality disorder. Rate also significantly increased for probable form of the disorder.
Coryell and Zimmerman (1988)	21 patients/80 relatives 38 controls/185 relatives	Blind Personal or telephone interview where possible	2.8 (MR)	2.5 (MR)	This study also failed to find an increased rate of schizophrenia in relatives of schizophrenics.
Frangos et al. (1985)	116 patients/572 relatives 116 controls/694 relatives	Blind Personal interview where possible	1.05	0.29	—
Maier et al. (1994)	101 patients/382 relatives 109 controls/419 relatives	Blind Personal interview where possible	2.1	0.3	—

Notes: All studies used RDC or DSM III/DSM-III-R criteria for schizophrenia.
MR – Morbid risk

The examination has been limited but its findings are telling. Patients can be diagnosed with DSM III schizotypal personality disorder when they are obviously suffering from other disorders, and a more than ten-fold variation has been found in its prevalence in the relatives of schizophrenic patients. These are the hallmarks of a disorder that either does not exist or whose criteria are excessively open to interpretation. The latter is particularly strikingly illustrated by the way in which 'Wash before wearing' could be made to fit DSM III criteria for schizotypal personality disorder. But when all is said and done patients are seen who show a lifelong pattern of personality abnormality which puts one immediately in mind of schizophrenia, and who are difficult to classify as having any other type of personality disorder. One such patient is described in Box 16.3.

Box 16.3 A patient with schizotypal personality disorder? (author's own case)

The patient was described as placid and content as a baby, but there were problems with feeding. She walked at the normal age but her speech was mildly delayed. As a child she was described as cheerful and demonstrative and she had temper tantrums up to three or four times a week if she could not get her own way. As a child she tended to play a lot on her own. At school she did not mix with other children, seemed frightened of them and also sometimes fought with them. As a result she was transferred to a residential school where she stayed until the age of 15. She hated lessons and did poorly academically, although she was of average intelligence on testing. However, she made some friends who she used to bring home with her on visits.

At age 5 she cut figures out of cardboard boxes and noticed that they were looking at her. She became interested in cats age 7 or 8 and started collecting pictures of cats, and drawing pictures of cat people. She was also interested in people with whiskers and pigtails. At the age of 13 she heard a record, 'Scarborough Fair' and started collecting as many different versions of it as she could find. She attributed magical properties to these records and her pictures and talked to them. She started carrying a record of the song with her at all times, and wore it on a piece of string round her neck. She also collected coloured flags that she called 'Georges'.

After leaving school she got a job in the office of a small company. At the age of 17 she was admitted to the Maudsley Hospital. Over the preceding two years she had become afraid of posters, pictures of the Statue of Liberty, the Esso Tiger, chimneys, coloured people, and 'men looking at her'. She had arguments with workmates and temper tantrums where she would shout and scream and throw herself about. On examination she was bizarrely dressed in short black trousers and red stockings with a plaid scarf dangling from her belt and multiple bangles on her wrist. She was wearing far too much make-up and her hair was in plaits, braided with lighter coloured extensions to her waist. When admitted she was wearing a gramophone record strung round her neck, which she later exchanged for a crucifix. Her affect was described as odd or inappropriate. She spoke at great length in an uninhibited way; there was no marked evidence of formal thought disorder, but she flitted from topic to topic. She occasionally used invented words ('Yes and I've got another word: *biggertheean* – it means unfancy or not sexy, or even unpleasant'). She was preoccupied with sadomasochistic sexual fantasies involving self-strangulation and putting fingers down her throat. She felt it was quite natural for her pictures and records to have magical properties and became resentful if any suggestion was made to the contrary. While in hospital she drew many pictures of bizarre cat people and would occasionally draw a beard or moustache or cats' whiskers on her face with black crayon.

A diagnosis of early schizophrenia was considered, but Sir Aubrey Lewis gave an opinion, and considered that she was 'a psychopathic personality – not antisocial – but a personality which was extremely distorted'.

She returned to her previous job and worked there for 25 years until the firm was taken over and she was made redundant. She had many boyfriends and one or two longer sexual relationships in later life. She began drinking excessively in her late twenties. From her twenties she also started complaining that she could see lines, curves and faces, e.g. on car bonnets, in picture rails, television aerials and chimneys. This symptom has persisted to the present day and is continually distressing. Treatment with neuroleptics for extended periods had no effect. No other psychotic symptoms were elicited other than hearing voices when half asleep. She made a number of suicide attempts from the age of 38, which were at least partly related to her visual symptoms.

About three years ago the patient's neuroleptics were withdrawn after she developed tardive dyskinesia. Several months later she had a brief period of apparent psychosis where she became loud, obviously thought-disordered and alluded to being possessed (but would not elaborate on this symptom). This improved over approximately three weeks on no treatment.

The patient is now in her sixties. She lives in sheltered accommodation near the hospital site, has multiple tattoos and wears bizarre 'gothic' make-up. For some time she has worn nothing but saris. Her conversation remains peppered with references to Scarborough Fair.

Borderline personality disorder

The tradition that began with latent schizophrenia did not end only with the modern concept of schizotypal personality disorder. After Kendler's familial and historical trends briefly merged to become borderline schizophrenia, they split again, with the other branch becoming the modern concept of borderline personality disorder. The association of this personality type with schizophrenia is now played down by many authors, but remains linked to it by virtue of the fact that one of its alleged features is short-lived episodes of psychosis.

The early history of borderline personality disorder

Gunderson and Singer (1975) and Mack (1975), who have given detailed histories of the borderline concept, identified American psychodynamic psychiatry as the driving force behind it, with papers published outside the United States actually being quite rare. The work of Hoch and Polatin (1949), described above, played a seminal role in the development of the concept, but more influential were Zilboorg (1941) and Schmideberg (1947). The former identified a group of patients who failed to integrate reality into their affective lives. He included psychopathic personalities, 'poor' personalities, transvestites, fetishists and other sexual perverts, murderers, as well as mild-mannered, quiet, unobtrusive and ineffective people who, however, were suffused with inner hatred and rage. Schmideberg was an early (but not the first) user of the term 'borderline personality', for individuals who had difficulty adapting to the real world and to whom something was always happening. Like Zilboorg, she grouped together psychopathic personalities, criminals, alcoholics and paranoids, as well as various other acting-out suicidal individuals, who she described as being 'stable in their instability'.

By 1950 most psychodynamically oriented American psychiatrists were convinced they were seeing a large group of what were by this time being referred to as borderline cases or borderline reaction types. These patients were not overtly schizophrenic, but showed a level of disturbance approaching this, which was more severe than in patients referred to as 'psychoneurotic'. While there was agreement that such individuals exhibited serious character disturbances and 'emotional infantilism', their traits were otherwise varied and poorly described.

A degree of order was brought to the concept, at least from the psychoanalytic point of view, in two papers by Knight (1954a, b). He detailed the kinds of ego defences and disturbances of object relationships such patients showed, and recommended that a complete inventory of ego functioning be undertaken before making the diagnosis, while also cautioning that the defence mechanisms employed by the ego could not always be explicitly correlated with particular fixations and points of regression in the development of the libido. Kernberg (1967) developed this line of reasoning further, arguing specifically that patients with what he called 'borderline personality organisation' employed a characteristic defence mechanism of 'splitting'.

Whatever else this work clarified, it was not the presenting clinical picture, which could be quite variable as Mack, quoting Chase and Hire, put it, borderline patients entered treatment following suicide attempts, disturbed behaviour ('marked regression'), severe depression, confusional states, depersonalisation and loss of reality, at the one extreme, to less dramatic and less acute manifestations at the other, such as a longstanding inability to form satisfying relationships, psychosomatic reactions to stress, or concerns about episodic or impulsive acting out. They could show a facade of maturity and be endowed with high intellectual ability and great creative gifts, but lived with a precarious psychic equilibrium because of a deficient development of reality sense and sense of self.

Mack considered that the modern literature on borderline personality was marked by a shift away from characterising borderline personality with reference to psychotic illnesses. However, Gunderson and Singer cited numerous references attesting to the fact that 'the borderline person's capacity to develop regressive psychotic symptoms may be a pathognomonic feature'. Both agreed that such states were reversible and transient, and developed in times of stress, in the setting of intolerable rage, or under the influence of drugs like cannabis and LSD. The symptoms also tended to be limited: they were often described as unsystematised and 'ego-alien', and clear, stable delusions or hallucinations were generally felt to be absent, although there were a few dissenting opinions. Some authors also emphasised derealisation, depersonalisation and dissociation, in much the same imprecise way as these terms were also later used in the DSM III description of schizotypal personality disorder (before they were dropped in DSM-III-R).

The DSM III concept of borderline personality disorder

When Spitzer and his colleagues on the APA Task Force on Nomenclature and Statistics (Spitzer *et al.*, 1979) came to consider borderline conditions for inclusion in DSM III, they found a large literature that used the term in contradictory and often obscure ways. However, within this two main usages were apparent. One was exemplified by the term borderline schizophrenia, which they went on to define criteria for and renamed schizotypal personality disorder. The other referred to a constellation of relatively enduring personality features, with most descriptions emphasising instability in affect, interpersonal relationships, job functioning and sense of identity. As by this time they thought it was important to avoid using the term 'borderline' altogether, they chose the term 'unstable personality' to describe this.

After consulting with Gunderson, Kernberg and other authorities, the Task Force produced a set of items that they thought would be adequate to capture the features of the syndrome. These are shown in Table 16.5.

Table 16.5 Features of unstable (borderline) personality disorder developed by the APA Task Force

---

Identity disturbance manifested by uncertainty about several issues relating to identity, such as self-image, gender identity, long-term goals or career choice, friendship patterns, values, and loyalties, e.g. 'Who am I?' 'I feel like I am my sister when I am good'.

A pattern of unstable and intense interpersonal relationships, e.g. marked shifts of attitude, idealisation, devaluation, manipulation (consistently using others for his own ends).

Impulsivity or unpredictability in at least two areas which are potentially self-damaging, e.g. spending, sex, gambling, drug or alcohol use, shop-lifting, overeating, physically self-damaging acts.

Inappropriate intense anger or lack of control or anger, e.g. frequently loses temper, always angry.

Physically self-damaging acts, e.g. suicidal gestures, self-mutilation, recurrent accidents, or physical fights.

Work history or school achievement unstable or below expected on basis of intelligence, training, or opportunities.

Affective instability: marked shifts from normal mood to depression, irritability, or anxiety, usually lasting hours and only rarely for more than a few days, with a return to normal mood.

Chronic feelings of emptiness or boredom.

Problems tolerating being alone, e.g. frantic efforts to avoid being alone, depressed when alone.

Note: The item concerning work history or school achievement was eliminated in DSM III.

Source: Spitzer *et al.* (1979).

They tapped concepts of identity disturbance, unstable and intense inter-personal relationships, impulsive and self-damaging behaviour, anger dyscon-trol and affective instability, problems tolerating being alone, and chronic feelings of emptiness and poor work or school achievement. The items were subjected to a sensitivity and specificity exercise similar to that for schizotypal personality disorder, but this time carried out on a group of 33 patients undergoing therapy in New York, 18 with and 15 without a borderline diag-nosis. Using a cut-off of presence of three or more items, a sensitivity of 100 per cent and a specificity of 80 per cent was achieved. Further analyses led to the removal of the item 'Work history or school achievement unstable or below expected on basis of intelligence, training, or opportunities', because it was found to be more predictive of schizotypal personality disorder than unstable personality disorder. The remaining items formed the criteria used in DSM III, where, however, the name reverted back to borderline personality disorder.

Borderline personality disorder and psychosis

Noticeably absent from Spitzer *et al.*'s set of items was anything pertaining to psychotic symptoms. This denial was less absolute in DSM III where the accompanying text allowed that 'during periods of extreme stress transient psychotic symptoms of insufficient severity or duration to warrant an additional diagnosis may occur'. Some of this coyness reflected a rising tide of opinion that borderline personality was unrelated to schizophrenia. However, the concept of regression into a psychotic state under conditions of stress was still a central feature of the concept to many, and in any case attempting to play this down could be regarded as disingenuous, even deceptive. If individuals with a certain form of personality organisation can develop psychotic symptoms under conditions of stress, this has supremely important implications for the nature of psychosis itself, and challenges the mainstream view that schizophrenia is a biological brain disease.

Despite, or possibly because of, its importance, the literature on this point is very small. The decision as to whether borderline patients develop short-lived episodes of psychosis currently stands or falls on just two studies which, needless to say, have had contradictory findings.

Gunderson's group (Zanarini *et al.*, 1990) rated psychotic and psychosis-like symptoms in 50 patients who met DSM III criteria for borderline personality disorder, 55 age- and sex-matched individuals who met criteria for a wide range of other personality disorders (including 8 with schizoid, paranoid or schizotypal personality disorder), and 46 normal controls. These were assessed using the Revised Diagnostic Interview for Borderlines, which contains items for disturbed but non-psychotic thought, such as magical thinking, superstitiousness, 'sixth sense', recurrent illusions, depersonalisation and derealisation, non-delusional paranoia and ideas of reference. It also contains items for 'quasi-psychotic experiences' – delusions or hallucinations that are judged to be transient (less than two days' duration), circumscribed (affecting only one or two areas of the patient's life) or atypical of psychotic disorders (possibly reality based, or not totally fantastic in content). All these symptoms were rated over the preceding two years. The subjects were also assessed with a conventional structured psychiatric interview for the lifetime occurrence of 'true' psychotic episodes.

The borderline patients were found to have significantly higher scores on most of the 'disturbed but non-psychotic' items than those with other personality disorders, who in turn had higher scores than the normal controls. 'Quasi-psychotic experiences' were virtually restricted to borderline patients: 20 of the 50 (40 per cent) had experienced quasi-delusions or quasi-hallucinations or both over the previous two years, in comparison to only 1 of 55 (2 per cent) of the other personality disorder group and none of the normal controls. Seven (14 per cent) of the borderline patients had also experienced psychotic episodes lasting more than two days, compared to two (4 per cent) of the other personality disorder patients and none of the normal subjects. In two of the borderline patients the episode occurred in the context of hallucinogenic drug abuse, in one it followed chronic amphetamine use, and in the remaining four the symptoms developed during a concurrent major depressive episode.

Pope *et al.* (1985) reviewed the case-notes of 33 patients who had a DSM III diagnosis of borderline personality disorder and who had been hospitalised. One of the investigators noted any psychotic symptoms that were recorded during the index admission and, based on this and other available information, assigned a DSM III diagnosis for the psychotic state. Another of the investigators followed up those patients who had experienced psychotic symptoms 4–7 years later and carried out a personal or telephone interview blind to the original diagnosis of the psychotic state.

Twenty of the 33 patients (61 per cent) were found to have exhibited psychotic symptoms during the index admission. One patient experienced these for several days before admission in the context of heavy use of multiple unknown drugs. His symptoms disappeared promptly after hospitalisation and remained absent during a 5-year follow-up. Seven patients appeared to display psychotic symptoms only at times when they also displayed either a full manic or full depressive syndrome. Six of these patients were also given a diagnosis of definite or possible major affective disorder on follow-up 4–7 years later. The remaining 12 patients were considered to meet DSM III criteria for factitious disorder. Pope *et al.*, acknowledged that such a diagnosis was controversial and had to be considered tentative, particularly when it was made on the basis of a case-note review. However, they defended their position with two examples, which are reproduced in Box 16.4.

Conclusion

The Achilles heel of the three main concepts of schizophrenia-related personality discussed has always been their overinclusiveness. For much of their history they have found it difficult to maintain their own separate identities, and they have been in constant danger of being broadened into a synonym for an attenuated form of whatever model of schizophrenia was adhered to. However, the apprehension expressed at the beginning of this chapter turns out not to be justified. All three types of personality disorder are now diagnosed according to the same kind of rigorous diagnostic criteria as other forms of psychiatric disorder. Consequently, they are in a position to be judged independently and on their own merits.

Schizoid personality, in the modern usage of the term, does seem to genuinely, although modestly, predispose to the development of schizophrenia. However, as its use has narrowed down, it has come to face another problem. This is that what is being described is no longer distinguishable from Asperger's syndrome. This problem is illustrated perfectly by a study by Wolff and Chick cited in the last chapter: after defining schizoid personality in childhood by clinical features of emotional detachment, solitariness, rigidity,

---

Box 16.4 Two cases of factitious psychosis in borderline personality disorder (from Pope *et al.*, 1985)

Case 1
During her index admission, Ms A, a 19-year-old woman with borderline personality disorder, claimed to hear the voices of her 'good self' and 'bad self' talking to her. She later conceded that these were not really voices, but rather 'internal' thoughts that she could control. Thus the index rater diagnosed them as factitious psychotic symptoms. In the follow-up interview, she told the rater that she could see figures of people floating in space whom she could 'will to be there'. However, she denied having more typical psychotic symptoms such as ideas of reference or paranoid delusions. There seemed to be no apparent goal of the symptoms other than to assume the 'patient' role. Thus she was independently diagnosed by the follow-up rater as having factitious psychotic symptoms. Interestingly, the follow-up rater also noted factitious neurological symptoms (conversion disorder) in the form of factitious seizures. During one 'seizure' she threw a desk across a room. Results of a detailed neurological workup of the 'seizures' had been negative.

Case 2
On follow-up interview, Ms B, a 32-year-old woman with borderline personality disorder, described visions of 13 women dressed as judges filing into her room. At other times she claimed to be floating free in space and looking at herself. She also described periods when she could recognise only children and not adults. However, she denied having typical psychotic symptoms such as ideas of reference or auditory hallucinations. She displayed no apparent goal for the symptoms other than to assume the 'patient' role. On the basis of the fantastic and non-stereotypic nature and course of the symptoms, the follow-up rater diagnosed her as having factitious psychosis. Interestingly, the index admission rater, although not noting factitious psychotic symptoms, did note factitious neurologic symptoms: during her admission, a neurologist had diagnosed factitious anaesthesia, present in a non-anatomic distribution. The treatment response rater noted that she failed to respond to chlorpromazine, thioridazine, lithium carbonate, and amitriptyline.

---

circumscribed interests, sensitivity, suspiciousness and paranoid ideation, lack of empathy, odd ideation, metaphorical use of language and marked lack of guardedness, they then went on to give one of the pioneering contemporary accounts of Asperger's syndrome.

Whereas schizoid personality disorder has been around so long that it is part of the furniture, schizotypal personality in its current sense is a recent arrival. What seems clear from the otherwise murky tradition that gave birth to it, is that unusual personality characteristics in the relatives of patients with schizophrenia – with both positive and negative consequences for them – are a part of the genetic puzzle that cannot be ignored. What is less clear is whether these characteristics would cluster together in any identifiable form in the kind of analysis carried out by Tyrer *et al.* (1988). Every psychiatrist will have seen typical examples of schizoid, paranoid, obsessional, hysterical, antisocial, asthenic and hyperthymic personalities, and so on. There will also be any number of word portraits of them in textbooks and articles. As often as not there will be famous historical examples of such personalities, and characters in novels who show all the attributes, even though the authors have not recognised this. To date none of these statements apply to schizotypal personality. The only thing that can be said with any certainty is that the existing diagnostic criteria do not seem to capture what is being described very well.

Even when it is defined in terms of clinical features rather than ego functions, there is a reluctance to accept the concept of borderline personality outside America. It also seems at least as unlikely that it would emerge as a recognisable cluster in an exercise of the Tyrer *et al.*, type. If the syndrome does exist, there is still a stark choice to be made with respect to its point of contact with schizophrenia, its association with brief episodes of psychotic symptoms. Either one accepts the view of Gunderson and co-workers that they can genuinely occur, which entails a radical reformulation of views about the nature of psychosis along psychosocial or even psychodynamic lines. Or one puts one's faith in the findings of Pope and his contrarian co-workers, which are reassuring for mainstream views on schizophrenia, but which imply that Gunderson's group have been at the very least naive, and makes one wonder why the challenge that was thrown down has not been responded to.

References

Abbott, R.J. and Loizou, L.A. (1986). Neuroleptic malignant syndrome. *British Journal of Psychiatry*, 148, 47–51.

Abi-Dargham, A., Gil, R., Krystal, J., Baldwin, R.M., Seibyl, J.P., Bowers, M. *et al.* (1998). Increased striatal dopamine transmission in schizophrenia: Confirmation in a second cohort. *American Journal of Psychiatry*, 155, 761–767.

Abi-Dargham, A., Mawlawi, O., Lombardo, I., Gil, R., Martinez, D., Huang, Y. *et al.* (2002). Prefrontal dopamine D1 receptors and working memory in schizophrenia. *Journal of Neuroscience*, 22, 3708–3719.

Abrams, R. and Taylor, M. (1973). First-rank symptoms, severity of illness, and treatment response in schizophrenia. *Comprehensive Psychiatry*, 14, 353–355.

Abrams, R.A. and Taylor, M.A. (1976a). Mania and schizo-affective disorder, manic type: A comparison. *American Journal of Psychiatry*, 133, 1445–1447.

Abrams, R. and Taylor, M.A. (1976b). Catatonia: A prospective clinical study. *Archives of General Psychiatry*, 33, 579–581.

Abrams, R. and Taylor, M.A. (1978). A rating scale for emotional blunting. *American Journal of Psychiatry*, 135, 226–229.

Achte, K.A. (1967). On prognosis and rehabilitation in schizophrenic and paranoid psychoses. *Acta Psychiatrica Scandinavica*, Supplement, 196, 1–217.

Achte, K.A., Hillbom, E. and Aalberg, V. (1969). Psychoses following war brain injuries. *Acta Psychiatrica Scandinavica*, 45, 1–18.

Ackner, B., Harris, A. and Oldham, A.J. (1957). Insulin treatment of schizophrenia: A controlled study. *Lancet*, i, 607–609.

Addonizio, G. and Susman, V.L. (1991). *Neuroleptic malignant syndrome: A clinical approach*. St Louis, Mo: Mosby.

Adler, C.M., Goldberg, T.M., Malhotra, A.K., Pickar, D. and Breier, A. (1998). Effects of ketamine on thought disorder, working memory and semantic memory in healthy volunteers. *Biological Psychiatry*, 43, 811–816.

Aita, J.A. and Reitan, R.M. (1948). Psychotic reactions in the late recovery period following head injury. *American Journal of Psychiatry*, 105, 161–169.

Akbarian, S., Sucher, N.J., Bradley, D., Tafazzoli, A., Trinh, D., Hetrick, W.P. *et al.* (1996). Selective alterations in gene expression for NMDA receptor subunits in prefrontal cortex of schizophrenics. *Journal of Neuroscience*, 16, 19–30.

Alberts, J.L., Francois, F. and Josserand, F. (1985). Etude des effets secondaires rapportes a l'occasion de traitements par dogmatil. *Semaine Hôpital Paris*, 61, 1351–1357.

Alexander, M.P., Benson, D.F. and Stuss, D.T. (1989). Frontal lobes and language. *Brain and Language*, 37, 656–691.

Al-Khani, M., Bebbington, P., Watson, J. and House, F. (1986). Life events and schizophrenia: A Saudi Arabian study. *British Journal of Psychiatry*, 148, 12–22.

Allderidge, P. (1974). *Richard Dadd*. London: Academy Editions.

Almeida, O.P., Howard, R., Forstl, H. and Levy, R. (1992). Should the diagnosis of late paraphrenia be abandoned? *Psychological Medicine*, 22, 11–14.

Almeida, O.P., Howard, R.J., Levy, R., David, A.S., Morris, R.G. and Sahakian, B.J. (1995). Cognitive features of psychotic states arising in late life (late paraphrenia). *Psychological Medicine*, 25, 685–698.

Altshuler, L.L., Conrad, A., Kovelman, J.A. and Scheibel, A. (1987). Hippocampal pyramidal cell orientation in schizophrenia: A controlled neurohistologic study of the Yakovlev Collection. *Archives of General Psychiatry*, 44, 1094–1098.

Andreasen, N.C. (1979a). Thought, language and communication disorders: I. Clinical assessment, definition of terms and evaluation of their reliability. *Archives of General Psychiatry*, 36, 1315–1321.

Andreasen, N.C. (1979b). Affective flattening and the criteria for schizophrenia. *American Journal of Psychiatry*, 136, 944–947.

Andreasen, N.C. (1982). Negative symptoms in schizophrenia: Definition and reliability. *Archives of General Psychiatry*, 39, 784–788.

Andreasen, N.C. (1999). A unitary model of schizophrenia: Bleuler's 'fragmented phrene' as schizencephaly. *Archives of General Psychiatry*, 56, 781–787.

Andreasen, N.C. and Bardach, J. (1977). Dysmorphophobia: Symptom or disease. *American Journal of Psychiatry*, 134, 673–676.

Andreasen, N.C. and Olsen, S. (1982). Negative v. positive schizophrenia: Definition and validation. *Archives of General Psychiatry*, 39, 789–794.

Andreasen, N.C., Rice, J., Endicott, J., Coryell, W., Grove, W.M. and Reich, T. (1987). Familial rates of affective disorder. *Archives of General Psychiatry*, 44, 461–469.

Andreasen, N.C., Swayze, V.W., Flaum, M., Yates, W.R., Arndt, S. and McChesney, C. (1990). Ventricular enlargement in schizophrenia evaluated with computed tomographic scanning. *Archives of General Psychiatry*, 47, 1008–1015.

Andreasen, N.C., Rezai, K., Alliger, R., Swayze, V.W., Flaum, M., Kirchner, P. *et al.* (1992). Hypofrontality in neuroleptic-naive patients and in patients with chronic schizophrenia. *Archives of General Psychiatry*, 49, 943–958.

Andreasen, N.C., Arndt, S., Alliger, R., Miller, D. and Flaum, M. (1995). Symptoms of schizophrenia: Methods, meanings, and mechanisms. *Archives of General Psychiatry*, 52, 341–351.

Angrist, B. and Sudilovsky, A. (1978). Central nervous system stimulants: Historical aspects and clinical effects. In L.L. Iversen, S.E. Iversen and S.H. Snyder (Eds.), *Handbook of psychopharmacology, Vol. 11, Stimulants*, pp. 99–166. New York: Plenum.

Angrist, B. and van Kammen, D.P. (1984). CNS stimulants as tools in the study of schizophrenia. *Trends in Neuroscience*, 7, 388–390.

Angrist, B.M. and Gershon, S. (1970). The phenomenology of experimentally induced amphetamine psychosis – preliminary observations. *Biological Psychiatry*, 2, 95–107.

APA (American Psychiatric Association) Task Force (1979). *Tardive dyskinesia: Report of the American Psychiatric Association task force on the late neurological effects of antipsychotic drugs*. Washington, DC: American Psychiatric Association.

Aparicio-Legarza, M.I., Davis, B., Hutson, P.H. and Reynolds, G.P. (1998). Increased density of glutamate/N-methyl-D-aspartate receptors in putamen from schizophrenic patients. *Neuroscience Letters*, 241, 143–146.

Arevalo, J. and Vizcarro, C. (1989). 'Emocion expresada' y curso de la esquizofrenia en una muestra española. *Analisis y Modificacion de Conducta*, 15, 3–23.

Arieti, S. (1974). *Interpretation of schizophrenia*, 2nd edn. London: Crosby Lockwood Staples.

Arnold, S.E., Franz, B.R., Gur, R.C., Gur, R.E., Shapiro, R.M., Moberg, P.J. *et al.* (1995a). Smaller neuron size in schizophrenia in hippocampal subfields that mediate cortical–hippocampal interactions. *American Journal of Psychiatry*, 152, 738–748.

Arnold, S.E., Gur, R.E., Shapiro, R.M., Fisher, K.R., Mober, P.J., Gibney, M.R. *et al.* (1995b). Prospective clinicopathological studies of schizophrenia: Accrual and assessment. *American Journal of Psychiatry*, 152, 731–737.

Arora, A., Avasthi, A. and Kulhara, P. (1997). Subsyndromes of chronic schizophrenia: A phenomenological study. *Acta Psychiatrica Scandinavica*, 96, 225–229.

Arseneault, L., Cannon, M., Witton, J. and Murray, R.M. (2004). Causal association between cannabis and psychosis: Examination of the evidence. *British Journal of Psychiatry*, 184, 110–117.

Arthur, A.Z. (1964). Theories and explanations of delusions: A review. *American Journal of Psychiatry*, 121, 105–115.

Asarnow, J.R. (1988). Children at risk for schizophrenia: Converging lines of evidence. *Schizophrenia Bulletin*, 14, 613–631.

Asarnow, R.F., Nuechterlein, K.H., Fogelson, D., Subotnik, K.L., Payne, D.A., Russell, A.T. *et al.* (2001). Schizophrenia and schizophrenia-spectrum personality disorders in the first-degree relatives of children with schizophrenia: The UCLA family study. *Archives of General Psychiatry*, 58, 581–588.

Asperger, H. (1944). Die 'Autistic Psychopathen' im Kindeshalter. *Archiv für Psychiatrie und Nervenkrankheiten*, 117, 76–136. (Trans. U. Frith as 'Autistic Psychopathy' in childhood. In U. Frith (Ed.), *Autism and Asperger syndrome*, pp. 37–93. Cambridge: Cambridge University Press.)

Astrup, C. (1979). *The chronic schizophrenias*. Oslo: Universitetsforlaget.

Astrup, C. and Noreik, K. (1966). *Functional psychoses: Diagnostic and prognostic models*. Springfield, IL: Thomas.

Astrup, C., Fossum, A. and Holmboe, R. (1959). A follow-up study of 270 patients with acute affective psychoses. *Acta Psychiatrica et Neurologica Scandinavica*, 34, Supplement, 135, 11–65.

Ayd, F.J. (1961). A survey of drug-induced extrapyramidal reactions. *Journal of the American Medical Association*, 175, 1054–1060.

Ayd, F.J., Coyle, J.T., Hollister, L.E., Simpson, G.M., Carpenter, W.T., Casey, D.E. *et al.* (1984). Tardive dyskinesia and thioridazine. *Archives of General Psychiatry*, 41, 414–416.

Barnes, T.R.E. and Braude, W.M. (1985). Akathisia variants and tardive dyskinesia. *Archives of General Psychiatry*, 42, 874–878.

Baron, M., Gruen, R., Asnis, L. and Kane, J. (1982). Schizoaffective illness, schizophrenia, and affective disorders: Morbidity risk and genetic transmission. *Acta Psychiatrica Scandinavica*, 65, 253–262.

Baron, M., Gruen, R., Rainer, J.D., Kane, J., Asnis, L. and Lord, S. (1985). A family study of schizophrenia and normal control probands: Implications for the spectrum concept of schizophrenia. *American Journal of Psychiatry*, 142, 447–455.

Barrelet, L., Ferrero, F., Szigethy, L., Giddey, C. and Pellizzer, G. (1990). Expressed emotion and first-admission schizophrenia: Nine-month follow-up in a French cultural environment. *British Journal of Psychiatry*, 156, 357–362.

Barrera, A., Hodges, J.R., McKenna, P.J. and Berrios, G.E. (2005). Formal thought disorder in schizophrenia: An executive or a semantic deficit? *Psychological Medicine*, 35, 121–132.

Barrowclough, C. and Tarrier, N. (1992). *Families of schizophrenic patients*. London: Chapman and Hall.

Baruk, H. (1959). Delusions of passion. In S.R. Hirsch and M. Shepherd (Eds.) (1974), *Themes and variations in European psychiatry*, pp. 375–384. Bristol: Wright.

Basso, M.R., Nasrallah, H.A., Olson, S.C. and Bornstein, R.A. (1998). Neuro-psychological correlates of negative, disorganized and psychotic symptoms in schizophrenia. *Schizophrenia Research*, 31, 99–111.

Bateson, G., Jackson, D.D., Haley, J. and Weakland, J. (1956). Toward a theory of schizophrenia. *Behavioral Science*, 1, 251–264.

Bearden, C.E., Rosso, I.M., Hollister, J.M., Gasperoni, T.L., Sanchez, L.E., Hadley, T. *et al.* (2000). A prospective cohort study of childhood behavioral deviance and language abnormalities as predictors of adult schizophrenia. *Schizophrenia Bulletin*, 26, 395–410.

Beasley, C.M., Dellva, M.A., Tamura, R.N., Morgenstern, H., Glazer, W.M., Ferguson, K. *et al.* (1999). Randomised double-blind comparison of the incidence of tardive dyskinesia in patients with schizophrenia during long-term treatment with olanzapine or haloperidol. *British Journal of Psychiatry*, 174, 23–30.

Bebbington, P., Wilkins, S., Jones, P., Foerster, A., Murray, R., Toone, B. *et al.* (1993). Life events and psychosis: Initial results from the Camberwell Collaborative Psychosis Study. *British Journal of Psychiatry*, 162, 72–79.

Beck, A.T. (1952). Successful outpatient psychotherapy of a chronic schizophrenic with a delusion based on borrowed guilt. *Psychiatry*, 15, 305–312.

Beer, M.D. (1996). Psychosis: A history of the concept. *Comprehensive Psychiatry*, 37, 273–291.

Beigel, A. and Murphy, D.L. (1971). Assessing clinical characteristics of the manic state. *American Journal of Psychiatry*, 128, 688–694.

Bell, M.D., Lysaker, P.H., Beam-Goulet, J.L., Milstein, R.M. and Lindenmayer, J.-P. (1994). Five-component model of schizophrenia: Assessing the factorial invariance of the Positive and Negative Syndrome Scale. *Psychiatry Research*, 52, 295–303.

Benes, F.M. (1988). Post-mortem structural analyses of schizophrenic brain: Study designs and the interpretation of data. *Psychiatric Developments*, 6, 213–226.

Benes, F.M., Sorensen, I. and Bird, E.D. (1991). Reduced neuronal size in posterior hippocampus of schizophrenic patients. *Schizophrenia Bulletin*, 17, 597–608.

Bennett, D. (1983). The historical development of rehabilitation services. In F.N. Watts and D.H. Bennett (Eds.), *Theory and practice of psychiatric rehabilitation*, pp. 15–42. Chichester: Wiley.

Bennett, D.H. (1978). Community psychiatry. *British Journal of Psychiatry*, 132, 209–220.

Bennett, S. and Klein, H.R. (1966). Childhood schizophrenia: 30 years later. *American Journal of Psychiatry*, 122, 1121–1124.

Benson, D.F. (1973). Psychiatric aspects of aphasia. *British Journal of Psychiatry*, 123, 555–566.

Bentaleb, L.A., Beauregard, M., Liddle, P. and Stip, E. (2002). Cerebral activity associated with auditory verbal hallucinations: A functional magnetic resonance imaging case study. *Journal of Psychiatry and Neuroscience*, 27, 110–115.

Bentall, R. (2003). *Madness explained: Psychosis and human nature*. London: Allen Lane.

Bentall, R.P. (1990). The syndromes and symptoms of psychosis. In R.P. Bentall (Ed.), *Reconstructing schizophrenia*, pp. 23–60. London: Routledge.

Berg, E., Lindelius, R., Patterson, U. and Salum, I. (1983). Schizoaffective psychoses: A long-term follow-up. *Acta Psychiatrica Scandinavica*, 67, 389–398.

Berrettini, W. (2003). Evidence for shared susceptibility in bipolar disorder and schizophrenia. *American Journal of Medical Genetics, Part C (Seminars in Medical Genetics)*, 123C, 59–64.

Berrios, G.E. (1982). Tactile hallucinations: Conceptual and historical aspects. *Journal of Neurology, Neurosurgery and Psychiatry*, 45, 285–293.

Berrios, G.E. (1985). Positive and negative symptoms and Jackson. *Archives of General Psychiatry*, 42, 95–97.

Berrios, G.E. (1986). Presbyophrenia: The rise and fall of a concept. *Psychological Medicine*, 16, 267–275.

Berrios, G.E. (1987). Historical aspects of the psychoses: 19th century issues. *British Medical Bulletin*, 43, 484–498.

Berrios, G.E. (1991). Positive and negative signals: A conceptual history. In A. Marneros, N.C. Andreasen and M.T. Tsuang (Eds.), *Negative versus positive schizophrenia*. Berlin/Heidelberg: Springer Verlag.

Berrios, G.E. (1996). *The history of mental symptoms: Descriptive psychopathology since the nineteenth century*. Cambridge: Cambridge University Press.

Biehl, H., Maurer, K., Schubart, C., Krum, B. and Jung, E. (1986). Prediction of outcome and utilization of medical services in a prospective study of first-onset schizophrenics: Results of a five-year follow-up study. *European Archives of Psychiatry and Neurological Sciences*, 236, 139–147.

Biel, J.H. and Bopp, B.A. (1978). Amphetamines: Structure–activity relationships. In L.L. Iversen, S.E. Iversen and S.H. Snyder (Eds.), *Handbook of psychopharmacology, Vol. 11, Stimulants*, pp. 1–40. New York: Plenum.

Birchwood, M.J., Hallett, S.E. and Preston, M.C. (1988). *Schizophrenia: An integrated approach to research and treatment*. London: Longman.

Bird, E.D., Barnes, J., Iversen, L.L., Spokes, E.G.S., MacKay, A.V.P. and Shepherd, M. (1977). Increased brain dopamine and reduced glutamic acid decarboxylase and choline acetyl transferase activity in schizophrenia and related psychoses. *Lancet*, ii, 1157–1159.

Bird, E.D., Langais, P.J. and Benes, F.M. (1984). Dopamine and homovanillic acid in postmortem schizophrenic brain. *Clinical Neuropharmacology*, 7, Supplement, 1, 910–911.

Bird, E.S., Spokes, E.G.S. and Iversen, L.L. (1979). Increased dopamine concentrations in limbic areas of brain of patients dying with schizophrenia. *Brain*, 102, 347–360.

Birley, J.L.T. and Brown, G.W. (1970). Crises and life changes preceding the onset or relapse of acute schizophrenia. *British Journal of Psychiatry*, 116, 327–333.

Blair, D. (1940). Prognosis in schizophrenia. *Journal of Mental Science*, 86, 378–477.

Blanchard, J. and Neale, J. (1994). The neuropsychological signature of schizophrenia: Generalised or differential deficit? *American Journal of Psychiatry*, 151, 40–48.

Bland, R.C. and Orn, H. (1978). 14 year outcome in early schizophrenia. *Acta Psychiatrica Scandinavica*, 58, 327–338.

Blashfield, R.K. (1984). *The classification of psychopathology: Neo-Kraepelian and quantitative approaches*. New York: Plenum.

Bleuler, E. (1911). *Dementia praecox or the group of schizophrenias* (trans. J. Zinkin, 1950). New York: International Universities Press.

Bleuler, E. (1926). *Textbook of psychiatry* (trans. A.A. Brill). London: George Allen & Unwin.

Bleuler, M. (1974). The long-term course of the schizophrenic psychoses. *Psychological Medicine*, 4, 244–254.

Bleuler, M. (1978). *The schizophrenic disorders: Long-term patient and family studies* (trans. S.M. Clemens). New Haven, CT: Yale University Press.

Blumer, D. and Benson, D.F. (1975). Personality changes with frontal and temporal lobe lesions. In D.F. Benson and D. Blumer (Eds.), *Psychiatric aspects of Neurological Disease*, pp. 151–170. New York: Grune & Stratton.

Boeringa, J.A. and Castellani, S. (1979). Reliability and validity of emotional blunting as a criterion for diagnosis of schizophrenia. *American Journal of Psychiatry*, 139, 1131–1135.

Bogerts, B. (1997). The temporolimbic system theory of positive schizophrenic symptoms. *Schizophrenia Bulletin*, 23, 423–435.

Bonner, C.A. and Kent, G.H. (1936). Overlapping symptoms in catatonic excitement and manic excitement. *American Journal of Psychiatry*, 92, 1311–1322.

Bonner, H. (1951). The problem of diagnosis in paranoic conditions. *American Journal of Psychiatry*, 107, 677–683.

Borison, R.L., Hitri, A., Blowers, A.J. and Diamond, B.I. (1983). Antipsychotic drug action: Clinical, biochemical and pharmacological evidence for site-specificity of action. *Clinical Neuropharmacology*, 6, 137–150.

Bourne, H. (1953). The insulin myth. *Lancet*, ii, 964–968.

Bowman, K.M. and Raymond, A.F. (1931). A statistical study of delusions in the manic-depressive psychoses. In *Proceedings of the association for research in nervous and mental diseases*, Vol. 11. Baltimore, MD: Williams and Wilkins.

Boyes, J., Whalley, H.C., Lawrie, S.M., Johnstone, E.C. and Best, J.J. (2001). A MRI study of ocular hypertelorism in individuals at high risk of developing schizophrenia. *Schizophrenia Research*, 50, 1–2.

Boyle, M. (1990). *Schizophrenia: A scientific delusion?* London: Routledge.

Bradbury, T.N. and Miller, G.A. (1985). Season of birth in schizophrenia: A review of evidence, methodology, and etiology. *Psychological Bulletin*, 98, 569–594.

Braff, D.L. and Saccuzzo, D.P. (1985). The time course of information-processing deficits in schizophrenia. *American Journal of Psychiatry*, 142, 170–174.

Braff, D.L., Heaton, R., Kuck, J., Cullum, M., Moranville, J., Grant, I. *et al.* (1991). The generalised pattern of neuropsychological deficits in outpatients with chronic schizophrenia with heterogeneous Wisconsin Card Sorting Test results. *Archives of General Psychiatry*, 48, 891–898.

Brandon, S., Cowley, P., McDonald, C., Neville, P., Palmer, R. and Wellstood-Eason, S. (1985). Leicester ECT trial: Results in schizophrenia. *British Journal of Psychiatry*, 146, 177–183.

Bredkjaer, S.R., Mortensen, P.B. and Parnas, J. (1998). Epilepsy and non-organic non-affective psychosis. National epidemiological study. *British Journal of Psychiatry*, 172, 235–238.

Breier, A., Schreiber, J.L., Dyer, J. and Pickar, D. (1991). National Institute of Mental Health longitudinal study of chronic schizophrenia: Prognosis and predictors of outcome. *Archives of General Psychiatry*, 48, 239–246.

Breier, A., Su, T.P., Saunders, R., Carson, R.E., Kolachana, B.S., deBartolomeis, A. *et al.* (1997). Schizophrenia is associated with elevated amphetamine-induced synaptic dopamine concentrations: Evidence from a novel positron emission tomography method. *Proceedings of the National Academy of Science, USA*, 94, 2569–2574.

Brekke, J.S., DeBonis, J.A. and Graham, J.W. (1994). A latent structure analysis of the positive and negative symptoms in schizophrenia. *Comprehensive Psychiatry*, 35, 252–259.

Bridge, T.P., Kleinman, J.E., Karoum, F. and Wyatt, R.J. (1985). Postmortem central catecholamines and antemortem cognitive impairment in elderly schizophrenics and controls. *Neuropsychobiology*, 14, 57–61.

Broadbent, D.E. (1958). *Perception and communication*. London: Pergamon.

Brockington, I. (1996). *Motherhood and mental health*. Oxford: Oxford University Press.

Brockington, I.F., Kendell, R.E. and Leff, J.P. (1978). Definitions of schizophrenia: Concordance and prediction of outcome. *Psychological Medicine*, 8, 387–398.

Brockington, I.F., Kendell, R.E., Wainwright, S., Hillier, V.F. and Walker, J. (1979). The distinction between the affective psychoses and schizophrenia. *British Journal of Psychiatry*, 135, 243–248.

Brockington, I.F., Kendell, R.E. and Wainwright, S. (1980a). Manic patients with schizophrenic or paranoid symptoms. *Psychological Medicine*, 10, 73–83.

Brockington, I.F., Kendell, R.E. and Wainwright, S. (1980b). Depressed patients with schizophrenic or paranoid symptoms. *Psychological Medicine*, 10, 665–675.

Brockington, I.F., Cernik, K.F., Schofield, E.M., Downing, A.R., Francis, A.F. and Keelan, C. (1981). Puerperal psychosis: Phenomena and diagnosis. *Archives of General Psychiatry*, 38, 829–833.

Brockington, I.F., Perris, C. and Meltzer, H. (1982a). Cycloid psychoses: Diagnostic and heuristic value. *Journal of Nervous and Mental Disease*, 170, 651–656.

Brockington, I.F., Perris, C., Kendell, R.E., Hillier, V.E. and Wainwright, S. (1982b). The course and outcome of cycloid psychosis. *Psychological Medicine*, 12, 97–105.

Brown, A.S., Cohen, P., Greenwald, S. and Susser, E. (2000). Nonaffective psychosis after prenatal exposure to rubella. *American Journal of Psychiatry*, 157, 438–443.

Brown, A.S., Cohen, P., Harkavy-Friedman, J., Babulas, V., Malaspina, D., Gorman, J.M. *et al.* (2001). Prenatal rubella, premorbid abnormalities, and adult schizophrenia. *Biological Psychiatry*, 49, 473–486.

Brown, G.W. (1985). The discovery of expressed emotion: Induction or deduction? In J. Leff and C. Vaughn (Eds.), *Expressed emotion in families: Its significance for mental illness*, pp. 7–25. London: Guildford Press.

Brown, G.W. and Birley, J.L.T. (1968). Crises and life changes and the onset of schizophrenia. *Journal of Health and Social Behavior*, 9, 203–214.

Brown, G.W., Carstairs, G.M. and Topping, G.C. (1958). The post hospital adjustment of chronic mental patients. *Lancet*, ii, 685–689.

Brown, G.W., Monck, E.M., Carstairs, G.M. and Wing, J.K. (1962). The influence of family life on the course of schizophrenic illness. *British Journal of Preventative and Social Medicine*, 16, 55–68.

Brown, G.W., Bone, M., Dalison, B. and Wing, J.K. (1966). *Schizophrenia and social care*, Maudsley Monograph, No. 17. London: Oxford University Press.

Brown, G.W., Birley, J.L.T. and Wing, J.K. (1972). Influence of family life on the course of schizophrenic disorders: A replication. *British Journal of Psychiatry*, 121, 241–258.

Brown, K.W. and White, T. (1992). Syndromes of chronic schizophrenia and some clinical correlates. *British Journal of Psychiatry*, 161, 317–322.

Brune, M. (2005). 'Theory of mind' in schizophrenia: A review of the literature. *Schizophrenia Bulletin*, 31, 21–42.

Buchanan, R.W., Strauss, M.E., Kirkpatrick, B., Holstein, C., Breier, A. and Carpenter, W.T. (1994). Neuropsychological impairments in deficit vs nondeficit forms of schizophrenia. *Archives of General Psychiatry*, 51, 804–811.

Buchanan, R.W., Breier, A., Kirkpatrick, B., Ball, P. and Carpenter, W.T. Jr. (1998). Positive and negative symptom response to clozapine in schizophrenic patients with and without the deficit syndrome. *American Journal of Psychiatry*, 155, 751–760.

Buchkremer, G., Stricker, K., Holle, R. and Kuhs, H. (1991). The predictability of relapses in schizophrenic patients. *European Archives of Psychiatry and Clinical Neurosciences*, 240, 292–300.

Buchsbaum, M.S., Ingvar, D.H., Kessler, R., Waters, R.N., Cappelletti, J., van Kammen, D.P. *et al.* (1982). Cerebral glucography with positron tomography. *Archives of General Psychiatry*, 39, 251–259.

Buhrich, N., Crow, T.J., Johnstone, E.C. and Owens, D.G.C. (1988). Age disorientation in chronic schizophrenia is not associated with pre-morbid intellectual impairment or past physical treatments. *British Journal of Psychiatry*, 152, 466–469.

Buka, S.L., Tsuang, M.T. and Lipsitt, L.P. (1993). Pregnancy/delivery complications and psychiatric diagnosis. *Archives of General Psychiatry*, 50, 151–156.

Burns, A., Jacoby, R. and Levy, R. (1990). Psychiatric phenomena in Alzheimer's disease. *British Journal of Psychiatry*, 157, 72–85.

Burt, D.R., Creese, I. and Snyder, S.H. (1977). Antischizophrenic drugs: Chronic treatment elevates dopamine receptor numbers. *Science*, 196, 326–328.

Byrne, M., Browne, R., Mulryan, M., Scully, A., Morris, M., Kinsella, A. *et al.* (2000). Labour and delivery complications and schizophrenia: Case-control study using contemporaneous labour ward records. *British Journal of Psychiatry*, 176, 531–536.

Byrne, M., Clafferty, B.A., Cosway, R., Grant, E., Hodges, A., Whalley, H.C. *et al.* (2003). Neuropsychology, genetic liability, and psychotic symptoms in those at high risk of schizophrenia. *Journal of Abnormal Psychology*, 112, 38–48.

Cade, J.F.J. (1970). The story of lithium. In F.J. Ayd and B. Blackwell (Eds.), *Discoveries in biological psychiatry*, pp. 230–243. Philadelphia, PA: Lippincott.

Cahn, W., Hulshoff Pol, H.E., Lems, E.B., van Haren, N.E., Schnack, H.G., van der Linden, J.A. *et al.* (2002). Brain volume changes in first-episode schizophrenia: A 1-year follow-up study. *Archives of General Psychiatry*, 59, 1002–1010.

Caine, E.D. and Shoulson I. (1983). Psychiatric syndromes in Huntington's disease. *American Journal of Psychiatry*, 140, 728–733.

Caldwell, A.E. (1970). *Origins of psychopharmacology: From CPZ to LSD*. Springfield, IL: Charles C. Thomas.

Calev, A. (1984a). Recall and recognition in mildly disturbed schizophrenics: The use of matched tasks. *Psychological Medicine*, 14, 425–429.

Calev, A. (1984b). Recall and recognition in chronic nondemented schizophrenics: Use of matched tasks. *Journal of Abnormal Psychology*, 93, 172–177.

Calev, A., Berlin, H. and Lerer, B. (1987a). Remote and recent memory in long-hospitalised chronic schizophrenics. *Biological Psychiatry*, 22, 79–85.

Calev, A., Korin, Y., Kugelmass, S. and Lerer, B. (1987b). Performance of chronic schizophrenics on matched word and design recall tasks. *Biological Psychiatry*, 22, 699–709.

Calloway, P. (1993). *Soviet and western psychiatry: A comparative study*. Keighley, Yorks: Moor Press.

Cameron, N. (1938). Reasoning, regression and communication in schizophrenics. *Psychological Monographs*, 50, 1–34.

Cameron, N. (1939). Schizophrenic thinking in a problem-solving situation. *Journal of Mental Science*, 85, 1012–1035.

Cameron, N. (1944). Experimental analysis of schizophrenic thinking. In J.S. Kasanin (Ed.), *Language and thought in schizophrenia*, pp. 50–64. Berkeley: University of California Press.

Cannon, M., Caspi, A., Moffitt, T.E., Harrington, H., Taylor, A., Murray, R.M. *et al.* (2002). Evidence for early-childhood, pan-developmental impairment specific to schizophreniform disorder: Results from a longitudinal birth cohort. *Archives of General Psychiatry*, 59, 449–456.

Cannon, T.D. and Mednick, S.A. (1993). The schizophrenia high-risk project in Copenhagen: Three decades of progress. *Acta Psychiatrica Scandinavica*, Supplement, 370, 33–47.

Cannon T.D., Rosso, I.M., Hollister, J.M., Bearden, C.E., Sanchez, L.E. and Hadley, T. (2000). Childhood cognitive functioning in schizophrenia patients and their unaffected siblings: A prospective cohort study. *Schizophrenia Bulletin*, 26, 379–393.

Canton, G. and Fraccon, I.G. (1985). Life events and schizophrenia: A replication. *Acta Psychiatrica Scandinavica*, 71, 211–216.

Cardno, A.G. and Gottesman, I.I. (2000). Twin studies of schizophrenia: From bow and arrow concordances to Star Wars Mx and functional genomics. *American Journal of Medical Genetics*, 97, 12–17.

Carlson, G.A. and Goodwin, F.K. (1973). The stages of mania: A longitudinal analysis of the manic episode. *Archives of General Psychiatry*, 28, 221–228.

Carlsson, A. (1977). Does dopamine play a role in schizophrenia? *Psychological Medicine*, 7, 583–597.

Carlsson, A. and Lindqvist, M. (1963). Effect of chlorpromazine and haloperidol on formation of 3-methoxytyramine and normetanephrine in mouse brain. *Acta Pharmacologica et Toxicologica*, 20, 140–144.

Caroff, S.N. (1980). The neuroleptic malignant syndrome. *Journal of Clinical Psychiatry*, 41, 79–83.

Carone, B.J., Harrow, M. and Westermeyer, J.F. (1991). Posthospital course and outcome in schizophrenia. *Archives of General Psychiatry*, 48, 247–253.

Carpenter, W.T., Bartko, J.J., Carpenter, C.L. and Strauss, J.L. (1976). Another view of schizophrenic subtypes. *Archives of General Psychiatry*, 33, 508–516.

Carpenter, W.T., Buchanan, R.W., Javitt, D.C., Marder, S.R., Schooler, N.R, Heresco-Levy, U. *et al.* (2005). Testing two efficacy hypotheses for the treatment of negative symptoms. *Schizophrenia Bulletin*, 31, 478.

Carpenter, W.T. Jr and Strauss, J.S. (1974). Cross-cultural evaluation of Schneider's first-rank symptoms of schizophrenia: A report from the International Pilot Study of Schizophrenia. *American Journal of Psychiatry*, 131, 682–687.

Carpenter, W.T. Jr, Strauss, J.S. and Muleh, S. (1973). Are there pathognomonic symptoms in schizophrenia? An empiric investigation of Kurt Schneider's first-rank symptoms. *Archives of General Psychiatry*, 28, 847–852.

Casey, D.E. (1989). Clozapine: Neuroleptic-induced EPS and tardive dyskinesia. *Psychopharmacology*, 99, Supplement, S47–S53.

Caspi, A., Reichenberg, A., Weiser, M., Rabinowitz, J., Kaplan, Z., Knobler, H. *et al.* (2003). Cognitive performance in schizophrenia patients assessed before and following the first psychotic episode. *Schizophrenia Research*, 65, 87–94.

Cazzullo, C.L., Bressi, C., Bertrando, P., Clerici, M. and Maffei, C. (1989). Schizophrenie et expression emotionelle familiale: Etude d'une population Italliene. *Encephale*, 15, 1–6.

Chadwick, P.D. and Lowe, C.F. (1990). The measurement and modification of delusional beliefs. *Journal of Consulting and Clinical Psychology*, 58, 225–232.

Chaika, E. (1974). A linguist looks at 'schizophrenic' language. *Brain and Language*, 1, 257–276.

Chaika, E. (1996). Intention, attention and deviant schizophrenic speech. In J. France and N. Muir (Eds.), *Communication and the mentally ill patient: Developmental and linguistic approaches to schizophrenia*, pp. 18–29. London: Jessica Kingsley.

Chaika, E. and Lambe, R.A. (1989). Cohesion in schizophrenic narratives, revisited. *Journal of Communication Disorders*, 22, 407–421.

Chaika, E.O. (1990). *Understanding psychotic speech: Beyond Freud and Chomsky*. Springfield, IL: Charles C. Thomas.

Chakos, M.H., Alvir, J.M., Woerner, M.G., Koreen, A,, Geisler, S., Mayerhoff, D. *et al.* (1996). Incidence and correlates of tardive dyskinesia in first episode of schizophrenia. *Archives of General Psychiatry*, 53, 313–319.

Chapman, L.J. and Chapman, J.P. (1973). *Disordered thought in schizophrenia*. New York: Appleton-Century-Crofts.

Chiu, L.P.W. (1989). Transient recurrence of auditory hallucinations during acute dystonia. *British Journal of Psychiatry*, 155, 110–113.

Christison, G.W., Casanova, M.F., Weinberger, D.R., Rawlings, R. and Kleinman, J.E. (1989). A quantitative investigation of hippocampal pyramidal cell size, shape, and variability of orientation in schizophrenia. *Archives of General Psychiatry*, 46, 1027–1032.

Chua, S.E. and McKenna, P.J. (1995). Schizophrenia – a brain disease? A critical review of structural and functional cerebral abnormality in the disorder. *British Journal of Psychiatry*, 166, 563–582.

Chuang, H.T. and Addington, D. (1988). Homosexual panic: A review of its concept. *Canadian Journal of Psychiatry*, 33, 613–617.

Chung, R.R., Langeluddecke, P. and Tennant, C. (1986). Threatening life events in the onset of schizophrenia, schizophreniform psychosis and hypomania. *British Journal of Psychiatry*, 148, 680–685.

Ciompi, L. (1980). The natural history of schizophrenia in the long term. *British Journal of Psychiatry*, 136, 413–420.

Clare, A. (1980). *Psychiatry in dissent*, 2nd edn. London: Tavistock Publications.

Claridge, G. and Davis, C. (2003). *Personality and psychological disorders*. London: Arnold.

Clark, D. (1981). *Social therapy in psychiatry*, 2nd edn. Edinburgh: Churchill Livingtsone.

Clayton, P., Pitts, F.N. Jr. and Winokur, G. (1965). Affective disorder: IV. Mania. *Comprehensive Psychiatry*, 6, 313–322.

Cobb, J. (1979). Morbid jealousy. *British Journal of Hospital Medicine*, 21, 511–518.

Cohen, W.J. and Cohen, N.H. (1974). Lithium carbonate, haloperidol, and irreversible brain damage. *Journal of the American Medical Association*, 230, 1283–1287.

Comings, D.E. (1991). *Tourette syndrome and human behavior*. Duarte, CA: Hope Press.

Connell. P. (1958). *Amphetamine psychosis*, Maudsley Monograph, No. 5. London: Oxford University Press.

Conrad, A.J., Abebe, T., Austin, R., Forsythe, S. and Scheibel, A.B. (1991). Hippo-campal pyramidal cell disarray in schizophrenia as a bilateral phenomenon. *Archives of General Psychiatry*, 48, 413–417.

Cooper, A.F., Garside, R.F. and Kay, D.W.K. (1974). A comparison of deaf and non-deaf patients with paranoid and affective psychoses. *British Journal of Psychiatry*, 129, 532–538.

Cooper, J.E., Kendell, R.E., Gurland, B.J., Sharpe, L., Copeland, J.R.M. and Simon, R. (1972). *Psychiatric diagnosis in New York and London*, Maudsley Monograph, No. 20. London: Oxford University Press.

Copolov, D.L., Seal, M.L., Maruff, P., Ulusoy, R., Wong, M.T., Tochon-Danguy, H.J. *et al.* (2003). Cortical activation associated with the experience of auditory hal-lucinations and perception of human speech in schizophrenia: A PET correlation study. *Psychiatry Research: Neuroimaging*, 122, 139–152.

Coryell, W. (1986). Schizoaffective and schizophreniform disorders. In G. Winokur and P. Clayton (Eds.), *The medical basis of psychiatry*, pp. 102–14. Philadelphia; PA: Saunders.

Coryell, W. and Zimmerman, M. (1988). The heritability of schizophrenia and schizoaffective disorder. A family study. *Archives of General Psychiatry*, 45, 323–327.

Coryell, W., Lavori, P., Endicott, J., Keller, M. and van Eerdewegh, M. (1984). Outcome in schizoaffective, psychotic, and nonpsychotic depression. *Archives of General Psychiatry*, 41, 787–791.

Costall, B. and Naylor, R.J. (1981). The hypothesis of different dopamine receptor mechanisms. *Life Sciences*, 28, 215–229.

Coward, D.M. (1992). General pharmacology of clozapine. *British Journal of Psychiatry*, 160, Supplement 17, 5–12.

Craddock, N. and Owen, M.J. (2005). The beginning of the end for the Kraepelinian dichotomy. *British Journal of Psychiatry*, 186, 364–366.

Crane G.E. (1972). Pseudoparkinsonism and tardive dyskinesia. *Archives of Neuro-logy*, 27, 426–430.

Creese, I., Burt, D.R. and Snyder, S.H. (1976). Dopamine receptor binding predicts clinical and pharmacological potencies of antischizophrenic drugs. *Science*, 192, 481–483.

Crilly, J. (2007). The history of clozapine and its emergence in the United States market: A review and analysis. *History of Psychiatry*, in press.

Critchley, M. (1964). The neurology of psychotic speech. *British Journal of Psych-iatry*, 110, 353–364.

Crow, T.J. (1980). Molecular pathology of schizophrenia: More than one disease process? *British Medical Journal*, 280, 66–68.

Crow, T.J. (1986). The continuum of psychosis and its implication for the structure of the gene. *British Journal of Psychiatry*, 149, 419–429.

Crow, T.J. (1991). The failure of the Kraepelinian binary concept and the search for the psychosis gene. In A. Kerr and H. McClelland (Eds.), *Concepts of mental disorder: A continuing debate*, pp. 31–47. London: Gaskell/Royal College of Psychiatrists.

Crow, T.J. and Mitchell, W.S. (1975). Subjective age in chronic schizophrenia: Evidence for a sub-group of patients with defective learning capacity. *British Journal of Psychiatry*, 126, 360–363.

Crow, T.J., Deakin, J.F.W. and Longden, A. (1977). The nucleus accumbens – possible site of antipsychotic action of neuroleptic drugs. *Psychological Medicine*, 7, 213–221.

Crow, T.J., Baker, H.F., Cross, A.J., Joseph, M.H., Lofthouse, R., Longden, A. *et al.* (1979). Monoamine mechanisms in chronic schizophrenia: Post-mortem neurochemical findings. *British Journal of Psychiatry*, 134, 249–256.

Crow, T.J., MacMillan, J.F., Johnson, A.L. and Johnstone, E.C. (1986). The Northwick Park study of first episodes of schizophrenia I. A randomised controlled trial of prophylactic neuroleptic treatment. *British Journal of Psychiatry*, 148, 120–127.

Csernansky, J.G., Mahmoud, R. and Brenner, R. (2002). A comparison of risperidone and haloperidol for the prevention of relapse in patients with schizophrenia. *New England Journal of Medicine*, 346, 16–22.

Cuesta, M.J. and Peralta, V. (2001). Integrating psychopathological dimensions in functional psychoses: A hierarchical approach. *Schizophrenia Research*, 52, 215–229.

Cummings, J.L. (1991). Behavioral complications of drug treatment of Parkinson's disease. *Journal of the American Geriatric Society*, 39, 708–716.

Cunningham Owens, D.G. (1999). *A guide to the extrapyramidal side-effects of neuroleptic drugs*. Cambridge: Cambridge University Press.

Cutting, J. (1980). Physical illness and psychosis. *British Journal of Psychiatry*, 136, 109–119.

Cutting, J. (1985). *The psychology of schizophrenia*. Edinburgh: Churchill Livingstone.

Cutting, J. (1987). The phenomenology of acute organic psychoses: Comparison with acute schizophrenia. *British Journal of Psychiatry*, 151, 324–332.

Cutting, J. and Dunne, F. (1989). Subjective experiences of schizophrenia. *Schizophrenia Bulletin*, 15, 217–231.

Cutting, J. and Shepherd, M. (1987). *The clinical roots of the schizophrenia concept*. Cambridge: Cambridge University Press.

Cutting, J.C., Clare, A.W. and Mann, A.H. (1978). Cycloid psychosis: An investigation of the diagnostic concept. *Psychological Medicine*, 8, 637–648.

Dalby, M.A. (1975). Behavioral effects of carbamazepine. In J.K. Penry and D.D. Daly (Eds.), *Complex partial seizures and their treatment*, Advances in Neurology, Vol. 11. New York: Raven Press.

Dale, R. (1991). *Louis Wain: The man who drew cats*, 2nd edn. London: Michael O'Mara.

Dalman, C., Thomas, H.V., David, A.S., Gentz, J., Lewis, G. and Allebeck, P. (2001). Signs of asphyxia at birth and risk of schizophrenia. *British Journal of Psychiatry*, 179, 403–408.

Dalman, C., Allebeck, P., Cullberg, J., Grunewald, C. and Köster, M. (1999). Obstetric complications and the risk of schizophrenia: A longitudinal study of a national birth cohort. *Archives of General Psychiatry*, 56, 234–240.

Darby, J.K. (1976). Neuropathological aspects of psychosis in childhood. *Journal of Autism and Childhood Schizophrenia*, 6, 339–352.

Davé, M. (1994). Clozapine-related tardive dyskinesia. *Biological Psychiatry*, 35, 886–887.

David, A.S. (1993). Cognitive neuropsychiatry? *Psychological Medicine*, 23, 1–5.

David, A.S., Malmberg, A., Brandt, L., Allebeck, P. and Lewis, G. (1997). IQ and risk for schizophrenia: A population based cohort study. *Psychological Medicine*, 27, 1311–1323.

David, A.S. and Prince, M. (2005). Psychosis following head injury: A critical review. *Journal of Neurology, Neurosurgery and Psychiatry*, 76, Supplement 1, i53–i60.

David, G.B. (1957). The pathological anatomy of the schizophrenias. In D. Richter (Ed.), *Schizophrenia: Somatic aspects*, pp. 93–130. Oxford: Pergamon.

Davidson, M., Harvey, P.D., Powchik, P., Parrella, M., White, L., Knobler, H.Y. *et al.* (1995). Severity of symptoms in chronically hospitalised geriatric schizophrenic patients. *American Journal of Psychiatry*, 152, 197–207.

Davis, J.M. (1975). Overview: Maintentance therapy in psychiatry: I. Schizophrenia. *American Journal of Psychiatry*, 132, 1237–1245.

Davis, J.M. (1985). Antipsychotic drugs. In H.I. Kaplan and B.J. Sadock (Eds.), *Comprehensive textbook of psychiatry*, 4th edn, pp. 1481–1512. Baltimore, MD: Williams and Wilkins.

Davis, J.M., Chen, N. and Glick, I.D. (2003). A meta-analysis of the efficacy of second-generation antipsychotics. *Archives of General Psychiatry*, 60, 553–564.

Davison, K. and Bagley C.R. (1969). Schizophrenia-like psychoses associated with organic disorders of the central nervous system: A review. *British Journal of Psychiatry*, Special Publication 4, 113–183.

de Clérambault, G. (1942). *Oeuvre psychiatrique*. Paris: Presses Universitaires de France.

De Mol, J., Violon, A. and Brihaye, J. (1987). Post-traumatic psychoses: A retrospective study of 18 cases. *Archivio di Psicologia, Neurologia e Psichiatria*, 48, 336–350.

de Vries, P., Honer, W.G., Kemp, P.M. and McKenna, P.J. (2001). Dementia as a complication of schizophrenia. *Journal of Neurology, Neurosurgery and Psychiatry*, 70, 588–596.

Deakin, J.F.W. (2000). Glutamate, GABA and cortical circuitry in schizophrenia. In M.A. Reveley and J.F.W. Deakin (Eds.), *The psychopharmacology of schizophrenia*, pp. 57–69. Oxford: Oxford University Press.

Dean, C. and Kendell, R.E. (1981). The symptomatology of puerperal illness. *British Journal of Psychiatry*, 139, 128–133.

Debray, Q. (1975). A genetic study of chronic delusions. *Neuropsychobiology*, 1, 313–321.

Delay, J. and Deniker, P. (1955). Hibernotherapies et cures neuroleptiques en psychiatrie. *Bulletin de la Academie Nationale de Medicin*, 139, 145–147.

Delay, J. and Deniker, P. (1968). Drug-induced extrapyramidal syndromes. In P.J. Vinken and G.W. Bruyn (Eds.), *Handbook of clinical neurology, Vol. 6, Diseases of the basal ganglia*, pp. 248–266. New York: Wiley.

Delay, J., Deniker, P. and Harl, J.-M. (1952). Traitement des états d'excitation et d'agitation par une methode medicamenteuse derivée de l'hibernotherapie. *Annales Medico-Psychologique*, 110, 267–273.

Delay, J., Deniker, P., Ropert, R., Beek, H., Barande, R. and Eurieult, M. (1959). Syndromes neurologiques experimentaux et therapeutique: Effets neurologique d'un nouveau neuroleptique majeur le 7843 RP. *Presse Medicale*, 67, 123–126.

DeLisi, L.E., Sakuma, M., Tew, W., Kushner, M., Hoff, A.L. and Grimson, R. (1997). Schizophrenia as a chronic active brain process: A study of progressive brain structural change subsequent to the onset of schizophrenia. *Psychiatry Research: Neuroimaging*, 74, 129–140.

Delva, N.J. and Letemendia, J.J. (1982). Lithium treatment in schizophrenia and schizo-affective disorders. *British Journal of Psychiatry*, 141, 387–400.

Dencker, S.J., Lepp, M. and Malm, U. (1980). Do schizophrenics well adapted in the community need neuroleptics? A depot withdrawal study. *Acta Psychiatrica Scandinavica*, Supplement, 279, 64–66.

Dening, T.R. and Berrios, G.E. (1990). Wilson's disease: Psychiatric symptoms in 195 cases. *Archives of General Psychiatry*, 46, 1126–1134.

Despert, J.L. (1968). *Schizophrenia in children*. New York: Brunner/Mazel.

Deutsch, H. (1942). Some forms of emotional disturbance and their relationship to schizophrenia. *Psychoanalytic Quarterly*, 11, 301–321.

Diem, O. (1903). The simple dementing form of dementia praecox. In J. Cutting and M. Shepherd (Eds.), *The clinical roots of the schizophrenia concept*, pp. 25–34. Cambridge: Cambridge University Press.

Dierks, T., Linden, D.E.J., Jandl, M., Formisano, E., Goebel, R., Lanferman, H. *et al.* (1999). Activation of Heschl's gyrus during auditory hallucinations. *Neuron*, 22, 615–621.

DiSimoni, F.G., Darley, F.L. and Aronson, A.E. (1977). Patterns of dysfunction in schizophrenic patients on an aphasia test battery. *Journal of Speech and Hearing Disorders*, 42, 498–513.

Docherty, N., Schnur, M. and Harvey, P.D. (1988). Reference performance and positive and negative thought disorder: A follow-up study of manics and schizophrenics. *Journal of Abnormal Psychology*, 97, 437–442.

Docherty, N.M. and Gordinier, S.W. (1999). Immediate memory, attention and communication disturbances in schizophrenia patients and their relatives. *Psychological Medicine*, 29, 189–197.

Docherty, N.M., Cohen, A.S., Nienow, T.M., Dinzeo, T.J. and Dangelmaier, R.E. (2003). Stability of formal thought disorder and referential communication disturbances in schizophrenia. *Journal of Abnormal Psychology*, 112, 469–475.

Dohrenwend, B.P., Levav, L., Shrout, P.E., Link, B.G., Skodol, A.E. and Martin, J.L. (1987). Life stress and psychopathology: Progress with research begun with Barbara Snell Dohrenwend. *American Journal of Community Psychology*, 15, 677–713.

Dollfus, S. and Everitt, B. (1998). Symptom structure in schizophrenia: Two-, three- or four-factor models. *Psychopathology*, 31, 120–130.

Dollfus, S., Everitt, B., Ribeyre, J.M., Assouly-Besse, F., Sharp, C. and Petit, M. (1996). Identifying subtypes of schizophrenia by cluster analysis. *Schizophrenia Bulletin*, 22, 545–556.

Done, D.J., Crow, T.J. and Sacker, A. (unpublished). Intellectual abilities in children who develop adult psychopathology. Does general intelligence act as a protective mechanism?

Done, D.J., Johnstone, E.C., Frith, C.D., Golding, J., Shepherd, P.M. and Crow, T.J. (1991). Complications of pregnancy and delivery in relation to psychosis in adult life: Data from the British perinatal mortality survey sample. *British Medical Journal*, 302, 1576–1580.

Done, D.J., Crow, T.J., Johnstone, E.C. and Sacker, A. (1994). Childhood antecedents of schizophrenia and affective illness: Social adjustment at ages 7 and 11. *British Medical Journal*, 309, 699–703.

Donohoe, G. and Robertson, I.H. (2003). Can specific deficits in executive functioning explain the negative symptoms of schizophrenia? A review. *Neurocase*, 9, 97–108.

Dracheva, S., Marras, S.A.E., Elhakem, S.L., Kramer, F.R., Davis, K.L. and Haroutunian, V. (2001). N-methyl-D-aspartic acid receptor expression in the dorso-lateral prefrontal cortex of elderly patients with schizophrenia. *Amercan Journal of Psychiatry*, 158, 1400–1410.

Drevets, W. and Rubin, E.H. (1989). Psychotic symptoms and the longitudinal course of senile dementia of the Alzheimer type. *Biological Psychiatry*, 25, 39–48.

Duffy, L. and O'Carroll, R. (1994). Memory impairment in schizophrenia – a comparison with that observed in the alcoholic Korsakoff syndrome. *Psychological Medicine*, 24, 155–166.

Dulz, B. and Hand, I. (1986). Short-term relapse in young schizophrenics: Can it be predicted and affected by family (CFI), patient and treatment variables? An experimental study. In M.J. Goldstein, I. Hand and K. Hahlweg (Eds.), *Treatment of schizophrenia: Family assessment and intervention*, pp. 59–75. Berlin: Springer Verlag.

Durham, R.C., Guthrie, M., Morton, R.V., Reid, D.A., Treliving, L.R., Fowler, D. *et al.* (2003). Tayside-Fife clinical trial of cognitive-behavioural therapy for medication-resistant psychotic symptoms. Results to 3-month follow-up. *British Journal of Psychiatry*, 182, 303–311.

Dwork, A.J. (1997). Postmortem studies of the hippocampal formation in schizophrenia. *Schizophrenia Bulletin*, 23, 385–402.

Dwork, A.J., Susser, E.S., Keilp, J., Waniek, C., Liu, D., Kaufman, M. *et al.* (1998). Senile degeneration and cognitive impairment in chronic schizophrenia. *American Journal of Psychiatry*, 155, 1536–1543.

Eaton, W.W., Tien, A.Y. and Poeschla, B.D. (1995). Epidemiology of schizophrenia. In J.A. Den Boer, H.G.M. Westenberg and H.M. van Praag (Eds.), *Advances in the neurobiology of schizophrenia*, pp. 27–57. Chichester: Wiley.

Eckman, P.S. and Shean, G.D. (2000). Impairment in test performance and symptom dimensions of schizophrenia. *Journal of Psychiatric Research*, 34, 147–153.

Eggers, C. (1978). Course and prognosis of childhood schizophrenia. *Journal of Autism and Childhood Schizophrenia*, 8, 21–36.

Eitinger, L., Laane, C.L. and Langfeldt, G. (1958). The prognostic value of the clinical picture and the therapeutic value of physical treatment in schizophrenia and the schizophreniform states. *Acta Psychiatrica et Neurologica Scandinavica*, 33, 33–53.

Ekbom, K., Lindholm, H. and Ljungberg, L. (1972). New dystonic syndrome associated with butyrophenone therapy. *Journal of Neurology*, 202, 94–103.

Ellingson, R.J. (1954). The incidence of EEG abnormality among patients with mental disorders of apparently nonorganic origin: A critical review. *American Journal of Psychiatry*, 111, 263–275.

Elliott, R., McKenna, P.J., Robbins, T.W. and Sahakian, B.J. (1995). Neurospychological evidence of frontostriatal dysfunction in schizophrenia. *Psychological Medicine*, 25, 619–630.

Elsasser, G. and Grunewald, H.-W. (1953). Schizophrene oder schizophrenieähnliche Psychosen bei Hirntraumatikern. *Nervenarzt*, 190, 134–140.

Endicott, J., Nee, J., Coryell, W., Keller, M., Andreasen, N. and Croughan, J. (1986). Schizoaffective, psychotic, and nonpsychotic depression: Differential familial association. *Comprehensive Psychiatry*, 27, 1–13.

Enoch, D. and Ball, H. (2001). *Uncommon psychiatric syndromes*, 4th edn. London: Hodder Arnold.

Erlenmeyer-Kimling, L. and Cornblatt, B. (1987). High-risk research in schizophrenia: A summary of what has been learned. *Journal of Psychiatric Research*, 21, 401–411.

Esquirol, J.E.D. (1838). *Les maladies mentales*. Paris: Baillière.

Essen-Moller, E. (1941). Psychiatrische Untersuchungen an einer Serie von Zwillingen. *Acta Psychiatrica*, Supplement 23.

Evans-Jones, L.G. and Rosenbloom, L. (1978). Disintegrative psychosis in childhood. *Developmental Medicine and Child Neurology*, 20, 462–470.

Everitt, B.S., Gourlay, J. and Kendell, R.E. (1971). An attempt at validation of traditional psychiatric syndromes by cluster analysis. *British Journal of Psychiatry*, 119, 399–412.

Ey, H. (1952). *Etudes psychiatriques*, Vol. 1. Paris: Desclée de Brouwer.

Faber, R. and Reichstein, M.B. (1981). Language dysfunction in schizophrenia. *British Journal of Psychiatry*, 139, 519–522.

Faber, R., Abrams, R., Taylor, M.A., Kasprison, A., Morris, C. and Weisz, R. (1983). Comparison of schizophrenic patients with formal thought disorder and neurologically impaired patients with aphasia. *American Journal of Psychiatry*, 140, 1348–1351.

Faergeman, P.M. (1963). *Psychogenic psychoses*. London: Butterworth.

Farde, L., Wiesel, F.-A., Hall, H., Halldin, C., Stone-Elander, S. and Sedvall, G. (1987). No D2 receptor increase in PET study of schizophrenia. *Archives of General Psychiatry*, 44, 671–672.

Farde, L., Wiesel, F.-A., Nordstrom, A.-L. and Sedvall, G. (1989). D1- and D2-dopamine receptor occupancy during treatment with conventional and atypical neuroleptics. *Psychopharmacology*, 99, Supplement, S28–S31.

Farde, L., Wiesel, F.-A., Stone-Elander, S., Halldin, C., Nordstrom, A.-L., Hall, H. et al. (1990). D2 dopamine receptors in neuroleptic-naive schizophrenic patients: A positron emission tomography study with [^{11}C]raclopride. *Archives of General Psychiatry*, 47, 213–219.

Farde, L., Nordstrom, A.L., Wiesel, F.-A., Pauli, S., Halldin, C. and Sedvall, G. (1992). Positron emission tomographic analysis of central D1 and D2 dopamine receptor occupancy in patients treated with classical neuroleptics and clozapine. *Archives of General Psychiatry*, 49, 538–544.

Farmer, A.E., McGuffin, P. and Spitznagel, E.L. (1983). Heterogeneity in schizophrenia: A cluster analytic approach. *Psychiatry Research*, 8, 1–12.

Feighner, J.P., Robins, E., Guze, S., Woodruff, R.A., Winokur, G. and Munoz, R. (1972). Diagnostic criteria for use in psychiatric research. *Archives of General Psychiatry*, 26, 57–62.

Feinberg, I. (1978). Efference copy and corollary discharge: Implications for thinking and its disorders. *Schizophrenia Bulletin*, 4, 636–640.

Fenton, W.S. (2000). Prevalence of spontaneous dyskinesia in schizophrenia. *Journal of Clinical Psychiatry*, 61, Supplement 4, 10–14.

Feuchtwanger, E. and Mayer-Gross, W. (1938). Hirnverletzung und Schizophrenie. *Schweizer Archiv für Neurologie und Psychiatrie*, 41, 17–99.

Fink, M. (1984). Meduna and the origins of convulsive therapy. *American Journal of Psychiatry*, 141, 1034–1041.

Fink, M. and Taylor, M.A. (2003). *Catatonia: A clinician's guide to diagnosis and treatment*. Cambridge: Cambridge University Press.

Fischer, M. (1973). Genetic and environmental factors in schizophrenia. *Acta Psychiatrica Scandinavica*, Supplement, 238, 1–158.

Fish, F. (1958a). Leonhard's classification of schizophrenia. *Journal of Mental Science*, 104, 943–971.

Fish, F. (1960). Senile schizophrenia. *Journal of Mental Science*, 106, 938–946.

Fish, F. (1964). The cycloid psychoses. *Comprehensive Psychiatry*, 5, 155–169.

Fish, F.J. (1957). The classification of schizophrenia: The views of Kleist and his co-workers. *Journal of Mental Science*, 103, 443–463.

Fish, F.J. (1958b). A clinical investigation of chronic schizophrenia. *Journal of Mental Science*, 104, 34–54.

Fish, F.J. (1962). *Schizophrenia*. Bristol: Wright.

Fitzgerald, M. (2004). *Autism and creativity*. Hove: Brunner-Routledge.

Folstein, S.E. (1989). *Huntington's disease: A disorder of families*. Baltimore, MD. Johns Hopkins University Press.

Frangos, E., Athenassenas, G., Tsitourides, S., Katsanon, N. and Alexandrakou, P. (1985). Schizophrenia among first-degree relatives of schizophrenic probands. *Acta Psychiatrica Scandinavica*, 72, 382–386.

Franzen, G. and Ingvar, D.H. (1975). Abnormal distribution of cerebral activity in chronic schizophrenia. *Journal of Psychiatric Research*, 12, 199–214.

Fraser, W.I., King, K.M., Thomas, P. and Kendell, R.E. (1986). The diagnosis of schizophrenia by language analysis. *British Journal of Psychiatry*, 148, 275–278.

Freeman, H.L. (1978). Pharmacological treatment and management. In J.K. Wing (Ed.), *Schizophrenia: Towards a new synthesis*, pp. 167–188. London: Academic Press.

Frith, C.D. (1979). Consciousness, information processing and schizophrenia. *British Journal of Psychiatry*, 134, 225–235.

Frith, C.D. (1987). The positive and negative symptoms of schizophrenia reflect impairments in the perception and initiation of action. *Psychological Medicine*, 17, 631–648.

Frith, C.D. (1992). *The cognitive neuropsychology of schizophrenia*. Hove: Erlbaum (UK) Taylor and Francis.

Frith, C. (1994). Theory of mind in schizophrenia. In A.S. David and J.C. Cutting (Eds.), *The neuropsychology of schizophrenia*, pp. 147–162. Hove: Erlbaum.

Frith, C.D. and Done, D.J. (1988). Towards a neuropsychology of schizophrenia. *British Journal of Psychiatry*, 153, 437–443.

Frith, C.D. and Done, D.J. (1989). Experiences of alien control in schizophrenia reflect a disorder in the central monitoring of action. *Psychological Medicine*, 19, 359–363.

Frith, U. (2003). *Autism: Explaining the enigma*, 2nd edn. Oxford: Blackwell.

Fromkin, V. (1975). A linguist looks at 'A linguist looks at schizophrenic language'. *Brain and Language*, 2, 498–503.

Fromm-Reichmann, F. (1948). Notes on the development of treatments of schizophrenics by psychoanalytic psychotherapy. *Psychiatry*, 2, 263–273.

Funding, T. (1961). Genetics of paranoid psychoses of later life. *Acta Psychiatrica Scandinavica*, 37, 267–282.

Galderisi, S., Bucci, P., Mucci, A., D'Amato, A.C., Conforti, R. and Maj, M. (1999). Simple schizophrenia: A controlled MRI and clinical/neuropsychological study. *Psychiatry Research. Neuroimaging*, 91, 175–184.

Gao, X.-M., Sakai, K., Roberts, R.C., Conley, R.R., Dean, B. and Tamminga, C.A. (2000). Ionotropic glutamate receptors and expression of n-methyl-d-aspartate receptor subunits in subregions of human hippocampus: Effects of schizophrenia. *American Journal of Psychiatry*, 157, 1141–1149.

Garety, P.A. and Freeman, D. (1999). Cognitive approaches to delusions: A critical review of theories and evidence. *British Journal of Clinical Psychology*, 38, 113–154.

Garnett, E.S., Firnau, G. and Nahmias, C. (1983). Doapmine visualized in the basal ganglia of living man. *Nature*, 305, 137–138.

Gattaz, W.F., Gasser, T. and Beckmann, H. (1985). Multidimensional analysis of the concentration of 17 substances in the CSF of schizophrenics and controls. *Biological Psychiatry*, 20, 360–366.

Gaupp, R. (1914). The scientific significance of the case of Ernst Wagner. In S.R. Hirsch and M. Shepherd (Eds.) (1974), *Themes and variations in European psychiatry*, pp. 121–133. Bristol: Wright.

Gaupp, R. (1938). The illness and death of the paranoid mass murderer, schoolmaster Wagner: A case history. In S.R. Hirsch and M. Shepherd (Eds.) (1974), *Themes and variations in European psychiatry*, pp. 134–152. Bristol: Wright.

Gerlach, J. (1979). Tardive dyskinesia. *Danish Medical Bulletin*, 46, 209–245.

German, G.A. (1972). Aspects of clinical psychiatry in sub-Saharan Africa. *British Journal of Psychiatry*, 121, 461–479.

Gershon, E.S., Hamovit, J., Guroff, J.J., Dibble, E., Leckman, J.F., Sceery, W. *et al.* (1982). A family study of schizoaffective, bipolar I, bipolar II, unipolar and normal control probands. *Archives of General Psychiatry*, 39, 1157–1167.

Gillberg, C. (1991). Outcome in autism and autistic-like conditions. *Journal of the American Academy of Child and Adolescent Psychiatry*, 30, 375–382.

Gillberg, C. and Coleman, M. (1992). *The biology of the autistic syndromes*, 2nd edn, Clinics in Developmental Medicine, No. 126. London: MacKeith Press.

Gillberg, C., Gillberg, I.C. and Steffenburg, S. (1992). Siblings and parents of children with autism: A controlled population-based study. *Developmental Medicine and Child Neurology*, 34, 389–398.

Gjessing, R. (1938). Disturbances of somatic functions in catatonia with a periodic course and their compensation. *Journal of Mental Science*, 84, 608–621.

Gold, D.J. Jr (1984). Late age of onset schizophrenia: Present but unaccounted for. *Comprehensive Psychiatry*, 25, 225–237.

Goldberg, S.C. (1985). Negative and deficit symptoms in schizophrenia do respond to neuroleptics. *Schizophrenia Bulletin*, 11, 453–456.

Goldberg, S.C., Klerman, G.L. and Cole, J.O. (1965). Changes in schizophrenic psychopathology and ward behaviour as a function of phenothiazine treatment. *British Journal of Psychiatry*, 111, 120–133.

Goldberg, T.E., Weinberger, D.R., Berman, K.F., Pliskin, N.H. and Podd, M.H. (1987). Further evidence for dementia of prefrontal type in schizophrenia? A controlled study of teaching the Wisconsin Card Sorting Test. *Archives of General Psychiatry*, 44, 1008–1014.

Goldberg, T.E., Kelsoe, J.R., Weinberger, D.R., Pliskin, N.H., Kirwin, P.D. and

Berman, K.R. (1988). Performance of schizophrenic patients on putative neuro-psychological tests of frontal lobe function. *International Journal of Neuroscience*, 42, 51–58.

Goldberg, T.E., Weinberger, D.R., Pliskin, N.H., Berman, K.F. and Podd, M.H. (1989). Recall memory deficit in schizophrenia: A possible manifestation of prefrontal dysfunction. *Schizophrenia Research*, 2, 251–257.

Goldberg, T.E., Ragland, J.D., Gold, J.M., Bigelow, L.B., Torrey, E.F. and Weinberger, D.R. (1990). Neuropsychological assessment of monozygotic twins discordant for schizophrenia. *Archives of General Psychiatry*, 47: 1066–1072.

Goldman, P.S. and Galkin, T.W. (1978). Prenatal removal of frontal association cortex in the fetal rhesus monkey: Anatomical and functional consequences in post-natal life. *Brain Research*, 152, 451–458.

Goldstein, G. (1978). Cognitive and perceptual differences between schizophrenics and organics. *Schizophrenia Bulletin*, 4, 160–185.

Goldstein, K. (1944). Methodological approach to the study of schizophrenic thought disorder. In J. S. Kasanin (Ed.), *Language and thought in schizophrenia*, pp. 17–40. Berkeley: University of California Press.

Gottesman, I.I. (1991). *Schizophrenia genesis: The origins of madness*. New York: Freeman.

Gottesman, I.I. and Shields, J. (1963). Schizophrenia in twins: Sixteen years' consecutive admissions to a psychiatric clinic. *British Journal of Psychiatry*, 112, 809–818.

Gottesman, I.I. and Shields, J. (1982). *Schizophrenia: The epigenetic puzzle*. Cambridge: Cambridge University Press.

Gould, L.N. (1948). Verbal hallucinations and activity of vocal musculature. *American Journal of Psychiatry*, 105, 367–372.

Gould, L.N. (1949). Auditory hallucinations and subvocal speech. *Journal of Nervous and Mental Disease*, 109, 418–427.

Gould, L.N. (1950). Verbal hallucinations as automatic speech. *American Journal of Psychiatry*, 107, 110–119.

Grahame, P.S. (1982). Late paraphrenia. *British Journal of Hospital Medicine*, 27, 522–527.

Gray, J.A., Rawlins, J.N.P., Hemsley, D.R. and Smith, A.D. (1991). The neuro-psychology of schizophrenia. *Behavioral and Brain Sciences*, 14, 1–84.

Green, M.F. and Kinsbourne, M. (1990). Subvocal activity and auditory hallucinations: Clues for behavioral treatments? *Schizophrenia Bulletin*, 16, 617–625.

Green, M.F. and Nuechterlein, K.H. (1994). Mechanisms of backward masking in schizophrenia. In A.S. David and J.C. Cutting (Eds.), *The neuropsychology of schizophrenia*, pp. 79–96. Hove: Erlbaum.

Green, P. and Preston, M. (1981). Reinforcement of vocal correlates of auditory hallucinations by auditory feedback: A case study. *British Journal of Psychiatry*, 139, 204–208.

Green, W.H., Campbell, M., Hardesty, A.S., Grega, D.M., Padron-Gayol, M., Shell, J. et al. (1984). A comparison of schizophrenic and autistic children. *Journal of the American Academy of Child and Adolescent Psychiatry*, 23, 399–409.

Greysmith, D. (1973). *Richard Dadd: The rock and castle of seclusion*. London: Studio Vista.

Griffith, J.D., Cavanaugh, J. and Oates, J. (1968). Paranoid episodes induced by drug. *Journal of the American Medical Association*, 205, 39, 46.

Grossman, L.S., Harrow, M., Fudala, J.H. and Meltzer, H.Y. (1984). The longitudinal course of schizoaffective disorders. *Journal of Nervous and Mental Disease*, 172, 140–149.

Grube, B.S., Bilder, R.M. and Goldman, R.S. (1998). Meta-analysis of symptom factors in schizophrenia. *Schizophrenia Research*, 31, 113–120.

Gunderson, J.G. and Singer, M.T. (1975). Defining borderline patients: An overview. *American Journal of Psychiatry*, 132, 1–10.

Gur, R.C. and Gur, R.E. (1995). Hypofrontality in schizophrenia: RIP. *Lancet*, 345, 1383–1384.

Gur, R.E., Cowell, P., Turetsky, B.I., Gallacher, F., Cannon, T., Bilker, W. *et al.* (1998). A follow-up magnetic resonance imaging study of schizophrenia. Relationship of neuroanatomical changes to clinical and neurobehavioral measures. *Archives of General Psychiatry*, 55, 145–152.

Gureje, O. and Adewunmi, A. (1988). Life events and schizophrenia in Nigerians. A controlled investigation. *British Journal of Psychiatry*, 153, 367–375.

Gutierrez, E., Escudero, V. and Valero, J.A. (1988). Expresion de emociones y curso de la esquizofrenia: II. Expresion de emociones y curso de la esquizofrenia en pacientes en remision. *Analisis y Modificacion de Conducta*, 14, 275–316.

Guze, S.B. (1980). Schizoaffective disorders. In H.I. Kaplan, A.M. Freedman and B.J. Sadock (Eds.), *Comprehensive textbook of psychiatry*, 3rd edn, pp. 1301–1304. Baltimore, MD: Williams and Wilkins.

Guze, S.B., Woodruff, R.A. and Clayton, P.J. (1975). The significance of psychotic affective disorders. *Archives of General Psychiatry*, 32, 1147–1150.

Hadju-Gaines, L. (1940). Contributions to the etiology of schizophrenia. *Psychoanalytic Review*, 27, 421–438.

Hakim, R.A. (1953). Indigenous drugs in the treatment of mental diseases, VIth Gujarat and Saurashtra provincial medical conference, Baroda, 1953. *Journal of the Indian Medical Association*, 22, Supplement, 85.

Hall, A.J. (1924). *Epidemic encephalitis*. Bristol: Wright.

Halligan, P.W. and David, A.S. (2001). Cognitive neuropsychiatry: Towards a scientific psychopathology. *Nature Reviews: Neuroscience*, 2, 209–215.

Hamilton, J.A. (1962). *Post-partum psychiatric problems*. St Louis, MD: Mosby.

Hamilton, M. (1984). *Fish's schizophrenia*, 3rd edn. Bristol: Wright.

Hanson, D.R. and Gottesman, I.I. (1976). The genetics, if any, of infantile autism and childhood schizophrenia. *Journal of Autism and Childhood Schizophrenia*, 6, 209–234.

Harding, C. (1988). Course types in schizophrenia: An analysis of European and American studies. *Schizophrenia Bulletin*, 14, 633–644.

Hare, E.H. (1973). A short note on pseudohallucinations. *British Journal of Psychiatry*, 122, 469–476.

Harnryd, C., Bjerkenstedt, C., Gullberg, G., Oxenstierna, G., Sedvall, G. and Wiesel, F.-A. (1984). Clinical evaluation of sulpiride in schizophrenic patients – a double-blind comparison with chlorpromazine. *Acta Psychiatrica Scandinavica*, 69, Supplement, 311, 7–30.

Harrison, G. and Mason, P. (1993). Schizophrenia – falling incidence and better outcome? *British Journal of Psychiatry*, 163, 535–541.

Harrison, G., Hopper, K., Craig, T., Laska, E., Siegel, C., Wanderling, J. *et al.* (2001). Recovery from psychotic illness: A 15- and 25-year international follow-up study. *British Journal of Psychiatry*, 178, 506–517.

Harrison, P.J. (1999). The neuropathology of schizophrenia: A critical review of the data and their interpretation. *Brain*, 122, 593–624.

Harrow, M. and Quinlan, D.M. (1985). *Disordered thinking and schizophrenic psychopathology*. New York: Gardner Press.

Harrow, M., Grossman, L.S., Herbener, E.S. and Davies, E.W. (2000). Ten-year outcome: Patients with schizoaffective disorders, schizophrenia, affective disorders and mood-incongruent psychotic symptoms. *British Journal of Psychiatry*, 177, 421–426.

Harvey, P.D. (1983). Speech competence in manic and schizophrenic psychoses: The association between clinically related thought disorder and cohesion and reference performance. *Journal of Abnormal Psychology*, 92, 368–377.

Hasan, S. and Buckley, P. (1998). Novel antipsychotics and the neuroleptic malignant syndrome: A review and critique. *American Journal of Psychiatry*, 155, 1113–1116.

Hassett, A.M., Keks, N.A., Jackson, H.J. and Copolov, D.L. (1992). The diagnostic validity of paraphrenia. *Australian and New Zealand Journal of Psychiatry*, 26, 18–29.

Haug, O.J. (1962). Pneumoencephalographic studies in mental disease. *Acta Psychiatrica Scandinavica*, Supplement, 165, 1–114.

Hawks, D.V. and Payne, R.W. (1971). Overinclusive thought disorder and symptomatology. *British Journal of Psychiatry*, 118, 663–670.

Hay, G.G. (1970). Dysmorphophobia. *British Journal of Psychiatry*, 116, 399–406.

Heaton, R.K., Baade, L.E. and Johnson, K.L. (1978). Neuropsychological test results associated with psychiatric disorders in adults. *Psychological Bulletin*, 85, 141–162.

Heckers, S. (1997). Neuropathology of schizophrenia: Cortex, thalamus, basal ganglia and neurotransmitter-specific projection systems. *Schizophrenia Bulletin*, 23, 403–421.

Heckers, S., Goff, D., Schacter, D., Savage, C.R., Fischman, A.J., Alpert, N.M. et al. (1999). Functional imaging of memory retrieval in deficit vs nondeficit schizophrenia. *Archives of General Psychiatry*, 56, 1117–1123.

Hegarty, J.D., Baldessarini, R.J., Tohen, M., Waternaux, C. and Oepen, G. (1994). One hundred years of schizophrenia: A meta-analysis of the outcome literature. *American Journal of Psychiatry*, 151, 1409–1416.

Hemsley, D.R. (1975). A two stage model of attention in schizophrenia research. *British Journal of Social and Clinical Psychology*, 14, 81–89.

Hemsley, D.R. (1977). What have cognitive deficits to do with schizophrenic symptoms? *British Journal of Psychiatry*, 130, 167–173.

Hemsley, D.R. and Garety, P.A. (1986). The formation and maintenance of delusions: A Bayesian analysis. *British Journal of Psychiatry*, 149, 51–56.

Hemsley, D.R. and Richardson, P.H. (1980). Shadowing by context in schizophrenia. *Journal of Nervous and Mental Disease*, 168, 141–145.

Henry, J.D. and Crawford, J.R. (2005). A meta-analytic review of verbal fluency deficits in schizophrenia relative to other neurocognitive deficits. *Cognitive Neuropsychiatry*, 10, 1–33.

Herbert, M. and Jacobson, S. (1967). Late paraphrenia. *British Journal of Psychiatry*, 113, 461–469.

Herbert, R.K. and Waltensperger, K.Z. (1980). Schizophrasia: Case study of a paranoid schizophrenic's language. *Applied Psycholinguistics*, 1, 81–93.

Heritch, A.J. (1990). Evidence for reduced and dysregulated turnover of dopamine in schizophrenia. *Schizophrenia Bulletin*, 16, 605–615.

Herman, E. and Pleasure, H. (1963). Clinical evaluation of thioridazine and chlorpromazine in chronic schizophrenia. *Diseases of the Nervous System*, 24, 54–59.

Heston, L.L. (1966). Psychiatric disorders in foster home reared children of schizophrenic mothers. *British Journal of Psychiatry*, 112, 819–825.

Heston, L.L. (1970). The genetics of schizophrenic and schizoid disease. *Science*, 167, 249–256.

Hietala, J., Syvälahti, E., Vuorio, K., Nagren, K., Lehikoinen, P., Ruotsalainen, U. *et al.* (1994). Striatal D2 receptor characteristics in neuroleptic-naive schizophrenic patients studied with positron emission tomography. *Archives of General Psychiatry*, 51, 116–123.

Hill, K., Mann, L., Laws, K.R., Stephenson, C.E., Nimmo-Smith, I. and McKenna, P.J. (2004). Hypofrontality in schizophrenia: A meta-analysis of functional imaging studies. *Acta Psychiatrica Scandinavica*, 110, 243–256.

Hillbom, E. (1951). Schizophrenia-like psychoses after brain trauma. *Acta Psychiatrica et Neurologica Scandinavica*, Supplement, 60, 36–47.

Hillbom, E. (1960). After-effects of brain-injuries. *Acta Psychiatrica et Neurologica Scandinavica*, Supplement, 142, 1–195.

Himmelhoch, J.M., Fuchs, C.Z., May, S.J., Symons, P.H.B.J. and Neil, J.F. (1981). When a schizoaffective diagnosis has meaning. *Journal of Nervous and Mental Disease*, 169, 277–282.

Hirsch, S.R. and Leff, J.P. (1971). Parental abnormalities of verbal communication in the transmission of schizophrenia. *Psychological Medicine*, 1, 118–127.

Hirsch, S.R. and Leff, J.P. (1975). *Abnormalities in parents of schizophrenics*, Maudsley Monograph, No. 22. London: Oxford University Press.

Hirsch, S.R. and Shepherd, M. (1974). *Themes and variations in European psychiatry*. Bristol: Wright.

Ho, B.-C., Andreasen, N.C., Nopoulas, P., Arndt, S., Magnotta, V. and Flaum, M. (2003). Progressive structural brain abnormalities and their relationship to clinical outcome. *Archives of General Psychiatry*, 60, 585–594.

Hoch, A. (1921). *Benign stupors: A study of a new manic-depressive reaction type*. New York: Macmillan.

Hoch, P.H. and Polatin, P. (1949). Pseudoneurotic forms of schizophrenia. *Psychiatric Quarterly*, 33, 248–276.

Hodges, A., Byrne, M., Grant, E. and Johnstone, E. (1999). People at risk of schizophrenia. Sample characteristics of the first 100 cases in the Edinburgh High-Risk Study. *British Journal of Psychiatry*, 174, 547–553.

Hoenig, J. (1983). The concept of schizophrenia: Kraepelin-Bleuler-Schneider. *British Journal of Psychiatry*, 142, 547–556.

Hoff, A.L., Sakuma, M., Wieneke, M., Horon, R., Kushner, M. and DeLisi, L.E. (1999). Longitudinal neuropsychological follow-up study of patients with first-episode schizophrenia. *American Journal of Psychiatry*, 156, 1336–1341.

Hoffman, R. and Sledge, W. (1984). A microgenetic model of paragrammatisms produced by a schizophrenic speaker. *Brain and Language*, 21, 147–173.

Hoffman, R.E. and Sledge, W. (1988). An analysis of grammatical deviance occurring in spontaneous schizophrenic speech. *Journal of Neurolinguistics*, 3, 89–101.

Holden, N.L. (1987). Late paraphrenia or the paraphrenias? A descriptive study with a 10-year follow-up. *British Journal of Psychiatry*, 150, 635–639.

Hole, R.W., Rush, A.J. and Beck, A.T. (1979). A cognitive investigation of schizophrenic delusions. *Psychiatry*, 42, 312–319.

Hollis, C. (1995). Child and adolescent (juvenile onset) schizophrenia: A case control study of premorbid developmental impairments. *British Journal of Psychiatry*, 166, 489–495.

Holmboe, R. and Astrup, C. (1957). A follow-up study 255 patients with acute schizophrenia and schizophreniform psychoses. *Acta Psychiatrica et Neurologica Scandinavica*, 32, Supplement, 115, 1–61.

Honey, G.D., Sharma, T., Suckling, J., Giampietro, V., Soni, W., Williams, S.C.R. *et al.* (2003). The functional neuroanatomy of schizophrenic subsyndromes. *Psychological Medicine*, 33, 1007–1018.

Hong, C.J., Chen, J.Y., Chiu, H.J. and Sim, C.B. (1997). A double-blind comparative study of clozapine versus chlorpromazine on Chinese patients with treatment-refractory schizophrenia. *International Clinical Psychopharmacology*, 12, 123–130.

Hopkinson, G. (1973). The psychiatric syndrome of infestation. *Psychiatria Clinica*, 6, 330–345.

Howard, R.J., Graham, C., Sham, P., Dennehy, J., Castle, D.J., Levy, R. *et al.* (1997). A controlled family study of late-onset non-affective psychosis (late paraphrenia). *British Journal of Psychiatry*, 170, 511–514.

Huber, G. (1967). Symptomwandel der Psychosen und Pharmakopsychiatrie. In H. Kranz and K. Heinrich (Eds.), *Pharmakopsychiatrie und Psychopathologie*, pp. 78–89. Stuttgart: Thieme.

Huber, G., Gross, G. and Schuttler, R. (1975). A long-term follow up study of schizophrenia: Psychiatric course of illness and prognosis. *Acta Psychiatrica Scandinavica*, 52, 49–57.

Huber, G., Gross, G., Schuttler, R. and Linz, M. (1980). Longitudinal studies of schizophrenic patients. *Schizophrenia Bulletin*, 6, 593–605.

Hulse, W.C. (1954). Dementia infantilis. *Journal of Nervous and Mental Disease*, 119, 471–477.

Hultman, C.M., Sparén, P., Takei, N., Murray, R.M. and Cnattingius, S. (1999). Prenatal and perinatal risk factors for schizophrenia, affective psychosis, and reactive psychosis of early onset: Case-control study. *British Medical Journal*, 318, 421–426.

Humphries, C., Mortimer, A., Hirsch, S. and de Belleroche, J. (1996). NMDA receptor mRNA correlation with antemortem cognitive impairment in schizophrenia. *Neuroreport*, 7, 2051–2055.

Huq, S.F., Garety, P.A. and Hemsley, D.R. (1988). Probabilistic judgments in deluded and non-deluded subjects. *Quarterly Journal of Experimental Psychology*, 40A, 801–812.

Huston, P.E. and Locher, L.M. (1948). Involutional psychosis: Course when untreated and when treated with electric shock. *Archives of Neurology and Psychiatry*, 59, 385–404.

Hyde, L., Bridges, K., Goldberg, D., Lowson, K., Sterling, L. and Faragher, B. (1987). The evaluation of a hostel ward: A controlled study using modified cost–benefit analysis. *British Journal of Psychiatry*, 151, 805–812.

Hymas, N., Naguib, M. and Levy, R. (1989). Late paraphrenia – a follow-up study. *International Journal of Geriatric Psychiatry*, 4, 23–29.

Hyttel, J., Larsen, J-J., Christensen, A.V. and Arnt, J. (1985). Receptor-binding profiles of neuroleptics. In D.E. Casey, T.W. Chase, A.V. Christensen and J. Gerlach (Eds.), *Dyskinesia – research and treatment*, Psychopharmacology Supplementum, No. 2, pp. 9–18. Berlin: Springer.

Ianzito, B.M., Cadoret, R.J. and Pugh, D.D. (1974). Thought disorder in depression. *American Journal of Psychiatry*, 131, 703–707.

Illowsky, B.P., Juliano, D.M., Bigelow, L.B. and Weinberger, D.R. (1988). Stability of CT scan findings in schizophrenia: Results of an 8 year follow-up study. *Journal of Neurology, Neurosurgery and Psychiatry*, 51, 209–213.

Ingvar, D.H. and Franzen, G. (1974). Abnormalities of cerebral blood flow distribution in patients with chronic schizophrenia. *Acta Psychiatrica Scandinavica*, 50, 425–462.

Inouye, E. (1961). Similarity and dissimilarity of schizophrenia in twins. In *Proceedings of the Third World Congress of Psychiatry*, Vol. 1., pp. 524–30. Montreal: University of Toronto Press.

Ishimaru, M., Kurumaji, A. and Toru, M. (1994). Increases in strychnine-insensitive glycine binding sites in cerebral cortex of chronic schizophrenics: Evidence for glutamate hypothesis. *Biological Psychiatry*, 35, 84–95.

Itil, T.M. (1977). Qualitative and quantitative EEG findings in schizophrenia. *Schizophrenia Bulletin*, 3, 61–79.

Ivanovic, M. and Vuletic, Z. (1989). Expressed emotion in families of patients with frequent types of schizophrenia and influence on the course of illness: Nine months' follow-up. Unpublished study presented at 19th congress of the European Association for Behaviour Therapy, Vienna.

Iversen, L.L. (1978). Biochemical and pharmacological studies: The dopamine hypothesis. In J.K. Wing (Ed.), *Schizophrenia: Towards a new synthesis*, pp. 89–116. London: Academic Press.

Iversen, S.D. and Fray, P.J. (1982). Brain catecholamines in relation to affect. In A.L. Beckman (Ed.), *The neural basis of behaviour*, pp. 229–269. New York: Spectrum.

Jablensky, A. (1987). Multicultural studies and the nature of schizophrenia: A review. *Journal of the Royal Society of Medicine*, 80, 162–167.

Jablensky, A. (1997). The 100-year epidemiology of schizophrenia. *Schizophrenia Research*, 28, 111–125.

Jablensky, A., Sartorius, N., Ernberg, G., Anker, M., Korten, A., Cooper, J.E. *et al.* (1992). Schizophrenia: Manifestations, incidence and course in different cultures. *Psychological Medicine*, Monograph, Supplement 20, 1–97.

Jacobs, S. and Myers, J. (1976). Recent life events and acute schizophrenic psychosis: A controlled study. *Journal of Nervous and Mental Disease*, 162, 75–87.

Jacobsen, L.K. and Rapoport, J.L. (1998). Research update: Childhood-onset schizophrenia: Implications of clinical and neurobiological research. *Journal of Child Psychology and Psychiatry*, 39, 101–113.

Jager, M., Bottlender, R., Strauss, A. and Moller, H.J. (2004). Fifteen-year follow-up of ICD-10 schizoaffective disorders compared with schizophrenia and affective disorders. *Acta Psychiatrica Scandinavica*, 109, 30–37.

James, I. (2003). Singular scientists. *Journal of the Royal Society of Medicine*, 96, 36–39.

Jaspers, K. (1959). *General psychopathology* (trans. J. Hoenig and M.W. Hamilton, 1963). Manchester: Manchester University Press.

Javitt, D.C. and Zukin, S.R. (1991). Recent advances in the phencycline model of schizophrenia. *American Journal of Psychiatry*, 148, 1301–1308.

Jelliffe, S.E. (1929). Psychological components in postencephalitic oculogyric crises. *Archives of Neurology and Psychiatry*, 21, 491–532.

Jelliffe, S.E. (1932). *Psychopathology of forced movements and the oculogyric crises of lethargic encephalitis*. Washington, DC: Nervous and Mental Disease Publishing Co.

Jeste, D.V., Lohr, J.B., Clark, K. and Wyatt, R.J. (1988). Pharmacological treatment of tardive dyskinesia in the 1980s. *Journal of Clinical Psychopharmacology*, 8, Supplement, 38S–48S.

Jeste, D.V., Harris, M.J., Krull, A., Kuck, J., McAdams, L.A. and Heaton, R. (1995). Clinical and neuropsychological characteristics of patients with late-onset schizophrenia. *American Journal of Psychiatry*, 152, 722–730.

Jeste, D.V., Eastham, J.H., Lacro, J.P., Gierz, M., Field, M.G. and Harris, M.J. (1996). Management of late-life psychosis. *Journal of Clinical Psychiatry*, 57, Supplement, 3, 39–45.

Johanson, E. (1958). A study of schizophrenia in the male. *Acta Psychiatrica et Neurologica Scandinavica*, 33, Supplement, 125, 1–132.

Johanson, E. (1964). Mild paranoia. *Acta Psychiatrica Scandinavica*, Supplement, 177, 1–100.

Johns, A. (2001). Psychiatric effects of cannabis. *British Journal of Psychiatry*, 178, 116–122.

Johnson, F.N. and Cade, J.F.J. (1975). The historical background to lithium research and therapy. In F.N. Johnson (Ed.), *Lithium research and therapy*, pp. 10–22. London: Academic Press.

Johnstone, E.C. (Ed.), (1991). Disabilities and circumstances of schizophrenic patients – a follow-up study. *British Journal of Psychiatry*, 159, Supplement, 13, 4–46.

Johnstone, E.C. (1994). *Searching for the causes of schizophrenia*. Oxford: Oxford University Press.

Johnstone, E.C., Crow, T.J., Frith, C.D., Husband, J. and Kreel, L. (1976). Cerebral ventricular size and cognitive impairment in chronic schizophrenia. *Lancet*, ii, 924–926.

Johnstone, E.C., Crow, T.J., Frith, C.D., Carney, M.W.P. and Price, J.S. (1978). Mechanism of the antipsychotic effect in the treatment of acute schizophrenia. *Lancet*, i, 848–851.

Johnstone, E.C., Crow, T.J., Frith, C.D. and Owens, D.G.C. (1988). The Northwick Park 'functional' psychosis study: Diagnosis and treatment response. *Lancet*, ii, 119–125.

Johnstone, E.C., Abukmeil, S.S., Byrne, M., Clafferty, R., Grant, E., Hodges, A. *et al.* (2000). Edinburgh high risk study – findings after four years: Demographic, attainment and psychopathological issues. *Schizophrenia Research*, 46, 1–15.

Johnstone, E.C., Lawrie, S.M. and Cosway, R. (2002). What does the Edinburgh High-Risk Study tell us about schizophrenia? *American Journal of Medical Genetics (Neuropsychiatric Genetics)*, 114, 906–912.

Johnstone, E.C., Ebmeier, K.P., Miller, P., Owens, D.G.C. and Lawrie, S.M. (2005). Predicting schizophrenia – findings from the Edinburgh High-Risk Study. *British Journal of Psychiatry*, 186, 18–25.

Johnstone, M., Evans, V. and Baigel, S. (1959). Sernyl (C1–395) in clinical anaesthesia. *British Journal of Anaesthesia*, 31, 433–439.

Jones, P. and Done, D.J. (1997). From birth to onset: A developmental perspective of schizophrenia in two national birth cohorts. In M.S. Keshevan and R.M. Murray

(Eds.), *Neurodevelopment and adult psychopathology*. Cambridge: Cambridge University Press.

Jones, P., Rodgers, B., Murray, R.M. and Marmot, M.G. (1994a). Child development risk factors for adult schizophrenia in the British 1946 birth cohort. *Lancet*, ii, 1398–1402.

Jones, P.B., Harvey, I., Lewis, S.W., Toone, B.K., Van Os, J., Williams, M. *et al.* (1994b). Cerebral ventricle dimensions as risk factors for schizophrenia and affective psychosis. *Psychological Medicine*, 24, 995–1011.

Jones, P.B., Rantakilli, P., Hartikainen, A.-L., Isohanni, M. and Sipila, P. (1998). Schizophrenia as a long-term outcome of pregnancy, delivery, and perinatal complications: A 28-year follow-up of the 1966 north Finland general population birth cohort. *American Journal of Psychiatry*, 155, 355–364.

Joyce, J.N. (1983). Multiple dopamine receptors and behavior. *Neuroscience and Biobehavioral Reviews*, 7, 227–256.

Jus, A., Pineau, R., Lachance, R., Pelchat, G., Jus, K., Pires, P. *et al.* (1976). Epidemiology of tardive dysinesia: Part I. *Diseases of the Nervous System*, 37, 210–214.

Kaczmarek, B.L.J. (1984). Neurolinguistic analysis of verbal utterances in patients with focal lesions of the frontal lobes. *Brain and Language*, 21, 52–58.

Kahlbaum, K.L. (1874). *Catatonia* (trans. Y. Levij and T. Priden, 1973). Baltimore, MD: Johns Hopkins University Press.

Kalant, O.J. (1966). *The amphetamines: Toxicity and addiction*, Brookside Monographs, No. 5. Toronto: University of Toronto Press.

Kallman, F.J. (1938). *The genetics of schizophrenia*. New York: Augustin.

Kallman, F.J. (1946). The genetic theory of schizophrenia: An analysis of 691 schizophrenic twin index families. *American Journal of Psychiatry*, 103, 309–322.

Kallman, F.J. and Roth, B. (1956). Genetic aspects of preadolescent schizophrenia. *American Journal of Psychiatry*, 112, 599–606.

Kamphuis, J.H. and Emmelkamp, P.M.G. (2000). Stalking – a contemporary challenge for forensic and clinical psychiatry. *British Journal of Psychiatry*, 176, 206–209.

Kane, J.M. and Smith, J.M. (1982). Tardive dyskinesia: Prevalence and risk factors, 1959–79. *Archives of General Psychiatry*, 39, 473–481.

Kane, J.M., Woerner, M., Weinhold, P., Wegner, J. and Kinon, B. (1982). A prospective study of tardive dyskinesia development: Preliminary results. *Journal of Clinical Psychopharmacology*, 2, 345–349.

Kane, J.M., Woerner, M. and Lieberman, J. (1985). Tardive dyskinesia: Prevalence, incidence and risk factors. In D.E. Casey, T.N. Chase and A.V. Christensen (Eds.), *Dyskinesia: Research and treatment*, pp. 72–78. Berlin: Springer.

Kane, J.M., Honigfeld, G., Singer, J. and Meltzer, H. (1988). Clozapine for the treatment resistant schizophrenic. *Archives of General Psychiatry*, 45, 789–796.

Kane, J.M., Woerner, M.G., Pollack, S., Safferman, A.Z. and Lieberman, J.A. (1993). Does clozapine cause tardive dyskinesia? *Journal of Clinical Psychiatry*, 54, 327–330.

Kane, J.M., Marder, S.R., Schooler, N.R., Wirshing, W.C., Umbricht, D., Baker, R.W. *et al.* (2001). Clozapine and haloperidol in moderately refractory schizophrenia: A 6-month randomized and double-blind comparison. *Archives of General Psychiatry*, 58, 965–972.

Kanner, L. (1943). Autistic disturbances of affective contact. *Nervous Child*, 2, 217–250.

Kanner, L. and Eisenberg, L. (1956). Early infantile autism 1943–1955. *American Journal of Orthopsychiatry*, 26, 55–65.

Kant, O. (1940). Types and analyses of the clinical pictures of recovered schizophrenics. *Psychiatric Quarterly*, 14, 676–700.

Kant, O. (1941a). Study of a group of recovered schizophrenic patients. *Psychiatric Quarterly*, 15, 262–283.

Kant, O. (1941b). A comparative study of recovered and deteriorated schizophrenic patients. *Journal of Nervous and Mental Disease*, 93, 616–624.

Kant, O. (1948). Clinical investigation of simple schizophrenia. *Psychiatric Quarterly*, 22, 141–151.

Kaplan, R.D., Szechtman, H., Franco, S., Szechtman, B., Nahmias, C., Garnett, E.S. *et al.* (1993). Three clinical syndromes of schizophrenia in untreated subjects: Relation to brain glucose activity measured by positron emission tomography (PET). *Schizophrenia Research*, 11, 47–54.

Kapur, S. and Seeman, P. (2001). Does fast dissociation from the dopamine D(2) receptor explain the action of atypical antipsychotics? A new hypothesis. *American Journal of Psychiatry*, 158, 360–369.

Kapur, S., Zipursky, R., Jones, C., Remington, G. and Houle, S. (2000). Relationship between dopamine D(2) occupancy, clinical response, and side-effects: A double-blind PET study of first-episode schizophrenia. *American Journal of Psychiatry*, 157, 514–520.

Karlsson, P., Farde, L., Halldin, C. and Sedvall, G. (2002). PET study of D(1) dopamine receptor binding in neuroleptic-naive patients with schizophrenia. *American Journal of Psychiatry*, 159, 761–767.

Karno, M., Jenkins, J.H. and de la Selva, A. (1987). Expressed emotion and schizophrenic outcome among Mexican-American families. *Journal of Nervous and Mental Disease*, 175, 143–151.

Kasai, K., Shenton, M.E., Salisbury, D.F., Hirayasu, Y., Lee, C.U., Ciszewski, A.A. *et al.* (2003). Progressive decrease of left superior temporal gyrus gray matter volume in patients with first-episode schizophrenia. *American Journal of Psychiatry*, 160, 156–164.

Kasanin, J. (1933). The acute schizoaffective psychoses. *American Journal of Psychiatry*, 13, 97–126.

Katz, M.M., Cole, J.O. and Lowery, H.A. (1969). Studies of the diagnostic process: The influence of symptom perception, past experience and ethnic background on diagnostic decisions. *American Journal of Psychiatry*, 125, 109–119.

Kavanagh, D.J. (1992). Recent developments in expressed emotion and schizophrenia. *British Journal of Psychiatry*, 160, 601–620.

Kay, D.W.K. (1959). Observations on the natural history and genetics of old age psychoses: A Stockholm survey, 1931–1937. *Proceedings of the Royal Society of Medicine*, 52, 791–794.

Kay, D.W.K. and Roth, M. (1961). Environmental and hereditary factors in the schizophrenias of old age ('late paraphrenia') and their bearing on the general problem of causation in schizophrenia. *Journal of Mental Science*, 107, 649–686.

Kay, D.W.K., Cooper, A.F., Garside, R.F. and Roth, M. (1976). The differentiation of paranoid from affective psychoses by patients' premorbid characteristics. *British Journal of Psychiatry*, 129, 207–215.

Kay, S.R., Opler, L.A. and Fiszbein, A. (1986). Significance of positive and negative syndromes in chronic schizophrenia. *British Journal of Psychiatry*, 149, 439–448.

Kebabian, J.W. and Calne, D.B. (1979). Multiple receptors for dopamine. *Nature*, 277, 93–96.

Keefe, R.S.E. (2000). Working memory dysfunction and its relevance to schizophrenia. In T. Sharma and P. Harvey (Eds.), *Cognition in schizophrenia*. Oxford: Oxford University Press.

Kemali, D., Maj, M., Galderisi, S., Milici, N. and Salvati, A. (1989). Ventricle-to-brain ratio in schizophrenia: A controlled follow-up study. *Biological Psychiatry*, 26, 756–759.

Kendell, R.E. (1975). *The role of diagnosis in psychiatry*. Oxford: Blackwell.

Kendell, R.E. (1986). The relationship of schizoaffective illness to schizophrenic and affective disorders. In A. Marneros and M.T. Tsuang (Eds.), *Schizoaffective psychoses*, pp. 18–30. Berlin: Springer.

Kendell, R.E. (1987). Diagnosis and classification of functional psychoses. In T.J. Crow (Ed.), *Recurrent and chronic psychoses*, British Medical Bulletin, 43, No. 3, pp 499–513. Edinburgh: Churchill Livingstone.

Kendell, R.E. (1991). The major functional psychoses: Are they independent entities or part of a continuum? Philosophical and conceptual issues underlying the debate. In A. Kerr and H. McClelland (Eds.), *Concepts of mental disorder: A continuing debate*, pp. 1–16. London: Gaskell/Royal College of Psychiatrists.

Kendell, R.E. and Gourlay, J. (1970). The clinical distinction between the affective psychoses and schizophrenia. *British Journal of Psychiatry*, 117, 261–266.

Kendell, R.E., Wainwright, S., Hailey, A. and Reed, R.S. (1976). The influence of childbirth on psychiatric morbidity. *Psychological Medicine*, 6, 297–302.

Kendell, R.E., Brockington, I.F. and Leff, J.P. (1979). Prognostic implications of six alternative definitions of schizophenia. *Archives of General Psychiatry*, 36, 25–31.

Kendell, R.E., Chalmers, J.C. and Platz, C. (1987). Epidemiology of puerperal psychoses. *British Journal of Psychiatry*, 150, 662–673.

Kendell, R.E., Juszczak, E. and Cole, S.K. (1996). Obstetric complications and schizophrenia. A case-control study based on standardised obstetric records. *British Journal of Psychiatry*, 168, 556–561.

Kendell, R.E., McInneny, K., Juszczak, E. and Bain, M. (2000). Obstetric complications and schizophrenia. Two case-control studies based on structured obstetric records. *British Journal of Psychiatry*, 176, 516–522.

Kendler, K.S. (1980). The nosologic validity of paranoia (simple delusional disorder). *Archives of General Psychiatry*, 37, 699–706.

Kendler, K.S. (1985). Diagnostic approaches to schizotypal personality disorder: A historical perspective. *Schizophrenia Bulletin*, 11, 538–553.

Kendler, K.S. and Tsuang, M.T. (1981). Nosology of paranoid schizophrenia and other paranoid psychoses. *Schizophrenia Bulletin*, 7, 594–610.

Kendler, K.S., Gruenberg, A.M. and Strauss, J.S. (1981). An independent re-analysis of the Copenhagen sample of the Danish adoption study of schizophrenia. II. The relationship between schizotypal personality disorder and schizophrenia. *Archives of General Psychiatry*, 38, 982–984.

Kendler, K.S., Liebermann, J.A. and Walsh, D. (1989). The structured interview for schizotypy (SIS): A preliminary report. *Schizophrenia Bulletin*, 15, 559–571.

Kendler, K.S., Masterson, C.C., Ungaro, R. and Davis, K.L. (1984). A family history study of schizophrenia-related personality disorders. *American Journal of Psychiatry*, 141, 424–427.

Kendler, K.S., Gruenberg, A.M. and Tsuang, M.T. (1985). Psychiatric illness in first-degree relatives of schizophrenic and surgical control patients: A family study using DSM III criteria. *Archives of General Psychiatry*, 42, 770–779.

Kendler, K.S., McGuire, M., Gruenberg, A.M., O'Hare, A., Spellman, M. and Walsh, D. (1993a). The Roscommon family study. I. Methods, diagnosis of probands, and risk of schizophrenia in relatives. *Archives of General Psychiatry*, 50, 527–540.

Kendler, K.S., McGuire, M., Gruenberg, A.M., O'Hare, A., Spellman, M. and Walsh, D. (1993b). The Roscommon family study. III. Schizophrenia – related personality disorders in relatives. *Archives of General Psychiatry*, 50, 781–788.

Kendler, K.S., McGuire, M., Gruenberg, A.M. and Walsh D. (1994). An epidemiological, clinical, and family study of simple schizophrenia in County Roscommon, Ireland. *American Journal of Psychiatry*, 151, 27–34.

Kenny, J.T. and Meltzer, H.Y. (1991). Attention and higher cortical functions in schizophrenia. *Journal of Neuropsychiatry and Clinical Neuroscience*, 3, 269–275.

Kernberg, O.F. (1967). Borderline personality organization. *Journal of the American Psychoanalytic Association*, 15, 641–685.

Kerr, A. and McClelland, H. (Eds.) (1991). *Concepts of mental disorder: A continuing debate*. London: Gaskell/Royal College of Psychiatrists.

Kerwin, R., Patel, S. and Meldrum, B. (1990). Quantitative autoradiographic analysis of glutamate binding sites in the hippocampal formation in normal and schizophrenic brain post mortem. *Neuroscience*, 39, 25–32.

Kessler, R.C., McGonagle, K.A., Zhao, S., Nelson, C.B., Hughes, M., Eshleman, S. *et al.* (1994). Lifetime and 12-month prevalence DSM-III-R psychiatric disorders in the United States: Results from the National Comorbidity Study. *Archives of General Psychiatry*, 51, 8–19.

Kety, S.S., Rosenthal, D., Wender, P.H. and Schulsinger, F. (1968). The types and prevalence of mental illness in the biological and adoptive families of adoptive schizophrenics. In D. Rosenthal and S.S. Kety (Eds.), *The transmission of schizophrenia*, pp. 345–362. Oxford: Pergamon Press.

Kety, S.S., Rosenthal, D., Wender, P.H. and Schulsinger, F. (1971). Mental illness in the biological and adoptive families of adopted schizophrenics. *American Journal of Psychiatry*, 128, 302–306.

Kim, J.S., Kornhuber, H.H., Schmid-Burgk, W. and Holzmuller, B. (1980). Low cerebrospinal fluid glutamate in schizophrenic patients and a new hypothesis on schizophrenia. *Neuroscience Letters*, 20, 379–382.

King, D.J. (1990). The effect of neuroleptics on cognitive and psychomotor function. *British Journal of Psychiatry*, 157, 799–811.

King, J.K. (1985). A visit to the home of lithium. *Bulletin of the Royal College of Psychiatrists*, 9, 90–91.

Kinon, B.J. and Lieberman, J.A. (1996). Mechanisms of action of atypical antipsychotic drugs: A critical analysis. *Psychopharmacology*, 124, 2–34.

Kirby, G.H. (1913). The catatonic syndrome and its relation to manic-depresssive insanity. *Journal of Nervous and Mental Disease*, 40, 694–704.

Kircher, T.T., Liddle, P.F., Brammer, M.J., Williams, S.C., Murray, R.M. and McGuire, P.K. (2001). Neural correlates of formal thought disorder in schizophrenia: Preliminary findings from a functional magnetic resonance imaging study. *Archives of General Psychiatry*, 58, 769–774.

Kitamura, T., Okazaki, Y., Fujinawa, A., Yoshino, M. and Kasahara, Y. (1995).

Symptoms of psychoses. A factor-analytic study. *British Journal of Psychiatry*, 166, 236–240.

Klawans, H.L. and Weiner, W.J. (1976). The pharmacology of choreatic movement disorders. *Progress in Neurobiology*, 6, 49–80.

Kleist, K. (1914). Aphasie und Geisteskrankheit. *Münchener Medizinische Wochenschrift*, 61, 8–12.

Kleist, K. (1930). Zur hirnpathologischen Auffassung der schizophrenen grundstörungen. Die alogische Denkstörung. *Schweizer Archiv für Neurologie und Psychiatrie*, 26, 99–102. (Translated as Alogical thought disorder: An organic manifestation of the schizophrenic psychological deficit, in J. Cutting and M. Shepherd (Eds.) (1987), *The clinical roots of the schizophrenia concept*. Cambridge: Cambridge University Press.)

Kleist, K. (1943). Die Katatonien. *Nervenarzt*, 16, 1–10.

Kleist, K. (1960). Schizophrenic symptoms and cerebral pathology. *Journal of Mental Science*, 106, 246–255.

Kline, N.S. (1954). Use of Rauwolfia serpentina Benth. in neuropsychiatric conditions. *Annals of the New York Academy of Sciences*, 59, 107–132.

Klonoff, H., Fibiger, C.H. and Hutton, C.H. (1970). Neuropsychological patterns in chronic schizophrenia. *Journal of Nervous and Mental Disease*, 150: 291–300.

Knight, J.G. (1982). Dopamine-receptor-stimulating autoantibodies: A possible cause of schizophrenia. *Lancet*, ii, 1073–1075.

Knight, R.P. (1954a). Borderline states. In R.P. Knight and C.R. Friedman (Eds.), *Psychoanalytic psychiatry and psychology*, Vol. I, pp. 97–109. New York: International Universities Press.

Knight, R.P. (1954b). Management and psychotherapy of the borderline schizophrenic patient. In R.P. Knight and C.R. Friedman (Eds.), *Psychoanalytic psychiatry and psychology*, Vol. I, pp. 110–122. New York: International Universities Press.

Koehler, K. (1979). First rank symptoms of schizophrenia: Questions concerning clinical boundaries. *British Journal of Psychiatry*, 134, 236–248.

Koehler, K., Guth, W. and Grimm, G. (1977). First rank symptoms in Schneider-oriented German centers. *Archives of General Psychiatry*, 34, 810–813.

Kokkinides, L. and Anisman, H. (1981). Amphetamine psychosis and schizophrenia: A dual model. *Neuroscience and Biobehavioral Reviews*, 5, 449–461.

Kolb, B. and Whishaw, I.Q. (1983). Performance of schizophrenic patients on tests sensitive to right or left frontal, temporal or parietal function in neurological patients. *Journal of Nervous and Mental Disease*, 171, 435–443.

Kolle, K. (1931). *Die primäre Verrücktheit*. Leipzig: Thieme.

Kolvin, I. (1972). Late onset psychosis. *British Medical Journal*, 3, 816–817.

Kolvin, I., Ounsted, C., Humphrey, M. and McNay, A. (1971). Studies in the childhood psychoses. II. The phenomenology of childhood psychoses. *British Journal of Psychiatry*, 118, 385–395.

Korboot, P.J. and Damiani, W. (1976). Auditory processing speed and signal detection in schizophrenia. *Journal of Abnormal Psychology*, 85, 287–295.

Kornhuber, J., Mack-Burkhardt, F., Riederer, P., Hebenstreit, G.F., Reynolds, G.P., Andrews, H.B. *et al.* (1989). [^{3}H] MK-801 binding sites in postmortem brain regions of schizophrenic brains. *Journal of Neural Transmission*, 77, 231–236.

Korpi, E.R., Kaufmann, C.A., Marnela, K.-M. and Weinberger, D.R. (1987). Cerebrospinal fluid amino acid concentrations in chronic schizophrenia. *Psychiatry Research*, 20, 337–345.

Kovelman, J.A. and Scheibel, A.B. (1984). A neurohistological correlate of schizophrenia. *Biological Psychiatry*, 19, 1601–1621.

Kraepelin, E. (1896). Dementia praecox. Trans. in J. Cutting and M. Shepherd (Eds.) (1987), *The clinical roots of the schizophrenia concept*, pp. 13–24. Cambridge: Cambridge University Press.

Kraepelin, E. (1905). *Lectures on clinical psychiatry*, 3rd English edn (trans. T. Johnstone, 1917). New York: W. Wood.

Kraepelin (1907). *Clinical psychiatry*, 7th edn (trans. A.R. Diefendorf, 1915). New York: Macmillan.

Kraepelin, E. (1909). *Lehrbuch der Psychiatrie*, 7th edn, Vol. 1, pp. 1025, 1040–1068. Leipzig: Barth.

Kraepelin, E. (1913a). *Dementia praecox and paraphrenia* (trans. R.M. Barclay, 1919). Edinburgh: Livingstone.

Kraepelin, E. (1913b). *Manic-depressive insanity and paranoia* (trans. R.M. Barclay, 1921). Edinburgh: Livingstone.

Kreiskott, H. (1980). Behavioral pharmacology of antipsychotics. In F. Hoffmeister and G. Stille (Eds.), *Handbook of experimental pharmacology, Vol. 55, Psychotropic agents, Part 1: Antipsychotics and antidepressants*, pp. 59–88. Berlin: Springer.

Kretschmer, E. (1925). *Physique and character: An investigation of the nature of constitution and of the theory of temperament*, 2nd edn (trans. W.J.H. Sprott). London: Kegan Paul, Trench, Trubner and Co. Ltd.

Kretschmer, E. (1927). The sensitive delusion of reference. Trans. in S.R. Hirsch and M. Shepherd (Eds.) (1974), *Themes and variations in European psychiatry*, pp. 153–196. Bristol: Wright.

Kringlen, E. (1967). *Hereditary and environment in the functional psychoses*. London: Heinemann.

Krystal, J.H., Karper, L.P., Seibyl, J.P., Freeman, G.K., Delanaey, R., Bremner, J.D. *et al.* (1994). Subanesthetic effects of the noncompetitive NMDA antagonist, ketamine, in humans. *Archives of General Psychiatry*, 51, 199–214.

Kuipers, E., Garety, P., Fowler, D., Dunn, G., Bebbington, P., Freeman, D. *et al.* (1997). London-East Anglia randomised controlled trial of cognitive-behavioural therapy for psychosis. I: Effects of the treatment phase. *British Journal of Psychiatry*, 171, 319–327.

Kulhara, P., Kota, S.K. and Joseph, S. (1986). Positive and negative subtypes of schizophrenia: A study from India. *Acta Psychiatrica Scandinavica*, 74, 353–359.

Kumra, S., Frazier, J.A., Jacobsen, L.K., McKenna, K., Gordon, C.T., Lenane, M.C. *et al.* (1996). Childhood-onset schizophrenia. A double-blind clozapine-haloperidol comparison. *Archives of General Psychiatry*, 53, 1090–1097.

Kumra, S., Giedd, J.N., Vaituzis, A.C., Jacobsen, L.K., McKenna, K., Bedwell, J. *et al.* (2000). Childhood-onset psychotic disorders: Magnetic resonance imaging of volumetric differences in brain structure. *American Journal of Psychiatry*, 157, 1467–1474.

Kutay, F.Z., Pogun, S., Hariri, N.I., Peker, G. and Erlacin, S. (1989). Free amino acid level determinations in normal and schizophrenic brain. *Progress in Neuropsychopharmacology and Biological Psychiatry*, 13, 119–126.

Laborit, H., Huguenard, P. and Alluaume, R. (1952). Un nouveau stabilisateur vegetatif (le 4560 RP). *Presse Medicale*, 60, 206–208.

Lahti, A.C., Holcomb, H.H., Medoff, D.R., Weiler, M.A., Tamminga, C.A. and Carpenter, W.T. (2001a). Abnormal patterns of regional cerebral blood flow in schizophrenia with primary negative symptoms during an effortful auditory recognition task. *American Journal of Psychiatry*, 158, 1797–1808.

Lahti, A.C., Weiler, M.A., Michaelidis, T., Parwani, A. and Tamminga, T.A. (2001b). Effects of ketamine on normal and schizophrenic volunteers. *Neuropsychopharmacology*, 25, 455–467.

Laing, R.D. (1965). *The divided self: A study of sanity and madness*. Harmondsworth: Penguin.

Laing, R.D. (1967). *The politics of experience*. Harmondsworth: Penguin.

Laing, R.D. and Esterson, A. (1964). *Sanity, madness and the family*, 2nd edn. London: Tavistock.

Landro, N.I., Orbeck, A.L. and Rund, B.R. (1993). Memory functioning in chronic and non-chronic schizophrenics, affectively disturbed patients and normal controls. *Schizophrenia Research*, 10, 85–92.

Lange, J. (1922). *Katatonische Erscheinungen in Rahmen Manischer Erkrankungen*. Berlin: Springer.

Langfeldt, G. (1937). The prognosis in schizophrenia and the factors influencing the course of the disease. *Acta Psychiatrica et Neurologica Scandinavica*, Supplement, 13, 7–228.

Langfeldt, G. (1956). The prognosis of schizophrenia. *Acta Psychiatrica et Neurologica Scandinavica*, Supplement, 110, 1–143.

Langsley, N., Miller, P., Byrne, M., McIntosh, A. and Johnstone, E.C. (2004). Dermatoglyphics and schizophrenia: Findings from the Edinburgh High-Risk Study. *Schizophrenia Research*, 74, 122–124.

Laruelle, M., Abi-Dargham, A., van Dyck, C.H., Gil, R., De Souza, C.D., Erdos, J. *et al.* (1996). Single photon emission computerized tomography imaging of amphetamine-induced dopamine release in drug free schizophrenic subjects. *Proceedings of the National Academy of Science, USA*, 93, 9235–9240.

Laruelle, M., Abi-Dargham, A., Gil, R., Kegelas, L. and Innes, R. (1999). Increased dopamine transmission in schizophrenia: Relationship to illness phases. *Biological Psychiatry*, 46, 56–72.

Lauritsen, M.B. and Ewald, H. (2001). The genetics of autism. *Acta Psychiatrica Scandinavica*, 103, 411–427.

Lawrie, S.M., Byrne, M., Miller, P., Hodges, A., Clafferty, R.A., Cunningham Owens, D.G. *et al.* (2001a). Neurodevelopmental indices and the development of psychotic symptoms in subjects at high risk of schizophrenia. *British Journal of Psychiatry*, 178, 524–530.

Lawrie, S.M., Whalley, H.C., Abukmeil, S.S., Kestelman, J.N., Donnelly, L., Miller, P. *et al.* (2001b). Brain structure, genetic liability, and psychotic symptoms in subjects at high risk of developing schizophrenia. *Biolological Psychiatry*, 49, 811–823.

Lawrie, S.M., Whalley, H.C., Abukmeil, S.S., Kestelman, J.N., Miller, P., Best, J.J.K. *et al.* (2002). Temporal lobe volume changes in people at high risk of schizophrenia with psychotic symptoms. *British Journal of Psychiatry*, 181, 138–143.

Laws, K. (1999). A meta-analytic review of Wisconsin Card Sort studies in schizophrenia: General intellectual deficit in disguise. *Cognitive Neuropsychiatry*, 4, 1–30.

Lay, R.A.Q. (1938). Schizophrenia-like psychoses in young children. *Journal of Mental Science*, 84, 105–133.

Leask, S.J., Done, D.J. and Crow, T.J. (2002). Adult psychosis, common childhood infections and neurological soft signs in a national birth cohort. *British Journal of Psychiatry*, 181, 387–392.

Lecours, A.R. and Vanier-Clément, M. (1976). Schizophasia and jargonaphasia: A comparative description with comments on Chaika's and Fromkin's respective looks at 'schizophrenic' language. *Brain and Language*, 3, 516–565.

Lee, T. and Seeman, P. (1980). Elevation of brain neuroleptic/dopamine receptors in schizophrenia. *American Journal of Psychiatry*, 137, 191–197.

Lee, T., Seeman, P., Tourtellotte, W.W., Farley, L.J. and Hornykiewicz, O. (1978). Binding of ^{3}H-neuroleptics and ^{3}H-apomorphine in schizophrenic brains. *Nature*, 274, 897–900.

Lees, A.J. (1985). *Tics and related disorders*. Edinburgh: Churchill Livingstone.

Leff, J., Wig, N.N., Ghosh, A., Bedi, H., Menon, D.K., Kuipers, L. *et al.* (1987). Influence of relatives' expressed emotion on the course of schizophrenia in Chandigarh. *British Journal of Psychiatry*, 151, 166–173.

Leff, J., Wig, N.N., Bedi, H., Menon, D.K., Kuipers, L., Korten, A. *et al.* (1990). Relatives' expressed emotion and the course of schizophrenia in Chandigarh. A two-year follow-up of a first-contact sample. *British Journal of Psychiatry*, 156, 351–356.

Leff, J.P. and Wing, J.K. (1971). Trial of maintenance therapy in schizophrenics. *British Medical Journal*, 3, 599–604.

Lennox, B.R., Park, S.B.G., Medley, I., Morris, P.G. and Jones, P.B. (2000). The functional neuroanatomy of auditory hallucinations in schizophrenia. *Psychiatry Research: Neuroimaging*, 100, 13–20.

Leonhard, K. (1961). Cycloid psychoses – endogenous psychoses which are neither schizophrenic nor manic-depressive. *Journal of Mental Science*, 107, 633–648.

Leonhard, K. (1979). *The classification of endogenous psychoses*, 5th edn (trans. R. Berman). New York: Irvington.

Letemendia, F.J.J. and Harris, A.D. (1967). Chlorpromazine and the untreated chronic schizophrenic. *British Journal of Psychiatry*, 113, 950–958.

Leucht, S., Kissling, W. and McGrath J. (2004). Lithium for schizophrenia revisited: A systematic review and meta-analysis of randomized controlled trials. *Journal of Clinical Psychiatry*, 65, 177–186.

Levenson, J.L. (1985). Neuroleptic malignant syndrome. *American Journal of Psychiatry*, 142, 1137–1145.

Levin, S. (1984). Frontal lobe dysfunctions in schizophrenia – II. Impairments of psychological and brain functions. *Journal of Psychiatric Research*, 18, 57–72.

Lewine, R.J., Fogg, L. and Meltzer, H.Y. (1983). Assessment of positive and negative symptoms in schizophrenia. *Schizophrenia Bulletin*, 9, 368–376.

Lewine, R.R.J. (1980). Sex differences in age of onset and first hospitalization in schizophrenia. *American Journal of Orthopsychiatry*, 50, 316–322.

Lewis, A. (1936). Patterns of obsessional illness. *Proceedings of the Royal Society of Medicine*, 29, 325–336. (Reprinted 1967, in *Inquiries in psychiatry*, pp. 141–156. London: Routledge and Kegan Paul.)

Lewis, A. (1970). Paranoia and paranoid: A historical perspective. *Psychological Medicine*, 1, 2–12.

Lewis, A.J. (1934). Melancholia: A clinical survey of depressive states. *Journal of Mental Science*, 80, 277–378.

Lewis, N.D.C. (1936). *Research in dementia praecox (past attainments, present trends, and future possibilities)*. New York: Committee on Mental Hygiene.

Lewis, S., Tarrier, N., Haddock, G., Bentall, R., Kinderman, P., Kingdon, D. *et al.* (2002). Randomised controlled trial of cognitive-behavioural therapy in early schizophrenia: Acute-phase outcomes. *British Journal of Psychiatry*, 181, Supplement, 43, s91–s97.

Lewis, S.W. (1989). Congenital risk factors for schizophrenia. *Psychological Medicine*, 19, 5–13.

Lewis, S.W. (1990). Computerised tomography in schizophrenia 15 years on. *British Journal of Psychiatry*, 157, Supplement, 9, 16–24.

Liberman, J.I. (1964). The influence of head injury in peace time on the development of schizophrenia: A statistical investigation. *Zhournal Nevropatologii Psikhiatrii I.M.S.S. Korsakova*, 64, 1369–1373.

Liddle, P.F. (1987a). The symptoms of chronic schizophrenia: A re-examination of the positive–negative dichotomy. *British Journal of Psychiatry*, 151, 145–151.

Liddle, P.F. (1987b). Schizophrenic syndromes, cognitive performance and neurological dysfunction. *Psychological Medicine*, 17, 49–57.

Liddle, P.F. (2001). *Disordered mind and brain*. London: Gaskell/Royal College of Psychiatrists.

Liddle, P.F. and Crow, T.J. (1984). Age disorientation in chronic schizophrenia is associated with global intellectual impairment. *British Journal of Psychiatry*, 144, 193–199.

Liddle, P.F. and Morris, D.L. (1991). Schizophrenic symptoms and frontal lobe performance. *British Journal of Psychiatry*, 158, 340–345.

Liddle, P.F., Friston, K.J., Frith, C.D., Hirsch, S.R., Jones, T. and Frackowiak, R.S.J. (1992). Patterns of cerebral blood flow in schizophrenia. *British Journal of Psychiatry*, 160, 179–186.

Lidz, T. and Blatt, S. (1983). Critique of the Danish-American studies of the biological and adoptive relatives of adoptees who became schizophrenic. *American Journal of Psychiatry*, 140, 426–434.

Lidz, T., Cornelison, A.R., Fleck, S. and Terry, D. (1957a). The intrafamilial environment of the schizophrenic patient: I. The father. *Psychiatry*, 20, 329–342.

Lidz, T., Cornelison, A.R., Fleck, S. and Terry, D. (1957b). The intrafamilial environment of the schizophrenic patient: II. Marital schism and marital skew. *American Journal of Psychiatry*, 114, 241–248.

Lidz, T., Blatt, S. and Cook, B. (1981). Critique of the Danish-American studies of the adopted-away offspring of schizophrenic parents. *American Journal of Psychiatry*, 138, 1063–1068.

Lieberman, J., Chakos, M., Wu, H., Alvir, J., Hoffman, E., Robinson, D. *et al.* (2001). Longitudinal study of brain morphology in first episode schizophrenia. *Biological Psychiatry*, 49, 487–499.

Lieberman, J.A. and Saltz, B.L. (1992). Tardive Tourette's: Tardive dyskinesia form fruste or a distinct clinical syndrome. In A.B. Joseph and R.R. Young (Eds.), *Movement disorders in neurology and neuropsychiatry*, pp 134–138. Boston, MA: Blackwell Scientific.

Lieberman, J.A., Phillips, M., Gu, H.K., Stroup, S., Zhang, P., Kong. L. *et al.* (2003). Atypical and conventional antipsychotic drugs in treatment-naive first-episode schizophrenia: A 52 week randomized trial of clozapine vs chlorpromazine. *Neuropsychopharmacology*, 28, 995–1993.

Lindenmayer, J.-P., Bernstein-Hyman, R., Grochowski, S. and Bark, N. (1995). Psychopathology of schizophrenia: Initial validation of a 5-factor model. *Psychopathology*, 28, 22–31.

Linn, M.W., Caffey, E.M., Klett, J., Hogarty, G.E. and Lamb, H.R. (1979). Day treatment and psychotropic drugs in the aftercare of schizophrenic patients. *Archives of General Psychiatry*, 36, 1055–1066.

Lishman W.A. (1998). *Organic psychiatry*, 3rd edn. Oxford: Blackwell Science.

Llorca, P.-M., Chereu, I., Bayle, F.-J. and Lancon, C. (2002). Tardive dyskinesias and antipsychotics: A review. *European Psychiatry*, 17, 129–138.

Lobova, L.P. (1960). The role of trauma in the development of schizophrenia. *Zhournal Nevropatologii Psikhiatrii I.M.S.S. Korsakova*, 60, 1187–1192.

Lohr, J.B. and Wisniewski, A.A. (1987). *Movement disorders: A neuropsychiatric approach*. Chichester: Wiley.

Lorr, M., Klett, C.J. and McNair, D.M. (1963). *Syndromes of psychosis*. Oxford: Pergamon.

Lorr, M., Klett, C.J. and McNair, D.M. (1966). Acute psychotic types. In M. Lorr (Ed.), *Explorations in typing psychotics*, pp. 33–75. Oxford: Pergamon.

Luby, E.D., Cohen, B.D., Rosenbaum, G., Gottlieb, J.S. and Kelley, R. (1959). Study of a new schizophrenomimetic drug – sernyl. *AMA Archives of Neurology and Psychiatry*, 81, 363–369.

Lund, C.E., Mortimer, A.M., Rogers, D. and McKenna, P.J. (1991). Motor, volitional and behavioural disorders in schizophrenia. 1: Assessment using the modified Rogers scale. *British Journal of Psychiatry*, 158, 323–327.

Luxenburger, H. (1928). Vorläufiger Bericht über psychiatrische serienuntersuchungen an Zwillingen. *Zeitschrift für die gesamte Neurologie und Psychiatrie*, 116, 297–326.

Lykouras, L., Oulis, P., Daskapoulou, E., Psarros, K. and Christodolou, G.N. (2001). Clinical subtypes of schizophrenic disorders: A cluster analytic study. *Psychopathology*, 34, 23–28.

McCarron, M.M., Schulze, B.W., Thompson, G.A., Conder, M.C. and Goetz, W.A. (1981). Acute phencyclidine intoxication: Clinical patterns, complications and treatment. *Annals of Emergency Medicine*, 10, 290–297.

McCreadie, R.G. and Phillips, K. (1988). The Nithsdale schizophrenia survey: VII. Does relatives' high expressed emotion predict relapse? *British Journal of Psychiatry*, 152, 477–481.

McCreadie, R.G., Thara, R., Kamath, S., Padmavathy, R., Latha, S., Mathrubootham N. *et al.* (1996). Abnormal movements in never-medicated Indian patients with schizophrenia. *British Journal of Psychiatry*, 168, 221–226.

McGhie, A. (1969). *Pathology of attention*. Harmondsworth: Penguin.

McGhie, A. and Chapman, J. (1961). Disorders of attention and perception in early schizophrenia. *British Journal of Medical Psychology*, 34, 103–106.

McGorry, P.D., Bell, R.C., Dudgeon, P.L. and Jackson, H.J. (1998). The dimensional structure of first episode psychosis: An exploratory factor analysis. *Psychological Medicine*, 28, 935–947.

McGrath, J. (1991). Ordering thoughts on thought disorder. *British Journal of Psychiatry*, 158, 307–316.

McGuffin, P. (1988). Genetics of schizophrenia. In P. Bebbington and P. McGuffin (Eds.), *Schizophrenia: The major issues*, pp. 107–126. Oxford: Heinemann/Mental Health Foundation.

McGuire, P.K., Quested, D.J., Spence, S.A., Murray, R.M., Frith, C.D. and Liddle, P.F. (1998). Pathophysiology of 'positive' thought disorder in schizophrenia. *British Journal of Psychiatry*, 173, 231–235.

McIntosh, A.M., Forrester, A., Lawrie, S.M., Byrne, M., Harper, A., Kestelman, J.N.

et al. (2001). A factor model of the functional psychoses and the relationship of factors to clinical variables and brain morphology. *Psychological Medicine*, 31, 159–171.

Mack, J.E. (1975). Borderline states: An historical perspective. In J.E. Mack (Ed.), *Borderline states in psychiatry*, pp. 1–27. New York: Grune and Stratton.

Mackay, A.V.P. (1982). Clinical controversies in tardive dyskinesia. In C.D. Marsden and S. Fahn (Eds.), *Movement disorders*, pp. 249–262. London: Butterworth.

Mackay, A.V.P., Doble, A., Bird, E.D., Spokes, E.G.S., Quik, M. and Iversen, L.L. (1978). ^{3}H-spiperone binding in normal and schizophrenic postmortem brain. *Life Science*, 23, 527–532.

Mackay, A.V.P., Iversen, L.L., Rossor, M., Spokes, E., Bird, E., Arregui, A. *et al.* (1982). Increased brain dopamine and and dopamine receptors in schizophrenia. *Archives of General Psychiatry*, 39, 991–997.

McKenna, P.J. (1984). Disorders with overvalued ideas. *British Journal of Psychiatry*, 145, 579–585.

McKenna, P.J. and Bailey, P.E. (1993). The strange story of clozapine. *British Journal of Psychiatry*, 162, 32–37.

McKenna, P. and Oh, T. (2005). *Schizophrenic speech: Making sense of bathroots and ponds that fall in doorways.* Cambridge: Cambridge University Press.

McKenna, P.J., Kane, J.M. and Parrish, K. (1985). Psychotic syndromes in epilepsy. *Americal Journal of Psychiatry*, 142, 895–904.

McKenna, P.J., Tamlyn, D., Lund, C.E., Mortimer, A.M., Hammond, S. and Baddeley, A.D. (1990). Amnesic syndrome in schizophrenia. *Psychological Medicine*, 20, 967–972.

McKenna, P.J., Thornton, A. and Turner M. (1999). Catatonia in and outside schizophrenia. In C. Williams and A. Sims (Eds.), *Proceedings of the 5th Leeds symposium on psychopathology*, pp. 105–135. Leeds: Leeds University Press.

McKenna, P.J., Ornstein, T. and Baddeley, A.D. (2002). Schizophrenia. In A.D. Baddeley, B.A. Wilson and M. Kopelman (Eds), *Handbook of memory disorders*, 2nd edn, pp. 413–436. Chichester: Wiley.

MacMillan, J.F., Gold, A., Crow, T.J., Johnson, A.L. and Johnstone, E.C. (1986). The Northwick Park study of first episodes of schizophrenia IV. Expressed emotion and relapse. *British Journal of Psychiatry*, 148, 133–143.

Mahendra, B. (1981). Where have all the catatonics gone? *Psychological Medicine*, 11, 669–671.

Maher, B. and Ross, J.S. (1984). Delusions. In H.E. Adams and P.B. Sutker (Eds.), *Comprehensive handbook of psychopathology*, pp. 383–410. New York: Plenum.

Maher, B.A. (1974). Delusional thinking and perceptual disorder. *Journal of Individual Psychology*, 30, 98–113.

Maher, B.A. (1983). A tentative theory of schizophrenic utterance. In B.A. Maher and W.B. Maher (Eds), *Progress in experimental personality research*. New York: Academic Press.

Maier, W., Lichterman, D., Minges, J., Hallmayer, J., Heun, R., Benkert, O. *et al.* (1993). Continuity and discontinuity of affective disorders and schizophrenia. *Archives of General Psychiatry*, 50, 871–883.

Maier, W., Lichtermann, D., Minges, J. and Heun, R. (1994). Personality disorders among the relatives of schizophrenia patients. *Schizophrenia Bulletin*, 20, 481–493.

Maj, M. (1985). Clinical course and outcome of schizoaffective disorders. *Acta Psychiatrica Scandinavica*, 72, 542–550.

Maj, M. (1988). Clinical course and outcome of cycloid psychotic disorder: A three-year prospective study. *Acta Psychiatrica Scandinavica*, 78, 182–187.

Malamud, N. (1959). Heller's disease and childhood schizophrenia. *American Journal of Psychiatry*, 116, 215–218.

Malamud, W. and Render, N. (1938). Course and prognosis in schizophrenia. *American Journal of Psychiatry*, 95, 1039–1057.

Malec, J. (1978). Neuropsychological assessment of schizophrenia vesus brain damage: A review. *Journal of Nervous and Mental Disease*, 166, 507–516.

Malzacher, M., Merz, J. and Ebnother, D. (1981). Einschneidende Lebenserreignisse im Vorfeld akuter schizophrener Episoden: Erstmals erkrankte Patienten im Vergleich mit einer Normalstichprobe. *Archiv für Psychiatrie und Nervenkrankheiten*, 230, 227–242.

Mann, S.C., Caroff, S.W., Bleier, H.R., Welz, W.K.R., Kling, M.A. and Hayashida, M. (1986). Lethal catatonia. *American Journal of Psychiatry*, 143, 1374–1381.

Manschreck, T.C., Maher, B.A., Milavetz, J.J., Ames, D., Weinstein, C.C. and Schneyer, M.L. (1988). Semantic priming in thought disordered schizophrenic patients. *Schizophrenia Research*, 1, 61–66.

Manton, K.G., Korten, A., Woodbury, M.A., Anker, M. and Jablensky, A. (1994). Symptom profiles of psychiatric disorders based on graded disease classes: An illustration using data from the WHO International Pilot Study of Schizophrenia. *Psychological Medicine*, 24, 133–144.

Marcé, L.V. (1858). *Traite de la folie des femmes enceintes des nouvelles accouchées et des nourricès*. Paris: Baillière et fils.

Marengo, J., Harrow, M., Sands, J. and Galloway, C. (1991). European versus U.S. data on the course of schizophrenia. *American Journal of Psychiatry*, 606–611.

Margo, A., Hemsley, D.R. and Slade, P.D. (1981). The effects of varying auditory input on schizophrenic hallucinations. *British Journal of Psychiatry*, 139, 122–127.

Marneros, A. and Pillman, F. (2004). *Acute and transient psychoses*. Cambridge: Cambridge University Press.

Marneros, A., Deister, A. and Rohde, A. (1990). Psychopathological and social status of patients with affective, schizophrenic and schizoaffective disorders after long-term course. *Acta Psychiatrica Scandinavica*, 82, 352–358.

Marsden, C.D. and Jenner, P. (1980). The pathophysiology of extrapyramidal side-effects of neuroleptic drugs. *Psychological Medicine*, 10, 55–72.

Marsden, C.D., Mindham, R.H.S. and Mackay, A.V.P. (1986). Extrapyramidal movement disorders produced by antipsychotic drugs. In P.B. Bradley and S.R. Hirsch (Eds.), *The psychopharmacology and treatment of schizophrenia*, pp. 340–402. Oxford: Oxford University Press.

Marsden, C.D., Tarsy, D. and Baldessarini, R.J. (1975). Spontaneous and drug induced movement disorders in psychiatric patients. In D.F. Benson and D. Blumer (Eds.), *Psychiatric aspects of neurologic disease*, pp. 219–266. New York: Grune and Stratton.

Marsh, L., Williams, J.R., Rocco, M., Grill, S., Munro, C. and Dawson, T.M. (2004). Psychiatric comorbidities in patients with Parkinson disease and psychosis. *Neurology*, 63, 293–300.

Martinot, J.L., Peron-Magnan, D., Huret, J.D. Mazoyer B., Baron, J.-C., Boulenger, J.-P. *et al.* (1990). Striatal D2 dopaminergic receptors assessed with positron emission tomography and ^{76}Br bromospiperone in untreated schizophrenic patients. *American Journal of Psychiatry*, 147, 44–50.

Mason, P., Harrison, G., Croudace, T., Glazebrook, C. and Medley, I. (1997). The predictive validity of a diagnosis of schizophrenia. *British Journal of Psychiatry*, 170, 321–327.

Mason, S.T. (1984). *Catecholamines and behaviour*. Cambridge: Cambridge University Press.

Mathalon, D.H., Sullivan, E.V., Lim, K.O. and Pfefferbaum, A. (2001). Progressive brain volume changes and the clinical course of schizophrenia in men: A longitudinal magnetic resonance imaging study. *Archives of General Psychiatry*, 58, 148–157.

Mathew, R.J., Duncan, G.C., Weinman, M.L. and Barr, D.L. (1982). Regional cerebral blood flow in schizophrenia. *Archives of General Psychiatry*, 39, 1121–1124.

May, P.R. (1968). *Treatment of schizophrenia*. New York: Science House.

Mayer, W. (1921). Über paraphrene Psychosen. *Zentralblatt für die gesamte Neurologie und Psychiatrie*, 26, 78–80.

Mayer-Gross, W. (1932). Die Schizophrenie. In O. Bumke (Ed.), *Handbuch der Geisteskrankheiten*, Vol. IX, pp. 534–578. Berlin: Springer.

Mayer-Gross, W., Slater, E. and Roth, M. (1969). *Clinical psychiatry*, 3rd edn. London: Baillière, Tindall & Cassell.

Meehl, P.E. (1962). Schizotaxia, schizotypy, schizophrenia. *American Psychologist*, 17, 827–838.

Meinertz, F. (1957). Schizophrenieähnliche Psychosen un Grenzzustände bei Hirnverletzen. In *Report of Second International Congress of Psychiatry*, Vol. 4. Zurich.

Mellor, C.S. (1970). First-rank symptoms of schizophrenia. *British Journal of Psychiatry*, 117, 15–23.

Meltzer, H.Y. (1991). The mechanism of action of novel antipsychotic drugs. *Schizophrenia Bulletin*, 17, 263–287.

Mendez, M.F., Grau, R., Doss, R.C. and Taylor, J.L. (1993). Schizophrenia in epilepsy: Seizure and psychosis variables. *Neurology*, 43, 1073–1077.

Mendlewicz, J., Fieve, R.R., Rainer, J.D. and Fliess, J.L. (1972). Manic-depressive illness: A comparative study of patients with and without a family history. *British Journal of Psychiatry*, 120, 523–530.

Menon, M., Pomarol-Clotet, E., McKenna, P.J. and McCarthy, R.A. (2006). Probabilistic reasoning in schizophrenia: A comparison of the performance of deluded and non-deluded schizophrenics and exploration of possible cognitive underpinnings. *Cognitive Neuropsychiatry*, 11, 521–536.

Menon, V., Anagnoson, R.T., Mathalon, D.H., Glover, G.H. and Pfefferbaum, A. (2001). Functional neuroanatomy of auditory working memory in schizophrenia: Relation to positive and negative symptoms. *Neuroimage*, 13, 433–446.

Merskey, H. (1995). *The analysis of hysteria*, 2nd edn. London: Gaskell/Royal College of Psychiatrists.

Mettler, F.A. (1955). Perceptual capacity, function of the corpus striatum and schizophrenia. *Psychiatric Quarterly*, 29, 89–111.

Mettler, F.A. and Crandell, A. (1959). Neurologic disorders in psychiatric institutions. *Journal of Nervous and Mental Disease*, 128, 148–159.

Miller, B.L., Cummings, J.L., Villanueva-Meyer, J., Boone, K., Mehringer, C. Lesser, I.M. *et al.* (1991). Frontal lobe degeneration: Clinical, neuropsychological, and SPECT characteristics. *Neurology*, 41, 1374–1382.

Miller, P., Byrne, M., Hodges, A., Lawrie, S.M. and Johnstone, E.C. (2002a). Childhood behaviour, psychotic symptoms and psychosis onset in young people at high risk of schizophrenia: Early findings from the Edinburgh High-Risk Study. *Psychological Medicine*, 32, 173–179.

Miller, P., Byrne, M., Hodges, A., Lawrie, S.M., Owens, D.G.C. and Johnstone, E.C. (2002b). Schizotypal components in people at high risk of developing schizophrenia – early findings from the Edinburgh High-Risk Study. *British Journal of Psychiatry*, 180, 179–184.

Miller, P., Lawrie, S.M., Byrne, M., Cosway, R. and Johnstone, E.C. (2002c). Self-rated schizotypal cognitions, psychotic symptoms and the onset of schizophrenia in young people at high risk of schizophrenia. *Acta Psychiatrica Scandinavica*, 105, 341–345.

Minzenberg, M., Ober, B.A. and Vinogradov, S. (2002). Semantic priming in schizophrenia: A review and synthesis. *Journal of the International Neuropsychological Society*, 8, 699–720.

Mirsky, A.F., Kugelmass, S., Ingraham, L.J., Frenkel, E. and Nathan, M. (1995). Overview and summary: Twenty-five-year followup of high-risk children. *Schizophrenia Bulletin*, 21, 227–239.

Mishara, A.L. and Goldberg, T.E. (2004). A meta-analysis and critical review of the effects of conventional neuroleptic treatment on cognition in schizophrenia: Opening a closed book. *Biological Psychiatry*, 55, 1013–1022.

Mitsuda, H. (Ed.) (1967). *Clinical genetics in psychiatry*, Bulletin of the Osaka Medical School, Supplement XII. Osaka: Osaka Medical College.

Mjones, H. (1949). Paralysis agitans: A clinical and genetic study. *Acta Psychiatrica et Neurologica Scandinavica*, Supplement, 54, 1–195.

Mlakar, J., Jensterle, J. and Frith C.D. (1994). Central monitoring deficiency and schizophrenic symptoms. *Psychological Medicine*, 24, 557–564.

Mohamed, S., Paulsen, J.S., O'Leary, D., Arndt, S. and Andreasen, N.C. (1999). Generalized cognitive deficits in schizophrenia: A study of first episode patients. *Archives of General Psychiatry*, 56, 749–754.

Moline, R.E., Singh, S., Morris, A. and Meltzer, H.Y. (1985). Family expressed emotion and relapse in schizophrenia in 24 urban American patients. *American Journal of Psychiatry*, 142, 1078–1081.

Monroe, R.R. (1982). Limbic ictus and atypical psychoses. *Journal of Nervous and Mental Disease*, 170, 711–716.

Montero, I., Gomez-Beneyto, M. and Ruiz, I. (1990). Emotional expressiveness and development of schizophrenia: A reply to the work of Vaughn. *Actas Luso-Españolas de Neurologia, Psiquiatria y Ciencias Afines*, 18, 387–395.

Moore, K.E. (1978). Amphetamines: Biochemical and behavioral actions in animals. In L.L. Iversen, S.E. Iversen and S.H. Snyder (Eds.), *Handbook of psychopharmacology, Vol. 11, Stimulants*, pp. 41–98. New York: Plenum.

Morgenstern, H. and Glazer, W.M. (1993). Identifying risk factors for tardive dyskinesia among long-term outpatients maintained with neuroleptic medications. *Archives of General Psychiatry*, 50, 723–733.

Morice, R. and Ingram, J.C.L. (1982). Language analysis in schizophrenia: Diagnostic implications. *Australian and New Zealand Journal of Psychiatry*, 16, 11–21.

Moritz, S. and Woodward, T.S. (2005). Jumping to conclusions in delusional and non-delusional schizophrenia patients. *British Journal of Clinical Psychology*, 44, 193–207.

Moritz, S., Andresen, B., Jacobsen, D., Mersmann, K., Wilke, U., Lambert, M. *et al.* (2001). Neuropsychological correlates of schizophrenic syndromes in patients treated with atypical neuroleptics. *European Psychiatry*, 16, 354–361.

Morrison, J.R. (1973). Catatonia: Retarded and excited types. *Archives of General Psychiatry*, 28, 39–41.

Mortimer, A.M. (1997). Cognitive function in schizophrenia: Do neuroleptics make a difference. *Pharmacology, Biochemistry and Behavior*, 56, 789–795.

Mortimer, A.M., Lund, C.E. and McKenna, P.J. (1990). The positive:negative dichotomy in schizophrenia. *British Journal of Psychiatry*, 156, 41–49.

Mortimer, A.M., McKenna, P.J., Lund, C.E. and Mannuzza, S. (1989). Rating of negative symptoms using the HEN scale. *British Journal of Psychiatry*, 155, Supplement, 7, 89–92.

Mozny, P., Petrikovitsova, A. and Lavicka, Z. (1989). Expressed emotions, relapse rate and utilization of psychiatric hospital care in schizophrenia. Unpublished study presented at 19th congress of the European Association for Behaviour Therapy, Vienna.

Mueller, H.T. and Meador-Woodruff, J.H. (2004). NR3A NMDA receptor subunit MRNA expression in schizophrenia, depression and bipolar disorder. *Schizophrenia Research*, 71, 361–370.

Mullen, P.E., Pathé, M., Purcell, R. and Stuart, G.W.J.H. (1999). Study of stalkers. *American Journal of Psychiatry*, 156, 1244–1249.

Munro, A. (1980). Monosymptomatic hypochondriacal psychosis. *British Journal of Hospital Medicine*, 24, 34–38.

Munro, A. (1999). *Delusional disorder: Paranoia and related illnesses*. Cambridge: Cambridge University Press.

Murphy, D.L. and Beigel, A. (1974). Depression, elation, and lithium carbonate responses in manic patient subgroups. *Archives of General Psychiatry*, 31, 643–648.

Murray, G.K., Leeson, V. and McKenna, P.J. (2004). Spontaneous improvement in severe, chronic schizophrenia and its neuropsychological correlates. *British Journal of Psychiatry*, 184, 357–358.

Murray, G.K., Jones, P.B., Moilanen, K., Veijola, J., Miettunen, J., Cannon, T.D. *et al.* (2006). Infant motor development and adult cognitive functions in schizophrenia. *Schizophrenia Research*, 81, 65–74.

Murray, R.M., Lewis, S.W. and Reveley, A.M. (1985). Towards an aetiological classification of schizophrenia. *Lancet*, i, 1023–1026.

Murray, R.M., Lewis, S.W., Owen, M.J. and Foerster, A. (1988). The neurodevelopmental origins of dementia praecox. In P. Bebbington and P. McGuffin (Eds.), *Schizophrenia: The major issues*, pp. 90–106. Oxford: Heinemann/Mental Health Foundation.

Murray, V., McKee, I., Miller, P.M., Young, D., Muir, W.J., Pelosi, A.J. *et al.* (2005). Dimensions and classes of psychosis in a population of cohort: A four-class, four-dimension model of schizophrenia and affective psychosis. *Psychological Medicine*, 35, 499–510.

Muscettola, G., Pampallona, S., Barbato, G., Casiello, M. and Bollini, P. (1993). Persistent tardive dyskinesia: Demographic and pharmacological risk factors. *Acta Psychiatrica Scandinavica*, 87, 29–36.

Naguib, M. and Levy, R. (1987). Late paraphrenia: Neuropsychological impairment and structural brain abnormalities on computed tomography. *International Journal of Geriatric Psychiatry*, 2, 83–90.

Nasar, S. (1998). *A beautiful mind*. London: Faber.

Nasrallah, H.A., Olsen, S.C., McCalley-Whitters, M., Chapman, S. and Jacoby, C.G.

(1986). Cerebral ventricular enlargement in schizophrenia: A preliminary follow-up study. *Archives of General Psychiatry*, 43, 157–159.

Neale, J.M. and Oltmanns, T.F (1980). *Schizophrenia*. New York: Wiley.

Neary, D., Snowden, J.S., Northen, B. and Goulding, P. (1988). Dementia of frontal lobe type. *Journal of Neurology, Neurosurgery and Psychiatry*, 51, 353–361.

Nelson, H. (1997). *Cognitive behavioural therapy with schizophrenia: A practice manual*. Cheltenham: Stanley Thornes.

Nelson, N.E. (1982). The National Adult Reading Test (NART). Windsor, Berks: NFER-Nelson.

Newcomer, J.W., Farber, N.B., Jevtovic-Todorovic, V., Selke, G., Melson, A.K., Hershey, T. *et al.* (1999). Ketamine-induced NMDA receptor hypofunction as a model of memory impairment and psychosis. *Neuropsychopharmacology*, 20, 106–118.

Nicolson, R., Brookner, F.B., Lenane, M., Gochman, P., Ingraham, L.J., Egan, M.F. *et al.* (2003). Parental schizophrenia spectrum disorders in childhood-onset and adult-onset schizophrenia. *American Journal of Psychiatry*, 160, 490–495.

NIMH (National Institute of Mental Health Psychopharmacology Service Center Collaborative Study Group) (1964). Phenothiazine treatment in acute schizophrenia. *Archives of General Psychiatry*, 10, 246–261.

Noga, J.T., Hyde, T.M., Herman, M.H., Spurney, C.F., Bigelow, L.B., Weinberger, D.R. *et al.* (1997). Glutamate receptors in the postmortem striatum of schizophrenic, suicide, and control brains. *Synapse*, 27, 168–176.

Norman, R.M.G., Malla, A.K., Morrison-Stewart, S.L., Helmes, E., Williamson, P.C., Thomas, J. *et al.* (1997). Neuropsychological correlates of syndromes in schizophrenia. *British Journal of Psychiatry*, 170, 134–139.

Novoa, O.P. and Ardila, A. (1987). Linguistic abilities in patients with prefrontal damage. *Brain and Language*, 30, 206–225.

Nuechterlein, K.H., Snyder, K.S., Dawson, M.E., Rappe, C.R., Gitlin, M. and Fogelson, D. (1986). Expressed emotion, fixed-dose fluphenazine decanoate maintenance, and relapse in recent-onset schizophrenia. *Psychopharmacology Bulletin*, 22, 633–639.

O'Grady, J.C. (1990). The prevalence and diagnostic significance of Schneiderian first-rank symptoms in a random sample of acute psychiatric in-patients. *British Journal of Psychiatry*, 156, 496–500.

Oh, T.M., McCarthy, R.A. and McKenna, P.J. (2002). Is there a schizophasia? A study applying the single case study approach to formal thought disorder in schizophrenia. *Neurocase*, 8, 233–244.

Ohnuma, T., Augood, S.J., Arai, H., McKenna, P.J. and Emson, P.C. (1998). Expression of the human excitatory amino acid transporter 2 and metabotropic glutamate receptors 3 and 5 in the prefrontal cortex from normal individuals and patients with schizophrenia. *Brain Research and Molecular Brain Research*, 56, 207–217.

Ohnuma, T., Tessler, S., Arai, H., Faull, R.L., McKenna, P.J. and Emson, P.C. (2000). Gene expression of metabotropic glutamate receptor 5 and excitatory amino acid transporter 2 in the schizophrenic hippocampus. *Brain Research and Molecular Brain Research*, 85, 24–31.

Okubo, Y., Suhara, T., Suzuki, K., Kobayashi, K., Inoue, O., Terasaki, O. *et al.* (1997). Decreased prefrontal dopamine D1 receptors in schizophrenia revealed by PET. *Nature*, 385, 634–636.

O'Leary, D.S., Flaum, M., Kesler, M.L., Flashman, L.A., Arndt, S. and Andreasen

N.C. (2000). Cognitive correlates of negative, disorganized and psychotic symptom dimensions of schizophrenia. *Journal of Neuropsychiatry and Clinical Neurosciences*, 12, 4–15.

Owen, F., Crow, T.J., Poulter, M., Cross, A.J., Longden, A. and Riley, G.J. (1978). Increased dopamine-receptor sensitivity in schizophrenia. *Lancet*, ii, 223–225.

Owen, M.J., Lewis, S.W. and Murray, R.M. (1989). Family history and cerebral ventricular enlargement in schizophrenia: A case control study. *British Journal of Psychiatry*, 154, 629–634.

Owens, D.G.C. (1990). Dystonia – a potential psychiatric pitfall. *British Journal of Psychiatry*, 156, 620–634.

Owens, D.G.C. and Johnstone, E.C. (1980). The disabilities of chronic schizophrenia – their nature and the factors contributing to their development. *British Journal of Psychiatry*, 136, 384–393.

Owens, D.G.C., Johnstone, E.C. and Frith, C.D. (1982). Spontaneous involuntary disorders of movement: Their prevalence, severity and distribution in chronic schizophrenics with and without treatment with neuroleptics. *Archives of General Psychiatry*, 39, 452–461.

Owens, D.G.C., Johnstone, E.C. and Frith, C.D. (1985a). Chronic schizophrenia and the defect state – a case of terminological inexactitude. In A.A. Schiff, M. Roth and H.L. Freeman (Eds.), *Schizophrenia: New pharmacological and clinical developments*, pp. 3–14. London: Royal Society of Medicine.

Owens, D.G.C., Johnstone, E.C., Crow, T.J., Frith, C.D., Jagoe, J.R. and Kreel, L. (1985b). Lateral ventricular size in schizophrenia: Relationship to the disease process and its clinical manifestations. *Psychological Medicine*, 15, 27–41.

Paris, J. (2005). *The fall of an icon: Psychoanalysis and academic psychiatry*. Toronto: University of Toronto Press.

Parker, G., Johnston, P. and Hayward, L. (1988). Parental 'expressed emotion' as a predictor of schizophrenic relapse. *Archives of General Psychiatry*, 45, 806–813.

Patrick, H.T. and Levy, D.M. (1922). Parkinson's disease: A clinical study of 146 cases. *Archives of Neurology and Psychiatry*, 7, 711–720.

Paulsen, J.S., Heaton, R.K., Sadek, J.R., Perry, W., Delis, D.C., Braff, D. *et al.* (1995). The nature of learning and memory impairments in schizophrenia. *Journal of the International Neuropsychological Society*, 1, 88–99.

Payne, R.W. (1973). Cognitive abnormalities. In H.J. Eysenck (Ed.), *Handbook of abnormal psychology*, pp. 420–483. London: Pitman.

Pearlson, G.D. (1981). Psychiatric and medical syndromes associated with phencyclidine (PCP) abuse. *Johns Hopkins Medical Journal*, 148, 25–33.

Peralta, V. and Cuesta, M.J. (2003). Cycloid psychosis: A clinical and nosological study. *Psychological Medicine*, 33, 443–453.

Peralta, V., Cuesta, M.J. and de Leon, J. (1994). An empirical analysis of latent structures underlying schizophrenic symptoms: A four-syndrome model. *Biological Psychiatry*, 36, 726–736.

Perlstein, W.M., Carter, C.S., Noll, D.C. and Cohen, J.D. (2001). Relation of prefrontal cortex dysfunction to working memory and symptoms in schizophrenia. *American Journal of Psychiatry*, 158, 1105–1113.

Peroutka, S.J. and Snyder, S.H. (1980). Relationship of neuroleptic drug effects at brain dopamine, serotonin, alpha-adrenergic, and histamine receptors to clinical potency. *American Journal of Psychiatry*, 137, 1518–1522.

Perris, C. (1974). A study of cycloid psychosis. *Acta Psychiatrica Scandinavica*, Supplement, 253, 1–76.

Perris, C. (1986). The case for the independence of cycloid psychotic disorder from the schizoaffective disorders. In A. Marneros and M.T. Tsuang (Eds.), *Schizoaffective psychoses*, pp. 272–308. Berlin: Springer.

Perry, T.L. (1982). Normal cerebrospinal fluid and brain glutamate levels in schizophrenia do not support the hypothesis of glutamatergic neuronal dysfunction. *Neuroscience Letters*, 28, 81–85.

Petty, L.K., Ornitz, E.M., Michelman, J.D. and Zimmerman, E.G. (1984). Autistic children who become schizophrenic. *Archives of General Psychiatry*, 41, 129–135.

Pfohl, B. and Winokur, G. (1982). The evolution of symptoms in institutionalized hebephrenic/catatonic schizophrenics. *British Journal of Psychiatry*, 141, 567–572.

Pfuhlmann, B., Stöber, G., Franzek, E. and Beckmann, H. (1998). Cycloid psychoses predominate in severe postpartum psychiatric disorder. *Journal of Affective Disorders*, 50, 125–134.

Pichot, P. (1982). The diagnosis and classification of mental disorders in French-speaking countries: Background, current views and comparison with other nomenclatures. *Psychological Medicine*, 12, 475–492.

Pichot, P. (1986). A comparison of different national concepts of schizoaffective psychosis. In A. Marneros and M.T. Tsuang (Eds.), *Schizoaffective psychoses*, pp. 8–17. Berlin: Springer.

Pilling, S., Bebbington, P., Kuipers, E., Garety, P., Geddes, J., Orbach, G. *et al.* (2002). Psychological treatments in schizophrenia: I. Meta-analysis of family intervention and cognitive behaviour therapy. *Psychological Medicine*, 32, 763–782.

Pilowsky, L.S., Costa, D.C., Ell, P.J., Verhoeff, N.P.L.G., Murray, R.M. and Kerwin, R.W. (1994). D2 dopamine receptor binding in the basal ganglia of antipsychotic-free schizophrenic patients: A [123]IBZM single photon emission tomography (SPET) study. *British Journal of Psychiatry*, 164, 16–26.

Planansky, K. (1966). Conceptual boundaries of schizoidness: Suggestions for epidemiological and genetic research. *Journal of Nervous and Mental Disease*, 142, 318–331.

Platz, C. and Kendell, R.E. (1988). A matched-control follow-up and family study of 'puerperal psychoses'. *British Journal of Psychiatry*, 153, 90–94.

Pogue-Geile, M.F. and Harrow, M. (1985). Negative symptoms in schizophrenia: Their longitudinal course and prognostic significance. *Schizophrenia Bulletin*, 11, 427–439.

Pogue-Geile, M.F. and Oltmanns, T.F. (1980). Sentence perception and distractibility in schizophrenic, manic and depressed patients. *Journal of Abnormal Psychology*, 89, 115–124.

Pollice, R., Roncone, R., Falloon, I.R.H., Mazza, M., De Risio, A., Necozione, S. *et al.* (2002). Is theory of mind in schizophrenia more strongly associated with clinical and social deficits than with neurocognitive deficits? *Psychopathology*, 35, 280–288.

Pollin, W., Allen, M.G., Hoffer, A., Stabeneau, J.R. and Hrubec, Z. (1969). Psychopathology in 15,909 pairs of veteran twins: Evidence for a genetic factor in the pathogenesis of schizophrenia and its relative absence in psychoneurosis. *American Journal of Psychiatry*, 126, 597–610.

Pomarol-Clotet, E., Honey, G.D., Murray, G.K., Corlett, P.R., Absalom, A.R., Lee, M. *et al.* (2006). Psychological effects of ketamine in healthy volunteers: Phenomenological study. *British Journal of Psychiatry*, 189, 173–179.

Pomarol-Clotet, E., Oh, T.M.S.S., Laws, K.R. and McKenna, P.J. (submitted). Semantic priming in schizophrenia: A meta-analysis. Submitted for publication.

Pope, H.G. and Lipinski, J.F. (1978). Diagnosis in schizophrenia and manic-depressive illness: A re-assessment of the specificity of 'schizophrenic' symptoms in the light of current research. *Archives of General Psychiatry*, 35, 811–828.

Pope, H.G., Lipinski, J.F., Cohen, B.M. and Axelrod, D.T. (1980). 'Schizoaffective disorder': An invalid diagnosis? A comparison of schizoaffective disorder, schizophrenia and affective disorder. *American Journal of Psychiatry*, 137, 921–927.

Pope, H.G., Jonas, J.M., Hudson, J.I., Cohen, B.M. and Tohen, M. (1985). An empirical study of psychosis in borderline personality disorder. *American Journal of Psychiatry*, 142, 1285–1290.

Poppelreuter, W. (1917). *Die psychischen Schaingungen durch Kopfschuss im Kriege, 1914–1916*. Leipzig: Voss.

Post, F. (1966). *Persistent persecutory states in the elderly*. Oxford: Pergamon.

Post, F. (1982). Functional disorders: I. Description, incidence and recognition. In R. Levy and F. Post (Eds.), *The psychiatry of late life*, pp. 176–196. Oxford: Blackwell.

Potkin, S.G., Alva, G., Fleming, K., Anand, R., Keator, D., Carreon, D. *et al.* (2002). A PET study of the pathophysiology of negative symptoms in schizophrenia. *American Journal of Psychiatry*, 159, 227–237.

Potter, H.W. (1933). Schizophrenia in children. *American Journal of Psychiatry*, 12, 1253–1270.

Potter, H.W. and Klein, H.R. (1937). An evaluation of the treatment of problem children as determined by a follow-up study. *American Journal of Psychiatry*, 17, 681–689.

Poulton, R., Caspi, A., Moffitt, T.E., Cannon, M., Murray R.M. and Harrington, H. (2000). Children's self-reported psychotic symptoms and adult schizophreniform disorder: A 15-year longitudinal study. *Archives of General Psychiatry*, 57, 1053–1058.

Povlsen, U.J., Noring, U., Fog, R. and Gerlach, J. (1985). Tolerability and therapeutic effect of clozapine. *Acta Psychiatrica Scandinavica*, 71, 176–185.

Prien, R.F., Caffey, E.M. and Klett, C.J. (1972). A comparison of lithium carbonate and chlorpromazine in the treatment of excited schizo-affectives. *Archives of General Psychiatry*, 27, 182–189.

Priest, R.G. (1976). The homeless person and the psychiatric services: An Edinburgh survey. *British Journal of Psychiatry*, 128, 128–136.

Pugh, T.F., Jerath, B.K., Schmidt, W.M. and Reed, R.B. (1963). Rates of mental disease relating to childbearing. *New England Journal of Medicine*, 268, 1224–1228.

Rabins, P., Pearlson, G., Jarayan, G. Steele, C. and Tune, L. (1987). Increased ventricle-to-brain ratio in late-onset schizophrenia. *American Journal of Psychiatry*, 144, 1216–1218.

Rachlin, H.L. (1935). A follow-up study of Hoch's benign stupor cases. *American Journal of Psychiatry*, 92, 531–558.

Ram, R., Bromet, E.J., Eaton, W.W., Pato, C. and Schwartz, J.E. (1992). The natural course of schizophrenia: A review of first admisssion studies. *Schizophrenia Bulletin*, 18, 185–207.

Rappaport, M. (1967). Competing voice messages: Effects of message load and drugs on the ability of acute schizophrenic patients to attend. *Archives of General Psychiatry*, 17, 97–103.

Raskind, M.A. and Storrie, M.C. (1980). The organic mental disorders. In E.W. Busse and D.L. Blazer (Eds.), *Handbook of geriatric psychiatry*, pp. 305–328. New York: Van Nostrand Reinhold.

Rathod, N.H. (1975). Cannabis psychosis. In P.H. Connell and N. Dorn (Eds.), *Cannabis and man: Psychological and clinical aspects and patterns of use*, pp. 90–106. Edinburgh: Churchill Livingstone.

Realmuto, G.M. and August, G.J. (1991) Catatonia in autistic disorder: A sign of comorbidity or variable expression? *Journal of Autism and Developmental Disorders*, 21, 517–528.

Rennie, T.A.C. (1942). Prognosis in manic-depressive psychoses. *American Journal of Psychiatry*, 98, 801–814.

Retterstol, N. (1966). *Paranoid and paranoiac psychoses*. Springfield, IL: Thomas.

Retterstol, N. (1970). *Prognosis in paranoid psychoses*. Springfield, IL: Thomas.

Reveley, M.A., Chitkara, B. and Lewis, S.W. (1988). Ventricular and cranial size in schizophrenia: A 4 to 7 year follow-up. *Schizophrenia Research*, 1, 163.

Reynolds, G.P. (1983). Increased concentrations and lateral asymmetries of amygdala dopamine in schizophrenia. *Nature*, 305, 527–529.

Richardson-Burns, S., Haroutunian, V., Davis, K., Watson, S. and Meador-Woodruff, J. (2000). Metabotropic glutamate receptor mRNA in the schizophrenic thalamus. *Biological Psychiatry*, 47, 22–28.

Riley, B., Asherson, P. and McGuffin, P. (2003). Genetics and schizophrenia. In S.R. Hirsch and D.R. Weinberger (Eds.), *Schizophrenia*, 2nd edn, pp. 251–276. Oxford: Blackwell.

Riley, B.P. and McGuffin, P. (2000). Linkage and association studies of schizophrenia. *American Journal of Medical Genetics*, 97, 23–44.

Rimon, R., Stenback, A. and Achte, K. (1965). A sociopsychiatric study of paranoid psychoses. *Acta Psychiatrica Scandinavica*, 40, Supplement, 180, 335–347.

Roberts, A.H. (1979). *Severe accidental head injury: An assessment of long-term prognosis*. London: Macmillan.

Robins, E. and Guze. S.B. (1970). Establishment of diagnostic validity in psychiatric illness: Its application to schizophrenia. *American Journal of Psychiatry*, 126, 983–987.

Robinson, D., Woerner, M.G., Alvir, J.M., Bilder, R., Goldman, R., Geisler, S. *et al.* (1999). Predictors of relapse following response from a first episode of schizophrenia or schizoaffective disorder. *Archives of General Psychiatry*, 56, 241–247.

Rochester, S. and Martin, J.R. (1979). *Crazy talk: A study of the discourse of schizophrenic speakers*. New York: Plenum.

Rogers, D. (1985). The motor disorders of severe psychiatric illness: A conflict of paradigms. *British Journal of Psychiatry*, 147, 221–232.

Rogers, D. (1992). *Motor disorder in psychiatry*. Chichester: Wiley.

Rollin, H.R. (1981). The impact of ECT. In R.L. Palmer (Ed.), *Electroconvulsive therapy: An appraisal*, pp. 11–18. Oxford: Oxford University Press.

Ron, M.A. and Logsdail, S.J. (1989). Psychiatric morbidity in multiple sclerosis: A clinical and MRI study. *Psychological Medicine*, 19, 887–896.

Rosanoff, A. (1914). A study of brain atrophy in relation to insanity. *American Journal of Insanity*, 70, 101–132.

Rosanoff, A.J., Handy, L.M., Plesset, I.R. and Brush, S. (1934). The etiology of so-called schizophrenic psychoses with special reference to their occurrence in twins. *American Journal of Psychiatry*, 91, 247–286.

Rosen, J. and Zubenko, G.S. (1991). Emergence of psychosis and depression in the longitudinal evaluation of Alzheimer's disease. *Biological Psychiatry*, 29, 224–232.

Rosen, W.G., Mohs, K.S., Johns, C.A., Small, N.S., Kendler, K.S., Horvath, T.B. *et al.* (1984). Positive and negative symptoms in schizophrenia. *Psychiatry Research*, 13, 277–284.

Rosenhan, D.L. (1973). On being sane in insane places. *Science*, 179, 250–258.

Rosenheck, R., Cramer, J., Xu, W., Thomas, J., Henderson, W., Frisman, L. *et al.* (1997). A comparison of clozapine and haloperidol in hospitalized patients with refractory schizophrenia. *New England Journal of Medicine*, 337, 809–815.

Rosenman, S., Korten, A., Medway, J. and Evans, M. (2000). Characterising psychosis in the Australian National Survey of Mental Health and Wellbeing Study on Low Prevalence (Psychotic) Disorders. *Australian and New Zealand Journal of Psychiatry*, 34, 792–800.

Rosenthal, D., Wender, P.H., Kety, S.S., Schulsinger, F., Welner, J. and Ostergaard, L. (1968). Schizophrenics' offspring reared in adoptive homes. In D. Rosenthal and S.S. Kety (Eds.), *The transmission of schizophrenia*, pp. 377–392. Oxford: Pergamon.

Rosenthal, D., Wender, P.H., Kety, S.S., Welner, P.H. and Schulsinger, F. (1971). The adopted-away offspring of schizophrenics. *American Journal of Psychiatry*, 128, 307–311.

Rosenthal, N.E., Rosenthal, L.N., Stallone, F., Dunner, D.L. and Fieve, R.R. (1980). The validation of RDC schizoaffective disorder. *Archives of General Psychiatry*, 37, 804–810.

Rosso, I.M., Bearden, C.E., Hollister, J.M., Gasperoni, T.L., Sanchez, L.E., Hadley, T. *et al.* (2000). Childhood neuromotor dysfunction in schizophrenia patients and their unaffected siblings: A prospective cohort study. *Schizophrenia Bulletin*, 26, 367–378.

Rostworowska, M., Barbaro, B. and Cechnicki, A. (1987). The influence of expressed emotion on the course of schizophrenia: A Polish replication. Unpublished study presented at 17th congress of the European Association for Behaviour Therapy, Amsterdam.

Roth, M. (1955). The natural history of mental disorder in old age. *Journal of Mental Science*, 101, 281–301.

Roth, M. and Morrissey J.D. (1952). Problems in the diagnosis and classification of mental disorders in old age. *Journal of Mental Science*, 98, 66–80.

Rowe, E.W. and Shean, G. (1997). Card-sort performance and syndromes of schizophrenia. *Genetic, Social, and Psychology Monographs*, 123, 197–209.

Rowlands, M.W.D. (1988). Psychiatric and legal aspects of persistent litigation. *British Journal of Psychiatry*, 153, 317–323.

Rubin, E.H., Drevets, W.C. and Burke, W.J. (1988). The nature of psychotic symptoms in senile dementia of the Alzheimer type. *Journal of Geriatric Psychiatry and Neurology*, 1, 16–20.

Rudin, E. (1916). *Zur Vererbung und Neuentestehung der Dementia Praecox*. Berlin: Springer.

Rumsey, J., Andreasen, N.C. and Rapoport, J. (1986). Thought, language, communication, and affective flattening in autistic adults. *Archives of General Psychiatry*, 43, 771–777.

Rumsey, J.M., Rapoport, J.L. and Sceery, W.R. (1985). Autistic children as adults: Psychiatric, social and behavioral outcomes. *Journal of the American Academy of Child Psychiatry*, 24, 465–473.

Rund, B.R. (1998). A review of longitudinal studies of cognitive functions in schizophrenia patients. *Schizophrenia Bulletin*, 24, 425–435.

Rupniak, N.M., Kilpatrick, G., Hall, M.D., Jenner, P. and Marsden, C.D. (1984). Differential alteration in striatal dopamine receptor sensitivity induced by repeated administration of clinically equivalent doses of haloperidol, sulpiride or clozapine. *Psychopharmacology*, 84, 512–519.

Rupniak, N.M., Jenner, P. and Marsden, C.D. (1986). Acute dystonia induced by neuroleptic drugs. *Psychopharmacology*, 88, 403–419.

Russell, A.J., Munro, J.C., Jones, P.B., Hemsle, D.R. and Murray, R.M. (1997). Schizophrenia and the myth of intellectual decline. *American Journal of Psychiatry*, 154, 635–639.

Russell, A.T., Bott, L. and Simmons, C. (1989). The phenomenology of schizophrenia occurring in childhood. *Journal of the American Academy of Child and Adolescent Psychiatry*, 28, 399–407.

Rutter, M. (1970). Autistic children: Infancy to adulthood. *Seminars in Psychiatry*, 2, 435–450.

Rutter, M. (1972). Childhood schizophrenia reconsidered. *Journal of Autism and Childhood Schizophrenia*, 2, 315–337.

Rylander, G. (1972). Psychoses and the punding and choreiform syndromes in addiction to central stimulant drugs. *Psychiatrica, Neurologica, Neurochirurgica*, 75, 203–212.

Saccuzzo, D.P. and Braff, D.L. (1981). Early information processing in deficit in schizophrenia: New findings using schizophrenic subgroups and manic control subjects. *Archives of General Psychiatry*, 38, 175–179.

Saccuzzo, D.P., Hirt, M. and Spenser, T.J. (1974). Backward masking as a measure of attention in schizophrenia. *Journal of Abnormal Psychology*, 86, 512–522.

Sachdev, P. (1995). *Akathisia and restless legs*. Cambridge: Cambridge University Press.

Sachdev, P. and Kruk, J. (1994). Clinical characteristics and predisposing factors in acute drug-induced akathisia. *Archives of General Psychiatry*, 51, 963–974.

Sachdev, P. and Tang, W.M. (1992). Psychotic symptoms preceding ocular deviation in a patient with tardive oculogyric crises. *Australian and New Zealand Journal of Psychiatry*, 26, 666–670.

Sacks, O. (1983). *Awakenings*. New York: Dutton.

Sacks, O.W. (1982). Acquired Tourettism in adult life. In A.J. Friedhoff and T.N. Chase (Eds.), *Gilles de la Tourette syndrome*, pp. 89–92. New York: Raven.

Sands, I.J. (1928). The acute psychiatric type of epidemic encephalitis. *American Journal of Psychiatry*, 7, 975–987.

Sarbin, T.R. and Mancuso, J.C. (1980). *Schizophrenia: Medical diagnosis or moral verdict?* New York: Pergamon.

Sartorius, N., Leff, J., Jablensky, A., Anker, H., Korten, A., Gulbinat, W. *et al.* (1987). The international pilot study of schizophrenia: Five-year follow-up findings. In H. Hafner, W.F. Gattaz and W. Janzarik (Eds.), *Search for the causes of schizophrenia*, pp. 107–113. Heidelberg: Springer.

Saykin, A., Shtasel, D., Gur, R., Kester, D., Mozley, L., Stafiniak, P. *et al.* (1994). Neuropsychological deficits in neuroleptic naive patients with first-episode schizophrenia. *Archives of General Psychiatry*, 51, 124–131.

Saykin, A.J., Gur, R.C., Gur, R.E., Mozley, P.D., Mozley, L.H., Resnick, S.M. *et al.* (1991). Neuropsychological function in schizophrenia: Selective impairment in memory and learning. *Archives of General Psychiatry*, 48, 618–624.

Schatz, J. (1998). Cognitive processing efficiency in schizophrenia: Generalized vs domain specific deficits. *Schizophrenia Research*, 30, 41–49.

Scheibel, A.B. and Kovelman, J.A. (1981). Disorientation of the hippocampal pyramidal cell and its processes in the schizophrenic patient. *Biological Psychiatry*, 16, 101–102.

Scherer, J., Tatsch, K., Schwarz, J., Oertel, W.H., Konjarczyk, M. and Albus, M. (1994). D2-dopamine receptor occupancy differs between patients with and without extrapyramidal side effects. *Acta Psychiatrica Scandinavica*, 90, 266–268.

Schiorring, E. (1981). Psychopathology induced by 'speed drugs'. *Pharmacology, Biochemistry and Behavior*, 14, Supplement, 1, 109–122.

Schmideberg, M. (1947). The treatment of psychopathic and borderline patients. *American Journal of Psychotherapy*, 1, 45–71.

Schneider, K. (1949). The concept of delusion. Trans. in S.R. Hirsch and M. Shepherd (Eds.) (1974), *Themes and variations in European Psychiatry*, pp. 33–39. Bristol: Wright.

Schneider, K. (1950). *Psychopathic personalities*, 9th edn (trans. M.W. Hamilton, 1958). London: Cassell,.

Schneider, K. (1958). *Clinical psychopathology*, 5th edn (trans. M.W. Hamilton, 1959). New York: Grune & Stratton,.

Schonecker, M. (1957). A strange syndrome in the oral area with application of chlorpromazine. *Nervenarzt*, 28, 35.

Schulz, S.C., Koller, M.M., Kishore, P.R. Hamer, R.M., Gehl, J.J. and Friedel, R.O. (1983). Ventricular enlargement in teenage patients with schizophrenia spectrum disorder. *American Journal of Psychiatry*, 140, 1592–1595.

Schwab, R.S., Fabing, H.D. and Prichard, J.S. (1951). Psychiatric symptoms and syndromes in Parkinson's disease. *American Journal of Psychiatry*, 107, 901–907.

Schwartz, S. (1982). Is there a schizophrenic language? *Behavioral and Brain Sciences*, 5, 579–626.

Sedler, M.J. (1985). The legacy of Ewald Hecker: A new translation of 'die Hebephrenie'. *American Journal of Psychiatry*, 142, 1265–1271.

Sedman, G. (1970). Theories of depersonalization: A reappraisal. *British Journal of Psychiatry*, 117, 1–14.

Seeman, P. (1980). Brain dopamine receptors. *Pharmacological Reviews*, 32, 229–313.

Seeman, P. (1987). Dopamine receptors and the dopamine hypothesis of schizophrenia. *Synapse*, 1, 133–152.

Seeman, P., Wong, M. and Lee, T. (1974). Dopamine receptor-block and nigral fiber impulse blockade by major tranquillizers. *Federation Proceedings*, 33, 246.

Seeman, P., Lee, T., Chau-Wong, M. and Wong, K. (1976). Antipsychotic drug doses and neuroleptic/dopamine receptors. *Nature*, 261, 717–719.

Sensky, T., Turkington, D., Kingdon, D., Scott, J.L., Scott, J., Siddle, R. *et al.* (2000). A randomized controlled trial of cognitive-behavioral therapy for persistent symptoms in schizophrenia resistant to medication. *Archives of General Psychiatry*, 57, 165–172.

Serra-Mestres, J., Gregory, C.A., Tandon, S., Stansfield, A.J., Kemp, P.M. and McKenna, P.J. (2000). Simple schizophrenia revisited: A clinical, neuropsychological and neuroimaging analysis of nine cases. *Schizophrenia Bulletin*, 26, 479–493.

Serretti, A., Macciardi, F. and Smeraldi, E. (1996). Identification of symptomatologic patterns common to major psychoses: Proposal for a phenotype definition. *American Journal of Medical Genetics*, 67, 393–400.

Serretti, A., Rietschel, M., Lattuada, E., Krauss, H., Schulze, T.G., Muller, D.J. *et al.* (2001). Major psychoses symptomatology: Factor analysis of 2241 psychotic subjects. *European Archives of Psychiatry and Clinical Neuroscience*, 251, 193–198.

Shagass, C. (1977). Twisted thoughts, twisted brain waves? In C. Shagass, S. Gershon and A.J. Friedhoff (Eds.), *Psychopathology and brain dysfunction*. New York: Raven.

Shalev, A. and Munitz, H. (1986). The neuroleptic malignant syndrome: Agent and host interaction. *Acta Psychiatrica Scandinavica*, 73, 337–347.

Shallice, T. (1988). *From neuropsychology to mental structure*. Cambridge: Cambridge University Press.

Shallice, T. and Burgess, P. (1991). Deficits in strategy application following frontal lobe damage in man. *Brain*, 114, 727–741.

Shallice, T., Burgess, P.W. and Frith, C.D. (1991). Can the neuropsychological case-study approach be applied to schizophrenia. *Psychological Medicine*, 21, 661–673.

Sheldrick, C., Jablensky, A., Sartorius, N. and Shepherd, M. (1977). Schizophrenia succeeded by affective illness: A catamnestic study and statistical enquiry. *Psychological Medicine*, 7, 619–624.

Shepherd, M., Watt, D., Falloon, I. and Smeeton, N. (1989). The natural history of schizophrenia: A five-year follow-up study of outcome and prediction in a representative sample of schizophrenics. *Psychological Medicine*, Monograph Supplement, 15, 1–46.

Shergill, S.S., Brammer, M.J., Williams, S.C.R., Murray, R.M. and McGuire, P.K. (2000). Mapping auditory hallucinations in schizophrenia using functional magnetic resonance imaging. *Archives of General Psychiatry*, 57, 1033–1038.

Shergill, S.S., Cameron, L.A., Brammer, M.J., Williams, S.C.R., Murray, R.M. and McGuire, P.K. (2001). Modality specific neural correlates of auditory and somatic hallucinations. *Journal of Neurology, Neurosurgery and Psychiatry*, 71, 688–690.

Shergill, S.S., Brammer, M.J., Amaro, E., Williams, S.C.R., Murray, R.M. and McGuire, P.K. (2004). Temporal course of auditory hallucinations. *British Journal of Psychiatry*, 185, 516–517.

Shorter, E, (1997). *A history of psychiatry: From the era of the asylum to the age of prozac*. New York: Wiley.

Shtasel, D.L., Gur, R.E., Gallacher, F., Heimberg, C., Cannon, T. and Gur, R.C. (1992). Phenomenology and functioning in first-episode schizophrenia. *Schizophrenia Bulletin*, 18, 449–461.

Shur, E. (1988). The epidemiology of schizophrenia. *British Journal of Hospital Medicine*, 40, 38–45.

Sigwald, J., Bouttier, D. and Courvoisier, S. (1959a). Les accidents neurologiques des medications neuroleptiques. *Revue Neurologique*, 100, 553–595.

Sigwald, J., Bouttier, D., Raymondeau, C. and Piot, C. (1959b). Quatre cas de dyskinesie facio-bucco-linguo-masticatrice à evolution prolongée secondaire à un traitement par les neuroleptiques. *Revue Neurologique*, 100, 751–755.

Silberswseig, D.A., Stern, E., Frith, C., Cahill, C., Holmes, A., Seaward, J. *et al.* (1995). A functional anatomy of hallucinations in schizophrenia. *Nature*, 378, 126–129.

Silva, P.A. and Stanton, W.R. (Eds.) (1996). *From child to adult: The Dunedin multidisciplinary health and development study*. New Zealand: Oxford University Press.

Silverberg-Shalev, R., Gordon, H.W., Bentin, S. and Aranson, A. (1981). Selective language deterioration in schizophrenia. *Journal of Neurology, Neurosurgery and Psychiatry*, 44, 547–551.

Silverman, J.M., Siever, L.J., Horvath, T.B., Coccaro, E.F., Klar, H., Davidson, M. *et al.* (1993). Schizophrenia-related and affective personality disorder traits in relatives of probands with schizophrenia and personality disorders. *American Journal of Psychiatry*, 150, 435–442.

Simpson, G.M., Lee, J.H., Zoubok, B. and Gardos, G. (1979). A rating scale for tardive dyskinesia. *Psychopharmacology*, 64, 171–179.

Simpson, M.D.C., Slater, P., Royston, C. and Deakin, J.F.W. (1992). Alterations in phencyclidine and sigma binding sites in schizophrenic brains. *Schizophrenia Research*, 6, 41–48.

Sims, A. (2002). *Symptoms in the mind*, 3rd edn. London: Saunders.

Singer, M.T. and Wynne, L.C. (1965). Thought disorder and family relations of schizophrenics III. Methodology using projective techniques. *Archives of General Psychiatry*, 12, 187–212.

Singer, M.T. and Wynne, L.C. (1966). Principles for scoring communication defects and deviances in parents of schizophrenics. Rorschach and T.A.T. scoring manuals. *Psychiatry*, 29, 260–268.

Slade, P.D. (1976). Hallucinations. *Psychological Medicine*, 6, 7–13.

Slade, P.D. and Bentall, R.P. (1988). *Sensory deception: A scientific analysis of hallucination*. London: Croom Helm.

Slater, E. (1953). *Psychotic and neurotic illness in twins*. London: Her Majesty's Stationery Office.

Slater, E. (1968). A review of earlier evidence on genetic factors in schizophrenia. In D. Rosenthal and S.S. Kety (Eds.), *The transmission of schizophrenia*, pp. 15–26. Oxford: Pergamon.

Slater, E., Beard, A.W. and Glitheroe, E. (1963). The schizophrenia-like psychoses of epilepsy. *British Journal of Psychiatry*, 109, 95–150.

Smith, D.A., Mar, C.M. and Turoff, B.K. (1998). The structure of schizophrenic symptoms: A meta-analytic confirmatory factor analysis. *Schizophrenia Resesarch*, 31, 57–70.

Smith, G.N. and Iacono, W.G. (1986). Lateral ventricular size in schizophrenia and choice of control group. *Lancet*, i, 1450.

Smith, J.M., Kuchanski, L.T. and Eblen, C. (1979). An assessment of tardive dyskinesia in schizophrenic outpatients. *Psychopharmacology*, 64, 99–104.

Smythies, J.R. (1983). The transmethylation and one-carbon cycle hypothesis of schizophrenia. *Psychological Medicine*, 13, 711–714.

Snaith, P. (1983). Pregnancy-related psychiatric disorder. *British Journal of Hospital Medicine*, 29, 450–456.

Sokolov, B.P. (1998). Expression of NMDAR1, GluR1, GluR7, and KA1 glutamate receptor mRNAs is decreased in frontal cortex of 'neuroleptic free' schizophrenics: Evidence on reversible up-regulation by typical neuroleptics. *Journal of Neurochemistry*, 71, 2454–2464.

Soni, S.D. and Freeman, H.L. (1985). Early clinical experiences with sulpiride. *British Journal of Psychiatry*, 146, 673.

Southard, E.E. (1915). On the topographical distribution of cortex lesions and anomalies in dementia praecox, with some account of their functional significance. *American Journal of Insanity*, 71, 603–671.

Spence, S.A., Brooks, D.J., Hirsch, S.R., Liddle, P.F., Meehan, J. and Grasby, P.M.

(1997). A PET study of voluntary movement in schizophrenic patients experiencing passivity phenomena (delusions of alien control). *Brain*, 120, 1997–2011.

Spencer, E.K. and Campbell, M. (1994). Children with schizophrenia: Diagnosis, phenomenology, and pharmacotherapy. *Schizophrenia Bulletin*, 20, 713–725.

Spitzer, M., Braun, U., Hermle, L. and Maier, S. (1993). Associative semantic network dysfunction in thought-disordered schizophrenic patients: Direct evidence from indirect semantic priming. *Biological Psychiatry*, 34, 864–877.

Spitzer, R.L., Endicott, J. and Robins, E. (1978). *Research diagnostic criteria for a selected group of functional disorders*. New York: Biometric Research, New York State Psychiatric Institute.

Spitzer, R.L., Endicott, J. and Gibbon, M. (1979). Crossing the border into borderline personality and borderline schizophrenia: The development of criteria. *Archives of General Psychiatry*, 36, 17–24.

Spitzer, R.L., Skodol, A.E., Gibbon, M., Williams, J.B.W. and First, M.B. (1981). *DSM-III case book*. Washington, DC: American Psychiatric Press.

Spitzer, R.L., Gibbon, M., Skodol, A.E., Williams, J.B.W. and First, M.B. (1989). *DSM-III-R case book*. Washington, DC: American Psychiatric Press.

Sponheim, S.R., Iacono, W.G. and Beiser, M. (1991). Stability of ventricular size after the onset of psychosis in schizophrenia. *Psychiatry Research: Neuroimaging*, 40, 21–29.

Sporn, A.L., Greenstein, D.K., Gogtay, N., Jeffries, N.O., Lenane, M., Gochman. P. *et al.* (2003). Progressive brain volume loss during adolescence in childhood-onset schizophrenia. *American Journal of Psychiatry*, 160, 2181–2189.

Sporn, A.L., Addington, A.M., Gogtay, N., Ordonez, A.E., Gornick, M., Clasen, L. *et al.* (2004). Pervasive developmental disorder and childhood-onset schizophrenia: Comorbid disorder or a phenotypic variant of a very early onset illness? *Biological Psychiatry*, 55, 989–994.

Spring, B., Weinstein, L., Freeman, R. and Thompson, S. (1991). Selective attention in schizophrenia. In S.R. Steinhauer, J.H. Gruzelier and J Zubin (Eds.), *Handbook of schizophrenia, Vol. 5: Neuropsychology, psychophysiology and information processing*. Amsterdam: Elsevier.

Stahlberg, O., Soderstrom, H., Rastam, M. and Gillberg, C. (2004). Bipolar disorder, schizophrenia, and other psychotic disorders in adults with childhood onset AD/HD and/or other autism spectrum disorders. *Journal of Neural Transmission*, 111, 891–902.

Steck, H. (1954). Le syndrome extrapyramidal et diencephalique au cours des traitements au largactil et au serpasil. *Annales Medico-Psychologique*, 112, 737–743.

Stein, Z., Susser, M., Saenger, G. and Marolla, F. (1975). Famine and human development: The Dutch hunger winter of 1944–45. New York: Oxford University Press.

Stephens, J.H. (1970). Long-term course and prognosis in schizophrenia. *Seminars in Psychiatry*, 2, 464–485.

Stephens, J.H. (1978). Long-term prognosis and followup in schizophrenia. *Schizophrenia Bulletin*, 4, 25–47.

Stephens, J.H. and Astrup, C. (1965). Treatment outcome in process and non-process schizophrenics treated by 'A' and 'B' type therapists. *Journal of Nervous and Mental Disease*, 140, 449–456.

Stevens, J. (1987). Brief psychoses: Do they contribute to the good prognosis and equal prevalence of schizophrenia in developing countries? *British Journal of Psychiatry*, 151, 393–396.

Stevens, M., Crow, T.J., Bowman, M.J. and Coles, R.C. (1978). Age disorientation in schizophrenia: A constant prevalence of 25 per cent in a chronic mental hospital population? *British Journal of Psychiatry*, 133, 130–136.

Stirling, J., Tantam, D., Thomas, P., Newby, D., Montague, L., Ring, N. *et al.* (1991). Expressed emotion and early onset schizophrenia: A one year follow-up. *Psychological Medicine*, 21, 675–685.

Stirling, J.D., Hellewell, J.S. and Quraishi N. (1998). Self-monitoring dysfunction and the schizophrenic symptoms of alien control. *Psychological Medicine*, 28, 675–683.

Stone, A.A., Hopkins, R., Mahnke, M.W., Shapiro, D. and Silverglato, H.A. (1968). Simple schizophrenia – syndrome or shibboleth. *American Journal of Psychiatry*, 125, 61–68.

Straube, E.R. and Germer, C.K. (1979). Dichotic shadowing and selective attention to word meaning in schizophrenia. *Journal of Abnormal Psychology*, 88, 346–353.

Strauss, J.S., Carpenter, W.T. and Bartko, J.J. (1974). The diagnosis and understanding of schizophrenia: III. Speculations on the processes that underlie schizophrenic symptoms and signs. *Schizophrenia Bulletin*, 1, 61–69.

Stuart, G.W., Pantelis, C., Klimides, S. and Minas, I.H. (1999). The three-syndrome model of schizophrenia: Meta-analysis of an artifact. *Schizophrenia Research*, 39, 233–242.

Suhara, T., Okubo, Y., Yasuno, F., Sudo, Y., Inoue, M., Ichimiya, T. *et al.* (2002). Decreased dopamine D2 receptor binding in the anterior cingulate cortex in schizophrenia. *Archives of General Psychiatry*, 59, 25–30.

Surridge, D. (1969). An investigation into some psychiatric aspects of multiple sclerosis. *British Journal of Psychiatry*, 115, 749–764.

Susser, E. and Lin S.P. (1992). Schizophrenia after prenatal exposure to the Dutch hunger winter of 1944–1945. *Archives of General Psychiatry*, 49, 983–988.

Susser, E., Neugebauer, R.N., Hoek, H.R., Brown, A.S., Lin, S., Labovitz, D. and Gorman, J.M. (1996). Schizophrenia after prenatal famine: Further evidence. *Archives of General Psychiatry*, 53, 25–31.

Suzuki, M., Nohara, S., Hagino, H., Takahashi, T., Kawasaki, Y., Yamashita, I. *et al.* (2005). Prefrontal abnormalities in patients with simple schizophrenia: Structural and functional brain-imaging studies in five cases. *Psychiatry Research: Neuroimaging*, 140, 157–171.

Swett, C. (1975). Drug-induced dystonia. *American Journal of Psychiatry*, 132, 532–534.

Szasz, T. (1971). *The manufacture of madness.* London: Routledge and Kegan Paul.

Szasz, T.S. (1960). The myth of mental illness. *American Psychologist*, 15, 113–118.

Tamlyn, D., McKenna, P.J., Mortimer, A.M., Lund, C.E., Hammond, S. and Baddeley, A.D. (1992). Memory impairment in schizophrenia: Its extent, affiliations and neuropsychological character. *Psychological Medicine*, 22, 101–115.

Tamminga, C., Thaker, G.K., Buchanan, R., Kirkpatrick, B., Alphs, L.D., Chase, T.N. *et al.* (1992). Limbic system abnormalities identified in schizophrenia using positron emission tomography with fluorodeoxyglucose and neocortical alterations with deficit syndrome. *Archives of General Psychiatry*, 49, 522–530.

Tantam, D. (1988). Lifelong eccentricity and social isolation. I. Psychiatric, social and forensic aspects. *British Journal of Psychiatry*, 153, 777–782.

Tantam, D. (1991). Asperger syndrome in adulthood. In U. Frith (Ed.), *Autism and Asperger syndrome*, pp. 147–183. Cambridge: Cambridge University Press.

Tarrier, N. and Wykes, T. (2004). Is there evidence that cognitive behaviour therapy is an effective treatment for schizophrenia? A cautious or cautionary tale? *Behavior Reseach and Therapy*, 42, 1377–1401.

Tarrier, N., Barrowclough, C., Vaughn, C., Bamrah, A., Porceddu, K., Watts, S. *et al.* (1988). The community management of schizophrenia: A controlled trial of a behavioural intervention with families to reduce relapse. *British Journal of Psychiatry*, 153, 532–542.

Tarrier, N., Beckett, R., Harwood, S., Baker, A., Yusupoff, L. and Ugarteburu, I. (1993). A trial of two cognitive-behavioural methods of treating drug-resistant residual psychotic symptoms in schizophrenic patients. I. Outcome. *British Journal of Psychiatry*, 162, 524–532.

Tarrier, N., Yusupoff, L., Kinney, C., McCarthy, E., Gledhill, A., Haddock, G. *et al.* (1998). Randomised controlled trial of intensive cognitive behaviour therapy for patients with chronic schizophrenia. *British Medical Journal*, 317, 303–307.

Tarrier, N., Wittkowski, A., Kinney, C., McCarthy, E., Morris, J. and Humphreys, L. (1999). Durability of the effects of cognitive-behavioural therapy in the treatment of chronic schizophrenia: 12-month follow-up. *British Journal of Psychiatry*, 174, 500–504.

Tarrier, N., Lewis, S., Haddock, G., Bentall, R., Drake, R., Kinderman, P. *et al.* (2004). Cognitive-behavioural therapy in first-episode and early schizophrenia. 18-month follow-up of a randomised controlled trial. *British Journal of Psychiatry*, 184, 231–239.

Tatetsu, S. (1964). Methamphetamine psychosis. *Folia Psychiatrica et Neurologica Japonica*, Supplement, 7, 377–380.

Taylor, M.A. (1972). Schneiderian first-rank symptoms and clinical prognostic features. *Archives of General Psychiatry*, 26, 64–67.

Taylor, M.A. and Abrams, R. (1973). The phenomenology of mania: A new look at some old patients. *Archives of General Psychiatry*, 29, 520–522.

Taylor, M.A. and Abrams, R. (1977). Catatonia: Prevalence and importance in the manic phase of manic-depressive illness. *Archives of General Psychiatry*, 34, 1223–1225.

Taylor, P. (1981). ECT: The preliminary report of a trial in schizophrenic patients. In R.L. Palmer (Ed.), *Electroconvulsive therapy: An appraisal*, pp. 214–225. Oxford: Oxford University Press.

Taylor, P. and Fleminger J.J. (1980). ECT for schizophrenia. *Lancet*, i, 1380–1382.

Thompson, P.A. and Meltzer, H.Y. (1993). Positive, negative and disorganisation factors from the Schedule for Affective Disorders and Schizophrenia and the Present State Examination: A three-factor solution. *British Journal of Psychiatry*, 163, 344–351.

Thornton, A. and McKenna, P.J. (1994). Acute dystonic reactions complicated by psychotic phenomena. *British Journal of Psychiatry*, 164, 115–118.

Tienari, P. (1963). Psychiatric illness in identical twins. *Acta Psychiatrica Scandinavica*, 39, Supplement, 171, 1–195.

Tienari, P. (1975). Schizophrenia in Finnish male twins. In M.H. Lader (Ed.), *Studies of schizophrenia*, pp. 29–35. Ashford, Kent: Headley Brothers.

Tienari, P., Wynne, L.C., Moring, J., Läksy, K., Nieminen, P., Sorri, A. *et al.* (2000). Finnish adoptive family study: Sample selection and adoptee DSM-III-R diagnoses. *Acta Psychiatrica Scandinavica*, 101, 433–443.

Toone, B.K. (2000). The psychoses of epilepsy. *Journal of Neurology, Neurosurgery and Psychiatry*, 69, 1–3.

Toru, M., Nishikawa, T., Mataga, N. and Takashima, M. (1982). Dopamine metabolism increases in postmortem schizophrenic basal ganglia. *Journal of Neural Transmission*, 54, 181–191.

Toru, M., Kurumaji, A., Kumashiro, S., Suga, I., Takashima, M. and Nishikawa, T. (1992). Excitatory amino acidergic neurones in chronic schizophrenic brain. *Molecular Neuropharmacology*, 2, 241–243.

Tramer, M. (1929). The biological significance of the birth month, with special reference to psychosis. *Schweizer Archive für Neurologie und Psychiatrie*, 24, 17–24.

Trimble, M.R. (1982). Functional diseases. *British Medical Journal*, 285, 1768–1770.

Tsai, G., Passani, L.A., Slusher, B., Carter, R., Baer, L., Kleinman, J.E. *et al.* (1995). Abnormal excitatory neurotransmitter metabolism in schizophrenic brains. *Archives of General Psychiatry*, 52, 829–836.

Tsuang, D. and Coryell, W. (1993). An 8-year follow-up of patients with DSM-III-R psychotic depression, schizoaffective disorder, and schizophrenia. *American Journal of Psychiatry*, 150, 1182–1188.

Tsuang, M.T, and Dempsey, M. (1979). Long-term outcome of major psychoses. *Archives of General Psychiatry*, 36, 1302–1304.

Tsuang, M.T., Woolson, R.F. and Fleming, J.H. (1979). Long-term outcome of major psychoses I: Schizophrenia and affective disorders. *Archives of General Psychiatry*, 36, 1295–1301.

Tsuang, M.T., Winokur, G. and Crowe, R.R. (1980). Morbidity risks of schizophrenia and affective disorders among first degree relatives of patients with schizophrenia, mania, depression and surgical conditions. *British Journal of Psychiatry*, 137, 497–504.

Tucker, G.J., Price, T.R.P., Johnson, V.B. and McAllister, T. (1986). Phenomenology of temporal lobe dysfunction: A link to atypical psychosis – a series of cases. *Journal of Nervous and Mental Disease*, 174, 348–356.

Tune, L.E., Wong, D.F., Pearlson, G., Strauss, M., Young, T., Shaya, E.K. *et al.* (1993). Dopamine D2 receptor density estimates in schizophrenia: A positron emission tomography study with ^{11}C-N-methylspiperone. *Psychiatry Research*, 49, 219–237.

Tuominen, H.J., Tiihonen, J. and Wahlbeck, K. (2005). Glutamatergic drugs for schizophrenia: A systematic review and meta-analysis. *Schizophrenia Research*, 72, 225–234.

Turner, S.W., Toone, B.K. and Brett-Jones, J.R. (1986). Computerised tomographic scan changes in early schizophrenia: Preliminary findings. *Psychological Medicine*, 16, 219–225.

Tyrer, P. and Alexander, J. (1988). Personality assessment schedule. In P Tyrer (Ed.), *Personality disorders: Diagnosis, management and course*, pp. 43–62. London: Wright.

Tyrer, P., Casey, P. and Ferguson, B. (1988). Personality disorder and mental illness. In P. Tyrer (Ed.), *Personality disorders: Diagnosis, management and course*, pp. 93–104. London: Wright.

Ulas, J. and Cotman, C.W. (1993). Excitatory amino acid receptors in schizophrenia. *Schizophrenia Bulletin*, 19, 105–117.

Ungvari, G.S. and Hollokoi, R.I.M. (1993). Successful treatment of litigious paranoia with pimozide. *Canadian Journal of Psychiatry*, 38, 4–8.

Vaillant, G.E. (1962). The prediction of recovery in schizophrenia. *Journal of Nervous and Mental Disease*, 135, 534–543.

Valmaggia, L.R., van der Gaag, M., Tarrier, N., Pijnenborg, M. and Slooff, C.J. (2005). Cognitive-behavioural therapy for refractory psychotic symptoms of schizophrenia resistant to atypical antipsychotic medication. Randomised controlled trial. *British Journal of Psychiatry*, 186, 324–330.

Van der Heijden, F.M., Tuinier, S., Kahn, R.S. and Verhoeven, W.M.A. (2004). Nonschizophrenic psychotic disorders: The case of cycloid psychoses. *Psychopathology*, 37, 161–167.

Van Krevelen, D.A. (1971). Early infantile autism and autistic psychopathy. *Journal of Autism and Childhood Schizophrenia*, 1, 82–86.

Van Os, J., Fahy, T.A., Jones, P., Harvey, I., Sham, P., Lewis, S. *et al.* (1996). Psychopathological syndromes in the functional psychoses: Associations with course and outcome. *Psychological Medicine*, 26, 161–176.

Van Os, J., Gilvarry, C., Bale, R., Van Horn, E., Tattan, T., White, I. *et al.* (1999). A comparison of the utility of dimensional and categorical representations of psychosis. *Psychological Medicine*, 29, 595–606.

Van Putten, T. (1975). The many faces of akathisia. *Comprehensive Psychiatry*, 16, 43–47.

Varma, S.L. and Sharma, I. (1993). Psychiatric morbidity in the first-degree relatives of schizophrenic patients. *British Journal of Psychiatry*, 162, 672–678.

Vaughan, K., Doyle, M. and McConaghy, N. (1992). The relationship between relatives' expressed emotion and schizophrenic relapse: An Australian replication. *Social Psychiatry and Psychiatric Epidemiology*, 27, 10–15.

Vaughn, C.E. and Leff, J.P. (1976). The influence of family and social factors on the course of psychiatric illness. *British Journal of Psychiatry*, 129, 125–137.

Vaughn, C.E., Snyder, K.S., Jones, S., Freeman, W.B. and Falloon, I.R.H. (1984). Family factors in schizophrenic relapse: Replication in California of British research on expressed emotion. *Archives of General Psychiatry*, 41, 1169–1177.

Velligan, D.I. and Bow-Thomas, C.C. (1999). Executive function in schizophrenia. *Seminars in Clinical Neuropsychiatry*, 4, 24–33.

Victor, G. (1984). *The riddle of autism*. Lexington: Gower Publishing/Lexington Books.

Volavka, J. (1985). Late onset schizophrenia: A review. *Comprehensive Psychiatry*, 26, 148–156.

Volavka, J., Czobor, P., Sheitman, B., Lindenmayer, J.P., Citrome, L., McEvoy, J.P. *et al.* (2002). Clozapine, olanzapine, risperidone, and haloperidol in the treatment of patients with chronic schizophrenia and schizoaffective disorder. *American Journal of Psychiatry*, 159, 255–262.

Volkow, N.D., Wolf, A.P., Van Gelder, P., Brodie, J.D., Overall, J.E., Cancro, R. *et al.* (1987). Phenomenological correlates of metabolic activity in 18 patients with chronic schizophrenia. *American Journal of Psychiatry*, 144, 151–158.

von Economo, C. (1931). *Encephalitis Lethargica: Its sequelae and treatment* (trans. K.O. Newman). London: Oxford University Press/Humphrey Milford.

Waddington, J.L. (1984). Tardive dyskinesia: A critical re-evaluation of the causal role of neuroleptics and of the dopamine receptor supersensitivity hypothesis. In N. Callaghan and R. Galvin (Eds.), *Recent research in neurology*, pp. 34–48. London: Pitman.

Waddington, J.L. (1989). Functional interactions between D–1 and D–2 dopamine receptor systems: Their role in the regulation of psychomotor behaviour, putative mechanisms, and clinical relevance. *Journal of Psychopharmacology*, 3, 54–63.

Waddington, J.L., Kapur, S., and Remington, G.J. (2003). The neuroscience and clinical psychopharmacology of first- and second-generation antipsychotic drugs. In S.R. Hirsch and D. Weinberger (Eds.), *Schizophrenia*, 2nd edn, pp. 421–441. Oxford: Blackwell Science.

Wahlbeck, K., Cheine, M., Essali, A. and Adams, C. (1999). Evidence of clozapine's effectiveness in schizophrenia: A systematic review and meta-analysis of randomized trials. *American Journal of Psychiatry*, 156, 990–999.

Walker, C. (1991). Delusion: What did Jaspers really say? *British Journal of Psychiatry*, 159, Supplement, 14, 94–101.

Walker, E. and Lewine, R.J. (1990). Prediction of adult-onset schizophrenia from childhood home movies of the patients. *American Journal of Psychiatry*, 147, 1052–1056.

Walker, E.F. (1994). Developmentally moderated expressions of the neuropathology underlying schizophrenia. *Schizophrenia Bulletin*, 20, 453–480.

Walker, E.F., Savoie, T. and Davis, D. (1994). Neuromotor precursors of schizophrenia. *Schizophrenia Bulletin*, 20, 441–451.

Ward, C.D. (1986). Encephalitis lethargica and the development of neuropsychiatry. *Psychiatric Clinics of North America*, 9, 215–223.

Watkins, J.M., Asarnow, R.F. and Tanguay, P.E. (1988). Symptom development in childhood onset schizophrenia. *Journal of Child Psychology and Psychiatry*, 29, 865–878.

Watt, D.C. and Seller, A. (1993). A clinico-genetic study of psychiatric disorder in Huntington's chorea. *Psychological Medicine*, Supplement, 23, 1–46.

Watts, F.N., Powell, G.E. and Austin, S.V. (1973). Modification of delusional beliefs. *British Journal of Medical Psychology*, 46, 359–363.

Weinberger, D.R. (1987). Implications of normal brain development for the pathogenesis of schizophrenia. *Archives of General Psychiatry*, 44, 660–669.

Weinberger, D.R. (1988). Schizophrenia and the frontal lobe. *Trends in Neuroscience*, 11, 367–370.

Weinberger, D.R., Torrey, E.F., Neophytides, A.N. and Wyatt, R.J. (1979). Lateral cerebral ventricular enlargement in schizophrenia. *Archives of General Psychiatry*, 36, 735–739.

Weinberger, D.R., DeLisi, L.E., Perman, G.P., Targum, S. and Wyatt, R.J. (1982). Computed tomography in schizophreniform disorder and other acute psychiatric disorders. *Archives of General Psychiatry*, 39, 778–783.

Weinberger, D.R., Berman, K.F. and Zec, R.F. (1986). Physiological dysfunction of dorsolateral prefrontal cortex in schizophrenia. *Archives of General Psychiatry*, 43, 114–135.

Weiner, R.U., Opler, L.A., Kay, S.R., Merriam, A.E. and Papouchis, N. (1990). Visual information processing in positive, mixed and negative schizophrenic syndromes. *Journal of Nervous and Mental Disease*, 178, 616–626.

Weiss, K.M., Chapman, H.A., Strauss, M.A. and Gilmore, C.C. (1992). Visual information decoding in schizophrenia. *Psychiatry Research*, 44, 203–216.

Weissman, A.D., Casanova, M.F., Kleinman, J.E., London, E.D. and De Souza, E.B. (1991). Selective loss of cerebral cortical sigma, but not PCP binding sites in schizophrenia. *Biological Psychiatry*, 29, 41–51.

Welner, A., Croughan, J., Fishman, R. and Robins, E. (1977). The group of schizoaffective and related psychoses: A follow-up study. *Comprehensive Psychiatry*, 18, 413–422.

Whitlock, F.A. (1967). The Ganser syndrome. *British Journal of Psychiatry*, 113, 19–29.

WHO (World Health Organization) (1973). *Report of the international pilot study of schizophrenia (WHO Offset Publication, No. 2)*. Geneva: World Health Organization.

WHO (World Health Organization) (1979). *Schizophrenia: An international follow-up study*. Geneva: Wiley.

Wielgus, M.S. and Harvey, P.D. (1988). Dichotic listening and recall in schizophrenia and mania. *Schizophrenia Bulletin*, 14, 689–700.

Wilson, B.A., Cockburn, J.M. and Baddeley, A.D. (1985). *The Rivermead behavioural memory test*. Bury St Edmunds, Suffolk: Thames Valley Test Co.

Wilson, M. (1993). DSM-III and the transformation of American psychiatry: A history. *American Journal of Psychiatry*, 150, 399–409.

Wilson, S.A.K. (1940). *Neurology*. London: Edward Arnold.

Wing, J. and Nixon, J. (1975). Discriminating symptoms in schizophrenia. *Archives of General Psychiatry*, 32, 853–859.

Wing, J.K. (1961). A simple and reliable subclassification of chronic schizophrenia. *Journal of Mental Science*, 107, 862–875.

Wing, J.K. (1963). Rehabilitation of psychiatric patients. *British Journal of Psychiatry*, 109, 635–641.

Wing, J.K. (1978). Clinical concepts of schizophrenia. In J.K. Wing (Ed.), *Schizophrenia: Towards a new synthesis*, pp. 1–30. London: Academic Press.

Wing, J.K. and Brown, G.W. (1970). *Institutionalism and schizophrenia: A comparative study of three mental hospitals, 1960–1968*. Cambridge: Cambridge University Press.

Wing, J.K., Birley, J.L.T., Cooper, J.E., Graham, P. and Isaacs, A.D. (1967). Reliability of a procedure for measuring and classifying 'Present Psychiatric State'. *British Journal of Psychiatry*, 113, 499–515.

Wing, J.K., Cooper, J.E. and Sartorius, N. (1974). *The measurement and classification of psychiatric symptoms*. Cambridge: Cambridge University Press.

Wing, L. (1980). *Early childhood autism*, 2nd edn. Oxford: Pergamon.

Wing, L. (1981). Asperger's syndrome: A clinical account. *Psychological Medicine*, 11, 115–129.

Wing, L. (1991). The relationship between Asperger's syndrome and Kanner's autism. In U. Frith (Ed.), *Autism and Asperger syndrome*, pp. 93–121. Cambridge: Cambridge University Press.

Wing, L. and Attwood, A. (1987). Syndromes of autism and atypical development. In D.J. Cohen and A.M. Donnellan (Ed.), *Handbook of autism and pervasive developmental disorders*, pp. 3–19. Silver Spring, Maryland: Winston.

Wing, L. and Shah, A. (2000). Catatonia in autistic spectrum disorders. *British Journal of Psychiatry*, 176, 357–362.

Winokur, G. (1977). Delusional disorder (paranoia). *Comprehensive Psychiatry*, 18, 511–521.

Winokur, G., Clayton, P.J. and Reich, T. (1969). *Manic-depressive illness*. St Louis, MO: Mosby.

Winters, K.C. and Neale, J.M. (1983). Delusions and delusional thinking in psychotics: A review of the literature. *Clinical Psychology Reviews*, 3, 227–253.

Wittenberg, N., Stein, D. Barak, Y. *et al.* (1996). Clozapine and tardive dyskinesia: Analysis of clinical trials. *Pathophysiology*, 3, 241–245.

Woerner, M.G., Kane, J.M., Lieberman, J.A., Alvir, J., Bergmann, K.J., Borenstein, M. *et al.* (1991). The prevalence of tardive dyskinesia. *Journal of Clinical Psychopharmacology*, 11, 34–42.

Wolfe, T. (1971). *The electric kool-aid acid test*. New York: Bantam Books.

Wolff, S. and Chick, J. (1980). Schizoid personality in childhood: A controlled follow-up study. *Psychological Medicine*, 10, 85–100.

Wolkin, A., Sanfilipo, M., Wolf, A.P., Angrist, B., Brodie, J.D. and Rotrosen, J. (1992). Negative symptoms and hypofrontality in chronic schizophrenia. *Archives of General Psychiatry*, 49, 959–965.

Wong, D.F., Wagner, H.N., Tune, L.E., Dannals, R.F., Pearlson, G.D., Links, J.M. *et al.* (1986). Positron emission tomography reveals elevated D2 dopamine receptors in drug-naive schizophrenics. *Science*, 234, 1558–1563.

Woodbury, M.A. and Manton, K.G. (1989). A new procedure for analysis of medical classifications. *Methods of Information in Medicine*, 21, 210–220.

Wragg, R.E. and Jeste, D.V. (1989). Overview of depression and psychosis in Alzheimer's disease. *American Journal of Psychiatry*, 146, 577–587.

Wright, I.C., Rabe-Hesketh, S., Woodruff, P.W.R., David, A.S., Murray, R.M. and Bullmore, E.T. (2000). Meta-analysis of regional brain volumes in schizophrenia. *American Journal of Psychiatry*, 157, 16–25.

Wynne, L.C. (1968). Methodologic and conceptual issues in the study of schizophrenics and their families. In D. Rosenthal and S. Kety (Eds.), *The transmission of schizophrenia*, pp. 185–200. Oxford: Pergamon.

Wynne, L.C. (1971). Family research on the pathogenesis of schizophrenia. In P. Doucet and C. Laurin (Eds.), *Problems of psychosis: International colloquium on psychosis*. Excerpta Medica Congress Series, No. 194. Amsterdam: Excerpta Medica.

Wynne, L.C. and Singer, M.T. (1963). Thought disorder and family relations of schizophrenics. *Archives of General Psychiatry*, 9, 191–196.

Wynne, L.C., Ryckoff, I., Day, J. and Hirsch, S. (1958). Pseudo-mutuality in the family relations of schizophrenics. *Psychiatry*, 21, 205–220.

Young, D. and Scoville, W.B. (1938). Paranoid psychosis in narcolepsy and the possible danger of benzedrine treatment. *Medical Clinics of North America*, 22, 637–646.

Zaidel, D.W., Esiri, M.M. and Harrison, P.J. (1997). Size, shape, and orientation of neurons in the left and right hippocampus: Investigation of normal asymmetries and alterations in schizophrenia. *American Journal of Psychiatry*, 154: 812–818.

Zanarini, M.C., Gunderson, J.G. and Frankenburg, F.R. (1990). Cognitive features of borderline personality disorder. *American Journal of Psychiatry*, 147, 57–63.

Zilboorg, G. (1941). Ambulatory schizophrenia. *Psychiatry*, 4, 149–155.

Zubin, J. (1967). Classification of the behavior disorders. *Annual Review of Psychology*, 18, 373–406.

Index

DATE DUE

APR 2 2 2009		
MAR 3 1 2009		
MAR 3 1 2010		
MAR 3 1 2010		

Demco, Inc. 38-293